The Life of Henry Moore

by the same author

GRAHAM SUTHERLAND: A BIOGRAPHY

THE LIFE OF
HENRY MOORE

ROGER BERTHOUD

A William Abrahams Book
E. P. Dutton
New York

A William Abrahams Book

Published in the United States
by E. P. Dutton,
a division of NAL Penguin Inc.,
2 Park Avenue,
New York, N.Y. 10016.

Originally published in Great Britain by
Faber and Faber.

Library of Congress Catalog Card Number: 87–71189

ISBN: 0–525–24563–4

OBE

1 3 5 7 9 10 8 6 4 2

First American Edition

Contents

Acknowledgements

This is the authorized biography of Henry Moore, in the sense that when started more than four years before his death it had his approval and co-operation, with permission to quote from his letters and written statements. So my first debt of gratitude is to my subject for giving the project his support and for patiently answering my questions for as long as he was fit enough to do so; and to his wife Irina, for contributing her memories of some episodes of their long life together. Thanks to their goodwill I was given access to much archival material, including many thousands of newspaper cuttings, boxes of letters, and all engagement diaries from 1955 onwards. Earlier archival material is largely in the possession of the sculptor's daughter Mary, who did not want to release it or co-operate unless she could control the final product, clearly an unacceptable condition.

My second debt is to the staff of the Henry Moore Foundation, and especially to Betty Tinsley, Ann Garrould, and David Mitchinson, for the many hours of help they gave me in answering questions and making material available; and to Alex Davis, the Foundation's librarian, without whose chronological filing of newspaper cuttings my task would have been much longer. I am also indebted to the Foundation's trustees for giving the book their initial support, though the text is in no sense officially approved: this is not an official biography.

Among those I interviewed I would like to mention with gratitude Frank Ambler, Maurice Ash, George Ablah, Elisabeth Ayrton, David Astor, Sir Ronald Arculus, Dennis Bult-Francis, Antony Bell, Alan Bowness, Anthony Blee, Gordon Bunshaft, Edmund Bovey, Harry Brooks, Hans and Walter Bechtler, Hans Peter Bruderer, Nicholas Brown, Raymond and Gin Coxon, Alfred Cohen, Elisabeth Collins, Robert Clatworthy, Jill Craigie, Anthony Caro, the late Ralph Colin, Bernard Cohen,

Giulio Cardini, Georg Eisler, Shelley Fausset, David Finn, Wolfgang Fischer, Frank and John Farnham, Terry Friedman, Sir Brinsley Ford, the late Geoffrey Grigson, Philip Givens, Sem Ghelardini, Olga Hirshhorn, the late Betty Howarth, the late Walter Hussey, Lord Houghton, Darryl Hill, Derek Howarth, Sir Denis Hamilton, Lady (Juliette) Huxley, Max Harari, Margrit Hahnloser, Sir William Keswick, Phillip King, Janie Lee, William Lieberman, Dr Gabriele Lavaggi, Bernard Meadows, Dorothy Miller, Pierre Marcel, Margaret McLeod, Michel Muller, Erich Milleker, I. M. Pei, Jack Pritchard, John Piper, the late Peter Powell, Roland Piché, Peter Palumbo, Aline Reed, John Russell, Véra Russell, John Read, Sir John Rothenstein, Sir James and Lady Richards, Eugene Rosenberg, Sir Norman Reid, Dr Heinz Roland, Robert Rowe, James Johnson Sweeney, Sir Stephen Spender, Sir Robert and Lady Sainsbury, David Sylvester, Lady Strauss, Hylton Stockwell, Willy and Marina Staehelin, Dr Alan Wilkinson, E. J. Winfield, William Withrow, John Weeks, Ruedi and Edi Wolfensberger, Dr Alan Webster, Malcolm Woodward, Desmond Zwemmer, Lord Zuckerman.

Letters from the following were especially helpful: Winnie Alker, C. G. Argan, Sir Harold Acton, Lauren Bacall, Margaret Barr, Francis Brennan. J. W. C. Boks, Muriel Beadle, Jørgen Bo, John Clarkson, Serge Chermayeff, Lynndon Clough, Giovanni Carandente, Theodora FitzGibbon, M. S. Farsi, Mathias Goeritz, Dick Hosking, Jack Hepworth, Gordon Hanes, Sir Fred Hoyle, Mikkel Hansen, Berthold Lubetkin, Gian-Carlo Menotti, William McNeill, William McVey, Georg Müller, Gordon Onslow-Ford, Walter Plumb, John Pollis, Sir Edward Playfair, Jacquetta Priestley, Vincent Price, John Rewald, Alma Ramsey, Cressida Ridley, Frank Stanton, Brian Toll, Hiram Winterbotham.

I would also like to thank staff of the following museums for help: the Leeds City Art Gallery; Wakefield City Art Gallery; Tate Gallery, London; Whitworth Art Gallery, Manchester; Imperial War Museum, London; National Gallery, Washington; Hirshhorn Museum, Washington; Metropolitan Museum, New York; Museum of Modern Art, New York; Albright-Knox Art Gallery, Buffalo, NY; Detroit Museum of Art; Dallas Museum of Art; Cranbrook Academy Museum; Boston Museum of Arts; Museum für Kunst und Gewerbe, Hamburg; Kunsthalle, Hamburg; Tel Aviv Museum; Auschwitz Museum.

My warm thanks go also to the British Council for its help in documenting its Henry Moore exhibitions, and especially to Margaret McLeod; to Isabel Johnstone of the Arts Council; to staff of the British Embassy in Warsaw and at Unesco headquarters in Paris; to the Library of the

University of Victoria, British Columbia; the Harry Ransom Humanities Research Center at the University of Texas; Castleford public library; Hubert Chesshyre of the College of Arms; J. M. Farrar, county archivist of Cambridgeshire; the library of *The Times*.

For permission to quote I am grateful to Dr Wolfgang Fischer and Dr Heinz Roland, from their diaries; to Leeds City Art Gallery, from Moore's letters to Jocelyn Horner; to Wakefield City Art Gallery, from Moore's letters to Albert Wainwright; to Ann Garrould, from Moore's letters to Alice Gostick; to Ben Read, from Moore's letters to Herbert Read; to the Coxons, from Moore's letters to them both; to the executors of the estate of Lord Clark, from Moore's letters to him; and to Joan Wyndham, from her early diaries published as *Love Lessons*.

Finally I would like to thank all those who helped eliminate errors by reading all or part of my typescript, especially Bernard Meadows and Ann Garrould; James Bishop, then editor of the *Illustrated London News*, for not infrequently allowing me to combine magazine business with Moore business on trips at home and abroad during my first two years as his deputy; and most especially my wife Joy, who helped research the chapter on Moore in the First World War, and daughters Lucy and Lottie, for putting up with my evenings, weekends and holidays spent pounding a typewriter.

Prelude

When I contemplated the scale of Henry Moore's achievement, the idea of writing his biography at first seemed foolhardy and presumptuous. Yet strangely, no full biography existed. An earlier request for permission to write one from Moore's friend and former neighbour, the Irish-American writer Constantine FitzGibbon, had been turned down. An American poet, Donald Hall, had written an engaging and stylish study of the sculptor's life and work, which had been published in Britain in 1965 after much of it had appeared in the *New Yorker*. It was quite short, though, and more in the nature of an extended profile than a detailed analysis. As suggested by the subtitle, 'The Life and Work of a Great Sculptor', the tone was hagiographical.

Among the many critical studies, those by Moore's friends Herbert Read, an incomparable supporter, and John Russell – also dating from the late 1960s – included much valuable biographical material up to the end of the Second World War. But both writers seemed to assume that once Moore had become successful and famous, his life had ceased to be interesting. Great success is, however, not easy to handle. A much lesser degree of fame has been the undoing of many talented artists: the temptation to avoid risks and churn out an identifiable and easily marketable product is strong. The British tend, moreover, to be envious of success, and their reactions can be destructive. For Moore to sustain his level of achievement, uneven though it sometimes was, against all the odds over half a century required toughness of mind, intelligence and deep resources of creativity.

I had been fortunate to know him for more than thirty years. We lived six miles apart when I was young, and had many mutual friends and acquaintances. Among them was Maurice Ash, later a trustee of the Henry Moore Foundation. He had introduced me to Moore when I was about sixteen, and later the Moores would come to a Sunday lunch or dinner when I was staying at the Ash home. It proved useful for this book that I had subsequently become closely acquainted with the London art world, and had travelled extensively abroad on behalf of *The Times*. My first biography had been of Moore's contemporary and friend Graham Sutherland, who was involved in many of the same events and institutions.

'Of course your book will be judged by your success in bridging the gap between the man and his work,' someone dauntingly observed after I had begun making the rounds of the sculptor's friends and associates. Moore and his creations did indeed seem very different. With his shortish, stocky physique, ruddy countryman's complexion, and tweedy taste in clothes, he might have been a well-to-do Yorkshire farmer. He had a lingering accent from his native county. No one could have been further from the popular conception of the artist as Bohemian, as Outsider or as obsessed egocentric than this down-to-earth family man with his preference for regular working hours, his extrovert, unpretentious manner, his sometimes slightly squeaky voice, unfinished sentences, and engaging giggle.

Many people must have asked themselves how a man who seemed so normal and straightforward could have produced such 'abnormal' and 'distorted' work, as it often seemed to those unfamiliar with it. Part of the answer was that Moore was more complex than he seemed. His appetite for work amounted to an addiction, and his restless hands betrayed inner tensions. He was genuinely modest in many ways, yet regularly bracketed himself with the greatest creative figures of Western civilization when answering questions. In many ways he was very generous, yet he rarely gave a work to a friend, unless it was to Kenneth Clark, who needed gifts least of all; and towards his assistants he tended to be penny-pinching. Although supremely self-confident, he was excessively worried about his place in the pantheon of greatness. Another partial explanation lies in the nature of his inspiration. Much of it came from a God-given source which he took pains to protect. But like most artists, writers, and musicians of note, he was also animated by the spirit of the times. He was a sensitive receiver of messages from the collective unconscious, and he lived through eighty-six years of a deeply troubled century.

His apparent normality as a human being helped people to accept the apparent abnormality of his sculpture. Since he was evidently a warm, genuine, and in many ways lovable man and not a poseur, prima donna, or intellectual snob, his work was often given the benefit of the doubt. Such a man was unlikely to be trying to pull a confidence trick on the public. Those who were beginning to appreciate his work were frequently swept into passionate enthusiasm by his personality, charm, and accessibility. From his transatlantic admirers especially a recurring comment was: '. . . and then we realized what a simply great human being he was!' They expected someone daunting. They found a small, almost cuddly figure who liked to be liked, who was approachable yet acute and had the kind of quick reaction to interesting facts and ideas which made them feel more intelligent than usual. He had a life-enhancing quality, and so, at its best, did his work. One felt the better for having talked to him or for having contemplated his creations. There was about him an innocence – probably a necessary attribute of any great artist – which sat oddly with his strong seam of Yorkshire realism. His interest in visitors and his charm were genuine, but they helped make him an outstanding salesman for his own work.

Appreciation for Moore the man and Moore the artist thus often became indivisible. His fame too, once achieved, cast a glow. In letter after letter, collectors and admirers expressed almost incredulous gratitude that he should have taken so much trouble to show them around his studios and talk to them. 'Can this really be me talking to the great Henry Moore?' they seemed to have asked themselves. The impact of his work and personality was particularly powerful in the USA and Canada where, Moore used to say, four-fifths of his output had come to rest – an exaggeration, though possibly true of his later bronzes. The Americans loved his directness, his seeming simplicity, his lack of pomposity, and his sense of humour and fun. He loved their enthusiasm, their willingness to take risks, their openness, and their ability to pay for his work even when his prices climbed into six figures.

Part of the Moore legend was the unchanging nature of his way of life, despite the wealth he eventually amassed. For the last forty-six years he lived at Hoglands, an old farmhouse one hour's drive north-east of London in the hamlet of Perry Green, near Hertfordshire's border with Essex. Paintings and drawings by Courbet, Millet, Degas, Vuillard, Cézanne, Seurat, and other artists, and fine carvings from many periods and civilizations were his sole indulgences. Apart from the addition of a largish sitting room at the back, the house remained unaltered. Only the garden grew and grew, and in time there were nine studios and a small sculpture park (Moores only) within the grounds. His holiday home on the Italian coast at Forte dei Marmi, in the Carrara marble-working area, was also very modest. That was the way he preferred to live. When he died in August 1986, the revenue from his work since the Henry Moore Foundation had been established in January 1977 – helped by a booming stock market – exceeded 30 million pounds.

During my first year of research I went to see him most Fridays with a list of questions. He would usually be drawing in the little graphics studio at the bottom of the garden, to which he could then still drive in his ancient yellow Rover. His back and legs gave him almost constant pain as a result of minor accidents which he had too often ignored in the interests of his work, and which were aggravated by arthritis. He could walk only with the aid of two sticks. But he never complained. Those sessions were frequently helpful though rarely revealing. Moore had long since worked out an edited version of his life and thoughts, no doubt to reduce the psychic drain of countless interviews. When I asked him questions calculated to guarantee a fresh response, he would – with a skill which one could but admire – steer his way back to one of the trusted old gramophone records with a couple of bridging sentences, only to break off with the words 'but I've told you that before, haven't I, Roger'. The rest of the morning I would spend going through some eighteen filing cabinets of newspaper cuttings, sent in from all over the world by cuttings agencies.

Since previous writers have on the whole accepted Moore's own version of events, one of my chief tasks must be to balance that with the memories and opinions of his friends and associates. Interviews with nearly a hundred of these, including former school friends, former students, collectors, dealers, architects, museum officials, neighbours, and former assistants have, I hope, provided a fuller and deeper portrait: Moore in the round, so to speak. From interviews in New York, Washington, Dallas, Houston, Toronto, Bonn, Zurich, and Paris as well as London and Yorkshire; from British Council reports from foreign cities where his work had been shown; from that mountain of newspaper cuttings, and from a few dozen related books, there emerged a picture of Moore as catalyst and initiator of dramas that affected the lives of individuals, of institutions, and even of whole cities.

What battles there were over the decades across England and the Western world between those who loved and loathed contemporary art, triggered as often as not by a Moore exhibition or a plan to buy a Moore bronze for a civic site. In Toronto the struggle between believers and 'philistines' helped shape the evolution of that city into the elegant and arts-conscious metropolis of today. As recently as in the late 1970s, the installation of a huge Moore sculpture in front of the architect I. M. Pei's dramatic, forward-sloping new city hall in Dallas strengthened the hand of those who saw excellence in the arts as vital for the much-maligned city's image and prosperity.

Moore's great exhibitions seemed on occasion to inspire a collective love affair with his work. The most famous example was the one staged in Florence through the summer of 1972, set in Michelangelo's Belvedere Fort overlooking the city and the great dome of Brunelleschi's cathedral. Moore emerged as a living embodiment of centuries of Western tradition. It was the high point of a career not lacking in climaxes. But subsequent, less publicized exhibitions in Zurich, Madrid, Mexico City, and Caracas, Venezuela were in their way as remarkable, both in attendance and impact.

Of the many individuals who have become obsessed by Moore's work, one of the most extraordinary has been George Ablah, whom I met in New York. Of Lebanese Christian origin but brought up in Wichita, Kansas, he made a lot of money from oil and property. Discovering art in middle age and starting with the Impressionists, he collected some eighty-five Moores within eighteen months in the early 1980s, stopping only when his total had reached a hundred and he had spent $22 million on the sculptor's work. Many of the larger pieces were shown in 1984 in New York in an officially backed exhibition called Moore in the Parks, which was intended to interest the non-museum-going public in contemporary sculpture. Ablah even had two small Moore pieces, along with others by Brancusi, Rodin, Marini, Giacometti, Arp, and Fernand Botero in his fourteen-seater executive jet: a sculptural cargo valued at $3 million. There is in Moore's later work in particular an affirmative spirit for which American entrepreneurs – optimists by nature – seem to feel a special affinity.

One of the pleasures in working on this book was to remind Moore, when his memory had faded, of some of the enjoyable trips he had made around the world, in earlier days often in the company of his friend Peter Gregory. 'How lucky I have been and what wonderful friends I have had,' he would say. After his prostate operation in summer 1983, following which he had for a time been critically ill, he could not even recall his visits in the 1950s to Mexico and the site of Auschwitz concentration camp in Poland. As often happens, however, childhood events seemed to remain reasonably clear. Talking to him at that stage gained from the presence of his wife Irina: she was often there in the sitting room, able to supply details of events or voyages with which she had been associated in their half-century of well-balanced marriage. For all his reduced state, Henry retained much of his old curiosity. When I asked to see the unicorn-like narwhal tusk which Sir William Keswick had given him, he was keen to know some facts about the mysterious whale's way of life. We debated how much the tits and finches weighed which fed at the bird tables outside the sitting-room windows; and he showed a lively interest in the technicalities of my job as deputy editor of the *Illustrated London News*.

It was a strange sensation to be writing the life of someone who was still alive yet unlikely to be in a fit state to read the end product, and might well not survive to see its publication, as indeed he did not. I found myself evolving a double relationship with my subject: an affectionate and, in his last year, purely social one with the frail old man in his chair in front of the sitting-room television set, and a more clinical and critical one with his tougher, earlier selves. One of my main difficulties was to strike the right balance between appreciation and judgement. When much that had been written was so eulogistic, a more astringent approach seemed to be needed. Many of Moore's written statements and printed interviews, often quoted as if they were immensely wise or revealing, do not stand up well to close scrutiny – nor, I am sure, were they intended to be treated as holy writ.

If I have sometimes been unduly severe, I ask his posthumous under-standing. A biographer perforce lives mentally with his subject, and for four years I could not have hoped for finer company. *The Life of Henry Moore* is a labour of love, written in the confident belief that to present his all too few shortcomings along with his many strengths will make him more rather than less lovable and interesting, and leave his stature undiminished.

Chapter I

Childhood and school

1898–1916

For some artists, insecurity is a spur. Moore was never of that type. As sculptor and man he was always confident of his value. It was one of his attractions. The basis of his confidence was the security and affection which he experienced as a child, and the firmness of his Yorkshire roots.

Henry Spencer Moore was born as the seventh of eight children on 30 July 1898 at 30 Roundhill Road, a modest, two-storey terrace house in the industrial town of Castleford in Yorkshire's West Riding. His father was Raymond Spencer Moore, a coalminer, who had been born in 1849 in the neighbouring county of Lincolnshire, where his father, Thomas Moore, was a labourer. Not having married till he was thirty-five, he was nearly fifty when Henry was born. According to family tradition, Raymond Moore's grandfather was from Ireland, but genealogical research by the College of Arms suggests that any Irish forebears were probably one generation further back at least.[1] His mother's name was Ann Spencer, and he was so proud of her that Spencer was included among the forenames of all his eight children.

As far as is known, Raymond Moore left school aged nine to work on the land like his father and grandfather. Scaring crows off the fields was, the family believe, one of his early tasks. He is assumed to have come to Castleford as a young man to escape the penury and bondage of farm work by going down the mines, which was relatively better paid. Surface coal had been used at Castleford for many centuries. A record of 1535 states that 'though heare be plenti of wode, yet the people burne much yearth cole, by cawse hit is plentifull and sold good chepe'.[2] Pottery making was, however, Castleford's oldest industry. David Dunderdale's famous pottery, established in the 1790s, was by no means the first, and in the nineteenth century the town also became a centre for the manufacture of glass bottles. Some 20 million of these were being made there each year towards the end of the century. Wheldale colliery, where Raymond Moore worked, had been opened in 1868 by a Dr Holt (the mines were then all privately owned) and was for years known as t' Doctor's pit.

Mary Baker, as Henry's mother was born, came from Burntwood in Staffordshire, to the south-west of Castleford across the Pennine hills, and was one of seven children. Her father too was a miner. She was twenty-seven, eight years younger than Raymond, when they married in April 1885 in the parish church of Methley, a village a couple of miles outside Castleford where she had been living. After that relatively late start, her eight children were born at fairly regular two- or three-yearly intervals. First there was Annie, who was to marry a tall, handsome glassblower called Albert Speight and have nine children, with twins at the end. Then there was Raymond, named after his father and, as it transpired, bearing a considerable resemblance to Henry, to a point where they were sometimes taken for each other (his daughter Aline, moreover, looks eerily like Henry when he was younger). Raymond was the first of the family to become a schoolteacher, in those days a classic escape route from manual labour for the intelligent child.

The third child, Henry's second brother, was Alfred. He left the country for Canada when he was seventeen or eighteen, probably to get away from a girl he had made pregnant. He was considered the black sheep of the family, and was not heard of again. Next came another boy, Willie, who was to die in infancy, possibly in Wales when Raymond Moore senior was sent there briefly to help open a pit at Ystalfera. They lived in a house on a mountain side, which Mrs Moore hated, and Willie died of the convulsions. Then there was Mary, a very bright all-rounder, who was born in Wales and nearly died later when five of the children, including Henry, contracted scarlet fever at the same time. She became a headmistress, and her next sister Betty, born in 1894, was another budding schoolteacher, and married one as well. Henry's birth in 1898 was followed three years later by the eighth child, Elsie. She was discovered, too late, to have had a weak heart which she fatally overstrained in a swimming competition when aged about twelve. Municipal swimming baths were just being opened at that time, and she was talented. Henry later regretted having egged her on. Her death may have affected him even more than he realized: a school of thought holds that in such cases of bereavement the closest surviving sibling sometimes seeks to perform or achieve for two.[3] Once again he was cherished as the youngest.

The linchpin of this large and happy family was Henry's mother, a woman of exceptional character, energy and determination. 'She was a very handsome woman,' one of her grandchildren recalled. 'She stood very straight, and she wore black all the time, and always clothes with a high neck. She had the kind of dignity that Henry's figures have.'[4]

If the dignity was tinged with vanity, she was also humorous and affectionate. Henry loved her female presence. To him she was 'absolutely feminine, womanly, motherly ... I suppose I've got a mother complex ...'[5] She was to me the absolute stability, the whole thing in life that one knew was there for one's protection. If she went out, I'd be terrified she wouldn't return. So it's not surprising that the kind of women I've done in sculpture are mature women rather than young.'[6] He remembered her stamina, often helping her husband to get ready for the 6 a.m. shift and kept busy till night with all the cooking, washing, housework and other tasks demanded by a large young family. So it went on until she was in her late fifties, and as a child he could not recall seeing her rest.

If Mary Moore inspired nothing but affection, Henry's relations with his father were properly respectful, as befitted the age. Raymond Moore was one of a proud generation of self-taught miners, high-minded, self-improving, self-respecting, conscious of the dignity of labour yet determined that his children should achieve a better and more fulfilling life. He had read the works of Shakespeare, taught himself the violin (later inflicting violin lessons on his protesting youngest son) and enough mathematics and engineering to qualify first as a pit deputy, then as an under-manager. But an injury to his eyes in a pit accident, probably a gas explosion, prevented him from taking up this position, and he focused his ambitions on his children the more fiercely. He had almost certainly worked at the coal-face as a young man: a surviving photograph of him, aged about twenty-two, suggests a powerful physique and no lack of self-confidence. A good deal has been made by Moore's commentators of the analogies between coal-mining and sculpting, both being hewing and tunnelling activities. The mining community's close links with the earth, and the constant dramas of the subterranean life, undoubtedly made their mark on young Henry's mind, leaving a lifelong fascination with holes, caverns, tunnels and other natural orifices; but by the time he was a small boy, his father had, according to Elsie's birth certificate, become a lampman, responsible for maintaining and distributing those vital items of equipment.

In his own old age Henry remembered his father with a measure of awe:

He was a kind of Victorian father. He had his own chair near the coal fire – miners got their coal at a very nominal cost – and nobody had to touch him as they went past. If we accidentally kicked his foot or something, he'd go for us, not physically but [and he imitated growling imprecations]. If he didn't like some food my mother gave him, he would say 'I'll throw this back of fire.' My mother would say 'All right, go on.' He never did. She called his bluff. He was a conscientious father who wanted his children not to have the suffering, the drawbacks and the restricted life he'd had, and he saw that we didn't.[7]

Moore's sister Betty also remembered their father as very strict:

He would line us up on a Sunday morning in front of him, and he would go through all the different things we had been doing. We had to know how to tell the time before we were five, and we had to know our tables ... he was very, very ambitious for us all. I think he expected too much, really.[8]

Of overt signs of affection from him there were none that she could recall. It was in character with this exacting, vicariously ambitious Victorian paterfamilias that he should have been an early trade unionist and friend of Herbert Smith, a Castleford man who became the first president of the Yorkshire Miners Union. Smith was later a governor of Castleford Secondary School, which Henry was to attend at the same time as Smith's son.

It was a measure of the strength of local trade unionism that a strike at Castleford's Fryston and Wheldale collieries should have lasted sixty-eight weeks, from 15 October 1902 to 30 January 1904.[9] The strike was essentially over wage levels, and Raymond Moore was a Wheldale man. Henry recalled that his father bought an iron last to save money by mending the shoes first of his extensive family (by no means an unusual practice in those days) and then, to earn something extra, of several neighbours. During this hard period, Mary Moore did some additional domestic work for the Clokies who owned one of the town's main potteries. They must have been decent folk, since Henry was sometimes asked to stay to tea when he went along with his mother.[10]

Roundhill Road, where Henry lived for his first twelve years, was uninspiring, but not miserably so. The red-brick houses are of the variety known as two-up and two-down, but they do not stand back-to-back with those of the adjacent street. Of the two smallish rooms on the ground floor, the front one was kept for special occasions, like visits from relatives on Sundays. Daily life centred on the back room, which was for eating, cooking and living. There, too, ablutions were performed in a tin bath in front of the fire. Mrs Moore would help remove the grime of the colliery from her husband. Upstairs were two somewhat larger rooms in which somehow the six surviving children and their parents managed to sleep. At the end of the small garden was the washhouse with a boiler in it. Water was drawn from a pump in the garden. Betty recalled: 'As soon as Henry saw my mother taking washing down there, he used to cry and scream. He knew that she wasn't going to look after him and that we would be doing so, and of course we pushed him around a bit. He hated wash days.'[11] Next to the washhouse were the coal shed and toilet. Human waste went down a chute to a pit into which ash and other refuse were thrown. A separate door opened at the back for it to be cleared once a week by the soil carts via the access streets running along the back of the garden. Electricity was too recent an invention to have reached such modest residences, and the pump was the only source of water.

Castleford's population was then around 20,000. Despite its unprepossessing appearance, it had a long history going back to Roman times when, as Legioleum or Legecium, it had been an important station: a Roman milestone stating that Eboracum (York) was twenty miles away was found in the grounds of a house near Roundhill Road not long ago. In Saxon times the settlement was known as Chesterford. Its geographical situation at least is pleasant: standing at the junction of the rivers Calder and Aire, it has fine countryside including woods and hills within a few miles. Visiting it now, it is not hard to imagine how it was in Henry's young day, without the rush of cars, but with many horse-drawn carts trundling along the rough roads; a great deal more smoke, but also a great deal more greenery. There were then fields in the immediate vicinity of Roundhill Road. In one of them was a large pond in which the young Moores sometimes swam with their neighbours' seven children. On one such occasion the farmer removed all their clothes and they had to walk home naked, to be put to bed in disgrace.[12]

Off Beancroft Road, where the Roman milestone was found, the Briggs brothers had a slaughterhouse, to which the cattle would often be walked from market in Leeds. Henry and his friends would sometimes watch them being dispatched:

Every Wednesday used to be killing day. It was an exciting but gory experience. The butcher would have the cow or bullock with a rope around its head and neck, which went through a ring on the wall. Then two or three men would pull on it till the cow was right up against the wall, so it couldn't move. The butcher aimed with his pointed axe (poleaxe) at the middle of the forehead. Then they put a stick in the hole to break up the brain and make sure it was insensate. It was dreadful but fascinating. Some butchers had the reputation for always getting the animal down in one. Some would fumble and fail to stun it.[13]

In a poem partly inspired by such a description, Moore's friend, Stephen Spender, juxtaposed the slaughterman stirring the brains and the sculptor taking a 'flat transparent stone thin as a bone' and cutting a hole through it, light penetrating darkness, implicitly ranking the experience as among the most seminal in Henry's life.[14] The artist himself regarded it more as a bygone substitute for the guilty excitements of watching violence on television.

Young Henry's schooling had begun at the age of three, when he was obliged to attend the infants department of the nearby Temple Street elementary school. For his first day there his mother had made him a khaki coat and trousers, his sister Betty recalled. 'He had white hair as a child, and was the pride and joy of my mother. We all dressed him up and took him to school. He yelled all the way. We did think him a nuisance!'[15]

It was family life in the full sense of the term. Grandmother Ann Spencer Moore lived in a cottage near the parish church, and come over every Sunday after matins, usually wearing a little black-sequined bonnet and a skirt which trailed along the floor. If Raymond Moore reprimanded his children when she was there, she would say, 'Now remember, Raymond, you were a bairn yourself one day.' She smoked a clay pipe, which her son would fill and light for her, and they would sit smoking their pipes together. Another frequent visitor was Raymond Moore's sister, Aunt Elsie. She was relatively well off, having married a farmer from Garforth near Leeds, but childless and much less agreeable. She would arrive on horseback, often bringing fresh eggs, and liked to make the children garters to keep their stockings up. A maternal aunt lived in the nearby village of Methley, where the fine church and its carvings were to make an impact on Henry's mind.

The rhythms of family life were disturbed by the shift system worked by the miners, including Raymond Moore senior. The shifts were from 6 a.m. to 2 p.m., 2 p.m. to 10 p.m., and 10 p.m. to 6 a.m. One of Henry's school friends, Frank Ambler, recalled that if one walked down the town's main street, Carlton Street, around 2.30 p.m., one could pick out the miners by their black faces.[16] There were no pithead baths until after the First World War. Many of the miners would be woken by Old Moss, the knocker-up, as he was called. He had a long pole with a cork on the end, which he would tap against the miner's bedroom window to rouse him at 4.30 a.m. or so, for the early shift. For Henry's father there was then a walk of a good mile to Wheldale Colliery, which employed about a thousand men; much of its coal was taken along the Aire and Calder Navigation Canal to the port of Goole, whence it was shipped to sea-going, coal-powered vessels. The sound of the miners' clogs as they walked to work while Henry lay in bed remained in his memory to old age.

When he was eight years old he was transferred to the main section of Temple Street school. Including infants (for whom provision was not often made at this period), it comprised some 850 boys and girls, many of whom left at the age of twelve to start work, while the brighter ones went on to grammar school. The art teacher there, John Holland, had noticed that Henry's brother Raymond had a natural facility for drawing, which he never lost: throughout his life Raymond enjoyed drawing both people and animals, and as a very small boy Henry used to ask him to draw horses and other beasts for him.[17] Holland was no doubt delighted to find that the youngest of the Moore boys shared the same talent. Henry was charged with designing a decorative border for the school timetable, and perhaps with other small tasks.[18]

At around ten or eleven years old, he had several experiences which he later came to regard as formative. Memory is of course highly selective, but the frequency with which he recounted these episodes, no doubt progressively polishing them, suggests that he saw them as genuinely significant. Perhaps the most repeated concerned Sunday school, an unwelcome feature of a day of the week marked by a Puritan banning of all pleasures. Off Henry and his sisters went each Sunday to the nearby Congregational chapel. It was not that the Moores were religious. They went only rarely to church, Elsie's funeral being one such occasion. But the children had been baptized into the Church of England, and it was good to get them out of the house on a Sunday afternoon.

The Sunday school superintendent liked to finish their sessions with an improving story. One such concerned Michelangelo, 'the greatest sculptor who ever lived'. Working one day in his stoneyard behind the cathedral in Florence on the head of a faun, he was interrupted by a cocky passer-by who commented: 'But you have given that faun all his teeth. If he's as old as he seems to be, he would have lost some of them.' Whereupon the great man knocked out two of the unduly perfect teeth. Henry was not so much impressed by Michelangelo's openness to advice in this garbled version of a famous incident, but he did feel strangely excited by the description of the Italian as 'the greatest sculptor who ever lived'. When he returned home he looked him up in his children's encyclopedia, and was fascinated by what he read. His imagination had been fired by those words. From then on (as he would later round off the reminiscence), when asked what he wanted to be in life, he would answer 'a sculptor'.[19] Be that as it may, he does not seem to have mentioned his ambition to his friends.

Another seminal episode concerned his mother's rheumatic or arthritic pains, resulting from her constant hard labour. She would rub her own knees with a soothing liniment, then call over Henry and ask him to rub her back with the pungent mixture which she had prepared herself. It made his eyes smart and caused him considerable embarrassment, but for a time he performed the rite two or three times a week. He never forgot the sensation of her flesh and bones, the one yielding (she was not slim), the other resistant beneath his kneading fingers.[20] In retrospect, he recognized it as one of his first specifically sculptural experiences, and with all its Oedipal undertones it doubtless played no small role in shaping his preoccupation with the female figure as a theme.

Two local and seasonal games were seen in later life to have provided Moore with his first activity as a carver. One was called tipcat, or piggy, the other knurr and spell. Both involved a stick or bat. With tipcat, the object to be hit (the piggy) was a piece of wood about one inch thick and five inches long, shaped at both ends. The idea was to tap it at one end so that it jumped up into the air, whereupon it had to be hit as far as possible with the stick or bat. The distance would then be paced out for comparison with rival efforts. In knurr and spell, the piggy was replaced by a little wooden ball, which was knocked up from a sloping platform of wood. Henry found that carving the piggy – and only a well-made piggy just the right shape at both ends would rise properly when tapped – was a very enjoyable activity. If the piggies were his first carvings, his first maquettes were the 'touchstone' ovens which he and his friends would make in the late autumn. There were several clay pits in Castleford, including one immediately behind Temple Street school, owned by a brick-making firm. With clay from these, the little ovens would be fashioned, looking like small boxes with a chimney and a hole on one side into which rotten wood was stuffed. This could then be lit, producing a wonderful glow which also kept the hands warm. Sometimes the boys decorated the sides of the ovens.[21]

And then there was Adel Crag. Just as the block and ball required for knurr and spell were later seen by Henry to have been the subconscious source of one of his cryptic carvings of the mid-1930s, the alabaster Bird and Egg of 1934, so this magnificent outcrop of stone above Leeds came back to the sculptor's mind's eye when pondering the sources of his first two-piece reclining figure of 1959.[22] The crag consists of two huge rocks, now patinated with moss and partially screened by silver birches, the leg-like lower part thrusting eighteen feet into the air. It was the focal point of some of the family's excursions and picnics, which ranged over the hills and dales not far from Castleford. The legacy of their wild and sensual contours in the child's receptive mind was of the utmost importance. For the rest of his life Yorkshire was his mental landscape. The slag heaps too left their mark. 'They had the scale of the pyramids and this triangular, bare, stark reality that was just as though one were in the Alps,' he later recalled a trifle hyperbolically. 'Perhaps these impressions when you're young are what count.'[23]

To secondary school

In 1910, when he was twelve years old, Henry was accepted at the second attempt by Castleford Secondary School (now Castleford High School) on a county minor scholarship. His brothers and sisters had made it first time. Henry ascribed his initial failure to his father's musical ambitions for him:

> I told my father I failed because he made me have violin lessons three nights a week, which cost a shilling a night. I hated the noise I made. So I said: 'Dad, you know why I failed, I haven't done the homework because three nights a week you made me do the violin.'[24]

The scholarships were awarded on the basis of examination results rather than parental need: those without them paid £2 3s. 4d. a term. The school had been established only four years earlier. Previously, scholars had had to travel to a secondary school in Leeds. The Castleford school

had started modestly in a hut in Wheldon Lane with 115 pupils and 6
staff. The new building in nearby Healdfield Road, a florid, much-gabled
construction in dark red brick with an impressive central hall for gath-
erings and performances, opened the summer before Henry arrived. A
swimming pool had been deleted from the plans on the grounds of
economy; but a gymnasium, then a novelty, and more eccentrically an
Eton fives court were installed. By the time of Henry's arrival there would
have been some 230 pupils of both sexes.

By far the most remarkable feature of the school was its headmaster
T.R. Dawes, affectionately known as Toddy or just TRD. A Pem-
brokeshireman, he had previously been head of Pembroke Dock County
School for twelve years, and was forty-one when he came to Castleford.
Henry was extremely fortunate to come under the pervasive spirit of this
remarkable man, who was a good quarter-century ahead of his time in
his ideas of a liberal education. Dawes was in love with history, languages,
and the arts. He brought with him more than a whiff of continental
culture, having studied at both Bonn University and the Sorbonne.

To new pupils he could seem alarming, especially in one of his rages,
when he might charge across the Hall, hands clenched, tattered and
slightly mildewed gown flapping, pince-nez gleaming above his ragged
moustache. But his anger spent itself rapidly, and often its object would
be given a mint humbug when the tirade was over. Hostile to formal
timetables, he had in him a strong streak of the impresario. Each school
term had its big day on which parents came to watch their offspring
perform. In the autumn term, it was the school concert; in spring, the
Eisteddfod, a good Welsh import; in summer, Speech Day. The school
concert was the big one. Each form had its own production, and Dawes
insisted that every pupil, however untalented, should have a part of
sorts. Some Shakespeare was always on the programme: *A Midsummer
Night's Dream* was a favourite, as was the trial scene from *The Merchant
of Venice.* Such items doubtless helped foster Henry's lifelong affection for
the theatre, which reached its climax when he became a member of the
board of the new National Theatre in London.[25]

Dawes liked to invite distinguished public figures and musicians to the
school for talks and performances. Every summer he went to Germany
on holiday, sometimes taking a group of staff and pupils; and shortly
before the First World War he took the Castleford Brass Band to Paris,
where it won first prize in a competition and marched down the Champs
Elysées blowing with tempestuous vigour, as he later described it.[26] From
1921 onwards, he brought school and town yet closer together by

organizing a series of local history pageants in which many miners joined.

Of more immediate relevance to young Moore's burgeoning artistic proclivities was Dawes's interest in English church architecture. On a fine summer's day he would sometimes say to his class: 'I think we ought to go for a walk today.' Off they would go, sometimes with Mrs Dawes too, to see an interesting church, especially those at Ledsham and Methley, where Henry's large stout maternal aunt lived. Although he may have been familiar from family visits with the church in which his parents had been married, it was no doubt Dawes who drew his attention to its finer details. The genial headmaster commended as a guide to the order of English architectural styles the sentence 'Some Never Eat Dirty Potatoes' – Saxon, Norman, Early English, Decorated, Perpendicular. What struck Henry most forcibly, however, were the Gothic corbels: over-life-sized carved stone heads about twenty feet above the choir near the altar. There are eight large ones and two smaller ones – a devil with horns, a hideous old man with a huge nose and open mouth, an old lady with an anguished look, all rather caricatural. In a nearby side chapel lie some much more overtly attractive fifteenth-century effigy figures. The stillness and simplicity of these recumbent knights and their ladies also impressed Henry, but it was the grotesque corbels which he attempted to capture in some drawings done for pleasure. The lesson from Dawes was clear, and the apt pupil never forgot it: sculpture by fine English craftsmen abounds in churches and other public places, if only we have eyes to see it.

Even more important than Dawes was to be the art teacher he recruited and who arrived at the start of Henry's second year at grammar school. He had taken against the woman who taught him during the first year, a Miss Dowding. Asked, as at his primary school, to design a classroom timetable, he had drawn two figures supporting a central panel. Miss Dowding complained that the feet hung down in a frontal position (as in some medieval manuscripts), and ridiculed them to the class. Would his enthusiasm long have survived such wounding treatment? Help was at hand in the shape of Miss Alice Gostick. Her mother, who came to share her half-timbered house near the school, was French, gave piano recitals at school, and liked to be called Madame. Alice Gostick was in her early to mid-twenties when she arrived, probably straight from qualifying as an art teacher: a pleasant-looking woman with brown hair, full of enthusiasm yet gentle and generous.

Henry was not the only one of her charges to show a strong talent. There was Arthur Dalby, who arrived the same year as Miss Gostick. As a schoolboy he was a good all-rounder too. Later he became an inspector of art schools for the Ministry of Education, and died in 1960. The most precocious and sophisticated was Albert Wainwright, an exact contemporary of Henry's, cruelly nicknamed Pussy Wainwright. He was fascinated by Aubrey Beardsley's virtuoso draughtsmanship, and under his influence Henry too went through a very Beardsleyesque phase. Wainwright went on to specialize in theatre design, but died, aged forty, while working in Leeds. These three were friendly rivals for any commissions from Miss Gostick for magazine covers, stage costumes, posters and suchlike, and they were by no means the only talented ones.

As a leading member of the progressive Art Teachers Guild, Miss Gostick favoured a freer approach than was then common and a practical knowledge of the applied arts, especially pottery. Parents as well as children were later drawn in to her evening pottery classes. A favourite feature of these was painting pottery from Clokie's, which would then be burnished and fired back at the works, along with pots which her pupils and adult students made. Thus, like Toddy Dawes, she too became a well-known local figure. She also removed the customary barrier between home and school by inviting her pupils to her home in Park Avenue. With her French background and connections, she had about her an aura of continental sophistication. In her sitting room were fascinating art books and such influential art magazines as *Studio*, which had a European circulation and reproduced the work of the continental avant-garde. With the Cubist movement in full swing at this stage, some of these reproductions must have looked baffling, if exciting, to teenagers who had not ventured far from Castleford. Such matters could be freely discussed in the Gostick salon, and with his art teacher Henry built up a warm and confiding relationship which endured to her death more than half a century later.

Though strictly average academically, he was a good games player. The school's boys were divided into three houses, called Red, White and Blue, which was Henry's. The houses helped them to mix with other age groups, and were a handy basis for football and cricket teams. As a child, indeed well into his twenties, Henry was called Harry. At school, he was often called Buck, a nickname first applied to brother Raymond. Miss Gostick sometimes called him Hal, and he occasionally signed his early drawings Hal S. Moore. His school friend, Frank Ambler, saw him thus:

He was quite an ordinary boy, was Henry Moore, games-loving and fun-loving. You wouldn't have singled him out as a future famous artist at all. He was quite a decent lad on the right wing at football. I remember he once objected to the way I tackled him: he seemed to think I was getting in front of him and obstructing him, quite good-naturedly though ... he was quite a popular lad.[27]

Another contemporary and friend, Winnie Testin (later Alker), who also had a talent for art, recalled him as 'quiet, a few close friends, rather unobtrusive ... the girls did not find him attractive, he was just *there*. He never threw his weight around, and no thought or talk of being a sculptor.'[28] Assessments of physical attractiveness are notoriously subjective. What is not in doubt is young Henry, Harry, Buck or Hal's interest in the opposite sex, and especially in the contours of the female form. In the morning assembly, for example, the girls stood in front of the boys. 'If their bodies and features had been hidden by a board below which only their legs showed from the knees down, I could still have given a name to each pair,' he told his great friend, Herbert Read, in later life.[29] The mature sculptor ascribed this teenaged talent to his growing sense of form. However, not only budding sculptors are interested in girls' legs, and others may have studied form as retentively.

Henry's first proper carving and sculptural commission came in 1913 when, no doubt at Miss Gostick's suggestion, he was asked to produce a notice-board for the newly formed school Scott Society. Captain Scott's trip to the Antarctic was among Toddy Dawes's myriad enthusiasms. During its preparatory stage in 1909, the school collected money for the purchase of a husky dog or some other necessity, and the school's name was inscribed on the timbers of the *Discovery*. When Scott died in 1912, Dawes made his pupils learn his last words by heart. The Scott Society was formed following a visit to the school by one of the surviving members of the trip, Apsley Cherry-Garrard, as a society of adventure and discovery. Henry incised the words SCOTT SOCIETY 13 (for 1913, presumably) into the tough oak board, a sound and pleasing bit of amateur craftsmanship. It survives in the study of the present headmaster.

Around 1911, the Moore family moved from the cramped confines of 30 Roundhill Road to a larger house at 56 Smawthorne Lane, just around the corner and a wider, busier and smarter street. Brother Raymond had by then been contributing to the family income from his wages as a teacher. Annie had left to marry. Alfred had disappeared into the vastness of Canada. The financial position was thus better, and there may have been some pressure from the girls to move to a marginally pleasanter environment. Certainly the new house was roomier, with a good kitchen, dining room and sitting room on the ground floor, and three bedrooms upstairs. When the present owner, also a miner, stripped the lining paper off the sitting-room ceiling, he found paintings of fruit in each corner.[30] It is nice to imagine Henry emulating his hero Michelangelo's endeavours in the Sistine Chapel in this rather smaller context. Opposite the house stood The Smawthorne, a pub-cum-hotel; just up the road was the Smawthorne Working Men's Club, a bastion of boozy male solidarity.

Dreary though Castleford was and is, it was home to Henry and he knew no better place. The countryside was at hand. His school friends included farmers' sons. Sometimes he would help with the harvest on their farms, a deeply satisfying activity with the added excitement of seeing rabbits, hares, rodents, and birds leaping in alarm out of the cut corn. Henry later remembered with regret the cruelty of his companions when they caught a small and helpless creature.[31] He also went bird's-nesting and, more originally, searching for moth chrysalises to hatch out in matchboxes.

At the age of fifteen or sixteen he attended confirmation classes and passed through a religious phase: 'I remember very clearly the day I was confirmed, feeling so good and saintly as I walked down the aisle that I didn't walk, I floated about four feet off the ground . . . Confirmation was a very important happening in my feelings and emotional outlook.'[32] His zeal waned after a few months, but he continued to go to church on Sundays spasmodically until he joined the army in 1917.

In May 1914, three months before the outbreak of the First World War, the Moores bought for £230 a house a quarter of a mile up the hill towards the dramatic silhouette of Glasshoughton Colliery, at 37 Briggs Avenue. If, as seems likely, and as Betty recalled, they moved into it, this was a further improvement in environment. Briggs Avenue is a pleasant road, and was then on the edge of the countryside. Henry's school career was nearing its end, and in 1915 he took the 'senior Cambridge' examination, a sort of junior A-level certificate. The right grades qualified the candidate for college or university. Winnie Testin, who took the exams at the same time, recalled:

Mr Dawes was so wrapped up in ideas for this and that, he forgot to enter us, so we had to wait and then go to Archbishop Holgate's School in York for a week. The art test was to design a tile and draw from a model of cubes, cones, etc. The light was fading before we had finished, so the superintendent wrote an explanation on each paper, for we needed the shadows thrown by the blocks. We both gained Distinction in art, and I remember Toddy Dawes assembling the school and giving us a half holiday. Dalby also gained Distinction.[33]

The schoolteacher

According to Henry's school attendance certificate, he left on 26 July 1915, four days before his seventeenth birthday. By then, thanks in part to Alice Gostick's guidance and encouragement, he was bent on a career as a professional artist. His father, however, was understandably disapproving. Where was the security in such a life? He wanted his youngest son to follow brother Raymond's example and qualify as a teacher, either at the York training college or at Leeds University. If after that he still wanted to be a sculptor, well and good. First, he should acquire a solid qualification. So Henry found himself, as Raymond had been before him, assigned as a student teacher to his old elementary school at Temple Street (now called Half Acres Middle School). Because some teachers had gone off to the war, he was at it virtually full time:

> I think this was the most miserable period of my life. I was too young to know when the children were going to make fun of me and pull my leg and do their little stunts ... the girls were infinitely worse than the boys. They knew just how to make a boy of seventeen embarrassed in all sorts of ways. They'd weep and cry and sob ...[34]

The miners' sons could be downright nasty. Once, when Henry had kept a few boys in during playtime for a misdemeanour, they waited around a corner of the school building, ready to throw stones at him as he went home.[35]

Links with Castleford Secondary School remained strong, and it was in 1916 that he was asked to carve the school's Roll of Honour [10], a much larger task than the Scott Society board. On it were eventually to be listed in gold paint the names of the ninety-one old boys who served in the Great War, eight of whom lost their lives. Towards the end of the list come H. S. Moore, Civil Service Rifles; A. Dalby, Royal Naval Volunteer Reserve; and A. Wainwright, Royal Flying Corps. Henry carved the inscription at the top: Castleford Secondary School ROLL OF HONOUR, and the dates 1914–19– below, the war's conclusion remaining uncompleted. Miss Gostick lent him her carving tools, and on the reverse side, he practised with a crudely incised ABCD, adding perhaps on completion DESIGNED AND EXECUTED BY H. S. MOORE. Underneath he outlined a telling little cartoon of T. R. Dawes. Carving the main inscription into the oak panel must have been hard work. Frank Ambler remembered visiting the school woodwork shop and watching him at it. For years the roll of honour hung in the school's entrance hall, not least because Dawes was intensely patriotic: early on in the war he read out a telegram he had received from Lord Kitchener congratulating Castleford on producing so high a proportion of volunteers.

To mark the tercentenary of Shakespeare's death in 1916 Henry, Dalby and Winnie Testin painted life-sized figures in pastel of Shakespearean characters. These were arrayed on the walls of the balconies at either end of the school hall, and gazed down on assemblies there for several years. Winnie Testin did Portia and Ophelia, and a girl who arrived in 1917, Connie Hardy (later McOwat), remembered a vigorous figure from *Julius Caesar* by the young Moore, perhaps Brutus or Mark Antony.[36] Henry and his friends from Alice Gostick's art class used to exchange autograph books and draw in them. One such drawing by the seventeen-year-old Moore was later cut out and presented to the Castleford public library. It is an able copy in pencil and water-colour, measuring some three by five inches, of a Turner painting called *Ulysses Deriding Polyphemus*, and successfully conveys the Turneresque sense of atmosphere and light. Signed and dated 19/2/16, it was presented to the library by a contemporary who became Mrs L. Clark and lived in Leeds. It is interesting that Moore's admiration for Turner, which led to him becoming President of the Turner Society, should have begun so relatively young. Winnie Testin recalled a more personal drawing he did in the autograph book of another friend called Pansy Brook. It showed his mother wearing a fancy hat and veil.

Such exercises, along with Alice Gostick's evening pottery classes, were a welcome diversion from the frustrations and tedium of teaching. For an ambitious young man conscious of the war raging across the Channel, it was a trying time. Yet looking back on Henry's first seventeen years, we can see how lucky he had been. It would be hard to imagine a better combination of security and stimulus: the bedrock of his mother's love, his father's frustrated ambitions and high esteem for knowledge, Miss Gostick's perceptive support and tuition, Toddy Dawes's internationalism and many enthusiasms, a sense of belonging to Castleford and Yorkshire.

The foundations for success were all there. But as Herbert Read put it, a sculptor is born, not made.[37] It required a spark of genius as well as much strength of character for Henry Moore to become a name famous far beyond the grime of his native town,

Chapter II

Briefly to war

1917 to early 1919

Henry was a soldier for just two years, from February 1917 to February 1919. His reactions to the experience, not just at the time but in later life, were surprising:

> For me, the war passed in a romantic haze of hoping to be a hero. Sometimes in France there were three or four days of great danger when you thought there wasn't a chance of getting through, and then all one felt was sadness at having taken so much trouble for no purpose; but on the whole I enjoyed the army ...[1]

That was the sculptor in his mid-sixties looking back. Can this be the same Moore who responded in adult life so swiftly to human suffering? Can this be the same war which killed 750,000 British citizens and which gave us such literary classics as *All Quiet on the Western Front, Goodbye to All That, Her Privates We,* and the poems of Wilfred Owen? If we could pinpoint the answer to those questions we might be nearer to understanding the contradiction between Moore's apparent normality as a personality and the extraordinary nature of his work and achievement. At a superficial level, there are numerous possible explanations for his apparent insensitivity: emotional immaturity resulting from his relatively protected, mother-bound childhood; a youthful taste for adventure sharpened by the excitement of getting away from Castleford and the bonds of the family; and sheer good luck in the brevity of his exposure in the front line. At a deeper level, it seems likely that his antennae were already more sensitive than they seemed, but that he thrust the messages they received straight down into his subconscious, where they helped nourish the sources on which he was to draw so long and deeply. Given a more intellectual education, background, and disposition, he might have reacted like his later friend, Herbert Read. He, more maturely, did not want to be a hero but became one, subsequently laying out his experiences in prose of almost unbearable poignancy.[2] Words were Read's medium, as they have been for so much of the flower of British genius. Moore created through stone, wood, and bronze. His work would have been the poorer if he had ever expressed his innermost thoughts through his pen rather than with gouge or chisel.

Compulsory conscription for unmarried men aged between eighteen and forty-one was introduced in January 1916, softened by a promise that no one should be called up before he was eighteen and a half. Raymond Moore senior reckoned it would be better for Henry to join a regiment of his choice as a volunteer than wait to be conscripted, probably into the King's Own Yorkshire Light Infantry based at Pontefract nearby. A London regiment would furthermore provide the young Moore with wider horizons and social contacts. And so in February 1917, when he was in fact just over eighteen and a half, and no doubt expecting the dreaded summons any day, Henry said farewell to the family and Castleford and caught a train to the metropolis, armed with the addresses of two or three regiments which seemed suitable.

On the train he met a genial youth of his own age, Douglas Houghton, who was later to become a Labour government Cabinet minister and a life peer. Houghton was London-bound on the same mission. The son of a Nottingham lace-maker, he had been working in the Inland Revenue, a reserved occupation. 'We agreed that in going the rounds of the regiments we wanted to join, we shouldn't be separated: they couldn't take one and reject the other,' Lord Houghton recalled.[3]

It was Henry's first visit to London, and February cannot have been an agreeable month in which to make the capital's acquaintance. After spending the night in a room at 38 Oakley Crescent (now Oakley Gardens) in Chelsea, where he paid 3s. 6d. for tea, supper, bed and breakfast, he and Houghton presented themselves the following day at several recruiting centres. His first choice, for obvious reasons, was the Artists' Rifles regiment, but they turned him down as too short; so did the Inns of Court Officer Training Corps.[4] Houghton was no taller. The Honourable Artillery Company, originally Henry's second choice because some student friends of his had joined it, apparently considered them both too young. Houghton recalls snobbery playing its part:

> Everywhere we went they asked: 'What is your father?' Well, his was a coalminer and mine was a lace-maker. We hadn't got the social background, and it's difficult in these days to imagine the

kind of social distinction that was drawn when applying for a commission or anything that might lead to a commission.[5]

They were not in fact applying for a commission, but at the HAC in particular there was probably some prejudice against the sons of north-country manual workers.

Since Houghton was a junior civil servant he suggested they should try the Civil Service Rifles, and there they were at last accepted. They stayed overnight at the drill hall of the CSR at Somerset House on the Strand, and next day went down to the training unit at Hazeley Down, near Winchester in Hampshire. There they were kitted out, a dispiriting experience as soft civilian clothes were replaced by a coarse, ill-fitting uniform and the recruit felt submerged in the khaki anonymity of the barrack room.

The Civil Service Rifles' origins went back to 1798 and the threat of invasion by Napoleon, but its identity as such dated from 1907, when it was assigned to the London Regiment as its 15th battalion in the reconstituted territorial army. As the 1/15th it had been mobilized in 1914 and soon saw active service in France and Belgium. Two further battalions were later formed, and it was the 3rd Battalion which Moore and Houghton had now joined for their training.[6]

If 534592 Private Moore, of Hut 16C, 3rd Platoon, A Company was in any way downcast by his induction in His Majesty's forces, his natural resilience seemed to be in the ascendant by 12 February. Writing to Miss Gostick, he described a weekend walk over the Downs to Winchester, where he had tea and went to the pictures. On the Sunday he had been caught by cookhouse fatigues, which came around only once every two months, and he had cleaned some two hundred tin plates and mugs, and twenty or thirty big pans. Now they were getting into the full swing of squad drill, he reported. Three days previously he had collected his first army pay, amounting to one shilling ... 'for that we had to march up to a table, come to attention, salute, say our number, take our money, salute again and walk off (all for 1s.).'[7] He was sending home for his drawing things, he told her, in the belief that he would be able to do something in his spare time.

Over the next few weeks inoculations, vaccinations, and mud were the main banes of his life, cheerfully enough borne. The worst part of the mud was having to clean their boots twice a day, he wrote; luckily their sergeant was a jolly old chap who had been through the whole of the Boer War and sported a moustache, the ends of which were quite visible from behind. With all his equipment on, Henry declared, he felt like a walking saddler's shop, all belts, buckles and straps. Yet despite all that and having to get up at 6 a.m. 'it is much more preferable to me than teaching in a stuffy classroom.' All the men were 'grand fellows' and they got on well together.[8]

When spring came he found time, he later recalled, to visit London and see the National Gallery and British Museum for the first time.[9] No comments have survived. The tone of his letters to Miss Gostick is generally jocular, but sometimes a gentler side peeps out, as when he sends her some wild flowers picked on a walk: 'I thought more people than myself should share the joy of them.' At various stages she sent him cigarettes – he had started smoking in the army – sweets and cakes, and his old art class collectively sent him a wrist watch. Sometimes he sounds wistful as he thinks of his Castleford friends enjoying themselves while he is drilling and marching, but he longs to have news of them all. His drawing makes little headway, and despite the spring weather, some indian ink sent from home has scarcely been used, he laments in one of his regular but often undated letters to Alice. He attempts a correspondence course in drawing with the Press Art School, but gets bogged down in lesson six. Asked whether he would like a party given for him when he comes home on leave (in May, seemingly), he replies with touching realism:

> Well, I don't think I do, you know I should feel so much out of it when all the boys could dance except me, the only dance I can do properly is the polka, every dance would have to be a polka, and I don't think everyone would agree to that.[10]

In the event, that first home leave left him momentarily disenchanted with life at Hazeley Down:

> It does seem a rotten place after seeing all my old friends in Castleford, but it is gradually wearing off, I suppose it's home sickness. I don't know, I've never had it before, however I think I shall be totally recovered by tomorrow night, after an anticipated good time in Winchester.[11]

He bounced back quickly, despite a route march under a terribly hot sun: 'by the help of two combined factors, water (cold) & rest (absolute) I am feeling alright again.' He was evidently proud to have come third in the General Musketry course, scoring 103 out of 170 points and thus qualifying as a first-class shot. 'After two years service this will entitle

me to an extra sixpence a day, so it looks promising for me in two years
time, doesn't it!' he reported with irony. Of more immediate use, he had
found he could, for a small fee, play tennis on the court of a vicarage half
a mile from camp, in the village of Morestead. The vicar was a nice chap
of about forty who had shown them his collection of roughly 1,000 birds'
eggs, 'so you see I am getting acquainted with the élite of society down
here'.[12]

In what seems to have been his last letter to Alice Gostick from Hazeley
camp, probably written in July, he regrets not having seen anything in
the newspapers about a Castleford man's VC, and concludes: 'Heigh
Ho! for France and a jolly old "blighty" [meaning a wound causing
repatriation], fine time in hospital & then – the end of the war!!' It was,
as time proved, a pretty good forecast.

To the Front in France

Up to early 1918 it was the practice not to send conscripts abroad until they
were nineteen. Henry reached that age on 30 July 1917, while Douglas
Houghton, who had been for most of their training in a different platoon,
was just twelve days younger. The latter's recollection was that they
went out to France together in mid-August, from the port of Southampton
not far away. On arrival they were separated, Henry being sent to a quiet
sector near Arras for training in trench warfare. Precisely where and
when Private Moore joined up with the 1st Battalion of the CSR is not
clear. But from regimental histories we know that the 1st Battalion
had been involved in the capture of Messines Ridge that June, and had
subsequently been in and out of the Ypres salient.[13] Much of August had
been spent recuperating and retraining at a camp behind the front lines.
Pte Moore seems to have been sent forward for his first taste of action in
the second half of September, since at the end of the month he felt able
to write to his old school friend Albert Wainwright, though without
giving his location for security reasons:

I'm now in the Front Line trenches, I continue in some amazing way
to get about two hours sleep every night, the rest of the time is
taken up in sentry duty on the firestep. Things were rather lively
... last night, both sides were strafing, I don't know if we did
much damage, but they did not. The afternoon strafing is just
subsiding (now about 3.30 p.m.). There she goes, one of ours, an
18-pounder.

Saw two aerial fights this morning and two aeroplanes brought down in flames, oh things are getting exciting ...[14]

He ended the letter in the mock high-flown style in which young men often delight: 'I quite agree with you, undoubtedly Tempus Fugit (except on sentry) therefore most noble and puissant youth, Cheerio...' A neat deflation.

His tone was still determinedly larky when he wrote to Alice Gostick a week later from five miles behind the lines, though he still calls her Dear Miss Gostick:

We had a spell of 8 days in, 4 in the support line and 4 in the front line. We had it very quiet the first few days but after that things smartened up a little, we had a few selections rendered by the German big guns, the chief feature in them being the whizz-bang. The noise even during a small 'strafe' is hellish ...[15]

What little sleep they got was in their clothes and equipment, in cubby holes dug into the sides of the trenches. Otherwise they did firestep sentry duty, two at a time, one looking over the top, the other seated on the firestep ready for an emergency:

If one likes to let one's imagination run ahead one can be quite convinced that the barbed wire posts are forming fours, or advancing in line towards your trench. The only thing to do in that case is to divert one's gaze to some other object and it's ten to one that will also become animated, however you've to put up with it (unless the other sentry also thinks they are Huns) until the hour's duty is up.

He lamented the destruction of a nearby cathedral which he had visited with some friends and which censorship forbade him to name, and even more so the bombardment of Rheims cathedral: 'It's an absolute shame that such places should be destroyed, the Germans deserve all we can give them, yes & more if possible.' A fortnight later he was back in the trenches, telling Miss Gostick that he was 'ever so much more comfy out here than I thought I should be'; but he admits to a twinge of nostalgia for Castleford, which despite its notoriety for dinginess and smoke, 'has a unique attraction when one is away from it'.[16] Comfy is not a word frequently applied to the trench war in France. But Henry was wonderfully adaptable, and on 14 November could even write that he was having a 'jolly good time' doing a course (unspecified) at the Brigade school. He was sorry not to have received the cigarettes she had sent, but 'some poor beggar may have got them who needed them much more so than I'.

On 18 November the battalion was taken by train to a camp at Ecoivres, where two days later, in the middle of a rugby match, news arrived of the 3rd Army's dramatically successful deployment of tanks in an ambitious assault on Cambrai. Tanks were still regarded as a brilliant new weapon, and four hundred of them had led the attack by the six divisions of Sir Julian Byng's 3rd Army. The Germans were taken by surprise, and the British forces achieved a deeper penetration than in any past offensive. But all Byng's forces had been thrown into the first assault. Adequate reinforcements were not forthcoming, and the advance was halted several miles short of Cambrai. A series of bitterly fought local actions ensued the following week as the Germans prepared their counterstroke. Along the northern flank of the new salient, the villages of Bourlon and Fontaine Notre Dame changed hands several times, and it was into this fiercely contested zone that the Civil Service Rifles were about to be pitched two days before the big German push.[17]

On 28 November, Henry's battalion moved up to relieve the 2nd Dismounted Cavalry and the 2/5th West Yorkshires at Bourlon Wood, which they reached at about 2 a.m. the following day. The four companies consolidated their positions through the 29th, at a cost of fifty-five casualties. The full-scale horror of a major German assault was then unleashed on the CSR. First came a short, heavy bombardment with gas and smoke. As one witness later described it:

> The gas in Bourlon Wood hung in the trees and bushes so thickly that all ranks were compelled to wear their respirators continuously if they were to escape the effects of the gas. But men cannot dig for long without removing them, and it was necessary to dig trenches to get away from the persistent shell fire. Throughout November 30th there was, therefore, a steady stream of gassed and wounded men coming through the regimental aid posts. Their clothes were full of gas . . .[18]

That morning the main waves of the enemy infantry were passing diagonally across the CSR's front, but the Germans' low-flying planes seemed to swarm 'like bees' over the area, inflicting many casualties with strafing machine-gun fire. It was probably one of these which inspired the incident Henry remembered most clearly from the attack on Bourlon Wood and which bulked largest, with minor variations, in his later reminiscences of those days:

I was the No. 1 with a Lewis gun team: it was a little machine-gun not as powerful as the big ones. Each gun had a corporal, a No. 1 and five others. The Germans were bombing and I was sure I could hit one. At last I got the officer to say yes, I could have a go, but I must move off to avoid drawing fire. We went 40 or 50 yards off. It was like trying to bring down a house that was moving over your head at 80 mph, except you could only hit one or two bricks: you had to get the pilot or the engine. We found a bottle of rum in one pothole. The corporal got tight and I had to take control. We had to take off one of the men who had got shell shock. I said, Come on, we are going to run. It looked as if *he* was pulling *me*! The lance corporal got the medal and I didn't. But I was young and it was all romantic, heroic excitement.[19]

Sometimes, as if conscious that the story showed a measure of thoughtlessness, he would add 'I was the daftest!'[20] Regret at not getting the medal shows through.

Precisely when this episode took place is uncertain, as is the basis of the statistic with which Henry would round off the story: that when the battle was over, only 52 of the 400 men of his regiment were able to muster. What is not in doubt is that he was exceedingly lucky to survive. Among the desperate actions of a desperate day was a bid by the CSR's Colonel Segrave to save some men on the battalion's left from being cut off and encircled. It involved moving the battalion HQ and A Company, to which Henry may well have belonged, in two waves across open country, under heavy fire. It was done like an exercise on Salisbury Plain, the colonel with his map in one hand and whistle in the other, giving his directions by signal.[21] The losses that day, according to the battalion's handwritten war diary, were 39 other ranks killed, 120 wounded and 40 missing, with 2 officers killed and 8 wounded.[22] By the time the 1st Surrey Rifles arrived in the night of 1 December, overall losses were put at 12 officers and 278 other ranks. The CSR battalion, its effective strength reduced from some 500 men to 200 of all ranks, withdrew to tents at Fémy Wood.[23]

That was the end of Henry Moore's active war service, a brief but grim experience. He was among those who had begun to feel and show symptoms of mustard-gas poisoning. After reporting to the regimental aid post he was obliged to walk some ten miles with his fellow sufferers to the field hospital in the rear. That helped to work the gas well and truly into his system, and after being put to bed he was sent back to

England as a stretcher case.[24] He had got his 'blighty', though probably not the sort he expected.

Convalescence and retraining

Moore was to spend the next six weeks or so recuperating in the Lansdowne Road hospital in Cardiff, South Wales. From there he wrote to Alice Gostick on 3 January 1918, perky as ever:

> You ask me how I'm 'suffering'. Well, I get up at half-past seven in the morning, breakfast at eight, write letters, read, smoke or do anything that takes my fancy until dinner at twelve. After dinner (which is generally A1), get ready and take a car into Cardiff. Picture houses, theatres, matinees, etc. Tea in Cardiff. Back in hospital (supposed to be) at five. Smoke and read or several of us sing (accompanied on the piano) in the corridor. Lights out 8 o'clock (supposition again).

The combination of smoking and singing does not sound ideal for a patient recovering from being gassed, and his voice was from then on prone to huskiness. In moments of strong emotion it sometimes failed him altogether.

A letter of six days later (Henry having by now graduated to addressing her as My dear Miss Gostick) suggests that he was about to be moved to a convalescent hospital near Swansea, and that his old art teacher was trying to get him into one nearer home.[25] No clear record or memory of his movements is available until we find him at a vast convalescent camp on the Downs at Shoreham-by-Sea in Sussex to which, coincidentally, Douglas Houghton had also been sent. Suffering from a medically baffling affliction called trench fever, Houghton had been repatriated to a hospital in Ipswich in early 1918. At Shoreham they both volunteered for a physical training course at Mill Hill School on London's north-western fringes. After two or three weeks at this preliminary course for instructors they transferred to the Army Headquarters gymnasium and physical instruction training centre at Aldershot in Surrey. 'Over the main entrance,' Lord Houghton recalled, 'was a legend which I once quoted in the House of Commons against Gerald Nabarro [a notoriously opinionated Conservative MP of the fifties and sixties and self-made millionaire]: 'Be not wise in your own conceit, there is more hope of a fool.'[26]

The course of about a month at Aldershot took their training as instructors several stages further, most of which the future chairman of the Parliamentary Labour Party found 'highly unpleasant':

> There were bayonet assault courses, jumping out of trenches, going
> over the top, open warfare, all that kind of thing, as well as the nor-
> mal exercises for physical fitness – running and jumping, the sort
> of thing one gets at school. Henry got quite a lot of fun out of our
> experiences. I was probably made unduly unhappy by physical
> discomfort and being pushed around.[27]

A passing-out photograph marking the end of the course shows Moore
and Houghton, nearing twenty but still looking youthful, with their
twelve fellow soldiers and the officer, sergeant-major and sergeant who
had instructed them, arms crossed to emphasize muscles, chest, and
shoulders perhaps. From Aldershot they both rejoined the training battalion of the CSR, which had by now moved from Hazeley Down to
Wimbledon, in suburban south London. Promoted to the acting rank of
lance-corporal, they there instructed two categories of soldiers: new
recruits, some now well into their thirties; and repatriated servicemen
from overseas needing to be restored to fitness before rejoining their unit
abroad. As Houghton recalled, the older age groups predominated, and
he and Henry noticed how much more supple the younger ones were.

L/Cpl Moore was a specialist bayonet instructor. Not only was the
battle course very tough, but the instructor had to put on a great show
of toughness:

> You jumped down into a trench, stabbed a sack of tight straw and
> climbed up the side of the trench again. I had to teach the recruits
> how to do it, viciously and violently. Sometimes they were young
> officers. One was so polite and gentle. Instead of getting down there
> and saying 'You bloody bastard' or something, he said 'Bother
> you!'[28]

He also started some off-duty boxing, having enjoyed bouts at school,
and was happy to do a few demonstration rounds. He could take a lot of
punishment without feeling any pain, and retained an active interest in
the sport well into middle age.[29]

Henry was lucky not to have been sent back to France himself when
fit enough. Apart from his continued survival, the main legacy of his six-
odd months at the Wimbledon training battalion was physical fitness. He
already had a good physique. Wimbledon gave him added strength and
enhanced the powers of endurance which he believed he had inherited
from his indefatigable mother. As Barbara Hepworth was to show, a

sculptor does not have to be of powerful stature. But physical toughness can be no disadvantage, especially when much lifting is involved.

Shortly before the Armistice was signed on 11 November 1918, Henry volunteered to return to his old battalion in France. He arrived soon after peace had broken out, and was billeted in the village of Ferfay, some 15 kilometres from Béthune and thus well north-west of the Cambrai area. Ferfay was 'squallid', he wrote to Albert Wainwright on 2 January 1919, some six weeks after his arrival. It had one main street consisting of shops, estaminets, chip shops, and barns, in which most of the soldiers were billeted. One 'palliative feature' was that it was in a mining district and so reminded him of home. Though he had lost his acting stripe as a lance-corporal on posting, he was billeted in greater comfort than the majority, at the home of M. and Mme Caron, who worked in the mines, and their son René:

> She is hard-working, goodhearted, generous, with a peasant sense of humour. She calls me each morning (when she does not forget) & before embarking on the sea of my ephemeral duties I partake of her hospitality in the shape of a steaming coffee ... In return I am general housemaid, I chop sticks, get water & coal, wash or wipe dishes & plates and shop. Every Tuesdays, Thursdays and Saturdays I go to the Boulangerie and return each time with four huge loaves – my French is improving perceptibly.[30]

A vivid pen sketch alongside showed Mme Caron at her sewing machine. With Henry *chez* Caron was a soldier called Allen, evidently monoglot and clodhopping, whose efforts to communicate with Madame were described – and illustrated – by Henry with relish: a neat drawing caught them gesticulating at each other.

As a teacher, and moreover one with a territorial rather than a regular regiment, Henry was entitled to early demobilization. He recalled being among the first batch of ten in his regiment to be sent home, played down to the railway station by the regimental band.[31] Having returned to England and Castleford in February 1919, he resumed teaching at Temple Street elementary school in March. There were no difficulties in keeping order now for the ex-PT and bayonet instructor: 'I had complete and absolute control.'[32]

Miss Gostick had found out all about ex-servicemen's grants. With her advice and help he successfully applied for one, and secured a place at Leeds School of Art for the forthcoming academic year. So that he would not arrive there 'absolutely raw' in September, he attended evening classes three nights a week during the remainder of the spring and summer terms. Part of the intervening summer vacation seems to have been spent with Alice Gostick, Albert Wainwright, and Arthur Dalby at Beaumaris on the east coast of Anglesey, north Wales.[33]

For Henry Moore it had been a lucky war, with little more than two months exposure off and on to front-line fighting, and only a few days' experience of the horrors of full-scale battle. Looking back in the 1940s on his army days he observed: 'It was in those years that I broke finally away from parental domination, which had been very strong.'[34] Two years away from home had matured him. His knowledge of human nature had been vastly enlarged by sharing the joys and sufferings of his fellow soldiers in barrack rooms, tents, and trenches, and by sizing them up as an instructor. The bedrock of common sense and realism which marked his career was being formed. Yet intellectually and in some other respects he was still unfledged and callow. Those letters from France, so refreshingly free from self-pity, showed a high degree of self-absorption and a curious unawareness of the wider tragedy of the war. No twenty-year-old with a trained mind and a cultivated background could have penned them. Artists, however, work with more than the front of their mind. It is impossible to answer the hypothetical question: would Moore's work have been significantly different if he had not fought in the First World War? He appeared to walk away from it entirely unscarred emotionally. Yet at the deepest level, it must have taken its toll. Arguably Moore's response to suffering, both personally and in his later work, would have been less impressive had he not seen so much of it in the front line in France. It is tempting to see a link between the fallen bodies of his army comrades and the cadaverous, hole-pierced forms of his reclining figures from the mid-thirties onwards.

Chapter III

Art student in Leeds

1919–21

Henry Moore was some six weeks past his twenty-first birthday when in September 1919 he walked (probably bounded) up the front steps of Leeds School of Art into its pillared entrance hall. It was a venerable age by normal art student standards. Yet he was several years younger than many war veterans who were then crowding into higher education. At Leeds, as at other art schools, students were also accepted when only fifteen or sixteen years old. That year's intake was therefore particularly varied.

Henry's eyes were already, at least as he later judged, roving ambitiously ahead:

> This was understood from the outset merely to be a first step. London was the goal. But the only way to get to London was to take the Board of Education examinations and win a scholarship ... Leeds school was very proficient in teaching tricks of getting through examinations.[1]

Impatient though he was, Henry was also grateful that the war had given him more confidence in his own judgement: 'I was very lucky not to have gone to art school until I knew better than to believe what the teachers said.'[2] Yet if the course was destined to be tediously academic, he knew that he had to acquire a body of examinable skills. True ability would win through, however grim the ordeal ahead.

At least the art school's building was exceptionally pleasant. Situated in Cookridge Street, a few minutes uphill from Leeds City Art Gallery and the monumental Victorian town hall in The Headrow, it was completed in 1903, and its clean, uncluttered lines reflect the Arts and Crafts movement's reaction against Victorian pomposity. Leeds itself was still Yorkshire's commercial metropolis, benefiting from cheap local coal, a good transport network, and fertile surrounding countryside. Trams plied down the main street of Briggate, though there was talk of removing them to make more room for carriages and motor cars. Away from the handsome if grimy centre there were rows of mean back-to-back houses. In such areas tuberculosis was still a scourge, bow-legged and under-nourished children played in cobbled streets, and 'rat fortnights' yielded large harvests. Fond son that he was, Henry decided to commute from home rather than take a room in the town, thus also saving money.

On his first day at college he met a slightly older fellow entrant called Raymond Coxon, who came from Rudyard in Staffordshire. They soon became like brothers:

> Harry and I met in the lavatory. We both had brand new serge suits on: it was a sort of mark of respectability. I thought his eye had a twinkle, and he was cheerful and had a nice taste for a smutty story. There was a sort of gaiety about us, but it didn't interfere with our will to get a lot done quickly. We were aiming at Michel-angelo and Titian, nothing less. We were trying to make up for the lost time in the army. We were young, and we were thankful to God Almighty that we had survived.[3]

Both Coxon and Moore were doing the two-year drawing course in one year. Among the disciplines involved were architectural drawing; drawing from memory, from the life and from the antique; and perspective drawing. Though some of these were valuable techniques to master, Henry was no doubt justified in resenting the narrow, technical spirit in which they were taught. The drawing teacher Walter Pearson had very strict rules. Shading had to be at an angle of 45 degrees – any other would be criticized. He knew what the Inspector wanted:[4]

> We were set to draw from the antique such things as the Boy and Goose, which is a late Roman copy of a Greek work, and we had to draw the Discobulus. Now I didn't have the slightest bit of interest in these sculptures, and there was a stage when in the first week or two at the school of art I thought: 'Well, is it me that doesn't know what sculpture is? Is there something wrong with me that I don't like these pieces?'[5]

Later he realized that they were indifferent sculptures, and that their contours had become blurred by twenty years of whitewashing.

The chief model was an elderly Italian who had been engaged from London and stayed with them the entire year. 'We got sick of the sight of him,' Coxon recalled; and Henry later wondered whether his over-exposure to this unappealing male figure helped predispose him to con-centrate almost exclusively on the female form.[6] There was considerable excitement at the beginning of the second year when a beautiful girl was hired. The students had to withdraw to their basement common room while Mr Pearson posed her. Then he would come down and announce with his stammer, 'Aaaah, the model is posing.' He was considered a decent and kindly man who did his best in his conscientious Quaker way for his students. His ambition was to get them to London, and in achieving that he was very successful. The principal was Hayward Ryder, in Moore's memory an eminence whom one saw rarely and who spoke little. Perhaps he had not recovered from losing his only son in the war.[7]

The art school's timetable meant a long day for the students, since there was a life-drawing class between 7 and 9 p.m. Henry would catch the 8.10 a.m. train from Castleford, always sitting in the front compartment with old school friends who were studying at Leeds Uni-versity. There was Frank Ambler, who was reading chemistry and eventu-ally became deputy headmaster of Castleford Secondary School; Donald Lawson, doing medicine, who became an ophthalmologist and married another school friend, Pansy Brook; and Kenneth Gee, who was reading languages and like Ambler became a teacher. The art school's day began at 9.30 a.m., stopped at 4 p.m. and started again at 7 p.m. Henry spent the three-hour gap with Coxon, who had lodgings in the Caledonian Road, and recalled:

> After perhaps watching a horse pulling a load of coal up the hill –
> we had to do drawings of figures in motion – we rushed back to
> Caledonian Road, where most of the university students lived. The
> first thing we did was to lie on the bed, exhausted and depressed
> by the gap between performance and ambition. It became a habit:
> silent, not a word spoken. Then the bell went in the basement and
> we went down and had a good Yorkshire tea, by the end of which
> we were back again full of ambition and tea; it was like an evening
> dinner, but with tea. Then we descended the hill to the school's
> reference library, where we studied the subjects which we thought
> we might need, history of art and so on.[8]

A surviving bundle of Henry's notes on the history of sculpture testifies to the seriousness of his studies. It covers the ground from Assyrian, Egyptian, Chaldean, and Babylonian sculpture to Greek and Roman, and there are also extensive notes on Greek, Roman, Byzantine, Renaissance, and Gothic architecture. He dwells on the intensity of Michelangelo's conceptions and the vitality of his ideas, which enabled him to express emotion in a monolithic mass; and notes approvingly that though Michelangelo excelled in painting, he chose sculpture for his revelation of fresh emotions – or rather 'unrealized aspects of emotions which are as old as civilization'.[9]

If Coxon's humour and ability helped to make him Henry's closest friend at Leeds, there were other students of talent and personality. One of the most attractive was Edna Ginesi, who came from Horsforth five miles away and had had an Italian great-grandfather. Since she hated the name Edna, she was always known as Gin. With Henry and Coxon, she would walk to Leeds railway station in the evenings. Henry would catch the 9.25 to Castleford, often doing homework till 1 a.m., while she returned to Horsforth and Coxon to his lodgings. Henry fell in love with her later, but she married Coxon. The triangular friendship survived.

Then there was Vivian Pitchforth, from Wakefield, who became a respected landscape painter and an outstanding teacher. He was three years older than Moore and had arrived the previous year, having lost his hearing in the artillery. Barbara Hepworth, also from Wakefield, arrived the following year three months before her eighteenth birthday. As if to demonstrate that all generalizations about the formation of serious sculptural talent are of doubtful value, she came from a very different background to the miner's son from Castleford: her father was the county surveyor of the West Riding of Yorkshire, and her mother a typically county woman, a social gap which would have been more noticeable in those days. Like Moore and Coxon, she did the drawing course in one year, then moved down with them, Gin and others in autumn 1921 to the Royal College of Art in London. She was a slim, attractive girl with a forehead bulging with intelligence, and Henry had a 'little flirtation' with her at Leeds.[10] In the thirties, she was to become, in a quiet way, his only serious competitor among his English contemporaries, a situation he did not entirely welcome. Others who came down to the Royal College were Horace Brook, known as Buggins, and Jack Elvin, a dark-haired, cheerful ex-sailor who was a talented draughtsman. Moore and Coxon were, however, the stars. At the end of that first year of drawing, there was a competitive exhibition of students' work, assessed without identification. Three prizes were awarded for each of nine categories, and Moore and Coxon won a third of them. Henry accounted for five, including that for dress design: he had a conspicuously good and slightly Victorian sense of pattern. 'It was his versatility which impressed me. It was marvellous,' Coxon recalled.[11]

That confident sense of design was also deployed at Alice Gostick's Castleford Peasant Pottery classes, which Coxon too sometimes joined. A few pieces decorated with considerable panache have survived. During weekends and holidays Henry remained involved in the cosy Castleford scene, playing football, tennis, and even some Eton fives at his old school, and winning the mixed tennis doubles of the Old Legiolians (named after the Latin name for Castleford) with his elder sister Mary against Frank Ambler and his sister Dorothy. He was active too in the field of theatre, in which Toddy Dawes had so effectively aroused his interest, even to the point of writing and starring in a play.

Narayana and Bhataryan by 'Harry Spencer Moore', with costumes and stage pictures by Albert Wainwright, was heavily influenced by the incantatory orientalism of James Elroy Flecker, then fashionable. It was performed for the first time at Castleford Grammar School in 1920. Henry designed the programme cover and played Bhataryan. His sister Mary was his stage sister Narayana, whom he was to save from being sacrificed to the hippopotamus goddess Chandrasati, heroically dispatching the hippo himself. A senior teacher Miss N.D. Lloyd, known as Pap on account of her large breasts, played his mother. Toddy Dawes had a small part, and the chemistry master was in charge of the gas lighting, which involved mirrors, a stick of burning carbon, and messenger boys plying between the projectionist and the stage manager.

The prologue, spoken by Albert Wainwright, set the tone all too clearly:

> It is the sad tale of Zabibi, And of her daughter, Naryana, And of her son, Bhataryan – Journeying through the arid desert From a land of singing-birds, And scented winds, Journeying to a land of rock-bound temples, Devout priests, A king And councillors, Carven Gods and Goddesses, Sacred Fruits and Flowers – A land of strange happenings – of sacrifice and song. Of death and celestial life. Listen to this strange story, Look upon these strange sights, And when your heart is turned to pity, Forget ... perhaps it is only A dream!

One of the boys roped in to help with the complicated lighting arrangements was E.J. Winfield, later Castleford's public health officer and a keen amateur actor. The play was considered very avant-garde, he remembered, and was the subject of much ribaldry in the fourth form:

For some weeks afterwards people would call out to one another: 'Is the great red moon purple tonight, my son?' It was a sign of death, but it became a kind of catch-phrase. The reply would come back: 'No, mother, the moon is still red.'[12]

The play was staged again in 1922 at the Easter Social of the Royal College of Art, as an entertainment put on by the first-year students or Freshers. This time Henry produced it and designed the sets.[13] Coxon played a prominent part, no doubt to hilarious effect. It is by no means clear how seriously Moore intended it to be taken. A recent revival in Leeds, staged as an act of homage, left the impression that it could have been very funny if camped up.[14] Connie Hardy, who was at school at the time of the Castleford production, reckoned that Henry had helped Wainwright design and paint the scenery, and that it had been used for an earlier school production of *The Merchant of Venice*. She recalled too a poster he executed for a Wainwright production of *Julius Caesar* in 1921, and a demonstration of batik which the same two old boys gave the art class shortly afterwards, using pure silk, wax candlegrease, and dyes of brilliant hues.[15]

Some early influences

If Moore's career as a sculptor did not deprive the world of letters of a major talent, this was a phase when reading meant much to him. Having absorbed every novel of Thomas Hardy's when he was seventeen or eighteen, he was now greatly excited by the masters of the Russian novel, especially Dostoevsky, and by the work of that other, very different, miner's son D. H. Lawrence: *Sons and Lovers* had appeared in 1913, *The Rainbow* (which was prosecuted for obscenity) two years later, and *Women in Love* in 1921. All these writers had a considerable influence, Henry reckoned, in shaping his outlook and intellectual development.[16]

Undoubtedly such reading helped to accelerate the maturing process. Of more direct relevance to his artistic evolution were his contacts with the most remarkable figure in the cultural life of Leeds, Professor Michael Sadler, Vice-Chancellor of Leeds University from 1911 to 1922. Sir Michael, as he later became, was exceptional in his day for having a passionate appreciation of modern painting and sculpture and for collecting it with great discernment. He had bought the work of Cézanne, Gauguin, Daumier, Courbet, and others before 1914, and in 1912 had visited Wassily Kandinsky, one of the pioneers of abstract painting, in

Bavaria and bought several of his works. He had even persuaded his son, who became a well-known novelist, to translate Kandinsky's influential theoretical tract *Über das Geistige* ('*The Art of Spiritual Harmony*').[17] Works by these and other modern masters hung in his Leeds residence. There were, for example, six Matisses which he had bought after helping to organize an exhibition of that artist's work at the Leicester Galleries in London in 1918.[18] Sir Michael also collected African art: thanks in part to the studies of German academics, this had by now been a source of excitement and inspiration to artists on the Continent, and especially in Paris, for more than two decades, without making much impact in insular Britain.

With such enthusiasms it was natural for him to invite the most talented students from the school of art to share his pleasure with them. At the Sadler home, Moore had his first contact with fine original examples of modern art, being particularly struck by the work of Van Gogh and Gauguin.[19] Later, Sadler became one of his patrons, buying several early carvings and drawings and, as Master of University College, Oxford, introducing such undergraduates as Stephen Spender to the wide-ranging delights of contemporary art.[20]

His contribution to Leeds was well summarized by the art critic and painter Roger Fry, whose writings were to help shape Moore's development:

> Every time I came to Leeds I got more and more impressed with the work Sir Michael was doing. He had civilized a whole population. The entire spirit had changed from a rather sullen suspicion of ideas to a genuine enthusiastic intellectual and spiritual life. He showed what *can* be done, but rarely is, by education.[21]

Fry had become the leading protagonist in England of modern French painting when he staged two sensational shows of post-Impressionist work in London in 1910 and 1912 respectively. The first had included twenty-one Cézannes, thirty-six Gauguins, twenty-two Van Goghs, some work by the Fauves, oils and bronzes by Matisse, and two Picassos. The second ran to forty-one Matisses and sixteen Picassos, including Cubist works. The tremors from these seismic explosions of Parisian genius must have reached Miss Gostick's sitting room in Henry's school-days. Sadly, but inevitably, the Great War had snuffed out the spirit of adventure and discovery which they had helped engender in British art in the pre-war period; but Fry now returned to the charge with a collection of essays which was to influence a generation of young talent. Leeds's reference library acquired its copy of *Vision and Design*, as the seminal work was called, in January 1921, just a few weeks after publication.

Reading Fry's essays even today is a stimulating experience, since they are written with an enviable blend of fluency, liveliness, and erudition. In Henry's day, when so much of their content was heretical and icono-clastic, it must have been intoxicating. He came across the book while searching for something else – 'the most lucky discovery', he later called it.[22] As we have seen, he had already been troubled by his response, or lack of it, to the Graeco-Roman tradition as represented by the art school's plaster casts. Here, especially in Fry's essays on primitive sculpture, he found confirmation of the soundness of his instincts. The famous essay on Negro sculpture had started as a review of an exhibition in 1920 at the Chelsea Book Club in London. It opened stirringly:

> What a comfortable mental furniture the generalizations of a century ago must have afforded! What a right little, tight little, round little world it was when Greece was the only source of culture, when Greek art, even in Roman copies, was the only indisputable art, except for some Renaissance repetitions![23]

Fry went on to argue, more headily still, that 'certain nameless savages' possessed the power to create plastic form to a higher degree than the English had ever possessed it, even in the Middle Ages. African sculpture, for example, made fuller use of the special qualities of sculpture: 'They have complete plastic freedom: that is to say, these African artists really conceive form in three dimensions.' That three-dimensionality, often underlined by exaggerations of form, and the black man's 'exquisite taste in his handling of material' were to be crucial concepts for Moore in his early years as a sculptor, as they had been already for continental artists like Picasso, Matisse, and Modigliani, alerted to them by visits to the Musée de l'Homme, and by ethnologists.

Linking *Vision and Design* to what he later saw at the British Museum, Henry was to comment: 'Once you'd read Roger Fry, the whole thing was there.'[24] Some of Fry's theorizings are confusing and contradictory. But his broad message was clear enough: the telling use of formal relation-ships is the principal source of aesthetic enjoyment. Form becomes 'sig-nificant' when it reflects the artist's effort to convey his passionate convictions through some intractable material. The doctrine of expressive or significant form, which the critic Clive Bell also espoused, linked the high points of art together. It led Fry to savour, for example, the impact of Masaccio's frescoes in Florence in the same manner as the tightly knit massiveness of Cézanne, both subsequently so dear to Moore's heart and art.

By the time Henry came upon the Fry book he was well into his second year, after his prize-laden completion of the drawing course. Instead of moving on to painting, like Coxon – his experiments with oil paint and canvas had not excited him – he asked to do sculpture. That created some difficulties. The sculpture department had evidently been closed down during the war, and none existed. So a young graduate of the Royal College of Art in London was brought in to start one up. That was probably not done solely with Moore in mind, since Reginald Cotterill also took part-time students and evening classes. He had been in the army, and, Henry reckoned, was probably about five years older than his main full-time pupil:

> He looked after me like a child. He was always breathing down my neck, but in a way this was a help, because I got through the two-year course in one year, as well as winning a Royal exhibition [scholarship] ... Cotterill was an intelligent person and a good teacher.[25]

Henry could thus master all the tricks of the trade which Cotterill had learned in London, but the emphasis was almost exclusively on modelling in clay. Carving was not taught. Two small, painted plasters from those Leeds days have survived. One shows a well-muscled but elderly man with knees half bent and head twisted around on to his right shoulder, a somewhat contrived pose. The other is a fully modelled figure of a seated, brooding young man of melancholy mien, arms crossed on raised knees. It is wholly conventional.[26] Even so, the signs of talent were there. As part of his final examination he had to model a hand; later, if his memory was correct, this was sent around to other art schools to show how it should be done.[27] But then he had been fortunate, he admitted, in having the undivided attention of his teacher, unlike those in the painting school.

The scholarship, one of ten awarded annually from the proceeds of an exhibition of Queen Alexandra's wedding gifts, was worth £90 a year. That would make him one of the better-off students at the RCA; Raymond Coxon, for example, received a miserable £50 for his bursary from Staffordshire County Council. Details like this helped boost his already surging morale. By the time he left Leeds, he knew he was good. But was he good simply by Leeds standards? How would he measure up against his contemporaries in the capital? He had still done no carving, and his drawing and modelling showed as yet no hint of what was to come. London, in those days, was not just the centre of creative activity, but drained off the best talent from the provinces. Henry Moore was impatient to be there.

Chapter IV

Student in London and abroad

1921–5

For an able and ambitious Yorkshire lad, to be in London in the early 1920s must have been an exhilarating experience. The Great War, whose horrors were fading in the public memory, had paved the way for some liberating social changes. Women had done men's work in the factories and were in no mood to return to their old status. Morals and underwear had loosened, hemlines were rising. It was the time of bobbed hair, sun-bathing, the Charleston, jazz, swing, and the Bright Young Things. Cars gave a new freedom of movement: there were half a million in Britain by 1925, though horse-drawn vehicles were still widespread. Radios brought entertainment to the masses throughout the country. A certain determined enjoyment was in the air, and no doubt it served to heighten Henry's delight at being alive and in the centre of all good things:

For the first year I was in a dream of excitement. When I rode on the open top of a bus I felt I was travelling in Heaven almost, and that the bus was floating in the air. And it was Heaven all over again in the evening, in the little room that I had in Sydney Street. It was a dreadful room, the most horrible little room that you can imagine, and the landlady gave me the most awful finnan haddock for breakfast every morning, but at night I had my books, and the coffee stall on the Embankment if I wanted to go out to eat, and I knew that not far away I had the National Gallery and British Museum and the Victoria and Albert with the reference library where I could get at any book I wanted. I could learn about all the sculptures that had ever been made in the world. With the £90 a year that I had in scholarships I was one of the real rich students at the College and I had no worries or problems at all except purely and simply my own development as a sculptor.[1]

Though Henry was not to know it, the Royal College of Art in South Kensington was a place of solid, unglamorous endeavour. Its origins went back to 1837, when it was founded at Somerset House in the Strand as the government-sponsored school of design. It moved to its present site by the then still unbuilt Victoria and Albert Museum in 1863, finally becoming the Royal College of Art in 1896. There were four schools: architecture, painting, sculpture, and design, and the aim was to provide three-year full-time courses for students who had done at least three years' training elsewhere. The sculpture school was a brisk ten- to fifteen-minute walk from the main buildings, located then as now half-way down Queen's Gate in some hutments built to receive casualties of the Boer War, and used for the same purpose in the First World War.

In the decades before Henry's arrival the Royal College had been eclipsed by the Slade School of Fine Art, which produced most of the leading painters of the time including Augustus and Gwen John, William Orpen, Harold Gilman, Wyndham Lewis, Matthew Smith, Duncan Grant, C. R. W. Nevinson, Mark Gertler, Stanley Spencer, Edward Wadsworth, Paul Nash, Ben Nicholson, and David Bomberg. That pre-eminence was largely due to the high standards and pulling power of Professor Henry Tonks, an irascible advocate of fine draughtsmanship. The Slade did not however award the diplomas required for teaching.

In 1919 H. A. L. Fisher, President of the Board of Education under Lloyd George, decided the prestige of the Royal College should be raised, and invited his old friend William Rothenstein, who believed in excellence, to become its principal. The two men had met in Paris, where Rothenstein (fresh from the Slade) was honing his precocious gifts as a portraitist at the Académie Julian and getting to know such painters and writers as Degas, Pissarro, Whistler, Bonnard, Vuillard, Verlaine, and Mallarmé. Most of these he also drew. Though not in the front rank as an artist himself, he had an unerring eye for quality in others. He was a small man, slightly simian in appearance, of wit and charm, though his tongue could be too sharp for a sensitive student's good, and intense energy. Like Henry, he was a Yorkshireman, albeit of German–Jewish extraction: his father Moritz Rothenstein had come to Bradford following the failure of the 1848 revolution and prospered in the textile industry. Will's brothers Charles, a substantial art collector, and Albert, a gifted artist and designer, had both changed their names to Rutherston in 1916 to avoid anti-German feeling.

It was typical of Henry's luck that this gifted man should have taken over at the Royal College in autumn 1920, the year before he arrived (not, as he liked to assert, at the 'very same time that I arrived as a student').[2] Rothenstein believed that the college should be 'a true University of the Arts, a refuge away from the market place, where students and staff can pursue truth for its own sake. Here we may learn to piece together the fragments of rich clothing which the human spirit has worn in past times, and learn to weave a garment in which to dress the living spirit in the fashion of our day.'[3] He was, however, no out-and-out modernist. He had doubts about Matisse's value, and while recognizing Picasso's prodigious talents, regarded him as an aesthetic rake who spent each weekend with a new style.[4] Even if he tended to balance his more imaginative staff appointments with safely academic practitioners, he brought an entirely new outlook to an institution which had become primarily a teachers' training college. Suddenly there was a whiff of cosmopolitan sophistication in its corridors.

Fairly soon after settling down in Sydney Street, Henry took the train to Salisbury to see Stonehenge, having been fascinated since childhood by those primeval monoliths. He arrived in the early evening, but after finding a hotel room, decided to make his first visit straight away, even though it was getting dark:

As it was a clear evening I got to Stonehenge and saw it by moonlight. I was alone and tremendously impressed. (Moonlight, as you know, enlarges everything, and the mysterious depths and distances made it seem enormous). I went again the next morning, it was still very impressive, but that first moonlight visit remained for years my idea of Stonehenge.[5]

Late October found him writing to his old Leeds School of Art friend, Jocelyn Horner:

I meant my voice to be heard before now – but I've been so terribly busy enjoying life that I've been unable to find any time for letter writing except home.

When I'm not at College I'm hockeying or Tate-ing or Museuming, or at a theatre or supping at the coffee stall on the embankment – occasionally I'm invited out to tea (once I was invited out to Dinner!)

I've got the scalps of four plays and two operas dangling from my girdle ... Yesterday I spent my second afternoon in the British

Museum with the Egyptian and Assyrian sculptures – An hour before closing time I tore myself away from these to do a little exploring and found – in the Ethnographical Gallery – the ecstatically fine negro sculptures … How wonderful it is to be in London (says country-bred Harry) … At times, in my little room here, I get touches of homesickness – usually it comes upon me in bed …[6]

Primitive versus academic

He took to visiting the British Museum on Wednesday and Sunday afternoons. For the first three months it seemed to offer a new world at every turn. Initially he was struck by the monumental impressiveness of the Egyptian galleries, but then much of what he saw there came to seem too stylized and hieratic, with the later works showing a rather stupid love of the colossal. He admired the contained, bull-like grandeur and energy of some Assyrian sculpture, and relished the seemingly inexhaustible jumble of the Ethnographical Room (now coherently displayed at the Museum of Mankind off Bond Street). He noted that the African carvers in wood had contrived to free the arms from the body in their figures and to create a space between the legs, giving a more three-dimensional effect than other primitive artists. Yet he also admired the 'thin flicker' of Oceanic carvings and the subtle modelling and simplicity of the slim figures from Greece's Cycladic islands, executed around 3000 BC.[7]

All this was tremendously exciting, and could have been overwhelmingly so, not least because his taste for the primitive was in direct conflict with what he was being taught at the Royal College:

> For a considerable while after my discovery of the archaic sculpture in the British Museum there was a bitter struggle within me, on the one hand between the need to follow my course at college in order to get a teacher's diploma and on the other, the desire to work freely at what appealed most to me in sculpture. At one point I was seriously considering giving up college and working only in the direction that attracted me. But thank goodness I came to the realization that academic discipline is valuable. And my need to have a diploma, in order to earn a living, helped.[8]

Eventually he worked out a compromise: academic work during the term time, and during holidays 'a free rein to the interests I had developed in the British Museum'. It became a sort of double life, drawing and modelling from life in college during working hours; and in the evenings, at weekends and during vacations working out his own destiny as a carver whose imagination had been set alight by what he had seen at the BM.

From the professor of sculpture at the college, Derwent Wood, he received little more than occasional technical guidance. Wood, a scholarly academic sculptor and skilled modeller, was heavily involved in commissions for war memorials. He left many of his duties to an unmemorable assistant, Will Coxon (no relation to Raymond). Barry Hart, the instructor in stone carving, was different. He came from a family of professional stone masons and carvers, experts at using pointing machines to copy or enlarge in stone or marble the plaster or clay casts modelled by Royal Academicians and others of similar approach. These machines have calibrated arms enabling measurements to be transferred from one medium to another with extreme fidelity, and have been in use with minor variations for centuries. Henry believed that their soulless accuracy, and the encouragement they gave sculptors to conceive their work in a medium wholly different to the final one, had helped make the output of academicians so uninspired and dead: 'Had we students been allowed to carve more freely, there might have been more quality of stone about our work.'[9]

None the less he and Hart, a tall, red-headed fellow, got on well enough for Hart eventually to be best man at Henry's marriage; and there was nothing to stop Henry attempting some direct carving in his own time. This he first did (allowing for the fallibility of memories) in the Christmas holidays after his initial term at the Royal College. Forty years later he discovered the end product in an old box of pebbles. It was to have been a very small – only four and a half inches high – mother and child. But the Cornish Serpentine stone proved too tough, and too small to hold, and he abandoned it unfinished.[10] An example also survives of the very different work which he did in college and in no way despised. It is a realistically modelled clay head [16] of an old man who bears a slight resemblance to Moore in old age. He found such modelling from the life 'tremendously interesting: there was a period when I wouldn't have minded if I had had to concentrate on it for some years', he later commented.[11]

Of Moore's recurring themes, that of mother and child was the first to attract him. It worked at several levels, having been a universal subject for sculptors and one which expressed the basic experiences of being child and parent. In formal terms it challenged the sculptor to express the relationship of a large form to a small one, and the dependence of the small form on the larger.[12] Given his own devotion to his mother, it also expressed something of his own feelings in transmuted form. His notebook from this period includes a drawing of a North American Nootkan wood carving of a mother and child from the British Museum. In this, he later said, there was a great feeling of maternal protectiveness, yet it was not at all sentimental.[13]

His first completed (and surviving) mother and child is also his first known 'free' carving. Standing just under a foot high, it reeks of the British Museum, and in particular of those Mexican carvings which were beginning to appeal to him above all others:

> Mexican sculpture, as soon as I found it, seemed to me true and right, perhaps because I at once hit on similarities in it with some eleventh-century carvings I had seen as a boy on Yorkshire churches. Its 'stoniness', by which I mean its truth to material, its tremendous power without loss of sensitiveness, its astonishing variety and fertility of form-invention, and its approach to a full three-dimensional conception of form, made it unsurpassed in my opinion by any other period of stone sculpture.[14]

In this instance an Aztec figure, thought to be of the God Xochipilla, seems to have been an inspiration. In Moore's figure [14] the seated mother broods mournfully, heavy arms crossed on heavy raised legs, while in an almost humorous touch the head and arms of a plump, angry-looking baby are seen struggling to emerge, nipped between the maternal knees and body. Both from an exaggerated respect for the stone and fear of weakening it, Henry was reluctant at this stage to try opening out his carving. Hence, as he later explained, the block-like quality of several early pieces.[15]

Carving in stone could unfortunately only be done away from London, since it made too much mess. After his first term lodging alone in Sydney Street, he had decided to move in with Raymond Coxon, now studying at the painting school behind the Victoria and Albert Museum. In early 1922 they took a large bedsitting room somewhat further westwards at Seymour Place (now Seymour Walk), near the Fulham Road. They had to share a huge double bed, and there was just room for Moore to carve in wood in one corner and for Coxon to paint in another. But the place stank of cats. Before long they moved again, this time to an unfurnished flat in Acworth Road, Wandsworth, which lay yet further west. They rented it for ten shillings and sixpence a week, and furnished it with two cheap beds from Gamages department store, and other minimal bric-à-brac. An open veranda was one of its attractions. Coxon, who tended to take the lead in such matters (Henry having been cosseted by his women-folk at home), found it and recalled:

> There was an elderly lady in the flat above who asked if she could 'do' for us. She did our washing, she knocked us up in the morning – 'Time gentlemen please'. She had been a ballet mistress, and she gave me a silk dressing gown that was so grand that I didn't dare wear it. She got us half a pint of ale every Saturday morning. All that was free. She took us over.[16]

Not far up the road was the Lyric Theatre, Hammersmith, where John Gay's *The Beggar's Opera* had become a fixture. Moore and Coxon were soon obsessed with it. When they were a bit bored they would drop in to see it yet again, and eventually they knew most of it by heart. There was much singing while they worked, and during trips up north. For a time they would address each other as Peachum, who was the father of MacHeath's girlfriend Polly Peachum.

A first taste of Paris

If Moore's memory is correct, it was at Whitsun 1922 (Coxon put it a year later) that they decided they would go to Paris and see some great modern painting at first hand, especially the work of Roger Fry's favourite, Cézanne.[17] Rothenstein gave them an introduction to the sculptor Aristide Maillol, and commended to them the collection of Auguste Pellerin, a margarine manufacturer who had more than a hundred Cézanne oils at his house in Neuilly. They stayed in the Hotel Celtique off the Boulevard Montparnasse, and were very cautious with their money. The mornings were spent visiting museums, the afternoons and part of the evenings drawing at Colorossi's or La Grande Chaumière, two studio art schools. After that they rewarded themselves with a drink.

There was no instruction at these *croquis* or sketching classes. Those who wanted to join them bought a book of inexpensive tickets for the afternoon or evening sessions. At the former, the model held a pose for an hour or two, so a drawing could be quite fully worked. In the evenings, each pose was shorter than the one before, ending with several of one minute each. The more tired you became, the faster you had to work. That appealed to Moore's competitive instincts, and forced him to focus rapidly on the essential lines of the pose.[18]

There were thousands of art students in Paris at that time. Many were Americans. They would drift in to the session, and if they did not fancy the model, drift out again. Such levity shocked the Yorkshire lads, who seem to have missed, on this and subsequent visits, the Paris of all the talents discovered by many of their compatriots. At the Dôme, the Coupole or the Rotonde they might have come across James Joyce, Hemingway, Modigliani, Picasso, Giacometti, Zadkine, Cocteau, Utrillo, Chagall, and many others. Perhaps they were too poor, too shy, too provincial, and too bad at French to join the unprecedentedly rich and international cultural life of Paris at this era.

Moore was even too diffident to make use of Rothenstein's introduction to Maillol. He got to the door, then thought, 'Well, he's working and he won't want to be bothered,' and turned away.[19] If only more of his own admirers had been as considerate in later life! But he and Coxon did just make it to the Pellerin collection, arriving by taxi just after it closed and having to pay extra to get in. Pellerin had progressed to Cézanne via Corot, the Impressionists, and Manet in particular, by whom he had some fifty oils and pastels before switching to the founder of modern painting.[20] The house was crammed with Cézannes, but the one which made the greatest impact on Moore was the monumental *Grandes Baigneuses*, now in the Philadelphia Museum of Art. The female nude bathers are shown in perspective, lying, standing, and seated under an arch of branches 'as if they'd been sliced out of mountain rock', as he later described it. Coming upon it there in Pellerin's entrance hall was 'like seeing Chartres Cathedral'.[21] Spiritually enriched if financially impoverished they returned to London, looking 'absolutely decrepit' when Edna Ginesi met them at Victoria Station. Indeed, Henry was briefly detained as he went through the barrier and asked whence he came. It was evidently thought he might be some Bolshevist infiltrator. He was piqued that Coxon did not also arouse suspicions.[22]

It was a wonderful friendship, with no dissembling. At one of the parties they gave at their Hammersmith flat they thought they would test the effect of alcohol on art, having heard that Augustus John did his best work under the influence. Seven or eight fellow students, all male, took part. Paper was pinned to the walls, and a list of sacred and profane subjects posted on the mantelpiece. A drink between subjects was obligatory. 'They got better and better to half way, then they began to get worse.' Coxon recalled. 'It was very noisy and we thoroughly enjoyed it.'[23]

They even lured William Rothenstein over to the Acworth Road room for tea and crumpets and to see their work, and they, in turn, were invited along with other bright students to the principal's open Sunday

1. Mary Moore, Henry's mother, drawn by him in 1927, when she was nearly 70

2. Henry's father, Raymond Moore, in his twenties

3. Henry's mother Mary at 52

4. Raymond Moore in 1909, aged 60

5. Henry in 1909, aged 11, the only surviving picture of him as a child

6. Castleford around 1900

7. Moore's birthplace at 30 Roundhill Road, Castleford (second door from right). It was demolished in 1974

8. T. R. Dawes, headmaster of Castleford
Secondary School, as he was in 1931

9. Alice Gostick (far right) in December 1919, with her evening pottery class: Henry at
her knees, Arthur Dalby (left front) and Raymond Coxon (rear right)

10. The school's Roll of Honour, carved by Moore in 1916. His own name was added later in the third column

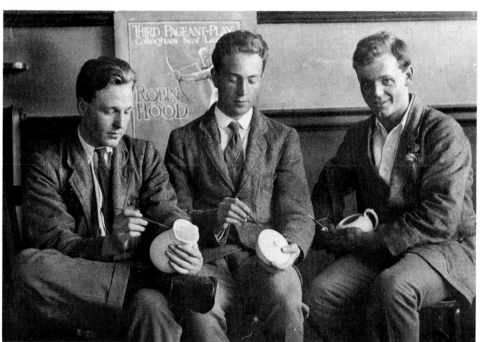

11. Henry Moore, Raymond Coxon and Arthur Dalby in 1919

12. Private Moore shortly after he joined
the army in 1917, aged 18

13. Moore (seated far right) and his platoon of the Civil Service Rifles, Winchester 1917

14. Moore (back row, far left) with Douglas (later Lord) Houghton next to him, on completion of their physical training course at Aldershot, summer 1918

15. Moore convalescent in spring 1918, in the Eton fives court of Castleford Secondary School

16. *Portrait Bust*, 1921, 15 inches high, clay: Moore's first sculpture at the Royal College of Art, subsequently destroyed

17. *Head of the Virgin*, 1922–3, 21 inches high, carved direct in marble, after a relief by Domenico Rosselli in the Victoria and Albert Museum

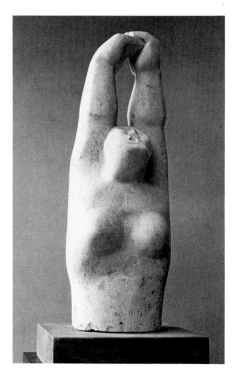

18. *Woman with Upraised Arms*, 1924–5,
17 inches high, Hopton-wood stone,
Henry Moore Foundation.
An uncharacteristically
expressionistic carving

19. *Mother and Child*, 1924–5,
$22\frac{1}{2}$ inches high, Hornton
stone, Manchester City Art
Gallery. Moore's power begins to
emerge

20. *Head and Shoulders*, 1927, 18 inches high, Verde di Prato, collection of Dr Heinz
Roland, England. A first minor masterpiece

21. *Reclining Woman*, 1927, 25 inches long, cast concrete

22. *Suckling Child*, 1927, 17 inches long, cast concrete. An economical yet tender image of maternity

23. Moore aged about 29 at No. 3 Grove Studios, Adie Road, Hammersmith

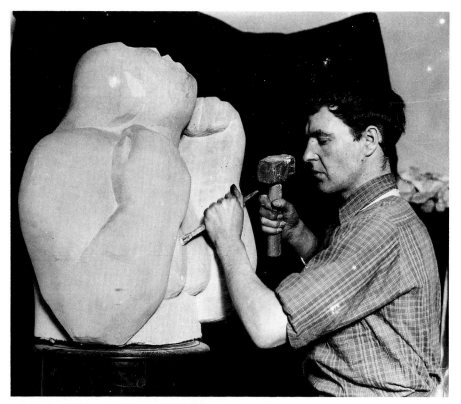

24. Moore at work in 1928, when he was already hailed as a genius. The carving, evidently influenced by Epstein's work, has not survived

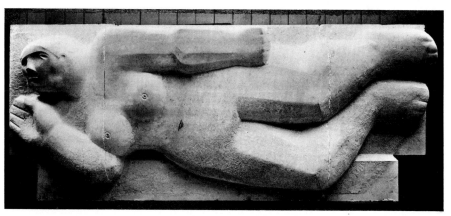

25. *West Wind* (sometimes called *North Wind*), 1928–9, 96 inches long, Portland stone, still to be seen high up on the façade of the old London Underground headquarters at St James's Park station

26. *The Artist's Sister Mary*, 1926, $13\frac{3}{4}$ inches by $9\frac{1}{2}$ inches, pen and ink

27. A full-lipped, Bohemian-looking Moore at the time of his first one-man show in London in 1928

28. Jacob Epstein, around 1920

29. William Rothenstein, Principal of the Royal College of Art

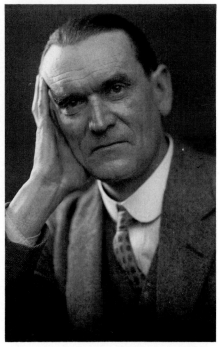

30. Francis Derwent Wood, Professor of Sculpture at the Royal College of Art when Moore started there

evenings at Airlie Gardens, Campden Hill, Kensington. There they might meet such Rothenstein friends as Arnold Bennett, Gordon Craig, T. E. Lawrence, Max Beerbohm, Lady Cunard and G. K. Chesterton. Henry particularly remembered encountering the poet Walter de la Mare, who positively radiated goodness, and Ramsay MacDonald, who became Prime Minister in 1924 and held artists and writers in high regard:

> Meeting MacDonald was another bit of education for someone like me. I remember being left alone with him and standing waiting for him to begin the conversation. He did say one or two things to me, and I remember feeling that it was all perfectly ordinary and natural. I wasn't awed or anything; and so Rothenstein gave me the feeling that they was no barrier, no limit to what a young provincial student could get to be and do, and that's very important at that age.[24]

A letter written to Albert Wainright a few weeks after arrival in London suggests that initially at least he was less confident than that memory from his early sixties might suggest. Looking forward to meeting the likes of the Indian philosopher and poet Rabindranath Tagore *chez* Rothenstein, he lamented: 'I wish I weren't a "Fresher" and naturally diffident with strangers – I must overcome it unless it wears off pretty quickly.'[25] Evidently it did.

The move to Norfolk

The web of happy memories and relationships that bound him to Castleford was torn in early July 1922 when his family moved to north Norfolk. The intention was to transplant Henry's father, who had had several minor strokes, from the industrial pollution of grimy Castleford to the salubrious, well-ventilated climes of East Anglia. The burden fell on their daughter Mary, who was unmarried, just thirty years old and head of a large primary school in Yorkshire. She sacrificed this job in favour of the vacant headship of a Church of England primary school in the village of Wighton, set in unexpectedly rolling, pretty countryside near the coast. The solid brick-and-flint schoolhouse had plenty of room for her parents, and Henry in holiday-time too. Wighton was, moreover, a pleasant little village of some three hundred souls, then supporting two bakers and butchers, three village shops and pubs, all now gone, and a fine old church. Next door to Mary's school, which catered for about fifty children, was a mixed farm owned then as now by a family called Temple.

A greater contrast to Castleford could scarcely be imagined.

The move turned out to have been too late. Raymond Moore barely left his bedroom after his arrival there, and died in August after being removed to a nursing home or hospital in Walsingham. Henry would be all right, he acknowledged on his deathbed, satisfied that his son's studies would provide a secure base of teaching qualifications. Most of the other children were teachers or married to teachers, so they would be all right too.[26] As he died, Raymond Moore said to his wife, using her pet name: 'Polly, why don't you come with me?' 'I can't,' she replied. 'I have to look after all the children, don't I?' 'Yes,' he assented, and died.[27] Had he lived another decade he would have had some inkling of his son's potential fame.

Norfolk soon became the new focal point of the Moore family. Betty had married a teacher and settled some thirty miles south, at Mulbarton near Norwich. Raymond, Henry's brother, became headmaster of a school at Stoke Ferry not far off. Much mutual visiting took place, and if Henry generally spent holidays at Wighton, he also liked to stay with Betty and Rowland Howarth at Mulbarton, where he soon executed a tender drawing of their baby son Peter. Carving was generally done in the garden at Wighton, often holding smaller blocks between his feet, sometimes lodging them in the ground: if held in a vice, they would not survive the impact of hammer and chisel. The area was rich in flint stones, which he began to collect. Their Moore-ish shapes would always appeal to him. A blurred photograph shows him in the garden, broad-shouldered and slim-waisted in shirt sleeves and braces, near him that first mother and child in Portland stone, a carving of a dog, and a piece of white marble from which a head and shoulders were beginning to emerge. This piece was found buried when the present owners of the schoolhouse were levelling the garden in the early 1980s. When shown it, Moore recalled that he had tried to saw the bottom, and there was the mark.[28]

If as a student he was conscious of the Jekyll and Hyde nature of his sculpting activities in college and out of it, the conflict between training and artistic development was less acute where drawing was concerned:

> My first few months at College had rid me of the romantic idea that art schools were of no value and I'd began to draw from life as hard as I could. A sculptor needs to be able to understand and see three-dimensional form correctly, and you can only do that with a great deal of effort and experience and struggle ... The construction of

the human figure, the tremendous variety of balance, of size, of rhythm: all those things make the human being much more difficult to get right in a drawing than anything else. It's not only a matter of training – you can't understand it without being emotionally involved ... it really is a deep, strong, fundamental struggle to understand oneself as much as to understand what one's drawing.[29]

The life-drawing classes were held for two hours every afternoon except Wednesdays in the painting school. Given the pleasure which Henry derived from drawing and his awareness of its importance, it is not surprising that he rarely missed one, and sometimes he drew in modelling classes too. Fortunately one of Rotherstein's appointees as a part-time drawing instructor, Leon Underwood, was a fine artist, an engaging personality, and outstanding teacher. Indeed he earned the accolade from Moore of being 'the only teacher I learned anything from in a useful way'.[30] Underwood discouraged meticulous shading, and laid emphasis in his forceful way on the rendering of volume, mass, and direction with the greatest possible economy. Heretically for those times, students were encouraged to ignore contours in favour of form: the shape of the object was permanent, Underwood would say, even if the light falling on it might vary. They must use their brains as well as their eyes. As Henry was to discover, his favourite teacher was not only an accomplished painter but a sculptor who believed in direct carving and who had begun collecting African sculpture several years previously. A few year later his enthusiasm for Mayan and Aztec art was to take him across Mexico.

Underwood helped to confirm Moore in the rightness of his instincts (often the most important part of teaching). So in a much more explosive way did the drawing, sculpture, and writing of the young French genius Henri Gaudier-Brzeska. Like so many artists of that time, he too had discovered primitive and archaic art in Paris before settling in London in 1911. There he met Jacob Epstein and the American writer Ezra Pound, joined Wyndham Lewis's Vorticist group, produced some remarkable sculpture, and made hypnotic contributions to Wyndham Lewis's magazine *Blast* before being killed fighting with the French army at Neuville-St-Vaast in 1915, aged twenty-four.

Moore later has said that he was aware of Gaudier-Brzeska, Brancusi, Modigliani, and early Epstein, and all that direction in sculpture stood for, when he came to London in 1921.[31] But it was probably not till 1922 that he came upon Ezra Pound's anthology/memoir *Gaudier-Brzeska*, published in 1916, which brought the whole Gaudier phenomenon into focus, both in words and pictures. There he could read the Frenchman's lapidary credo:

> Sculptural energy is the mountain.
> Sculptural feeling is the appreciation of masses in relation.
> Sculptural ability is the defining of these masses by planes.[32]

In the same article in *Blast*, reproduced by Pound, Gaudier had written:

> The fair Greek saw himself only. He petrified his own semblance. His sculpture was derivative, his feeling for form secondary. The absence of direct energy lasted for a thousand years ... Plastic soul is intensity of life bursting the plane.

In the second *Blast*, Gaudier had promised: 'I shall present my emotions by the arrangement of my surfaces, the planes and lines by which they are defined.' In a famous gloss on these apophthegms, Pound himself wrote: 'We have again arrived at an age when men can consider a statue as a statue. The hard stone is not the live coney. Its beauty cannot be the same beauty'; and he approvingly quoted the poet Laurence Binyon, then Keeper of Prints and Drawings at the British Museum: 'Art is not an adjunct to existence, a reproduction of the actual. For indeed it is not essential that the subject matter should represent or be like anything in nature: only it must be alive with a rhythmic vitality of its own.' Within a decade Moore was commending in print the 'removal of the Greek spectacles from the eyes of the modern sculptor' and stating his admiration for sculpture which was 'strong and vital, giving out something of the energy and power of great mountains'.[33]

He was impressed too by Gaudier's commendation of craftsmanship and of truth to material: 'Every inch of the surface is won at the point of a chisel – every stroke of the hammer is a physical and mental effort. Not mere arbitrary translations of a design in any material,' the Frenchman had written, instancing Brancusi's great pride in his accomplished workmanship.[34] We may smile today at the moral superiority ascribed to the strenuous wielding of hammer and chisel. In those days it represented a healthy reaction to the fussiness and would-be verisimilitude of much academic sculpture. Modernists claimed truth to material as their own doctrine, though a concern for the properties of different stones and woods was far from rare across the creative spectrum, from craftsmen to Royal Academicians. For Moore it meant 'not making stone look like flesh or making wood behave like metal'.[35] Before long he realized that out of exaggerated respect for the material he was limiting the power of his sculpture, and he felt free to take greater liberties.

Gaudier's evangelical fervour, shared by Pound, was to be expected. In that epoch, bringing modern art to the philistines, reactionaries, and faint-hearts was a crusade against numerically vastly superior forces, and one in which Moore was soon to be honourably scarred. The scene of battle was the lecture theatre of the Victoria and Albert Museum adjoining the painting school. There the monthly compositions of the students were pinned, with the one considered best in the middle. Each month one of the professors would give his views on them. Towards the end of Henry's first year it was the turn of Beresford Pite, the professor of architecture, an excellent lecturer but a man of narrow ideas. Moore's 'comp' on the theme of Night had been partly inspired by the lid of an Etruscan tomb in the British Museum (subsequently pronounced a forgery) showing the reclining figures of a man and woman. Pite, no admirer of primitive art, gave Moore's effort a slating which included a sentence his victim never forgot: 'This student has been feeding on garbage, anyone can see that.' Henry was most distressed, and walked around Hyde Park wondering whether he should give up college and go his own way as an artist. Next morning he was summoned by Rothenstein, who had witnessed the verbal assault. Coxon's work had also been savaged, and he came along too. 'I hope you weren't too upset,' the principal said. 'These things are bound to happen, you know. We all have our opinions and likings. You'll have this all through your life, and you'll have to learn to put up with it.'[36] The advice was as sound as the forecast was accurate.

At the end of his first year at college, as he departed for his first holiday at Wighton, Henry had plenty to think about. The report of the sculpture professor Derwent Wood was not quite the ringing endorsement which he might have hoped for: 'His life work shows improvement. Design not to my liking. Is much interested in carvings.'[37] Pite's bite had hurt; and the 'garbage' on which he had been feeding at the British Museum was wonderful but confusing. His own work was progressing slowly: to achieve something worthwhile would perhaps take longer than he had hoped. Had he died now, at the same age as Gaudier-Brzeska, he would have left nothing behind (and had Gaudier survived and stayed in London, the face of English sculpture might have been quite different). Among the many positive aspects of his life, however, was Rothenstein's faith in his talents, due in part to 'Rothy's' periodic use of the shed-like studio which Henry used at the sculpture school. There, while the principal worked on an experimental model of a head in clay, they came to know each other better; later Sir William, as he became, even did a portrait drawing of Moore.[38]

Not the least of his kindnesses to his talented student was to introduce him to his first patron, in the shape of his brother Charles Rutherston, who ran the family firm in Bradford. Probably in early 1923 Rutherston bought two smallish wood carvings by Moore: a faintly Modigliani-esque, negroid *Head of a Girl*, nine and a half inches high, and a much more ambitious *Standing Woman*, a foot high and in polished walnut, showing the influence of Gaudier-Brzeska. These exciting first sales brought in £7 and £10 respectively, worth around £105 and £150 in today's money.[39] They were the more cheering for having been made to a discriminating collector.

In August 1923 Rutherston invited his young protégé to spend four days with him in Bradford. Shortly afterwards ('I had my *25th* birthday only three weeks ago!') he described the experience in a letter from Wighton to his old Leeds friend Jocelyn Horner. In between spells of 'work', i.e. looking at his host's collection of ancient Chinese, Negro, Scythian, Siberian, Archaic Greek, and Egyptian art, busts by Epstein and Frank Dobson, and paintings and drawings by French and English contemporary artists, they had been for several motor drives through industrial and agricultural Yorkshire.[40]

The letter reflects the turmoil which Henry's exposure to so many stimuli, and his natural but still unchannelled inventiveness, had created. He was about to tackle a block of beautiful green marble which his carving teacher, Barry Hart, had given him:

> The trouble is that I've too many ideas, many only half conceived, that have mounted up during the past year, & which all cry out to be given a full chance, the problem of choosing and giving preference is very difficult, & the days composing this, the only long holiday of the year, pass by so annoyingly quickly.

Just when he was beginning to sift out his ideas, and to discard 'false masks', college with its hand-to-mouth, timetable existence, would recommence:

> I feel I can gain much yet out of College with its numerous facilities and advantages – but this constant changing of gears doesn't do the engine any good (see what my bit of motoring with Rutherston does for me). Art institutions can be crutches, too long. I feel that once I'm free from them I shall do much more worthwhile ... and

for this reason I'm seriously thinking of eschewing all such things as Prix de Romes, etc. – of forgoing all the glory which such things mean in student circles ...

Since Moore was always a very competitive person, it went against the grain not to make a bid for the Prix de Rome, which was divided into sections for painting, engraving, etc., and tenable for three years at the British School in Rome. Yet in his later career he was always reluctant to expose himself to the danger of not winning. He eschewed not only the Prix de Rome, but all competitions. John Skeaping won it in the year when Moore would have tried, 1924, from the Royal Academy Schools. Barbara Hepworth was runner-up (as the better artist tended to be), met Skeaping in Rome, and married him.

Tacking uneasily between the constraints of college work and the frustrations of his private carving, Henry decided to prove to himself that his hard-won skills as a carver could be used for conventional purposes. An opportunity came when Professor Wood required him to copy a Renaissance head. Moore asked whether he could carve it directly into marble. No, that would not produce an accurate copy, he was told. He must make a plaster model, and use the pointing machine to translate it into marble. Henry persuaded his friend Barry Hart to let him do it direct. The work chosen was a relief by Domenico Rosselli in the Victoria and Albert Museum, called *Virgin and Child with Three Cherub Heads*. Henry's version [17] of the Virgin's head is more three-dimensional and a virtuoso feat of carving. To complete the deception, he peppered the Virgin's face with tiny holes like those left by the pointing machine. Derwent Wood was taken in, and well pleased with the result. So, naturally, was Henry.[41] Later he gave the carving to the Coxons. A relief head in slate with negroid features and intense eyes, a bit Gauguinesque and done that same year, represented the private side of Moore's evolution.

In the summer of 1923, the Royal College lost the services of Leon Underwood, the only teacher Henry really respected. It happened when Rothenstein, who could be insensitive, strode unannounced into Underwood's drawing class and told the students to draw a bundle of foliage which he had brought along. Furious at this interruption, the volatile Underwood wrote out his resignation on the spot.[42] Later that June, Moore, Coxon, Pitchforth, and a few other students called on Underwood at his studio in Girdles Road, Hammersmith, and persuaded him to give them evening classes. They said they would pay two shillings and sixpence a week, leave him their best drawings, keep the studio tidy, and look after the stove. Underwood's view was that there were no 'best' drawings. Out of politeness he accepted them, but destroyed them all.

During his last student year Henry's free carving was marked by a steady gain in power but a continuing inability to digest his influences. A little Hopton-wood stone *Maternity*, showing an infant at the breast of a powerfully brooding mother, owed something to Epstein's earlier treatment of the same theme on a grander scale, as well as to the Ethnographical Room. *Woman with Upraised Arms* [18], started in the same year, had its origins in a large arm in the British Museum's Egyptian section.[43] It was rare in Moore's entire output in showing an expression of outright anguish, reminiscent of Rodin's *Prodigal Son*.

Early that year Moore carried out his first public commission, albeit a modest one which was probably part of a collective student effort. It involved some heads, probably in plaster, for the cotton exhibit in the Palace of Industry at the British Empire Exhibition which was opened by King George V in April at Wembley.[44] Art schools were much involved in the huge task of decorating the pavilions. The entire exhibition covered 216 acres of what was then rural Middlesex, recently connected to the capital by underground railway. Like its spiritual offspring, the 1951 Festival of Britain, it was a form of celebration six years after a world war. In five months it attracted 27 million visitors. At least a few thousand must have noticed the Moore heads perched up at the intersection of the arches. Whether or not he witnessed such highlights as 12,000 performers in the Stadium re-enacting scenes from the Empire's history, Henry was fascinated on visiting the exhibition to see some African carvers at work. He had greatly admired the three-dimensionality of African sculpture, and the way the carvers never worked in outline, seeming always to look into the middle of their subject. Seeing them at work, he reckoned it was their use of the adze, a cross between a chisel and an axe, which enabled them achieve that effect. So he designed one to use himself. According to his not infallible memory, this adze bounced off the wood on to his leg, leaving a small scar for life.[45] The plaster heads from Wembley did not survive.

At the end of the summer term of 1924 Moore achieved his Diploma, which qualified him as an art-school teacher, and even earned the praise of Professor Wood, who wrote in his final report: 'Has shown great improvement in all branches, hard-working, his life-work shows promise, altogether a good student.'[46] He was also given a six-month travelling scholarship, awarded for each of the college's four main subjects by an eminence called The Visitor.

Teaching at the Royal College of Art

Henry doubtless planned to take up the scholarship that autumn. But two weeks before the college was due to reassemble for the autumn term, Derwent Wood resigned after a disagreement with Rothenstein, taking his assistant, the unmemorable Coxon, with him. The principal thereupon summoned his ablest recent ex-student:

> I came down to London and he said 'Moore, you may not be surprised to know that Derwent Wood has left. I want you to look after the school as best you can and see that it runs until we get a new professor.' As there were only five or six sculpture students, maybe eight or nine, it wasn't all that difficult.[47]

Both Rothenstein, in his memoirs, and Henry claim to have suggested Jacob Epstein as Wood's successor. It was a bold idea, since although the American-born sculptor's portrait busts were generally admired, his carvings had already been the subject of outcry and scandal. The Permanent Under-Secretary at the Board of Education was quick to scotch the incendiary suggestion:

> To appoint Epstein would be a very perilous experiment and might cause us considerable embarrassment. For a Professor we would want not only a genius (as to which I am no authority) but also character: and I am not sure that character in a place of this kind is not of greater importance.[48]

Moore being of unflamboyant character and not yet seen as a genius, there were no difficulties over his appointment as assistant in the sculpture department. Eric Gill and Frank Dobson were two other potential nominees for the professorship, being more cautious modernists in work if not temperament; but eventually, on the advice of the eminent engraver Muirhead Bone, Rothenstein offered the post to Ernest Cole, a Royal Academician. Cole had been hailed as a young genius in the less reactionary academic circles. Henry became his part-time assistant.

It was a crucial moment in his career. The post of assistant carried a salary of £240 a year (some £4,000 in today's money) for teaching two days a week. Allowing for holidays, that meant a mere sixty-six days a year, leaving 299 days to pursue his own development. He was spared the pain of questing around for a steady basic income, or of trying to work without one. 'I couldn't have dreamed of better conditions,' he commented later. Rothenstein was justified in saying to him: 'Moore, you've got the ball at your feet.'[49]

The appointment was for seven years, so he had security combined with a large measure of freedom. It was the ideal combination. Carving away at No. 3 Grove Studios, Hammersmith, which he now shared with Raymond Coxon, he could feel optimistic, even if there were some initial difficulties when Cole took up his post:

> To begin with, he was very against what I had been doing when teaching – telling people to go to the British Museum and look at negro sculpture. He didn't like it, being a typical academician. But he was quite a decent person and had a bit of a mind; so we argued in rest-time and lunch-time, and gradually he became more so-called Bolshevik than me. He began to let the students do all sorts of things ... he chucked up the academic thing, but he wasn't good at the other thing.[50]

The travelling scholarship

Cole's establishment as professor left Henry free to take up his travelling scholarship, a not unmixed blessing. The award had to be spent in Italy. Only there could the money be made available. So when Moore suggested that he might go instead to Paris or Berlin, where primitive art could be best studied, his request was rejected. It was stressed, moreover, that the scholarship was for the study of Old Masters:

> I thought I knew enough about Renaissance art and Greek art (which I didn't), the Old Masters, the kind of traditional art; I was fighting just like a young person trying to get free from the authority of his parents, to live his own life, to have his own outlook.[51]

There is some youthful arrogance in the young Moore at this stage, and not a little insularity too. He set off feeling he was being diverted from his true business, though a few months in Italy were surely not so grim a prospect for a young man with open eyes and mind. Even Paris failed to pass muster on his way through in early February 1925. A letter to Raymond Coxon from their old favourite, the Hotel Celtique off the Boulevard Montparnasse, conveys his negative mood:

> You were right about Paris, it's a dull hole, nothing of any interest seems to be going on, & the place itself hasn't the variety of London –

I've given up all notions I had of wanting to settle down here for a few months or a year – no, a week is enough ...[52]

The unfamiliarity with the city implied by these comments, not to mention the continued ignorance of its seething cultural life, is hard to square with assertions that he visited the French capital regularly once or twice a year from 1922.[53] Perhaps it was his second or third visit. Certainly he was excited to explore the Musée Guimet, which 'Rothy' had recommended, and was much struck by its Indian collection. One room in particular, he told Coxon, was a 'real stunner', with a standing male nude which even in plaster-cast form was one of the finest pieces he had ever seen. He and Norman Dawson (a college contemporary who had won the painting department's equivalent scholarship) had spent most of their time at the Louvre, which was 'no better, if as good, as our National'. The big experience there had been Mantegna. They had drawn a couple of evenings at Colorossi's. Dawson was 'all right', but he wished to goodness Coxon were there instead. They were off the following night by train to Rome via Turin, Genoa, and Pisa. He asked to be remembered to various girls at the college: 'My opinion of the Paris women is lower than ever.'

Moore never gave a full account of the ensuing Italian journey. Perhaps it was too unsettling an experience. Yet he came to realize that, disorienting though it was in the short term, it was ultimately enriching. It made him reassess his artistic loyalties and vastly enlarged his frame of reference. In the longer term it helped to make him determined to take his place in the mainstream of European culture.

Having been a late developer intellectually, he had come a long way in the six years since he had left the army. Those letters from the front line have a boyish innocence, lost forever in the painful process of forging a mature personality. Artists, whose fate it is to expose their inner selves at least to some extent in their work, are obliged to be self-conscious. At this stage, Henry was painfully so, as a letter he wrote to Will Rothenstein from Florence in March demonstrates. Above all it shows the protégé desperately anxious to impress his benefactor and employer. He had, he said, been moving with the speed of an American tourist. After Paris, where the Guimet and its contents had stood out like cypress trees in an Italian landscape, he had stopped at Genoa, Pisa, and Rome:

In Italy the early wall paintings – the work of Giotto, Orcagna, Lorenzetti, Taddeo Gaddi, the paintings leading up to and including Masaccio's are what have so far interested me most. Of great

sculpture I've seen very little – Giotto's painting is the finest sculpture I met in Italy – what I know of Indian, Egyptian and Mexican
sculpture completely overwhelms Renaissance sculpture – except
for the early Italian portrait busts, the very late work of Michelangelo and the work of Donatello, though in the influence of
Donatello I think I see the beginning of the end – Donatello was a
modeller, and it seems to me that it is modelling that has sapped
the manhood out of Western sculpture. . . .[54]

So far, he says, Giotto has made the most impression on him, perhaps
because he is the most English of the primitives! His plans were to see
the Giottos at Assisi and Padua, then to return home via Ravenna,
Venice, Munich, and Paris. He reckoned he was getting England into
perspective and would return a violent patriot:

If this scholarship does nothing else for me, it will have made me
realize what treasures we have in England – what a paradise the
British Museum is ... how choice is our National Collection, and
how inspiring is our English landscape. I do not wonder that the
Italians have no landscape school – I have a great desire – almost
an ache for the sight of a tree that can be called a tree – for a tree
with a trunk.

How touchingly, despite the apparent arrogance, Henry was clinging to
the archaic gods he had come to worship at the British Museum, and to
all things British. But Renaissance humanism did not call to him entirely
in vain from the walls of Italy's churches and museums. He was moved
in particular by the scenes from the lives of the apostles painted in the
early fifteenth century on the walls of the Brancacci chapel in the Carmelite church in Florence. The drama, humanity, and sculptural quality
of the scene called *The Tribute Money* he found especially enthralling:
Masaccio strove for realism yet retained a primitive grandeur and simplicity.[55] He took to visiting the chapel in the morning for ten to fifteen
minutes, before other activities, perhaps following the advice of the great
chronicler of artists' lives, Vasari: 'All the most renowned sculptors and
painters who have lived from that time to this have become wonderfully
proficient and famous by studying and working in that chapel.'[56] Moore
never forget those frescoes, and in later life ranked Masaccio (who died
at the age Henry was when he first saw them, twenty-six) among the
greatest artists of the Western world.

Apart from the glories of Giotto and Masaccio, this first Italian trip
enabled him to see such classics of cultural tourism as the leaning tower

of Pisa, where he strained to discover the famous carvings atop the
nearby Baptistery by Giovanni Pisano, but they were just silhouettes
against the sky;[57] the Roman Forum, virtually a sculpture pierced by sky;
and Michelangelo's Sistine Chapel ceiling. When Henry suggested to
someone at the Prix de Rome headquarters that they should visit the
latter together, the reply was 'I've been once.' This became a standing
joke between Henry and Coxon back in London. If one of them suggested
a visit to the National Gallery or British Museum, the other would reply:
'No, I've been once.'[58]

By the time Moore got to Florence, there were four other Royal College
ex-students or students there: from the painting school, Edna Ginesi,
Norman Dawson, and Robert Lyon, who had taken a flat there with his
wife Mabel; and from the design school, the delightful Eric Ravilious, who
had arrived at the Royal College in the following year's intake along with
Edward Bawden, Edward Burra, and Barnett Freedman. Ravilious was
even more thrown than Henry by over-exposure to Renaissance painting.
He sought equilibrium in long walks along the banks of the river Arno,
where Henry too did some drawing.[59] There were moments when they
took collective action to counter their visual indigestion and the frustrations of looking rather than doing, as Henry recalled:

> Some of us decided to have a really splashy meal to show the
> Italians how Englishmen could eat and drink. I think I must have
> been the drunkest, because I can remember shouting that Epstein
> was only a modeller and *I* was a carver. I remember standing up
> and shouting: 'I'm the best sculptor.'[60]

(From the same memory he could have deduced that he was the most
conceited rather than the drunkest. Epstein was in fact a magnificent
carver.)

Sustained tourism was not his natural bent, however fine the subject
matter. His only artistic activity in his two or so months in Florence
consisted of sketching, mainly from the works of the masters: some
evidence of zeal had to be taken home. His unhappiness was aggravated
by being in love with his best friend's fiancée. Edna Ginesi had been
engaged to Raymond Coxon for the past three years, so Henry had
inevitably seen a good deal of her. In Florence, or possibly before, his
feelings for her had changed from affection to something more intense.
Drawings of her proliferated in his sketchbook, and one day in mid-March
he confessed his love. With Yorkshire directness Gin said that she wanted
to go back to Raymond a better person than when she started the journey.

Henry was suitably mortified and wrote a contrite letter to Coxon saying he hoped he would meet someone who would help him get over his feelings for Gin, and that they could all stay together as before. 'The wonderful thing was that we did stay together,' Gin recalled. 'Raymond was wonderful, and so was Harry.'[61] But it all added to the misery of that time for Henry:

> I knew, we all three knew. I was very fond of Ray, and Ray was very fond of me: we were true friends and very attached. This made the thing with Gin worse ... it might have been almost wanting to share. That may have been part of the tie, both of us liking Gin.[62]

When the Coxons were married the following year, he was best man. All three believed that Henry came back to England from Italy for a brief break to recover from the emotional strain before returning. The slightly nightmarish quality of those days must have been heightened by the spectacle of Fascism in action. Mussolini had taken over as dictator in January 1925, and his Blackshirts spread a chill of fear when they appeared in the streets. In view of Henry's later espousal of democratic socialism, it is odd that he never alluded to those early contacts with Fascism, which provided a sinister counterpoint to the glories of Italian cultural history.

Venice, where the last instalment of his scholarship money was to be handed over, proved memorable not just for its architecture, setting, and museums. He arrived there expecting the money to be waiting for him, but it was not, and he had virtually none left:

> I was taken by gondola from the train to a hotel on the Lido. I had no idea that the Lido was one of the most expensive parts of Venice. After one day I asked how much my room cost and discovered that I hadn't enough money to pay for it. I couldn't leave, so I sent urgent letters to Wellington, the Registrar, and just hung on ... I was there for about a fortnight and all the time the bill was mounting up. As a result I didn't really enjoy Venice – not half as much as I could have done.[63]

Twelve weeks abroad had evidently not taught this traveller the wisdom of asking the price of hotel rooms before rather than after settling into them.

Just three and a half months after leaving Paris he was back there in late May, using a poisoned cut in a hand to justify an accelerated return to England. He was seriously concerned about it, he wrote to Wellington at the Royal College, felt it needed careful attention, and had therefore decided to return to Norfolk immediately to consult his own doctor. Did he seriously believe that worthy practitioner to be superior to any Parisian doctor? He told Wellington that since he had undertaken to make the scholarship last till mid-June, he would return to Paris around 10 June and stay for a fortnight before returning to college. Wellington accepted this with a good grace, while pointing out that 'attention and skill of the highest order can be found in Paris'.[64]

The poisoned hand reflected his run-down state, bringing the odyssey to a symbolic conclusion. Once again, as from the battle of Cambrai, he was returning to Blighty from France for medical treatment, mentally gassed by an excessive ingestion of high culture. Much later he was to comment that his time in Italy as a student was the nearest he had come to a nervous breakdown.[65] Remarkably, his experiences there in no way coloured his later relationship with Italy, which was supremely happy and prolonged, reaching its apotheosis in the triumphant exhibition of his work in Florence in 1972. Like many unhappy experiences, the Italian journey was formative. The mental conflict which it helped cause was to continue; but being a true artist, Moore would turn it to his own benefit.

Chapter V

Public débuts and teaching

1925–8

Within three years of his return from Italy in a confused and depressed
state, Moore's career would be launched with a successful one-man show.
Any such eventuality must have seemed very remote in that summer of
1925, as he attempted to re-establish his sense of equilibrium. Looking
back some forty years later, it was a very dismal phase:

> For about six months after my return I was never more miserable
> in my life. Six months' exposure [it must have felt that long] to the
> master works of European art which I saw on my trip had stirred
> up a violent conflict with my previous ideals. I couldn't seem to
> shake off the new impressions, or make use of them without denying
> all that I had devoutly believed in before. I found myself helpless
> and unable to work. Then gradually I began to find my way out of
> my quandary in the direction of my earlier interests. I came back
> to ancient Mexican art in the British Museum...[1]

The conflict between Renaissance masterpieces and the archaic art to
which he had pledged his artistic allegiance was not the only source of
unhappiness. He was still at least half in love with Gin; and in his absence
abroad there had been another family move. That Easter his sister Mary
had married George Garrould, who worked at Barclay's Bank in the
nearby townlet of Wells-next-the-Sea. They were to live there, at No. 2
Church Street, for eighteen months. George Garrould was then posted to
Colchester in Essex, and they moved yet again.

Writing in mid-August to Gin ('My dear lassie') from the refuge of
Betty's house at Mulbarton, Henry showed how much he disliked no
longer being the only male about the place. He did not feel at home in
Wells as he had in Wighton:

> In Wighton ... there was but mother, Mary and myself, and I had meals how & when I liked & had a large stock of stones in the back garden and mucked up the premises as much as I liked – I can't be as selfish as I was then, but I'm thankful I'm not having to spend my holidays in London as I thought I might be obliged to do – I'm thankful for these two spots in Norfolk where I can sit in the open air, crosslegged on patches of grass & chip stone – though I was nearly sent loopy this afternoon by the incessant lowing of a cow that the farmer next door is starving for killing.[2]

Perhaps as a constant reminder of his feelings for her, he had sent Gin a sheepdog puppy as a present. It had arrived safely by rail, to his relief, and his tender but never overtly loving letter was full of sage advice about the pup's diet, how short its tail should be docked and suchlike. Later he added from a beach near Yarmouth:

> I've just had a grand dip in the sea & am now sunbathing half in the altogether – soaking in the ultra-violet rays – & enjoying the general view! At the moment it's a good life, simple, easy & but slightly clouded, except that I'm obliged to smoke a pipe, having no cigarettes and no money ...

Evidently he had barely started to resume carving: hence the far from despondent tone. To his annoyance, his stock of stone at Wighton had been left there, most of it being disposed of by Mary's successor. He had managed to obtain one or two bits from local masons, and had begun to do a little work, he had told Raymond Coxon from Wells a fortnight earlier. Commenting on the possibility of another visit to Charles Rutherston and the latter's apparent unhappiness despite his wealth, he wrote revealingly:

> If I were in his position I should take myself into a country district in England, somewhere like Wighton or Walsingham, and stay there until I'd found and wedded one of those richly formed, big-limbed, fresh faced, full blooded country wenches, built for breeding, honest, simple minded, practical, common sensed, healthily sexed lasses that I've seen about here.[3]

The mouth-watering relish with which he described these girls suggests that his subsequent portrayal in both sculpture and drawings of generously proportioned female bodies was influenced by personal taste as well as formal considerations. It also squares with his predilection for Cézanne's sculpturesque bathing ladies, Renoir's pneumatic late nudes, and the ample flesh of Rubens's women. In fact Rutherston was then becoming engaged to Essil Elmslie, a painter who managed the Redfern Gallery in Cork Street, W1. Coincidentally or not, Henry and several Royal College contemporaries including Pitchforth, Hepworth, Burra, Percy Horton, and Charles Tunnicliffe had shown a few works each at the Redfern in April–May 1924: Moore's first public exposure, but one without repercussions.

His tenderness, charm, and spoilt-son's lack of domesticity come over in a letter written to Gin from London in early September, when he was acting as metropolitan guide to the Norfolk chapter of the family:

> Mother and Mary say they'll be about 2 minutes before they are ready, that means 10 minutes at the least – I can't think of anything better or that I'd rather do more than write to you ... I brought Betty and her husband Rowland here on Sunday and rushed them off their feet ... the place was in a nell (*sic*) of a state when we got here (not in my eyes, but in theirs). Betty thoroughly enjoyed herself on Sunday morning with kettles of hot water in the back premises...[4]

He signed off when Mary and Mother started putting on their hats with a 'Cheerio – All of everything – God bless you. Yrs Harry.'

Despite such agreeable distractions and the responsibilities of his teaching, he managed with considerable difficulty to finish a *Mother and Child* started before his Italian journey. Standing almost two feet high and executed in Hornton stone, this was his most accomplished work to date. Thanks to his fear of weakening the stone, it is still rather blockish, with the scowling child stuck on to the mother's neckless head. Yet it has the authentic brooding quality and slow majesty which mark so much of his mature work.

First Reclining Figure

If the full catalogue (five volumes, with one to come) of Moore's work is accurate, he had first tackled the dominant theme of his career, the reclining figure, just before departing on his travelling scholarship. The prototype of hundreds of recumbent females was in fact male, twelve inches long and done in Mansfield stone.[5] Sadly, Moore's sole reclining male nude has not survived: it is catalogued as 'destroyed', probably by accident rather than intent, since Henry destroyed many unsatisfactory drawings but few completed sculptures. Its maleness probably derived from its apparent source, the Mayan idol called Chacmool, the Rain Spirit. The particular version which so impressed him was a life-sized limestone carving from the fifteenth century found in Chichen Itza in Mexico. He had first seen it reproduced in a German publication, then on one of his two visits to Paris in 1925 had come upon a plaster cast of it or a similar version in the Trocadéro Museum (later called the Musée de l'Homme). What struck him was not just its hypnotic stare, but its curious reclining posture: on its back, with knees drawn up and head twisted to the right. Mexico was very much in fashion in the 1920s in England. Nine years of upheaval had ushered in a new and seemingly attractive social order, and Aldous Huxley, Middleton Murry, and D.H. Lawrence had all been there in search of the noble savage. Designers responded to the new enthusiasm: stepped wireless cabinets echoed Aztec temples, and prickly cacti drove aspidistras from many a mantelpiece. Moore's response to the Chacmool was thus partly conditioned by the prevailing intellectual climate. The reclining figure, too, was a theme of the day. Painters like Duncan Grant, Matthew Smith, and Mark Gertler were filling canvases with ripely recumbent nudes, and they could look back to Velasquez, Ingres, Courbet, and Gauguin among many great artists who had dealt memorably with the same subject. In sculpture Matisse had tackled it in some bold bronzes before 1910, while at home Frank Dobson, twelve years Henry's senior, was to produce a finely sensual reclining *Marble Woman* in 1925, which can be seen in the Courtauld Institute Galleries in London. Moore's own first two reclining females emerged the following year (1926). One is in painted plaster and survives only as a photograph, the other is a sixteen-inch-long bronze: apart from a small horse done as a student, his first essay in this medium. Though the position of the first is Chacmoolish, both figures are notably sensual, with large thighs parted invitingly.

In drawing on ethnic art for much of his inspiration and in aiming to emulate its intensity, Henry was encouraged by the example of Jacob Epstein, whom he first met around this time. Epstein, a New Yorker who had settled in London in 1905 after three years in Paris, was then at the height of his notoriety. Although this was the heyday of the School of Paris, led by Picasso and Matisse, and Expressionism was in full cry in Germany tempered by its spiritual antithesis, the Bauhaus, in England modernism in any guise remained deeply suspect in all but the most avant-garde circles. In 1925, when Epstein was forty-five, his memorial panel to the writer W. H. Hudson was unveiled in Hyde Park by the Prime Minister, Stanley Baldwin. This innocuous depiction of Rima, the heroine of *Green Mansions*, as a naked young woman with arms raised and surrounded by birds, was greeted in the press with a hate campaign of great venom and spite. The monument was described as obscene, an atrocity, a nightmare in stone, a 'bad dream of the Bolshevist in Art'. Hilaire Belloc, Sir Arthur Conan Doyle, Sir Philip Burne-Jones, and Alfred Munnings were among those who wrote to the *Morning Post* demanding its removal. Ranged on the other side, defending Epstein and his Rima in a letter to *The Times*, were Bernard Shaw, Arnold Bennett, Augustus John, Michael Sadler, Hugh Walpole, Ramsay MacDonald, and 170 students of the Royal College of Art, supported no doubt by Rothenstein and Moore.[6] Among other works to have brought vilification on Epstein's head were his monument to Oscar Wilde in a Paris cemetery, and the statues he had carved (without assistance) for the headquarters of the British Medical Association in the Strand.

The brooding, often negroid features with which he frequently endowed his carvings, even those on Christian themes, seemed to forge an unholy alliance between British philistinism and racism. Henry was conscious all his life how much modern British sculpture – as well as he himself – owed to this courageous man:

> He took the brickbats, he took the insults, he faced the howls of derision with which artists since Rembrandt have learned to become familiar. And as far as sculpture in this century is concerned, he took them first. We of the generation that succeeded him were spared a great deal, simply because his sturdy personality and determination had taken so much. Sculpture always arouses more violent emotions than, say, painting, simply because it is three-dimensional. It cannot be ignored. It is there. And I believe that the sculptors who followed Epstein in this country would have been more insulted ... had the popular fury not partially spent itself on him ...[7]

At the personal level Moore admired his warmth, vitality and broad-shouldered, sturdy presence. Epstein for his part was quick to spot Henry's ability and made several purchases over the next three years. On one occasion,

> he jumped into a taxi with a piece of sculpture of mine which he had just bought from me, even though I did not regard it as completely finished, because it was his and therefore he wanted it

there and then ... he was strong and immediate in his likes, and also in his dislikes.[8]

Epstein invited Henry to the tea parties he gave at his home in Hyde Park Gate, where he had a fine collection of African, Egyptian, and other 'primitive' art; and took to dropping in at the Royal College to see how Moore and his pupils were progressing. The set-up at the sculpture school was ideal. There were no constraints on Moore now. He could do what he wanted in his studio, and he could choose the models and set their poses. At first he found teaching enjoyable and even helpful:

> The first two or three years of teaching your own subject is as much a way of learning for the teachers as for the students themselves. I remember I used to be very surprised quite often at the things I discovered while teaching, the actual sentences I used .... after a few years of teaching ... there comes a stage when you have to repeat things that you think are fundamental in the training of a sculptor. They become a deadening thing.[9]

The situation at the sculpture school was marred only by the unsympathetic nature of the successive professors. Ernest Cole resigned in 1926, to be succeeded by Gilbert Ledward, a neo-classical sculptor ten years Moore's senior whose work is heavily represented in London (the *Guards Memorial* at Horse Guards Parade, the Imperial War Museum, Sloane Square, and so on). Since Moore's work was far from being to the taste of all students, Rothenstein's practice of employing a more academic sculptor as professor had its logic. Jack Clarkson, for example, who arrived as a student in 1927, found both Moore and Ledward to be pleasant, gentle personalities, but inclined more to Ledward's style. None the less he found Henry's teaching very helpful:

> He would take me to the edge of the life room, where we would sit on the floor, gaze at the model and compare what we saw with my work viewed from the same angle. He taught me to see the human figure not as an outline but in masses, tilting this way and that. He had what I call his matchbox trick. He would refer to the upper and lower parts of the human torso as being like two matchboxes, and he would produce them to demonstrate that the only time they are in alignment is when a soldier is at attention or a body is in a coffin: in life they are in movement. Demonstrated with a living model present, it was very convincing and helpful in establishing the correct balancing of form in a living figure. At this period we

were in the habit of applying clay in pieces (as opposed to the
Lanteri 'lick and spit' method). We started with great lumps, finally
applying small pellets. I am afraid I began to get quite finicky and
mannered in this respect, and Moore would say 'Stop clerking,
Clarkson.' This illustrates, I think, his feeling that what mattered
most was the form rather than the surface appearance.[10]

Another student from the same year, Alma Ramsey, recalled that they
spent three days a week modelling from the life, one doing free composition and carving, and another on a craft. To save the trek to the
main building for the daily life-drawing class in the late afternoon, the
sculpture school now had its own model (usually chosen by Henry):

> I was very aware that Henry Moore was a great sculptor, so much
> so that I was rather in awe of him, and therefore not able to get on
> friendly terms ... He always took our work seriously and prefaced
> criticism with 'at the stage you are in ...' Students were expected
> to get on by themselves most of the time and to be technically
> competent. At that time technique was unfashionable, and we
> hacked and muddled and agonized. HM's teaching that I managed
> to digest had a lifelong and deep effect on me ... I remember dancing
> with him once at a Friday hop and he remarked that I felt more
> well-built (or words to that effect) than I looked – all quite serious
> and no suggestion of flirtation. I should rate him C in sex appeal, I
> think because he was so immersed in his own sculpture and not
> interested in silly young students.[11]

The belle of the class of 1928, Elizabeth Ramsden, by contrast considered
him 'rather splendid and sturdy'. She had a Yorkshire father and an
American mother, had been to Leeds School of Art and found Moore to
be already a legend there. Later she married the painter Cecil Collins.
Henry's slogan, she recalled, was 'Hit it with a stick' (i.e. don't fiddle
around), the stick being seventeen inches long and one and three-quarter
inches wide and intended for knocking clay into shape. Though Ledward
was diffident where Moore was confident, she considered him 'the end'.
'I remember telling him with all the cruelty of youth, "We don't really
want to learn from you at all." He was a sensitive man, and he was really
upset.'[12] By then the class had swelled to some twenty students, about
half of each sex. A large Australian girl called Ola Cohn, to whose ample
bosom a Welsh student called Gapper felt tempted to apply the calipers
used for measuring the models, later made a name as a portraitist in

bronze. Many became art-school teachers, but not one became known at the national level in Britain: no reflection on Moore's teaching, since, by this stage, talent could be encouraged but not discovered.

For his own work, remaining close to the great South Kensington museums was valuable. At the nearby Geological Museum he found an exciting range of stone on display. Sometimes he would note the name of a quarry from which one came and write off for some random blocks for his students and himself. Over the next two decades he worked in a rich variety of stone and wood, from Portland, Mansfield, Hornton, Darley Dale, Ham Hill, Ancaster stone, alabaster and Cumberland alabaster, Verde di Prato, Styrian jade, Armenian marble, and travertine, as well as elm, beech, walnut, box, lignum vitae, Pynkado, and ebony. He would visit stonemasons' yards, pick up 'random blocks' and store them in his studio, waiting for an idea which suited the shape and texture of a particular stone. At the Natural History Museum he could study bones, whose structural strength and subtle evolutions of shape he admired, shells and other natural forms. Consciously or unconsciously, all were to be valuable sources of inspiration – as they were to contemporary artists of very different persuasion. It might almost have been Moore who, in 1929, wrote: 'I found inspiration more than ever in natural forms, the treasures of the sea, fishes of all kinds, and every class of molluscous and crustacean life, the crab, lobster and such like.' In fact it was Sir Alfred Gilbert, former darling of Queen Victoria's court and creator of the Eros statue in Piccadilly.[13]

Moore's notebooks from the mid-1920s show the deep seriousness of his approach. In 1926, for example, we find him adjuring himself: 'Development of sculpture from now, not back to Maillol and archaic Greek & modelling . . . sculpture in relation to masses, etc., etc., modelling is undulation of surfaces . . . what I am attempting to express – connection with my own life – and vision. Make a sketch each night of something observed during the day. Keep ever prominent the world tradition – the big view of sculpture.'[14] Another entry urges: 'Go to V & A & get out Chinese Sculpture by Osvald Siren Volume 4 – Plates . . . Ancient Egyptian Works of Art – Arthur Weigall,' and so on.

His growing success in digesting his varied sources and making his work more personal was marked in 1927 by a beautiful *Head and Shoulders*, eighteen inches high and carved in Verde di Prato marble [20]. If the *Mother and Child* of 1925 was the first substantial Moore in terms of quality, this work (long in the collection of the former London dealer Dr Heinz Roland) has justly been called his first masterpiece, being fully three-dimensional and memorable from virtually any aspect.[15] There are Cubist distortions in the asymmetrical eyes, and Herbert Read suspected that the elongated nose might have been influenced by a Modigliani head which had been presented to the Victoria and Albert Museum in 1922.[16] Yet it has a new and moving blend of tenderness and strength. A trace of the same tenderness is to be seen in *Suckling Child* [22], completed in summer 1927 and one of a number of pieces done in cast concrete: an exciting new material which Henry moulded while still malleable. The child clutches the single bell-shaped breast as it hungrily sucks, an eloquent and sensual microcosm of the maternity theme.

First one-man exhibition

Before the test of his first one-man show in early 1928, Moore exhibited in a mixed show in 1926 at the St George's Gallery in Grosvenor Street, and helped to form a small group of painters and sculptors who showed at the Beaux-Arts Gallery in 1927. Of neither has any traceable review or comment survived. His solo début, the climax of any artist's early career (and not always so early) was to take place in late January 1928 at the Warren gallery, Maddox Street, W1. Henry's first patron Charles Rutherston, who had died in the previous year all too soon after his marriage, had effected the introduction to Dorothy Warren. Moore remembered her as a woman of great flair, energy, and courage, which she certainly needed the following year when, in one of the most celebrated police raids in history, the allegedly pornographic paintings of D. H. Lawrence were seized from the walls of her gallery.[17]

It was natural that in his later life Moore should have remembered the hostile notices which his first one-man show prompted, rather than the favourable and constructive ones. One wounding review is liable to be more memorable than ten laudatory notices. Sheer volume is important too. In the event his début attracted widespread attention in both the national and provincial press; by today's standards it was an almost ideal balance of praise, vituperation, and controversy.

The Times's serious and by no means brief review reflected his growing reputation in what would today be called the art world:

> In order to do justice to the sculpture and drawings of Mr Henry Moore it is necessary to remain with them for some little time, and to take the side of the materials rather than that of what is called 'nature' ... you might prefer that the forms were carried further

towards the imitation of nature, but you cannot deny that they are consistent with themselves and each other and loyal to the substances of which they are made. Indeed a refusal to be seduced from his loyalty to the capacities of his materials is Mr Moore's most striking characteristic. His actual sense of form is not yet very highly developed, and the number of his works ... suggests that he does not wait long enough to be sure that a conception is worth while before he carries it out. There is nothing hasty or scamped about the workmanship, but the conceptions themselves would gain by longer consideration.[18]

Henry had mustered forty-two sculptures and fifty-one drawings. Among the former were the *Recumbent Male Figure* in Mansfield stone, the little bronze *Horse* and the concrete *Suckling Child*, which Epstein bought. *The Times*'s anonymous critic commented on the range of materials used. He found the drawings nearer to nature, and mentioned ten as 'particularly fine'.

In the *Observer*, P. G. Konody found some inconsistency between Moore's sensitively carved torsos and the 'clumsy formula' of inflated limbs and square feet. *Suckling Child*, a general favourite, was again praised, as was a severely stylized (and probably Brancusi-like) *Bird* in polished bronze, since vanished, and the draughtsmanship 'of a very high order' of the wash, pen, and chalk drawings.[19]

There was praise too in the popular press. The *Daily Herald* announced:

MINER'S SON AS ARTIST

SCULPTURES THAT ARE STAGGERING

HIS GENIUS

The story traced the rise of the miner's son through 'ordinary Board School' where his schoolteacher, Miss Alice Gostick, discovered his gifts, to art college in London. Some of his early drawings were said to recall the 'graceful work of Fragonard', but graceful was the last word anyone would dream of applying to the simply staggering sculpture. 'Many of the figures have been done with a minimum of carving ... A very "advanced" show and one that will shock the orthodox, it contains much sculpture of almost overwhelming power.'[20] Some of this 'primitive vitality' derived, the *Yorkshire Evening Post* shrewdly surmised, from the 'sturdy mining stock from which the artist springs'.[21] Support from the Yorkshire newspapers was to be a steady feature of Moore's career.

His 'statuary' was, however, not at all to the taste of the critic of the *Morning Post*, who said with unconcealed malice that the exhibition 'must raise furious thoughts in the minds of those responsible for the teaching at the Royal College of Art ... A master in a national art school should be a man of taste with a keen sense of form.' Yet in the *Suckling Child*, though the head of the baby was admirably modelled, the mutilated breast was 'revolting'. Other statues were 'lumpy masses bound by clumsy contours ... the best of the drawings are quite ordinary; nothing shall be said of the worst.'[22] Under the heading 'Distortions in Stone. Sculpture that displeases', the *Westminster Gazette*'s critic deplored the tortuous twistings of stone, marble and wood, finding them 'grotesque, and not even amusingly grotesque. The women seem to me to be suffering from elephantiasis.' The writer did, however, concede that Moore had his appreciative and intelligent followers, and regretted that the work made him feel a philistine.[23]

There it was at the beginning in microcosm; the polarization of opinion, the praise and the vilification, in one instance made the nastier by a deliberate attempt to undermine Henry's teaching post. Rothenstein's loyalty was proof against such attacks on his staff. Eventually £90-worth of Moore's work was sold, equivalent to some £1,800 today, including thirty drawings at £1 each (£19 today). He was even more pleased by the identity of the buyers, who apart from Epstein included the artists Augustus John and Henry Lamb. The latter had already purchased the 1925 *Mother and Child* which he later gave to Manchester City Art Gallery. Like the novelist Hugh Walpole, a compulsive collector who had acquired a white marble snake, he lent it back for the exhibition.[24] For Henry to have attracted the support of his peers was the most pleasing aspect of the exercise. Having achieved encouraging sales and a modest *succès d'estime et de scandale*, Moore could be well pleased with the outcome. It was not fame overnight, but it put him firmly on the map as an artist to be reckoned with.

Only a few weeks later the *Evening Standard* was reporting that a 'little cargo' of work by 'Mr Augustus John, Mr Paul Nash, the designer, and Mr Henry Moore, the sculptor, together with a few lesser lights' was on its way to be shown in Berlin.[25] No record survives of how the Berliners reacted to what must have been tame fare by the standards of Expressionism and *Neue Sachlichkeit*. Equally problematical was Moore's contribution that June to a British Independent Society of Artists show at the Redfern Gallery on the theme 'Gentlemen Prefer Blondes'. 'Mr Henry S. Moore's unclothed scene of rustic dalliance is classic in conception but

Piccadilly Circus in Execution,' commented the *New Age* cryptically.[26]
Coxon and Pitchforth also took part.

First public commission

Next in this *annus mirabilis* of 1928, shortly after his thirtieth birthday,
came Moore's first big public commission. It was to carve a relief sym-
bolizing the West Wind for the handsome new headquarters of the
London Underground Railway at 55 Broadway, not far from St James's
Park and Westminster. The architect of the huge (for those days), fourteen-
storey and cruciform building was Charles Holden, the same austere
Quaker who had provoked uproar by commissioning Epstein to carve his
eighteen figures for the British Medical Association building in the Strand.
Undaunted by that row of twenty years earlier, Holden now invited
Epstein to execute two groups representing Night and Day to stand
above prominent street-level doorways of the building. Throughout, the
architect enjoyed the support of the redoubtable Frank Pick, the Underground's managing director, whose imaginative use of the best
contemporary artists to design his posters was a landmark in public
patronage. Epstein, in turn, recommended Moore as one of the six other
sculptors who would be invited to execute eight reliefs symbolizing the
four winds. These were to be located, less than ideally, on a band of stone
eighty feet above street level, at a point where the wings of the buildings
were stepped back towards the tower. Eric Gill, six years Henry's senior,
was asked to do three of them, the remainder going to Moore, A. H.
Gerrard, Allan Wyon, Eric Aumonier and F. Rabinovitch, who as Sam
Rabin later achieved a name as boxer, opera singer, and painter. Moore
later admitted that he had had reservations about tackling *West Wind*:

> Relief sculpture symbolized for me the humiliating subservience of
> the sculptor to the architect, for in 99 cases out of 100, the architect
> only thought of sculpture as a surface decoration, and ordered a
> relief as a matter of course. But the architect of the Underground
> building was persuasive, and I was young, and when one is young
> one can be persuaded that an uncongenial task is a problem that
> one doesn't want to face up to.[27]

None the less he tackled the commission with great thoroughness, and
the dozens of drawings with which he filled his sketchbook even indicate a
measure of excitement. Doubtless at Holden's suggestion, all six sculptors
used the human figure as their symbolic subject matter, some male,

others – as with Henry's *West Wind* – female. The challenge was to endow a horizontal lady with a sense of speed and of flying. This Moore achieved rather successfully [25] by tilting her legs upwards and placing the arms in a swimming position, one palm outwards by the head, the other stretched along the top flank towards the feet. The scale was vastly bigger than anything he had so far attempted: nine feet six inches long, three feet six inches high. He consequently had to carve the Portland stone in three squareish sections, which meant dividing the West Wind's substantial right breast evenly between the head and torso sections. In his studio at the sculpture school, where he virtually completed the commission, he installed a mirror on the floor to give him an impression of how the relief would look seen from below.[28]

In January 1929, when the work was nearly done, the blocks were raised and fixed into position on the northern face of the building's east wing. By this stage winter had set in, and a wind less amiable than Henry's was blowing:

> I completed the carving on a scaffolding platform where there was only about three feet to stand on, and at first I was alarmed. It was so high up. But when I got down and looked at it from the ground, I realized that the figure's navel couldn't be seen properly. This was terrible, because the umbilical area is absolutely central to me – the cord attaches you to your mother, after all. By this time the scaffolding had been dismantled, so I went up again in a cradle, winching it up myself from side to side until I reached the carving. But once there, I found I couldn't carve properly. Every time I struck a blow, the cradle shot back from the figure. So in the end I got out some charcoal and shaded the navel in ... the cradle zigzagged all over the place on the return journey as well. Epstein watched me. After I'd come down he said: 'I wouldn't have done that for all the money in the world.'[29]

Enough London soot soon gathered in the navel for it to satisfy the most Oedipal eye. Shortly afterwards Moore took his niece Aline Reed along to see Epstein working on *Day*. Later they stood in the road looking up at *West Wind* to judge the effect it made. A stranger came and gazed with them. 'What do you think of that? Who did it?' the stranger asked. 'A man called Henry Moore,' Henry replied. 'Bloody awful, isn't it!' said the stranger. 'I rather like it,' said Henry pleasantly.[30]

The commission brought Moore a steady trickle of publicity. Epstein praised it to the *Evening Standard*'s art critic R. H. Wilenski, saying: 'It seems to me to suggest volition in space quite remarkably well.'[31] *The Times*'s critic adjudged the whole exercise a conspicuous success, but thought that Moore's contribution, though well modelled, was too bulky and 'suffers from the lack of drapery to connect it with the lines of the building'[32] (whereas to modern eyes it is the simplicity of *West Wind* which makes it harmonize best of all with the severity of the building). A brisk correspondence, mainly hostile, ensued. The *Morning Post*'s critic once again gunned for Moore's job and that of A. H. Gerrard, who taught at the Slade: 'It is almost unbelievable that men occupying positions of this high responsibility should execute such figures as serious works of art.'[33]

Epstein's work was again savaged for its 'debased Indo-Chinese style, half Buddha, half Mummy'.[34] Angry letters from shareholders to the board of the Underground company almost forced its removal, and Epstein was obliged to shorten the penis of the boy in Day by an inch and a half. Night was tarred and feathered by vandals.[35] It was one of those many instances where Epstein drew most of the fire of the philistines and neo-Victorians.

Given Moore's reservations about relief sculpture, it is ironic that his first private commission should also have been in this not fully three-dimensional genre, and once again from an architect. In The Vale, Chelsea, Gordon Holt was designing a house for a Mr and Mrs Reckitt. Probably while executing *West Wind* (since the drawings follow in the same sketchbook), Henry was asked to decorate two large *jardinières*, each six foot eight inches tall. Once again, the material was Portland stone. He responded by carving voluptuous standing and seated female nudes in relief on three sides of the upper portion of each of these decorative flower pots. The Reckitts later took them with them to a house in Marryat Road, Wimbledon. That house was in turn bought in 1961 by the great British viola player Lionel Tertis, then aged eighty-four. Knowing they were believed to be by Henry Moore, he invited the sculptor to come and see them. Partly because they had never been recorded in any catalogue of his work, Henry had completely forgotten about them. His immediate and very typical comment was: 'Oh yes, that's me – not bad, is it?!'[36] In 1964 they were knocked down at Sotheby's for £5,200 to the Bond Street dealers Marlborough Fine Art.[37] They sold them to Sophia Loren and Carlo Ponti, both keen Moore collectors. The *jardinières* ended up indoors, on either side of the sitting-room fireplace of the Ponti villa outside Rome, where Henry eventually saw them again.

Frustrating though the medium may have been, these reliefs show a delight in the contours of the female figure which had not previously found expression in his carving. Partly this reflected his growing technical assurance, partly his emotional and artistic development. At last his sculpture as well as his drawing was beginning to bear the impress of personal experience, not just of aesthetic discoveries. It may or may not have been a coincidence that his personal life was about to take a crucial turn. The larky but ambitious provincial lad was soon to give way decisively to the successful young sculptor well on the road to national fame from the secure base of a happy marriage.

Chapter VI

Marriage and a masterpiece

1929–31

Henry Moore at thirty: an ambitious, dedicated, outward-going, zestful young man, with the Yorkshire shrewdness just below the surface; good-looking, a fine physical specimen (as they used to say), full of vitality, attractive to women, despite the varying testimony of his students. Certainly there had been no shortage of girlfriends. But with none, apart from Gin, does he seem to have been seriously in love. One of them disliked taking second place to his carving; another was too free with his money.[1] Most of his emotional energies he ploughed into his work.

Irina Radetzky was different. She had been a painting student at the Royal College for a couple of years before Henry spotted her. It was in the autumn term of 1928, and she was walking over to the students' common room in a Nissen hut near the sculpture school. The building also served as a dining room, and every term there was a dance in it. When Henry took in Irina's beauty he said to himself: 'I am going to dance with that girl at the next hop.' Being Moore, he did. They had about three dances running, he recalled, after which she said that she had better get back to her friend:

> I found out later she was engaged to this fellow, but they had had a tiff, a little lover's quarrel, and weren't talking when I had asked. Otherwise she might have said 'I'm sorry'. I even said 'Can I see you home?' . . . and I found this fellow she had been sitting next to was also hanging around. When she came out of the girls' cloak-room, coat at the ready, we walked all three down Queen's Gate, but I didn't know what connection poor old Leslie, his name was, had with her, and he walked in the gutter. Before that I had argued with all my friends that really serious artists shouldn't get married, they should be married to their art: Michelangelo and Beethoven

weren't married, and so on. After meeting Irina I began to say
Rembrandt was married, Bach had twenty children . . .[2]

Irina Anatolia Radetzky had been born in Kiev in Russia in March
1907. Her father was probably Russian but from an Austrian or Austro-
Polish background, upper-class and rich, her mother mainly Russian but
partly Polish. A few weeks after Irina was born they moved from Kiev and
lived either in Moscow or St Petersburg, with summers in Yalta and
other resorts of the wealthy. Her father was lost in the chaos and blood-
shed of the 1917 Revolution, and she was parked by her mother with
her grandmother in the Crimea. Then the grandmother died of cancer,
a traumatic experience for Irina, who was about eleven years old. It was
also a time of acute hunger. A teacher of deaf and dumb children
befriended her, together they went on a seemingly endless journey to
Moscow by train, and there Irina helped teach the handicapped children.[3]

Meanwhile her mother, who was beautiful, restless, and singularly
unmaternal, had been evacuated along with other White Russians,
mainly women and children, by the French military mission, which had
been helping the anti-Bolsheviks of the south in the civil war while the
British did the same in Siberia. With the French mission that autumn of
1919 was a British officer, Captain (perhaps Major) Norman Bult-Francis.
According to his son Dennis, he would then have been in his mid-thirties.[4]
It is not clear whether Irina's mother and the gallant Briton, who spoke
excellent French, had met on Russian soil or whether their romance was
of the shipboard variety. Certainly they settled in Paris, and through the
Polish embassy there they managed to have Irina traced and smuggled
out on a Polish passport. By now around thirteen, and at first showing
such symptoms of malnourishment as very thin legs and a distended
stomach, she spent between two and three years in the French capital,
attending school, and getting to know her stepfather, as he may have
become.

Both Irina's mother and Norman Bult-Francis, who had divorced his
first wife around 1917, were rolling stones. Perhaps because their own
relationship was crumbling – he went off to the USA alone, and for good,
in 1923 – they decided around 1921–2 to bring Irina to England and
settle her with his parents, George Bult-Francis and his wife. So when
she was about fifteen, Irina found herself once again living in some style
in a large Georgian property called Fern House near Little Marlow
in Buckinghamshire, thirty-odd miles from London. Step-grandfather
George was chairman of the family pharmaceutical firm of Heron, Squire

and Francis, which later became British Drug Houses and was eventually bought by Glaxo. Irina's memory was that later on her step-grandfather lost a great deal of his money.[5]

Such losses are relative. Meanwhile Fern House was a pleasant place for a teenager. It had about nine bedrooms, and in the garden was a reconstructed Japanese house which the Bult-Francises had had brought back after spending their honeymoon in Japan.[6] The grandchildren, who enjoyed playing in it, had mixed feelings about this Russian girl suddenly thrust into their midst. Such a deeply unsettling background might have wrecked the life of a lesser person, but it seemed to leave her with a clear view of what was really important, and that she never lost.

When she went to study at the Royal College on a Monday morning, she took the train from Bourne End to Paddington, and then walked across Hyde Park to the college. She spent the following four nights in lodgings in Hendon. When Henry met her she was a well-proportioned young woman of nicely rounded beauty and great grace: Henry liked to tease her by saying that he had married her just for her shoulders. Her English was still imperfect, and was delivered in a delightful Russian accent. She was known to her friends as Nitchka, short for Irinitchka, and had a very Russian blend of mystery, warmth, gaiety, and down-to-earth common sense, the latter evidently not inherited from her mother. A fellow student, Dick Hosking, remembered her warm, friendly manner and peaceful charm. Her main interest seemed to be in making furnishing screens decorated with scenes of Russian peasants in traditional costumes, performing ritual dances, he recalled.[7]

The courtship proceeded apace, with Henry wasting no time. He was a good letter-writer, Irina found:

> He began with 'dear so and so' and then his next letter with 'my dear', and on the next he put 'dearest'. The first letter he ended 'with my best wishes', and then 'with love', and then 'with love and kisses'. By the time the holiday was over, we were thick.[8]

Henry was eventually invited to Fern House to be looked over by step-grandfather, whose wife had died of cancer a couple of years previously.

When Irina had first met Henry he was working on the *West Wind* commission, she recalled.[9] The nature of her new admirer's work greatly surprised her, since she had grown used to paintings by the likes of Alma-Tadema on the walls of the Bult-Francis home. There followed the great Leeds *Reclining Figure*, to which we will revert. Having known each other for about nine months, Henry and Irina were married shortly before

his thirty-first birthday in late July 1929, Irina being twenty-two. The
ceremony took place at St John's, West Hendon. Perhaps because Henry
did not want to drag the Coxons down to London during the vacation,
Raymond Coxon was not invited to be best man, which hurt him, Barry
Hart (Henry's old carving instructor) fulfilling the role instead. The
reception was held in the nearby home of Irina's step-uncle Alan Bult-
Francis, a solicitor, and was quite noisy, thanks to the Royal College
element.[10]

The miner's son with the secure working-class background and the
upper-class Russian girl who had experienced so many childhood vicissi-
tudes went off for their honeymoon to a little boarding house at Start
Point on the Cornish coast, just south of Tintagel. The husband of
the family which ran it, a fisherman, had been drowned, and his two
daughters were in charge. Their name was Trout, and Ella Trout did the
fishing while her sister did the cooking. Henry and his bride went out to
fish for mackerel, which they greatly enjoyed, and for dab, which was
less fun. The boarding house could only be reached by boat. It was all
very romantic.[11]

After returning to London they set off by train for Suffolk, where they
had rented a cottage in the heart of Constable country, near Dedham –
not far from Henry's mother and sister Mary at Colchester. At Liverpool
Street Station in London Irina tried to lift Henry's suitcase, but could not
move it. He had packed a 'small' block of alabaster. This he duly carved
while they were at Cuckoo Cottage, later selling it for £65 to the dealer
and collector Lucy Carrington Wertheim.[12] The Coxons came to stay,
harbouring no resentments, and found the whole place seething with
wasps. Among them was Irina, trying to make plum jam and constantly
being stung. Henry would periodically stride across a cabbage field to do
the shopping. He and Irina loved the gently undulating countryside.

To Hampstead, nest of artists

Since the Coxons' marriage in 1926, Henry had been living alone at No.
3 Grove Studios, Hammersmith: the same studio which he had shared
with Raymond before the latter moved next door on wedding Gin. Prior
to his own marriage Henry lived briefly in St John's Wood[13] in north-west
London, near the military barracks there: hence perhaps their decision
to make their first married home nearby in Belsize Park, a pleasant area
within a few minutes of Hampstead proper, with the more down-at-heel
Kentish Town to the south. The accommodation they found was at 11A

Parkhill Road, a street of spacious Victorian villas with, in this instance, an extension tacked on to one side. 11A consisted of a ground-floor studio and bathroom with curved, cast-iron outdoor steps to a two-roomed flat above. Although encouraged to carry on by Henry, Irina gave up painting: 'You can't paint if you are looking after someone like Henry.'[14] She proved adept at helping to move sculpture, using ropes tied around the staircase banisters and putting rollers under the stands – in addition to cleaning, washing, cooking, posing and polishing the sculpture too. Henry greatly valued her views on his work, which she gave with complete candour.

They had found the studio-cum-flat through Barbara Hepworth. She had moved the previous year with her first husband John Skeaping, from St John's Wood to 7 The Mall Studios, a tree-shaded alley of cabin-like studios off Parkhill Road. Cecil Stephenson, a good but underrated painter, was at No. 6, with his model railway which ran out into the garden at the back. The writer Herbert Read, who settled in the same alley in 1933, was to refer to the area as 'a gentle nest of artists', virtually a contradiction in terms. Certainly Hampstead and its environs were to be home to a large number of artists, designers, architects, and even collectors in the 1930s, as we shall see. Cecil Stephenson was gentle, and so was Herbert Read, but many of the others were disputatious and dogmatic.

Among the most creative and entertaining but least easy was Ben Nicholson, whose father Sir William was a distinguished painter of portraits and still lifes. Ben Nicholson met Barbara Hepworth in 1931, when her marriage to John Skeaping was breaking up, and before long moved into No. 7 in his stead. That summer the two of them, plus Henry, Irina, the painter Ivon Hitchens, who lived nearby in Adelaide Road, and Barbara's friends Mary and Douglas Jenkins spent a happy holiday together at a farm which Hepworth had rented at Happisburgh on the Norfolk coast, just above the Broads. There they talked, walked, bathed, played cricket, and worked.[15]

Nicholson and Moore had in common a devotion to work, mutual respect and, eventually, acknowledged leadership in Britain of their respective fields. Those considerations apart, they were very different. Moore was down to earth yet a romantic, endlessly enraptured by the dramas of nature and of organic form, fascinated by primitive cultures, obsessed with a desire to charge his works to the uttermost with the energy and intensity of these two sources. In the field of art he was incorrigibly eclectic: here a bit of Picasso, Brancusi or Modigliani might be detected, there a strong whiff of the British Museum, progressively fused into a more personal mixture. Nicholson was a much more fastidious and perfectionist spirit, a juggler with words, a fancier of fast cars, a champion at diabolo, a fiend at table tennis, and as an artist a lyrical classicist who sought his effects in the subtlest balance of volume, tone, and line. All artists have to be fairly egocentric, but Nicholson was more self-centred than most, and easily bored. 'Irina knew how to deal with Ben best,' Henry recalled. 'She would say "Now, Ben, when you're bored and you want to go home, don't hesitate, go!" '[16]

No one looking at the carvings of Henry Moore and Barbara Hepworth executed between 1928 and the mid–1930s could fail to be struck by the overlap in their styles. They were living very close to each other, had many mutual friends, were open to the same contemporary influences, and seem to have maintained a friendly yet fruitfully competitive relationship. Certainly Henry continued to think of her as his junior in every way. It was a bit as if he had a stimulating younger sister who sometimes, as young sisters will, wanted to share the limelight with him. When he saw her doing masks, heavy-limbed women and, before long, mothers with children around 1929–30, it must have felt as if imitation was the most annoying form of flattery. Hepworth for her part has recorded how great an impression her own *Pierced Form* of 1931 made on Moore when he saw it, implying that she was the first to pierce such a hole clean through the middle of a carving.[17] In 1934–5 both were producing largely abstract sculpture, sometimes with incised Nicholsonian lines, which was remarkably similar. Hepworth's first stringed figure came in 1934, Moore's in 1937. Yet as their later careers were to emphasize, they were at heart very different artists: where Moore was dynamic, disturbing and many-layered, Hepworth was serene and classical in spirit. Hers was an exclusive art while his was inclusive, as John Russell has expressed it.[18] As for holes, Archipenko had pioneered them in Paris two decades earlier, albeit not in stone.

It is nice to think of Henry and Barbara bickering together over which was being derivative of the other, as Solly Zuckerman, a young South African biologist recently arrived at the Zoological Society of London in Regent's Park remembered them doing (he had got to know first Hepworth and Skeaping, then Henry, when they came to sketch birds and beasts at the Zoo, as Gaudier-Brzeska and many other artists had before them).[19] But it is a side-issue. When Moore pulled out all the stops, as he was to do with increasing frequency, he was utterly his own man.

There had been a promising development of the reclining figure theme in the summer of 1927, when he produced a roundly sensual *Reclining Woman* in cast concrete [21]. Her 'grandiose curve of hip, great lumbar expanse and ample thickness of thigh' attracted favourable notice when she was shown in a mixed exhibition in Liverpool in June 1929, not long before Henry's wedding, though the *Liverpool Echo*'s headline – 'The Curved Lady in Concrete. Remarkable Example of Sculpture' – made her sound like a fairground exhibit.[20] Leaning on her right elbow and side, breasts squeezed upwards, left thigh tipped voluptuously over right, she looks sultrily alluring.

The Leeds Reclining Figure

Moore's work took a qualitative leap forward with a *Reclining Figure* [36] on which he worked between March and May 1929, basing himself on preparatory drawings for the garden reliefs.[21] His material was a once-random block of richly veined brown Hornton stone from Edge Hill in Warwickshire. In this figure, almost three feet long, his admiration for the Chacmool figure found its most overt expression. Yet if the position of the head, with its strange protuberance (of hair?) from one side, and the staring intensity of the eyes are all reminiscent of the Mayan rain god, the differences are also marked. The figure is not just female rather than male, but quintessentially so. Leaning on her right elbow, though less voluptuously than her concrete sister, she has none of what Herbert Read has called the hieratic rigidity of the Chacmool.[22] Smallish rounded breasts with pierced nipples rise from the torso; the left arm is raised almost questioningly to the head, a formal device which produces a swooping line between armpit and raised left thigh. While exploring this, the eye is tugged towards the head, with its scooped-out eyes of staring intensity. For the first time in Moore's work the human body was here unequivocally used to evoke an undulating landscape. The analogy is heightened by the veining of the stone, which suggests aeons of geological development.

As one of Moore's friendly critics has pointed out, the idea of woman as landscape is not new: in *The Song of Solomon* she is the land flowing with milk and honey; John Donne invokes her as 'my America! my new-found-land!', while in the work of the Norwegian painter, Edvard Munch, her energy sometimes generates the turbulence of land and sky.[23] Another critic has speculated that Moore may have been emboldened to use the body-as-landscape metaphor by Roger Fry's essay on Michelangelo's *Tondo* in the Uffizi, Florence:

When we find a group of figures so arranged that the planes have a sequence comparable in breadth and dignity to the mouldings of the earth, mounting by clearly felt gradations to an overtopping summit, innumerable instinctive reactions are brought into play.[24]

Regardless of the sources of the idea, what matters is that Moore applied it to sculpture with great power and, in this instance particularly, considerable subtlety. His ability to bring into play 'innumerable instinctive reactions' lies at the heart of the wide appeal of his work. In the Leeds *Reclining Figure* which was acquired by the City Art Gallery in 1941, he pioneered in sculpture a romantic fusion of the eternally feminine and the spirit of the land. This aspect of his work has inevitably been seized on by Jungian interpreters, one of whom, Eric Neumann, has justifiably claimed that as Moore's work develops, 'the female reclining figure becomes more and more clearly the archetype of the earth goddess, nature goddess and life goddess.'[25]

If we may see something of the rolling Yorkshire dales of Henry's youth in the Leeds figure's contours, its face was a pure derivation from the Mexican-style masks with which he was experimenting around this period. He liked the way masks isolate the facial expression, and had first tried his hand at one in 1924. Usually his main aim was to give the eyes the maximum intensity, but sometimes he repeated a Mexican trick of making each one different, thus emphasizing the asymmetry found to a greater or lesser extent in all faces.[26]

Thanks in part to the fruitful influence of Irina, this was also a vintage period for Moore's life drawings, which rank among his finest works. Again, influences can be discerned. The most obvious is the series of heavy-limbed nudes, often bathing, which Picasso had produced in the early 1920s. These were clearly also the inspiration for a very tender terracotta, *Woman Combing her Hair*, which Moore had done in 1927. That same tenderness suffused many of these life drawings, along with a serenity and grave strength suggesting a high degree of emotional fulfilment. Not surprisingly, in view of the vastly greater intractability of stone, the drawings of this early phase are ahead of the carvings in consistent originality and maturity.

With his Warren Gallery exhibition and the *West Wind* commission behind him, Moore was by 1930 already considered one of England's leading artists. That summer he was chosen, with Epstein and John Skeaping, to represent British sculpture at the Venice Biennale. William Rothenstein was among the painters shown in the British pavilion, along with Augustus John, Wilson Steer, Roger Fry, Walter Sickert, C. R. W. Nevinson, and others. Nine of Epstein's works were included, with seven each by Moore and Skeaping. There was also a selection of contemporary gold and silver assembled by the Goldsmiths' Company.

The Biennale had been founded in 1895, mainly as a showcase of Italian art. In the national pavilions, mixed exhibitions were the custom, rather than the one-man shows which have dominated since the Second World War. Mussolini was a pioneer in the use of art as a propaganda weapon. In the winter of 1929–30, London had been treated to a staggering selection of Italian Old Masters at the Royal Academy: perhaps the finest group of such works ever gathered together in one place. At the 1930 Biennale one of the main Italian artists to be shown was Modigliani, who had spent most of his career in Paris before dying there in 1920, and was Jewish and, by later Fascist standards, degenerate in every sense. Those were pre-British Council days: the Council was formed in 1934 to counter German rather than Italian Fascist propaganda. The British Pavilion was, however, for the first time under government patronage. Sir Joseph Duveen, art dealer extraordinary and benefactor of the Tate Gallery, paid all costs.[27]

The Biennale ran from early May to October, so many thousands of Italians and a useful number of foreign museum directors of all nationalities were able to see Moore's work. It was probably as a consequence of this showing that the 1929 *Reclining Figure* was included in a mixed exhibition at the Kunsthaus in Zurich the following year. Although his Venice debut had no detectible repercussions in London, it is odd that no one alluded to it when he became the only living British artist to be shown there at the 1948 Biennale.

In London his participation in mixed exhibitions multiplied during 1930. Groups with which he showed ranged from the Modern English Water-colour Society and the Young Artists (under forty) to the broadly modernist and very durable London Group, which staged a sculpture show on the roof-top of Selfridges, the Oxford Street department store opened a couple of decades earlier. Epstein and Dobson were co-exhibitors, leading the *Scotsman*'s critic to regret that 'the old affectations of elegance are replaced by the new affectations of distortion. Massiveness is now the rule, and excessive simplification of all forms, human and animal.'[28] He particularly disliked a 'block-like, unalluring Woman with triangular eyes' by Moore. That autumn the same three leading sculptors showed their drawings together at the Zwemmer Gallery in Litchfield Street in an exhibition mainly devoted to the work of Gaudier-Brzeska. The

Zwemmer Gallery was a tributary of the already well-known art bookshop which Anton Zwemmer, a Dutch immigrant, had built up around the corner in Charing Cross Road and which had become a favourite browsing spot for Moore and other artists and art students on their way to the National Gallery.[29] Zwemmer was the sole agent and distributor for fine art magazines like *Minotaure, Cahiers d'Art* and *Verve,* and also sold unprecedentedly good reproductions of the Impressionists and post-Impressionists printed in Germany by Piper and Hanfstaengl. The gallery was started partly to show these more effectively, but became a focal point of the modern movement specializing in lithographs and other original graphics. It was directed by Robert Wellington, son of the Royal College's registrar Hubert Wellington.

This show witnessed the emergence in print of an unsung hero of Moore's early years, the *Evening Standard*'s art critic R. H. Wilenski.[30] It is odd that Henry never acknowledged the powerful support he gave him. Wilenski had visited Moore's studio in spring 1930 to gather material for a series of lectures he was to give on modern art at Bristol University, which he hoped to repeat in London. His plan was, he told Henry, to shock his audience by showing them a slide of a Moore work at the start of the lectures, educate them by showing them later Renoirs, Maillols, Dobsons and so forth in the intermediate lectures, and then show them 'your thing' right at the end of the sixth lecture, by when he hoped they would be able to appreciate it.[31] Unfortunately the plan misfired: at the end the wrong slide appeared, and Wilenski, totally thrown, fluffed his final tribute. Henry urged him not to worry – 'I am only too grateful for all you have done to help me already.'[32] Wilenski bought a few of Henry's drawings that summer, and in the December issue of the art magazine *Apollo* published what seems to have been the first major critical assessment of Moore's work. It was somewhat wordy, in the style of those days, making much of the new internationalism of art. The new conception of sculpture, he wrote, was concerned with the aesthetic disposition of masses and with the rhythmic relations divined by artists in the organic world. He was confident that sculptural masterpieces of this kind were about to be created, and 'one of the artists who, I believe, may produce them is Henry Moore'.

That article, resonantly entitled 'Ruminations on Sculpture and the work of Henry Moore', infuriated among others the *Morning Post*'s venomous art critic, who resumed his efforts to get Moore dislodged from his teaching job. Under the headline 'Ugliness In Art' and a photograph of Moore's *Reclining Woman* of 1930 in Green Hornton stone (now in the

National Gallery, Ottawa) he referred to current discussion 'regarding the prevalence in certain art circles of unconventional or what is called "Bolshevist" art, especially in sculpture'. Mentioning Wilenski's article in praise of the 'statuary of Mr Moore', he offered the opinion of three 'famous' sculptors on creations of this sort:

> Sir William Goscombe John: 'It is beneath contempt.'
> Mr S. C. Jagger: 'The sort of people who do it merely seek an easy road to notoriety; all they seek is the limelight. I do not think that this rubbish will have a serious effect on real art. Like every other epidemic, it will die a natural death.'
> Mr Albert Toft: 'Such aimless creations are beyond my comprehension. What end can there be to such a negation of truth and nature but a pit or a precipice?'[33]

Alas for Messrs Toft and John. It is their work which has fallen into the pit of oblivion. Jagger, who designed the huge Royal Artillery monument at Hyde Park Corner in London, has fared better, at least as the designer of a more humane class of war memorial. Their anger is not entirely incomprehensible: the *Reclining Woman* with the sandcastle-style breasts and parted thighs is among Henry's most provocative yet least appealing treatments of this theme.

The attack was taken up a fortnight later by the President of the Society of Art Masters. There should be the closest scrutiny before allowing susceptible talent to be influenced by a teacher whose ideal was represented by such 'vulgar and repulsive distortions', he said in his presidential address. Moore commented to the *Evening News*, which reported the diatribe: 'I work for myself and for those people whose views I value.'[34] The attacks of the philistines no longer wounded him deeply. Indeed, they stimulated him: 'I felt I was fighting a crusade, and it gave one a head of steam.'[35]

Yet he could not be impervious to the attempts to undermine his position at the Royal College. He owed much to William Rothenstein, and perhaps felt he should no longer be an embarrassment to him. Precisely how the fateful sequence of events unfolded is far from clear. Henry remembered Professor Ledward saying to Rothenstein in 1930: 'Either Moore goes or I go,' to which the principal pointed out that Moore's seven-year contract had not yet expired.[36] The episode sounds out of character for such a mild man, but certainly Ledward had left before the autumn term of 1930, well before the present wave of assaults on Moore was launched. He was succeeded by Richard Garbe, whose prejudices were said by Herbert Read (presumably on the basis of Moore's recollection) to be even stronger.[37] We may note parenthetically that Garbe was, in the words of his *Times* obituary in 1957, 'before everything a carver', a craftsman whose affinities were with Oriental and Gothic carvers, and whose work was always based on the qualities of the materials employed.[38] In short he was an artist who believed in direct carving and truth to material. But because he was not a modernist, he was thought to be firmly in the enemy camp. Since he much admired Japanese netsuke, those thimble-sized ivory figures, he may well have found Moore's work thoroughly *lumpen*, and have seized the opportunity presented by these attacks to urge on Rothenstein that Moore really must go. If it is also true that the college's old students' association, which included many teachers, protested to the same effect, the eventual outcome is not so surprising.[39]

Adding to the rag-bag of fallible evidence the memories of Raymond Coxon, generally a sound witness, it seems that the following may have happened. Henry felt he was becoming a burden to Rothenstein. Coxon, who had been teaching at Richmond School of Art, had moved to Chelsea School of Art, and had suggested to its new head, H. S. Williamson, that Moore should be invited to start its sculpture school. Having had such an approach, Henry went to Rothenstein and suggested that it might be helpful if he found another job elsewhere. Rothenstein was all compliments and reassurance, and it took Moore some time to realize that his semi-resignation had been accepted.[40] 'My dear Moore,' Sir William (as he had just become) wrote on 14 January 1931,

> It is with particular regret that I accept your decision to give up your work at the College. Under the circumstances, however, I feel this to be inevitable. I should like to take this opportunity of telling you how sensible I am of your services to the Sculpture School of the College. I know that everything you have told the students has come from your own inner experience, and ever since you have been at the College, I have recognized your single mindedness and sincerity...[41]

Precisely when his resignation took effect is also not clear: possibly there and then, perhaps at the end of the summer term. College records show that his successor in the autumn term of 1931 was Herbert W. Palliser.

To supplement his college earnings, half of which now went on rent, Henry had set himself a target of thirty sculptures a year. Twenty-two survive from 1930, with reclining figures and mothers-and-children

BOARD OF EDUCATION.

Please address your reply
to the Registrar and quote
No ....

ROYAL COLLEGE OF ART,

SOUTH KENSINGTON, LONDON, S.W.7.

14th January 1931.

Telephone :—WESTERN 6371.

My dear Moore,

It is with particular regret that I accept your decision to give up your work at the College. Under the circumstances, however, I feel this to be inevitable. I should like to take this opportunity of telling you how sensible I am of your services to the Sculpture School of the College. I know that everything you have told the students has come from your own inner experience, and ever since you have been at the College, both as a student and as a member of the staff, I have recognised your single mindedness and sincerity.

I hope and believe you will make the best possible use of the fuller working hours freedom from teaching will bring you. I am sending your letter to the Board with my own personal expressions of regret.

Believe me, my dear Moore,

Ever yours sincerely,

W. Rothenstein

H.Moore,Esq., A.R.C.A.,
    11a, Studio,
        Park Hill Road,
            Hampstead,
                N.W.3.

Letter from William Rothenstein accepting Moore's resignation predominating. One of the most interesting of the former is in the collection of Sir Robert Sainsbury; it is a seven-inch long lady [47] who seems to be clasping her right ear as if in pain. The material was ironstone, and Moore took advantage of its strength to pierce it clean through for the first time, forming an oval hole between arm, neck and upper torso. This deliberate use of space was quite different in kind from the more incidental-looking gap created by the raised arm of the Leeds reclining figure; but it still fell short of piercing the torso itself.

Leicester Galleries début

By spring 1931 Moore had accumulated enough work for his second one-man show, held at the Leicester Galleries in Leicester Square in mid-April. Of the ten or so London art galleries sympathetic to the modern movement, this was much the most enterprising and the best known. Founded in 1902, it had put on one-man shows between 1917 and 1926 of, among others, Epstein, Gaudier-Brzeska, Matisse, and Picasso (their first in London), van Gogh, Cézanne, and Renoir. Such discriminating and active collectors as Sir Michael Sadler, Sir Hugh Walpole, Samuel Courtauld, Hugh Blaker, and Sir Edward Marsh were among their regular clients. Oliver Brown, son of the founder, had been impressed by Moore's 1928 show at the Warren Gallery, as much by the drawings as by the sculpture. Eventually he visited Parkhill Road in the hope of arranging a larger showing.[42]

Henry was thus in the best of hands, but the timing of the show was hardly propitious. Following the crash of 1929, which wiped out stock exchange values across the Western world, unemployment was climbing towards its 1932 record level of 3,750,000 in Britain. Times were hard for most artists, and not good even for wealthy collectors. The top price among Henry's thirty-four sculptures was £200 for the *Reclining Woman*, now in Ottawa, the more famous Leeds figure being £50 cheaper, or the equivalent of £3,000 in today's money: a snip, but no one bought it. The smaller items were about £25 each, the eighteen drawings between £7 and £9 each (£140–£180 today).

Epstein helped with a foreword to the tiny, minimally informative catalogue:

> Before these works I ponder in silence ... If sculpture is truly 'the relation of masses', here is the example for all to see. Henry Moore, by his integrity to the central idea of sculpture, calls all sculptors

to his side ... Forces from within the works project upon our minds what the sculptor wishes to convey. Here is something to startle the unthinking out of their complacency ... For the future of sculpture in England, Henry Moore is vitally important.

It was portentous and provocative stuff, calculated to infuriate opponents by bracketing them with the 'unthinking'. Press reaction ranged again from the hysterically abusive to the seriously appreciative, and once more the former stuck more firmly in Moore's memory. Yet *The Times*'s critic was impressed by his 'remarkable invention in the composition of masses' and his 'unusual capacity for feeling his masses in terms of the material he happens to be using'.[43] The *Manchester Guardian* urged: 'Nobody anxious to discover what the modern sculptor is trying to achieve should miss this exhibition...'[44] In the *Observer* doughty young Wilenski hailed the show as 'a landmark in the history of English sculpture'.[45] The *Jewish Chronicle* went furthest, under a headline proclaiming 'A Genius Of The First Order':

> Good sculptors are so extremely rare, especially in England, that when one appears we find it hard to resist hailing him with all the superlatives that should be reserved for genius... It is impossible to foresee where the development of this extraordinarily vital art will stop ... that it should be produced by so young a man, and in England, in the present century, is almost incredible ... Three of the greatest names in present-day sculpture are Jewish names – Epstein, Zadkine, and Lipchitz. No admirer of these should neglect the opportunity of seeing an exhibition which constitutes the most serious challenge they have yet received.[46]

The Luftwaffe destroyed the records which might have revealed the identity of this perceptive reviewer.

Once again the *Morning Post* led the attack:

> The cult of ugliness triumphs at the hands of Mr Moore. He shows an utter contempt for the natural beauty of women and children ... aesthetic detachment is bound to atrophy soul and vision and lead to revolting formlessness such as offends sensitive people.[47]

He was on the offensive again two days later, reiterating that 'Mr Moore's work is a menace from which the students at the Royal College should be protected.' Of a reclining figure in Corsehill stone, since lost, he said there was nothing more depraved from the 'natural or aesthetic point of view' in all primitive art: 'It is almost impossible to believe it came from the hands of a man of normal mentality.'

A series of published letters congratulated this assault on Moore's 'freak potato' art. The popular and provincial press took up the chase, for example 'Merry Andrew' in the *Daily Mirror*:

> 'Before these works I ponder in silence.' Personally I could not restrain one or two short, sharp yelps of pain, but some people may be stunned into silence by Mr Moore's ponderous imagination.[48]

For the *Bournemouth Echo* it represented 'nothing more nor less than Bolshevism in art ... foisted on us in malice prepense by foreigners ... the critics and writers who uphold it are in almost every instance aliens.'[49] The authentic voice of middle-class bigotry and racism!

For the future, much the most important review was by Herbert Read in the *Listener*, the influential weekly magazine of the BBC of which he was the art critic. It brought Moore into touch with a fellow Yorkshireman who was to be one of his closest friends and most powerful advocates: Read became in many respects the Roger Fry of the pre- and post-Second World War periods, and his influence as the guru of modernism lasted into the 1960s. He was a tall, shy, handsome man of considerable complexity. After an idyllic early childhood on the family farm in the Yorkshire dales, he had lost his father at the age of nine and been sent for five years to a Leeds orphanage school. Subsequently he worked in a savings bank, then enrolled at Leeds University where he came under the influence of Frank Rutter, director of the City Art Gallery and protagonist of the post-Impressionists. In 1915 he joined the army. The diffident poet, philosopher, aesthetician, and gentle anarchist ('Life must be so ordered that the individual can live a natural life, attending to what is within')[50] won the DSO and MC as an infantry captain in France. Entering the Treasury on demobilization, an odd choice, he moved to the Victoria and Albert Museum in 1922. Books, initially mainly on English literature, soon flowed from his pen.

Read and Moore first met around 1929, when Sir Eric Maclagan, the V and A's director and a Moore collector, introduced them at his office.[51] Shortly before the 1931 exhibition Read asked whether he might come and see Henry's work in Hampstead. The Moores gave him some supper and showed him the available sculpture and drawings. Read remained silent, and Henry and Irina wondered whether he had been utterly bored. Next morning (such was the postal service then) they received a letter from Read saying how interested and impressed he had been, and that he would be writing an article on Moore's work in the *Listener* of the following week. 'I was surprised, absolutely staggered when the article came out at the amount of appreciation and understanding he'd got out of that experience,' Henry recalled.[52]

The *Listener* article was a fine piece of propaganda, full of what now seem shameless over-simplifications and excessive denigration of Moore's sculptural forebears in England:

> For the past four hundred years artists have said: We will carve a block of stone or marble into the very image of Alderman Jones, or of Miss Simpkins posing as Venus, of a dying lion or a flying duck, and man has marvelled at the ingenuity with which the artist has accomplished this difficult aim. The aim of a sculptor like Henry Moore has nothing in common with this. He has no regard at all for the appearance of the object (if there is one) which inspires his work of art ... Sculpture is not a *reduplication* of form and feature; it is rather the translation of meaning from one material to another ... Henry Moore, in virtue of his sureness and consistency, springs straight to the head of the modern movement in England.[53]

Yet Read had almost uncannily good judgement, and showed an unmatched understanding of what the boldest contemporary artists were trying to do in those days. Such polemics were part of the crusade of modernism against closed and prejudiced minds. Later that year the *Listener* article was reprinted virtually verbatim in the book which made Read's name in the English-speaking world, *The Meaning of Art*.[54] It helped to spread Moore's growing fame through the Commonwealth.

Having again enjoyed a *succès d'estime et de scandale*, the Leicester Galleries exhibition brought total sales of £385, or about £7,700 in today's money. When about a third was subtracted for dealer's commission and the costs of material and transport, it was not a munificent return on three years' work. However, Henry told Oliver Brown that he was 'quite pleased with the result, considering the bad times',[55] and indeed it must have been a valuable addition to his teaching income.

Among the purchasers was the first museum director to buy one of his sculptures – and of a German museum at that. Max Sauerlandt, head of the Museum für Kunst und Gewerbe (Art and Crafts) in Hamburg, visited Moore in Hampstead shortly before the exhibition opened, and bought eight items – a charming little ironstone head in profile and seven drawings, all for the special price of £20.15s. The drawings were studies for sculpture, and three were in water-colours.[56] Dr Sauerlandt was a

strong supporter of such contemporary German artists as Nolde,
Kirchner, and Heckel, and also of a sculptor called Gustav Heinrich Wolff,
who worked in an idiom not dissimilar to Moore's. Wolff came to England
in 1930 and met Herbert Read, who urged him to visit Moore. The
German sculptor swiftly recognized Henry's quality, and in turn pressed
Sauerlandt to visit this English discovery. Sauerlandt did so, making his
purchases in time for the museum to be listed in the Leicester Galleries
catalogue as an owner. On 21 April Henry wrote to thank him for the
cheque he had received, adding:

> It makes me very proud to know that my work is represented in
> your museum. My Exhibition at the Leicester Galleries is meeting
> with more success than I let myself hope for – (knowing how bad
> the financial depression is everywhere). But what pleases me more
> than the sales is that many people seriously interested in painting
> & sculpture & fellow artists have taken the trouble to tell me that
> they have seen the work and liked it.[57]

When Hitler came to power in 1933, Dr Sauerlandt, who was one of
those courageous conservative Germans who opposed the upstart Führer,
was sacked. All so-called degenerate art was removed from display,
Moore's naturally included, to be finally confiscated (and probably
destroyed) in 1937. A water-colour portrait of Sauerlandt by his friend,
Emil Nolde, was among a few items hidden by a commissionaire and
later recovered. Nothing else has since been seen. Sauerlandt himself had
died of cancer on New Year's Day 1934.[58]

Though the Hamburg museum was the first to purchase a Moore
sculpture, an English museum, the Whitworth Art Gallery at Manchester
University, had already acquired four handsome Moore drawings. Thanks
either to its director Dudley Wallis or its chairman Sir Thomas Barlow,
it had bought for two guineas *Study of a Seated Woman* from the Warren
Gallery in 1927, the year before his first one-man show there. In the
same year Dorothy Warren herself presented a nude study in black and
white chalks; and in the following year two further drawings came
from a major Whitworth benefactor, A. E. Anderson, a shy, shabby little
bachelor with a keen eye who gave the museum more than four hundred
works of art.[59] There were more remarkable collectors of contemporary
art (though Anderson's taste was very wide) in those days in Britain than
is generally appreciated.

In the collective Moore memory it was a legacy which came to Irina
rather than any profits from the Leicester Galleries show which enabled

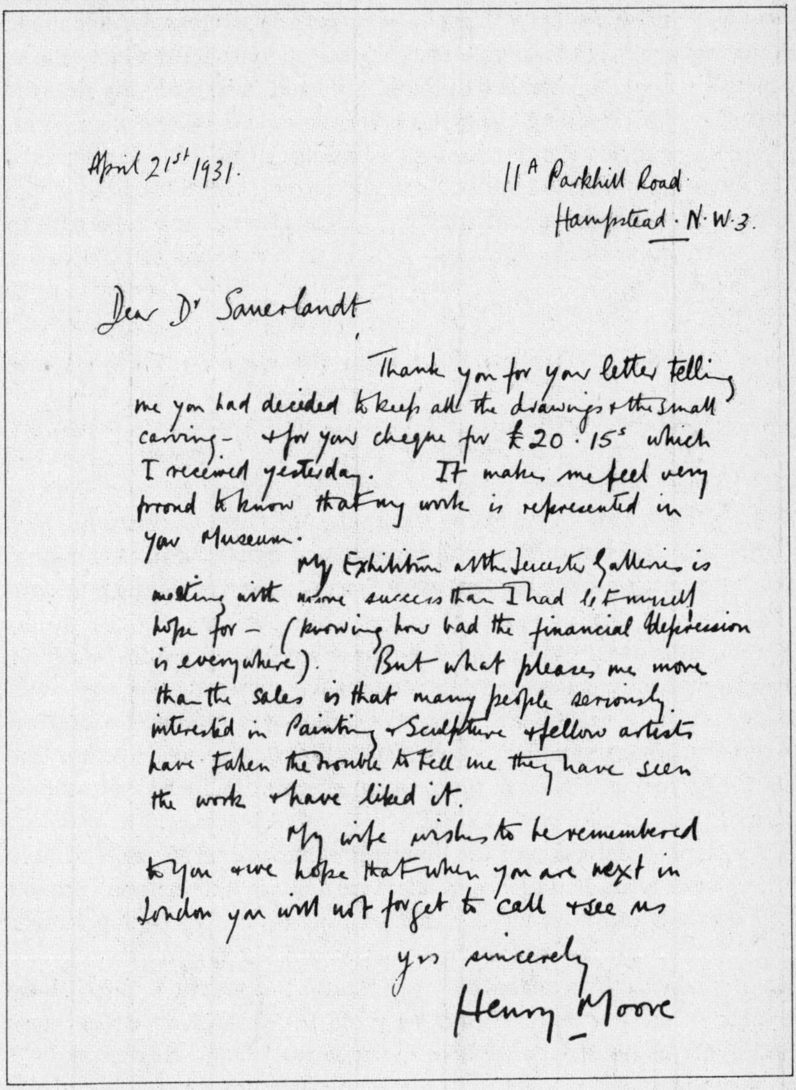

April 21st 1931.
11A Parkhill Road.
Hampstead · N·W·3.

Dear Dr Sauerlandt,

Thank you for your letter telling me you had decided to keep all the drawings & the small carving — & for your cheque for £20·15s which I received yesterday. It makes me feel very proud to know that my work is represented in your Museum.

My Exhibition at the Leicester Galleries is meeting with more success than I had let myself hope for — (knowing how bad the financial depression is everywhere). But what pleases me more than the sales is that many people seriously interested in Painting & Sculpture & fellow artists have taken the trouble to tell me they have seen the work & have liked it.

My wife wishes to be remembered to you & we hope that when you are next in London you will not forget to call & see us

yrs sincerely
Henry Moore

Letter from Moore to Dr Sauerlandt

them in 1931 to acquire a cottage in Kent. At heart, as we have seen,
Henry was a countryman. He had enjoyed working out of doors in
Norfolk. The studio in Hampstead was small and crowded, and there
were many social distractions. They had got to know Kent when visiting
Moore's sister Betty and her husband Rowland, who had moved to the
port of Deal. Before long Henry's mother settled nearby at Waldershare.
The cottage which Henry and Irina found and acquired for £80 was in
the hamlet of Barfreston, not far from Canterbury and within easy reach
of Dover. It is a pretty, gently rolling area, still unspoilt and full of sunken
lanes – so much so that it comes as a shock to find the Kentish coal mines
not far away, an oddly sited reminder of Henry's youth. Jasmine Cottage
consisted (and still does) of two labourers' cottages knocked into one. On
the ground floor Henry and Irina removed a wall to create a decent-sized
sitting room, and at the back they made a small studio with a pitched-
glass roof overlooking the garden. Upstairs are two matching bedrooms.
The garden, about sixty feet long, runs down to the churchyard of
St Nicholas, Barfreston, a jewel of Norman architecture with some of
England's finest surviving Norman carvings. Just over the fence between
the cottage and the churchyard stands a yew tree in which the church
bell hangs, summoning the faithful with a rather disappointing note, and
the pub next door is called The Yew Tree. Not long ago the oldest
inhabitant of Barfreston could still remember heavy vehicles rumbling
down the narrow lanes to collect Moore's larger pieces.[60] For their own
transport Henry acquired a motorbike. When he commuted to London
to teach in the summer, Irina went with him on the pillion seat to the
station and drove it back, the procedure being reversed when she fetched
him.[61]

For the rest of the decade the three agreeable poles of Moore's life were
Hampstead, Kent, and Chelsea, where he took up his new appointment
at the School of Art in the autumn term of 1931. His association with
the Royal College as student and teacher had lasted exactly ten years.
Even if none of the professors of sculpture had taught him anything
significant, he had much cause for gratitude: to William Rothenstein
above all, for his support, encouragement and worldly advice, and for
giving him the invaluable security of his first teaching job; to Leon
Underwood, for his eye-opening drawing lessons; to Barry Hart, for
some useful instruction in carving techniques; and to his friends and
contemporaries – Coxon, Hepworth, Bawden, Ravilious et al., for their
stimulus. Art students usually learn most from each other.

From Moore's point of view, though he never expressed it,

Rothenstein's flaw was his reluctance to commit himself and the college to the modern movement. Sir William's urbanity and the width of his interests made him anxious to keep a foot in every camp. By placating both traditionalists and modernists with his appointments, he created tensions which took their toll on Henry. Chelsea was an altogether more homogeneous establishment, and therefore much happier for the teaching staff.

Chapter VII

Hampstead, Chelsea and Kent

1931–6

Developments in politics and the arts usually reflect each other, though not always predictably. Despite the superficial glamour of the jazz age, the 1920s had been essentially a time of recovery from the First World War, of retrenchment, reconstruction, and quiet individual achievement. In the London art world there was little of the spirit of experiment and openness to foreign stimuli which had marked the pre-war years.

The tone of the 1930s was set by the formation in September 1931, following the financial crisis leading to the end of the gold standard, of the national coalition government under Ramsay MacDonald, who had led Britain's first, short-lived Socialist government of 1924. It was to be a decade of pulling together, despite much squabbling; of social concern aroused by the effects of the Depression; and of growing awareness of the appalling impact of Fascism, first in Germany, then also in the Spanish Civil War. Hitler's persecution of Germany's finest creative spirits, by no means all of whom were Jewish, led to the arrival in London of many brilliantly talented refugees. Among them were such seminal figures as Walter Gropius, Marcel Breuer, and László Moholy-Nagy, who brought with them the spirit of the Bauhaus school: art was not a self-contained activity, but intimately related to design, architecture, the machine age, and indeed to social well-being. Sheer economic necessity too drove artists into the design field, and rarely this century have the fine and applied arts been so fruitfully interwoven.

For Henry Moore the 1930s were the most inventive, productive, and arguably the happiest years of a very long career. At no other time was he so much at the heart of all that was liveliest and best in contemporary British art and so in touch with creative spirits in other fields. To be modern in the thirties was a heady experience. There were arguments and dissensions both artistic and political, sharpened as the decade wore on by events on the continent and the strong admixture of refugees. For a brief period, before many of the latter moved on to New York, London rivalled Paris as a focal point of all-round creativity; and in London the action centred on Hampstead. Henry was in the thick of it, adept at making a full contribution yet somehow remaining above the sound of battle.

Compared with many of their Continental peers, British artists lack a developed polemical spirit. Abstract theorizing and the formation of movements do not come naturally to them. None the less, feeling as they did the hostility of the academicians as well as of the general public, the more modern artists had since the 1880s banded together in such groupings as the New English Art Club, the Camden Town Group, the Allied Artists Association, the London Group, the idiosyncratic Vorticists, and the Seven and Five Society.

When the latter had been formed in 1920 with seven painters and five sculptors as its members, its initial statement of intent exemplified the spirit of that post-war era:

> A periodic explosion is essential in Art as in all other forms of organized activity, to blow away the crust of dead matter that time inevitably accumulates. The SEVEN & FIVE are grateful to the pioneers, but feel that there has of late been too much pioneering along too many lines in altogether too much of a hurry, and themselves desire the pursuit of their own calling rather than the confusion of conflict . . . Individual members have their own theories of Art, but as a group the SEVEN & FIVE has none.[1]

Leon Underwood, Ivon Hitchens and H. S. Williamson, later principal of Chelsea School of Art, were among the founding members who subscribed to this ringing plea for a quiet life. All that changed in 1924 when Hitchens rashly introduced Ben Nicholson to the group. He became a member, and showed an abstract painting (dubbed a 'dadaistic futility' by P. G. Konody in the *Daily Mail*)[2] in the society's fifth exhibition at Patersons in Old Bond Street. Nicholson became chairman in 1926, and it was probably as a result of their holiday together at Happisburgh in 1931 that Moore became a member that year. In a group show the following February his contribution prompted the *Scotsman* to comment sourly:

> Henry Moore shows a variety of carvings of the type which at a recent show in these galleries won for him a *succès de scandale*. He was fortunate, for probably the best thing that can happen to an

artist nowadays is to be attacked or ridiculed in the Press. His reputation as a 'genius' is then established.[3]

In that year the constitution of the Seven and Five was redrafted, a ruling being passed that members should be voted on each year rather than every three years and must receive a straight majority. Those of whom Nicholson disapproved could thus be the more easily purged. In 1934, continuing to use what now look like the committee techniques of the militant left, he manipulated the acceptance of a ruling that only non-representational (i.e. abstract) works could be shown under the society's aegis. Five members resigned or were voted out, including Edward Bawden, Frances Hodgkins, and Percy Jowett (who eventually succeeded Rothenstein at the Royal College of Art). Only ten members were left, and the society's show in October 1935 at the Zwemmer Gallery was its last. Anthony Blunt, the *Spectator*'s blatantly Marxist critic, later unmasked as a Soviet agent, scornfully described the group as a 'whole bedful of dreamers ... Miss Hepworth snores à la Brancusi; Mr Piper à la Picasso. There are signs that Mr Moore is regaining consciousness.'[4] For a few years, thanks to Nicholson, the Seven and Five had shown some of the finest artists of the day; but the man who made it also broke it, through an excess of doctrinal zeal for abstraction.

Contact with Ben Nicholson in Hampstead no doubt played its part in a significant loosening up of Moore's sculptural style in 1931, though Picasso is the most obvious influence. Hitherto his work had been marked by a certain massiveness and blockishness, stemming in part from its ethnographical inspiration and in part from caution in 'releasing' the form from the block of stone. Then suddenly Moore produced a carving in Hornton stone [45] which showed a new confidence in technique and whose organic shape placed it in the mainstream of European art. It was called *Composition*, and he regarded it as 'an important stage in my development as a sculptor'. This strange piece mixes here an egg shape, there a sort of head, the whole ambiguous creation looking half-human, half-juglike.[5] At last he was beginning to escape the tyranny of his material. Equally striking, and also from 1931, is a small reclining figure in lead [44], with a hollowed-out chest traversed by three bars, and a tiny, simplified head presiding over an acrobatically twisted body. Its sinuous rhythms are far removed from the ponderous grace of earlier treatments of the same theme. As John Russell has commented: 'Consistent it is not, but it crackles with confident invention.'[6]

Another obvious influence on the growing fluidity of Moore's work in the early 1930s was the Alsatian sculptor Hans Arp, whose sinuous, sexual fusion of landscape and the human form had made a deep impression on Barbara Hepworth when she visited him with Ben Nicholson in Meudon in 1932.[7] On the way back they called on Picasso, who showed them 'a miraculous succession of large canvases ... from which emanated a blaze of energy in form and colour'. Such experiences would have been shared with Henry in Hampstead.

The traffic was by no means all one way. When the Moores visited Jacques Lipchitz in Paris around 1932, he told them how impressed he had been by the Leeds *Reclining Figure* which he had seen at the recent Kunsthaus, Zurich exhibition. Some Moores were shown at the Musée des Beaux Arts in Brussels in 1931, and in a substantial exhibition of contemporary British art at the Hamburg Kunstverein (Art Society) in June 1932. This included such painters as David Bomberg, Edward Burra, Stanley Spencer, and Ben Nicholson; and Hepworth, Skeaping, and Underwood among the sculptors. German critics were reported to be impressed by the recovery of British art from its earlier sentimentality.[8]

Like Hepworth and Nicholson, Moore was by 1932 moving towards a more abstract and international style. His last fling for a few years in a broadly naturalistic vein produced one of his finest works: a three-foot-high *Mother and Child* in Green Hornton stone [46], a carving of marvellous tension and vitality. Completed in 1932, it was bought the following year from the Leicester Galleries by Robert Sainsbury, then aged twenty-seven and working in the family grocery business. He had met Moore at a party just before the exhibition opened, and clinched the deal before the private view. 'Henry used to say that the £160 I paid him for it was the equivalent of half a year's income,' Sir Robert recalled:

> The *Mother and Child* was in our hall from the time we bought it. There is no doubt that it was the exception for anyone to like it. Most people thought it was funny – and those were educated people. Even in those days there was a bias towards the arts among our friends.[9]

Stylistically this piece looks both forwards and backwards, having something of the alert intensity of the Leeds *Reclining Figure*, yet also foreshadowing the genuinely maternal feel of the post-Second World War madonnas and family groups. At last the inspiration from the British Museum had been fully absorbed.

A more organic period lay ahead, with the Natural History Museum providing some valuable stimuli. During his earlier holidays in Norfolk,

Henry had been strongly attracted by the sculptured shapes of the local flintstones, and had collected them with enthusiasm. The surrealist movement, which under the leadership of André Breton had been gathering strength in France through the 1920s, had endowed found objects with a new artistic sanctity. 'Biomorphic' art, deriving its forms from organic life, was a natural tributary of that broad surrealist river which flowed into British art in the 1930s. With its emphasis on the promptings of the subconscious and the association of ideas, it merged – often very subtly – with the British Romantic tendency to endow nature with human characteristics. Blake and Samuel Palmer had suffused nature with radiance and mystery. Henry's friend and sometime Royal College colleague, Paul Nash, delighted in strange juxtapositions. Graham Sutherland, who was on the staff of Chelsea School of Art when Moore joined in 1931, was before long to discover amid the 'exultant strangeness' of Pembrokeshire in Wales that 'landscape is not necessarily scenic, but that its parts have an individual figurative detachment'.[10] Stones, pebbles, twigs, bones, shells: Henry began to collect them all, to study their equivalents at the Natural History Museum, and to sketch them in his notebooks. As he drew them, a bone became a reclining figure, a stone was transformed into a head and shoulders.

Sometimes drawing was, in the best surrealist tradition, a form of automatism. With no preconceived ideas he would apply pencil to paper. As the lines took shape, an idea would crystallize, and a process of ordering would take place. Often he adopted this approach in the evenings. In the mornings by contrast he would start with a definite idea, perhaps to draw a seated figure. As many as thirty variations might appear on a single page, all within a few hours. One might then hold his attention as a potential sculpture.[11] The fertility of his imagination was prodigious, and would remain so. All his early carvings were done direct from drawings. Only around 1935 did he start to work from a preliminary small-scale model in plaster or clay, itself derived from a drawing.[12]

Henry's life was now without any tensions from having to work with incompatible colleagues. Chelsea School of Art provided company of Hampstead standards. The principal, H. S. Williamson, was a sound, cautiously modernist painter and a very good commercial artist. He designed many excellent posters, and also the long-lived packet for Smarties chocolate drops. Sutherland was already on the staff when he took over in 1930, recruited by his predecessor Percy Jowett; but he brought in Raymond Coxon and Moore, in 1932 adding Robert Medley, the painter and stage designer, and in 1938 the painter Ceri Richards.

Charged with starting up a proper sculpture school, Henry taught some life drawing as well at first, thereafter concentrating on modelling from life. It was all very small-scale:

> To begin with I only had three or four students who wanted to do sculpture, and I think there was some exam in which (other) students were supposed to do a bit of modelling. My class was in a tiny room at the bottom of the corridor. You couldn't have got more than seven or eight stands around the model.[13]

With one exception all the students of sculpture in his nine years at Chelsea were female, many of them débutantes of small talent picking up a smattering of art. Serious painting students however could and did come in and try their hand.

With its good company, agreeable lunches in nearby King's Road pubs and abundance of pretty girls, Chelsea was a pleasant environment even if the repetition involved in continuous teaching became wearisome. The action was in Hampstead. In 1932 Moore was caught up in the formation of a new group. The initiator was Paul Nash, who lived nearby: a stylish, articulate, well-travelled, and versatile man. Nash felt it was time to bring like-minded artists and architects together in mutual support and promotion of the modern spirit. Wells Coates, a gifted and energetic Canadian engineer-turned-architect, had recently formed the Modern Architectural Research Group (MARS) of progressive architects and planners. It seemed sensible for artists and architects to make common cause. Most of the artists whom Nash had in mind had shown in 1931 in an exhibition which he had helped organize at Arthur Tooth and Sons.[14]

Unit One's formation

In a letter to Moore of 17 January 1933, Nash suggested the two of them should get together with Edward Wadsworth and Wells Coates as 'the most stable and least biased members of the rather difficult collection of people who are likely to constitute the group'. He believed the other members they had agreed on were John Armstrong, Edward Burra, John Bigge, and Ben Nicholson, to whom he was writing guardedly about other possible members: 'Ben is a good fellow, but I do not regard his judgement as entirely sound, and I believe you agree on this.' Hepworth, Frances Hodgkins, and another architect, Colin Lucas, were eventually added.

The birth of Unit One, as it was dubbed in an attempt to combine the ideas of individuality and unity, was announced in, of all places, the letters column of *The Times* that June.[15] It was a neat bit of public relations which took advantage of a recent correspondence on nature and art. 'Unit One,' Nash proclaimed, 'may be said to stand for the expression of a truly contemporary spirit, for that which is recognized as peculiarly *of today* in painting, sculpture and architecture.' He pinpointed 'lack of structural purpose' as the crippling weakness of English art, allied to a tendency to revert to the 'nature cult'. The members of Unit One, he said, were at variance with the Great Unconscious School of Painting (apparently a reference to expressionism rather than surrealism)[16] and seemed to lack reverence for nature. More engrossing for them, he wrote, were design considered as a structural pursuit, and imagination explored apart from literature and metaphysics.

This was cryptic and misleading stuff. Apart from Nicholson and perhaps Wadsworth, none of the artists involved showed a marked taste for structure, while several of them including Moore and Nash himself certainly revered nature. Nash had furthermore a strong taste for literary inspiration. Herbert Read, whom Moore had introduced to the group in the spring of 1933, more convincingly if less specifically described its aims as 'to form a point in the forward thrust of modernism in architecture, painting and sculpture, and to harden this point in the fires of criticism and controversy'.[17] In the event, nowhere were these to burn more briskly than within the disparate ranks of Unit One.

The group's base was to be the Mayor Gallery, which had recently moved from Sackville Street, W1, to Cork Street around the corner. Freddie Mayor, who had opened it in 1925, aged twenty-two, was the son of two painters and a convinced advocate of contemporary art. The inaugural Cork Street show, in April 1933, brought Francis Bacon into the public eye for the first time. Moore was represented by four carvings, amid works by such major continental figures as Picasso, Masson, Ernst, Arp, and Klee. Mayor's own sharp eye for quality was reinforced by that of the gallery's chief backer, a wealthy young man of Australian forebears called Douglas Cooper who later became a malevolent critic of English art in general and Moore's in particular.

There followed in October 1933 an exhibition at the Mayor Gallery linked to the publication of Herbert Read's new book *Art Now*. This analysis of the main streams of art since Impressionism carried illustrations of four Moores, two Nicholsons, and one Hepworth, which Henry must have felt was about the right ratio. Most of the Unit One artists were represented in the exhibition, along with such distinguished foreigners as

Braque, Léger, Miró, Kandinsky, Dali, Soutine, and Giacometti.

The first exhibition devoted solely to Unit One members was held at the Mayor Gallery in April 1934. It was arranged by Douglas Cooper, was intended to be the first of a series, and subsequently toured the provinces, stopping in municipal galleries in six cities, including Liverpool, Manchester, Swansea, and Belfast. Much controversy was aroused along the way. In London it coincided with yet another book edited by Herbert Read, called *Unit One*, to which each member contributed a statement. Moore's listed five qualities in sculpture which he said were of fundamental importance to him: truth to material; full three-dimensional realization; observation of natural objects; vision and expression; and vitality and power of expression.

Except for truth to material, all were to be lifelong preoccupations. Of immediate relevance to the debates of the time were his emphasis on the human figure, organic and natural forms, asymmetry, and the psychological element. His distaste for the geometric was made clear, and abstraction was put firmly in its place:

> All art is an abstraction to some degree ... abstract qualities of design are essential to the value of a work, but to me of equal importance is the psychological human element. If both abstract and human elements are welded together in a work, it must have a fuller, deeper meaning.[18]

For the longer term, the most important passages concerned Henry's notion of vitality and power, which in sculptural terms he deemed to be 'a pent-up energy, an intense life of its own, independent of the object it may represent':

> Beauty, in the later Greek or Renaissance sense, is not the aim in my sculpture. Between beauty of expression and power of expression there is a difference of function. The first aims at pleasing the senses, the second has a spiritual vitality which for me is more moving and goes deeper than the senses. Because a work does not aim at reproducing natural appearances it is not, therefore, an escape from life – but may be a penetration into reality ... an expression of the significance of life, a stimulation to greater effort in living.

The first three sentences of the last passage were to be displayed in large type at dozens of Henry Moore exhibitions after the Second World War, in an attempt to persuade visitors unfamiliar with modern art to forget their preconceived notions of what constitutes beauty.

The Unit One book was the group's most solid monument, but the members' contributions brought out their fundamental differences. It had from the start been an oddly assorted selection of talent, with some veering to abstraction, others to surrealism, the architects to functionalism. The first exhibition turned out to be the last, and the end was not long in coming. In early 1935 Nash was persuaded, perhaps by the incorrigible Nicholson, that there should be a secret ballot on who should remain members. According to Nash, the vote had to be unanimous, and only he and Moore survived. Henry's more probable version was that members needed to attract more than half the available votes, and only he succeeded in doing so. As he later put it: 'I was Unit One.'[19]

Nash seemed to find it hard to believe that his brainchild was dead, writing to Moore from his beloved Swanage in Dorset:

> Douglas [Cooper] tells me you are the sole survivor of that crazy ballot. Very well, now it seems to me that the proper next step is for us to agree upon an architect who agrees about us . . . We could then announce that the result of the ballot has been the election of one sculptor and one painter and that they had agreed upon one architect.[20]

Wiser counsels, perhaps Moore's, prevailed and no attempt at resuscitation was made. The year 1935 thus witnessed the demise of both the Seven and Five and Unit One. Abstract art was moving into the ascendant. Ben Nicholson had started to produce his white reliefs in 1933. In the same year he and Hepworth joined *Abstraction-Création*, a Paris exhibiting society devoted to non-figurative art, and the following year underwent the spiritual experience of visiting Piet Mondrian in his Paris studio, emerging with 'an astonishing feeling of quiet and repose'.[21] In January 1935 Myfanwy Piper, as she soon became, produced the first issue of the magazine *Axis*, which was at the outset committed to abstract art but later came out against all factionalism.

From 1934 Moore's work too was to veer increasingly towards abstraction while never entirely losing its detectably human or organic basis. His second show at the Leicester Galleries, in early November 1933, found him at the end of a phase of opening out his reclining figures. Jasmine Cottage, so blessedly free from distractions, was proving to be a boon for productivity, as he told the Coxons in a letter of 3 September 1933:

This cottage idea was a good one, for me. For without it and a show in the offing, I should have had to have stayed sweating in the Hampstead studio, as it is I've averaged, according to Irina's reckoning, 8 hours carving a day, & yet have had the best part of a day once or twice a week at the sea, a game of tennis every two or three days at Waldershare, occasional trips to Canterbury or Dover & other odd jaunts on the motor bike, with spare spells of gardening (handyman to Nitchka) house decorating and repairing. We get up at six and go to bed soon after 9, and the day seems twice as long.

So far, he wrote, he had done four bits of sculpture, one of them quite large, and six or seven drawings, and was hoping to do a further three small carvings in the three weeks and three days left before 'blasted teaching again, & then, soon after, my show – both of 'em I hate to think about ... I admit I'm a bit worried now the time's getting near, that unpleasant keyed-up feeling is growing. What I'd like to see, Peachum, is the end of this teaching in sight.'

Moore's third one-man show was a smaller and less controversial affair than the first two. Productivity had evidently been well below target, two years' work having yielded eighteen sculptures and nineteen drawings (though some may well have been sold privately meanwhile, and not lent back). The sculptures were in the usual wide range of materials including lead and concrete – no bronzes – and priced between £20 and £175, the drawings at £7–£10. Despite the reduced choice, it did better than its predecessor, £700-worth of work being sold (about £14,000 in today's money). In addition to Robert Sainsbury, who had bought the *Mother and Child* for the top price, buyers included Sir Michael Sadler, now Master of University College, Oxford; Mrs Fanny Wadsworth, wife of the wealthy Unit One painter; and E. C. ('Peter') Gregory, a genial printer whom Henry had met through Charles Rutherston in Bradford and who was to become one of his closest friends.

The Times was sympathetic to the new work, preferring the more naturalistic forms and the more abstract ones to those in between, in which 'it is not the unlikeness but the likeness to Nature, the effect of deformed realism, that alienates sympathy ... he is a most interesting sculptor, with a real sense of form in the abstract and he is a most accomplished craftsman.'[22] In a lyrical review in the *Spectator*, Adrian Stokes likened Moore's last, opened-out concrete reclining figure, an astonishing creation with jutting breasts echoed by pointed knees, and

a single Cyclopean eye, to an image of Cleopatra reclining in the stern
of an Egyptian barge.[23]

The first book on Moore

It may have been the success of this second Leicester Galleries show
which, probably in late 1933, inspired the Charing Cross Road bookseller,
Anton Zwemmer, to suggest to Moore that the time had perhaps come
for a little book about his work. The latter naturally thought that an
excellent idea, and mentioned it to Peter Gregory, joint managing director
of the Bradford printing firm of Lund Humphries. The progressive Yorkshire firm, of which Gregory was also the chief shareholder, had latterly
opened an office with its own design department in Bedford Square, a
few minutes from Zwemmer's. According to Moore, Gregory agreed to
give Zwemmer an extended credit covering the cost of the printing. The
Yorkshire triangle was completed when Read was brought in to write
the text. He had finally moved to London that summer after two years
of lecturing in Edinburgh, settling in the Mall Studios after borrowing 11A
Parkhill Road from the Moores while they were spending the vacation in
Kent. He was paid £20 for his introduction of a few thousand words.
With a contribution from Henry himself towards the costs, the deal was
complete.[24]

The first of dozens of books on Moore's work was an attractive
production, with thirty-six full-page plates including six of drawings, and
a cover showing a Madonna-like beechwood figure of 1931 (now in the
Tate Gallery). By today's standards, the text is turgid, two-thirds being
devoted to theorizing about the merits of direct carving and inveighing
against the classical concept of beauty. Only after that did Read come to
Henry and his work, stressing his subject's close study of natural forms
and his truth to material. The sculptor's whole art, he wrote, was to
effect a credible compromise between the forms natural to the material
and the concepts of his imagination. He concluded:

> The life of an original artist of any kind . . . is hard; only an unfailing
> integrity of purpose can carry him through those years of financial
> failure, of public neglect or derision, which are his inevitable lot.
> All but a few are compelled to compromise. There has been no
> compromise in the life of Henry Moore, and now, in the fullness of
> his powers, he offers us the perfected product of his genius.

Since Moore was still young and not very well known, it was a courageous endorsement by Read, and one which Moore was bound greatly to appreciate. In the climate of the times, such public support was of inestimable value: confident though he was in so many ways, Henry always welcomed reassurance about the level of his achievement, and however famous he became, he remained anxious about how his work would ultimately be judged. The immediate response to the book's publication was however most disappointing, as Zwemmer's son Desmond recalled:

> Father had no machinery for distributing it, and he went around London himself subscribing it to Hatchard's, Foyles, Bumpus, Selfridges and so on. He said he got a miserable figure of sixteen subscriptions, and it certainly sold under a hundred copies on publication. Generally the booksellers looked through it and said, 'Oh my God, I suppose this is modern art. Oh no, we haven't got those sorts of clients.'[25]

According to Moore, Allen Lane, who was to found Penguin Books in 1936, was at that time a young travelling salesman working for his uncle, 'going around the provinces with an attaché case full of sample books, one of them being *Henry Moore*'.[26] It's a nice image, but in fact Lane was then thirty-two and managing director of the Bodley Head. He may, however, have assisted with the distribution. Foreign sales eventually helped disperse the edition, amounting as Moore remembered it to 1,500 copies. The book would have been remaindered, Desmond Zwemmer recalled, had not the big Japanese booksellers, Maruzen, placed a series of orders for five or more copies. Japan too had its surrealist movement, several of whose activists had begun to write about Moore's work around 1935.

The art critics in London reacted favourably, even Anthony Blunt treating it to a long, discursive review in the *Spectator* which began: 'There are few contemporary English artists to whom it would be worth devoting a monograph, but Mr Henry Moore is certainly among them.'[27] An appreciative article in the *Architectural Review* helped to establish a lifelong friendship between Moore and its author, J. M. Richards, who was soon to become the magazine's deputy editor. Henry liked the piece, and shortly afterwards the two men met by chance at a cricket match at Lords, to which the sculptor had gone with Raymond Coxon, Vivian Pitchforth, and Eric Ravilious. The latter introduced them, and Richards became a regular visitor to Parkhill Road, recalling:

Henry was very interested in everything, with a very sharp eye for what was going on, extremely serious about his work: I think he had by then a sense of his own value, as it were, even though he was struggling and little known. The great thing, I remember, was how open-minded he was, unlike so many avant-garde artists: he wouldn't only think of the movement he belonged to, and only admire the people who thought as he did. He was always a very good critic.[28]

They would have met before long in any event, since Hampstead was becoming the focal point for the great Bauhaus refugees, a twist of history owing much to an enterprising and catalytic spirit called Jack Pritchard. He had become a devotee of modernism, and had commissioned the Unit One architect, Wells Coates, to design a block of apartments in Lawn Road, Hampstead. The Isokon flats, as they were called after the company which Pritchard had formed, were one of the first fruits of the modern movement in architecture in Britain. They were novel not just in their long, low, rather liner-like lines with only porthole-style windows on the street side, but also in their intended use as single and double apartments for young professional people. Fitted kitchens were among the innovations provided. Tenants tended to be civil servants, lawyers, academics, and writers, including Agatha Christie and Nicholas Monsarrat, who later wrote *The Cruel Sea*.[29]

Before Pritchard had risked all by branching out on his own he had worked for Venesta. His searches across Europe for new uses for plywood, which the firm made, had brought him into contact with the Bauhaus and its presiding genius, the architect Walter Gropius. When Hitler came to power in 1933 Gropius's life was in danger, and Pritchard helped him to get out of Germany, brought him and his new wife Ise to Hampstead, and provided them with one of the Lawn Road flats. Soon afterwards they were joined there by the Hungarian Marcel Breuer, former director of the Bauhaus's furniture workshop, who before long designed his famous Long Chair in bent plywood for Pritchard's company; and by Breuer's compatriot László Moholy-Nagy, polymathic graphic designer, photographer and painter, who had also taught at the Bauhaus.

Breuer's talents were soon put to use within the Lawn Road block, where he designed a club-restaurant on the ground floor. It was called the Isobar, and was managed after a false start by Philip Harben, later famous as the first TV cook. Henry and Irina, though not members, ate there frequently with friends who were. It was the sort of place where

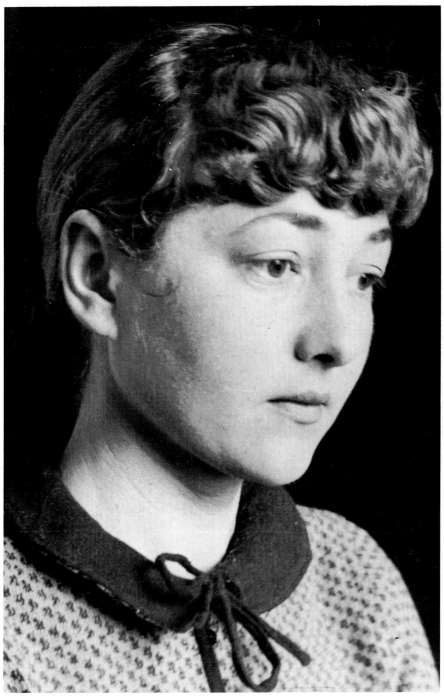

31. Portrait of Irina (Radetzky) by Henry Moore around the time of their marriage in summer 1929

32. Irina at the age of 6 in the Caucasus

33. Henry and Irina on their wedding day in 1929

34. Henry and Irina camping in Suffolk in the early 1930s

35. Moore's studio and home from 1929 to 1940 at 11A Parkhill Road, London NW3

36. *Reclining Figure*, 1929, 33 inches long, Brown Hornton stone, Leeds City Art Gallery. A masterpiece which remains arguably his finest stone carving

37. On holiday at Happisburgh, Norfolk, 1931: (left to right) Ivon Hitchens, Irina Moore, Henry Moore, Barbara Hepworth, Ben Nicholson and Mary Jenkins, whose husband Douglas took the picture

38. Moore and colleagues at the Royal College of Art, late 1920s: (left to right) Barry Hart (stone carving instructor); Professor Garbe (sculpture); Jack Clarkson (student); Henry Moore; and Alan Durst (wood-carving)

39. *Seated Nude*, 1929, $22\frac{1}{4}$ inches by 15 inches, Whitworth Art Gallery, Manchester

40. Dr Max Sauerlandt, director of the Museum für Kunst und Gewerbe in Hamburg, with Moore's *Head* in ironstone, purchased in 1931: Moore's first sale to a museum

41. Jasmine Cottage, Barfrestone, Kent, as it is today (with the author taking notes)

42. Henry and Irina's second cottage in Kent, Burcroft at Kingston, with some of its land

43. Moore in April 1931 with a stone carving, *Standing Girl* of 1926, later destroyed or lost

44. *Reclining Figure*, 1931, $16\frac{1}{2}$ inches long, lead

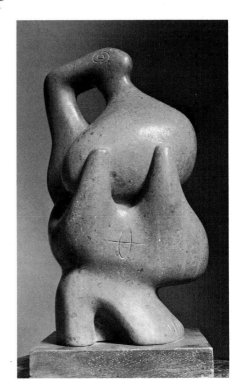

45. *Composition*, 1931, 19 inches high,
Blue Hornton stone. A Picasso-esque
departure marking a new freedom of style

46. *Mother and Child*, 1932, 35 inches high, Green Hornton stone, Robert and Lisa Sainsbury Collection for the Visual Arts, University of East Anglia, Norwich

47. *Reclining Figure*, 1930, 7 inches long, ironstone, collection of Sir Robert Sainsbury, London

48. *Reclining Figure*, 1934–5, 24½ inches long, Corsehill stone

49. *Reclining Figure*, 1935–6, 36 inches long, elmwood, Albright-Knox Art Gallery, Buffalo, New York. The first of the great elmwood reclining figures

50. *Reclining Figure*, 1936, 42 inches long, elmwood, Wakefield City Art Gallery. Feeling the grain of the wood is almost irresistible

51. *Reclining Figure*, 1937, 33 inches long, Hopton-wood stone. Like a nippled shoe-tree, it is one of Moore's most mysterious pieces

52. *Reclining Figure,* 1938, 13 inches long, lead (and later bronze), from which the huge version for Singapore was enlarged in the 1980s

53. *Recumbent Form,* 1938, 55 inches long, Green Hornton stone, Tate Gallery, London. An unprecedented opening-out of the stone

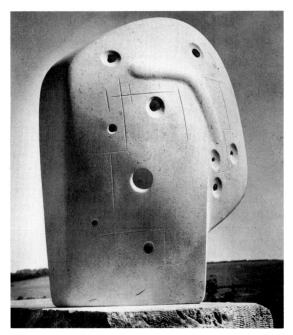

54. *Head*, 1937, 21 inches high, Hopton-wood stone, an enigmatic but intriguing presence

55. The object from the British Museum which inspired the *Head*: an Old Babylonian clay model of a sheep's liver divided into sections, annotated for the purposes of divination or omen-reading

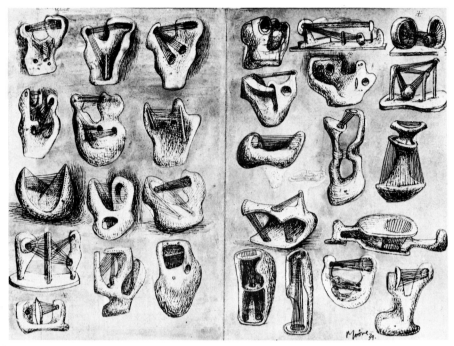

56. *Ideas for Sculpture in Metal and Wire*, 1939, $10\frac{3}{4}$ inches by 15 inches, pencil, pen and ink, and watercolour. Moore could produce such variations almost *ad infinitum*

57. *Ideas for Sculpture in a Setting*, 1938, 15 inches by 22 inches, charcoal, chalk and Indian ink: one of many claustrophobic, prison-like interiors from just before the Second World War

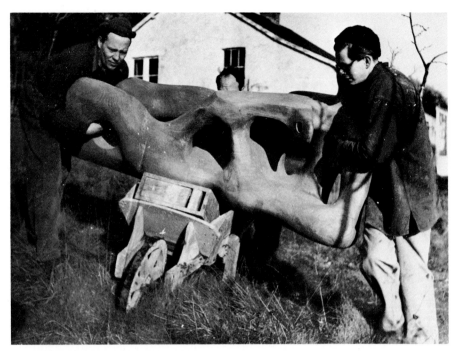

58. Bernard Meadows (right), Moore (centre), and an unknown helper moving the great elmwood Reclining Figure at Burcroft, Kent, 1939

59. The studio at 11A Parkhill Road around 1934

60. Moore in the 1930s

they might meet Hampstead locals like the zoologist Julian Huxley and his delightful Swiss-born wife Juliette; the Marxist physicist J. D. Bernal; the Russian-born architect Serge Chermayeff, soon to play a part in Moore's life; or Raymond Postgate, the Socialist writer who later founded *The Good Food Guide*.

Henry recalled earnest discussions between himself and other Hampstead friends on the one hand and Moholy-Nagy and Gropius on the other, with the latter bandying about all kinds of new ideas on how to link art with technology. Moholy-Nagy would insist that an artist should be able to order his work by telephone from a factory according to specifications. Gropius would counter with stories of the devotion of Bauhaus students to the classes of Klee and Kandinsky, even after being told by another lecturer that oil painting was an anachronism.[30]

A sprinkling of poets further enlivened the Hampstead world of art and architecture. Geoffrey Grigson, then living in Keats Grove and editing his magazine *New Verse*, was a frequent visitor to Parkhill Road and the Mall Studios. Nicholson, Read, Moore, and also Piper were among his best friends, and after the latest private view there would be discursive suppers in Soho: 'That was very marvellous at that stage of life,' Grigson recalled nostalgically.[31]

Stephen Spender came to know Moore in 1934, having for some time heard his work being discussed by such friends as Grigson and Herbert Read. He finally met the sculptor, uniquely, through a portrait commission:

> There was a magazine called *The London Mercury*, which used to have drawings by some rather terrible 'house' artist of living writers and poets, and they wrote to me asking whether this artist could come and do a drawing of me. I replied, rather arrogantly, that I would only allow Henry Moore to draw me.[32]

Spender was then twenty-five, and old enough to know that Moore did not do portraits. The editor, however, wrote to the sculptor, who – perhaps intrigued – agreed to have a go. Henry did a number of drawings, partly with the idea, which he subsequently abandoned, of amalgamating several done from different angles into a single composite portrait.[33] Most were in pencil, but one was in green ink, and there was a page of thumbnail sketches. The two most finished ones have hung on either side of the Spender grand piano in St John's Wood, showing the poet in three-quarter profile [62]. A certain intensity but not much character come through. The likeness is good and the pale eyes are well caught.

Normally Henry and Irina retreated from all the distractions of Hampstead to Barfreston in the vacations. In the summer, for a change and because Henry liked the east coast, they would sometimes rent a cottage at Sizewell, just above Aldeburgh in Suffolk (and later the site of an early nuclear power station), for a month or so with friends. The Coxons would come, and perhaps Blair Hughes-Stanton, a painter and etcher who had attended Leon Underwood's classes from the Royal Academy Schools, or their Hampstead neighbour Ivon Hitchens. Hitchens was a gentle, rather indecisive bachelor, and a bit of a fusspot. There would be long discussions about whether they should go to the beach for the day, or somewhere else. Hitchens was equally tentative about women, Henry recalled with an affectionate laugh, and used to wonder whether making love would be good for his painting. 'It wasn't for its own sake ... Oh dear, dear old Ivon!'[34] There would be games of cricket on the beach. On one occasion, which Henry liked to recall to illustrate how Irina often saved him from himself, someone challenged him to jump over a fence of spiked sticks wired at top and bottom. Irina realized what it might do to him and stopped him when he was about to try.

In the late summer of 1934, the Moores and the Coxons went on a motoring holiday to the Continent in the Coxons' old convertible Sunbeam tourer. The idea was to 'do' the cave paintings of the Dordogne and northern Spain.[35] The Coxons tended to be the initiators in such matters, but Henry helped with the preparations. 'I've found out where the Altamira caves are,' he told them proudly in a letter written on 30 July, his thirty-sixth birthday: a very pretty girl at a Spanish tourist agency in Piccadilly had located them in a travel book while he was on a visit to London from Kent. 'We go first to Santander ... at Barreda turn right to visit Santillana ... and three kms south-west of Santillana are the caves of Altamira ... The Paul Nashs have lent us a Spanish conversation book, which we'll have to start swotting up, & also they've sent us a prescription for some stuff to make you immune from Malaria, etc.'

What drew Moore to the caves was not just his long-standing interest in primitive art, but 'the mystery of the hole – the mysterious fascination of caves in hillsides and cliffs', as he described it.[36] Since the Ice Age that same fascination has lured men into the innermost recesses of the earth, perhaps in search of its secrets, perhaps to worship in the womb of the great Earth Mother. Coxon's memory is that they drove straight down to Bordeaux, crossed over the border and headed for Pamplona, thereafter taking the coastal road to Santander and the Altamira caves, by whose ochreous yellowness they were much struck. Having enjoyed this Royal

Academy of cave painting, as they jokingly called it, they headed for Madrid, spending a night sleeping within view of the great Escorial Palace. They travelled very simply, Henry recalled:

> It was a very close foursome. The two girls slept in the car: you could take the seats down and sleep in the back. We had a sleeping bag each and slept by the side of the car each night, like camping without a tent. The weather was very kind to us. I don't think we ever got badly wet, though there were some heavy downpours.[37]

As they set off for Madrid, there was a sinister noise from the left front wheel. With the help of a volunteer interpreter, a local garage explained that a hub screw was cracked, and that it would take a week to get one from England. Eventually they agreed to forge one themselves. While this was being done the English party took a bus to Toledo to see the El Grecos, including the great *Burial of Count Orgaz*: El Greco's use of distortion for expressive effect had made him a sort of honorary godfather of the modern movement. In Madrid they visited the Prado in an exhausted state, and went to a bullfight. A Spaniard took a fancy to Henry and insisted on showing them behind the scenes. 'They always take Henry for a sucker,' Irina commented disapprovingly.[38]

Not sparing themselves or the reinvigorated Sunbeam, they headed across to Barcelona on the Mediterranean coast. There the main target was the Museo Episcopal at Vic (or Vich) just north of the Catalan capital, with its fourteenth-century paintings and sculptures. On the return journey they paused in the Dordogne, latterly favoured by the English for its green and rolling countryside, forests, and rivers. The interest of the travelling quartet naturally focused on those caves where Magdalenian man's artistic talents had seemed to reach their zenith. The finest known cave paintings, at Lascaux, had not yet been discovered. But there were moving examples to be seen, interspersed with those very evocative bear claw marks, at Rouffignac, Les Eyzies, and Font de Gaume, the latter two of which Moore remembered. Before bearing west to Calais they paid a sentimental visit to the battlefield of Cambrai and Bourlon Wood, where Henry had been gassed seventeen years earlier. There was not much debris of war visible, until Coxon spotted two inches of pointed steel sticking out of the roadside. Pulling it out he found it was a bayonet, which thereafter did duty as a poker at their home by the Thames in Hammersmith. Irina, who had done most of the catering on the trip, prepared a superb final picnic which they consumed on the beach at Calais. Gin had done almost all the driving.[39]

From Jasmine Cottage to Burcroft

Almost a year later, in August 1935, Henry and Irina sold Jasmine
Cottage at Barfreston for £350, and paid £500 for a much larger property
six miles to the west at Marley, near Kingston. It had five acres of land
shelving down into a valley, with hills on the far side: 'Any bit of stone
stuck down in that field looked marvellous, like a bit of Stonehenge,' he
commented later.[40] The house was called Burcroft – 'just an ordinary
modern bungalow, but much lighter and brighter to live in & easier to
keep clean than Jasmine Cottage,' he told the Coxons, urging them to
come and stay and reminiscing about the Spanish trip and the discovery
of the bayonet a year back.[41] Before long he had a studio-workshop
erected, and a greenhouse for Irina's plants and cacti. Reflecting their
growing sense of security, they sold the motorbike and bought a new
Austin Seven on hire purchase, thanks to a persuasive salesman. They
had originally planned to spend just £30 on a second-hand one.

The move from Barfreston to Kingston was a nice example of life
directly affecting art. As Moore put it:

> Living at Burcroft was what probably clinched my interest in trying
> to make sculpture and nature enhance each other. I feel that the
> sky and nature are the best setting for my sculpture. They are
> asymmetrical, unlike an architectural background with its verticals
> and horizontals. In a natural setting, the background to a sculpture
> changes if you move only a very small distance.[42]

In later life Moore preferred to ignore the fact that much of his finest
work, including the great elmwood carvings, is indoor sculpture; and
that some of his best bronzes look very well indeed in architectural
settings. He liked to deal in homespun, quotable verities. On this theme
the most frequently cited utterance dates from 1951:

> Sculpture is an art of the open air. Daylight, *sunlight*, is necessary
> to it, and for me its best setting and complement is nature. I would
> rather have a piece of my sculpture put in a landscape, almost any
> landscape, than in, or on, the most beautiful building I know.[43]

That is an archetypal Moore statement. It looks good, it sounds good. It
makes you feel: Isn't he wise, simple and down-to-earth, unlike all those
pretentious old critics! Yet the harder you scrutinize each sentence, the
less convincing it seems. The opening generalization is bold, eye-catching,
memorable, but obviously true of only about fifty per cent of all sculpture,

if as much, and is not even valid, for the reasons of size and materials already mentioned, for a great deal of Moore's own work. If all the carvings in the British Museum, the Museum of Mankind, and the Victoria and Albert Museum were exposed out of doors, a majority would not only rapidly disintegrate but would look much the worse, designed as they were for church or cathedral interiors or the dim habitations of primitive peoples. Nor is it difficult to think of natural settings in which Moore's own work would look pretty terrible: bogland, scrubland, pine plantations ... the point need not be laboured. If he had said 'Most of my larger bronzes look better in a natural setting than against buildings, however good,' it would have been more accurate and more modest, but less striking.

It was almost certainly in this summer of 1935 that Henry enjoyed for several weeks the services of a first assistant. His name was Jack Hepworth, and he was a first cousin of Barbara's (his father being her father's younger brother). After a spell at St Martin's School of Art in the Charing Cross Road, he had attached himself to Ben Nicholson as a pupil after the latter had moved to 7 Mall Studios with Barbara. 'Although my main interest was in painting,' Hepworth junior recalled, 'I was already spending some of my time at Mr Gumbrell's mason's yard in Lismore Circus, trying my hand at carving and masonry, and I occasionally helped Barbara with some roughing out.'[44] Working there and living in a succession of rooms in and around Parkhill Road, he naturally came to know Henry, who was thirteen years his senior, and Irina. Eventually they suggested that he come down to Burcroft and lend a hand with some of the basic initial carving which is pure drudgery for the accomplished practitioner. He remembers being considered good enough to be entrusted with a large block of white Carrara marble, and it was presumably this same block which became the almost completely abstract and attractively cryptic *Sculpture* of 1935 (later acquired by the Chicagoan collector of Moore's work, Joel Starrels), since it is the only surviving white marble piece from that immediate period. Hepworth found the Moores extremely kind. They took him around with them, even on a visit to Henry's mother at Waldershare, who struck him as 'a dear old lady of great character'. Despite the unique experience of working for Britain's two leading sculptors he remained primarily a painter, showing before long with the Circle group under the name of Arthur Jackson, to avoid confusions of identity. Later, with the encouragement of Leslie and Sadie Martin, he turned to architecture.

For Henry the experiment was evidently a success, since in early 1936 a meeting with three young students from Norwich School of Art led him to take one of them on. They were introduced to him by a former Royal College pupil, Elizabeth Raikes, herself a friend of a Norwich School of Art teacher. One of the youthful trio was Bernard Meadows. He had brought some of his work to show Moore, and could scarcely believe his luck when next day he received a postcard asking whether he would like to work with him. For the next eighteen months he assisted Henry during vacations from Norwich, subsequently moving his base to a room in Hampstead which he shared with a Norwich friend. Down in Kent he lived with the Moores as a member of the family: full board and lodging, in effect, but no pay. It was to be by far Henry's most enduring relationship with another artist, lasting with only a few gaps for the rest of his life, in one form or another. Both of them looked back on those Burcroft years as a sort of prolonged, hard-working but intensely enjoyable idyll, destined to be destroyed first by the war and then, beyond recall, by the pressures of fame and the sophistication of modern communications and travel.

The house had two bedrooms, a kitchen, and bathroom, but no electricity or piped gas. Lighting was by oil or pressure lamps, and water was heated by bottled gas. Irina kept dozens of chickens, and many eggs were consumed, usefully supplemented by the local fauna, as Meadows recalled:

We used to shoot rabbits and other people's pheasants and partridges with a double-barrelled 12-bore and a single-barrelled 4·10. There was a copse along one side of the field, and at dusk there were hundreds of rabbits. We used to swim two or three times a week in the summer, chiefly at Dover, occasionally at Deal, and then go to the cinema. I have never seen so many bad films in my life, and a lot of good ones, of course. Irina would never go to foreign films. Henry was like a boy, jokey, singing bawdy army songs he had learnt in the First World War. There was a *simplicity* about him, not a naiveté. We used to have trials of strength. He was always stronger than I was. He was very tough. We used to stand on our hands against a wall, and he would do a press-down and take a match-box off the ground in his teeth: he was that sort of character. We often used to get up at 5 a.m. to start work. To wake ourselves up we would throw buckets of cold water over each other, dry off and have breakfast and start work right away. One year when he was preparing for an exhibition we worked from 7 a.m. to 3 the next morning *for three weeks!*[45]

Moore had previously been spending two or three whole days preparing a large piece of stone for carving – knocking the corners off and so on, a straight labouring job. From Michelangelo to Rodin, sculptors had employed assistants to do much of the preliminary work, and Henry had no hesitation in following their example. Just how much of the work the assistant executed depended on many factors, including the degree of trust established. Generally Moore allowed Meadows to carve down to within a quarter of an inch of the final surface: no closer partly for reasons of safety (a mistake would probably ruin the block); and partly because Henry lost interest if Meadows left too little to be done. If they were not working on the same piece, they worked alongside each other, discussing work and politics the whole time. Generally Meadows – at twenty-one when he joined almost seventeen years younger than Moore – took the more youthfully dogmatic line, Henry seeing the more human aspects of the issue. After a hard day's carving Henry would sometimes draw late into the night.

For Meadows it was a matchless education, and one which led ultimately to him becoming professor of sculpture at the Royal College, a nice irony of fate, and a well-known artist in his own right. One of his duties at Burcroft was to help Moore to photograph his own work. Henry had recently started to do this to save himself from the expense and, as he saw it, incompetence of professional photographers. He took enormous care, Meadows recalled:

> I used to suffer great pangs of impatience while he fiddled around getting the camera in the right place, getting it focused and the light right on the sculpture, with me holding up sheets of paper to reflect it, and so on – always with a plate camera: it's a direct image, you know exactly what you are going to get. He took just one shot. All his early photos are very factual. His aim was to get as near the actual existence of the thing as possible.[46]

Moore was also, from the start, interested in certain photographic effects: by taking a close-up of a small carving only a few inches long against the sky or a distant landscape, it could be made to seem monumental, thus demonstrating that scale is not just a matter of size. Henry would later cite this to justify his belief that small pieces could be enlarged, with some necessary adjustments, to enormous dimensions and gain thereby. He was however already thinking big. As he expressed it in 1937:

> If practical considerations allowed me, cost of material, of transport, etc., I should like to work on large carvings more often than I do.

The average in-between size does not disconnect an idea enough from prosaic everyday life. The very small or the very big take on an added size emotion ... carving in the open air, I find sculpture more natural than in a London studio, but it needs bigger dimensions. A large piece of stone or wood, placed almost anywhere at random in a field, orchard or garden immediately looks right and inspiring.[47]

As so often, this raises more questions than it answers. How big did he mean by large? In using the phrase 'more often', he suggests the size of his larger pieces of this period, i.e. around three feet long or tall: by later standards, relatively small. As it is, his work of the 1930s never gives the impression of being grossed up just to make an impact. Working on a modest scale may have stimulated his inventiveness, for from 1932 onwards he produced a strikingly diverse range of carvings. Some are almost completely abstract though always with organic roots like *Bird and Egg* of 1934, which relates to the childhood game of knurr and spell; or *Two Forms* of the same year, in which a scooped-out and pierced oval form seems to incline protectively over a much smaller form resembling an avocado pear stone, evidently a metaphor for the mother and child theme. Among the most remarkable is a *Reclining Figure* of 1935 in Corsehill stone [48]. It resembles an old stone bedwarmer: the human form is reduced to a small head, two tiny mounds for breasts, from which a strange fin leads to the larger mound of the feet. In others, such as the Arp-like *Mother and Child* of 1936, the human reference is a little more explicit. In this year a chunkier phase begins, squareish or rectangular forms with many incised surface markings seeming to indicate a reversion to blockishness; yet these are blocks transformed into mysterious, often powerful yet strangely elegant utterances in stone. From some of them, like *Head* of 1937 [54, 55], an almost religious aura emanates. While many of the later bronzes have a blandness which makes them go stale quickly, these more cryptic and complex carvings of the 1930s withstand endless scrutiny without yielding up all their secrets.

The first elmwood masterpiece

With so much successful experimentation behind him, Moore had – probably in late 1935 or early 1936 – felt able to tackle a major treatment of the reclining figure theme in wood for the first time. From a Canterbury timber merchant he obtained a large trunk of elm, a wood which, though inclined to crack, has a beautiful grain which can add greatly to the flow and tactile quality of a carving. Such a piece must be tackled layer by layer so that the wood can dry out progressively. If too much is done at one time, it is liable to crack. So it would have been several months before the piece was completed. Feeling able to take greater liberties with wood than with stone, and in the later stages with Meadows' assistance, he opened out the figure of this reclining woman in a way that he had previously attempted only in lead and, to a lesser extent, moulded concrete. The complete elmwood lady [49] is a magnificent creature measuring three feet long, lying on her left elbow and flank, small rounded breasts poised high between powerful rounded shoulders and above a cave-like hole in lieu of a chest. The viewer's eye follows the undulating grain of the wood down over her tapered waist, past the tiny mound of her navel to the gaping hills that are her legs, then into the shadow-filled valley between them. *Reclining Figure* (1936) is one of Moore's landmark works and the first of six elmwood variations on the same theme spanning thirty years, none of them less than superb.

Yet for almost three years she found no purchaser, and it took an American to summon the necessary nerve and resources. The man who fell for her in spring 1939 was Gordon Washburn, director of the Albright (later Albright-Knox) Art Gallery in Buffalo, near the Niagara Falls, a museum which after the Second World War was to acquire one of the best collections of contemporary art in the world. Since opening in its Greek Revival building in 1905, it had been devoted to Old Masters, but in 1939 Washburn opened a Contemporary Art Room, for which the Moore was intended. The price paid was £150. Thanking him for his cheque, Henry said he looked forward to their next meeting in London – 'or when my wife and I make the visit to America we intend to make one day'.[48]

Thanks to the outbreak of war, the first visit did not take place till 1946. Yet if a suggestion from a British Consular official in Chicago, John Thwaites, had been accepted, Moore would have had cause to visit that city as early as 1937. Thwaites, who later became an influential art critic, tried in that year to persuade the Foreign office to support an exhibition of Moore's work in the USA. The Foreign Office sent him a memorandum stating that it had 'no official money for this purpose', but that the British Council (then three years old) might conceivably help. Since counteracting Nazi propaganda had been the British Council's main mission, and since its officials believed that 'the Americans object most strenuously to any form of foreign propaganda', it felt unable to be of any assistance.[49] It is interesting to speculate whether such an exhibition held in 1937 might have significantly affected Moore's career.

Washburn's purchase for the Albright-Knox was not the first to be made by an American museum. He had been pipped to the post in 1936 by Alfred Barr, the first director of the Museum of Modern Art in New York. Barr had met Moore on a visit to London in 1928, when he was struck by the sculptor's admiration for the Chacmool. Barr revisited London, and Moore, in 1935 and 1936, partly to collect work for an exhibition held in 1936 at MOMA called *Cubism and Abstract Art*. For this Henry lent him *Two Forms* in Pynkado wood – the two-part piece of 1934 relating to the mother and child theme, mentioned earlier. Before long Barr decided that this carving should be a part of the Museum's permanent collection. Questing around for funds, with which MOMA then seems to have been far from amply supplied, he asked Moore whether there might be anyone in England ready to help the museum to acquire it. Henry suggested Sir Michael Sadler, who sent the money so that the museum itself could be the purchaser rather than he the donor.[50]

Among other Americans who visited Moore in the 1930s were James Johnson Sweeney, later a leading figure in the museum world but then living in Paris, in Hampstead in 1932; Sturgis Ingersoll, a Philadelphia lawyer who became a substantial collector, in Hampstead in 1934; and the painter, poet, and collector Gordon Onslow-Ford, in Kent in 1939 before making what turned out to be a seminal purchase.[51]

The 'Buffalo' reclining figure was almost immediately followed by a sister figure [50] which was later purchased by the Wakefield City Art Gallery. Also in elmwood and seven inches longer than her predecessor, the second carving took the opening-out process even further. The evolution of the characteristic Moore hole had gone through three phases. First there had been the void created almost incidentally – and not particularly originally – by a raised limb, as with the arm of the Leeds *Reclining Figure* of 1929. Then in the early 1930s came the little semi-abstract pierced carvings and terracottas, many of them simply called *Composition*, some in several parts. These have, as noted, a strong affinity in many instances with work being done by Barbara Hepworth. It was the union of hole and human figure, in this third phase marked by the first two great elmwood carvings, which represented Moore's first major stylistic contribution to sculpture.

The top halves of the 'Buffalo' and 'Wakefield' figures are not dissimilar, but in the second carving the treatment of the legs is more naturalistic and also more sculpturally consistent: the two parts of the body echo each other, void calling to void, and the grain of the wood is even more beautifully used. It is hard to choose between the two: 'Buffalo' is perhaps more mysterious, her gaping legs seeming almost threatening. 'Wakefield', though more opened out, seems chunkier and more cheerful. Her charms, however, did not make a very immediate impact on the purchasing committee of Wakefield City Art Gallery. Henry showed her there in the South-West Riding Artists' Exhibition in November 1938 (only a few miles from his native Castleford). She was then priced at 300 guineas, but he offered to halve this to £150 to enable the museum to buy it there and then. The Victoria and Albert Museum in London offered to help, and Peter Gregory said he would raise £50. But even with these inducements Ernest Musgrave, the gallery's director, could not persuade his committee to acquire the work. It took the plunge only in 1942, for the same modest price, of which it had to find just £30 from its own funds.[52]

From now on the hole – space – became part of Moore's sculptural language. In 1937 he was to apostrophize the hole in almost lyrical terms:

> The first hole made through a piece of stone is a revelation.
> The hole connects one side to the other, making it immediately more three-dimensional.
> A hole can itself have as much shape-meaning as a solid mass. Sculpture in air is possible, where the stone contains only the hole, which is the intended and considered form.
> The mystery of the hole – the mysterious fascination of caves in hillsides and cliffs.[53]

Henry's idea that space has its own identity and significance was not always very easily assimilated, even perhaps by his admirers; and it does require a small mental adjustment. If we look at the silhouette of a tree in winter, we are struck by the shape of the branches outlined against the sky. Yet the impact of those shapes derives to a considerable extent from the configuration of the spaces which branches and twigs define. Chunks of pure blue sky glimpsed through the columns of the Parthenon at Athens or the ruins of some old abbey: their shape and their vividness are an essential part of the memory we carry away. So it is with many of Moore's sculptures. Space penetrates them as they penetrate space. That is one reason why he liked the larger ones to be viewed in a natural

setting and preferably against a background of sky. There, without inter-
ference from other works of man, solid form and space could mutually
embrace.

Chapter VIII

Surrealism, constructivism and socialism

1936–9

At no other time in this century have history and Britain's intellectual life been as closely intermeshed as in the last three years of the 1930s. Indeed the sensitivity of British writers and artists to events abroad provided an exemplary contrast to the behaviour of the British government. First under Stanley Baldwin, who had replaced Ramsay MacDonald as Prime Minister in 1935, and then under Neville Chamberlain, it equivocated in the face of Fascism's onward march, yielding supinely to the popular yearning for peace at any price.

The middle-class intelligentsia, by contrast, had been alerted to the full significance of developments on the Continent if not by their own travels then by the arrival in London of that steady stream of impressive refugees. If Hitler's accession to power in January 1933 had first set in motion the internationalizing and radicalizing of London's cultural life, the process was sharpened and accelerated by the outbreak of the Spanish Civil War in July 1936. It has been convincingly said that no foreign question since the French Revolution so excited and divided British intellectual opinion.[1] While all those of left-of-centre, socialist and communist sympathies naturally supported the Republican government, some Roman Catholics and anti-communists far from sympathetic to German Nazism favoured General Franco and his regular army forces. The war took on an international dimension when Mussolini and Hitler sent military aid to Franco, to which the Soviet Union replied by reinforcing the Republic whose armed workers had so unexpectedly held Franco's forces at bay. Unenthusiastic about the Republic and fearing a general war, the British and French governments proposed a European pact of non-intervention. To this they ignobly adhered while Germany, Italy and Russia flagrantly flouted it.

Henry himself was much affected by the appalling events in the country which he had so recently visited, writing to the Coxons: 'Of course one would be moved in any case by the happenings in the Spanish revolution, but our trip there makes the picture of it twenty times as vivid.'[2] His sympathies, like those of his friends, were unequivocally on the Republican side. Although generally suspicious of ideological entanglements, he had two years earlier given his support to the Marxist-oriented Artists International Association. The Artists International, as it was first and more explicitly called, had been founded in 1933 by a talented group of painters, cartoonists and designers, several of whom had been to Russia (i.e. Clifford Rowe and Pearl Binder). Its stated aim was to mobilize 'the international unity of artists against Imperialist War on the Soviet Union, Fascism, and Colonial oppression'.[3] Behind this political front compassionate and indignant hearts beat in sympathy with the victims of unemployment and poverty at home and of Fascism abroad. In retrospect one of the AI's most interesting achievements was to bring together out-and-out modernists and artists of more conventional, academic and, in many cases, social-realist persuasion. Their social consciences were stronger than their artistic differences, which means they must have been very strong indeed.

Moore was among the mixed bag who showed at the AI's first exhibition in September and October 1934. It was called *The Social Scene*, and was held in a large shop in Charlotte Street off Tottenham Court Road. Many of the works were overtly propagandist, depicting the hardships of the proletariat, starving children and the brutality of the police as well as straightforward scenes from working life. Interspersed among paintings, drawings, cartoons, and photographs on such themes were items by Moore, Paul Nash, Edward Burra, and Henry's Chelsea colleague Robert Medley. Though Moore seems to have had few if any qualms about being identified with the far left in this exhibition, there is no reason to believe that he joined the Communist Party, as has sometimes been suggested. 'I was approached by the Communists in the 1930s,' he recalled, 'when a lot of people did join them. But I didn't go that far. To be a member of the Communist Party was an active role which I didn't want to have.'[4]

In 1935 the Artists International sought to broaden its appeal by adding the word Association to its name and adopting as its aim the 'unity of artists against Fascism and War and the suppression of culture'.[5] Its second exhibition, called *Artists against Fascism and War*, coincided with Mussolini's invasion of Abyssinia and brought together artists from across the spectrum: as one commentator put it, 'Those whom art politics have put asunder, an exhibition against War and Fascism has joined together.'[6] Thus Moore, the Nicholsons, Piper, Léger, Zadkine, and Marcel Gromaire, among other members of the avant-garde, rubbed shoulders with such subsequent pillars of the Royal Academy as Augustus John, Laura Knight, Ethel Walker, James Fitton, and Charles Cundall. More than 6,000 visitors paid threepence each to marvel at this artistic diversity.

Soon after the outbreak of the Spanish Civil War an AIA member, the painter Felicia Browne, became the first British woman to be killed in action there. Several other members suffered a similar fate with the British Battalion of the International Brigade, for which the AIA made a banner. Fund-raising efforts proliferated, and the war was one of the main topics discussed at the first British Artists' Congress in the first half of 1937. This was held at the Conway Hall in London in parallel with an exhibition also organized by the AIA. The name of Henry Moore featured prominently in a box on the front page of the Congress's agenda, as one of the 'well-known artists and critics' supporting the twin ventures. His friends Herbert Read, Edward Wadsworth, Eric Ravilious, and Raymond Coxon were among the thirteen others listed.

The Congress again brought together artists of widely diverging views in discussion of such matters as a possible trade-union style of organization for the profession, the patronage of art by the state, and some aesthetic questions. The accompanying exhibition, held at 41 Grosvenor Square, was divided into sections, and Moore exhibited with the British Surrealist Group, to whose formation we will shortly come. This was the occasion which prompted the publication of a famous broadsheet attacking the British government's policy of non-intervention of Spain. Moore was not only one of the fifteen signatories, but designed the front page. Headlined 'We ask your attention', it featured what looks like a trombonist (no doubt playing a fanfare) overlaid on the type. The group pointed to the far from neutral effects of the government's policy and its move to make the recruitment of volunteers illegal, insisted that pacifism had been discredited by events in Spain, and warned of the growth at home of something it called 'Fascism by deceit'. As if anxious to reinforce the unconvincing tenor of this phrase, it concluded by inviting sympathizers to intervene 'as poets, artists and intellectuals by violent or subtle subversion and by stimulating desire'.[7]

October 1937 found Henry signing letters to provincial newspapers, with Epstein, Nash, Read, and others, to drum up support for the British section of the International Peace Campaign: a national congress, prompted partly by the resumption of the Sino-Japanese war, was held later that month. In early 1938 he came near to active involvement, having been invited to Spain by the Republicans with a small delegation including Epstein, Rose Macaulay, Charlotte Haldane, Stephen Spender, and the American singer Paul Robeson. 'The idea was,' Henry recalled, 'that we were going to tour the Spanish towns and report on the Republican government's attitude towards art, artists, and museums.'[8]

More significantly perhaps, the visit would have been an act of solidarity. The refusal of the Foreign Office to give them the necessary permits to travel (apparently because they did not fit into any of the permitted categories) was presumably based on the government's non-intervention policy and the group's leftish sympathies. Epstein commented: 'If the invitation had come from Franco we should probably have got our visas.'[9] Being a very law-abiding fellow, Moore did not try slipping over the border illicitly, as did Stephen Spender and the artist S. W. Hayter. Spender recalled:

> Henry always took the line, very sensibly I think, that his art expressed his feelings and was therefore in some mysterious way anti-fascist and humanistic, which I would agree with. I would never have pressed him at all to do the kind of boring things I did.[10]

None the less Moore did at this stage show a degree of commitment to the cause of freedom and democracy (rather than any ideology) unmatched at any other phase of his life. With the Italians in Abyssinia, the Japanese in China, and the increasing brutality of the Hitler regime in Germany, Spain was not the only focus of his concern. In March 1938 he was the sole signatory of a long and impassioned letter to the *Yorkshire Post*, calling for support for a demonstration in Leeds in favour of a collective security pact by the 'peace-loving powers' to defend any country which became the victim of aggression:

> We are witnessing in Europe, in Africa, in Asia, three large-scale wars which are being carried on, despite the deeply shocked protests of the whole civilized world, with an inhuman totalitarian ferocity which may well make us despair ... France is being surrounded; our own line of communication with the Colonies and Dominions, both by the Mediterranean and the African coast, is being menaced ... Are we to stand aside while these forces complete the wreck of our civilization?[11]

Later that year he was busy drumming up funds as a member of the Artists Refugee Committee to help settle German artists who had fled to

Czechoslovakia and were now in great danger there as a direct result of the Munich agreement between Hitler and Chamberlain. Some of these, like the brilliant satirist John Heartfield, subsequently lodged for a while in Hampstead. To Britain's shame, many of them were interned after the outbreak of the Second World War.

By bringing British artists into closer touch with domestic and international events and making them feel part of their times, the AIA did much to force them out of their enclaves and into closer touch with each other and the man in the street: quite literally, in the case of its *Art for the People* show at the Whitechapel Gallery in the East End in February 1939. To dissociate the event from the mystique of West End galleries and the glamour of some private views, a passer-by from Whitechapel High Street, who turned out to be unemployed, was called in to open it. Moore was among the customary mixed gaggle of exhibitors, ranging from the abstract to the academic. The exhibition attracted a remarkable 40,000 visitors.[12]

Surrealist involvement

As has been noted in the case of the 1937 AIA exhibition and the manifesto on Spain, the British Surrealist Group found itself strongly in sympathy with the AIA's leftist and anti-establishment ethos. Surrealism had come late to England, perhaps because – as the group's first statement defensively indicated – the English are a nation of individualists whose social life favours equivocations and disguises, and whose capitalism is rich enough to put a good face on poverty with philanthropy.[13] When Herbert Read commented that a nation which had produced 'super-realists', as he initially called surrealists, like William Blake and Lewis Carroll was 'to the manner born', he unintentionally implied that the English imagination did not need a surrealist movement: it already had a developed surrealist streak.

Certainly surrealism was from its birth in the mid-1920s strongly literary. The poet Apollinaire had coined the word *surréaliste* in 1917, and the poet and essayist André Breton became its leading theoretician. The purpose of surrealism, he said, was 'to resolve the previously contradictory conditions of dream and reality into an absolute reality, a super-reality'. He also defined it as 'pure psychic automatism through which we undertake to express, in words, writing or any other activity, the actual functioning of thought, thoughts dictated apart from any control by reason or any aesthetic or moral consideration. Surrealism rests upon belief in the higher reality of specific forms of associations, previously neglected, in the omnipotence of dreams, and in the disinterested play of thinking.'[14] Since neither painting nor, in particular, sculpture lent themselves readily to automatism, much emphasis was laid by surrealist artists on dreams, the suggestive juxtaposition of unconnected objects, and on ambiguous images.

No doubt all this was familiar to Moore by the early 1930s, not just from his periodic trips to Paris but also from exhibitions in London of work by such surrealists as de Chirico, Ernst, Miró, and Dali, all exhibited in commercial galleries between 1928 and 1936; and from articles in Geoffrey Grigson's magazine *New Verse*. However the full impact of the movement did not hit Hampstead until Roland Penrose arrived in Downshire Hill in 1934 fresh from thirteen years in Paris. This charming and relatively wealthy collector and painter had come to know such leading artists as Picasso, Max Ernst, Miró, and Man Ray, and was amazed to discover that the English had seen little of their achievements. In Paris he had also met the poet David Gascoyne, who was about to publish a *Short Survey of Surrealism*. Together they determined to remedy British ignorance with a proper surrealist exhibition, and to work towards the formation of an English Surrealist Group, akin to those already formed in Belgium, Yugoslavia, Spain, Japan, and numerous other countries in addition to France, *mère des arts*.

To gather together works for the proposed exhibition Penrose – with the help, almost inevitably, of Herbert Read – visited some twenty London artists, turning them into surrealists virtually overnight, as Julian Trevelyan has remarked.[15] Among those elected were Cecil Collins, Robert Medley, and Graham Sutherland, none of whose work was surrealist in any real sense of that flexible word. Moore was a borderline case. His work *is* surrealist, like much good art, in that it springs from and appeals to deeper layers of the mind and of the subconscious and makes use of richly ambiguous images. As has already been described, in his drawing, seedbed of his work, he often practised a form of automatism before beginning the process of ordering.

Meanwhile André Breton and his fellow poet Paul Eluard were selecting work from across the Channel for the big show in London. The International Surrealist Exhibition, as it was styled, opened at the New Burlington Galleries in the West End on 11 June 1936. There were some pioneering 'happenings'. Salvador Dali nearly asphyxiated while delivering a lecture on Paranoia from inside a diving suit. At the private view a girl wore a fencing mask covered with red roses. A real kipper attached to a painted one gave off a strong smell. Not surprisingly, such exhibitionist side-shows diverted even the art critics from the strength of the work displayed. Moore was represented by three drawings and four sculptures. In vain did Herbert Read urge in his catalogue introduction:

> Do not judge this movement kindly. It is not just another amusing stunt. It is defiant, the desperate act of men too profoundly convinced of the rottenness of our civilization to want to save a shred of its respectability.[16]

Such more-radical-than-thou hyperbole lent itself to ridicule, and James Boswell obliged with a brilliant cartoon in the *Left Review* of July 1936, setting Read's words against fleshy, befurred members of the bourgeoisie, who are seen inspecting the exhibits without a trace of alarm. There lay the paradox of surrealism. It was intended to shock and disturb, yet it was embraced by the middle classes and became the most popular art movement between the wars; the styles of exponents like de Chirico, Dali, and Magritte were swiftly and for ever absorbed into the repertoire of commercial and especially advertising art.

The London exhibition itself cannot have done much to convince Moore that surrealism would flower vigorously in British soil. Much of its fantasy world of dripping watches and bizarre juxtapositions (as in the Comte de Lautréamont's famous definition of beauty as 'the chance meeting of a sewing machine and an umbrella on a dissecting table')[17] struck him as altogether too glib. Much of the work of the British exhibitors, like John Banting, John Bigge, Eileen Agar, and Reuben Mednikoff, now has a somewhat contrived and second-rate look. It was overshadowed in the New Burlington Galleries by the work of the genuine Continental practitioners, of whom – in addition to Dali – Magritte, Miró, Tanguy, and Ernst came to London. Whether Picasso, Klee, and Miró, whose paintings were also shown, are considered authentic surrealists is a matter of taste. Moore himself can only have been enriched by the human and artistic contacts which the exhibition provided; but he had already absorbed what he needed from the movement into his work. If de Chirico's influence seems detectable in some of his drawings of 1938–40, with their cloistral, Kafkaesque interiors, Moore might have absorbed that from the Italian artist's shows in London in 1928 and 1931.

The abstract camp

Surrealism's unconvincing evolution in London coincided with the growth of abstract art, and in particular of its 'constructivist' wing. The moving force behind the latter was Naum Gabo, a Russian émigré who had arrived in Hampstead in 1935 from Germany. In 1920 Gabo and his brother Antoine Pevsner had issued a 'constructivist' manifesto in Russia, renouncing volume and mass as sculptural elements and seeking to explore space with new forms and materials. In its belief that art must be a dynamic element in everyday life, constructivism overlapped with the Bauhaus philosophy and its goal of a classless, machine-age synthesis of all the arts.

Gabo and Moore showed together, along with Nicholson, Piper, Mondrian, Léger, Alexander Calder, and numerous others, at an important exhibition in 1936 called *Abstract and Concrete*. This was organized by the art historian Nicolete Gray, sponsored by the Pipers' journal *Axis*, and held first in Oxford, then London (at the Lefevre Gallery), Liverpool, and Cambridge. As noted in the previous chapter, *Axis* had done pioneering work since 1935 as a very literate quarterly journal setting British abstract art in an international context. 'Henry was quite sympathetic to *Axis* and all its goings-on,' John Piper recalled, 'more so than Paul Nash, for instance, who wrote an article called "For but not with", which Henry would never have done.'[18] (The Moores quite frequently visited the Pipers' farmhouse at Fawley Bottom, near Henley-on-Thames.)

Axis lasted only eight issues but left behind a solid monument in the form of a book entitled *The Painter's Object*, edited by Myfanwy Piper and published in 1937.[19] Among some unexpectedly entertaining essays by fifteen artists, including Léger, Kandinsky, and Moholy-Nagy, were Moore's 'Notes on Sculpture', first published shortly beforehand in the *Listener* magazine as 'The Sculptor Speaks'.[20] He began with some advice which he was himself to ignore with great frequency: 'It is a mistake for a sculptor or painter to speak or write very often about his job. It releases tension needed for his work.' He was illuminating about Brancusi's 'special mission' to rid sculpture of surface accretions and make us once more shape-conscious; yet in doing so the Rumanian had, he reckoned, refined and polished a single shape 'to a degree almost too precious'. On the same theme he said – and it must have read like a form of tribute to surrealism: 'There are universal shapes to which everybody is subconsciously conditioned and to which they can respond if their conscious control does not shut them off.' Equally, he considered that 'actual physical size has an emotional meaning ... An exact model to one-tenth scale of Stonehenge, where the stones would be less than us, would lose all its impressiveness.' Conversely, he said, a carving might be several times over life-size yet small and petty in feeling. 'There is a right physical size for every idea.' (Why then did he produce his later bronzes in three or four sizes? It was a question he never properly answered.)

As for current controversies, he contrived to sound both statesmanlike and disdainful:

> The violent quarrel between the abstractionists and the surrealists seems to me quite unnecessary. All good art has contained both abstract and surrealist elements, just as it has contained both classical and romantic elements – order and surprise, intellect and imagination, conscious and unconscious.

Again, that is not a statement which withstands close scrutiny: the equations are too glib. But it was by rising above the battle in this very self-assured way that Moore was able – if the metaphor can take the strain – to keep a foot in both camps. The only other major figure to do so at this time was Herbert Read, who later likened his position to that of a circus rider with his feet planted astride two horses. 'Such dialectical oppositions are good for the progress of art,' he wrote, 'and ... the greatest artists (I always had Henry Moore in mind) are great precisely because they can resolve such oppositions.'[21]

Underpinning much abstract art of this period was the belief that simplicity and clarity of design reflected a larger vision of social organization. That was particularly true of the constructivist camp, which the *Abstract and Concrete* exhibition had notably strengthened by bringing together Naum Gabo, Ben Nicholson, and the architect Leslie Martin. These three combined in 1937 to collect and publish a collection of essays entitled *Circle: International Survey of Constructive Art*.[22] One of its aims was to emphasize the positive (hence constructive rather than constructivist) nature of art. Another was to strengthen the position of the abstract artist by association with other fields of endeavour. Thus Lewis Mumford wrote on concepts of the city, Siegfried Giedion on engineering, Jan Tschichold on typography, Leonard Massine on choreography, and the physicist J. D. Bernal on art. In his comments Gabo wrote: 'Art and Science are two different streams which arise from the same creative source and flow in to the same ocean of the common culture ... the force of Art lies in its immediate influence on human psychology and in its active contagiousness.' Here, too, we may note an irony of history: just as surrealism was embraced by those it sought to shock, so the almost clinical purity of constructivism alienated those it sought to involve.

Moore was among the many other contributors to *Circle*, as were Mondrian, le Corbusier, Breuer, Herbert Read, and the architect Maxwell Fry. Perhaps feeling threatened by the quality of all those designers and architects, Henry drew some very obvious distinctions between their activities and his:

> Sculpture, more naturally than architecture, can use organic rhythms. Aesthetically, architecture is the abstract relationship of masses. If sculpture is limited to this, then in the field of scale and size, architecture has the advantage; but sculpture, not being tied to a functional and utilitarian purpose, can attempt much more freely the exploration of the world of pure form.

These remarks reflect the competitive feeling which marked his attitude to architects and their products for much of his life. None the less constructivism and its philosophy of art as an enrichment of life reinforced his own convictions, which he had expressed in 1934 and now repeated:

> Because a work does not aim at reproducing natural appearances it is not, therefore, an escape from life – it may be penetrating into reality; not a sedative or drug, not just the exercise of good taste, the provision of pleasant shapes and colours in a pleasing combination, not a decoration to life – but an expression of the significance of life, a stimulation to a greater effort in living.[23]

That idea of art as a moral activity was to remain with Moore throughout his career. All great art had a moral dimension, he would say, and therefore all great artists had an element at least of moral greatness. The unspoken implication was that he did too: the man and his art reflected each other. Anyone arguing with him that many great artists have been flawed human beings was liable to receive short shrift.

Gabo's belief that the exploration of space (preferably using transparent materials) was one of the fundamental attributes of sculpture doubtless encouraged Moore to produce his most overtly constructivist works: some sixteen stringed figures in lead or wood, completed between 1937 and early 1940. Although they are at first sight largely abstract, most of these stringed pieces refer to the human or other natural forms, and often foreshadow works of the 1950s and beyond. Their origin went back to the mathematical models which Henry had admired at the Science Museum near the Royal College of Art, devised to show the intermediate shape between a circle and a square (for example) by means of string or wire threaded between a similar number of holes in each shape. 'The string seemed to add new tenseness and vitality to the form by contrasting, in its tautness, with the rounded wooden form and the swirling grain of the wood,' he subsequently explained.[24] 'It wasn't the scientific study of those models but the ability to look through the strings as with a bird cage, and to see one form within another which excited me.'[25] Eventually the excitement wore off, as he recalled in 1962:

> I could have done hundreds. They were fun, but too much in the nature of experiments to be really satisfying ... When the war came, I gave up this type of thing. Others, like Gabo and Barbara Hepworth have gone on doing it. It becomes a matter of ingenuity rather than a fundamental human experience.[26]

That was self-congratulatory, ungenerous, and wide of the mark. Strings formed a much more integral part of Barbara Hepworth's pieces than they did in the case of Moore's, while Gabo's work was mainly concerned with such ingenious and poetic explorations of space. Henry was using his own practice as a yardstick of excellence. Some of his own stringed pieces are not very interesting. The most convincing are *Bird Basket*, of 1939 [71], in which a pattern of angled strings can be seen through a fine mesh of straight ones; and *The Bride*, of 1939–40 [70], in which the strings seem to provide a veil for a totem-like figure foreshadowing the *Standing Forms* of the mid-1950s.

Constructivism, surrealism, and socialism were not his only points of contact with the intellectual life of the 1930s. Through his two days a week of teaching at Chelsea he became friendly with Robert Medley, who had joined the staff in 1932 to teach life drawing and a bit of painting. Medley was an old and close friend of the poet W.H. Auden, with whom he had been at school, and of Rupert Doone, a former ballet dancer of considerable ability. Doone had a vision of a more contemporary and creative form of theatre in which actors, painters, singers, dancers, and members of the audience could collaborate. In 1932 Group Theatre was formed to put these ideas into practice, and over the next five years gave the first performances of works by Auden, Christopher Isherwood, Louis MacNeice, T.S. Eliot, and Stephen Spender. They were generally performed at the Westminster Theatre, near Buckingham Palace. Medley designed the sets, and from 1935 Benjamin Britten wrote much of the music.

Henry became involved in Auden's first play, *The Dance of Death*, for which he provided a mask (it is not clear which one). Since Doone was on stage throughout, Tyrone Guthrie co-produced it, and the play was a considerable success when performed in February and March 1934. Bertolt Brecht came and was impressed by its blend of cabaret, poetry, and dance, and the following year it was teamed in a double bill with Eliot's *Sweeney Agonistes*. Subsequent Group Theatre productions included the Auden–Isherwood plays *The Dog Beneath the Skin* and *The Ascent of F6*. These were pioneering works, and Henry shared the excitement – mingled with frustration, since Doone's ability to animate his collaborators was not matched by administrative skills – of those more closely involved. With Britten and Eliot, Moore was to remain in sporadic contact: Eliot was very friendly with Herbert Read and, less predictably, with Peter Gregory, two Moore intimates.

Henry taught at Chelsea on Thursdays and Fridays. For a time Bernard Meadows joined his modelling classes, and found him, superficially at any rate, very encouraging to his pupils:

> His standard way was to go along to a student's work and say 'That's marvellous, that's fine,' and then he would start talking about it, and by the end you wondered what the hell was fine about it! There were a few people, I remember, who came along with sort of sub-Henry Moores, and he was very quick to jump on that. He said he didn't expect to see substitute Henry Moores, he expected to see their own work.[27]

One of his ablest students was Joyce Salmond, who later married the principal, H. S. Williamson. Another, less gifted, was the actor-to-be Dirk Bogarde, who attended some of Moore's life-drawing classes and tried his hand unsuccessfully at modelling. He recalled Henry, smocked and wearing a woolly tie, moving quietly and gently among his pupils, 'correcting and suggesting here and there, patient with the slow, glowing with the more advanced of us, wanting to share his obvious delight and love of the Human Body'.[28]

In summer 1937, just before the vacation began, Henry went to Derbyshire to make a bulk purchase of two tons of Hopton-wood stone. He described the aftermath in a letter to the Coxons from Burcroft in Kent:

It took the boy [Bernard Meadows] & me, best part of the first
fortnight he was here, squaring up a face on each of them, making
concrete blocks to stand them on, in one corner of the field, &
getting them up – when they were up it looked a little like a
miniature Stonehenge, still does & will do for a year or two until
they're all carved.[29]

In the same letter he described in an engagingly modest way how he had
saved a woman from drowning while they were swimming at Reculver
on the Kent coast:

We'd just bathed & were still in our bathing costumes, eating lunch
of sandwiches, when there was a shout for help, from the next
breakwater division, & it wasn't until I was swimming back with
her (just as I'd seen it done in demonstrations!) that I realized I was
still chewing a mouthful of sandwich.

One of the first fruits of the bulk purchase of stone was a mysterious
Reclining Figure [51] almost three feet long, somewhat resembling a
shoe tree which has sprouted various bizarre protuberances. This he
photographed at close range against the sky, making it look like something from *Gulliver's Travels*. At first sight, such pieces may seem too
cryptic and hermetic to be of wide interest or appeal. Yet, as observed
earlier, they wear uncommonly well, while some of the more attractive
pieces show less staying power.

Opening out the figure

By 1938 Moore's work was entering a more naturalistic phase, which
was to last for the next twenty years. There would be some exceptions,
like the stringed figures, and the striking little *Three Points* of 1939–40
[73]. But in the two years preceding the Second World War, the reclining
figure was once again a frequent preoccupation, and in recognizable form
at that. His next major work was to combine toughness, innovation and
a fair measure of appeal. Called *Recumbent Figure* [53] and completed in
1938 in Hornton (rather than Hopton-wood) stone and measuring fifty-
five inches long, it was to be another of those landmark works.

The starting point was a tentative commission from Serge Chermayeff,
one of the most imaginative of the Russian-born architects in London.
Educated at Harrow and married to an English girl, he was building
himself a house of advanced design at Halland in Sussex. He asked Moore
whether he could envisage one of his carvings standing at the intersection

of terrace and garden, specifying the dimensions of the base which would receive the figure.[30] Almost twenty years later Henry recalled:

> It was a long, low building and there was an open view of the long, sinuous lines of the Downs. There seemed to be no point in opposing all these horizontals ... so I carved a reclining figure for him, intending it to be kind of focal point for all the horizontals; and it was then that I became aware of the necessity of giving outdoor sculpture a far-seeing gaze. My figure looked out across a great sweep of the Downs, and her gaze gathered in the horizon. The sculpture ... had its own identity and did not *need* to be on Chermayeff's terrace, but it so to speak *enjoyed* being there, and I think it introduced a humanizing element. It became a mediator between modern house and ageless land.[31]

A fee of £300 had been agreed, and Chermayeff paid £50 as a deposit. The finished product was delivered in September 1938. 'No money changed hands after its delivery,' the architect confirmed not long ago. 'Instead came *war*, and I returned it to Henry with much regret – we had to sell our house ... and left England in New Year 1940,' (for the USA, where he flourished).[32] Henry returned the deposit to Chermayeff, whose finances tended to be overstretched: in fact the piece seems to have reverted to Moore after only six months, as will become evident later.

With its doughnut-like hole encircled by breast, arms and pelvis, the *Recumbent Figure* is by far the most opened out of all Moore's larger stone carvings. It is indeed hard to envisage how he and Meadows achieved so large a hole without fatally weakening the strength of the stone, all the more so since Hornton stone can only be quarried in a limited thickness. The piece had therefore to be made of three horizontal layers of stone which were then dowelled and cemented together.[33] The next years severely tested its durability. First Kenneth Clark suggested to the Museum of Modern Art in New York that they might like to buy it, but they were unable to do so. So he commended it to the Contemporary Art Society, which had been presenting contemporary works of art to national and provincial galleries since 1910. Since Clark was that year (1939) the CAS's chief buyer, the purchase was made and *Recumbent Figure* was presented to the Tate Gallery as its first Henry Moore. Quixotically, however, the Tate decided to lend it to the World Fair in New York in the summer of 1939. There it was trapped by the outbreak of war, and found refuge in the sculpture garden of the same Museum of Modern Art which had failed to buy it. In New York it suffered not only the extremes of heat and cold but from the attention of vandals, being pushed from its base in 1944 and decapitated. Given the nature of its layered structure, the damage might have been a lot more severe than it was. The repair shows, but not to a disfiguring degree. The sculpture was repatriated in 1945.

The evidence suggests that Kenneth Clark had entered Moore's life in early 1938. By then he had been director of the National Gallery for four years, yet was only thirty-four years old, being five years younger than Henry almost to the day. Bernard Meadows believes Clark's first visit to Burcroft was shortly after he had been knighted in the New Year's Honours of 1938: Henry was all of a flutter at being visited by the great man, and called him Mr Clark rather than Sir Kenneth. The sculptor had suggested to his assistant that he should give their guest a demonstration of carving with a small axe-like chopper. Meadows declined, fearing his own nervousness might lead him to injure himself.[34] The occasion went very well however, as such occasions virtually always did with Henry: he was extemely good at putting himself across. No doubt his teaching had helped to make him articulate in explaining his work, and the enthusiasm and charm of his manner naturally helped.

At that stage Clark was already friendly with Graham Sutherland, John Piper, and several other British artists: Moore was relatively late in entering the charmed circle. It was the height of the 'Clark Boom'. After two years working for the famous art historian Bernard Berenson near Florence, the handsome and wealthy young prodigy (an ancestor had invented the cotton spool) had become Keeper of Art at the Ashmolean Museum in Oxford, and was now much lionized by London hostesses in addition to presiding over the fortunes of the national collection in Trafalgar Square. The house at which he and his wife Jane entertained the great in Portland Place, W1, and at Lympne in Kent (some forty-five minutes' drive from the Moores' bungalow at Kingston) were hung with Impressionist and contemporary works.

In his delightful but unreliable autobiography Clark wrote of Moore that 'from the first minute I saw his work in an exhibition at the Warren Galleries in 1928 I had recognized that something extraordinary and completely unexpected had happened in English art.'[35] That may be literally true, but whether he liked what he saw as instantaneously as suggested is in doubt: the collective memory of his artist friends, like the Sutherlands, was that he appreciated Moore's drawings, one of which he bought at the Warren Gallery show, much more quickly than the sculpture, which at one stage he would liken to hot-water bottles.[36] At the human level the friendship which was to last more than forty years seems to have begun quite slowly, though Clark was not backward in using his matchless connections on Moore's behalf: before long the highly esteemed Rosenberg & Helft gallery in Bruton Street (London offshoot of a well-known Paris gallery) was offering him a show of his drawings, at Clark's prompting. But the sculptor had to reply ('Dear Sir Kenneth') that he was committed to a similar exhibition at the Mayor Gallery early the following year.[37]

There is no doubting the real affection which the two men from such startlingly different backgrounds came to feel for each other. In a sense they were complementary. Superficially Clark had everything: money, looks, position, a strikingly attractive wife. Yet his childhood had been miserable and had stunted his emotional life. He had no real roots. Henry by contrast was, at that stage, poor in material terms, and his reputation as an artist was far short of its peak. But with his happy childhood and his firm Yorkshire roots, he was vastly more secure emotionally. Clark, the Wykehamist aesthete (a rare flower indeed) with the keen intellect and pellucid and supremely elegant prose style, may have envied Henry his bursting creative energy. Within a few years he came to regard the sculptor as one of his two dearest friends, the other being Maurice Bowra, the Oxford classicist and Warden of Wadham College. To Clark, the sculptor was 'always himself, gay, confident, strong in the head and with a disposition to look on the best side of everything and everybody. The deep, disturbing well from which emerged his finest drawings and sculpture was never referred to, and no one meeting him could have guessed at its existence.'[38]

For Henry, the support and friendship of by far the most influential man in the London art world was of enormous value both psychologically and in practical terms. Though Moore was well established by the time they met, Clark's patronage in wartime was to give his reputation a big boost. Read was more powerful as a shaper of opinion on contemporary art. But Clark bridged the gap between the great artists of the past and those of the present. Read's opinion would cut no ice with the upper middle classes. If, however, the director of the National Gallery, and one as well connected as Clark, thought there was something in that fellow Moore, well, perhaps there was. Some of Moore's friends believe that Clark was at least partly responsible for Henry's habit of implicitly equating himself with such masters as Titian, Rembrandt, Michelangelo, by referring to them when answering questions about himself. Certainly the admiration of so eminent a figure, with his fine eye and deep knowledge, must have been irresistible and deeply flattering; just as for Clark the friendship of the miner's inspired son was to provide close contact not just with England's 'greatest living artist' but with a classless Yorkshireman (as Henry came to seem) from a social layer with which he rarely consorted on equal terms; which is not to suggest that any such considerations were *consciously* entertained on either side...

When Clark paid that first visit to Burcroft, Moore and Meadows were working on their third elmwood reclining figure. This one was to be almost twice as long, at eighty-one inches, as the larger, Wakefield figure. It had been half commissioned by the gifted Russian-born architect Berthold Lubetkin, who had arrived in London from Paris in 1930, causing a stir before long with the gorilla house and penguin pool which he and his Tecton partnership designed for the Zoo in Regent's Park. For human habitation he had conceived a beautifully simple-looking eight-storey block of flats in Highgate called High Point, in which he had himself taken a penthouse apartment. He suggested to Moore that he should create something special for an alcove, without apparently providing much information about the site. The famous architect recalled quite recently that Henry had produced a small model of the proposed carving, intended to be seen at eye level. The shelf on which it was to recline was in fact eight feet off the ground, and Lubetkin felt obliged to conclude that the figure proposed by Moore would be both too large and too high to be seen to advantage.[39]

Henry was not deterred. He had never considered it a formal commission anyway, and pressed on with its completion. The result [61] was to rank as one of his very finest works: arguably indeed his masterpiece. In no other sculpture did he more mysteriously and evocatively use the female form to portray both woman and earth at once. The sinuous yet majestic figure is pierced not just by one or two holes but by a series of cave-like voids, as if eroded by swirling waters. The projecting breast, like the head animated by a single small hole and jutting sideways over the eroded chest, looks from certain angles like an eagle with wings spread. It was perhaps this carving in particular that André Breton had in mind when he wrote:

Apollinaire had dreamed of a unique statue, one that would be a hollow wrought within the earth itself: this is the statue which Moore's art has succeeded in wedding to its opposite, the solid statue, so that they embrace each other in perfect harmony.[40]

Henry himself came to feel that in this *Reclining Figure* he had for the first time achieved complete unity between solid form and space, while at the same time retaining the tensions of the human figure.[41] None the less this great work has a somewhat spectral or skeletal quality, a product perhaps of the sculptor's sensitivity to the doom-laden atmosphere of the months preceding the outbreak of war.

When Kenneth Clark heard that Lubetkin had dropped out as purchaser, he cabled the Museum of Modern Art that they could have a masterpiece for £300 (then around $1,500). Partly because Alfred Barr had not actually seen it, the opportunity was once again passed up.[42] At Moore's show in February 1940, at the Leicester Galleries, it was priced at £500 but failed to find a buyer. Among those who greatly admired it there was the painter Gordon Onslow-Ford, an original member of the Surrealist Group in Paris who had arrived in London in September 1939.

Onslow-Ford had been down to see the Moores in Kent, where he turned the pages – not one had been removed for sale – of some marvellous sketchbooks and purchased a small lead figure, one of several which Moore had recently made with Meadows' help. His first sight of the great elmwood figure impressed him deeply, as he remembered almost half a century later:

> The surface was subtle and invited the touch. As one walked around the carving, one could catch the essence of well-loved rolling landscapes that had been transposed into anthropomorphic forms. I felt that I was in the presence of the Mother Earth Goddess. With the help of a photographer I took some photographs of the *Reclining Figure*, and for an article in the London *Bulletin* I made a collage using a cutout of the figure pasted onto a reproduction of a Dutch landscape painting. The collage was composed so that a church showed through one of the holes in the carving and the horizon through another. At the Surrealist exhibition at the Zwemmer Gallery in May 1940 [actually June], the *Reclining Figure* was shown on the floor on a red earth-coloured blanket; behind, there was a painting of mine called *Cyclotomania*, and I like to think there was a play between them. Henry Moore may not have been entirely pleased with these presentations of his work, but he never reproached me.[43]

Knowing that the sculptor was still very hard up, Onslow-Ford purchased the *Reclining Figure* – 'as much as an act of friendship as out of admiration for that great work' – and was glad to learn that Henry had used the £300 cheque as a down-payment for Hoglands, destined to be home for the rest of his life. To complete the saga of the carving: after living in a remote valley in Mexico for six years, Onslow-Ford settled in 1947 in his wife's native California. Probably in early 1965 he sold the *Reclining Figure* to the Marlborough-Gerson Gallery, as it then was, in New York, when he disposed of much of his notable art collection. The £22,000 which he thereby gained went towards the purchase and preservation of the wooded, remote Californian valley where at the time of writing he still lived and painted. Moore was keen that the carving should come to rest in a public collection: preferably in England, otherwise in a really good foreign museum. In the event it was sold direct to the Detroit Institute of Arts in late July 1965.[44]

Slow off the mark though the Museum of Modern Art in New York had been where this carving was concerned, it did acquire one of the best of the eighteen-odd lead figures which, as noted, were produced at Burcroft in 1938 and 1939. Most of them were fluent and rhythmic reclining figures of about one foot in length. When Moore was in his eighties the MOMA piece was, at the suggestion of the architect I. M. Pei, enlarged to a length of thirty-five feet for a site at the base of a bank designed by Pei in Singapore.

For Moore the advantage of lead was that it has a low melting point and is very malleable. He and Meadows would light a fire in a makeshift kiln of firebricks, sited to catch the prevailing wind. The model would be made of wax, then packed into a special mixture containing ground pottery, and subsequently melted out in the kiln. The lead had meanwhile been reduced to liquid in one of Irina's long-suffering saucepans on a primus stove, and would be poured in to replace the melted wax: the so-called lost-wax or *cire perdue* form of casting, practised for centuries.

Onslow-Ford, with his artist's eye, had picked perhaps the finest of all these lead creations, so opened out that it resembled a drawing in space, and exuding energy. Like many others, it was cast in bronze in an edition of nine in the late 1950s. In the perspective of Moore's later work, the most significant of the lead figures was a small *Helmet* [72], completed in January 1940 and bought before long by Roland Penrose. It was the first of Moore's works in which an outer figure contained an inner one. The helmet itself is womb-like and slightly sinister, and it is hard to say whether the nervous, spaghetti-like creature within is being protected or imprisoned. With overtones both of war and of the mother and child theme, it is very Moore-ish in its rich and many-layered suggestiveness.

Many of Moore's drawings of this period express his deep disquiet in even stronger (or more obviously strong) terms. A number of them show either sculptural creations, including stringed figures [56], or human figures placed in prison-like settings [57], with bleakly geometrical window openings high above them. Even the sculptural creations look profoundly lonely. Commentators have noted the affinity with the eerie perspectives of de Chirico's urban scenes; but as Moore's Jungian interpreter, Ernst Neumann, has pointed out, whereas in the Italian's work the haunted quality usually comes from the unending openness of the scenes portrayed, Moore's interiors seem stiflingly claustrophobic.[45] Yet sometimes Henry achieves his impact by contrast. In *Sculptural Object in Landscape* (1939), for instance, a skeletal, surrealist form is rendered the more baleful by being placed against a pastoral landscape in which three cows graze.

There were some lighter moments amid the encircling gloom, such as a trip to Paris in May 1937, when Henry and Irina paid a memorable visit to Picasso's studio, as he recalled to John and Véra Russell:

> There was a big lunch with Giacometti, Max Ernst, Paul Eluard, André Breton, and Irina and me, and it was all tremendously lively and I think that even Picasso was excited by the idea of our going to his studio. But when we got there he lightened the mood of the whole thing, as he loved to do. *Guernica* was still a long way from being finished. It was like a cartoon, just laid in black and grey, and he could have coloured it as he coloured the sketches. You know the woman who comes running out of the cabin on the right with one hand held in front of her? Well, Picasso told us there was something missing there, and he went and fetched a roll of paper and stuck it in the woman's hand, as much as to say that she had been caught in the bathroom when the bombs came. That was just like him – to be so tremendously moved about Spain and yet turn it aside as a joke.[46]

Penrose, who was also there, quotes Picasso saying, as he pinned a long piece of toilet paper to the woman's hand: 'That shows clearly enough the commonest and most primitive effect of fear.'[47] About a year later Penrose brought Max Ernst to Moore's studio in Hampstead. The German-born surrealist was much impressed by the way the work stood around the studio draped mysteriously in white sheets, so that each piece could be unveiled at the sculptor's discretion. 'Never can you do that with paintings,' he complained: quite unjustifiably, since paintings can be withdrawn from a rack and placed on an easel in front of a visitor with equally dramatic effect.[48]

In summer 1938 Moore was asked by his old patron, the architect Charles Holden, to tackle another commission. It was just ten years since he had carved the *West Wind* relief for Holden's London Underground building. Now the architect was masterminding the centralization and development of London University in Bloomsbury in west central London, and wanted Henry to do a set of reliefs for his fine Senate House in Malet Street, near the British Museum. Once again, however, the carvings were to be sited some fifty to sixty feet up. Henry took the proposition seriously, as his sketchbook of the time shows. He filled half a dozen pages with drawings and self-admonitions, such as 'Think of subject matter ... mother and child – university the mother, child the students & try abstract subjects ... keep it all architectural and *big* ... figure protecting young wisdom ... a university gives a haven from commercialism'; and, rather wistfully, 'Imagine that one was doing it for oneself or say for a Wells Coates building.'

Among his sketches were seated female figures reading a book, one with a bookshelf behind her, and some abstract symbols representing the arts and sciences. He reached the stage of making some models, as he later recalled:

> Eight seated figures were wanted, on eight separate stones. But I couldn't sustain any excitement about it. I was trying at this time to achieve form in the round, making figures which occupied real space, and I preferred to forgo the commission rather than work for a long time on a kind of sculpture that went against the grain – and that would be too high up to be seen properly anyway. The architect said he would go ahead anyway and put up the stones in case I altered my mind. The eight stones, cut to the proportions of my drawings, are there high up on the Senate House, but they remain blank to this day.[49]

The preliminary work was not wasted. When he came to do the Unesco commission in the later 1950s, he was the better equipped for having already examined the problem of how to render the idea of education in three-dimensional form.

In that spring of 1938 Moore and his Chelsea colleagues had been involved in a ludicrous episode in which the central figure was Peggy Guggenheim. That wealthy and in some ways outrageous New Yorker, who loved artists as much as art, had settled in England in the 1930s after several years in Paris, establishing an art gallery in Cork Street called Guggenheim Jeune. While helping her to assemble an exhibition of contemporary sculpture, Marcel Duchamp had sent her a consignment of works by his brother Raymond Duchamp-Villon, Gabo's brother Antoine Pevsner, Arp and his wife Sophie Tauber-Arp, Brancusi, Henri Laurens, and the American Alexander Calder. Moore was to represent England in this honourable company. No difficulties were expected, least of all from the aesthetic sensibilities of the English customs authorities. Puzzled as to whether the bizarre objects being imported were works of art, they consulted the director of the Tate Gallery, J. B. Manson, for a ruling. Manson, himself a minor artist and former secretary of the Camden Town Group of low-key post-Impressionist painters, said they were not. In effect the power of veto had been conferred on him in such instances by the government under legislation intended to protect British stonecutters from being undercut by imported tombstones and the like.

As in a similar case eleven years earlier in New York involving Brancusi's wonderful bronze *Bird*, the Guggenheim sculptures could thus only be imported as pieces of bronze, marble, wood or whatever, on which duty must be paid. Moore, Medley, Coxon, Sutherland, and H. S. Williamson, the principal, wrote a letter to the *Daily Telegraph*, concluding: 'Are the new regulations ill-defined and at fault in placing upon one man the responsibility of making the necessary decisions, or is Mr J. B. Manson ignorant of the international reputation of these artists?'[50] Leading art critics sent a letter to Manson demanding that he change his decision, which he did. ' "Banned Sculpture" May Now Be Seen,' a headline in the *Daily Mail* shrieked a fortnight later, 'But Most Of It Is "Comical" '.[51] Manson himself did not survive long at his post. Shortly afterwards he became drunk and disorderly at a luncheon in Paris held to mark the opening of an exhibition of British painting at the Louvre, and was obliged to resign. He was succeeded by Sir William Rothenstein's son John, who had been director of the city art galleries of Leeds and Sheffield.

Manson had been an implacable opponent of Moore's work. For example, early in 1938 he had asked Robert Sainsbury whether the Tate might borrow a study of Eve by the French sculptor Charles Despiau. 'Yes,' Sainsbury replied, 'providing you show the *Mother and Child* of my friend Henry Moore.' Manson replied, 'Over my dead body will Henry Moore ever enter the Tate.'[52] It was a far more natural state of affairs that the Tate's director should be an admirer of Moore's work, which John Rothenstein had been since coming to know Henry as one of his father's favourite students at the Royal College. None the less the acquisition of the *Recumbent Figure* which Chermayeff had returned was not easily accomplished, even as a gift from the Contemporary Art Society. Both Clark and Rothenstein had to lobby the trustees to ensure they would accept it: to the latter's surprise, several of them showed signs of hostility and seemed likely to vote against it.[53]

Writing to Clark in March 1939 (still as 'Dear Sir Kenneth' but now signed 'Yrs Ever, Henry') the sculptor said he was very pleased indeed that the Tate's board had agreed by a majority to accept the piece if presented: he had hoped that would happen, he wrote, ever since Chermayeff, 'to release himself from feeling too bad about not knowing when he'd be able to pay me for it', had suggested it should go to America for the World Fair marked for sale. 'It might be a long time before I'm able to do another stone figure capable perhaps by its size of standing up to the scale of the Tate's new sculpture gallery, & one which I'm as generally satisfied with as that one.'[54] He confessed to being surprised by the prices charged by Dobson, Skeaping, and (Maurice) Lambert, and reckoned he would have charged £500 for it had it been going into his next Leicester Galleries show, but would be well satisfied with £300 (the original price to Chermayeff) from the CAS. A fortnight later he feared he might have seemed greedy and cut it to £250, and was 'very happy indeed' when Clark dismissed the idea.[55]

Moore was thus forty years old when the first of his works entered the national collection of modern and British art. Happily it was a major example, though one might have wished for it a more propitious setting than the vast stone hall which constituted the new sculpture gallery, opened in 1937 with funds from Lord Duveen. In the event it was, as we have seen, to have an adventurous five and a half years in the USA before settling there in 1945. The Tate's acquisition represented a measure of acceptance of Moore's stature by the art establishment. Clark was certainly influential in bringing this about. Moore was even asked to appear with him on a Sunday television discussion: since transmissions had only started in 1936, that was scarcely an everyday invitation. But Henry turned it down because he and Irina had planned five days in Kent – 'there's so much to be done in the garden which Irina can only do at this time of year.'[56] Modesty? Arrogance? Fear of the new medium? Loyalty to Irina? Probably more a very Yorkshire refusal to be impressed by any new-fangled invention and a desire to get on with his own work.

There is a strong sense of foreboding about the growing crisis in Europe in his letters to Clark in 1939 (scrappy though they tend to be). As the tension mounted he worked full stretch down at Kingston in Kent. It was not just the sense of impending doom which drove Henry on: he needed to produce enough work for his next show at the Leicester Galleries, due in early 1940. So he concentrated on making lead pieces, which was much quicker than carving, completing nine or ten in a month.

On the day war was declared, 3 September, he went swimming with Irina and Bernard Meadows by Shakespeare Cliff at Dover, an experience which he transmuted before long into one of his most eloquent drawings [74]. Executed in wax crayon, pen and ink, pencil and water-colour (already a favourite mixture), it shows eight women standing chest-high in blood-red water against a background of cliffs. Some of them seem to be wearing gasmasks, and they are gazing alertly and perhaps fearfully out to sea. Apprehension is the keynote. He called the drawing simply *September 3 1939*.

The declaration of war threw everything into doubt. Although at forty-one Moore was just over the age for military service, he could not be sure whether his teaching job would still be available as a tiresome but regular source of income. Would the Leicester Galleries show take place as scheduled? Could they continue to live in Kent, directly in the line of any likely German invasion? The most inventive and, in terms of his work, consistently interesting decade of his career was drawing to a close. Nothing was certain except that the outbreak of war would disrupt the happy continuity of a supremely productive period.

Chapter IX

Shelter drawings and the Northampton *Madonna*

1940–4

In later life Moore tended to suggest that he was still little known in 1940. It was part of his probably unconscious myth-making: miner's son wins through against heavy odds. Equally he liked to indicate that in the 1930s it was the foreigners, and especially the Americans, who had the perspicacity to support him as collectors. In fact, as we have seen, by 1940 he was considered to be well-known both by the serious and the popular press. In the mid-1930s, for example, one is not surprised to find such comments as: 'Henry Moore's fame is so considerable that the show of his drawings at the Zwemmer Gallery is an event of some note';[1] or apropos a Leicester Galleries show: 'In formal invention he is, excepting Picasso, perhaps the most fertile artist in Europe.'[2] He was, moreover, increasingly known on the Continent, showing for example with the likes of Klee, Mondrian, Léger, and Brancusi at the Stedelijk Museum in Amsterdam in April 1938, and in Paris that November with other contemporary British artists at the Salon d'Automne.

Most of his early work was, moreover, bought in the first instance by English collectors, even if many were friends or acquaintances. They included Lady Norton, Sir Michael Sadler, Lucy Wertheim, Philip Hendy, Stephen Spender, Roland Penrose, Peter Gregory, Charles Rutherston, Colin Anderson, Michael Ventris, Fanny Wadsworth, Heinz Roland, Robert Sainsbury, Henry Lamb, Peter Watson, Augustus John, Maynard Keynes, Robert Birley, and Eric Maclagan. A handful only of Americans was involved, and some of them, like Peggy Guggenheim and Dorothy Elmhirst, lived in England.

It is true, however, that the years of the Second World War gave Moore's popular reputation at home a much broader base, and also helped establish his name among American collectors. By the end of hostilities he was on his way to becoming a national institution at home, even if some of his fame rested on the cartoonist's mockery.

A likelier prospect in autumn 1939 was that the outbreak of war would bring serious artistic endeavour to a halt. A visit to Burcroft from his slightly younger Northern Irish sculptor friend, F. E. McWilliam, made him realize just how lucky he was not to be in London, as he told Kenneth Clark:

> According to him [McWilliam], most of the people he and I both know, when they're not trying to get jobs, find they're talking interminably round and round the war situation. Because he hoped I might still be working, he came down here to get a short respite from it. I am very thankful we got this cottage ... Of course, before long the war atmosphere might get closer and so intense that to keep the state of mind for working won't be possible, & so there'd be nothing for it but to seek actively a way of taking part in it. For I hate intensely all that Fascism and Nazism stand for, & if it should win it might be the end in Europe of all the painting, sculpture, music, architecture, literature which we all believe in ...[3]

There was no teaching at Chelsea that term, though it resumed for two terms in early 1940 before the school was evacuated later that summer to Northampton, at last severing Henry from his teaching obligations. He was fortunate to have in hand the £300 for the Tate Gallery's *Recumbent Figure* and to have recently sold a number of drawings at the Mayor Gallery. As an economy measure, he told Clark, he had given three months' notice to leave the Parkhill Road studio flat. On the debit side, they had recently bought a new car, a Standard 8, and wished they hadn't. He was worried, too, about the framing and transport costs of the Leicester Galleries show to be held in February 1940, the war permitting. Clark was meanwhile taking his own precautionary measures. As director of the National Gallery he supervised the removal of its paintings to a vast cave in a Welsh slate quarry; and at the domestic level he sold the grand house in Portland Place where the private lift had so impressed Henry. The house at Lympne, vulnerably sited on the Kent coast, was abandoned in favour of a large rented Georgian house near Tetbury in Gloucestershire.

The first nine months of the war, the so-called phoney war, left Britain physically unscathed while Hitler's armies planned and then carried out the invasion of much of northern Europe. For Moore it was a fruitful period which saw the completion of the great elmwood reclining figure and of the lead figures and drawings. Despite the menace of the war, it was in its way an idyllic period. His show at the Leicester Galleries, the fourth, ran to twenty sculptures and thirty-one drawings and passed off without dramas. The ever-attentive *Times* critic considered the elmwood reclining figure a noble work and 'the finest thing he has done on a large scale ... it should find a home in the new sculpture hall of the Tate Gallery'.[4] The *Surrealism Today* show at which the carving was exhibited that June virtually coincided with the fall of France. In the gallery's window, an armchair upholstered in the shape of a fat negro mammy stood next to a child's bed with rumpled sheets transfixed by a dagger. 'Shocking bad taste', commented the *Sunday Times*; 'seems unnecessary at a moment like this', said the *Manchester Guardian*.[5] At last surrealism had managed to offend.

With the Germans now just across the Channel in France, the invasion of England seemed likely, almost inevitable. Kent being the obvious landing point, much of it became a restricted area, and in its skies many of the fiercest duels of the Battle of Britain were fought that summer. Special permission was required for non-residents to enter the sensitive zones. The Clarks suggested that Henry and Irina should join them in Gloucestershire in the safer south-westerly area, and persuaded their neighbour Hiram Winterbotham, who came from a prosperous cloth-making family, to take them in temporarily if things got worse, while they looked for a nearby cottage. 'Will you tell your friend how nice it is of him to agree to this,' Henry wrote to Jane Clark on 15 June, 'and that if it became necessary we should be glad to take advantage of his goodness ... I saw a friend yesterday who was in Paris a fortnight ago to see a Picasso exhibition. He said Paris looked wonderful in the glorious weather. It's unbearable to think of the Germans there now.'

In the event, the Moores seem to have spent at most a couple of weeks *chez* Winterbotham. In the house there lived also a Canadian of great charm called Alan Jarvis, who later became director of the National Gallery in Ottawa. Winterbotham, who was at that time in charge of 20,000 personnel in some twenty aircraft factories, found the sculptor very down-to-earth, calm, and practical: 'One might have taken him for a village schoolmaster from Yorkshire.'[6] Henry and Irina subsequently paid several visits to the Clarks at their Tetbury residence, shared throughout 1940 with Graham and Kathy Sutherland and the writer and musicologist Edward Sackville-West, whose verse drama *The Rescue* Moore was to illustrate in 1944.[7]

Around May–June 1940 Moore and Graham Sutherland, who had become friendly as colleagues at Chelsea School of Art, came to feel that they should be making a direct contribution to the war effort. So they responded to an advertisement for a government-sponsored course at Chelsea Polytechnic in munition gauge-making, a branch of the precision tool industry, for which Sutherland, as a former apprentice engineer, was particularly well qualified. They were told to await a call; but as the weeks went by, it became clear that the course had been over-subscribed.

Teaching at Chelsea continued, and the school was even taking on new students. One of them was Joan Wyndham, whose published wartime diaries vividly evoke the feeling of *carpe diem* inspired by the sense of impending doom in those spring and summer months before the Blitz. Henry made a strong impact on the susceptible seventeen-year-old when they met on 1 April, the day she enrolled:

> The great man is small and brown with magnetic blazing blue eyes … he had rather flat brown hair, wore a navy sweater, and smoked. I checked a morbid desire to address him as 'Maître' … [he] knocked me up an armature, flung a lump of clay and some calipers at me, and told me to enjoy myself.[8]

On 25 April she wrote: 'Modelling with Henry Moore. He theorized for hours about sculpture and it was very interesting. When he comes into a room it's like a spark being struck.' By 15 May her frivolity was proving infectious:

> Holland surrendered today. Henry Moore said he was surprised and pleased at the way I'd got on with my first figure, so felt terribly exhilarated. I do hope I'm not going to get a crush on him. He really looks amazing at the moment, in a violet shirt with a lemon yellow tie, and his face all ruddy and shining. We played the fool a bit, flicking hard clay pellets at the model's twimmock, using our modelling tools as catapults.

6 June found her succumbing:

> Growth of strong immoral passion for Henry Moore. Today he hammered his thumb doing something to my armature and said 'Bugger'. There was blood all over the clay.[9]

Such youthful crushes on Moore were probably not infrequent, fading like this one as rapidly as they bloomed. He was not one to succumb to complicating entanglements with students, even if he was far from impervious to the charms of pretty girls. He respected Irina, who was his antidote to success and excess, and she knew how to be sharp with him.

That summer term at Chelsea was the last before the school was evacuated, with several other London art schools, to Northampton. London's ordeal by bombing began on 7 September. The Battle of Britain had been intended to deprive the RAF of air superiority and thus make possible a sea-borne invasion. In its second, most dangerous phase the Luftwaffe had concentrated its attacks on the fighter bases in Kent. Partly in retaliation against British night-bombing raids on German towns which had begun in late August, Hitler switched his own bombers from the airfields to the capital itself: bad news for Londoners but good for the RAF. London was bombed every night from 7 September to 2 November, and spasmodically, but often intensively, thereafter until May 1941.

The shelter drawings

It was not long after that first full day-and-night offensive that Henry's new Standard 8 was providentially out of action. After dinner with some friends in the West End he and Irina returned to Belsize Park by Underground on the Northern Line:

> As a rule I went into town by car and hadn't been by Tube for ages. For the first time that evening I saw people lying on the platforms at all the stations we stopped at. When we got to Belsize Park we weren't allowed out of the station for an hour because of the bombing. I spent the time looking at the rows of people sleeping on the platforms. I had never seen so many reclining figures, and even the train tunnels seemed to be like the holes in my sculpture. Amid the grim tension, I noticed groups of strangers formed together into intimate groups and children asleep within feet of the passing trains.[10]

The official bomb shelters having proved inadequate, Londoners had taken to rolling their blankets together in the evening and settling down there on the Underground platforms, safe in the bowels of the London clay. It was, in its way, as Erich Neumann has pointed out with some Jungian hyperbole, a return to primitive cave life, with human beings crawling for shelter like worms into the womb of the earth.[11] Moore found himself riveted by the scene, not just as a spectacle but as a human situation. Nothing similar had happened before, he reckoned, except possibly in the bowels of slave ships from Africa to America.[12]

Some ten months earlier, in November 1939, the War Artists' Advisory Committee had been formed. Its aim, following the First World War precedent, was to produce a record of Britain's involvement in the war and to bolster morale by exhibiting the results up and down the country. Kenneth Clark, who was appointed chairman, hoped to keep good artists in work and to prevent them from being killed. In that he was not entirely successful: Henry's friend Eric Ravilious was lost, aged thirty-nine, when flying over Iceland in September 1942; in 1945 Albert Richards died in Normandy, and Thomas Hennell in Java. Clark naturally invited those artists whom he particularly cherished, like Moore, Sutherland, and Piper, to join the scheme. Henry at first declined, feeling that he had seen enough of war during his spell at the front in 1917 and having been unimpressed by the phoney war. But the sight of the shelterers had been a revelation, and when he showed Kenneth Clark his first sketches, his friend observed that he could no longer refuse to become an official war artist. The prospect of a reliable source of income was no doubt an added inducement to sign on the dotted line.

Had Moore been purely a sculptor, he would not have been considered eligible, and it was ironic that his drawings rather than his sculpture should have first enabled him to live by his art alone. Abstract artists, too, were considered to be out of the running, in the unlikely event of their wanting to be considered as war artists. Ben Nicholson and Barbara Hepworth had left London for the relative safety of St Ives, Cornwall, with their triplets, a nursemaid, and cook in late August 1940, not long after the Luftwaffe had begun to bomb the English interior. Henry and Irina seized the opportunity to take over No. 7 Mall Studios from them. It was just a few yards from their previous home in Parkhill Road, and appreciably cheaper.

The first shelter sketches were thus executed in the new studio. It did not, however, remain the Moores' London home for long. One weekend in October they went to stay with friends, the Labour MP Leonard Matters and his Polish wife, who lived in a twisty lane at Perry Green, a hamlet near Much Hadham in Hertfordshire lying about an hour's drive north-east of London. The capital was particularly fiercely bombed that weekend – they could see the glare of the fires from Perry Green – and when they returned to Mall Studios on Monday morning, they found the area cordoned off. A policeman or air-raid warden made a sweeping horizontal gesture in reply to their inquiry, indicating that the studio had been flattened by a bomb. Henry persisted, and found that although No. 7 had suffered badly from the blast and was a shambles of broken glass, only one sculpture had been damaged. The Leeds *Reclining Figure* of 1929 was among those which had survived intact. Gas and water supplies were cut off, and it was a mountaineering job climbing over the debris. There could be no question of staying there, so they telephoned Leonard Matters. The MP was happy to put them up while they looked for somewhere to live in that area, which had struck them as attractive and convenient for London.

Very soon they found half of a charming but run-down early seventeenth-century house called Hoglands to let in Perry Green. 'I think we may stay here for some time,' Henry wrote to Jane Clark on 3 November in what turned out to be a notable understatement:

> Irina has full use and control of the very neglected garden ... It's easy to get to London & I go up once or twice each week when there's anything to be seen to – & perhaps also out of morbid curiosity, & a strange subdued excitement there is in being in London now ... I've joined the Home Guard here and go out on night duty patrolling the country lanes twice a week. My battle-dress uniform is very warm, but the trousers are six inches too long & the tunic too tight under the arms. As I was a bayonet instructor for a time in the last war I'm told I shall be asked to instruct our squad in it. But I shall make an awful mess of it, I've forgotten it all.

The name of the pretty if dilapidated farmhouse suggested that it had once been associated with the rearing of pigs, and certainly the garden at the back was to prove a rich source of often inspirational animal bones. In the other half of the divided house there was a Jewish family from London: the mother was one of those rare people Henry could not stand. They left after about a year, and ended up in Israel. When the Moores had been there for a few months the owner, a Mr Britton, offered them the whole house for £900, a substantial sum in those days. Providentially Henry had just received his cheque for £300 from Gordon Onslow-Ford for the elmwood figure: just the amount required for the deposit. Never was a cheque more welcome. In the long task of getting the house into shape he and Irina were hampered by the restrictions on the sale of building materials.

Since the Luftwaffe did not generally bomb London by day, Henry would sometimes spend an entire night in the Underground on his visits to London, returning to Hoglands at dawn in the Standard 8 (courtesy of his war artist's petrol allowance) with his mind seething with material.

The conditions endured by the shelterers were appalling: with only a few buckets serving as toilets for hundreds of people, the stench and the fug were so vile that it was sometimes a relief to get out among the bombs. Moore became a connoisseur of Underground stations:

> I used to go quite often to Cricklewood, and I was fascinated by a huge shelter at Tilbury which was in fact the basement of a [paper] warehouse. But Liverpool Street Underground extension was the place that interested me most. The new tunnel had been completed except for the rails, and at night its entire length was occupied by a double row of sleeping figures.[13]

The resulting drawings, with reclining figures lining both sides of the deeply receding tunnel, as in real life but far more rhythmically arranged, were to be among his most famous. Realism was not part of his aim, nor could direct sketching from life be part of his method. To have openly drawn people dressing or sleeping would have been to intrude on their privacy and also to invite abuse or hostility. So he made only a few surreptitious notes in discreet corners. If anxious to retain a particular scene, he would walk past it several times, imprinting it on his excellent visual memory. Then on his return to Hoglands he would work in his shelter sketchbooks 'from the memory of actuality'.[14] The usual self-admonitions proliferated, such as: 'Remember figures seen last Wednesday night (Piccadilly Tube). Two sleeping figures (seen from above) sharing cream-coloured thin blankets (drapery closely stuck to form). Hands and arms. Try positions oneself.' He was also concerned, though to a much lesser extent, with the effects of the bombing above ground. *The Morning after the Blitz* [75], for example, shows groups of men standing around in a street covered with glass; *Gash in Road*, also from 1940, shows a larvae-like group of shelterers seen from outside.

Moore's correspondence with the all-important War Artists' Advisory Committee did not open till January 1941. On the committee sat representatives of the armed services, government departments and the art world, with Clark in the chair. The second most important man was the secretary, E. M. O'R. Dickey, a former Ministry of Education Inspector for Art and member of the London Group. Henry's technique was to treat Dickey's suggestions with the utmost politeness, but generally to ignore them: Clark would back him if there was any trouble. Thus the first letter from Dickey confirms the purchase of four shelter drawings for 32 guineas (i.e. £32 and as many shillings) and passes on the committee's recommendation that he should do a series of drawings of Civil Defence subjects for 50 guineas. Moore gave them more shelter scenes, and they bought ten for 70 guineas.[15] That August they tried to get him to draw certain specified First Aid Posts 'suggested to Sir Kenneth Clark by Lady Louis Mountbatten and Mrs Reginald McKenna'.[16] Henry tactfully accepted this powerfully backed commission, but never carried it out.

Selections of war artists' work were periodically shown at the National Gallery where, like the famous lunchtime piano recitals of Dame Myra Hess, Clifford Curzon, and other instrumentalists, they drew large crowds. Other selections toured the provinces, the Commonwealth and the USA, and they were reproduced in books and booklets introduced by well-known writers. There was a great hunger for culture. At the Churchill Club, where the Clarks were among the moving spirits, there were poetry readings and discussions which Henry often attended. Of those years Stephen Spender was to comment: 'Civilized values and activities acquired a kind of poignancy because they were part of what we were fighting for and the reason for which we were fighting . . . a little island of civilization surrounded by burning churches – that was how the arts seemed in England during the war.'[17] The *Sunday Times*'s influential critic, Eric Newton, reflected the new role which art suddenly played in the life of the nation when he wrote, somewhat portentously:

> It is my considered opinion that the opening of a new roomful of war pictures at the National Gallery is one of the most important single events that has happened in British art for three-quarters of a century. The pictures are not at all revolutionary, but about sixty per cent of them are charged with the electric current that can be generated only by passionate experience . . . Paul Nash's *Totes Meer*, a moon-haunted, grey-green sea of twisted metal that once was German bombers, Stanley Spencer's new panels showing riveters and welders working with the consecrated energy of devils in a medieval Last Judgement, Graham Sutherland's paintings of architectural wreckage, Henry Moore's unearthly studies of a white, grub-like race of troglodytes swathed in protective blankets in underground shelters – these may or may not be works of genius. What matters is that they are works of utter sincerity.[18]

In the cold light of today it is evident that utter sincerity is not a significant ingredient in works of art. Generally speaking the work of the Second World War's artists is remarkable not for its passion or sense of involvement but for its note of low-key, elegiac melancholy. War had become impersonal, death was delivered from long range.

With their strong sense of compassion, and even of indignation over sufferings endured, Moore's shelter drawings are very different. Clearly they have some documentary quality; but to compare them with, for example, Bill Brandt's photographs of similar scenes is to appreciate how thoroughly Henry transmuted reality into art. Brandt's photographs deal with the particular, with the here and now. Even when Moore focuses on a particular shelterer, he is portraying the ordeals of the victims of war as a whole. The sleeping woman into whose open mouth and vulnerable nostrils we seem to gaze in sympathy might be anywhere in Europe, one hand clawing at her blanket, the other thrown back across her head, while the arm of her companion rests protectively on the blanket covering her breast. The over-pretty colouring of these *Pink and Green Sleepers* [76], and of some other shelter drawings, reveals a lurking tendency to sentimentality. But sometimes, as in the Liverpool Street Station scenes, Moore reaches further beyond his immediate subject to grasp the charnel-house horror of genocidal warfare, and to anticipate the barely animate skeletal remains of humanity which were to be discovered when the concentration camps were 'liberated' at the end of the war, as John Russell has pointed out.[19]

Because of their actuality, their coherence as a group, and because they endowed the sufferings of Londoners with an epic dimension, the shelter drawings were, and have remained, extremely popular; but as works of art they are less satisfying than many of his more purely imaginative drawings. Francis Bacon's comment, that they looked like knitting with the needles pulled out, was malicious, but had just enough truth to make it score.[20] They were, however, important in Moore's development, tugging him away from the aesthetic preoccupations of the 1930s, with their pressures towards abstraction, back towards humanity. Once again Henry saw a close connection between his life and his art: 'Without the war, which directed one to life itself,' he told Alan Wilkinson, 'I think I would have been a far less sensitive and responsible person – if I had ignored all that and went on working just as before. The war brought out and encouraged the humanist side in one's work.'[21] (There is more pantheism than humanism in Moore's art. He used the term as shorthand for 'concerned with humanity' or 'going back to the Renaissance'. 'The word humanism is modern cant,' Kenneth Clark was to observe. 'This usage ought not to be allowed.')[22] The old admiration felt for Giotto, Masaccio, Titian, El Greco, and others on his trips to Italy, Spain, and Paris, long suppressed, had at last been allowed to find its way into his work.

In mid-1941, just when his sense of emotional involvement with the London shelterers was beginning to wane, his connections with Yorkshire were briskly revived by a major exhibition near Leeds. It was held at Temple Newsam, a superb Tudor-Jacobean house presented to Leeds City Art Galleries by Lord Halifax in 1922. To this vast mansion, set high in fine rolling countryside, the contents of the main art gallery in Leeds had been removed for safety in 1939. Its director, Philip Hendy, was, like Clark, an enthusiast for modern as well as old masters. A more open and vulnerable man than Clark, whom he was to succeed at the National Gallery, Hendy was tall, handsome, energetic, charming, slightly vain, and thin-skinned. He had started his career at the Wallace Collection in London, and had come to Leeds in 1934 from Boston, Mass., where he had been curator of paintings at the Museum of Fine Arts. In late 1938 he had conceived the idea of showing together in Leeds the work of three artists he greatly admired: Moore, Sutherland, and John Piper. Henry had suggested there should be a retrospective flavour, reckoning he could muster thirty or forty worthwhile pieces.[23] Now, despite the war, this plan was reaching fruition. With thirty-nine sculptures and fifty-six drawings, it was to be his biggest exhibition so far.

Rather generously, Hendy invited Kenneth Clark to come up and open the show of his three friends' work. The artists and their wives made the train journey north too, along with their collective friend Colin Anderson of the P & O shipping company and his wife Morna. Jane Clark had equipped the men with braces decorated with mermaids and prepared a picnic, which they washed down with a dozen half-bottles of Orvieto Secco. It was like a school outing, with the worries of the war forgotten. The weather was warm and jackets were taken off. When the ticket collector saw the mermaids, the glowing faces and the empty bottles, he said: 'You be careful, or you won't be able to do your act this evening.'[24] The party was still in high spirits when greeted by an entirely sober Hendy at Leeds railway station.

The exhibition, described by Clark in his opening speech as 'a very great landmark in the history of English art', attracted 55,000 visitors, a remarkable total considering the museum's relative inaccessibility.[25] Part of it then toured the provinces under the auspices of the newly created Council for the Encouragement of Music and the Arts (CEMA), the forerunner of the Arts Council. Clark opened it again when it reached the City Literary Institute in London in February 1942. Hostility as well as excitement was aroused along the way: a none too literate correspondent of the *Harrogate Advertiser*, for example, complained of the 'horrible Mongolian type of statuary debasing the human form, the likes of which has never been seen or discovered, outside the brains of the above exhibition and mental art quacks, fills me with nausea, disgust, mingled with much pity.'[26] Quite like old times.

By the end of July Henry had been involved with his shelter drawings for almost a year. The government had been progressively moving in on the once-improvised scene, providing bunks, canteens, and sanitary arrangements. With such developments much of the early drama and strangeness receded. Fresh subject matter was needed, yet none of the War Artists' Advisory Committee's ideas had much appeal. Then Herbert Read had an inspiration: why not tackle coal-mining as a subject? Britain's Underground Army was considered to be doing work of national importance. Henry's father had been a miner. There was a subterranean analogy with the shelter drawings.

Coal-mining drawings

Moore was formally commissioned to do some coal-mining drawings on 29 August 1941, for the niggardly sum of 29 guineas, plus third-class travelling expenses and £1 a day maintenance allowance (when abroad, war artists were treated as officers with the rank of captain; at home the Treasury was cheeseparing). As always, though particularly ludicrously in this instance, he was enjoined not to show what he did even to friends before it was submitted to censorship. Asked by Dickey whether he had any particular place in mind to visit, he replied that he had thought of going to his home town of Castleford, which had several coal-mines, and there was also one at Temple Newsam which he would like to look at.[27] A septic right hand, damaged while putting down a concrete floor in a shed at Hoglands, caused delays while arrangements were made for him to go down a mine at the Wheldale Colliery, where his father had worked.

Since the family moved to Norfolk in 1922 he had only infrequently revisited Castleford, the last time being in 1938, when he was guest of honour at a school reunion. There was such a thick fog when he arrived there now in early December that he had some difficulty finding the small hotel into which he had been booked. Next morning the colliery manager asked a deputy to give Henry a tour of the mine's main features. Thirty years later the memory was still painfully vivid:

> Crawling on sore hands and knees and reaching the actual coal-face was the biggest experience. If one was asked to describe what

Hell might be like, this would do. A dense darkness you could touch, the whirring din of the coal-cutting machine, throwing into the air black dust so thick that the light beams from the miners' lamps could only shine into it a few inches – the impression of numberless short pitprops placed only a foot or two apart, to support above them a mile's weight of rock and earth ceiling – all this in the stifling heat. I have never had a tougher day in my life, of physical effort and exertion – but I wanted to show the Deputy that I could stand as much as the miners.[28]

In fact on that first tour he was required to walk and crawl much further than a working miner. No wonder it seemed like Dante's Inferno. For the first few days he familiarized himself with the road and tunnels, the positions of the miners at work, the pit ponies and so on. Then he began sketching: there need be no inhibitions about doing it on the spot this time, since the miners knew he had been commissioned to record their work. For the first time in his mature career he was dealing not just exclusively with male figures, but with violent action, though the movement was generally only from the waist upwards. Both in sculpture and drawing, his preference had always been for the static and monu-mental. He found it far from easy:

> There was first the difficulty of seeing forms emerging out of deep darkness, then the problem of conveying the claustrophobic effects of countless pitprops ... receding into blackness, and of expressing the gritty, grubby smears of black coal-dust on the miners' bodies and faces at the same time as the anatomy underneath.[29]

He was not then aware of Seurat's wonderful 'black' drawings, of which he later acquired three fine examples. But he was reminded by the way the whites of the miners' eyes showed up against the grime of their faces [77] of Masaccio's frescoes in Florence, where the same feature was emphasized.[30]

Writing after Christmas to Herbert Read, whose idea it had all been, Moore reported that he had spent five or six days in Castleford on that first trip,

> and then came home to play about in a small sketchbook trying to fix some of the first impressions, & I now know more or less what in particular I'd like to look at over again. It's a strange and rather exciting world down the pit, and I'm not so sure just how easy it's going to be to make good drawings of it.[31]

He returned to his home town on 30 December for nine days: seven down the pit and a weekend with Read's friend Bonamy Dobrée, professor of English for many years at Leeds University, and his wife Valentine. On two days, however, there was a partial strike, and when Russian trade union delegates paid a visit, the red flag with hammer and sickle hung next to the Union Jack in the canteen, he told Read.[32] Another day there was a photographer from *Illustrated* magazine, which had caught wind of his trip. Though at that stage diffident about being photographed, Henry thought some coverage might be good propaganda. Two pages of admirable photo-reportage resulted, showing him sketching an ostler posing with a pit pony, a miner hewing the Silstone seam 2,000 feet underground, four miners waiting to come to the surface after their shift, with lamps gleaming in the dark 'like giant fireflies'; and 'artist-sculptor' Henry Moore squatting in the lift cage.[33]

On his return to Hoglands he worked up his on-the-spot notebook drawings first into two sketchbooks and then into about twenty more finished drawings in the 'mixed media' technique which he had devised in the mid-1930s, somewhat by chance: when playing around with the cheap wax crayons from Woolworths brought by a visiting young niece, he noticed that if these were applied first, a subsequent wash of water-colour simply slid off them on to the background. To give greater defin-ition to the forms, indian ink could then be used, and if the waxed surface was too greasy for that to register, it could be scraped down with a knife.[34]

Despite the family involvement in mining and his sympathy for the miners' hardships, he did not find the project as fruitful as the shelter drawings. As he later explained, the latter had come about after he had been moved by experiencing the shelters during a bombing raid, whereas the coal-mining drawings were 'more in the nature of a commission coldly approached': a difficult task, but 'something I am glad to have done'.[35] It is true that they do not have the same emotional impact as the shelter drawings, or the same popular appeal. Erich Neumann may well have been right in attributing Moore's feeling of detachment to his strong preference for women as subject matter, and in deducing that miners 'could not activate the unconscious archetypal connection between the world underground and the feminine'.[36] None the less these drawings demonstrate Henry's remarkable skill in capturing the physical and psychological realities of mining, and have a sombre dignity and power that is impressive. They were also to prove significant in his artistic evolution. Through them he discovered, or rediscovered, the male figure

which he had not drawn since his student days, and the thematic possibilities of the body in action. Without them, later bronzes like the *Falling
Warrior* series and the broad-backed king of the *King and Queen* might
never have evolved.

Dickey's committee in no way shared Moore's reservations about their
value. 'Your coal-mining subjects were received with acclamation at
yesterday's meeting,' Dickey wrote on 28 May 1942. 'The committee
have recommended that four of the pictures should be accepted for 25
guineas.' A fortnight later he was voted an additional 30 guineas for the
eight drawings which he had by then delivered, and three more followed.
When some of them were shown with other war drawings at the National
Gallery that October, the *Daily Herald*'s well-known columnist Hannen
Swaffer rather oddly described them as 'a pitiless exposure of the perils
and hardships of cramped life far below the surface'.[37] More pitying than
pitiless, surely.

By June 1942 Moore had completed his mining drawings and shot his
bolt as a war artist. The War Artists' Advisory Committee attempted –
sporadically, right up to July 1945 – to interest him in such projects as
a collection of objects dropped from the air and a bomb museum, but
without success. He wanted to get back to sculpture after two years in
which he had, in effect, worked as a painter, albeit not in oils. His financial
position now seemed more secure. In 1941 the great Brown Hornton
stone *Reclining Figure* of 1929 had at last found a buyer for £220 in the
Leeds City Art Gallery, thanks to Philip Hendy, and in the following year
Wakefield City Art Gallery had finally mustered the £150 needed to
secure the elmwood recliner of 1936. The shelter drawings, though
theoretically all the property of the committee which commissioned them,
were selling briskly to collectors like Clark himself, Colin Anderson, and
the economist John Maynard Keynes. Irina too swelled the family income
with some teaching in this period, taking art classes for five- to eight-
year-olds at a school in Much Hadham: she felt she ought to make a
contribution, but found she was not a born teacher.[38]

Before returning to sculpture, however, Henry submerged himself
again in the populous world of his own imagination, emerging with a
magnificent series of unrelated drawings – again in a mixture of media –
many of which showed future sculptural projects in a landscape or
interior setting. For example, *Reclining Figure and Pink Rocks* prefigured
another major elmwood carving completed in 1946. The most remarkable however, was the purely pictorial *Crowd Looking at a Tied-Up Object*
[87], perhaps his most famous drawing. It was probably inspired, he told

Alan Wilkinson, by a spectacle common at the Royal College of Art: a sculpture covered in a damp cloth to keep the clay moist, and tied around with string. But the indefatigable Wilkinson has convincingly shown that the source was more probably a photograph in one of Moore's books on primitive art showing a group of Nupe tribesmen in northern Nigeria standing around two tall, veiled cult objects.[39] As an image of stirring yet mysterious power, Henry's drawing (which Clark snapped up) is even more impressive than *September 3 1939*, with its anxious swimmers off the cliffs of Dover. The identity of the wrapped object remains a matter for conjecture. In a bleak landscape compressed by a leaden sky, the tightly grouped crowd gazes up at its looming, sinister presence.

First show in the USA

Many of these largish drawings were destined to be exhibited first in the USA, thanks to one of the most important letters which Moore ever received. It came from a New York art dealer of whom he had heard little or nothing called Curt Valentin, who said he wanted to buy some drawings for an exhibition at his Buchholz Gallery:

> Several people of whom I inquired spoke highly of him ... and unlike my present habit I answered the letter the very same day... He asked whether he could have forty drawings for sure, and I said yes. By the afternoon post ... came a letter from another New York dealer suggesting the same thing. If I had not answered Valentin that morning, I would have agreed to his suggestion, since I knew all about him.[40]

The second letter was from Pierre Matisse, son of Henri and a dealer of some renown and prestige. Yet Henry never regretted his rare burst of letter-writing zeal. Valentin was as lovable as a human being as he was inspired as a dealer. Disgusted by Nazism and saddened by the death of the great Arthur Flechtheim, for whose gallery in Berlin he had worked, he had settled in New York in 1937, and opened his gallery on 57th Street two years later. Modern sculpture was his particular passion, along with the work of his old friend Paul Klee, and he did more than anyone else to spread enthusiasm for such sculptors as Barlach, Lehmbruck, Arp, and Marini through the American art world (another of his artists, Lipchitz, had commended Moore's work to him). Valentin was rare among dealers in being highly respected by museum directors and art historians. Among his friends, of whom Henry became one of the closest, he inspired

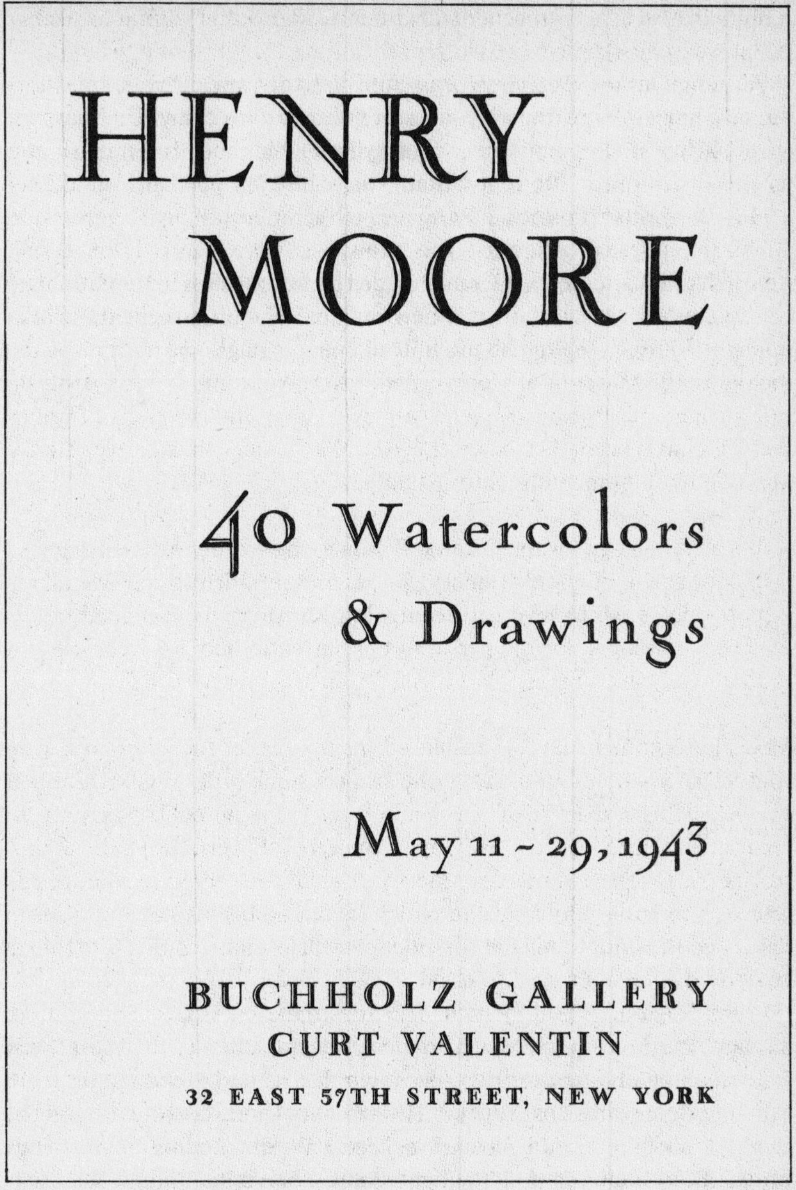

HENRY MOORE

40 Watercolors & Drawings

May 11 ~ 29, 1943

BUCHHOLZ GALLERY
CURT VALENTIN
32 EAST 57TH STREET, NEW YORK

Catalogue cover of Moore's first exhibition in the USA.

a high level of affection, being warm-hearted and entertaining as well as intuitive and perceptive.[41]

Although a few American museum directors and private collectors already knew Moore's work, Valentin's show of his drawings, many of them shelter studies, and one reclining figure, did much to establish and spread his transatlantic reputation. The exhibition opened in mid-May 1943, the British Council having helped arrange transport across the submarine-infested Atlantic. The drawings were insured for £398. Kenneth Clark and Herbert Read provided prefatory notes to the catalogue to explain Moore's work to this new public. Valentin bought the works outright himself, selling about half of them straight on to museums, including the Museum of Modern Art in New York and the Art Institute in Chicago, and to New York private collectors. The reactions of critics seem to have been mixed. In the *New York Sun*, for example, Henry McBride wrote somewhat patronizingly:

> It's a bit of a test for the Entente Cordiale, these drawings by Henry Moore at the Buchholz Gallery, for Mr Moore is British and we all, naturally, wish to love British art, but Mr Moore is also abstract. This is not a test for me personally, I hasten to add, for I got used to abstract art long ago, but it is for you, Mr Average Citizen.[42]

McBride reckoned that Moore placed his figures on the stage in a way that fastened attention, making one suspect something tragic was afoot, yet veiled his terrors in a gentlemanly air of remoteness, seeming to recommend us to 'brood mistily upon the general overtones of the affair'. In *Art News* of the same day, Martha Davidson seemed to admire the 'great crepuscular ambience' in which he placed his figures, but disliked his 'hideous, almost malicious manner of transforming women into things composed of all body and no mind'.

From Valentin's gallery two dozen of the drawings, including six already bought from the New York dealer, went across to the West Coast to the gallery of a pioneering Californian dealer, Earl Stendhal, at 3006 Wilshire Boulevard, Los Angeles. He sold only three, one of which went to the anglophile Santa Barbara collector Wright Ludington. Reviews ranged from the puzzled to the appreciative, one critic finding the existence and work of men such as Moore to be like 'heartening rockets in the night assuring us that man is still capable of creating art'.[43] All in all it was a good American début. Writing to Lilian Somerville of the British Council to thank her for their help, Henry said he was 'most pleased about it in every way.'[44] Since Valentin had bought the drawings, it was of no importance financially that a fair number had not been resold by the gallery. As in Britain, those clients who did buy (like James Johnson Sweeney) were of known discernment.

Madonna and Child

The shelter drawings had meanwhile precipitated a commission which provided, as it transpired, an ideal return ticket to carving and produced another landmark sculpture: the *Madonna and Child* [85, 86], executed for the large, late-Victorian parish church of St Matthew's in the Midlands town of Northampton. Its vicar, the Revd Walter Hussey, wanted to celebrate the church's fiftieth anniversary in 1943 in a worthy manner, and had strong views about the need for the Church to patronize good modern music and art, rather than the sugary and undemanding variety almost universally favoured. Benjamin Britten had agreed to write a cantata, and Hussey was now casting around for an artist of comparable power. On seeing a war artists' exhibition at the National Gallery in 1942 it struck him that Moore, of whom he had not heard, might be his man: the dignity and three-dimensional quality of the shelter drawings made everything around them seem flat and dull, he found.[45]

Harold Williamson, principal of the Chelsea School of Art evacuated to Northampton, confirmed his judgement, adding that Moore would also be very cheap. The artist happened to be coming to Northampton the following week to judge an art competition. Williamson showed Moore the church, and afterwards the three men dined together at the Angel Hotel. There the project for a madonna and child was broached. Henry said he would be interested, but added understandably that he couldn't say whether he could, or would want, to do it. The historic precedents were, after all, daunting, the current state of church art depressing. For several months he shrank from committing himself; to produce a sanctified version of his first theme, the mother and child, cannot furthermore have seemed a very enterprising form of sculptural comeback. A gentle reminder or two from Hussey was deflected with references to the pressure of preparing the New York exhibition.

By the time he met Hussey for lunch in London in early May 1943 he had done some notebook sketches, and when asked whether he liked the idea of doing the commission, he replied: 'Oh yes, it's the sort of thing that would happen in an ideal world.'[46] Thereafter progress was swifter.

By late June, Moore had made four clay models of about four inches high, and was planning to add four or five more. In late July, Hussey went to Kenneth Clark's office at the National Gallery to see five models short-listed with Clark's help. Moore himself and Jasper Ridley, the genially patrician chairman of the trustees of the Tate Gallery, were also there. 'It is the most exciting sight I have ever seen,' said Clark as he surveyed the maquettes, adding that Ridley wanted to commission the model chosen as the best if Hussey didn't, or indeed another one (as he later did).

Afterwards, over tea with Hussey nearby, Henry agreed to undertake the commission for £300 or £350, according to the current price of stone and transport: for exhibition it would have cost £500, he said. To do it slightly over life-size, as he felt the site required, would need about a two-ton block of brown Hornton stone, and would take some six weeks of hard work, ten or twelve hours a day. In a subsequent statement intended to help Hussey gain the approval of the Parochial Church Council for the commission, Henry explained how a Madonna and Child might differ from a carving of a Mother and Child: it should, he believed, have 'an austerity and nobility and some touch of grandeur (even hieratic aloofness) which is missing in the everyday Mother and Child idea'.[47] The chosen model had, he thought, a 'quiet dignity and gentleness' and he had tried to convey a sense of 'complete easiness and repose'. The Madonna would be seated on a low bench, facing the direction from which she would be first seen, while the Infant looked straight ahead.

Having no assistant, he had to set to work unaided when the large block of stone arrived at Hoglands only a couple of weeks before the original fiftieth-anniversary deadline of 21 September. He soon realized that he could not hope to complete it in less than two full months, and in the event it took five. Hussey took a few chips off the block himself when inspecting progress in early November 1943, to get a sense of the physical act of carving, carefully preserving them. Clark advised on some adjustments to the base, and due attention was paid to lighting arrangements in the church.

On 10 February 1944 the completed *Madonna and Child* was transported to Northampton by truck, with Moore aboard. After spending the night *chez* Hussey and adding some finishing touches next morning, he left the sculpture covered, returning nine days later for the dedication and unveiling by the bishop of Peterborough and Sir Kenneth Clark respectively. With him came Irina, the Clarks and the Sutherlands:

Hussey wanted to place a strong painting on the wall opposite the *Madonna and Child,* and Moore had recommended Sutherland as the most suitable of the suggested candidates. The resulting anguished *Crucifixion* was the perfect complement.

It was to be a far less jolly train journey than the one to Leeds. The weather was very cold, the train unheated and without lavatories. After some thirty minutes it stopped: the line had been bombed. They remained stationary for two hours, arriving an hour after the service was due to begin, frozen and in a state of acute discomfort, to find a congregation approaching the end of its patience.[48] Clark none the less delivered a felicitous address, save for a warning that the figure he was about to unveil 'may worry some simple people, it may raise indignation in the minds of self-centred people, and it may lead arrogant people to protest' (who, his listeners may reasonably have wondered, was being arrogant?). But – generous touch – he added that he felt there were many in the congregation who would sense its beauty more and more every day, and its great harmony, even tenderness of feeling.[49]

Clark's pre-emptive strike was almost certainly counter-productive. Though no work of Moore's now seems to us more accessible and natu-ralistic than the *Madonna and Child,* none aroused as much anger, dismay, and disgust when first shown to the public. 'Simplicitas' – the *nom de plume* was doubtless a dig at Clark's patronizing reference to 'simple people' – probably spoke for many when he wrote to the *Northampton Chronicle and Echo*: 'This sculpture may be great art without beauty, or it may be beautiful in the eyes of an initiated few, but it warps a mental picture of an ideal which has remained unchanged for 2,000 years.'[50] Less temperate correspondents suggested that the Madonna had elephantiasis, was wearing jackboots and would have made a better doorstop. Others found it a fine sermon in stone, and commended Moore's avoidance of conventional prettiness.

When the more obviously controversial *Crucifixion* by Graham Suth-erland was unveiled (with the Moores and Clarks present) in St Matthew's two and a half years later, it aroused much less indignation. Pondering this riddle, the *Northampton Independent* was surely right in surmising that 'whereas in the popular mind there are rigid limits to an artist's licence in dealing with womanhood and motherhood, there can be none when his subject is as imponderable as agonized death'.[51] It was not just a conventional image of womanhood and motherhood which Moore had broken: both the mother and child were very special, their images sacrosanct. The sculpture became a sort of sensation, Hussey recalled:

Thousands of people came to see it from all over the country ...
What pleased me was that not one member of the Church Council
ever ratted. There was enthusiasm from all sorts of people who saw
it, and all the opposition came from outside the parish ... one got
all sorts of comments that were sheer imagination. I remember one
aesthetically educated person who said 'Oh yes, the *Madonna and
Child*, that's got the holes in the funny places.'[52]

Henry paid a return visit to Northampton about a week after the unveiling, and in the crowded bus from the station asked Hussey how it was
going. The cleric replied that a week ago probably no one on the bus
would have heard of him. Now there was probably not a soul who hadn't.
Henry seemed alarmed at this transformation. The friendly relationship
between the two men survived an episode which revealed the sculptor's
blend of generosity and Yorkshire realism. As a gesture of thanks for the
commission, Henry promised to give Hussey the clay model on which
the carving was based, but subsequently also promised it to Clark, who
had been so helpful. With his developed sense of *Realpolitik*, Moore
was always likely to resolve such a dilemma in favour of the more
powerful patron and closer friend, rather than on the basis of moral
obligation. When he tried to do so, Hussey stood up for his rights, backing down only when Moore offered him a bronze cast instead. Henry was
obliged, however, to ask Hussey to pay the cost of the casting (£5),
explaining that he simply did not have the money himself: this at the
age of forty-six, when he was already well known.[53] A total of seven
casts was made before long, the first instance of a Moore bronze being
'editioned'.

Stylistically the Northampton *Madonna* linked Henry's past and future
work. The theme of mother and child went back to his beginnings as a
direct carver, and the strength of his early primitive vein is still there,
tempered, however, by two elements: first, the skills in carving and in
the disposition of masses acquired in his mature career; and secondly, a
warmth and humanity new to his sculpture, deriving doubtless from the
experience of the shelter drawings, but also perhaps from having finally
digested the lessons of the great Italian masters whose work he had
contemplated in Italy, Spain, Paris, and London. The same sources must
also have inspired his first significant sculptural use of drapery, hitherto
only adumbrated. In this, as in her serenity, the Madonna looks forward
to much of Moore's impending work.

The *Madonna* speaks straight to the heart, and the shiny darkness of her oft-touched knees is eloquent of her tactile qualities too. Henry was pleased by the directness of her appeal, of which he gave Hussey a touching example. A couple he knew had a daughter in a Northampton mental home. When they visited her, they always went to see the carving, because it gave them such reassurance and tranquillity. That, he said, meant more to him than the warmest critical review.[54]

A developed skill in combining carefully ordered design with emotional impact was pinpointed as one of Moore's greatest strengths in a short study of his work by Geoffrey Grigson published by Penguin in April 1944. Author and subject were Hampstead friends, and in 1939 Moore had provided Grigson with a drawing for the jacket of his first volume of poetry, *Several Observations*. The short study of Moore's work was one of the first batch of four in a new series, *Penguin Modern Painters*, a title which restricted the illustrations to Moore's drawings. The books were the brainchild of the ubiquitous Clark, who had suggested the series to his friend William Emrys Williams, then editor-in-chief of Penguin Books, and had been asked to choose the subjects and authors (the other three were devoted to Graham Sutherland, Paul Nash and Duncan Grant). The books were well designed, with sixteen high-quality colour plates, sixteen in black and white, and a dozen short pages of text. Grigson's was a great deal sprightlier and more vividly perceptive than Herbert Read's pioneering study of a decade earlier.

Probably with Henry's encouragement, Grigson gave pride of place among the early influences on Moore to the 'hard solemnity' of Mexican carving and to Masaccio's figures, both of which combined deliberation with a 'held-in immensity of life'. He explored his friend's pantheistic relationship to landscape and natural objects, and discoursed rather freely on the effect of contemporary knowledge on artists. Like the great inventors, he wrote, Moore 'balances his road between the theorem and the heart . . . In the mess and muddle and fecundity of life, which he finds wonderful and mysterious, Moore puts together shapes by which all that life is both ordered and symbolized.'[55] The series was hugely popular, the Moore volume being reprinted that November. 'If anyone has a quarrel with so-called "distortion" in art, let him read this book,' said *The Times Educational Supplement*, among many enthusiastic reviews.[56]

Clark played an important part in another venture that year: a film about war artists called *Out of Chaos*, directed by Jill Craigie, who later married the Labour MP and future party leader Michael Foot. The fact that it was her first film, though she had written some scripts for documentaries, and that she was suspiciously pretty, aroused doubts about its likely value. But once Clark had agreed to take part, all the artists approached (they included Moore, Sutherland, Nash, and Stanley Spencer) except John Piper fell into line. Sutherland turned out to be a very self-conscious performer, while the scruffy and rather strong-smelling Spencer delighted in shocking people. 'Of course all my painting is masturbation,' he would say loudly in a crowded train compartment on the way to Clydeside, where he had so memorably painted the shipyard workers. Jill Craigie and her large crew repaired to Hoglands to film Moore with his shelter drawings (he was also shown among sleeping shelterers at Holborn Underground station) and he 'bowled them over', she recalled, with his grasp of what was required and of the complex lighting system. When the call for action came, he drew seemingly invisibly in white wax crayon on a sheet of white paper, then put on a wash of dark water-colour which did not take on the wax:

> Magically, a powerful impression of two women restlessly asleep in the Underground appeared, the whole creating an atmosphere of oppression beyond the scope of a photograph. The execution of the work was so beautifully timed and adapted to a medium devised for action – it was shot in one take – that Henry's conquest of the film unit was complete.[57]

Over tea he described how his interest in three-dimensional form had been aroused by massaging his mother's hip to ease her lumbago, demonstrating first on his own hip and then on that of the enchanting Jill Craigie. 'To have Henry Moore rub one's hip is not an experience anyone would be likely to forget,' she found. The film ran for twenty-eight minutes, with music by Lennox Berkeley. Released shortly after being shown to the press in December 1944, it was considered well-intentioned but in parts heavy-handed and patronizing.

Family groups

By the time Moore's achievements as draughtsman were being celebrated in book and film, he was back in full cry as sculptor. Soon after finishing the Northampton *Madonna* he tackled an expanded version of the same theme: the family group, including a father and in some cases an extra child. The idea came from the charismatic educationalist Henry Morris, who wanted a major Moore sculpture for the second of his revolutionary village colleges, at Impington in Cambridgeshire. As the young secretary of that county's education committee, Morris had produced a memorandum in 1924 persuasively arguing that in rural areas primary, secondary, and adult education should be brought together under one roof: no one would ever really leave school, and the college would be a focal point for neighbouring villages too. The idea was accepted, and the first college had been opened in 1930 at Sawston by the Prince of Wales, later Edward VIII. Architecturally it was disappointing. In 1934 Jack Pritchard, who had recently commissioned the Lawn Road flats, took Morris's visual education in hand and introduced him to Gropius, who designed the Impington College with Maxwell Fry.

At much the same time Moore too was introduced to Morris and was much taken by the educator's explanation of the village college concept. 'The *Family Group* in all its differing forms,' he later wrote, 'sprang from my absorbing his idea of the village college – that it should be an institution which could provide for the family unit at all its stages.'[58] Impington's birth proved difficult. The county authorities objected to paying an outside architect when they had their own, and there were difficulties in raising funds. The college was finally opened in late 1939, well after Gropius's departure for the USA; later the building strongly influenced post-war British school architecture. Moore received no firm go-ahead for his commission at that time, but in 1944 Morris reckoned he could now get enough money together for the sculpture if Moore would still like to do it. The sculptor accepted, made some notebook drawings, and from them came a number of small maquettes: mostly ideas for stone carvings, but some for bronze.

Like so many enthusiasts, Morris had been over-optimistic, and failed to raise the necessary money. Furthermore, the Cambridge councillors who had bilked at Gropius were unlikely to be devotees of contemporary art. In his biography of Henry Morris, Harry Rée says that a first maquette was sent to Morris, who was eager to have it executed; but 'for the Cambridge county councillors of the time, Moore, and the price asked, were too much. They refused to order it.'[59] Two years later, Henry's adoptive county of Hertfordshire commissioned the piece (to Morris's fury), thanks to an initiative of a Morris admirer, John Newsom, who had become Hertfordshire's education director in 1940.

Meanwhile Moore's work on the maquettes was far from wasted. Ten of the little terracotta models, mostly five to eight inches high but in two cases some eighteen inches tall, were cast in bronze in editions of seven or nine each. The sculptor had quickly grasped the benefits of the process, and five of the Madonna and Child maquettes were also cast in editions of seven. Taking a few other pieces into account, around 140 small Moore bronzes were cast between 1943 and 1947. Their sale to collectors and museums around the world and in Britain (the Tate bought seven in 1945) helped further to establish Moore's fame. According to Herbert Read, however, there were some devotees who thought this multi-plication reflected a loss of integrity.[60] For the artist it represented an attractively easy way of recouping the time and effort spent on a major project like the Northampton *Madonna*. The old disciple of 'truth to material' had come a long way. 'There I've changed,' he acknowledged in 1957:

> I still think it's tremendously important, but I used to exaggerate the importance. That's partly due to the state sculpture was in in this country thirty or forty years ago – it had become almost entirely representational and decorative. So it was necessary to get back to first principles and emphasize them afresh. But it's impossible for a sculptor to keep lots of pieces of stone lying around his studio, or to go about constantly searching for the right piece to embody each idea that's working in his mind.[61]

The brisk sale of his little bronzes ended the nagging constraint of a barely adequate income. Slowly but inexorably he was henceforward to move towards the dubious privilege of being among Britain's highest taxpayers. It must have saddened him that his mother, the rock on which his life had been built, did not survive long into this more prosperous era. In May 1944 she died, aged eighty-six, in a Woking nursing home. Henry was much affected by the sight of her body in death:

> She had such a dignity, such an eternity feeling about her, that to me it was beautiful but terribly, terribly moving ... there's some-thing about a dead body which is statuesque. It's like a sculpture. The foreheads are cold. If you touch a dead forehead it's like touching marble.[62]

Gathered together for the cremation, Henry's brothers and sisters turned to the most successful member of the family to put her death in perspec-tive. It was important to grieve, he told them – less of a truism then than now; but later they must put her death behind them and live in the present and for the future.[63]

The war had taught Moore much about humanity. His mother's death was another bridge between the personal and the universal: a loss which could also be a gain.

Chapter X

Via New York and Venice to international fame

1945–8

In the First World War, soldiers had been the main victims; in the Second, civilians suffered worst, and their ordeal was to continue. Rejoicing was short-lived when first Germany and then Japan surrendered to the Allies in May and August of 1945 respectively. The mind of mankind was scarred by the horrors of the liberated German concentration camps and by the nuclear bombs dropped on Hiroshima and Nagasaki. The suffering of the European continent was prolonged by its division between East and West, prompting millions of ethnic Germans to flee from Eastern Europe to the hope of freedom in the West.

Though Britain continued to endure austerity and rationing, it was spared the fratricidal tensions of countries which had been occupied by the Germans. Hopes of creating a more equitable social order, to which Henry Moore ardently subscribed, found expression in the huge majority with which the Labour Party was voted to power in the general election of July 1945. If photographs, films, and reports of the fate of Hitler's victims in Europe induced a sense of despair about man's inhumanity to man, and if the rise of a new totalitarianism in eastern Europe boded ill, at least in our island kingdom there seemed to be a small chance of creating a better world.

It was thus a time of relief, horror, anxiety, and hope. In his personal life Moore was an optimist, but he was also a man of spontaneous and ready compassion. Especially through his drawings he had, since the late 1930s, shown his sensitivity as a receiver and retransmitter of signals from suffering humanity. All serious artists are open to the spirit of the times, and in this respect Moore was as sensitive as any. With his deep feeling for the human form he must have been particularly affected by

61. *Reclining Figure*, 1939, 81 inches long, elmwood, Detroit Institute of Arts.
Commissioned by Berthold Lubetkin and first bought by Gordon Onslow-Ford, it remains
the quintessence of Moore's contribution to the language of sculpture, with claims to be
ranked as his finest work

62. *Portrait of Stephen Spender*, 1934,
pencil and chalk

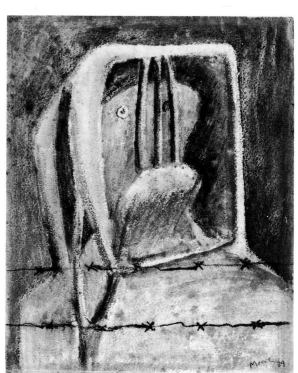

63. *Spanish Prisoner*, 1939,
$14\frac{1}{2}$ inches by $12\frac{1}{4}$ inches,
a mixed media drawing for
Moore's first lithograph

64. Wells Coates

65. Marcel Breuer

66. Walter Gropius

67. Paul Nash

68. Serge Chermayeff

69. Berthold Lubetkin

70. *The Bride*, 1939–40, $9\frac{3}{4}$ inches high, lead and wire, Museum of Modern Art, New York. Often considered the best of the stringed works

71. *Bird Basket*, 1939, $16\frac{1}{2}$ inches long, lignum vitae and string

72. *The Helmet*, 1939–40, 12 inches high, lead and later bronze. Roland Penrose bought the original version. Jacques Lipchitz had done a remarkably similar *Head* (though without the interior form) in 1932, of which the Tate Gallery has a version

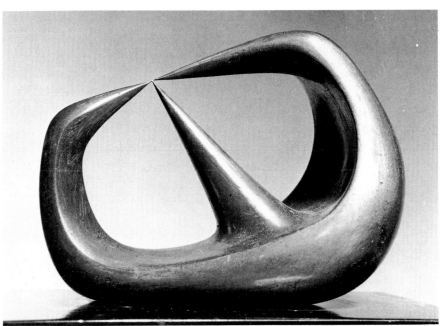

73. *Three Points*, 1939–40, $7\frac{1}{2}$ inches long, cast iron (originally lead). In his later years Moore was to produce many variations on this theme, but none as tense and economical

74. *September 3rd 1939*, 1939, 12 inches by $15\frac{3}{4}$ inches, pencil, wax crayon, coloured crayon and Indian ink. Moore was bathing near Dover when war broke out, and recreated this scene of women gazing anxiously across to France

75. *Morning after the Blitz*, 1940, 25 inches by 22 inches, mixed media. One of Moore's few above-ground wartime drawings

76. *Pink and Green Sleepers*, 1941, 15 inches by 22 inches, mixed media. One of Moore's most famous shelter drawings

77. *Miners' Faces*, 1942, $9\frac{3}{4}$ inches by 7 inches, pen, watercolour and crayon, from a sketchbook

78. Moore sketching two Castleford miners as they erect a Tupping machine 1400 feet below ground, January 1942

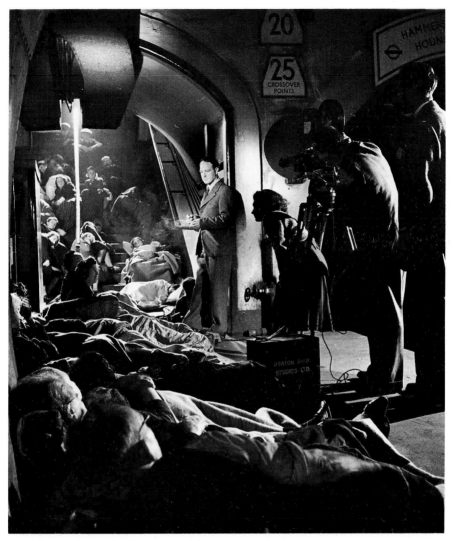

79. Moore as an official war-artist revisiting the London Underground in September 1943, with Jill Craigie (leaning over), for the filming of *Out of Chaos*

80. Hoglands, the Moores' home at Perry Green in Hertfordshire from 1940, where Henry died in 1986, seen here as immaculately restored

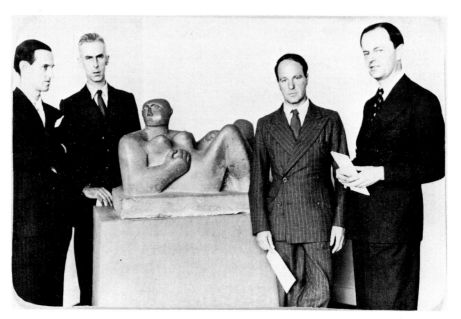

81. Moore with Graham Sutherland (left), John Piper and Kenneth Clark at Temple Newsam, Leeds, in 1941 at the time of their joint exhibition

82. Henry Moore in 1942

83. Irina Moore in 1940

84. The Revd Walter Hussey, vicar of St Matthew's Church, Northampton, later Dean of Chichester

85. The Northampton *Madonna and Child* in progress, initially a heavy labouring job, for which he had no assistance

86. *Madonna and Child*, 1943–4, 59 inches high, Hornton stone, St Matthew's Church, Northampton. Its stormy reception helped make Moore famous

87. *Crowd Looking at a Tied-Up Object*, 1942, $5\frac{3}{4}$ inches by $6\frac{1}{4}$ inches, mixed media, formerly in Kenneth Clark's collection. One of Moore's most haunting images

88. Terracotta models for family groups, 1945

89. Moore in his studio, a converted stable at Hoglands, in July 1945

90. Moore with Pat Strauss of the London County Council and Aneurin Bevan, Minister for Health, admiring *Three Standing Figures* of 1947–8, 84 inches high, Darley Dale stone, at Battersea Park Open Air Sculpture Exhibition, 1948

91. *Memorial Figure*, 1945–6, 56 inches long, Hornton stone, Dartington Hall, Devon. The most elegiac of Moore's major works

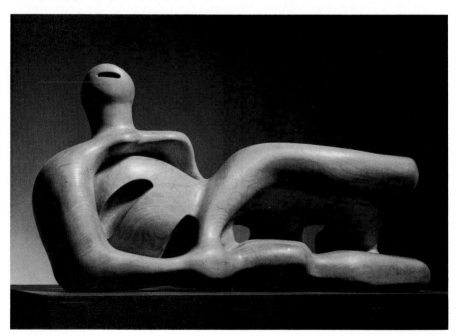

92. *Reclining Figure*, 1945, 75 inches long, elmwood, J. B. Speed Art Museum, Louisville. Fourth of the great elmwood reclining figures, it was destined to break several auction records

the haunting images from the extermination camps in Poland. Since the later 1930s many of his reclining figures had had an eviscerated and skeletal quality, and a sense of death filled many of his shelter drawings. Having drawn heavily on his positive, tender or Apollonian vein for his madonnas and family group studies, he now had every reason to give expression to the darker, tougher, and more Dionysiac side of his artistic character.

Starting in autumn 1945, he was to work for the next year in parallel on two carvings which reflected both aspects of his nature. The 'tough' one was his fourth major elmwood reclining figure, the 'tender' one a stone memorial to Christopher Martin, a gentle friend who had died in 1944 of TB after ten years as head of the Arts Department at Dartington Hall in Devon. It was commissioned by Dorothy and Leonard Elmhirst, the New York heiress and Yorkshireman who had created at Dartington a community embracing light industry, agriculture, education and the arts, with a fourteenth-century manor house as its focal point. Henry's initial contact seems to have been through Kenneth Clark and Philip Hendy, whom he had assisted in a Dartington-backed inquiry into the prospects for the arts in Britain.[1] The fifty-six-inch-long *Memorial Figure* [91], as it was called, is perhaps the most serene and elegiac piece of Moore's entire career, perfectly balanced and harmonious from the unusually detailed head with its far-seeing gaze, down through the rhythmically handled drapery and up to the sharply raised hill of the right knee. The position of the figure has something in common with the Leeds *Reclining Figure* of 1929, with its Chacmool parentage, but the mood could scarcely be more different. Seen *in situ*, the Dartington figure is the more poignant for the striking beauty of its surroundings, especially when viewed against the background of a giant Scots fir which frames the grassed and terraced tiltyard and the austerely handsome Hall. Thirty years have given the Hornton stone a patina of lichen growths, and there has been some erosion caused by rain dripping from the overhanging trees. Happily there are no scars from an incident in 1968 when someone drew in eyes and a cigarette.[2]

As with the Northampton *Madonna and Child*, Moore carved the Dartington figure single-handed, or virtually so. Bernard Meadows, stalwart support of the later 1930s, returned to the Royal College of Art in 1946 after five years in the RAF, later taking Moore's old job at the Chelsea School of Art. With typical loyalty, Henry helped to restart Chelsea's sculpture school after the war, continuing to appear in a visiting capacity into the early 1950s. The sculptor Elisabeth Frink was one of those who benefited from his visits and appreciated his patience, encouragement, and the feeling he gave his students of having his full attention.[3] He performed the same valuable service at the Slade from 1949 to 1952.

In the event, Henry found his first post-war assistant not through Chelsea or Meadows but via a chance encounter in a tweed shop on the way to Cambridge. Buying some cloth there for a jacket or suit, he fell into conversation with the writer Hugh l'Anson Fausset, who mentioned that his son Shelley wanted to become a sculptor. So it happened that when the latter had finished his land service (he had been a conscientious objector), he went and lived with Henry and Irina in Hoglands itself: the first and last assistant to do so. The arrangement had its snags, since he was expected to double up as houseboy for such tasks as laying fires. His artistic background was not ideal. He had studied graphic design at the Central School of Art and Design in London, and had briefly apprenticed himself to a stonemason, but otherwise he had no training as a sculptor. His sense of form was on his own admission rudimentary, and when he helped Henry with the big elmwood reclining figure, he very nearly ruined it:

> The wood was green, with the sap squirting out. It is very easy to cut when it is green. If you take enough of the heart of the wood out sufficiently evenly, as it contracts you don't get damaging cracks, called 'shakes', when it seasons and dries out. The tension holding all those rings together is spectacular. Henry had ordered a very big gouge, about two and a quarter inches wide. I had never used one more than just over one inch across. I was roughing out the top of the upper leg, and at one point I cut too much. I cut it into a trough, and at that stage it looked horrifying ... instead of blowing his top, which he would have been perfectly entitled to do, he said 'Right, now you and I have to see how much is left.'[4]

Careful measurements were taken, and to the enormous relief of both men the affected part was found to be still 'proud'. When finished without further mishaps in autumn 1946, this large piece, at seventy-five inches long just a little shorter than its predecessor which Onslow-Ford had bought, turned out to be the most richly ambiguous of all Moore's eight large wood carvings. [92] The sculptor himself interpreted the large slit oval beneath the pectoral shelf as a heart, remarking on one occasion: 'For me, [it] had great drama, with its big beating heart like a great pumping station.' On another occasion he said of the same piece: 'The artist can make his point, reveal his love for his fellows just by suggesting, as I tried to do in my *Reclining Figure* in elmwood of 1945–6, the operations, the palpitations of a human heart.'[5] Kenneth Clark likened the 'heart' to a crusader's head burrowing in the hollow breast, 'the whole figure with averted thorax and open legs, struggling out of the earth like a tree, not without a powerful suggestion of sexual readiness.'[6] Yet much of the disturbing power of this carving comes surely from the ambiguity of the 'heart', which seems also to be the head of a child eating out the mother's breast, the great shelving legs seeming to do duty for both of them.

Mary's birth

Life became intertwined with art when on 7 March 1946, Irina gave birth to a daughter, who was named Mary after Henry's mother and sister. Henry was forty-seven, Irina thirty-nine. Mary was in every sense a 'precious' baby, since Irina had suffered many miscarriages in earlier years. To be on the safe side in this instance she stayed for a few weeks before the birth in one of the Lawn Road flats, within easy reach of the Belsize Park clinic where the child was safely delivered. Henry was from the first an active and doting father, and played a full part in helping to look after his beloved daughter. As a small child Mary was to be enchanting but spoilt.

Some of Moore's commentators have suggested that the addition of a child to the Hoglands scene renewed his interest in the mother and child theme or in family groups: as John Russell puts it, with the birth of a daughter 'the image of the family took on a new, leaping, unpredictable intensity'.[7] In fact the happy event crowned the readoption of a favoured motif of the mid-to-late twenties rather than triggering it, the *Madonna and Child* and the maquettes for the family groups having been completed in the preceding two years. Apart from some drawings and the charming little bronze rocking-chair studies of mother and child of 1950–2, the theme fades away for many years as an inspiration for major new work, with one or two notable exceptions. The most striking of these is the Tate Gallery's sinisterly barbaric-looking *Mother and Child* of 1953 [108], in which a birdlike child snaps, beak agape, at the breast of a mother with a serrated head, who in turn holds the serpentine neck of her would-be devourer tightly enough to strangle it.

So exceptional a work, more reminiscent of Picasso than Moore, has naturally prompted many interpretations. Neumann calls it 'a negative modulation of the old motif ... a picture of the terrible Mother, of the primal relationship fixed forever in its negative aspect'.[8] Herbert Read comments that the group is 'so close an illustration of the psychoanalytical theories of Melanie Klein that it might seem the sculptor had some first-hand acquaintance with them; but the artist assures me that this is not so'.[9] Equally true to form, Dr Wilkinson explains that the immediate source of inspiration is a bas-relief on a Peruvian pot reproduced in a book in Moore's library.[10] The question remains: *why* was Henry attracted to this image? The answer seems to be that, initially at least, he was alarmed at the sight of Mary feeding at Irina's breast. Within the family the bronze mother came to be known as Nora, since whenever someone asked the sculptor whether the child was trying to devour her, Henry would say: 'No, gnaw her.'[11]

The great elmwood *Reclining Figure,* completed in October 1946, was sold to Curt Valentin, who did not find a buyer for it till 1952. While languishing under wraps on a balcony at his gallery it was then shown to William McVey, a sculptor who taught at Cranbrook Academy of Art at Bloomfield Hills, Michigan, and whose nine-foot tall statue of Winston Churchill stands outside the British Embassy in Washington. The price, Valentin told him, was $6,500. McVey, much impressed by the sculpture, commended it to the director of Cranbrook's own museum, Eva Gattling. Though her annual budget was only $10,000, buy it she did, to the consternation of the museum's trustees, who wanted to know who had recommended 'that big splinter'.[12]

For twenty years the carving enriched the lives of students and teachers at this community of artists and craftsmen, being exhibited in the main galleries of the museum. In 1972 the once-affluent academy needed to raise some capital and, after much heart-searching, the Moore sculpture and some other works were auctioned on 1 March at Sotheby Parke Bernet in New York. The price paid, $260,000 (£101,562), was a record for a sculpture by a living artist. The buyer was Fischer Fine Art: after more than two decades as a founding director of Marlborough Fine Art in London, Harry Fischer was setting up his own gallery in St James's, and this was an opening coup. Just ten years later it was consigned for auction, again at Sotheby's in New York, by the Italian businessman who had purchased it from Fischer. This time the price was an even more staggering $1,265,000 (£641,740), and the buyer was another London dealer, Thomas Gibson, who sold it that evening, over a good dinner, for an extra ten per cent to Wendell Cherry, the Louisville collector and head of the Humana private hospital group.[13] Cherry in turn lent it to the J. B.

Speed Art Museum in Louisville. That auction price was then the highest ever paid for the work of a living artist, painter or sculptor.

Both the Dartington and Cranbrook figures were shown at Henry's fifth exhibition at the Leicester Galleries in October 1946, which came near to selling out within a few days of opening. The drawings, at £21-36, were particularly popular, as were the small bronze maquettes for the Impington family group project (£105 each, or some £1,200 in today's money). The stylistic contrast between the two main exhibits was the subject of some rather crass critical comment. Only Maurice Collis in the *Observer* seemed to appreciate that the Dartington figure's serenity derived in part from the nature of the commission, while the elmwood carving was quintessential Moore:

> It was as if, with profane eyes, one had come unawares upon the earth spirit in her lair of the woods and that she had looked up and was about to do what no man could conceive. Henry Moore has acquired the power to bewitch. The formula of the bewitchment will be given by the erudite – curves, holes, pressures, balances – but its essence, and why it should act so, is a secret only he knows.[14]

In this end-of-war period Moore's work seemed to be in mixed shows everywhere: at the Berkeley Galleries in Davies Street, W1, where Vincent Price, the actor, started a lifelong admiration for Henry's work by buying a small bronze and a drawing;[15] at the Lefevre gallery, where Francis Bacon stole the limelight for the first time with his *Three Studies at the Base of a Crucifixion*, which caused outrage; and at the British Council's offices in the Champs Elysées, Paris, where the French critics reacted snootily to a pot-pourri of contemporary British art. Very different emotions were aroused by a selection of modern works (Moore's included) from the Tate Gallery which toured the continent in 1946. For hundreds of thousands of war-shattered and culturally starved citizens in cities like Brussels, Amsterdam, Vienna, Prague, Warsaw, and Rome, it was a first chance to see the work of artists such as Moore, Sutherland, Piper, Pasmore. In every capital save Paris, there was astonishment that so mature and diverse a school of artists should exist in England. In Warsaw enthusiasts emerged from the cellars where they were still living to witness the artistic vitality of the nation which had attempted to stand by Poland's side.[16]

If Kenneth Clark is to be believed, Picasso was more impressed by Moore's work than the Paris critics. Shortly after the Germans left the French capital, and not long before he resigned as director of the National

Gallery, he showed Picasso the volume on Henry's work which Lund Humphries had published in 1944. Picasso took it in a spirit of derision. *'C'est bien, il fait le Picasso,'* he remarked after his first glance. Then he became worried, left the lunch table, and took the book to the far corner of their hostess's room. There he remained for the rest of the meal, Clark recalled, 'turning the pages like an old monkey that has got hold of a tin he can't open', eventually handing it back without a word.[17]

Though Moore was by now mature enough to be relatively impervious, Picasso was overwhelmingly the dominant influence on British painting at this juncture, being likened in a correspondence in the *New Statesman* to a Dracula sucking the lifeblood from young talent. Henry met him again in Paris in November 1945, when he also visited Brancusi. Picasso was selecting some fifty works for an exhibition, shared with Matisse, which created a sensation when it opened at the Victoria and Albert Museum in London in December. The great man was due to have been the guest of honour at a dinner given on the eve of the opening by the French ambassador, René Massigli. Moore, Sutherland, Read, and Penrose, with whom Picasso was to stay in Hampstead, were among those waiting for his arrival. At the last moment, he sent word that he could not make it. He did, however, visit London in November 1950 (just thirty years after his previous visit with the Diaghilev Ballet), this time on his way to a Peace Congress in Sheffield. Because the Labour government was hostile to this Communist-backed event, he refused to attend a large party given for him by the Arts Council; but he did appear for one the following evening at the huge studio in Maida Vale, W9, of the Polish-born painter Feliks Topolski, and was particularly friendly to the assembled artists, who included Epstein, Moore, Pasmore, and Sutherland. Fernand Léger also came over that year. This time the ambassador had better luck with his dinner party, and Moore was inevitably again there. As Léger left, he shook the sculptor by the shoulders and said to John Rothenstein, director of the Tate Gallery: *'Type sympathique, hein?'*[18]

It was probably at about this time that Braque paid a memorable visit to Hoglands. Naturally Henry showed him around, but Braque took little interest in his work, and kept on staring at his host's trousers, to such an extent that the sculptor thought his flies must be open. Discovering that all was in order, he asked Braque what it was that interested him. 'Where did you get those splendid trousers?' the Frenchman asked. Henry explained that he had bought the corduroy trousers in question in the 1920s in the Caledonian Market in London.[19] The cookery writer

Theodora FitzGibbon, who had settled with her husband, Constantine FitzGibbon, nearby at Allen's Green in 1950 and become very friendly with the Moores, has an even better version of this story. Henry had been much struck by a pair of the local moleskin trousers which she had given to her rumbustious husband, and so she gave him a pair too – and it was these which Braque had so admired.[20]

In October 1945 Leeds University bestowed on Moore the first of some two dozen honorary degrees which he was to receive from British and foreign universities: seals of official approval which the academic establishment, not without an element of self-congratulation, confers on those who balance their achievements with the right admixture of respectability. It was appropriate that Leeds, whose Vice-Chancellor Michael Sadler had encouraged Moore while he was at the nearby art college, should have been first off the mark in making him an Honorary Doctor of Letters, and that Bonamy Dobrée, with whom he had stayed after doing the mining drawings, should have presented him to the distinguished gathering. The best known of those being honoured was Anthony Eden, later Lord Avon, the former wartime Foreign Secretary and, in earlier years, occasional columnist for the *Yorkshire Post*, of which his father-in-law Sir Gervase Beckett was a director. The man who as Prime Minister was to send British troops into battle over President Nasser's seizure of the Suez Canal warned those assembled that 'unless the nations of the world are willing to work constructively together for peace, there will be an explosion which will blow them all to smithereens'.[21]

Eight years later Leeds was followed by London University, with a doctorate of literature. Next came Harvard in 1958, Reading and Cambridge in 1959, with Oxford limping in two years later, tailed by West Berlin's Technical University, Hull, Sussex, Sheffield, York, Yale, St Andrews, Toronto, Manchester, Warwick, Durham, Leicester, Columbia (USA), and Bradford. Only the American universities could muster an honorary Arts degree. The rest were in literature, letters, law and engineering (Berlin). Moore was also made an Honorary Fellow by Lincoln College, Oxford, and Churchill College, Cambridge. With many of these institutions the sculptor had no particular connection, but he was happy to accept the compliment: 'You can't throw kindness back in people's faces,' he would say. 'It would be an insult. Who the hell is one to be above something?'[22] Initially at least he had no doubt felt the honour was being bestowed on modern art as a whole and not just on himself. Yet an artist like Francis Bacon would have no time for such Establishment fripperies. Henry liked to be reassured about his own place, and the place of the artist, in the established order of society.

He believed, too, that he should do his duty as a public figure; and so he sacrificed a considerable amount of time to serve for two terms as a trustee of the Tate Gallery, from 1941 to 1948 and 1949 to 1956; as a founder member of the art panel of the Council for the Encouragement of Music and Art (CEMA) from December 1942, and then with its successor body, the Arts Council, from 1945 to 1949, again from 1955 to 1959, and on the Arts Council itself from 1963 to 1967; as a trustee of the National Gallery from 1955 to 1963 and from 1964 to 1974; and as a member of the Royal Fine Art Commission, that misnamed watchdog of the built environment, from 1947 to 1971, probably a record span. More surprisingly he was also a member of the National Theatre board from 1962. Although not by nature a committee man, his views were always forthright, sensible and usually broad-minded. Meetings were far from being pure penance for him, since he was gregarious by nature, enjoyed and benefited from the good company on these bodies, and was obliged by his responsibilities to keep more in touch with current developments in the art world than he would otherwise have done in Hertfordshire.

The New York retrospective

If Mary's birth and the completion of the Dartington and Cranbrook figures had already made 1946 an *annus mirabilis*, the most important development for Moore's career was yet to come. On 24 November he embarked for New York for the first major retrospective exhibition of his work, due to open in mid-December at the Museum of Modern Art: the first such show to be devoted to a British artist, and the sculptor's first trip to the USA. With him went his staunch friend and fellow Yorkshireman, the publisher Peter Gregory: it was, a colleague of Gregory's recalled, like seeing two young children going off with bucket and spade to the beach.[23] They travelled aboard the *SS America* on its maiden westbound voyage after a £2 million conversion from its wartime role as a troopship. From start to finish of his five-week trip away from the enduring austerities of England, Henry was amazed by all the food that was available, and found it difficult to choose.[24]

Thus revictualled, they arrived in New York (how dramatic its skyscrapers then looked, being without parallel in Europe) on 1 December. Curt Valentin whisked them via their hotel, the New Weston, to the

Museum of Modern Art, where preparations for the opening on 17 December were proceeding against considerable odds. The past three years had been a period of tribulation for the senior staff of the fine art department. In 1943 Alfred Barr, director of MOMA since its foundation in 1929 and an internationally respected figure, had been abruptly relieved of his duties by the chairman of the board of trustees, the autocratic millionaire collector Stephen C. Clark. Barr stayed on in a research position in the library, being partially reinstated as director of museum collections in 1947. He had also been curator of painting and sculpture, in which position he was succeeded first by the intellectually brilliant James Thrall Soby, and then, in January 1945, by Moore's old acquaintance from the 1930s, James Johnson Sweeney.

Soby's resignation had been a great blow to staff already sickened by Barr's dismissal. Sweeney, who was rich and no leader of men, was less loved, and he too left after some contretemps, just half-way through the preparations for the Moore exhibition. The show had been largely his idea. He had selected the works, prepared the catalogue and written its prefatory essay. The man in charge when Moore arrived was René d'Harnoncourt, an immensely tall (six feet eight inches) Austrian aristocrat who had arrived penniless in New York in the 1930s after a spell in Mexico, establishing himself as a master of installation with an exhibition at MOMA in 1941 called Indian Art of the United States.[25] In 1944 he had been appointed an executive administrator with the title of vice-president. As director between 1949 and 1968 he was to preside over the museum's period of greatest growth.

These comings and goings, and the resulting bitterness, caused Henry some embarrassment:

> People were saying 'Henry, you should insist that the exhibition is put on by Jim Sweeney or refuse to have it.' But it was Sweeney who said no to that. I remember him telling me 'I have left the museum. I don't want to enter into any sort of squabble about the show or make any problems for you.' He insisted on letting things work themselves out. Very nice of him. Of course he took me around and I saw a lot of him and his wife Laura.[26]

All Henry's correspondence had been with Sweeney. Now he found himself dealing with d'Harnoncourt and Dorothy Miller, an attractive and able young woman who was to become director of painting and sculpture. It was she who took him along to d'Harnoncourt's dismal flat by the top of Central Park, where he was recovering from 'flu. 'Henry was adorable,' she recalled. 'In the taxi he clutched my hand and said "I am terrified. I have never been here before, and I am absolutely terrified of this big exhibition." I said, "Don't be scared, everything is going to be fine, we like you." '[27] D'Harnoncourt, who always arranged his shows on paper, had done a floor-plan to scale showing the location of each piece. Henry was delighted by it all.

There followed four of the most hectic weeks of his life, probably the longest stretch in his productive years in which he did nothing creative. Every morning Curt Valentin would call him at 8.30 to discuss the day's programme. Part of each day before the opening was spent helping with the installation. The rest was given over to meeting people and looking at works of art. When it came to drinking Valentin set a stiff pace, and Henry recalled falling asleep in a taxi one evening with his head in Martha Graham's lap.[28] During a session with the poet e.e. cummings in Greenwich Village a smashed table landed on his foot. He went to see Walter Lippmann, thinking this was his chance to understand American politics. When he had fired off some questions the great commentator said 'Of course I could tell you what you want to know, but if I were you I wouldn't bother my head with it. Just get on with your work, Mr Moore.'[29] Not only the English were patronizing.

Among the museums which he visited in New York were the Metropolitan, the Frick Collection, and the Pierpont Morgan Library, where the director showed him some important Romanesque English illuminated manuscripts, including a leaf from the Winchester Bible. Moore was deeply moved, and at one point exclaimed: 'Here England was great, and it will be great again!'[30] With Peter Gregory he travelled to Boston, where he saw the Museum of Fine Arts, the Fogg and Peabody museums, and enjoyed a warm reunion with Walter Gropius, who had settled in Massachusetts. There were also brief visits to Washington, where he visited the National Gallery and the Phillips collection; to Dumbarton Oaks; and to Philadelphia for the fabled collection of Impressionist and modern paintings of Dr Alfred Barnes, including the great Cézanne *Bathers* which he had so admired in the Pellerin collection in Paris in 1922.

Barnes was notoriously curmudgeonly. Moore had come armed with an introduction from Kenneth Clark, only to be warned it would be fatal to use it. One day d'Harnoncourt introduced them at MOMA. Henry confessed he was about to write to him 'since I would love to come, if I may, to see your fabulous collection'. After a short silence Barnes said: 'Such exaggerated flattery makes me sick.' Even his bodyguards looked aghast, as another silence ensued. Eventually Barnes asked when he would like to come. Any time, said Henry meekly. Whether deliberately or not, Barnes suggested the day of Moore's opening. The sculptor swallowed, then accepted providing he could be back by 7 p.m. Barnes promised to see to it, and did. He proved to be the perfect host, escorting Henry around the entire collection, giving him lunch, and sending him off in good time with a bottle of whisky and a copy of his book *The Art of Renoir*.[31]

On the previous evening, when MOMA gave a party for Henry to meet fellow artists and others, his voice deserted him, as occasionally happened at times of stress and exhaustion. Among artists he met then or on other occasions were Jackson Pollock, Arshile Gorky, Mark Tobey, Georgia O'Keefe, John Marin, Marc Chagall, his old friend Sandy Calder, and Jean Arp, who was visiting. When Nelson Rockefeller, whose mother had helped found the museum, gave a dinner in his honour, Henry realized he had no dinner jacket. Valentin sent his over to the museum, and Henry retired behind one of his carvings to try it on while Dorothy Miller stood guard. Valentin being portly, it was no good. Dorothy Miller's husband, Holger Cahill, offered his, but that was no good either. So he had to hire one on Broadway; but he did wear Cahill's black shoes.[32]

Among those working on the staff of MOMA was the young William Lieberman. Thirty-seven years later he was to organize the second major retrospective of Moore's work in New York, at the time of his eighty-fifth birthday, this time at the Metropolitan Museum. Back in 1946 Lieberman introduced the sculptor to his mother, who eccentrically observed that Moore should visit a Mayflower Coffee Shop. 'Why should I do that, Mrs Slattery?' he asked politely, as Lieberman *fils* blushed with mortification. 'Because they have your motto,' she replied, and recited:

> As you go through life, brother,
> Whatever be your goal,
> Keep your eye upon the doughnut
> And not upon the hole!

'I nearly dropped dead,' Lieberman recalled. 'Henry roared with laughter.'[33]

Although New Yorkers visited the 1946 exhibition in vast numbers – 158,000 in three months – there was no immediate and general acceptance of his work. 'It's hard to believe now, but it was very far out in 1946,' Dorothy Miller recalled not long ago:

Almost immediately it wasn't far out any more. Now you can show anything. But then it was quite avant-garde, and there were many people who did not like it and who wrote letters, and all those letters were handed to me. There were only a few I could answer. Most were from nuts.[34]

The press was quite enthusiastic, with general agreement that the fifty-eight sculptures and forty-eight drawings had been presented to excellent advantage, and virtually unanimous praise for the drawings. In the *New York Times*, Edward Alden Jewell called the show an 'unusually interesting and challenging survey', and found the shelter drawings to be 'packed with terror and pathos and unconquerable hope'.[35] Emily Genauer, then of the *New York World Telegram*, admired the 'rhythmic, undulating flow of his forms, the exquisite balance between one form and another ... the counterpoint he creates between the strong jutting angles of reclining figures ... even more than the monumental, elemental strength and dignity of his conceptions ...'[36] Marion Summers, in the *New York Daily Worker*, considered his mining drawings 'as stirring as any done in our time'.[37] The most lavish praise came from Alfred M. Frankfurter, publisher and editor of *Art News.* Today we could clearly see, he wrote, that what seemed the vast revolutionary strides of Rodin and Brancusi were but steps pointing the way to one 'whose inherent greatness of vision and the innate power to realize it in full makes him the formative force of the twentieth century'.[38] There was extensive coverage in *Newsweek, Time, Life,* and *Vogue* magazines, and in newspapers from Tampa, Florida to Zanesville, Ohio: all this before the show proceeded to Chicago and then San Francisco.

On the eve of Henry's departure for England after Christmas (which he had spent in Gordonville, Virginia, with Mr and Mrs George Dix, anglophile collectors), Jim Sweeney gave a small farewell dinner for him. Among the guests was Francis Taylor, director of the Metropolitan Museum, to whom Henry regretted that he had not, thanks to all his engagements, spent more time at the Metropolitan. Taylor abruptly left the table, and on returning said: 'I've arranged that in about an hour's time they'll be waiting for us. We can all go, and you, Henry, can have a private viewing of the Metropolitan along with all your friends here.' Off they went in two cars, with a vastly impressed Moore trying to imagine the whole of the National Gallery in London being opened up in the middle of the night for a distinguished visitor.[39]

On 17 April 1947, just a month after closing in New York, the same

Moore retrospective opened at the Chicago Art Institute, to a rather mixed press reception. It made an enormous impression, however, on the students of the institute (whose magnificent public galleries had evolved from the art school's collection). Among them was Alfred Cohen, who almost forty years later bought the school house at Wighton in Norfolk, to which Henry's parents had moved with their daughter Mary from Castleford in 1922. Cohen recalled:

> Most of the male students were ex-servicemen on the GI Bill of Rights, and the war years had been a complete black-out as far as anything new that had been going on outside America was concerned. The exhibition was a feast – a strong, fresh wind blowing across the Atlantic. I remember the Shelter drawings made a very strong impression ... we lost no time in trying to acquire the techniques of Moore's drawings, and there was a rush for wax crayons and indian inks. The sculpture classes were bowled over – the pierced and stringed forms, the exciting surfaces and inventive treatment of drapery. We were fortunate that our classrooms were in the main Art Institute building, and this gave us easy and continuous access to the retrospective. A lot of time was spent absorbing its lessons.[40]

Hundreds of students also visited the exhibition from Midwestern universities and colleges, on their own and in groups. After just a month in Chicago it travelled on to San Francisco, where it opened towards the end of June for two and a half months at the city's Museum of Art.

The American showings had aroused the interest of public gallery directors in Australia, who had made direct approaches to Moore. He referred them to the British Council, under whose auspices a severely reduced version of the MOMA exhibition (fifteen sculptures but no large carvings, and twenty-seven drawings) went for a ten-month tour to Australia, embracing the public galleries in Melbourne, Adelaide, Perth, Hobart, and Sydney. By the time these well-travelled items returned to England in Autumn 1948, their lenders had been deprived of them for almost two years, a sacrifice made more tolerable by their desire for Moore's true value to be accepted more widely.

The British Council shared this desire. It was the first time they had toured the work of an artist who was to become, along with the English language, Shakespeare, Margot Fonteyn, Laurence Olivier, and British orchestras, a major cultural export. The Council's chief representative in Australia, Charles Wilmot, stamped official approval firmly, if a trifle defensively, on Moore's work in his catalogue introduction, in which he wrote: 'Henry Moore is widely regarded as one of the most vitally creative figures in British art today. As usually happens with products of imaginative genius, his work will raise controversy. So much the better.' It was thus official: Moore had genius. Of course he had more than proved himself by this stage; and he was after all in his fiftieth year, by which age nowadays many famous young artists are slipping back into obscurity. The British Council did not make Moore's name, but it did much to spread it far and wide. Some able artists who were almost totally ignored by this powerful promotional body, like John Piper, had good cause to feel wistful.

The Australians' first reactions to Moore's work were similar to those of provincial Britons. The critics in general applauded and tried to lead the public to appreciation rather than outrage, of which there was plenty. A profile in the *Melbourne Age*, for example, described him as 'the one true sculptor upon a big scale who has matured in England since the Middle Ages,' while the *Herald* welcomed the show as 'splendid evidence of a vital and significant British art, flourishing despite manifold difficulties'.[41] But a letter-writer to the *Argus* in the same city thought it 'high time a death blow was dealt to this pernicious tomfoolery'.[42] Opening the show in Adelaide, Mr Justice Mayo reminded his audience that at one stage Keats' poems had been greeted with laughter, Wagner's operas with catcalls, and Cézanne's paintings regarded as an impudent joke. The warning failed to ensure Henry a uniformly respectful reaction. One *Adelaide Advertiser* reader complained of the inane giggles of exhibition viewers, and comments like 'Isn't it awful!' Although in Sydney the *Sun*'s critic called it 'the most important exhibition of its kind ever held in Australia,' the Sydney *Morning Herald*'s critic found Moore's work both too intellectual and too tasteful: 'he is a man of talent, not genius.'[43] Despite the wide range of reactions, Wilmot hailed the tour as a considerable success. It had, he reported to the British Council in London, been an inspiration to Australian artists, and created a demand for more shows of work by contemporary British artists.[44] So Moore was not alone in benefiting.

In the late 1940s everything Henry touched seemed to turn to fame. Back from New York he tackled a project destined to make a mark on Londoners: the large *Three Standing Figures* [90] now in Battersea Park. Henry had been told the Museum of Modern Art in New York would like a big sculpture from him. So he decided to carve it in exceptionally hard Darley Dale stone, which seemed ideal for the harsh New York climate.

When the Contemporary Art Society decided they would like to offer it to the London County Council for Battersea Park, MOMA agreed to wait. Later it acquired instead a cast of the *Family Group*.

The three standing ladies started off in 1945 as a monumental-looking little terracotta maquette, eight and a quarter inches in height, and ended up eighty-four inches tall in stone three years later. They were, Henry later explained, an expression in stone of the group feeling with which he had been concerned in the shelter drawings. To create a unified mood in three identifiably female rather than abstract figures was far from easy, especially as he wanted to overlay the hint of apprehension with a sense of release, creating figures 'conscious of being in the open air – they have a lifted gaze, for scanning distances'.[45]

The mood is established in the maquette, with apprehension uppermost. Translating it into stone at well over life-size was a major task. Meadows responded to a call for help and carved most of the left-hand figure. Shelley Fausset, still Henry's assistant, did the basic carving of the middle lady. Leslie Lawley, a young stonecutter from Pickering in Yorkshire, also helped out. When Moore was worried about finishing on time, he brought in Reg Butler, who lived not far off, for three weeks of hard labour on the right-hand figure. Butler, who before long was to acquire his own measure of fame, had trained as an architect and worked as a blacksmith. So hard was the Darley Dale stone, Fausset remembered, that they had to use silicone carbide-tipped chisels. 'To polish it we had a hose running over each of the figures, and several grades of carborundum block. My fiancée and Reg Butler and a few neighbours all joined in and were polishing away by arc light one evening.'[46]

The *Three Standing Figures* have been variously interpreted. For Neumann they evoke the three Norn virgin goddesses of Norse mythology and are 'the most magnificent portrayal of the Fate Goddesses yet known to sculpture ... here the spiritual core of the feminine archetype has been reached and shaped in stone ... they have the rock-like dependability of the Great Mother, but their steadfastness includes death and disaster as well as life and its duration.'[47] John Russell convincingly relates them to the theme of watcher or witness pioneered by W. H. Auden in the 1930s. In carving women looking apprehensively towards the skies, he adds, Moore consciously or otherwise drew on the stored memories of the millions for whom the skies had been a source of catastrophe, from the Spanish Civil War onwards. None the less he finds the swathed cylindrical figures suffer from the same 'decorative and linear stylization' which Moore had criticized in later Sumerian art.[48]

The eventual resting place of this striking if not entirely successful work, Battersea Park on the south bank of the Thames, was to be the site in 1948 of England's, indeed by all accounts the world's first big, public open-air sculpture exhibition. For centuries sculpture had been created for specific out-of-doors sites, but the idea of showing large quantities of recent works *al fresco* was novel. It was hatched by Patricia Strauss, a Labour member of the London County Council (for Lambeth North) and chairman of the LCC's parks committee. She had been a professional artist's model – one of Russell Flint's favourites – and then a journalist; she was married to a wealthy Labour MP, George Strauss, and became a keen collector of contemporary art. The state of London's parks depressed her. Most of them had been used, at least partly, for allotments during the war years. 'They looked dreadful with all the little huts,' she recalled. An open-air sculpture show would cheer everyone up and help upgrade the concept of the park:

> Everyone said, Oh what a silly idea, the woman is dotty! Who wants sculpture in a park! As you would expect, the fiercest opposition came from the Labour members, who looked on all art as soppy, and sculpture as particularly soppy because it hasn't got any nice colour. I had to go and put my idea to the Leader of the LCC, Charles Latham, a man of some culture, and get his backing for this matter of policy. To my surprise he supported me, and said he thought it would be a good idea ... but if it hadn't been for the Tories, I would never have got it through my parks committee.[49]

The Arts Council joined in the organization. Kenneth Clark lent his authority to an *ad hoc* committee whose two most active members, Pat Strauss recalled, were Henry Moore and, balancing him from the academic flank, his old Royal College of Art superior, Gilbert Ledward. Moore showed both enthusiasm and patience, especially in helping site the selected works, and seemed to get along well with Ledward. The *Three Standing Figures* were favourably placed with a background of trees and lake; and the Tate Gallery lent (among many works) his *Recumbent Figure* which had lost its head briefly in New York. By today's standards, the selection of works was eclectic to the point of incoherence: Royal Academicians such as Charles Wheeler, William Reid Dick, and Ledward himself were very adequately represented, striking an incongruous note in the proximity of such artists as Modigliani, Laurens, Matisse, Epstein and Zadkine. Theoretically the show was international and covered the last fifty years, but there were plenty of notable omissions, among them Brancusi, Picasso, Gaudier-Brzeska, and Calder.

None the less, this was a pioneering venture – with pedagogic overtones, demonstrations of carving and modelling being provided by London art-school students, in a marquee near the main entrance when the weather was bad. The Duke of Wellington opened the exhibition on 13 May 1948, and it soon proved to be an overwhelming success, attracting 150,000 visitors at one shilling each over the next four months. Moore's *Three Standing Figures* aroused predictable hostility: a *Yorkshire Evening Post* reporter picked up such comments from viewers as 'monstrous', 'an attempt to out-Epstein Epstein', and 'an affront to womanhood'.[50]

News of the offer of the controversial carving to the LCC from the Contemporary Art Society drew a typically barbed letter to *The Times* from the art historian Douglas Cooper, erstwhile secretary of Unit One and backer of the Mayor Gallery:

> This offer was unexpectedly made in a speech from the platform, to the obvious surprise both of the Chairman of the London County Council and of the Mayor of Battersea. One could only sympathize with their embarrassment and hope that they will have the strength of will to suggest some alternative recipient.[51]

The painter-critic Patrick Heron singled out the Moore group for praise in the *New Statesman*, while in the *Spectator* M. H. Middleton proclaimed Moore to be 'the Michelangelo of our times'.[52] The exhibition aroused tremendous press interest, not least from Continental and American publications; yet its very success resulted in Pat Strauss losing her chairmanship of the parks committee and being exiled to the chair of the supply committee. Hard to believe though this became in the heyday of Labour's Ken Livingstone in the mid-1980s, there was then a strict rule against personal publicity for LCC activities, which she was considered to have infringed.

The Venice Biennale of 1948

Just two weeks separated the Battersea opening and Moore's departure for the Venice Biennale, which was to provide another landmark in the rise of his international reputation. Surprisingly perhaps, the Biennale had been held in 1940 and 1942, with the participation of the USA, Holland, and Yugoslavia as well as of a number of neutral and Fascist countries. The decision to revive it after what would be a six-year gap was taken only in late 1947. There was no time to assemble the cocktail of contemporary works which Britain had generally shown, as when Moore had been included in 1930. The British Council had to move fast. Sir Eric Maclagan, the former director of the Victoria and Albert Museum and chairman of the Council's fine arts advisory committee, appointed the painter and collector Edward le Bas and three critics, Clive Bell, Alan Clutton-Brock (of *The Times*), and the inevitable Herbert Read, to decide who should represent Britain. Moore had been in and out of the Council's offices in connection with the Australian leg of his American exhibition, and it was known that enough of his work was available. An exhibition of J. M. W. Turner's paintings, drawn from the Tate Gallery's vast holding, was touring the Continent and could easily be rerouted to Venice. So it was decided that Britain's greatest living and greatest dead artist should be deployed.

The Biennale takes place in the Giardini di Sant'Elena, and the British pavilion is pleasantly situated on top of a little hill. John Rothenstein, the Tate's director, went out as 'commissioner' in charge of the British pavilion, arriving on 27 May to supervise the installation. Henry followed on 31 May, again with Peter Gregory. He spent the first two days adding some finishing touches and sightseeing, the remaining three talking to the press, other artists and critics. 'He had the wonderful gift of being able to make himself understood without knowing the language,' the British Council's representative Ronald Bottrall, the poet and anthologist, reported. 'His visit to Venice was undoubtedly one of the most important factors in the resounding success of the British pavilion.'[53] Henry's sightseeing included expeditions with Gregory and Rothenstein to see Giotto's frescoes in the Arena Chapel in Padua, last glimpsed twenty-three years earlier on his travelling scholarship, and to the magical island of Torcello. In the evenings there were dinners and drinks with such pioneering artists as the Futurist Gino Severini, Carlo Carra (co-founder with de Chirico of so-called metaphysical painting), the brilliant draughtsman (and Communist) Renato Guttuso, and Giorgio Morandi, himself as withdrawn and meditative as his still lifes.[54] With dealers, artists and critics from all over the Western world congregating in the evenings in the cafés and restaurants in the environs of St Mark's, the Biennale in its heyday was like an extended party for the brightest and best, with a healthy leavening of charlatans and parasites.

At the British pavilion, the only real hitch was over the catalogues. Those for the Turner show had been translated in Rome into commercial Italian, no doubt to hilarious effect, and the rewritten version arrived twelve days after the opening. Moore's came two days after the press day, on the eve of the opening, a delay benefiting sales of the first foreign monograph on his work, by Giulio Carlo Argan.

Signor Argan could surely not exist in the Anglo-Saxon world: a Communist art historian who became mayor of Rome. In 1945 he had contrived, against the odds, to secure in Italy a copy of the shelter drawings sketchbook published that year by Poetry London. He was struck by the beauty of the drawing and the feeling of tenacity they expressed: they seemed to him 'an ode to the spirit of collective heroism' which inspired British resistance to the German bombardment.[55] While working at the Warburg Institute in London in 1946 he visited Moore in Perry Green, and an enduring friendship resulted. Hearing about the planned Biennale show of Moore's work, he decided to publish in book form an essay he had written for an Italian magazine. It sold out in a few weeks, and in 1971 he published a fresh and much longer assessment. The first version was very slim, and notable for a tortuous but flattering comparison between Moore's work and Picasso's, likening Picasso to a cicada and Moore to an ant, ('Picasso e la cicala, Moore la formica'). Kenneth Clark later expressed the same thought more clearly when he wrote in The Nude: 'Where Picasso is volatile, Moore is tenacious. Picasso swoops, Moore burrows.'[56]

In Italy it is normal for senior political figures to be deeply interested in the arts. When President Einaudi was shown around the British pavilion, he astonished the officials there by recognizing several Turners from his visits to the Tate, and by spotting among the Moore drawings one which he had seen at a contemporary art exhibition in Rome. From the bridge of a small visiting British warship the senior representatives watched the President return to the mainland in his magnificent state gondola, accompanied by others representing the ancient guilds of the republic, all with brilliantly liveried gondoliers. It was, as Rothenstein observed, like a Canaletto come to life.[57]

In those post–war years the focal point of Biennale gossip was the award of the main prizes. They were for the best foreign painter and sculptor (500,000 lire each or £500); the best Italian painter and sculptor; and the best foreign and Italian engraver (100,000 lire each). Rothenstein reckoned that Moore was clearly the best sculptor, but hoped that he would not, as the British member of the International Jury, have to propose him. The Italian representative obliged, stating flatly that Moore was the obvious choice. The suggestion was accepted without dispute, but there was uproar over the rival claims of Braque and Rouault to the main painting prize, even though they were both French. Braque prevailed, Manzù won the prize for Italian sculpture, and Chagall was considered the best foreign engraver.[58] Moore's one serious rival was the Frenchman Henri Laurens. Only a few of his works were shown, however, and inevitably they lacked the intensity of Moore's.

Today, when works of art of all sizes are flown around the globe for exhibitions and anyone can hop on a plane to keep abreast of trends in New York, Tokyo, Paris, or Rome, it is easy to forget how important the Biennale was in making and sometimes breaking reputations internationally (in 1950 the Venetian light proved cruel to Matthew Smith's painting). Moore's sculpture prize, and the great impact of the show on visiting museum directors, dealers and critics, transformed his reputation in Europe as suddenly as the MOMA show had in the USA. Henry always recognized this, and it confirmed his view that 'the British Council did more for me as an artist than any dealer'.[59] He was particularly grateful to Lilian Somerville, head of the Council's fine arts department from shortly after the Biennale to 1970 and a formidable advocate of his work. Dealers had cause for gratitude too: not a few civic purchases of a big bronze followed a Council exhibition, especially in Germany. Indeed, his shows seemed to do everyone a power of good. 'Undoubtedly he is by far the most important British artist in the world of modern art in Italian eyes,' Bottrall enthused in his report to headquarters. 'The Henry Moore exhibition has done much to raise the prestige of contemporary British art in Italy ... it is by far and away the most important artistic event undertaken by the British Council in Italy.' Even the British Ambassador in Rome, Sir Victor Mallet, who had graced the opening, managed a tepid endorsement, reporting to the Foreign Office in London: 'The Henry Moore exhibition is a matter of taste, and although I am too old-fashioned to enjoy it, I was glad to notice that all the many people who like, or profess to like modern art, were wildly enthusiastic.'[60]

Before leaving Italy, Henry paid brief homage to the Masaccio frescoes in the Brancacci chapel in Florence, and called on Bernard Berenson at I Tatti, the famous villa nearby where Kenneth Clark had worked as a young man. The art historian's distaste for Moore's work survived the encounter, as he made abundantly clear to Rothenstein a few days later:

The two most destructive personalities in European art today are Picasso and Moore [he said], Picasso consciously destructive and Moore unconsciously... How strange it should be so, for I've never received a visitor who showed such knowledge and perception

about my sculpture, not a piece of which he'd ever seen before. But
I think his work monstrous, as bad as Picasso's, and it only needs
a considerable artist to appear to blow Picasso and Moore sky-
high.[61]

In ranking Moore with Picasso, however negatively, Berenson paid him
a high compliment. Though eighty-three, 'BB' went soon afterwards to
Venice, where Rothenstein took him around Moore's sculptures and
drawings. He expressed further astonishment, but conceded, 'He's an
honest fool, whereas Picasso is a rogue.' Berenson's dislike of Moore's
work once prompted Kenneth Clark to observe to Alfred Barr's wife
Margaret:

> The question of taste is so difficult! and I think it has to do with
> age. I did my best over the years to make BB admire Henry Moore,
> but he *wouldn't*. And I myself feel the same way: I can only go so
> far and no further. I can only go as far as Rothko.[62]

Lauded in America, controversial in Australia, prize-winning in Venice:
Moore returned home from his five days in Italy a stage further in his
emergence as a National Treasure. 'It is impossible not to be glad at this
recognition of a distinguished sculptor who happens to be an Englishman,' modestly murmured a leading article in the *Manchester Guardian*.[63]
While enjoying the recognition, he was not a man to rest on his laurels.
The gap between his reputation and recognized greatness was still wide.
With his fiftieth birthday looming, there was no time to be wasted in
closing it.

Chapter XI

Execration and celebration

1949–51

The art world is a harsh place in which popular acclaim and the esteem of fellow artists rarely survive together for long. By the time the public has caught up, artists in the vanguard have moved on. A gap opens up: the more famous the artist, the less relevant he seems to his peers. One cause of this is the difficulty for any painter or sculptor, Picasso being the notable exception, of remaining for long in touch with the spirit of the times. He or she is liable to be identified irrevocably with a particular era when the flame seemed to burn brightest and most illuminatingly. For example, Graham Sutherland's Pembrokeshire landscapes of the late 1930s and war years were seen to have helped shape the elegiac romanticism of much British painting of that era, and many admirers regard them as his finest works. Among artists prominent in the early 1950s, John Bratby was rapidly and enduringly identified with the emerging 'kitchen sink' school of realism. The sculptors Lynn Chadwick and Kenneth Armitage enjoyed their finest hour as spearheads of the new, *Angst*-ridden group which created such an impact at the Venice Biennale of 1952, and of which Moore's old associate Bernard Meadows formed a part.

In this respect Moore fared much better than most. For a good twenty years, roughly from 1930 to 1950, he enjoyed growing public acclaim *and* the unstinted admiration of fellow artists. In those two decades his work reflected the most vital art movements of the day and, especially in the war years, the fears and hopes of his fellow men; yet at the same time it retained a power, a mystery and an archetypal dimension which added up to greatness. At the end of this period of integration came the *Three Standing Figures* of 1948 and the *Standing Figure* of 1950, to which we shall come: works permeated by the same Cold War anxieties which shaped the spiky creations of the younger generation of sculptors. They can be taken as marking the end of Moore's acutest 'contemporaneity'. From then on there was not necessarily a decline in his achievements *sub specie aeternitatis*; but in the eyes of his juniors, grateful though they were for what he had done in making modern art more acceptable and respected, his sculpture ceased to be of much relevance to their own efforts. As he became a public institution, his work went its own way: inventive, often courageously tackling new approaches, but increasingly divorced from the mainstream of contemporary art as it continued to evolve.

Such subtle shifts were not evident to the opponents of modernism who, in Britain if not on the Continent, were still fighting a vicious rearguard action from the academic trenches. For them Moore was still the enemy, and an increasingly famous and redoubtable one. Their commander-in-chief at this hour was to be Sir Alfred Munnings, President of the Royal Academy since 1944 and now aged seventy-one. Like Constable, whom he so admired, Munnings was the son of a Suffolk miller, and had painted in a pleasant sub-Impressionist manner before churning out the horse-racing scenes which made him popular and rich. Though in many ways engagingly eccentric, Sir Alfred had a vindictive streak, of which Henry was now to become the target.

It happened for the first time in late April 1949, when the traditional annual pre-Summer Show Royal Academy banquet was being revived after the years of austerity. Munnings had decided to retire as President, so it would be his last as well as his first Presidential address. To his right sat the Duke of Gloucester, the Lord Chief Justice Lord Goddard and the equally reactionary Archbishop of Canterbury Lord Fisher, and Lord Montgomery of Alamein; to his left, Sir Winston Churchill and many other distinguished public figures. The speeches were being broadcast live on radio. Sir Alfred, who spoke fifth, told his guests that he found himself president of a body of men 'who are what I call shilly-shallying: they feel there is something in this so-called modern art'. He attacked experts 'who think they know more about art than the men who paint the pictures', and mentioned Anthony Blunt, then Surveyor of the King's Pictures, whom he had once heard say that Reynolds was not as good as Picasso. 'What an extraordinary thing for a man to say!' When he made a disparaging reference to Matisse and 'aesthetic juggling' there were shouts of 'beautiful' and 'lovely work'.

Coming nearer to home, Munnings referred to some of the recent Battersea Park exhibits as 'foolish drollery', adding in an obvious reference to Moore, 'People were disgusted and angered, just as they were with this mother and child in a church in Northampton ... My horses may be all wrong ... but I'm damned sure that isn't right.' There were more hostile shouts, and Sir Alfred said heatedly: 'I hear other members interrupting me. I am the President and I have the right to speak. I shall not be here next year, thank God!' And with that he sat down. Immediately the BBC's main switchboard was besieged with callers objecting to the broadcast and the swear-words used.[1] Henry had not listened, and was not to be drawn by reporters seeking a reaction. Next day Philip Hendy, who had succeeded Clark as director of the National Gallery in 1946, pointed out publicly that Moore had been awarded the prize as best sculptor at the Venice Biennale. Henry emerged from discretion to say that 'a lot of silly remarks were made at the dinner. But it is well known that Sir Alfred is a violent critic of contemporary art. I do not care what his opinions are.'[2] Unfortunately both Munnings and Moore belonged to the Athenaeum Club in Pall Mall, where Munnings liked to hold forth to his cronies in the long drawing room. As Moore climbed the staircase one day with his friend J. M. Richards, *The Times*'s architectural correspondent, the painter and cronies came towards them. 'There's that fellow Moore,' Munnings said in a loud voice. 'What's a bloody charlatan like him doing in this club?' The charlatan, who had joined because it offered facilities for women, took no notice.[3]

Now that the Royal Academy has become almost touchingly anxious to clasp modern art to its ever more eclectic bosom, it is easy to forget how bitter the struggle between the modernists and academicians was, continuing right into the 1960s. The turning point came in 1966, when the abstract painter Sir Thomas Monnington, who was also the most decent of men, took over as president from the diehard sculptor Sir Charles Wheeler. In the real world, even in Munnings's day the balance of power had shifted in favour of the moderns. It was now the Arts Council, the British Council, the senior officials of the Tate Gallery, and in the cases of Clark and Hendy the directors of the National Gallery, who represented the art establishment. The mastodons of the RA were a threatened species: hence perhaps some of their bitterness. Henry's friends had become far more powerful than his enemies. His own appointment in July 1949 to a second seven-year term as a trustee of the Tate Gallery (theoretically a government decision) was taken as official support for the modernists as the Munnings row rumbled on.[4]

No academic artist could have hoped to have promotion remotely comparable to Moore's. Philip Hendy and Leeds had done him proud in 1941 at Temple Newsam. Now it was the turn of Wakefield, a smaller town also very near Castleford, to initiate the biggest exhibition to date of his work in England. In terms of scale the scorecard now read:

Temple Newsam, Leeds, 1941	36 sculptures	59 drawings
MOMA, New York, 1946	58 sculptures	48 drawings
Wakefield City Art Gallery, 1949	53 sculptures	73 drawings

Both in Wakefield and at its next stop, Manchester's City Art Gallery, Philip Hendy performed the opening honours. To doubting Yorkshiremen and Lancastrians, it must have been reassuring to have the director of the National Gallery's word that Moore had strong claims to be regarded as the (world's) greatest living sculptor. He went up just before the opening, and was soon winning over doubting hearts and minds. One elderly visitor was asked by an Arts Council lecturer what he made of it all. 'It's rum stuff,' he confessed in broad Yorkshire. 'I can't make much on it.' 'Well,' said the kindly lecturer, 'I'll introduce you to someone who can explain it.' She took him along to the sculptor, who showed him around for an hour. 'It's been the greatest thrill of my life,' he told the lecturer afterwards (she was Helen Kapp, soon to be director of the same gallery).[5] When the exhibition closed after seven weeks, it had been seen by 9,995 visitors, easily a record for Wakefield, even if many came purely out of curiosity, like a small, bespectacled lady overheard saying to her companion: 'I wouldn't give tuppence for the lot,' to which a languid youth nearby observed 'Morons.'[6]

From Manchester, virtually the same exhibition went on to cross the Channel. Australia apart, it was the British Council's first extended tour of Moore's work, and so played its part in strengthening his European reputation. Yet from its first stop in Brussels through Paris, Amsterdam, Hamburg, Düsseldorf, and Berne, it was a far from triumphal procession. Open hostility was at its strongest in the Belgian capital, but in each city there was considerable resistance to Moore's work, and public attendance was modest, from an apathetic 2,000 in Berne to 10,000 in Amsterdam.[7]

Henry went over for most of the openings – his first visit to almost all the cities concerned. With him went Geoffrey Grigson, who had been invited by the British Council to lecture on Moore's work as it toured. This was to be a common practice. Philip Hendy and Herbert Read were sometimes pressed into service as evangelists, and of course such talks served to reinforce the official endorsement of the importance of his work. Belgian reactions were lively, to say the least. Some sixty-six articles on his work appeared in the press, thirty-four in French, thirty in Flemish, and two in English. They ranged from the appreciative and understanding through the sarcastically patronizing to the downright vicious. One of three attacks in the right-wing newspaper *Libre Belgique*, headed 'A Scandal!', set new standards in venom:

> 'Tiriri, zaboum, crolabulito, pim, pom, warzibou calatalato-lacristoli' – ... imagine a whole novel written in this gibberish ... and that it had been sent abroad officially to give a small idea of our national talents ... these words are to literature what Henry Moore is to the plastic arts ... one pays ten francs to see ... these giant vermicelli, these iguana collarbones, these gorilla sketches, in a word this polished and glacial charnel house. A heavy schoolboy's nightmare, that is Henry Moore's contribution to contemporary art.[8]

It was among the classiest abuse to which his work was subjected. Other critics, however, inclined to the view of a leading Belgian sculptor Philip van der Swaylens, who commented after seeing the show: 'Henry Moore has accomplished for the prestige of British art what Nelson did for the British navy.'[9]

In Paris, the timely arrival of Kenneth Clark saved the exhibition from disaster. The old Musée National d'Art Moderne on the Avenue President Wilson is a difficult 'space'. Clark arrived two days before the opening to find Moore deeply depressed by the design of the exhibition. Sir Kenneth asked the museum's director Jean Cassou whether a few changes could be made, but was told no staff was available to move such heavy pieces. Clark telephoned his friend Georges Salles, director of France's national museums, who promised: 'I will send you the *équipe* from the Louvre.' The men arrived shortly, and within the afternoon he and Henry had rearranged the entire exhibition, so that it looked – in Clark's view, at any rate – stunning.[10]

Through his Venice triumph Moore had played his part in helping to break the old dominance of the School of Paris over contemporary art, which the Americans were now so powerfully challenging. Piqued though they may have been by such developments, the French critics responded well to Henry's exhibition. Frank Elgar, of the literary weekly *Carrefour*, had been scathing about the British Council's 1945 mixed exhibition. 'The work of all these artists floats in a halo of sentimentality, fussiness and tasteless romanticism,' he had written. '... If Moore has more humanity in his work, he owes it to the influence of his continental masters.' Four years later he now saw Moore as 'the only real master England possesses – he is without doubt the first sculptor of our time'.[11] From a Frenchman that was a remarkable tribute. Parisians seem not to have been great exhibition-goers in those post-war years: Moore's exhibition drew only some 250 a week, or a total of around 3,000, yet that was more than Matisse, Léger, and Klee exhibitions had recently attracted, and four times as many as fellow sculptor Zadkine's.

Geoffrey Grigson has given a lively account of Henry's next stop, Amsterdam, where the exhibition was shown at the Stedelijk Museum, directed by the redoubtable Dr Willem Sandberg. On their way to see the van Goghs at the Kröller-Müller Museum out in a region of pine and dune, the two old Hampstead friends and Roger Hinks, the British Council representative, played the game of picking the artist they could most do without. They agreed on Frans Hals. Henry spoke of Turner's greatness, and reproved Grigson for unduly admiring Klee, a miniaturist in his eyes. (Being human, the sculptor admired most in other artists' work those qualities which he hoped to find in his own: grandeur, intensity, serenity, compassionate humanity, a certain greatness of soul. Klee's quirky humour was utterly alien to Moore's work, which entirely lacks the sculptor's own sense of fun).

They went together to the Rijksmuseum, where Moore hardly allowed Grigson to pause on the way to Rembrandt's *Night Watch* and *Anatomy Lesson*, believing that one should look long and hard at one masterpiece or two rather than gain a fleeting impression of many. Sandberg took them to Amsterdam's red-light district, where the girls show themselves in lighted windows. One of them was fat, unprepossessing, and doing some knitting. 'She'll finish that jumper before she gets a customer,' Henry remarked.[12] Some of the Dutch critics were cool towards the Moore exhibition, but few were hostile and many appreciative. Sandberg's presentation was considered excellent. Including attendance on free evenings, the official total of 8,538 visitors probably topped 10,000, making it by far the most successful stop.

Political tensions affected the exhibition's reception in Hamburg. Its opening in the down-at-heel and inconveniently located Kunsthalle coincided with the attempted demolition by the British of the largest dock in Hamburg, a subject of bitter dispute between the Germans and their British overlords (as they still were). The Germans maintained that the destruction of the dock would endanger a tunnel under the river Elbe. To allay German fears, the British regional commissioner was sitting in the tunnel when he should have been opening the Moore exhibition. The subsequent nadir in local Anglo-German relations may have affected attendance, which was less than 3,000 in a month.[13] Yet the critics welcomed the show as a chance to widen their long-restricted cultural horizons. Their notices reflected Germany's own traumas under the double impact of Hitler and Allied bombing. *Die Welt*'s reviewer, for example, believed that Moore's work represented 'all of us in our Western impotence against mass and the machine ... man hunted by the machine taking refuge in the earth'.[14] When the exhibition reached Düsseldorf in late April 1950, the *Rheinische Post*'s critic compared Moore's work to that of Lehmbruck, also a miner's son, who had trained in Düsseldorf and killed himself in 1919, aged thirty-eight. He concluded that whereas to Lehmbruck 'shapes are no more than a means to make his deadly melancholy visible ... Henry Moore tries to find a way out of our age of robots, to win back lost nature with a new creative intensity'.[15] The tour ended in Berne, the Swiss capital, with Moore again in attendance. Despite a generally favourable press, it drew barely 2,000 visitors. The Swiss had not yet come to terms with contemporary sculpture. All in all, Europe had reacted cautiously, but the seeds of future enthusiasm had been sown, and before long the British Council would be able to harvest a full crop.

Back at Hoglands, the struggle went on to fulfil commitments on the one hand, and on the other to achieve those feats of self-renewal with which the long-distance artist must maintain momentum and belief in his own work. Having completed the Battersea figures, Moore had focused his attention on two commissions arising from previous projects. The first was to carve another *Madonna and Child*. Sir Jasper Ridley, who had been in Kenneth Clark's office when the maquette for Northampton was selected, had taken the plunge and chosen another model to be enlarged as a memorial to his son and three other villagers killed in the Second World War. The Ridleys lived at Mockbeggars Hall near the small Suffolk village of Claydon. The Claydon *Madonna*, as the carving came to be called, was destined for a site in the south transept of St Peter's church there. Carved from the same honey-coloured Hornton stone as her Midlands sister, she was at four feet tall a good deal smaller. As first completed, Moore reckoned she lacked sufficient majesty, so he added a crown, building it up over several days with ground stone and fixative.[16] The mother's gently moulded features have a great sweetness, which cannot be said for the somewhat doltish-looking child's. In 1978, after St Peter's had become redundant, Henry supervised the removal of the sculpture to the larger parish church in the adjacent village of Barham. It has aroused more interest there, being better lit and more prominent.

If the appealing and isolated Claydon *Madonna* was unlikely to provoke much hostility, the large bronze *Family Group* [93] which Moore completed from one of the Impington maquettes faced the full ordeal of trial by press and public opinion. As mentioned earlier, John Newsom, Hertfordshire's imaginative county education officer, was an admirer of Henry Morris and knew that Moore still had the models for the Impington project up his sleeve. So apparently did the architect F. R. S. Yorke, who had been commissioned to design a new secondary school suitable for the brave-new-world aspirations of England's first post-war new town, Stevenage. Newsom had persuaded his committee that a fraction of one per cent of each school's budget should be set aside for the provision of works of art. Moore, whose home was after all in the same county, was among those who advised informally on how it could best be spent.[17]

Yet even with such progressive spirits as Newsom at the helm, the sailing was far from plain. The approval of the county education committee had to be gained, presumably on the basis of the maquette and photographs; and inevitably it did not prove easy, as Eugene Rosenberg, the architect in charge of the building of Barclay School, recalled:

> At one meeting at which I was present, there was the usual argument: 'it's a waste of money; what is it?' – that sort of thing. There was an elderly lady on the committee and she said, 'I don't know what it is about, but my grandson aged two will like it.' That remark really did tip the balance and literally clinched the decision. Without that old lady, and Newsom, it wouldn't have happened.[18]

All Moore's previous large works, whether commissioned or not, had been carvings either in wood or stone. This was to be the first bronze, necessitating the construction of a full-scale plaster model based on an armature of, in this instance, wood and plaster, which Bernard Meadows built up limb by limb. From this the bronze cast would be made in two or three pieces, then welded together. The sculptor went to see the site while the school was still under construction, taking with him a full-sized cardboard cut-out of the five-foot-tall group. The architect wanted it to stand in front of a curved baffle wall on the left of the main entrance and, for security reasons, not far from the building. They stood it as far away from the wall as possible; but Henry always regretted that it could only be seen from a limited number of views. No sudden revelations from unexpected angles were possible. In such circumstances, he thought, a turntable might sometimes be used, so that another view could be presented every month or so.[19]

Novice as he still was where large bronzes were concerned, he entrusted the casting to a London foundry which could not adequately handle it. There were many difficulties which caused much worry, and it took a year to be satisfactorily completed.[20] In September 1950 it was installed without warning at the school. Not surprisingly, the public was taken aback. 'School gives new family a poor reception,' a *Daily Graphic* headline reported. Most of the school's governors disliked the 'statue', according to one of them, Dr Margaret Swayne, who added: 'We were particularly annoyed because we were not told when it was to be erected. It appeared overnight.'[21] ' "Belsen" statue came in the night,' trumpeted the *Daily Dispatch* five weeks after the event, quoting postman Robert Lapworth's first reaction: 'I looked and almost let the letters drop from my hands. I thought it was something from Belsen Camp,' The newspaper consulted Sir Alfred Munnings for a dispassionate view. 'Distorted figures and knobs instead of heads get a man talked about these foolish days,' the old sage commented. 'Anyone can do round balls for heads. Few can chisel the features of a face.'[22]

Even the *Financial Times*'s Men and Matters column sneered: 'One county education authority has recently thought it more worthwhile to buy a lumpish piece of sculpture by Mr Henry Moore than to raise its teachers' salaries.'[23] In fact Henry's fee had struck the education committee as excessive. So he reduced it to what he reckoned was cost price, about £750, covering casting, transport, materials, enlargement, etc., on the understanding that he could make extra casts and dispose of them himself: a concession from which he was overwhelmingly the gainer. He was not a Yorkshireman for nothing. Half the cost to the education authority was in fact met by private subscribers.

The further casts were made in Paris over the following couple of years. The second eventually went to the Tate Gallery; the third to the Museum of Modern Art in New York (as an alternative to the *Three Standing Figures*), and the fourth to the garden of Nelson Rockefeller's country house. In 1979 this last cast was sold to the Hakone Open Air Museum between Tokyo and Mount Fuji. In 1985 George Ablah, the Kansan collector who was still in the middle of his buying spree, tried unsuccessfully first to buy the Stevenage cast and then to persuade the Henry Moore Foundation to have another cast made for him to buy. Since any extra cast made after the original edition is deemed to devalue those already sold, the prior permission of existing owners is required. In the case of Ablah, such consent was not forthcoming. Whether the artist has the right to make an extra cast for himself is a delicate issue which appears never to have been codified. Certainly there appeared to be nothing wrong in a practice which developed in the late 1950s, in which the owner of a unique piece by Moore – like one of the 1930s lead pieces – might be offered a sum of money and/or an extra cast in bronze if he or she would permit an edition of nine or so to be made from it. Everyone gained, but a whiff of commercialization hung in the air.

How one responds to a work like the *Family Group* is ultimately a matter of personal taste. The design is ingenious, with the child (as Moore only subsequently realized) seeming to form a knot connecting the arms of the parents.[24] Yet the group as a whole is somewhat stiff, and the general and the particular, happily married in the Northampton *Madonna*, never quite fuse. Though parents and child are given features, they remain symbols, and the facial details are banal. John Russell puts it elegantly in saying that the piece is 'less successful than the Northampton *Madonna and Child* in negotiating the dangerous ground between simplicity and flatness'. Moore's basic gift, he concludes, is 'more for the telling analogy and the multiple reference than for the identifiable human situation'.[25] It is a thought to be borne in mind in dealing with some of Henry's almost story-telling works of the 1950s.

Meanwhile the serious newspapers, those makers and breakers of reputations, stood four-square behind him, whether the enemy was the Royal Academy or the philistinism of Fleet Street's tabloids. Portrait Gallery in the *Sunday Times*, for example, showed 'the quiet, good-tempered, intelligent genius from Yorkshire' with a maquette of the *Family Group*. The hero-worshipping tone was sustained:

> 'Take it or leave it,' says the owner of that serious, sensitive face ... Looking at the *Family Group*, the thoughtless philistine might be tempted to say, 'Thank you; I'll leave it'; but looking back at the man who created that strange harmony of form he finds he can't bring himself to utter the thoughtless phrase ... Mercifully, the world is not entirely populated by philistines. Henry Moore is liked and his sculpture is considered miraculously satisfying by quite nice, ordinary people all over Europe and America.[26]

One could scarcely wish for a better example of the close link in the public mind between Moore's success and his personality; or indeed of the sycophantic praise which was bound to stick in the craw of the younger generation of artists.

Fortunately the 'quiet genius' was by no means always good-tempered with those who worked with him at Hoglands; and he was about to produce a work which would discomfort anyone rejoicing prematurely

'With any luck we should be through by Thursday.' *Punch*, 28 July 1948

at the greater naturalism of his recent major works, from madonnas to families. Nothing he had previously done prepares us for the ferocious, wiry energy of the *Standing Figure* (originally called *Striding Man*) of 1950 [106]. The barely recognizable human frame is split into three sections

From *Low Life and High Life*, Harvill Press, 1952

joined at shoulder, hip and knee, with shield-like triangular wedges in place of shoulders and two reptilian heads on stalk-like necks in place of one. Based on one of ten alternative figures in a *Drawing for Metal Sculpture* of 1948, it is Picasso-esque in its tense vitality.

The siting of this bronze of just over seven feet high was to prove revolutionary. Not long after the first cast had come back from the foundry, Moore had a visit at Hoglands from a substantial City figure, William Keswick (always known as Tony, later knighted), who lived a few miles away in a Georgian rectory at Theydon Bois. Keswick, no expert on contemporary art, had a very mundane domestic commission in mind for this well-known sculptor chap, whom he found closeted with distinguished academics from Harvard or Yale. When he saw the *Standing Figure* outside the studio, he was so taken by it that he commissioned another cast after a pleasant conversation with its creator: a surprising decision, since it is a relatively 'difficult' work. Indeed, when Keswick sent it up to his huge estate at Glenkiln, near Dumfries in Scotland, the gamekeeper who opened the crate mistook it for some new form of tractor attachment, and sent it off to a different farm on the estate. Yon figure, as the gamekeeper called it, was sited after much reflection on a rock in the middle of a grousemoor – by Keswick himself, without Henry's assistance, as Keswick recalled:

> I had theories about placing things. There was a very nice rock up there, about double the size of the chair you're sitting on, which looked as if it wanted an ornament. So I put it on the rock. Henry was very flattered that it should be put outside in nature, where it had all the advantages of being seen against the sky, and where the light bounces like mad off the planes of the sculpture. It's very important that sculpture should possess its surroundings: in a gallery the eye is constantly being diverted. In the open it's there with the grouse and the sheep and the rain and the clouds.[27]

Henry and Keswick became firm friends, and at Easter 1954 the director of Jardine, Matheson, of the Hudson's Bay Company, and later of the Bank of England took the miner's son up to Glenkiln. Henry was thrilled to see his figure standing there like a sentinel on the bleak moor. He reported back to Keswick's old school friend from Winchester days, Kenneth Clark: 'It's a most glorious place for it, very wild and surprisingly right for that particular piece.'[28] Clark had at first been opposed to the idea of a Moore among the grouse. He thought it was 'silly', Keswick remembered, and told the sculptor that he 'should not let Tony have any more things for Scotland'.[29] The idea of placing works of art in the wild must indeed have gone against all Clark's curatorial training. Later he changed his tune. For Henry, the spectacle clinched his view that nature made the best setting (though for larger pieces only, presumably). As he once put it: 'There is no background better than the sky, because you are contrasting solid form with its opposite – space. The sculpture then has no competition, no distraction from other solid objects . . .'[30]

As it happened, he was also very pleased with the siting when the *Standing Figure* made its debut at the second Battersea Park open-air sculpture show in summer 1951 – by the lake, where it seemed 'a gaunt figure rising in agitated verticals from the verge of a calm, flat sheen of water that seemed the very essence of horizontalism'.[31]

Moore was fortunate at this stage, *circa* 1950, in having two very able assistants: Oliffe Richmond, from Tasmania, who had taken over from Shelley Fausset in 1948, and a New Zealander, Alan Ingham, who had more recently arrived. They had built a little foundry at the bottom of the garden. The fire-box was, however, too big, and it was difficult even when the bellows were strenuously pumped to get the bronze hot enough. None the less they succeeded in using it to cast the little rocking-chair figures, some striking heads with a lattice-like, open-weave skin of bronze, and some new treatments of the old helmet head theme. For one summer vacation, probably in 1951, they were joined by Robert Clatworthy, who had met Moore while a student first at Chelsea and then at the Slade, to which he had rather naively gone on Henry's advice in preference to the livelier Royal College. He turned up for his first day at Hoglands at 8 a.m., starry-eyed and enthusiastic:

> The effect was a healthy dose of realism about the world. The pace of work was leisurely. Things got done but no one was killing themselves. To my naive and rather puritan eyes, Henry was more involved in the PR and meeting people bit than I thought proper. He should have been in there getting on with things ... the degree of control even when I was there was inadequate, I thought. But he was enormously friendly, and he had a great influence on me.[32]

Anthony Caro as assistant

Not long after Richmond left, he was replaced (later in 1951) by a bright young sculptor from the Royal Academy Schools who was to come nearest, in later years, to challenging Moore's pre-eminence: Anthony Caro. Bored with the RA and all it stood for, he had asked himself who was the best artist around, and concluded it was Moore. So he got into his little open Morris, and was soon knocking on the door of Hoglands. 'You should have made an appointment,' said Henry when the young man explained he would like to come and work for him. But he asked him in for a cup of tea, and after looking at some of Caro's work he urged him to ring six months later. When Caro did so, asking 'Do you remember me and can I come and work for you,' Henry replied: 'Yes I do, and you can.'

After working in the studio of Charles Wheeler, president-to-be of the Royal Academy, what a contrast Caro found:

> Henry had a mind that was a pleasure to meet, extraordinary, so inquiring, and he was quite prepared to throw the ball in the air and see if you caught it: 'Who is your favourite sculptor? If you could have three paintings in the world, which would you choose?' ... My impression of him was of a very open-minded man, quite amazingly open to the possibilities in sculpture and anything else really; and fun too, with a nice sense of humour.[33]

Caro, who was to remain as an assistant for two years, lodged initially with Alan Ingham in a council house in Perry Green. Henry evidently appreciated his quick and sensitive mind (honed at Cambridge), for the two established an affectionate master-pupil relationship that was unique in the Hoglands annals. 'Borrow my books,' Moore would urge. Caro would bear off one on modern art, and one on African, Oceanic, Mexican or some other form of primitive art. At the RA there had been just the Renaissance and Greece. Caro knew there was something called surrealism. He had heard Augustus John talking about Picasso with a sneer. Henry explained, and gave eye-opening demonstrations of how to draw properly: the laws of light, perspective, intensity, and especially life-drawing – his approach was a revelation. There was also the broader question of how an artist should live and work:

> Henry came at a crucial time in my development. I had gone into sculpture thinking I would be one of the chaps who does statues of Montgomery, or the very highest thing was Epstein. Then you suddenly realize there are better people to look at. I think I took the very best model. Had I taken a less good artist, my standards wouldn't have been as high ... the Henry Moore attitudes stayed a long time in the work, and in the way I conducted my studio and my life.[34]

For Moore, 1951 was destined to be, like 1946 and 1948, another *annus mirabilis*. But it started badly with a week in bed with 'flu – 'the first illness I've had to go to bed with for thirty years', he wrote to Jane Clark on 17 February. He had been cheered, however, by news from the Clarks that the celebrated actor, Edward G. Robinson, had some Moores in his fine art collection. Henry was engagingly susceptible to the glamour of the film world. 'He's an awfully good actor – I've always enjoyed his films, but I shall see them with a new interest now,' he told the Clarks.

He was excited too, he indicated, at the prospect of his first visit to Greece (aged fifty-two), where the British Council was arranging for the show which had toured the Continent to be seen at the Zappeion Gallery in Athens. This had been suggested by the professor of art history at Athens Polytechnic, A Procopiou, who had discovered Moore's work in England in 1948. Henry arrived with Irina in Athens in late February. They stayed at the British Embassy residence with the ambassador, Sir Clifford Norton, and his wife Noel, always known as Peter, a lady as forceful as her husband was gentle. In the 1930s she had run a West End gallery devoted to contemporary art (the London Gallery), and she had many artist friends and a fine collection. The Moores could not have been in better hands, and Peter Norton soon whisked them up to the Acropolis. He found it 'wonderful – more marvellous than ever I imagined', he wrote back to the Clarks. 'The Parthenon against a blue sky – the sunlight, and the scale it gets against the distant mountains can't be given by any photograph. It is the greatest thrill I've ever had.'[35]

The great sites too made their impact, as he later described. At Mycenae, for example,

> I felt I understood Greek tragedy and – well, the whole idea of Greece – much more completely than ever before. And Delphi, though I did feel it had a touch of theatricality, as if the eagles were flying around to order, and Olympia, with the idyllic sense of lovely living that you get there ... the Greek landscape was another revelation to me: that stark, stony quality, with the feeling that the sea may be around the next corner. I can understand why they were sculptors. The stone just had to be used, it was the only thing they had to hand.[36]

He was struck, as everyone is, by the light. Instead of being half absorbed into the object, as in England, in Greece the object seemed to give off light, as if lit from within.

The Athens exhibition was an overwhelming success. More people (3,400) saw it on its first day than during the whole of its six weeks in Paris. Attendance averaged 1,000 on weekdays, climbing to 7,000 or 8,000 on Sundays, and the total – in excess of 34,000 – was a record to date for Moore in Europe. Led by Procopiou, the critics ranged from the enthusiastic through the thinkingly hostile to the abusive. Nationalist papers in particular spoke of 'a denial of our Hellenism', 'an affront to the Acropolis' and so on.[37]

Before long the Greek visit would make itself felt in Moore's work. On his return, however, he faced a gruelling springtime. It included the completion of a big commission for the forthcoming Festival of Britain, his first Tate Gallery retrospective, another show with Curt Valentin in New York, and the first British film about his work. The New York show of recent sculpture and drawings produced some handsome reviews. An advance notice by the faithful Henry McBride in Art News threw a sugary light on the role Moore's personality played in his American success:

He has two countries completely sewn up, for New Yorkers look
upon his work with almost the unquestioning faith of the
Londoners, and love him personally as much, for he has been over
here and captivated everybody with his sweetness, simplicity and
decency. What Paris thinks of him I have not heard, but I imagine
it still holds him off a bit. In Paris, essential decency is not too
potent a factor in establishing reputations as it is in London and
New York.[38]

All credit to the Parisians, one may well think. With their clear minds
they could see that it was the work that mattered, not the man. Many
major artists – at home, Ben Nicholson or Francis Bacon would serve as
examples – have lacked Moore's 'sweetness', and Henry himself, though
often very generous and thoughtful, was not without that measure of
egocentricity which is essential for sustained achievement in virtually
any field.

The Festival of Britain commission came from the Arts Council, Moore
being the best known of a dozen sculptors similarly approached, and
painters too made their contribution. In retrospect the Festival, marking
the centenary of the 1851 Great Exhibition, seems a bright and determinedly cheerful hymn to the welfare state which the post-war Labour
government had tried to create. With its fresh new architecture, Skylon
monument, Dome of Discovery, Battersea Funfair and much else, it
attracted more than 8.5 million people through the summer.

Henry's commission faced stiff competition from a multiplicity of more
frivolous and eye-wrenching attractions. For a fee of £1,750 (some
£10,000 today) the Arts Council suggested a carving, possibly but not
necessarily a family group symbolizing Discovery.[39] With two years'
notice, Moore characteristically said he was ready to agree to that as a
subject if necessary – and then gave them a reclining figure in bronze;
an outstanding one, however, ninety inches long, unprecedentedly
opened out for a bronze on this scale and magnificent in its sinuous and
sexual tenseness [104]. It was his first conscious effort, the sculptor later
said, to make space and form absolutely inseparable. Creating space in a
stone sculpture was more difficult: making the hole was such a conscious
effort that it became a thing in itself, and the shape of the surrounding
stone sometimes suffered because its main purpose was to enclose the
hole. There was consequently no true amalgamation of form and space,
which in this work he felt he had achieved.[40] Both the flowing lines of

the figure and its tactile qualities were enhanced by fine raised lines or ridges, which added a calligraphic touch to the surface. They were achieved by fixing string to the plaster model before casting.

At the Festival the great bronze reclined in pride of place opposite the main entrance of the South Bank site. With good reason Moore came to regard it as one of those works which were specially important to him, along with the Tate's *Recumbent Figure* of 1938; the Lubetkin/Onslow-Ford/Detroit elmwood *Reclining Figure* of 1939; the *King and Queen* of 1952; the *Warrior with Shield* of 1954; the first large *Two-piece Reclining Figure* of 1959; and the *Reclining Mother with Child* of 1961 ('obviously there are others', he added, as if the list of his special pieces could not possibly be so short).[41] That November, when the Festival of Britain was over and the commissioned works of art were distributed to national and provincial museums, the *Reclining Figure* was lent by the Arts Council for five years to Leeds City Art Gallery. There it was placed in the grounds of Temple Newsam, to a chorus of protests. One correspondent of the *Yorkshire Post* saw it as 'a human form in an advanced stage of decomposition which has been disembowelled, partially decapitated and had both feet severed', and likened it to the victims of Belsen and Hiroshima. To others less in tune with history it was simply scrap metal.[42] One night just two years later it was daubed with blue paint.

The first Tate show

The Festival of Britain was in its way also a Festival of Moore. Not far down the Thames from the *Reclining Figure,* his *Standing Figure* stood etched against the lake in Battersea Gardens' festival sculpture exhibition. Across the river at the Tate Gallery, London's first Moore retrospective exhibition had opened on 1 May, two days before the Festival itself. It was touch and go whether the works from the Athens exhibition would be back in time: the elmwood *Reclining Figure* of 1945, not yet sold by Valentin to the Cranbrook Academy, had made the trip to Greece, and duly became the star of the Tate show.

This time the Arts Council, the official domestic sponsor of the fine and performing arts, was in charge and painfully conscious that London had not yet seen a full-scale exhibition of Moore's work, unlike several American, European, and Australian cities, not to mention Wakefield, Manchester, and Leeds. Courageously the Director of Art, Philip James, entrusted the selection of works and catalogue to an up-and-coming young critic, David Sylvester, who had become a friend of the sculptor and even acted as his first secretary. Sylvester had written two articles about Moore's work in 1944, in the Labour journal *Tribune* and a Roman Catholic magazine. Henry had enjoyed them and had taken the initiative in contacting Sylvester. After they had come to know each other, Moore observed one day that he needed some secretarial help, and from spring to autumn of that year Sylvester put his minimal skills at his disposal. As he recalled:

> I took down letters in longhand or typed them straight onto the typewriter. He paid me £2 10s. a day, and I worked part-time. The whole thing was a ghastly failure from his point of view, as we used to talk so much. We had long arguments about art and aesthetics. What he needed was a shorthand-typing lady, but in those days he did things in a ramshackle way, out of the kindness of his heart.[43]

For Sylvester at least those months were educational, and he used his new knowledge and understanding to amplify two long articles he had prepared for the *Burlington Magazine* and to write an introduction to the catalogue of the 1949 Wakefield show.[44] Since Sylvester was just twenty-six in 1951, it was none the less a considerable act of faith on the part of both James and Moore to entrust the Tate retrospective to him, and not to interfere in its presentation: 'K. Clark, who was then chairman of the Arts Council's art panel, came in and moved one or two pieces at the last minute, but I think Henry hardly touched anything. It was the same with the catalogue.'[45]

No one seeing this 'elaborately arranged' show could fail to be impressed by Moore's remarkable mastery of a number of mediums and styles, *The Times*'s critic commented. But he was irritated by the proclamation of Moore in the catalogue foreword not just as 'our greatest living sculptor' but also as being 'widely held to be England's greatest living artist'.[46] His reaction was symptomatic. Too much lavish praise was bound to produce a backlash. In the *Observer*, whose critic Nigel Gosling hailed the show as the work of a craftsman, romantic, and poet of amazingly high standards, a profile of the sculptor referred disparagingly to the patrons of modern artists as sycophants and exploiters and to the 'eulogistic and fantastic jargon' of Moore's own interpreting priests.[47] In similar vein in the *Sunday Times*, John Russell surmised that if the exhibition was a reward for 'thirty years of lonely and unremitting application', that loneliness might now have ended almost too completely as 'assiduous functionaries engage in mortal combat for the possession of the last chip from Mr Moore's workshop'.[48]

Some of the same resentment against the official patronage of Moore surfaced when the BBC showed the first British film about his work (the Americans had done one about his 1946 MOMA show). In those days television was seen as pre-eminently a medium for live transmissions. Apart from news coverage, virtually everything came live from the BBC's studios. From the earliest days in 1936 there had been programmes on art, with lots of stills. Remarkably enough, the Moore film was the BBC's first all-film documentary on any subject. Timed to coincide with the Tate exhibition, it was directed by John Read, Herbert Read's son by his first marriage, who had lived mainly with his mother in Edinburgh. He thus knew Moore only casually from holidays spent with his father, who had four children by his second wife. John Read found Moore 'extraordinarily patient. I remember learning everything from him about photographing sculpture, and especially about the use of natural light for "modelling": he taught me, and I think the cameraman too. He was really a first-class photographer of sculpture.'[49]

The film was transmitted on 30 April 1951. 'Don't let's have any more, Mr Moore', a headline next morning in the *Daily Mail* recommended. Its critic J. Stubbs Walker thought the film sycophantic, and warned the BBC against stuffing art down the viewer's throat. He had a point. From the first words of its commentary ('Henry Moore is the most important of living sculptors') the film had a lecturing and reverential tone likely to irritate the unconverted. None the less it won a prize at the Venice Film Festival that summer, on the day Read's contract expired. He went on to make five more films about the sculptor for the corporation, developing a healthy regard for the reticence which Moore hid behind his affability. It was always difficult, he found, to get Henry away from his set pieces about his life and art. He would ration himself to giving out just one or two little gobbets of new information each time. Only once did the artist open up, and that was after dinner and a lot of wine in Italy.

There were probably two main reasons why Moore's achievements were constantly being trumpeted by his defenders. The public was still sceptical of modern art, and the academicians were still sniping. To build up Moore's reputation was an effective counter-gambit. It was moreover gratifying to find a home-grown success story. As a force in the world Britain had declined sharply. Was there anything at which Britons still excelled? There was: improbably in many ways, the arts. Moore's international success was a source of pride; to proclaim his greatness a patriotic act. Margot Fonteyn and Laurence Olivier, great performers that they were, benefited similarly, though their work could not be touted around without their own presence. For Moore, the pendulum was bound to swing in the opposite direction, if only among his fellow artists and the critics.

Chapter XII

Anthology pieces, and a trip to Mexico

1952–4

In these three years Moore was to produce some of his best-known and most popular works. A majority of them are quite closely related to the human figure, 'eloquent' and in some cases even story-telling in a way that broadened their appeal to the public but tended to put critics on their guard. Partly they are the spiritual children of the shelter sketches, the coal-mining drawings and of wartime suffering in a broad sense; partly they reflect the impact of the trip to Greece, and a desire, conscious or unconscious, for the sculptor to fulfil a public role. There is something of the public monument about them, as if Henry was adjusting his metaphors to meet public expectations.

It is not pure perversity that some of Moore's most knowledgeable admirers, by no means all of them critics, find that some of these pieces yield up their secrets rather quickly. The same attributes which make them attractive at first sight also make them wear less well on closer acquaintance. Compared with much of Moore's work, they are a bit obvious. Others by contrast went back for inspiration to the 1930s and were more cryptic, ambiguous and many-layered, and consequently in the long run often more satisfying.

The first to be conceived was certainly not 'obvious'. *Upright Internal/ External Forms* [111], another large elmwood carving, had begun life in 1951 as a maquette from which a two-foot high working model was soon developed. The plan was to enlarge it in wood to above life-size. But after waiting for over a year for a suitable piece, Moore had a full-sized (six feet seven inches high) plaster made for casting into bronze. It was about to be sent to the foundry when his timber merchant in Bishop's Stortford reported that a large elm tree which seemed ideal had just come in. Carving began in early 1953, not much more than a week after the tree had been felled. Such a trunk, five feet in diameter, would normally season at the rate of one inch a year, taking thirty years to dry out naturally to the middle. The danger of cracking was diminished by carving it slowly over two years, the final product being no more than five inches thick in any one part.[1]

The image of outer and inner form was clearly derived from the first *Helmet* of 1939–40, with its little spaghetti-like captive. Moore likened it to 'a mother and child idea, or the stamen in a flower: that is, something young and growing being protected by an outer shell'.[2] There is, however, an apparent contradiction in such a tender image taking such giant form: at eight feet six inches, the elmwood version is two feet taller than the bronze. But it greatly impressed Seymour Knox of the Albright-Knox Gallery in Buffalo, NY when he saw it at Hoglands in summer 1955. On his advice it was acquired soon afterwards, just in time to save it falling to Joseph Hirshhorn.

The womb-and-foetus theme greatly excited Erich Neumann:

> It is no accident that this figure reminds us of those Egyptian sarcophagi in the form of mummies, showing the mother goddess as the sheltering womb that holds and contains the dead man like a child again, as at the beginning. Mother of life, mother of death, and all-embracing body-self, the archetypal mother of man's germinal ego-consciousness – this truly great sculpture of Moore's is all these in one.[3]

In this instance the Jungian commentator seems more concerned with the idea than its execution. When Moore attempted a reclining bronze version, he abandoned the interior form which had emerged periscope-like from the working model.

1952 was the year in which King George VI died and was succeeded by the young Queen Elizabeth. Perhaps these events played their part unconsciously in the birth of the *King and Queen* [105], though Moore has mentioned the stories about kings, queens and princesses which he was reading at that stage to Mary, aged six.[4] One day he was playing with a piece of modelling wax when it began to resemble a horned, bearded, Pan-like head. It grew a crown, and he recognized it as the head of a king, so he gave it a body, using the strength of wax when it hardens to repeat the slender, aristocratic refinement he had found in the head. He made three attempts at adding a queen who harmonized before being satisfied.

What has caused this to be the most famous of all Moore's bronzes and the anthology piece which big collectors and museums most ardently seek? Perhaps it is the hieratic yet touching dignity of the two figures, seated side by side on their bench, heads turned to the left, alert and vulnerable. The contrast between the invented heads (the king's is vastly the more interesting) and the beautifully naturalistic hands and feet, a surrealist device, adds piquancy. Perhaps, too, some of their appeal lies in their undulating silhouettes, with light shining through the single eye pierced through each head. In the maquette version, which some close admirers feel to be better, Henry framed the royal couple within a goalpost-like structure. For Alan Bowness, the large version has 'a certain inflatedly portentous quality that is alien to the general run of Moore's work.'[5] David Sylvester too prefers the smaller size.[6]

The first potential buyer was the purchasing committee of the Open Air Sculpture Park at Middelheim near Antwerp in Belgium, where Moore had exhibited in 1951. They had approached the sculptor for a suitable work as a permanent addition to the park, and he had them in mind in enlarging the maquette. The possible purchase had become a controversial issue, and in late 1952 or early 1953 they paid a collective visit to Hoglands to inspect. Thanks to an impenetrable fog, they arrived at 4 p.m. rather than 10 a.m. By that time Henry had given them up and sawn the Queen's head off the plaster cast, feeling it was still not quite right. When the committee finally arrived, they were so proud of having survived their terrible experience that they gave the sculpture the most cursory glance and bought it without more ado.[7]

A second cast found its way via the São Paulo Biennale (of which more later) to Curt Valentin's gallery in New York. There it took the fancy of Percy Uris, president of a company which owned an apartment block at 380 Madison Avenue. Valentin agreed that before paying he could place it on an experimental basis in the lobby, where Uris bravely listened to the wisecracks of the tenants. He was appalled by what he heard, and decided it was no good trying to force people to like contemporary art just because it was to his own taste.[8] The bronze was returned to Valentin's gallery, where it was bought by Jo Hirshhorn. It now stands in the foyer of the Hirshhorn Museum in Washington.

The third cast was shown at the Leicester Galleries in February 1954, where it was priced at £3,000 and dominated a very successful exhibition. It remained unsold, however, for at least two weeks, when it was spotted by David Astor, editor of the *Observer* and bought over the telephone via his secretary. For some twenty years it graced the back lawn of his home in St John's Wood in north-west London; but he feared for its safety when the only other sculpture on the lawn, a piece by Siegfried Charoux, was hacked off at the ankles and stolen, seemingly for scrap. Wanting some capital to endow a charitable foundation, he sold it in 1976 through Thomas Gibson to the Norton Simon Museum in Pasadena, California.[9]

The fourth cast was destined to become the best known. It was bought before long by Tony Keswick with his Scottish estate in mind, but proved much more difficult to site than the *Standing Figure*. 'I tried it in five different places,' he recalled. 'I wanted perfection: sky, grass, water, hills and framing, all very important if you are going to have sculpture in the open.'[10] The *King and Queen* came to rest in 1955 on an outcrop of rock overlooking Glenkiln Loch, where they are visible from half a mile away and succeed regally in possessing their environment. It was a further attraction to Keswick that they should be looking south across the border from Scotland into England. Later he added two further Moores to his moors: the *Glenkiln Cross*, as it became known, which he and Henry sited together on a hill from which they had observed a shepherd and his dog watching their sheep below; and *Two-Piece Reclining Figure No. 1*, which Moore lent for sixteen years and then replaced with a fibreglass version; on this a Caesarian operation was performed to weight it down with rocks. The original had to be blasted off its base with explosive, so firmly had it been attached. Works by Epstein and Renoir were added, but no two pieces could be seen together.

Not everyone admires the result, and Keswick receives a number of abusive letters asking how he dare desecrate the countryside with hideous bits of metal, and the like. Grateful letters, especially from foreign visitors, predominate however. One museum director from Munich wanted to know how he could get his party of enthusiasts to the right spot. Keswick referred him to his 'keeper'. Assuming he was referring to a curator, the German wrote to inquire about his academic background. Keswick felt tempted to reply that he was highly trained in killing stoats and weasels.

Originally there were to have been four casts, plus an artist's cast for Moore's own patchy holdings of his life's work. An extra cast was made for the Tate Gallery in 1957, to whom it was presented by the Friends of the Tate Gallery with funds provided by Associated Rediffusion. Henry gave his own cast to his daughter Mary. By the early 1980s the *King and Queen* had become enormously valuable, and Mary and her husband in their unsentimental way sold it through the dealers Wildenstein to the Atami Museum in Japan for $500,000. Keswick too received offers for his cast from museums, but rejected them.

Projects for Time-Life

While the *King and Queen* was in gestation, Moore also became involved in a double commission for the new London headquarters of the Time-Life magazine empire. Designed for the Crown leaseholders, the Pearl Assurance Company, by an immigrant Viennese architect called Michael Rosenauer, the clean but unexciting building was nearing completion on a corner site in Bond Street. Time-Life wanted the interior at least to represent the flower of British creative talent, engaged Hugh Casson and Misha Black (fresh from their triumphs at the Festival of Britain) as design co-ordinators, and dispatched the cartoonist Francis Brennan from New York to monitor progress. Moore was first approached in November 1951 to do something substantial for the third-floor garden terrace. Greatly daring, Brennan suggested that perhaps water might be involved. 'In my mind's eye I could see a whole new Moore experience,' he recalled. 'Not a jetting fountain, to be sure, but water – gently pooling, even perhaps gently trickling from level to level ... but the great man politely vetoed the suggestion, and we settled for the "safer", more familiar reclining figure now in place.'[11]

Henry knew that the figure would be seen from the reception room, from which the sight of a nude out on the terrace in cold weather might seem incongruous. So he became preoccupied with the challenge of creating a draped figure [110] which exploited the fluidity of plaster. In his stone carvings, drapery had been a matter of large, simple creases and folds, but the modelling technique enabled him to build up what he called 'a host of small crinklings and rucklings of the fabric' which reminded him of a mountain range in close-up, or the skin of the earth. He applied, too, a lesson he had learnt in Greece: that drapery could be used to emphasize the tension of the inside form by making it seem tight at pressure points like shoulders, breasts, and thighs, and slack elsewhere.[12] Leaning on her elbows, the *Draped Reclining Figure* looks cramped on her balcony above Bond Street, and her facial expression is banal. At one stage magazine staff christened her 'the tired researcher'.[13]

While discussing this project Rosenauer mentioned to Moore the difficulties he was having with the Portland stone screen which was required to protect the balcony and connect the new building to its neighbour. There had been a competition, and all the entries showed a solid wall with reliefs depicting the story of the magazines. Henry said he thought they were all silly: a pierced wall was needed to show the open space behind it. So he was asked to suggest a solution himself. Eventually he came up with four alternative maquettes, in which between four and eight abstract but organic forms, aligned side by side, allowed plenty of light between them and their frame. Brennan watched part of the creative process:

> As we talked, Moore pulled down a battered old shoe-box from a shelf. It was brim-filled with old bones and weather-worn stones of wondrous shapes and sizes. Picking through them, he'd choose one, hold it up and turn it around in the light, much as a jeweller might show a gemstone. Finally he had a collection of a dozen or so laid out on his drawing board ... I began to see his idea for the screen – a quartet of icon-like images, mysteriously ancient in feeling, yet unmistakably modern in execution.[14]

The final carving [109] was based on the 'working model' enlargement of the maquette which best complemented the fenestration of the building. It was a huge undertaking, each of the eight-feet-tall figures being hewn from two superimposed blocks of Portland stone, for which a scaffolding had to be erected by the front-garden studio at Hoglands. To judge progress from a distance Moore had to go out on to the village green. His original hope that each of the carvings could be installed on a turntable and rotated regularly, projecting from the building 'like half-buried pebbles whose form one's eye instinctively completes,' was abandoned on grounds of safety and expense.[15] No one fancied a five-ton block crashing on to Bond Street's crowded pavements. The working model, of which a cast can be seen in the Time-Life foyer, reveals what a tough, rich, and subtle design Moore created for his first work to form a fixed part of a building since the *West Wind* relief of 1929. But the nuances of its rhythms and indentations, so reminiscent of the sculptor's 1930s work, are invisible to those walking thirty-odd feet below, should they ever think to raise their eyes from the jewellers and fashion boutiques. One day a better location may be found. In the late 1960s Henry expressed a desire to buy it back ('it looked so much better here in my garden')[16] and more recently it was suggested to Time Inc. by his friend David Finn that they might present it to the Tate Gallery for its new extension.

Both the Time-Life Moores were unveiled in May 1953. During the casting process, Henry had noticed how complete in itself the wax impression of the torso of the *Draped Reclining Figure* seemed. So he asked the foundry to make another, cut off at points which he specified. Previously he had considered that incomplete figures smacked of romanticism, but in the Acropolis Museum in Athens he had been struck by the spectacle of twenty or thirty over-life-sized torsos lying on the ground. They seemed to validate the idea of the fragment as sculpture. The result in this instance was *Draped Torso*, whose origins as an off-cut are hard to guess.

Remarkably traditional though this piece looks, it proved too modernistic for the city councils of Manchester and Bristol, both of which were to decide against purchasing it in 1954. It was perhaps a heartening sign that the art galleries of major British cities should at last, with Moore in his fifties, be taking the initiative to acquire one of his works; but public taste was not quite ready. In Manchester the City Art Gallery committee's proposal to buy the bronze for a special price of £765 prompted one alderman to comment after it had been rejected by a majority of two: 'It appeared to be abnormal and could only appeal to abnormal people. Fortunately, here in Manchester we have not many people like that.'[17] Another wished it had been a statue of Marilyn Monroe.

When the torso issue reached Bristol two months later in May, the divisions were within the city's art gallery committee rather than the council itself. Recent local elections having strengthened Labour's representation, six of the ten members voted against the purchase, and the bronze was sent back to Hoglands.[18] A similar furore in Birmingham in early 1955 over Moore's next major work, *Warrior with Shield* [107], went the other way, even though the cost was, at £1,500, appreciably higher. 'He has no left arm, no left leg, no right foot,' the *Birmingham Gazette* reported disapprovingly after the warrior's installation in the Central Art Gallery in March. 'His face is a sort of split nose, with a hole bored through it which runs from the forehead between the place where the eyes should be to the place where the mouth should be.'[19] Other casts were soon bought by public galleries in Toronto, Mannheim, and Minneapolis, and a fifth cast was made that autumn for the city of Arnhem in Holland. There the mutilated warrior, with his battered but defiant look, commemorated the Allied attempt eleven years earlier to take the town from the air.

The warrior is unusual not only in being male and mutilated but in being even more expressive than the consciously noble *King and Queen*. It was inspired, Moore has said, by a pebble he found which reminded him of the stump of a leg amputated at the hip. As he added to it, the leg became a reclining wounded warrior. A day or two later he introduced the shield and made the warrior sit up, wounded but defiant. In his eyes the head had a 'blunted and bull-like power, but also a sort of dumb animal acceptance and forbearance of pain'.[20] Enlarging this bony, tense male form was almost like discovering a new subject, he found. Again, the Grecian overtones are strong, with a dash of Rodin too. For Erich Neumann it was an image not of defiance but of defeat, 'the most devastating portrayal in all art of a suprapersonal castration complex; it shows complete capitulation before the forces of destruction'.[21] Understatement was not his way.

Warrior with Shield could be seen as a summary in bronze of Moore's feelings about war in general, made at a time when the Korean conflict was still taking its toll and Stalin was living out his last months. The tensions of that era were much in evidence in the very effective display of eight sculptors in the British pavilion at the 1952 Venice Biennale. In showing the work of Robert Adams, Kenneth Armitage, Reg Butler, Lynn Chadwick, Geoffrey Clarke, Bernard Meadows, Eduardo Paolozzi, and William Turnbull, the British Council told the world that Moore no longer stood alone (or alone with Barbara Hepworth); but a double version of his *Standing Figure* was placed at the entrance to the pavilion, to show that he was, as Herbert Read put it in the catalogue, 'in some sense the parent of them all'. The images of the younger generation, Read said, 'belong to the iconography of despair, or of defiance ... here are images of flight, of ragged claws "scuttling across the floors of silent seas", of excoriated flesh, frustrated sex, the geometry of fear ... The consistent avoidance of massiveness, of monumentality, is what distinguishes these epigoni from their immediate predecessor, Moore. They have seized Eliot's image of the Hollow Men ... and peopled the Waste Land with their iron waifs.' Looking back at those iron or bronze waifs through the bewildering variety of intervening styles, from kinetic and Pop to minimalist, they seem to have more in common with Moore's work now than they did in 1952.

Henry returned to Venice himself in September 1952 to serve, with Graham Sutherland, the composer William Walton, the poet Stephen Spender, the architect Ralph Tubbs, and the playwright Benn Levy as Britain's delegation to an International Conference of Artists organized by Unesco. Despite his lifelong dislike of public speaking, he agreed to give a long address on 'The Sculptor in Modern Society', which Herbert Read had helped him to prepare.[22] In Britain, he told his distinguished international audience, there were three main types of patron: the private connoisseur; museums and galleries buying on the public's behalf; and architects, town-planners and other bodies satisfying a sense of public duty or corporate pride. Too often in the latter instance, he said, the work of art was an afterthought. Collaboration should begin when a building was first conceived, since the placing of a piece of sculpture could radically alter a design as a whole. Such an integral conception characterized the great epochs of art, he maintained.

Being an artist was an intensely private activity, he said, yet the best artists had always had their roots in a definite social order. While rejecting communistic state control of the arts, he wanted to preserve or restore the relationship between the artist's freedom and his social function, which he admitted was 'somewhat paradoxical'. Unesco, he suggested, could contribute by investigating the social conditions over the centuries which had most favoured the flourishing of the arts.[23] Reading his speech today, we may feel that Moore had failed to address himself to the gap between much contemporary art, including his own, and public taste. That gulf was created by many complex historical factors, including surely the modern artist's conviction that art was essentially a private activity and that the artist's independence was sacred. Can great art be created while working within the limits imposed by public expectations? It would have been an interesting question to tackle.

Henry's dislike of constraints put paid to his involvement in the interior of the new Coventry Cathedral. What better site could there have been to recapture the medieval traditions of the artist-craftsman firmly integrated into the social order? The old cathedral had been destroyed by the Luftwaffe in November 1940, and the architect Basil Spence had won the competition to design its successor. Thanks to his dedication to the arts, it became another occasion, like a miniature Festival of Britain, for wholesale patronage: Graham Sutherland was to do the largest tapestry in the world, John Piper some stained-glass windows, Jacob Epstein a figure of St Michael; and Henry Moore could not be left out. Spence regarded him as 'a deep and sensitive thinker, with the mind of a classical sculptor, [who] turned to stone for his greatest creations'.[24]

The architect approached Moore for advice on the eight large (twelve feet square) relief carvings which he had planned for the well-lit recesses in the cathedral nave. In these 'hallowing places' the activities of man were to be depicted and thus hallowed in the service of God. The Reconstruction Committee had its doubts: the scenes might soon look obsolete. When Henry was consulted, he affirmed there was nobody in the country, including himself, who was equipped to do such reliefs. 'He positively deterred Basil from doing it,' Spence's son-in-law and partner Anthony Blee recalled. 'If Henry Moore had got the bit between his teeth in his own way, I think we would have relief sculptures there today. The doubts would have been swept away.'[25]

So effectively did Moore put Spence off the idea of relief carvings that the sculpture of St Michael and the Devil, also shown as a relief in the original plans, was commissioned as a three-dimensional bronze by Epstein. For the hallowing places, the architect turned to Ralph Beyer, whose father Oskar had been a founding professor of the Bauhaus. The cathedral's Provost selected biblical texts calculated to provoke the correct level of thought, and Beyer incised them into the local pink stone.

Another ecclesiastical project involved John Rothenstein, director of the Tate Gallery and an active Roman Catholic. As a member of Westminster Cathedral's new art advisory committee, Rothenstein proposed in autumn 1953 that Henry be commissioned to design some mosaics for the baptistery walls. The sculptor paced out the dimensions, noted the way the light fell, and seemed fascinated by the possibilities. But when Rothenstein formally proposed the commission at a committee meeting, the art historian Thomas Bodkin – who was later publicly to attack Birmingham's *Warrior with Shield* purchase – said he was determined to prevent charlatans like Moore from being considered for work in the cathedral. He abused Moore as a creation of dealers and officialdom, and the proposal was rejected. When Rothenstein was authorized to revive it about fourteen years later, Henry not surprisingly proved unresponsive.[26]

The Tate row

John Rothenstein, was not universally admired. By some of his colleagues he was considered to be too interested in social climbing and lacking in true enthusiasm for the most important aspects of twentieth-century art, like Parisian painting when it was dominant, and American abstract painting when it gained the upper hand in the 1950s. They could point to his record: from 1938, when he took over from J. B. Manson, to 1948 (when Moore's first term as a trustee ended), the Tate had bought 189 British works from gallery funds and only fourteen foreign ones.[27] Matisse and Picasso were then still barely represented. Rothenstein had been more concerned to plug the gaps in the modern British collection, with works by Moore, Nicholson, Pasmore, and so on.

Theoretically and formally, decisions about purchases are made by the ten trustees, who can and do turn down many of the works put forward for decision. But they are naturally influenced by the director's views.

Four of the trustees are usually artists: not always a recommendation, since their vision is often limited to compatible painters and sculptors. Moore's tastes were broad, but if he argued the case for the School of Paris to Rothenstein during his own first seven-year stint as a trustee, he did not do so very effectively. He could, however, claim at least one small success. In 1946 Norman Reid joined the Tate's staff in a temporary capacity, having ended the war as a major in the Argyll and Sutherland Highlanders. Soon afterwards Reid applied for one of two vacant posts as an assistant keeper, only to be ruled ineligible because he had, rather than the stipulated first- or second-class degree from a university, a diploma from Edinburgh College of Art. Henry was so incensed that the matter was pursued to the requisite level and the regulations changed. Norman Reid eventually succeeded Rothenstein as director in 1964.[28]

Moore had every reason to feel well-disposed to Rothenstein, who admired his work and had bought several pieces for the Tate, and whose father had been so supportive at the Royal College. Loyal man that he was, the sculptor was now to stand by Rothenstein during the two crisis years of the great Tate row of 1952–4. Since Moore, whose second term as a trustee had begun in 1949, played only a small role in this affair, we need not examine it in great detail. But because it engaged his emotions deeply, it cannot be ignored.[29]

The roots of the drama were nurtured by the second-class status which the Tate had endured since its foundation in 1897 as a branch of the National Gallery, mandated to house modern British art only. In 1917 it was promoted to become the national collection of British art of all periods, and also of modern (the word was not defined) foreign painting and sculpture. Though the Tate's keeper was advanced to director and it gained its own board of trustees, the collection remained the responsibility of the National Gallery's trustees, who could and did move any work they chose from Millbank to Trafalgar Square. Until 1946, when £2,000 of taxpayers' money was granted annually, there were no purchase grants; and one of the main bequests, the Chantrey Bequest, was spent on the Tate's behalf by the Royal Academy, and so had inevitably become a source of conflict.

The two issues underlying the Tate debate were Rothenstein's competence as director, and the related question of the powers which would pass from the National Gallery to the Tate when it gained full independence under the proposed National Gallery and Tate Gallery Bill. Rothenstein became vulnerable to attack when it emerged that certain funds from bequests had, purely through negligence, been used to buy works which did not fall within their terms, and that there was a great deal of discontent among the Tate's staff. There ensued a vicious campaign against Rothenstein, intended to show him as incompetent, frivolous, and provincial in his tastes. The attack was led by the art historian Douglas Cooper, who accused the director of missing fine opportunities to acquire works by the School of Paris. He was aided and abetted by, among others, Henry's fellow trustee, Graham Sutherland, and an unscrupulous South African, LeRoux Smith LeRoux, whom Rothenstein had with typical *naïveté* introduced on to the staff.

Two Moore-related incidents will give a flavour of those days. One concerned a bequest called the Kerr Fund, which was supposed to be used to acquire paintings only. Money from it went to help buy Henry's *Family Group* in 1950: a regrettable misapplication, but scarcely earth-shattering or justifying the subsequent hue and cry in the press. The second involved Henry's judgement and contacts. The Tate had the opportunity of buying from Marlborough Fine Art a complete set of Degas bronzes for about £30,000. Moore was against making so large an investment in what he acidly described as 'these painter-sculptors', but favoured the purchase of *Petite Danseuse de 14 ans* and of two or three others.[30] The dancer was duly bought, for £9,000. In this instance Moore was among Rothenstein's critics. He, Sutherland, and John Piper felt the price was excessive, and when they consulted Valentin in New York he reckoned it should cost no more than £5,000. Rothenstein's enemies insinuated unjustly that he had pocketed a large commission.

There were malicious attacks in the press by the Cooper faction; in the House of Commons the Liberal MP Jo Grimond spoke of the courage needed to enter the lion's den of art controversy by MPs living in 'the comparatively calm and impartial atmosphere of party politics'; and the trustees wrestled with the issues at lengthy meetings, one of which lasted into the small hours at the spacious Hampstead home of the chairman of the Tate's trustees, Colin Anderson. Moore stuck by his old friend when Rothenstein came within a single vote of being sacked. 'I was all against LeRoux Smith LeRoux and all against Douglas Cooper, and all on the side of Rothenstein,' he recalled.[31] The latter survived to punch Douglas Cooper hard in the face at a London party and to serve another ten years as director. LeRoux was sacked and later took his own life after being suspected of defrauding Lord Beaverbrook, who had employed him, of large sums of money. The Tate's administration was strengthened, and peace restored. Henry retained his deep loathing of Cooper, who let no opportunity slip to denigrate Moore's work in public, right up to his death in 1984. A few years after the Tate row, Henry commented apropos of Rothenstein's near-demise: 'When I think what we almost did to John! I can never remember it without horror.'[32]

There is often a touching contrast between the noble aims of artists on the one hand and the pettiness of their actions, the unscrupulousness of some of those who profit from them, and the incomprehension or hostility of the public. As Naum Gabo bitterly expressed it in a letter to Moore in April 1953, it can be 'a profession full of poison and jealousy among one's colleagues and abuse from the public'.[33] Emotions were to run high again in early 1953 in the concluding phases of a competition for a sculpture celebrating *The Unknown Political Prisoner.* An anonymous American, sometimes suspected of having been acting for the CIA or some similar organization, had put up £11,500 in prize money. The Institute of Contemporary Arts, by then five years old, was sponsoring it (in co-operation with the American backers), and Henry was advising the central organizing committee. Herbert Read, one of the ICA's moving spirits, was on the international committee, and there were pre-winnowed entries from seventy countries, excluding the Eastern bloc, which saw the theme as Cold War propaganda. Henry had been prominent at the competition's launch in January 1952, using his own semi-involvement and his commitments as reasons for not competing.[34] Epstein, Lipchitz, Zadkine, and Marini were among other well-known artists who similarly avoided the danger of not winning. Most of them probably also shared Moore's dislike of being pinned to a specific theme.

In fact the first prize of £4,525 went to the relatively little-known Reg Butler for an impressive maquette incorporating ambiguous references to cage, scaffold, cross, guillotine and watchtower. That was certainly cause for satisfaction. Not only had Butler helped finish the *Three Standing Figures,* but in 1950 Moore had successfully proposed him as the first sculptor to become a Gregory Fellow at Leeds University: through Peter Gregory's generosity, a poet, sculptor, painter, and musician were to enjoy the university environment for two years untroubled by financial worries. Moore was on the selection panel. Butler's maquette was soon smashed at the Tate Gallery by a stateless Hungarian refugee, László Szilvassy, an act reported with some relish by a generally hostile press. The model was easily replaced. A casual suggestion by Butler that a huge version might be erected on the cliffs of Dover prompted a minor storm in parliament.

Shortly after this brouhaha and in the middle of the Tate affair, Henry was ill enough to be in bed for more than two weeks. It started with a chill in his kidneys, which led to a 'very unpleasant' infection, he told Gabo, whose work he had been commending to his fellow Tate trustees; only after much streptomycin and continual injections of penicillin could his high temperature be reduced.[35] Having largely recovered by the end of May 1953, he was taken to University College Hospital in London a month later for the removal of a stone near the same troublesome kidneys. He was in the private wing for about two weeks, though well enough after a few days to do some sketching.

To Brazil and Mexico

The year ended on a tonic note, however, with a three-week visit to Brazil and Mexico, by far the most exotic trip of his career. In São Paulo he was the guest of the British Council, which was sponsoring a medium-sized show of his sculpture and drawings at the second São Paulo Biennale. The city, whose population had increased from 400,000 in 1900 to four million, was at its most dynamic, being in effect the industrial capital of Latin America. A heavy influx of Japanese and Chinese as well as European and American immigrants had contributed. To the sculptor from his rural fastness it was a revelation: 'It is a truly magnificent experience to see this great racial diversity,' he told a Brazilian journalist soon after his arrival by air on 30 November. 'It is a new emotion for me.'[36] He was also greatly impressed by the prodigality and vitality of the new architecture and the wealth and prestige enjoyed by architects. Among those he met was Oscar Niemeyer, during a trip to Rio, where he attended a press conference and gave a radio interview. Brazil had then produced no artists of equivalent calibre, and several architects tried to persuade Moore to stay in Brazil and work with them.[37]

Sir Herbert Read (just knighted) was a member of the international jury of the Biennale, and Moore won the international sculpture prize, worth about £700. A special international prize, open to all categories, went to the underrated French sculptor Henri Laurens, whom Henry had eclipsed in Venice. The international painting prize was shared by Alfred Manessier and the Mexican Rufino Tamayo, while Gropius was given a special prize for architecture. Brazilian newspapers and magazines hailed Moore as a 'vigorous, life-giving creator' and as the originator of 'the most personal style of our time'.[38]

His subsequent trip to Mexico, where he arrived on 15 December, was purely private. It was an unmissable opportunity to see the country whose art had so influenced him a quarter-century previously. He had, moreover, a correspondent there called Mathias Goeritz, a German-born architect and artist then aged thirty-eight. Goeritz had admired reproductions of Moore's work in pre-war Paris and post-war Madrid, and had published an article on it in a Barcelona magazine. A correspondence had developed, and in January 1950, not long after Goeritz had settled in Guadalajara in Jalisco state, Henry had written: 'It must be very exciting for you to be in Mexico – it is the one country in the world which I have always wanted to visit most. And one day I will certainly do so. Pre-Columbian Mexican sculpture has been the most important single influence on my sculpture – I should love to see it in its own environment.'[39]

A few weeks later, in February 1950, those words were printed inside an invitation to a show of Moore's drawings in a new gallery linked to Guadalajara's university, where Goeritz taught in the architecture faculty. 'Moore speaks in a language we believe we know,' one critic wrote:

> A man who has never been in Mexico ... becomes one of the best and most authentic representatives of ... the spirit of our ancestors, which also animates us today ... Confronted with his work, we know we are in the presence of an artist of genius, a great creator.[40]

This impact was achieved with thirty-seven drawings backed up by seven large photographs of major works, sent over by the British Council at the suggestion of Goeritz. The state governor expressed keen interest in the exhibition. Horrified incomprehension came only from the British community.

Hearing that Moore was representing Britain (with several painters) at the São Paulo Biennale, Goeritz had urged him to come on to Mexico City, to which he had meanwhile moved with his wife Marianne, a writer and photographer who died only four years later. The émigré German met his illustrious correspondent at the airport, and helped look after him for a week with the British Council's representatives, Lynndon Clough and Walter Plumb. With one or other, and on occasion a mutual friend like Tamayo, Henry embarked on an intensive round of sight-seeing. Within striking distance of the capital he saw the huge Toltec pyramids at Teotihuacan; the pyramid and Cortes Palace at Cuernavaca; the archeological site of Xichicalco; and the extinct volcano of the Nevado de Toluca. On one such expedition they passed through a brick-making area in the northern outskirts of Mexico City. There Indians packed clay by hand into large wooden frames, which were set up to dry in open layers before being baked in huge adobe stoves whose shape echoed the surrounding mountains. Moore was enormously impressed by this feast of brickyard shapes, Goeritz recalled.[41] In Mexico City itself one of the high spots was the national collection of art in the old part of the capital, the famous Anthropological Museum not being completed till 1964. A visit to a bullfight with Goeritz was not entirely happy. They sat near the front, and the bull was killed a few yards off. It did not want to die, and the *torero* pushed his sword again and again into its neck as it vomited blood. Henry concentrated his eyes on a woman of about thirty-five sitting nearby, who seemed greatly excited by the cruel scene. In a thoughtful voice he asked Goeritz: 'Would you ever consider marrying a girl like that?'[42]

Though the 1950s were a lively period in modern Mexico's cultural history, the work of the muralists of the late 1920s and 1930s remained its most notable contribution to twentieth-century art. Of the most famous muralists, José Orozco had died in 1949, but his contemporary Diego Rivera and the slightly younger David Siqueiros were still alive, with their Marxist political convictions intact. Perhaps in contemplating their work Moore reflected, à propos his recent Venice discourse, that these artists had succeeded in fusing elements of surrealism and cubism, of traditional Mexican art, of propaganda and genuine rage and indignation into a valid popular art form.

An audience with Rivera was arranged. Mexico's most famous painter, who was to die four years later aged sixty-nine, lived with his Hungarian-born wife Frida (who was also a gifted painter and had known Leon Trotsky well) in a house filled with Mexican antiquities as well as Rivera's powerful paintings. While waiting in an ante-room, Henry made sketches of some 'Judas' figures which were hanging there. These were later transferred, vastly enlarged, by a team of artists to masonite panels and fixed to the wall of a design workshop-cum-meeting place which Goeritz had conceived. Unfortunately his backer died. El Eco, as it was called, became first a restaurant, then a night club, finally a university theatre, and the 'Mooral' disappeared. Had Christmas not beckoned with all its family pleasures and duties, Moore might perhaps have stayed longer to see more distant relics of a culture which had so excited him when young. As it was, after stopping off in New York on the homeward journey his plane was late in London, and Christmas lunch at Hoglands became Christmas dinner.

Valentin's death

Moore's pre-1955 engagement diaries being in the possession of his daughter Mary, it is not clear whether Curt Valentin spent Christmas with the Moores that year, as he regularly had since 1947. If not, they must certainly have met at the party given for Henry and his New York friends by the *New York Times*'s art critic Aline Loucheim during his stop-over. Either meeting would have been their last. Valentin's health began to deteriorate in early 1954. That summer he stayed with Marino and Marina Marini at Forte dei Marmi on the Italian Riviera. On the morning of 19 August he was in good spirits, reading a Balzac novel and keen to discuss plans. A few hours later he was dead of an embolism or blood clot.[43]

Henry was shocked by the news, and wrote shortly afterwards to the dealer's chief assistant, Jane Wade:

> He kept to only a few artists and these he called his 'boys'. They were his family and he looked after them and felt towards them like a father ... I begin to realize, now that he is dead ... how much all the time one unconsciously counted on his steadfast support, on him being there, tirelessly working for the cause of the painters and sculptors he believed in. I loved him very deeply and shall miss him terribly.[44]

Moore paid his first visit to Forte dei Marmi when he went to attend Valentin's funeral at the nearby town of Pietrasanta at the foot of the Carrara mountains, focal point of the marble-hewing industry and of a colony of international sculptors. The burial had a welcome touch of the absurd, as the sculptor described to Nigel Gosling:

> It had to be in a wall, you know – he was a Jew. They made a big hole and they heaved the coffin up, and it stuck. It wouldn't go in. Somebody had left a projection, a bit of stone. It had to be chipped out. It took over an hour, and by that time we had all relaxed. I remember thinking Curt would have liked that. It had all become real, natural.[45]

When the stock of Valentin's gallery was eventually sold, around $3 million went to his two brothers and sister, who did not care for modern art. Ralph Colin, the dealer's lawyer, executor, customer, and friend, believed that much of the work would have gone to museums had

Valentin made another will on his return from Italy that summer, as he had said he would.[46] Instead a collection was taken up. Rodin's *Balzac* was bought with the proceeds and placed as a memorial in the garden of the Museum of Modern Art.

With Colin's astute guidance, Jane Wade ran the gallery till June 1955. A memorial exhibition of Valentin's artists was followed there in November 1954 by a substantial show of Moore's recent work. The *King and Queen* (returned by Uris, not yet bought by Hirshhorn), the *Warrior with Shield* and the double *Standing Figures* dominated, to mixed reactions. Thomas Hess attacked in the December *Art News*. Moore, he wrote, was wrongly considered in the US and Great Britain to be one of the world's great sculptors, thanks mainly to post-war British intellectuals who needed *chefs-d'école* who were

> native, yet Continental in style; metaphysical for metaphors, yet natural (i.e. connected with a country garden of the soul); verbally Socialist in human sympathies, yet aristocratic in stance. Britten in music, Sutherland in painting, and Moore had the luck to fit the bill perfectly ... A few little bronzes and sketches escape the cul-de-sac of Official Modernity and offer carefully observed human gestures translated into variations on Picasso.[47]

Clement Greenberg, a formidable foe, sniped from the pages of *Partisan Review*, accusing Moore of 'modernistic trickiness' and a lack of authentic feeling.[48]

For Moore, Valentin's death marked the beginning of the end of the era of the pioneering, individualistic dealers who had shown such faith in him. His relationship with the Leicester Galleries in London, where he had another exhibition of recent work in February 1954, survived fitfully, and he continued to sell a few pieces through other early supporters from less palmy days, like (in London) the Redfern Gallery; Roland, Browse and Delbanco; Gimpel Fils; the Mayor Gallery; and the Brook Street Gallery. But the long era of the big battalions and the big prices was beginning. It is easy to be cynical about successful art dealers, some of whom behave with greater decency than their artists. Henry liked to tell the story of the two gallery owners who went to see a dying painter. 'How do you feel?' they asked solicitously, standing on either side of the bed. 'Like Christ, between two thieves,' the painter replied.[49] Yet he was glad enough of their help, and with many of them he was genuinely friendly.

When Colin closed Valentin's Buchholz Gallery in 1955, he tried to place the artists with compatible dealers: Calder with Perls, Marini and Giacometti with Pierre Matisse, and so on. Some found a happy home with Otto Gerson, but he died in 1962; the following year Marlborough Fine Art, already dominant in London and flourishing in Rome, opened in New York as the Marlborough-Gerson Gallery with an exhibition of Valentin's artists called *A Tribute to Curt Valentin*.

Colin felt that Moore's work needed the space of a large gallery. Two lively and sympathetic young partners at Knoedler's, Harry Brooks and Coe Kerr, jumped at the chance of taking on such a big name whose work they greatly admired. Brooks and his chairman went over to Perry Green, and Moore agreed to the move, even though Knoedler's was associated mainly with Old Masters and Impressionists and showed only a few minor contemporary artists. They bought outright from Valentin's estate fifty-eight Moore drawings and twenty-six sculptures, including many smallish items. Henry seemed to be not very interested in money at that stage, Brooks recalled. He just wanted his work to get around, and was happy with his still modest London arrangements:

> We found it rather difficult, as the Leicester Galleries, a very nice gallery, had very low overheads. They were taking pieces on consignment, and if they made ten or fifteen per cent they thought they were making a very fair profit; whereas we were trying to bring Henry's prices up to a higher level. We found we would be offering a piece for $4,000 which the Leicester Galleries would be selling for $3,000. We would even buy pieces from them.[50]

Moore's attitudes to dealers reflected his temperament, which was more complex than it seemed. He always refused to be tied down by any formal contract. After Marlborough Fine Art had become his main London dealer, his continued relationships with the smaller fry sprang from real sympathy tinged perhaps with guilt. Having a different main dealer in New York enabled him, up to a point, to divide and rule. Yet even to them he felt far from beholden. If a client they had introduced turned up at his studio, he would cheerfully do a direct deal. Sometimes galleries would buy work, especially smaller pieces, outright; sometimes, to save on capital outlay, they would sell on commission, the percentage varying according to the value of the piece. In eliminating either the mark-up or the commission, Moore could charge more than he would receive from a gallery, while the client would pay still less than if he had gone to a dealer, and often much less. One dealer commented without a trace of bitterness: 'He was so affable with people: they would go to his studio, and before you knew it, he would sell them the piece he had promised to you.' To his friends Henry was consistently generous, and later on he never minded if they sold for a vast sum a piece he had let them have cheaply. For the rest, his tactics were influenced by a desire to keep some independence, much Yorkshire realism, and a genuine feeling for the little man.

Chapter XIII

Unesco, New Zealand and Auschwitz

1956–8

1956 was the year of the Anglo-French Suez invasion, of Khrushchev's crushing of the Hungarian uprising, and of the negotiation of the Treaty of Rome, under which the EEC was established the following year. In 1957 Anthony Eden resigned – a case of ill-health aggravated by folly – and Harold Macmillan became Prime Minister, paving the way for the 'never had it so good' era of economic expansion in the self-consciously Swinging Sixties.

Where art was concerned, *Angst* and kitchen-sink realism were on their way out, Pop Art and abstraction surging in. It would be hard to exaggerate the impact on the art world of the exhibition *Modern Art in the United States* when it opened at the Tate Gallery in 1956. Though it ranged widely, the final room was devoted to Abstract Expressionism, including work by Pollock, Kline, Motherwell, de Kooning, Gorky, and Rothko. The British painter Patrick Heron was typical in being 'instantly elated by the size, energy, originality, economy, and inventive daring of many of the paintings,' as he put it. 'Their creative emptiness represented a radical discovery, I felt, as did their flatness, or rather their spacial shallowness.'[1] Britain had its own school of abstract painters of a gentler, more landscape-related variety which had been emerging at St Ives in Cornwall and which shared Heron's elation.

Pop Art, admirably suited to the British taste for irony, had nothing in common with the new wave of abstract painting except energy. It was obsessed with the exciting new world of cheap consumer goods – ballpoint pens, transistor radios, long-playing records – of colour magazines and popular newspapers, modern technology, television, show business, and advertising. By celebrating ordinary life and popular culture in a relentlessly upbeat if often wry manner, it widened the audience for art in post-austerity Britain.

Sculpture was altogether slower to respond to these swirling currents. The anguish and alienation which had marked the work of the much-vaunted 'geometry of fear' school featured at the 1952 Venice Biennale gave way gradually to a more primeval and totemic imagery, rugged and massive at first, then refined by a sharp revival of interest in Brancusi's work. Bronze continued to hold its own as a medium, and Anthony Caro's figures still had a massiveness reflecting in part the influence of his two years at Hoglands. The revolution was yet to come.

To the younger, Pop-oriented painters emerging from the Royal College of Art, like David Hockney, Peter Blake, and Allen Jones, the static monumentality of Moore's work must have looked complacent and anachronistic; yet within the context of late-1950s sculpture it still seemed to be of its own era. The totem-like *Upright Motives* which Moore created in 1955–6 look quite happy in the company of contemporary works by such younger sculptors as Eduardo Paolozzi, Hubert Dalwood, and William Turnbull. These tall figures – five were enlarged to between six and eleven feet from among a dozen models – owed their birth partly to an abortive commission from Olivetti. Seeing a lone Lombardy poplar behind the long, low office building on a visit of inspection to Milan in 1954, Moore felt that a vertical work would be the right foil. Back in his studio he started balancing forms one on top of the other, as the North American Indians had done in their totem poles. The resulting figures had, with their wealth of orifices and nubbly protuberances, a new overtly erotic element hitherto only implicit in the tense curves or parted thighs of a reclining figure.

As the name attached to *Upright Motive No. 1* after its siting on the Keswick estate implies, the *Glenkiln Cross* [116] also resembled a crucifix – 'a kind of worn-down body and cross merged into one', as Henry called it.[2] John Russell considers it one of the sculptor's greatest achievements: 'as arresting an image as has been created in the twentieth century'.[3] With its complex associations and Celtic overtones, it wears uncommonly well; and when displayed between the more cryptic and organic companion pieces Nos. 2 and 7 (as at the Amon Carter Museum in Fort Worth, Texas and at the Kröller-Müller Museum, Otterlo, Holland), the three figures take on the aspect of a crucifixion scene: to their creator's eyes, 'as though framed against the sky above Golgotha'.[4] As for the Olivetti commission, he lost interest in it when he discovered that the sculpture would be virtually in a car park.

Some of the forms found in the *Upright Motives* were derived in turn from a dazzling variety of images inspired variously by organic and

93. *Family Group*, 1948–9, 60 inches high, bronze. Conceived for Henry Morris's village college at Impington in Cambridgeshire, it found a home at a school in the New Town of Stevenage in Hertfordshire

94. Moore with Roland Penrose (left), and E. C. ('Peter') Gregory in Venice for the 1948 Biennale

95. Moore with Constantin Brancusi in Paris, 1945. Henry had no doubt which of them was the greater artist

96. Moore (second from left) at Leeds University after receiving his first honorary degree in 1945. Anthony Eden, former Foreign Secretary and future Prime Minister, is fourth from the left

97. Moore with Cicely and Philip Hendy, Hoglands, probably mid-1940s. At Irina's right is Susan Simmons, a friend

98. Moore with his daughter Mary, 1948

99. Moore with Peter Gregory around 1950. This was the closest and most disinterested of Henry's friendships in the years of his success

100. Moore announcing details of the 'Unknown Political Prisoner' international sculpture competition at the Institute of Contemporary Arts in January 1952. Left to right: Roland Penrose, Herbert Read, Anthony Kloman and John Rothenstein. Their gloom was to be justified

101. Anthony Caro assisting Moore at Hoglands, 1951 or 1952

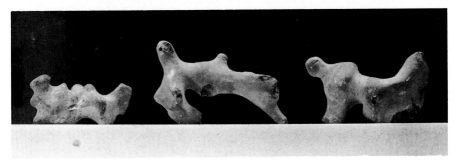

102. Reclining flints from Moore's collection

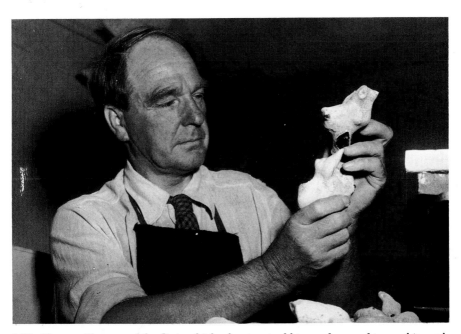

103. Moore with some of the flints which often inspired him and seemed to ape his work

104. *Reclining Figure*, Festival, 1951, 90 inches long, bronze, at the Scottish National Gallery of Modern Art, Inverleith House, Edinburgh. A different cast fetched $1.76 million at auction soon after Moore's death

105. *King and Queen*, 1952–3, 64½ inches high, bronze, at the Keswick estate in Scotland. The queen resembles Irina Moore, while Philip Hendy's hands and feet were models for the king's

106. *Standing Figure*, 1950, 87 inches high, bronze, the first sculpture to be sited on Sir William Keswick's Shawhead estate in Scotland

107. *Warrior with Shield*, 1953–4, 60 inches high, bronze. In telling its story of suffering and resistance, this sculpture has an old-fashioned appeal to the heart, as do Moore's fallen warriors

108. *Mother and Child*, 1953, 20 inches high, bronze. One of Moore's few images of active violence, it greatly excited his Jungian interpreter Erich Neumann

109. *Time-Life Screen*, 1952–3, 120 inches high by 318 inches long, Portland stone, Time-Life building, New Bond Street, London W1: rarely seen by pedestrians

110. *Draped Reclining Figure*, 1952–3, 62 inches long, bronze, seen to better advantage here in a Holland Park exhibition than on the Time-Life balcony

111. *Upright Internal/External Forms*,
1953–4, 103 inches high, elmwood,
Albright-Knox Art Gallery, Buffalo, New
York: Moore's finest rendering of a
recurring theme

112. Moore at work on the Unesco figure at Querceta, Italy, around spring 1958

113. *Unesco Reclining Figure*, 1957–8, 200 inches long, Roman travertine, at Unesco headquarters in Paris

114. Another view of the *Unesco Reclining Figure*

115. *Wall Relief*, 1955, $28\frac{1}{4}$ feet by 63 feet, red brick, Bouwcentrum, Rotterdam. A sunnier and more open location would have shown it off better, it was later realized

116. *Upright Motive No. 1: Glenkiln Cross,*
1955–6, 132 inches high, bronze, on the
Keswick estate in Scotland

117. Adel Crag near Leeds, which
impressed Moore as a child and may have
influenced *Two Piece Reclining Figure No. 1*

118. *Two Piece Reclining Figure No. 1,*
1959, 76 inches long, bronze, also on Sir
William Keswick's Scottish estate. The
cragginess can pall

119. Moore with some of his bronzes around 1958, including two casts of *Woman* (1957–8), *Draped Reclining Woman* (1957–8), three *Upright Motives* (1955–6) and *Reclining Figure: External Form* (1953–4)

120. Moore and Mathias Goeritz in
Mexico City, 1953

121. Henry and Irina Moore at home, 1954

122. Moore at the unveiling at Harlow, Essex, in May 1956, of his *Family Group* of 1954–5, 64½ inches high, Hadene stone, a gift of the Harlow Art Trust, subsequently much vandalized. On the right in a pale suit, Lilian Somerville of the British Council, a doughty supporter

123. Hermann Noack III, head of the West Berlin bronze foundry, Harry Fischer (then of Marlborough Fine Art in London) and Moore around 1960

124. A look of triumph from Moore, who had a remarkable eye for dimensions, after proving to an assistant with callipers that the enlargement of *Nuclear Energy* was, as he had thought, too wide by an inch or two in a crucial area

human forms and even (a touch of Paolozzi) tools and screws which he had evolved for a novel commission in Rotterdam. This was to design a wall relief [115] to be executed in red brick on the side of a new extension to Rotterdam's Building Centre (Bouwcentrum). The architect involved, J. W. C. Boks, had been asked to find a sculptor capable of designing decorative motives. Having admired Moore's work, he turned to him and, even though reliefs were involved, succeeded in the course of a visit to Hoglands in persuading him to accept the commission.[5] The novelty of the medium for Moore, its Gothic and Tudor tradition in Northern Europe and England, the free nature of his brief and Boks's assurance that the specialist bricklayers would be equal to any difficulty: all these no doubt helped him overcome his usual detestation of reliefs. In a typical burst of creativity he produced nine maquettes (each later cast in an edition of ten) on which Herbert Read counted at least sixty different motives.[6] The one chosen features five half-human, half-animal forms set within an attractive ribbed design. Henry went to Rotterdam in June 1955 to oversee the experimental enlargement of a small section, then again in October to inspect progress, but not for the unveiling in late December. He found the entire exercise stimulating, but considered the outcome only moderately satisfactory. The huge wall, twenty-eight feet high and sixty-three feet long, is in a narrow side street, so the relief gets little sunlight and it is hard to view the design from far enough away.[7]

Though (as we have seen) Moore was far from being without honour in his own country, the Time-Life screen, commissioned by Americans, was still the only one of his works on public view outdoors in central London apart from West Wind, and so it remained for a decade. That omission apart, he could not complain about lack of official support, of which many artists felt he had more than his fair share. Now, in the Queen's birthday honours of June 1955, the sculptor was named a Companion of Honour (CH), an honour limited at any one time to fifty distinguished Britons. The award seemed overdue: 'his country thus confers upon Mr Moore the distinction already conferred by world opinion,' the Yorkshire Post intoned in proud reproof.[8] It was not then known that a few years earlier, probably in 1951 or 1952, Moore had, greatly to his credit, turned down the offer of a knighthood. It took him two days to compose the letter of refusal: 'I didn't want to be rude, but titles change one's name and one's opinion of oneself. The initials aren't so bad. No one comprehends them,' he explained many years later.[9]

Henry felt that a knighthood would come between him and other people. He did not relish the idea of his assistants saying: 'Good morning,

Sir Henry!' Americans in particular could never understand that the CH, and to an even greater extent the Order of Merit which he received in 1963, were vastly greater honours than a knighthood. To them it seemed anomalous that Epstein could call himself Sir Jacob while Moore remained plain Mr. All explanations about the proliferation of knighthoods among backbench MPs and businessmen were wasted: no initials, however distinguished, had the courtly associations of a title. Plain Mr Moore (though he was constantly to be dubbed Sir Henry by careless journalists) was invested with the CH by the Queen at Buckingham Palace on 15 July 1955, the first of many contacts with the monarch.

It is worth noting that Francis Bacon, second to Moore in fame among Britain's contemporary artists, declined the CH twenty-two years later, saying: 'It might be fine for other people, but I want to stress I don't want anything for myself.'[10] The two artists could scarcely have been more different: Bacon the urban bachelor with his taste for Soho life and distaste for bourgeois morality; Moore the family and country man with his regular hours and strong desire to go quite early to his own bed. Bacon rejected the Establishment's embrace in all its forms: honours, honorary degrees, prizes, positions. Moore felt that a successful artist had his obligations, to the art world, to his less fortunate colleagues, and to society as a whole, and he liked to feel appreciated. Indeed, few artists can have been quite so concerned about how their work would ultimately be judged. Yet both pursued their path largely regardless of passing fashions, strongly armed with a sense of standing in the grand tradition of European culture. What Michelangelo was to Moore, Velasquez was to Bacon.

What could have been more alien to Bacon, a virtually propertyless man, than Moore's gradual emergence over the next quarter-century as the laird of Perry Green? Encouraged by Irina, who had a Russian feeling for land, and by his loyal neighbour, builder, and friend Frank Farnham, whom he generally used as an agent, he bought up seventeen local properties, including two substantial farms. The first and most important step came in spring 1955, when they acquired six acres adjoining the back garden. The smallholding had belonged to a Mr Kynaston, who grew vegetables and fruit there for sale in Muswell Hill, north London, and also kept about twenty pigs and a couple of cows. For fifteen years Moore had been obliged to use as a studio the former stables to the right of the Hoglands forecourt. It was too small and too low for large pieces, and made him vulnerable to every visitor arriving at the house. Now he could have Farnham build a larger studio well to the rear and work undisturbed, and he could eventually place his work in the grassed parkland between studio and house which Irina created, a perfect setting in which to assess and display it. Like most of the subsequent purchases, this one protected him from any troublesome adjacent development.

In his large new studio Henry and his assistants, of whom there were now four, worked on a big commission (its first) from the Harlow Arts Trust. This paternalistically enlightened body had been set up by a group of the sculptor's local friends, including Frederick Gibberd, the chief architect-planner of Harlow New Town; his wife-to-be Pat Fox-Edwards; Maurice Ash, an economist who had married the daughter of the Elm-hirsts of Dartington; and Philip Hendy, director of the National Gallery, who lived in London but was a frequent weekend guest with his wife Cicely at Hoglands. The aim was to endow the new town, then being built only a few miles from Perry Green, with some well-chosen open-air sculpture, thus enriching the lives of its brave settlers and counteracting the blandness of the architecture. Being a neighbour and famous, Moore was a natural choice for the first commission; and with young married couples predominating among the first inhabitants, a family group seemed appropriate.

One of the little Impington maquettes from 1944 was selected, a five-ton block of pale Hadene stone delivered to Hoglands, and the heavy work began. The assistants now consisted of two Tasmanians, Stephen Walker and Darryl Hill, another Australian called Lenton Parr, and a talented young Briton, Peter King, who died tragically two years later after a motorcycle accident. Walker was nearly sacked when he carved a hole in the Harlow group where no hole was intended. Moore found a way of overcoming the gaffe, and Walker left soon afterwards.[11]

The resulting group [122] – father with right arm around mother's shoulder, large baby on her left knee – is somewhat stiff and has more than a whiff of propagandistic uplift, as if to say 'Together we will go forward.' What looks like a length of towelling draped over the parents' knees strikes a bizarre note. The large carving, more than five feet tall, was unveiled in May 1956 by Clark, now chairman of the Arts Council and of the Independent Television Authority: he referred to it as a symbol of the new humanitarian civilization, of which Harlow was a complete expression: a delphic tribute.[12] A local purity squad, who had heard that the family had been shown nude, joined in the cheers when it was unveiled. Harlow's children proved less appreciative. In January 1957 it was found chipped by missiles and wearing a red tea cosy. In 1959 the heads were given green whiskers, after which the group was moved to a less exposed site. Then in July 1963 the child's head was severed. After a long gap, during which the group was removed and repaired – by Moore himself, who harboured no rancour over the treatment it had received – it was relocated on a high base in what passes for the town's central square. The Harlow Arts Trust was undeterred. The work of uplift went on, and fine sculptures by artists like Ralph Brown, F. E. McWilliam, Karel Vogel, and Willi Soukop were appreciated by many. In 1964 another Moore was added: one of the *Upright Motives*, a relatively vandal-proof bronze, sited in the Water Gardens.

The Unesco commission

While completing the Harlow group, Moore was turning his thoughts to the biggest commission of his career: to execute a huge piece for the new headquarters in Paris of the United Nations Educational, Scientific and Cultural Organization. Unesco had been founded in 1946 to promote the pursuit of knowledge in the cause of peace and mankind's welfare. Henry's old Hampstead friend Julian Huxley had been its first director-general and could give the sculptor a good briefing. To his successor, the Texan Dr Luther Evans, fell the task of building the new HQ on a site near the Ecole Militaire. Three architects had been chosen to design it: Marcel Breuer, of Hampstead memory, now an American; Pier Luigi Nervi, the Italian who put the poetry into concrete; and France's Bernard Zehrfuss. They came up with a graceful Y-shaped design, seven storeys high and standing on concrete columns or 'pilotis'.

At the United Nations in New York, member states had been asked to contribute works of art, with disastrous results. At Unesco they would do things better. A committee was set up to commission the best artists of the day. Among its members were Herbert Read and Clark's friend Georges Salles. The major commissions went to Picasso, Miró, Moore, Arp, Calder, Tamayo, and Noguchi, a judicious geographic spread. Moore was the first choice for the main sculpture, with the brothers Gabo and Pevsner as second and third.[13] The first approaches were made in May 1955, with a mid-1958 deadline for completion. In late November Moore came on a fact-finding mission to Paris, meeting Zehrfuss and Salles among others.

Given such a long delivery date, he found it hard to focus on the project. In addition to finishing the Harlow group, he completed an (uncommissioned) eight-feet long reclining figure in bronze which he then proceeded to stand upright, base and all, and carve in elmwood over the next four years. With only a few modifications, it became the *Upright Figure* now in the Guggenheim Museum in New York. In neither version does this exaggeratedly female figure, all bust and bottom, seem very successful.

On 7 August 1956 he wrote to Read that he had just started some notebook drawings to get his mind on to the Unesco problem:

> It's not going to be an easy commission. So far what ideas have come (some of them) might work out as sculpture purely for myself, but no one idea has turned up to concentrate on yet ... I have given up all my other work ... [but] the size and importance of the commission is such that I can't expect even the preliminary stages to be quick.

Henry's suggestion that some of his ideas might work out for his own purposes was an understatement, as it transpired: at least twenty-two of his subsequently completed works owed their origin to the Unesco gestatory process. He tried draped and undraped seated female figures, mothers with a standing child, figures on steps, figures reading. He was worried about the visibility of a bronze, darkened by urban pollution, against the glass windows of the main façade, so he provided some pieces with their own bronze background wall – only to realize they would thus be invisible from inside the building. Should his sculpture incorporate the idea of learning? His experiments had flirted with it, but such conceptualizing was not among his strengths, and he decided to abandon any attempt at a thematic approach. Unesco, he decided, should have an outsize reclining figure, a huge standard Moore, executed in the same Roman travertine stone which was being used at the top of the building and was pale enough to stand out against the windows.

On Jungian argumentation, the choice of a female figure was perfect: if the aggressiveness of our patriarchal culture had precipitated two world wars, Moore's figure was a reminder of the archetypal female role in developing man's social capabilities and more peaceable relationships. Some of the sculptor's critical admirers have, however, regarded it as an evasion of a challenge, a 'cop-out'. In the terms of the setting it is surprising that he even contemplated anything other than a single figure of large mass. At the practical level, a carving was evidently going to be a much tougher task than a bronze.

One day in early 1957 Henry arrived in Paris with four maquettes for scrutiny by representatives of the three architects and the art advisory committee. He was clear in his mind which maquette he preferred, the site architect Pierre Marcel recalled almost thirty years later, and said: 'If they choose a different one, I really will be very unhappy, I don't know what I shall do.' Leaving the models in Marcel's office, he went to look at the site. First Breuer arrived and said, 'Oh, there's no doubt, it's that one I prefer,' pointing to Moore's favourite. Georges Salles then did the same, independently. Marcel, who had no feeling for modern art, was worried but impressed by this unanimity:

> One of the other maquettes was more figurative. No one looked at it, though I thought I might have preferred it. I was amazed that three such important people should all think exactly the same. Then we had the meeting, and they all said 'That's the one.' M. Moore was very happy ... there was no discussion.[14]

Breuer in particular reckoned the final product should be eight metres long. Even Henry boggled at this, eight feet having till now been about his limit. 'I was a little nervous about making something larger than it should be, blowing it up more than it deserved,' he recalled later, when he had become less inhibited in this respect.[15] Five metres was large enough, he believed. To prove his point, he photographed the maquette and made a blown-up cut-out five metres long. On a dull, misty day in late March 1957 they tried it out for size and location in front of the Unesco building, having retreated to the far side of the Avenue de Ségur some hundred yards back. Henry won: five metres it would be. Later he admitted Breuer had been right. Bigger would have been better.[16]

He had envisaged carving the giantess at home in the large new studio. But it transpired that the cost of transport alone would swallow much of the fee of £16,000 (around £112,000 in today's money), which was intended to cover 'any and all other expenses involved in the execution, transport and final installation of the statue,' according to the final commissioning letter.[17] Henry's basic fee was £3,600, the same as Picasso's; the rest was for costs including the help of assistants. In the event, Unesco seems to have paid for both the stone and the transport, which came to a sum similar to the basic fee.[18]

The Italian firm which supplied Unesco's travertine was called Henraux, and had been founded in 1821 by G. B. Alexandre, a French-man sent by Napoleon to find marble for his grand edifices. It was located at the small town of Querceta at the foot of the Carrara mountains, a couple of miles from Forte dei Marmi and Pietrasanta, where Moore had been in 1954 for Valentin's funeral. Henraux not only worked the local white marble but marble and stone from all over the world, and they were now commissioned to bring a large block of honey-coloured travertine from a quarry north of Rome to Querceta. It weighed at least sixty tons, Henry believed, eventually reduced to thirty-nine tons when completed in four more manageable sections.[19] He planned to make sorties to Querceta to supervise the Henraux artisans as they did the roughing out, then complete the final stages in Paris *in situ*.

Visiting the Henraux works for the first time was for Henry like a child visiting a chocolate factory. *Entrare Adagio!* a large sign admonishes as the awed visitor drives *molto adagio* down avenues of huge, rough-hewn blocks of pink, green, black, white, grey or brown marble and stone, piled on top of each other, disappointingly destined in the main to be sliced into inch-thick cladding or flooring for office blocks. In one corner is the sculpture workshop-studio, representing a tiny fraction of the firm's activities and in the 1950s employing just four elderly artisans out of a work-force of about a thousand (subsequently reduced by mechanization to a third of that). Miró, Arp and Marini were then periodically using its facilities. Moore and his huge Unesco contract were a valuable boost to that department.[20]

Apart from many much smaller marble-working factories, the area abounds in ateliers where a dwindling number of artisans, many of them virtuoso carvers, produce everything from sentimental madonnas and figurines to serious works of art. These are often enlarged from the tiniest maquettes, with little or no supervision from the artist. Thanks to their skills and the abundant supply of cheap marble, Pietrasanta (meaning Holy Stone) has attracted what must be the largest international colony of sculptors in the world. Its members, some very able and established, others more amateurish, lead a hothouse, inbred existence, washing the marble dust and gossip down with *grappa* and coffee at the Bar Igea and the Bar Michelangelo. It was not a world with which Moore was to have any significant contact.

Towering above Pietrasanta and Querceta, and easily visible from Forte dei Marmi, are the Apuan mountains, which for two thousand years have yielded an inexhaustible supply of Carrara marble. On a clear day there seems even in midsummer to be snow on their upper flanks. It is marble chippings glinting in the sun, left by centuries of plunder. The sculptural Everest of these peaks, (5,129 feet high, but not, despite its name, the highest,) is Mount Altissimo, where Henraux has a number of quarries. To one of these Michelangelo had come to choose his material. Moore was quick to visit the hallowed spot. 'For me to enter the marble caves and look at some of the very stones Michelangelo had looked at was a terrific experience,' he recalled years later.[21] Being driven up to those distant white scars, as Henry was driven, is an experience to reduce the knees to jelly. Not only is the height vertiginous but there is a sporting chance of being brushed off the winding track by one of the firm's lorries thundering down with their massive cargo.

At these highest quarries the marble, forged by aeons of pressure on organic matter, is at its best. Here nature is all-powerful, the views stupendous, and man a puny intruder. The technology for removing the marble has improved over the centuries, but remains relatively primitive. In pre-explosive days, wooden wedges were driven into the natural fissures in the marble. These were then soaked in water, the force of their expansion enabling a slab to be prised off, then slid down the slopes with the aid of ropes or brought down in smaller pieces by ox-carts. Today small charges of explosive are used to disengage some sections, but mostly the marble is carved off with an apparatus of rotating wires which gnaw slowly through with the aid of water and abrasive sand. The huge blocks thus removed are then reduced to transportable dimensions.

According to Moore's recollection fairly soon afterwards, he would go over to Italy for three or four weeks at a time, then home for a month before returning. He would stay in a hotel in Forte dei Marmi, a pleasant seaside resort frequented by prosperous Florentines and Milanese, and sometimes he would bring Irina and Mary, then eleven. For them it was a holiday, and because they all enjoyed it so much, they continued to go there when the Unesco sculpture was finished.[22]

Assuming that work began at Querceta soon after he had completed a one-eighth scale model in July 1957, the massive figure was some fourteen months in the carving. At the end of December he told the *Sunday Dispatch* he was finding the stone the hardest piece he had come across, and feared he would not finish in time. 'I haven't begun to see the figures in the block yet. That will come later when I begin to rough-hew them,' he said.[23] In early March 1958 he told *The Times* that he was leaving for Italy to start work on the 'final stages', but two more longish visits would be needed.[24] Soon an Italian newspaper excitedly if belatedly announced that 'the Michelangelo of the twentieth century is working at Querceta for Unesco'.[25] In June he was said to have 'almost finished rough-hewing his figures', yet it was not until October that *The Times* could report that the thirty-nine-ton figure had been proudly set on its pedestal in Paris [112, 113, 114], the last to arrive of the eleven commissioned works of art and generally considered one of the best: 'Mr Moore's work stands high on the central lawn for all to see. The marble figure with its towering head affronts the visitor like a sentinel.'[26] To the *Daily Express*, the massive weight of the travertine goddess – sixty tons if the pedestal and supporting uprights were included – reposed on 'crushed taxpayers': Lord Beaverbrook, then the newspaper's proprietor, disapproved of subsidized culture.[27]

Henry was pleased with the siting and the way the sculpture caught the sun at all angles; and he was relieved that he had not done it in bronze, though the freshly chiselled travertine looked startlingly white at first. A few weeks of Paris's winter weather would soon mellow that, he accurately forecast. Asked whether the sculpture had any symbolic meaning, he said that he had spent six months pondering what Unesco stood for. Those thoughts had influenced his design, but the work meant whatever anyone wanted it to mean.[28] Late though he had delivered it after completion in Italy, it was in time for the inauguration of the Unesco building in early November. Typically, Henry did not attend: it was Mary's first half-term weekend at the boarding school, Cranborne Chase, to which they had sent her. Mary would have been so disappointed had they not gone, he explained to a friend, and he and Irina were relieved to find she was enjoying it.[29]

Herbert Read considered the Unesco figure one of Moore's greatest achievements, but his judgement may have been coloured by his involvement in the commission.[30] John Russell adopted a protective tone: it had never had the press it deserved, he wrote in his book on Moore, though it seemed to him to be 'the right answer to an impossible question'.[31] If the question was impossible, was it right to have tried to answer it? Probably yes, not least to provide the French capital with a major Moore, which it would never have acquired otherwise.

The real importance of the Unesco commission lay in its impact on Moore's life and work rather than in the actual sculpture which resulted, fine though that is. Being so much larger than anything he had hitherto attempted, it changed his ideas of scale, and also of what could be accomplished by assistants. Although it put him off carving for the next six years, it led to his discovery of the charms of Forte dei Marmi. His subsequent summer holidays there at the Hotel Byron, overlooking the sea, helped to restore his interest in carving, and culminated in the purchase of a holiday home some ten minutes' walk from the beach in 1965.

By this stage, indeed before it, Moore's life had become so busy that rigorous selectivity is required if a balance is to be maintained between the important and the interesting. We have passed over British Council tours of his work between 1952 and 1954, embracing Scandinavia and eight West German cities, which would have been major events in the careers of most artists. In March 1955 another British Council showing took Henry and Irina to Yugoslavia for almost two weeks. Relations between that country and its neighbour, Italy, were still strained by the dispute over Trieste, and the Italian coal of the train on which they travelled had to be changed to Yugoslav coal at the border, Irina recalled.[32] From Zagreb, where they arrived just before the exhibition closed, they went to the opening in Belgrade with an interpreter and a very bad driver. At one stage he left them on a hill and the car started to roll backwards. The roads were extremely rough, everything was short in the shops, and in the hotels people talked in a hush: civil war and Communism had taken their toll. The recommended escape was slivovitz, the local firewater, offered with coffee from 10 a.m. onwards. For entertainment they were taken to *King Lear*: it made a change from *Hamlet*, which Henry had seen in Greek, Spanish (in Mexico) and German. During the ambassador's speech at the Belgrade opening, a crowd of students burst through the doors shouting 'We want Moore,' and altogether 45,000 people saw the exhibition in Zagreb, Belgrade, Ljubljana and Skopje. Henry and Irina returned from Belgrade after visiting Split.[33]

New Zealand amazed

Much the same exhibition of two dozen sculptures and as many drawings, plus plaster casts of the *Standing Figures* (Battersea Park) and the *Draped Reclining Figure* (Time-Life), then toured Canada, New Zealand, and South Africa. If in Canada and South Africa the reactions were the familiar blend of excitement, appreciation, and abusive incomprehension, the impact on New Zealand was astonishing. Auckland's mayor, J. H. Luxford, played his part in its phenomenal success by declaring on the opening day: 'I never seen the art gallery so desecrated by such a nauseating sight . . . These figures, offending against all known anatomy, to me are repulsive.' An unidentified man then began to scream at the sculpture and ran from the gallery shouting 'That man ought to be shot' (Moore, not Luxford).[34]

In those days New Zealand was still a quiet, provincial, conservative country not often treated to such stirring events. News travelled quickly, and next day 2,187 visitors packed the Auckland Art Gallery, one girl commenting eloquently: 'At least it's a change from the Springboks.'[35] An attendant summed up the reactions: 'Up to forty-five, they can appreciate it; between forty-five and fifty they are a bit iffy; fifty and over, and they don't like it at all.' The exhibition became the main topic of conversation and debate, and even advertisements incorporated references to it. Eventually in twenty-three days it was seen by 36,738 people in a city with a population of 361,000 (a level of attendance probably only exceeded in Moore's career in Sri Lanka, then Ceylon, where three years later a small show of his work attracted 10,000 visitors *in three days* in the town of Galle, population 60,000). The director of the Auckland Art Gallery, Peter Tomory, reckoned that 'visual starvation' was the cause of the rush: apart from the scenery, New Zealanders had little else to excite them, he said. One woman who had commented 'I hate this stuff' came back five times.[36]

Christchurch, Dunedin, and Wellington reacted more calmly, but in each of the last two cities more than 9,000 people saw the exhibition, despite the relative inaccessibility of the public galleries. Total attendance in New Zealand was 61,000. The country had never known an artistic event like it.

When the Moore show arrived in Port Elizabeth, South Africa in early May 1957, it was described by the *Eastern Province Herald* as 'the most important, stimulating and astonishing display of art ever offered to the public'.[37] Two weeks later, after some minor controversy, the same newspaper displayed a Grahamstown gardener's arrangement of Five Standing Radishes in parody of the *Three Standing Figures*. Henry would have approved the analogy with nature. In Johannesburg the director of the City Art Gallery described the attendance of 11,000 in the first three weeks as 'fantastic', and eventually it clocked in 21,500, many from neighbouring African countries.[38]

During these far-flung excitements Moore worked on the Unesco project and on the generally uninspiring related figures, many of them seated. From one of these, the pregnant *Seated Woman* of 1957 – which Jo Hirshhorn so loved that he eventually bought two casts of it – he fashioned a far more striking piece, the *Falling Warrior*. Laying her on her back she just looked inert. To catch the act of falling, he used a shield in her flung-back left hand to support the torso just above the ground.[39]

In summer 1957 Henry took a ten-day break to stay with Maurice and Ruth Ash at their holiday villa at Cap d'Antibes on the French Riviera. Ash, then chairman of the Town and Country Planning Association, lived only a few miles from Perry Green, and loved good pictures, music, food, wine, and sailing. Every month or so Henry and Irina, often with

Philip and Cicely Hendy, would repair to the Ash home at Great Hallingbury for Sunday lunch or dinner. Over beef and good claret, they might discuss who was England's second greatest painter if Turner was accepted as No. 1. The claims of Stubbs, Constable, Gainsborough would be discussed with passion and humour.[40] When the Ash family moved to Devonshire in the 1960s they left a hole in Henry's life.

On the Côte d'Azur Henry seemed for once to forget his compulsion to work. There were expeditions on the boat which Ash shared with some friends. The sculptor was an entertaining companion, his host recalled: 'We'd go on picnics on the boat and he'd institute competitions to see who could blow the melon pips the furthest.'[41] They went to Monte Carlo, the Moores taking a fixed sum to gamble with. Henry soon lost his. Irina put hers on the number 10 and won a large sum, stopping there and then. The jellyfish rather spoiled the bathing, especially for Mary.[42]

Being keenly interested in philosophy as well as art, Ash has long ruminated on the true significance of Henry's work, which he collected in a modest way. His conclusion, argued roughly on the following lines, is that it is the opposite of humanistic:

> Since the time of Descartes and the Enlightenment, man has sought dominion over the natural world, not least through science and technology. In our century that attitude has begun to change. The Quantum Theory has undermined the old physics because it expresses the mutual dependence of the observer and the observed. Man's consciousness of his degradation of the environment has further emphasized this sea change in attitudes. By ambiguously mingling man and nature in his forms, Moore is saying that the self is part of the world, not separate from it. For this reason too, the individuality of a face is of no importance to him. Seeing a characteristic Henry Moore well sited in a natural environment, the observer is conscious of a three-way relationship between himself, nature and sculpture. All three are part of the same whole. In a museum, where the observer is consciously detached from the object, the sculpture cannot come fully alive. Moore's work thus reflects a historic shift in awareness and contributes to it.[43]

Because such thoughts are not easy to express in accessible language, it is all too easy to dismiss them as esoteric and obscure. Yet even if they often raise many questions – for example: are Moore's best pieces necessarily those which look best in nature? By no means so, surely – they can, like Erich Neumann's, prove highly illuminating. Genuinely fresh thought about Moore's work has been rare.

Had Henry himself been more cerebral and intellectual, that 'deep well' of his inspiration would no doubt have been shallower. He preferred ideas with clear outlines, such as that great creative men have also been great human beings, or that epic novelists were superior to more psychological ones ('Oh Flaubert – Balzac's your man, he's got real sweep,' he once told a neighbour's son revealingly). He enjoyed arguing, loved information, but was loath to change his mind on big issues, and he could be very dogmatic. It was perhaps a way of guarding the inner sanctum of his mind: he needed his true mental energy for his work. As he became more and more famous and the object of endless pilgrimages and interviews, his affability rarely flagged but he mentally economized by retelling the same old stories about his evolution as an artist, occasionally tossing in a fresh morsel for the connoisseur.

Judging an Auschwitz memorial

On one episode he seems never to have touched. Perhaps it was too painful, too first-hand, involving as it did a journey to Auschwitz, the vast extermination camp near Cracow in southern Poland where more than 4 million Jews, gypsies, Russians, Poles and other innocent victims of the Nazis' genocidal hatred were murdered in the biggest criminal act in history. His task – and it was an act of courage and self-sacrifice to undertake it – was to serve as chairman of an international jury which had been set an almost impossible task: to choose the winner of a competition for a monument to those mass murders, which had reached their peak only fifteen years previously.

Could any work of art commemorate such suffering, let alone such a crime? Six hundred and eighty-five artists from thirty-one countries took part in the competition, sending 426 projects for Moore and his fellow judges to consider. One of the latter was the French art critic Pierre Courthion, who later recalled, in true Gallic style, the sculptor's belated arrival at Auschwitz:

> Out of breath, fatigued and flustered because he had refused the plane for the train, he was six days behind us. Not very tall, closed in his language, hesitating before each word, his eyebrows lifted, the nose short, the eyes bright but sad, he profiled his imperial Irish face, miraculously escaped from the coal-mines of Yorkshire, against the barracks of the old death camps.[44]

Doubtless Henry had preferred to avoid the initial winnowing process, but there is no reason to believe that he missed the main judging days at the end of April 1958. With him went his Hertfordshire neighbour and friend, Constantine FitzGibbon, whose book on the London Blitz, illustrated with some of Moore's shelter drawings, had been well reviewed when published the previous autumn. Being an accomplished linguist, he was able to interpret for Henry when necessary. A few days after their arrival he described something of what they had seen in those 'ten square miles of hell' for the *Observer*:

> The five crematoria were blown up by the Germans just before they left, but the ruins, each as big as a London tube station, remain. Most of the wooden huts were burned, and a forest of brick chimneys stretches away for miles. Mountains of children's shoes – the ones not worth exporting to Germany and selling in the shops – are still to be seen, tons of human hair shaved by other prisoners from the heads of gassed women, are here, as well as bolts of cloth into which hundreds more tons were woven. It is preserved, all this disgusting horror, because it is believed that what happened here must never be forgotten.[45]

A method had been devised of hiding the nationality and identity of the competitors. Of the seven entries short-listed, three were from groups of Poles, three from Italians, and one from a solo West German. Having led his colleagues in this exhausting task and returned after a few days to his Hertfordshire haven, Henry went to Paris for a second session of the jury to Paris that November. It was held at Unesco headquarters, with him again in the chair. This time the short-list of six was whittled down to three: two Italian groups, one Polish. In a statement which he made at the end of this session, Moore touched on the question of whether a work of art could express the emotions engendered by Auschwitz:

> It is my conviction that a very great sculptor – a new Michelangelo or a new Rodin – might conceivably have achieved this. The odds against such a design turning up among the many maquettes were always enormous. And none did. Nor were any of the purely architectural – or predominantly architectural – projects fully satisfactory . . .[46]

Did his reference to a new Michelangelo or Rodin mean that he had not been able to prevent his own fecund imagination from toying with a solution? Yet not even he could have hoped to succeed. With a few exceptions like the falling and mutilated warriors, the direct expression of emotions had rarely been among his aims, and at Auschwitz the scale was too vast.

Each of the three final schemes was found to have a drawback. The exceptionally brilliant Polish project would, in the eyes of the former inmates represented on the committee, have too drastic an impact on the site. One of the Italian groups concentrated on a single element of the tragedy, the sealed trains which delivered the victims. The other was felt to lack emotional depth and would cut the camp in two. Eventually the jury, which also included two architects, decided that a worthy memorial was more important than choosing a winner. The three finalists were urged to fuse together their best ideas. The project resulting from this collaboration was adopted at the third and final jury meeting in Rome in May 1959, but without Moore's presence: he had written ten days earlier explaining that he was not well enough to attend. Conceivably he had concluded that he was being used to keep alive hatred of West Germany. The cornerstone of the monument was not laid till April 1965, and it was unveiled two years later.[47]

Moore's chairmanship of the jury may well have been a factor in the decision of the Polish authorities to permit an exhibition of his work to be shown in Warsaw and other Polish cities eighteen months later. His working-class origins also helped to make his work more ideologically acceptable: even though Poland had benefited from a mild political thaw since Gomulka's return as party leader in 1956, the impact of Moore's sculpture on the battered and culturally starved nation was bound to be electrifying. Leaving aside the post-war tour of modern British art from the Tate and his own début in Tito's Yugoslavia, it was the first Henry Moore exhibition in the communist world. The Poles soon showed their appreciation.

Thirty sculptures and as many drawings were involved, brought over by the British Council in association with the Ministry of Culture's Central Bureau of Art Exhibitions. In the first week at the Zachenta Gallery in mid-October 1959, attendance averaged 1,300–1,500 a day, breaking all records, and catalogues sent for the entire tour sold out before the exhibition closed in Warsaw. A Polish newsreel film was made of the exhibition, and a documentary film about Moore's work which incorporated BBC material was packed out at every showing.

Critical coverage was voluminous if divided. The official news agency PAP probably reflected public opinion accurately when it reported that the show had provoked 'great interest, warm admiration and expressions of condemnation and even indignation'.[48] As we have seen, such a combination of reactions was almost universal at this time, though the intensity of enthusiasm varied widely. For Ignacy Witz, art critic of the newspaper *Zycie Warszawy*, it constituted 'a virtual discovery of his incontestable greatness, his individuality … this great creativeness'.[49] Reproductions had given no idea of the dimensions or range of Moore's work, he wrote; nor indeed had the replicas and travesties made by Polish sculptors who believed that imitating him was 'an obligatory even if transient stage of their development'. Interestingly, given that Western critics often saw much death and decay in Moore's work, Witz admired his 'praise of life, his affirmative attitude', expressed not so much in themes like mothers with children or family groups as in his attitude to matter and medium.

The same enthusiasm greeted Moore's work when it passed on to Cracow, Poznan, Wroclaw, and Szczecin. The five-month tour had its political overtones. Visiting it was one way for Poles to show what they thought of official attacks on the decadence of Western culture. The British Council representative commented, rather oddly, that a major industrial organization launching a new product on the market could scarcely have exceeded the publicity Moore had enjoyed, and his was all free. Even before the public had seen his work Moore had been a legendary figure in Poland, he reported to London. 'Now it seems to us that he stands on a pinnacle apart, and what Dame Margot Fonteyn achieved for Britain last May [in Poland] in the world of ballet, Mr Moore has now accomplished, through his exhibition, in sculpture.'[50] Every such triumph helped build up Moore's formidable international reputation. When Cracow's Society of Friends of the Fine Arts sent Henry a gold medal and parchment shortly after his show there, brotherhood in art was affirmed across the ideological divide.

In June 1958, just a few weeks after his visit to Auschwitz, Moore had paid his first (and only) visit to the west coast of the USA. The main object had been to receive an honorary degree at Harvard, his first from an American university. From there he crossed the country to spend a weekend in San Francisco discussing the possibility of providing a major piece for a large new headquarters building for the International Longshoremen's and Warehousemen's Union. It was quite a coup by the architect, Henry Hill, to have persuaded the sculptor to come so far: however beautiful San Francisco might be, sightseeing was never high on Moore's priorities. In the course of his brief trip he also squeezed in a visit to his old friend of the late 1930s, the painter and collector Gordon Onslow-Ford, still in possession of the great 1939 elmwood *Reclining Figure*. The Long-shoremen's project came to nothing. Correspondence continued until 1960, but Henry seems to have considered the site unsuited to a large sculpture, and none was bought for that spot.[51]

Since he retained an innocent, schoolboyish enthusiasm for actors and show business ('There is something glamorous about film stars that makes one treat them as something special,' he told a Californian friend),[52] it is surprising he never visited Los Angeles. Hollywood and its environs teemed with Moore collectors and admirers, among them Burt Lancaster, Billy Wilder, Vincent Price, Hal Wallis, and Ray Stark. Despite many invitations, he resisted the potentially time-consuming embrace of the film world. Catching stars on the move in England was another matter. One who came to Hoglands in early September 1959 was fellow Yorkshireman Charles Laughton, a considerable collector since the 1930s of Impressionist and modern art. Actor and sculptor had admired each other for many years, and with Laughton's agent Taft Schreiber, they all had lunch together at a nearby restaurant. Later they went up to see the famous Laughton rendering of King Lear with the Royal Shakespeare Company at Stratford-upon-Avon. Taking Mary backstage afterwards, they found him lying on a couch, exhausted. Though a year younger than Moore, he died just two years after that visit, aged sixty-two.

For at least thirty years Henry could and did meet almost anyone in the arts and public life of his country who might interest him, and many of their equivalents in America too. Like most successful people, he admired success in others, providing it was accompanied by other qual-ities. But he rarely dropped names, and regarded almost any expression of opinion, however nondescript the source, as of interest, especially from children's fresh minds. With Irina as a corrective, he achieved a good compromise between his own gregariousness and his compulsion to achieve.

Chapter XIV

Good causes, big dealers, and Caro's thrust

1959–62

Many of those whose heart is, politically speaking, on the left lose their idealism in middle age and move to the right. Henry Moore never did. He remained a moderate Socialist, disgusted by the revelations about the Soviet Gulags and by the invasion of Hungary in 1956 (as by the Suez adventure), and loyal to leftish, liberal and humanitarian causes. For those involved in such issues, the late 1950s and early 1960s were heady years. Not since the 1930s had artistic and intellectual consciences been so active, and few prominent citizens can have signed as many letters to newspapers, principally *The Times* and *Manchester Guardian*, as Moore. The greater his fame, the more desirable his signature and the more duty-bound he felt to add his name.

Twenty years on, it is an almost Proustian evocation of lost times (and some lost causes) to recall the issues which attracted Henry's sympathy and signature. Starting in August 1955, they included: the abolition of capital punishment; the threat to Hungarian intellectuals; the defendants in the South African Treason Trials; nuclear testing by the (then) three nuclear powers; Lord Stansgate's struggle to shed his title and revert to being Anthony Wedgwood Benn, Labour MP; opposition to the Commonwealth Immigrants Bill; imprisoned Mexican intellectuals, including the painter David Siqueiros; the banning of bachelors from diplomatic postings abroad (on security grounds); restrictions on the liberty of Polish intellectuals (in 1964); and support for a multi-million pound conference, entertainment and arts centre in Covent Garden, happily stillborn: Moore was to have sat on its general council.[1]

But above all, this was the bright dawn of the Campaign for Nuclear Disarmament. CND was formed in 1958 largely as a result of the huge response to an article in the *New Statesman* in the previous November by J. B. Priestley called *Britain and the Nuclear Bomb*.[2] In 1960 Moore, who had remained friendly with Priestley and his wife, the archaeologist and writer Jacquetta Hawkes, was invited to become a founder member of the Committee of 100, an activist body officially launched that October with Herbert Read among its members and show business strongly represented. There was, however, none of Read's anarchist streak in Moore, who recoiled from the thought of 'direct action' as envisaged by the committee and declined the invitation:

> I said no because I thought it would be the wrong kind of propa-
> ganda for the idea ... civil disobedience would turn more people's
> sympathy away from the anti-nuclear thing than it would gain ...
> But anyhow I think it is necessary for the protests to be made, even
> if they're wrong-headed, to show that there are people who are not
> going to let things slide without expressing their feelings about
> them.[3]

Others might let off steam and break the law. Sculpture would remain his own chief form of expression. Yet CND retained his sympathies.

The same towering public reputation which made Moore desirable as a supporter of leftish causes made him irresistible to the most dynamic art dealers to have emerged in London since – well, Lord Duveen perhaps. By the late 1950s Marlborough Fine Art had established an extraordinary ascendancy in the London art world. The firm's origins went back to the Second World War, when Frank Lloyd and Harry Fischer, both refugees from Vienna, had met as volunteers in the Pioneer Corps, peeling potatoes. They got on well, and Lloyd said to Fischer: 'We will start up a business together after the war, because you have such an honest face.' They began with a mixture of antiques, rare books, and art in 1947. By 1950 they were already in Bond Street as Marlborough Fine Art. Their first big break came a few years later when they acquired the last complete set of Degas bronzes, including the little dancer in her muslin tutu who had featured in the Tate affair. In 1959 came the sale of thirty of the finest Impressionist and modern paintings from the collection of the Norwegian shipping magnate Ragnar Moltzau to the Staatsgalerie in Stuttgart for a reputed $10 million, other outstanding Moltzau items finding American homes. Those sales made the gallery a force to be reckoned with on the Continent.

Fischer, Lloyd and their partner David Somerset had complementary abilities: the handsome Somerset, heir to the Duke of Beaufort (which he now is) and married to the Marquess of Bath's daughter, moved naturally among the landed and pictured aristocracy, and was friendly with such foreign tribes of the very rich as the Agnellis, Niarchoses, and Kennedys. Lloyd had a brilliant business mind, while Fischer contributed charm and a wide knowledge and love of art, reinforced by his third wife Elfriede, a Berliner whose father had founded the art book publishing house, Rembrandt-Verlag. 'Harry really loved paintings,' Moore recalled. 'He wasn't just dealing for the money. He had good taste and he helped me a lot. I had some very good times with him.'[4]

Their first business contact took place, according to Fischer, when two of Moore's lead pieces from the 1930s were brought to Marlborough Fine Art for sale. Fischer telephoned Henry to tell him about them and to ask his permission to have a limited edition of bronzes cast from them, as a joint venture. The sculptor found the suggestion admirable.[5] Doubtless he had already been favourably prejudiced towards Marlborough by their exhibitions, at that stage mainly of Impressionists, and by Fischer's acquaintance with Valentin in pre-war Berlin. The Bond Street triumvirate had realized that more and more good Impressionists and post-Impressionists were leaving the market and being frozen, commercially speaking, in museums. So they decided to take on contemporary artists like Moore, Pasmore, Sutherland, and Bacon – selling a Bacon at that stage was far from easy. The first Moores to be seen at Marlborough were the recently completed *Falling Warrior* and *Seated Figure against a Curved Wall* in June 1958, just three years after his last show at the Leicester Galleries. That had been a crowded affair. The Leicester was too even-handed: one artist, one room, even if it were Moore. The Marlborough knew about display and had space. This mixed exhibition, not unflatteringly called *Nineteenth – and Twentieth – Century Masters*, also featured Braque, Munch, van Gogh, Picasso, and Klee.

Fischer's services to Henry included an introduction, thanks to his wife's connections, to the West Berlin bronze foundry of Noack, which had worked for German artists like Ernst Barlach and Käthe Kollwitz. For almost ninety years three generations of Hermann Noacks have led the firm on the same site in the bourgeois, suburban Fehlerstrasse. Once surrounded by cornfields, the foundry is now hidden behind apartments whose residents deplore the noise it creates. In the Nazi era the Noacks mixed courage with pragmatism, taking risks to do work for Barlach, yet ready to execute bronze eagles and busts of the Führer (often by quite good sculptors). When the war ended, the Russians dismantled and annexed the foundry's equipment, only to have it sent back from the USSR when they realized they could not match Noack's expertise. Hermann Noack III recalled:

The first thing they asked us to do was lettering for their huge cemeteries – millions of letters in cyrillic script; then many figures of soldiers, which are in Poland and elsewhere, and here in Treptow we did most of the huge (Soviet) memorial. The Russians paid in food at first: bread, vegetables, whole cows. It lasted till the currency reform of 1948, then they didn't have any more money ...[6]

All was not lost. In came the Americans and ordered a huge bronze cast of Dwight Eisenhower for West Point military academy. Business picked up again, and before Moore arrived on the scene, Noack remade Johann Schadow's vast Quadriga of horses and chariot on top of the Brandenburg Gate.[7]

According to the firm's records, Moore first sent over a plaster model, almost certainly of one of his draped figures, in 1958, and came over with Fischer the following year to inspect the result. 'All went very well. We surprised him,' Hermann III recalled. 'He was very struck by our gleaming patinas.' With blow-torch and a brush dipped into a pot of chemicals, Noack still does much of the patinating of art works himself. The mixture was passed down from Hermann I and Moore, intrigued, always called it the secret pot. Hermann II died of cancer shortly after that first visit, leaving Hermann III to take over in his mid-twenties. Moore soon established an excellent understanding with him and his craftsmen, exercising less supervision than one might expect, on Noack's evidence:

Generally he only came out for the larger ones. For the smaller ones, we did them as we thought they should be done. Often we changed quite a lot from the models: you live with it and you know how it ought to look – here we must polish a bit and so on. If it was to be sent direct from here to the customer, he would want to see it. He never changed anything, though he might say 'There the patina ought to be a bit brighter or darker' ...

The scope for error lay not so much in the form of the constituent parts of a large bronze, but in the accuracy and finesse with which these were assembled. With a lesser firm, for example, a head might perhaps be welded on at slightly the wrong angle, or the joins be too obvious. Randolph Meier, the master craftsman latterly in charge of the production side, said that occasionally (when Moore was in his prime) they would deliberately do something slightly wrong, like the easily remediable positioning of a two-figure piece, so the sculptor could have the satisfaction of saying 'That bit should come forward a little.'[8] Moore used Noack mainly for the larger bronzes, at which they excelled, while London foundries like Fiorini, Corinthian, and Morris Singer (which later moved to Basingstoke) coped well with the smaller ones. It was the shortcomings of Susse in Paris, then going through a difficult patch, and delays in delivery from British foundries which made Moore happy to use Noack. The patination could always be done or adjusted at Hoglands.

Moore was now formidably well set up, with Knoedler's as his dealers in New York, Marlborough in London, and Noack in Berlin as his main foundry. Fischer and Lloyd believed in keeping their big catch in front of the public eye, and in May 1959 proudly showed the bronze working model, almost eight foot long, of the Unesco carving. There it dominated another classy mixed exhibition, 'drawing attention away from the Picassos, the Matisses and the Klees ... and even from Cézanne's *Garçon Couche*', Alan Bowness wrote in the *Observer*.[9] Having seen in Moore's post-war work a trend towards the acceptance of Renaissance sculpture, the powerful bronze reassured the future director of the Tate that the 'hard-won ideals' of the 1930s were not being 'quietly surrendered'. The comment reveals how relatively low Moore's critical reputation had sunk.

Two-piece figure

In truth, nothing but an endless series of seated women had emerged from his studio since the Unesco figure, and the *Upright Motives* of 1955–6 had been his last significant new departure. By his standards, that represented a serious loss of momentum. A protean capacity for self-renewal was, however, to be a feature of Moore's later career. Perhaps sheer boredom with what he had been producing stimulated him to revive on a giant scale an idea he had had in the 1930s. As early as 1934 he had executed small carvings in which an abstracted version of the human body was divided into two, three and even four pieces. Now in 1959, when enlarging a maquette of a reclining figure, he realized that if he divided it into two parts – a torso and a leg section – many three-dimensional variations became possible, and from every different viewpoint the two pieces would have a fresh relationship.[10] The experiment completed [118], he found he had simplified and separated two characteristic features of his reclining figures: an upright head, neck, and sometimes torso which provided contrast to the horizontal direction of the whole sculpture, and a thrusting lower leg section which gave a sense of power.

Never before had Moore made the analogy between landscape and the female figure so clear. Indeed, while he was working on the uprearing and, from certain angles, decidedly phallic leg end, it began to remind him of a painting by Seurat of a cliff outlined against the sea, *Le Bec du Hoc* (1885), which he had long admired in Kenneth Clark's collection.[11] The same section was also strikingly reminiscent of Adel Crag, near Leeds, at which he had marvelled as a child. Four more *Two-Piece Reclining Figures* followed in 1960–2, followed by a series divided into three. In the former especially, the rugged, rock-like finish of the bronze emphasized, a trifle crudely perhaps, the landscape/woman metaphor. No. 2 features an eroded-looking arch which, as commentators never fail to point out, recalls Monet's rendering of *The Cliff at Etretat* (1883, in the Metropolitan Museum, New York), a favourite Impressionist subject. Although these two-piece sculptures of Moore's can now seem somewhat *lumpen* and self-conscious in their monumentality, they were an exciting new departure in the 1960s. The old inventive Moore was back.

Among his assistants at this time was another young sculptor who was to achieve a brilliant career. Phillip King joined the Hoglands team in January 1959, not long after finishing his studies at St Martin's School of Art in London under Anthony Caro, who effected the introduction. King could not help trying to introduce his own taste into the essentially mechanical process of enlarging maquettes into plaster models:

> Once you had finished, he would come in and make it his own, eradicating your influence ... He didn't criticize you for getting something out of proportion. He would take it from where you left it – in some cases he would alter it considerably. What I found interesting was when he altered it minimally yet there was a fundamental change. Often it was the head that he changed ... he told me that the angle of the head was the most crucial thing about a sculpture. The enlargements were supposed to be within two inches of the finished surface, but often one would go in front to the final surface itself with Henry Moore's approval; and when he worked it was always fascinating to me to see after a weekend the surface had dramatically come to life by making a slight depression here or smoothing down a protuberance there.[12]

In 1959 Moore started the penultimate in the series of elmwood reclining figures which are one of the greatest glories of his career. Majestic, sensual, tactile, even if lacking some of the mystery and power of her older sisters, she was five years in the making. In the early stages a crack appeared in her nether regions. It grew bigger, Henry became disheartened, and work stopped, later being resumed cautiously. Isaac Witkin, a young South African who was also to distinguish himself, was among those who worked on it after joining in May 1962. The extent of Moore's own involvement as carver is impossible to assess. According to King, his hands were 'not in a condition to do heavy work'.

In addition to the ex-art school students working for one, two or more years, there was (and still is) John Farnham, son of Frank Farnham, the master carpenter who lived on the green and built all Henry's later studios. John started off part-time, mainly making wooden bases or pedestals. Covered in copper sheeting, they looked like bronze but were cheaper and lighter to transport. Later, only bronze bases were used, and then it was his job to 'tap' the sculpture, making internal threads so it could be screwed firmly down at points of contact, thus preventing 'chattering'. He also did some patination: cleaning off surface oils, applying a coat of liver of sulphate, then adding a mixture of ammonium chloride and ferric chloride if the green finish was wanted. 'The way you do it, stippling it on with brushes, will give you lots of different colours,' he explained. 'It gives off some fumes and could be a health hazard if you didn't take care.'[13] John Farnham also became expert in making all the complex arrangements for transporting heavy bronzes from Perry Green to distant exhibitions. Cranes came from a local firm which initially built them on to army surplus gun carriages: primitive contraptions which had to be bolted together at either end of the journey. Now they are telescopic: you just order the right size and tonnage. Lighter transport was provided either by a London firm specializing in fine-art packing or local general removers.

Although Moore had now reached the age when civil servants and many other employees are obliged to retire, he remained addicted to work. By this stage he had, social life and London engagements apart, no other pastimes, no inner resources not related to work, and he was too restless to read for any length of time. As he explained once:

> I get depressed when I am not working enough. In fact, working is a way of not becoming depressed. Of course there are times when I am disappointed at not achieving some particular aim. But I don't accept, for instance, the general idea that artists are unhappy people ... if you can concentrate on work, it is a terrific recompense ... to be obsessed with some vision and to have the continuous

opportunity of working to realize that vision could be looked upon as God's greatest gift to anyone.[14]

There was always so much still to be attempted, so many peaks to scale. The kidney troubles had been an intimation of mortality, sound though his health had since been. There were others of a distressing nature. In 1959 there occurred the death, aged seventy-one, of his closest friend, Peter Gregory, and also of Sir Jacob Epstein, aged seventy-eight. In the *Sunday Times* Henry paid tribute to the sculptor who had supported him when he was young and first faced the brickbats and howls of derision of the philistines; and in *The Times*'s obituary columns he lamented the passing of Gregory, the bluff, kindly Yorkshireman who had so generously supported contemporary art and poetry, touching too on his qualities as a travelling companion: 'never ruffled or moody or upset by difficulties and ... ever fresh to visit a place or site or building or gallery that might contain objects of beauty'.[15]

A memorial show of Gregory's collection was held that summer at the ICA in Dover Street, W1, which he had helped to found: it was an uneven collection, Henry explained in a catalogue introduction, because Gregory had so often been concerned to help unknown artists. Given first choice of six works from it, the Tate Gallery selected among others two touching little early Moore carvings, and to Henry himself Gregory bequeathed a drawing by Modigliani.

Of the four friendships which Henry always said were the closest of his mature life, with Gregory, Clark, Hendy, and Read, the first was the warmest and most disinterested. Certainly Gregory helped in his capacity as chairman of the publishers Lund Humphries, assisting the birth of the 1934 Read monograph and then initiating what would become the six-volume catalogue of all Moore's sculpture. But that help was modest and no doubt replaceable compared to the contribution of the two successive directors of the National Gallery and the best-known expounder of modern art in the English language: only the British Council did more to spread and legitimize Henry's fame, and then often with their help. Their friendship with Moore also helped their own reputations. Such mutual benefit did not make the affection less genuine: artists often grow closest to those who understand their work and provide moral support and intellectual stimulus.

In July 1959 Moore had also lost one of his bitterest detractors, with the death at eighty of Sir Alfred Munnings. Since their antagonism symbolized the old mutual contempt of academicians and modernists, it was piquant that in coming years racing scenes by the former president of the Royal Academy constantly appeared, quite coincidentally, in the same auctions as Moore's bronzes and often fetched similar sums, even when they climbed into six figures.

A cherished link with his childhood was severed the following year when Alice Gostick, with whom Henry had kept in touch, died at her house in Sussex, aged eighty-seven. Touchingly but inappropriately, she left her house to her ablest pupil once her companion had died. The success whose roots she had nourished gave him little choice but to sell it.

By 1960 Henry had not had a one-man show in England for five years, a measure of the impact of the Unesco carving on his worthwhile output. An exhibition in December 1959 at the Arts Club in Chicago, consisting of thirty-eight of his sculptures and forty-three drawings drawn from private and public collections in the locality, demonstrated the strength of his growing American following. Two months earlier he had even made it to the cover of *Time* magazine, with a long profile inside dominating an assessment of what *Time* saw as an international renaissance of sculpture as an art form. Other sculptors featured were Picasso, Lipchitz, Giacometti, Manzù, Calder, and David Smith.[16]

Touring the Continent

The British Council had not been idle on Moore's behalf either. In 1959 it sent medium-sized shows of his work to Portugal and Spain. Since both were still dictatorships, the sculptor would not visit them. In the same year a smaller exhibition of fifteen sculptures and thirteen drawings gave the Japanese their first good look at his work, and brought Moore the oddly named Foreign Minister's (and top) prize at the Fifth International Art Exhibition in Tokyo. From the Metropolitan Art Gallery in the capital it went on to eight Japanese cities, including Hiroshima and Osaka, in most of them being squeezed ingeniously in the Japanese fashion into the galleries of department stores. No doubt the considerable popularity of this Japanese début laid the ground for Moore's later reputation there.

The Henry Moore exhibition which the Council showed on the Continent from May 1960 was its biggest to date. With fifty-five sculptures and sixty-two drawings it was to visit Hamburg, Essen, Zurich, Munich, Rome, Paris, Amsterdam, Berlin, Vienna, and Copenhagen. Moore and British prestige were not the only beneficiaries. In the British Council, Marlborough Fine Art had a state-supported public-relations operation on behalf of their client which the largest multinational corporation might indeed have envied. Trade followed the flag. From now on, in any prosperous city where Henry Moore's work was doing its bit for Britain, there would be Harry Fischer at the opening, and very often Harry Brooks of Knoedler too. Fischer, with his proprietorial manner and tendency to flap, was not always welcome. For example, Peter Powell, a British Council representative in West Germany, objected to the way the dealer behaved as if he had invented Moore 'whereas the Germans had known about him for years!'[17] The cream of local museum authorities and enthusiasts attended such official openings. How could Fischer resist all those wonderful contacts and all that reflected respectability? No wonder so many German cities ended up with a Henry Moore bronze in a main square, often sold by Fischer.

Hamburg had come a long way since the ill-starred 1950 exhibition, and the Hamburgers had recovered their traditional Hanseatic anglophilia. The director of the Kunsthalle, Alfred Hentzen, had admired Moore's work while still a prisoner-of-war in England in 1946. The two men had become friendly during his previous curatorship in Hanover, where he had installed the earlier British Council show of 1953–4.[18] Now in Hamburg he laid on a teutonically formal opening, with speeches lasting one and a half hours. Though the hall held 700 people, many had to be turned away. Press coverage was extensive and respectful, some headlines giving the flavour: 'Genius and Commonsense' (*Der Tagesspiegel*, Berlin); 'The Picasso among Sculptors' (*Lübecker Nachrichten*); 'Henry Moore – a Real Revolutionary' (*Hamburger Echo*); 'Half Man, Half Cliff' (*Neuss-Grevenbroicher Zeitung*). Visitors totalled 23,000 in six weeks. In Munich, where Henry did not attend the opening, though Fischer did – and Herbert Read gave an address beforehand – visitors topped 28,000 in five weeks.[19]

Paris reacted tepidly this time. The Musée Rodin was an unfortunate venue. Some of Rodin's works in the former chapel had to be left in place under the terms of his bequest. Moore was a well-known and respected figure, the British Council man reported mutedly, but he was not accepted by French taste without considerable reservations, and for the young he had no novelty value. His work seemed to be better understood and appreciated in northern countries.

The point, a good one, was amplified shortly after the Berlin opening by the art historian Will Grohmann, who had published a book on Moore's work in 1960. The Germans understood this English artist better than any other nation, he wrote in a Berlin newspaper. 'Moore is in the last analysis a man of the north, of a quality indeed that we have met hitherto only among the greatest English poets.'[20] (Yet the Yugoslavs, Greeks, Italians, Spaniards, Mexicans, and Venezuelans either had or would prove to be among his most enthusiastic admirers.) At the Berlin opening in the newly built Akademie der Künste, designed, suitably, by a former British Council scholar, Moore was perhaps startled to hear himself pressed into the ideological struggle: his work was, the British ambassador from Bonn, Sir Christopher Steel, told the private viewers, an expression of 'the Christian culture of Western Europe' and a 'symbol of Western unity and cultural life'.[21]

One of the purposes of bringing the Moore show to Berlin was to make an impact on the Soviet zone of Germany, within which West Berlin formed an enclave of freedom and prosperity. Henry had arrived (with Harry and Elfriede Fischer) on 21 July 1961 at a time when East–West tension was high. East Germany's Communist leadership had been losing the ideological battle with the West, and many of its best-educated and trained citizens had been voting with their feet for freedom. In the first week of the Moore exhibition, East Berliners helped swell attendance to 10,000, but the political climate was so thundery that Moore was advised to abandon a trip to the Pergamon Museum and its archaeological glories in the Eastern sector. Soon after his departure, in the night of 12–13 August, the infamous Wall was built. The chink in the Iron Curtain was closed. Hard by the border though the Akademie was, the exhibition remained in place till 3 September, but attendance dropped, eventually barely doubling the first week's. Fischer feared that access to Noack's foundry would become too difficult. But despite periodic delays on the autobahn, the air, road, and canal links remained intact.

In the front line of the ideological war though they were, not all West Germans were fully seized of Moore's pivotal role as a symbol of Christian and Western culture. A few weeks after his *Draped Seated Woman* had been purchased and publicly installed in the Ruhr town of Wuppertal, the imposing bronze was tarred and feathered, a placard around her neck reading 'Woman on the shelf! One hundred frying pans could have been made out of this.' A Sunday newspaper columnist back home commented that on the same principle the *Mona Lisa* would make a very smart little canvas handbag.[22] There were protests too in spring 1961 when Stuttgart's city fathers acquired the draped figure's reclining sister [119]. Some Stuttgarters were particularly incensed by the smallness of the head, a common cause of complaint: Moore used this formal device to make the rest look more monumental. The *Stuttgarter Zeitung* called it

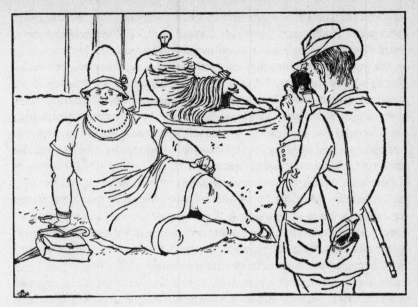

Art and Nature: 'Mariele, watch out. You're becoming fashionable.' *Stuttgarter Zeitung*, 6 May 1961

'more idol than ideal'.[23] Not long after being installed on a prominent stretch of civic grass between opera house and *Land* parliament, she was banished to a less exposed site in a park behind the state art gallery. In February 1984 she re-emerged to complement the front of James Stirling's new state gallery: a British sculpture for a British building.

Even over by the border with the German Democratic Republic, at the town of Wolfsburg known for its huge Volkswagen factory, the council was forced by local protests to reverse an earlier decision, taken by a narrow majority, to spend the entire annual budget for works of art, some £10,700, on a Moore reclining figure. Even so, by the mid-1960s West Germany already had civic or public Moores in Cologne, Essen, Recklinghausen, Hamburg, Hanover, Stuttgart, Wuppertal, and Munich. Eventually these eight were joined by others in Berlin (two), Bielefeld, Goslar, Freiburg, Duisburg (two), and Nuremberg, making at least fifteen in all. Only the USA, which has by far the most, and Britain would do better.

Rows over civic purchases were still in season at home: for example, in Huddersfield in Yorkshire. Henry had offered his *Falling Warrior* to the city art gallery for a paltry £1,500, yet many townsmen waxed indignant at so gross a misuse of public funds. The protests to local newspapers of 'Shocked', 'Magna est Veritas' and 'Warrior with Fallen Arches' were in vain. The council decided in November 1958 to buy it.

Perhaps the most entertaining controversy was, however, in Ireland. It had started in spring 1954 with the purchase by the Friends of the National Collections of Ireland of Moore's particularly cadaverous three-foot-long bronze *Reclining Figure No. 2*, done the previous year. Lady Dunalley led the protests at the society's annual meeting against the 'monstrosity', adding later that it obviously had leprosy and cancer. The ensuing 'cancer or art' debate caused much ink to flow while the Friends debated on whom to bestow their controversial largesse. When they picked Dublin's Municipal Art Gallery, it was rejected by the corporation's art advisory committee, along with a fine painting by Georges Rouault. Two years later this fatuous recommendation was rejected by the Dublin Corporation itself. In early May 1956 both the Moore and the Rouault went on view, to rejoicing by the philistine-bashers.[24]

Moore was not worried by such scenes. In their way, they were all good publicity. Yet he was very sensitive to attacks, even veiled and coded ones, from people he respected or liked. Criticism, implied or stated, was particularly painful when it came, as it now did, from someone he had, in a rather paternal fashion, helped to develop as an artist. Anthony Caro had been on a fateful journey to the USA in 1959. There he had communed long and fruitfully with the critic Clement Greenberg, who was no Moore admirer; the brilliant but doomed American sculptor David Smith, a virtuoso in welded steel; and the abstract painter Kenneth Noland. In 1960 he returned to his teaching post at St Martin's School of Art transformed and transforming. Back in the twenties and thirties, long before Smith, the Spanish-born sculptor Julio Gonzalez had worked, and then shown Picasso how to work, in welded iron. Now, inspired by Smith, Caro started to create abstract, open sculptures in welded and bolted steel, sometimes chunky and heavy at first, then increasingly light and even graceful, like abstract drawings in space. Some were painted in bright colours. All stood firmly on the ground, shorn of the theatricality of the pedestal. Caro's influence was pervasive. He and his colleagues and students at St Martin's set about questioning the basis of sculpture, rather as the pioneering modernists had done at the beginning of the century.

Caro had taken sculpture off its pedestal and placed it, unheroically, on the floor. Did he now feel tempted to do the same to his old hero Moore? The opportunity came when an exhibition of Moore's last ten years of work opened at the Whitechapel Gallery, then directed by Bryan Robertson, in November 1960. A well-informed adviser to the *Observer* newspaper had the mischievous idea of inviting Caro to write about it. The result was a masterpiece of taking with one hand and giving with the other. The article opened memorably:

> When you try to think clearly about Henry Moore you are deafened by the applause. The picture is not man-size, but screen-size. It is as if the build-up into a great public figure has got out of hand, and, like a film star's big 'front', has clouded our view of the real Moore.

Caro went on to pay tribute, as Moore had recently paid tribute to Epstein, for doing so much to win the battle for modern art in Britain, taking the brunt of uneducated insult and making many people think there must be something in modern art after all. All students of sculpture were indebted to him for providing an alphabet and a discipline within which to start to develop. His success had created a climate in which they could have confidence in themselves. However, Caro wrote, he felt Moore had paid heavily for his stardom. In his self-imposed isolation away from London and unable to have casual meetings with younger artists on neutral ground, Moore had grown out of touch with the post-war developments in art. Moreover, he went on:

> In his later works it sometimes appears that he is affected by a consciousness of his greatness. My generation abhors the idea of a father-figure, and his work is bitterly attacked by artists and critics under forty when it fails to measure up to the outsize scale it has been given. His own contemporaries, on the other hand, have constantly failed to offer any new or useful criticisms of his work, perhaps because his real success seems in some way to justify to them their own comparative failure. There is, in fact, for what you might call family reasons, a refusal by all of us in the art game to take Moore on his merits ... The truth is that, like that of most artists, the quality of his work varies considerably; at his best he has made some of the greatest twentieth-century sculptures.[25]

Caro seemed to be saying: 'Thanks a lot, Henry, you've done a great if patchy job; now it's time to hand over and fade out.' He had perhaps scored a valid point in touching on Henry's consciousness of his greatness; but there was much that was unfair in his feline attack. Even though Moore no longer lived in Caro's sacred metropolis, his teaching

appearances at Chelsea and the Slade, his trusteeships of the Tate and
National Gallery and his membership of the Arts Council's art panel and
of the Royal Fine Art Commission had brought him up to London once or
twice a week and kept him tolerably abreast of the art world. Did Caro's
generation expect to enjoy the benefits of Moore's success without facing
up to his continued activity? It was not Henry's way to defend himself
publicly on such an occasion; but his friends remember that he was hurt
by Caro's venture into journalism. He rated loyalty highly. His former
assistant, being more intellectual in his approach, probably felt that
personal feelings should not block the path of ideas. Happily the art critics
did not follow Caro's lead. 'The most profoundly disturbing, exhilarating,
presence-haunted single room in London at the moment is the great
light-filled hall of the Whitechapel Gallery, where sculptures by Mr Moore
done during the last ten years are assembled ...,' wrote the youthful
David Thompson of *The Times*.[26] An exhibition of Moore's early carvings
was even more warmly received at Marlborough Fine Art in June 1961 –
the gallery's first big effort on his behalf. Broadly speaking, the critics
always preferred the more personal, involved and craftsmanlike flavour
of the early carvings to the public Moore of the big bronzes.

It was entirely natural and healthy that Moore's reputation should
oscillate within the art world (that is to say, the world of contemporary
art). When a reputation becomes as great as his, it invites attack, and
younger artists were almost bound to see it as an obstruction. Moore's
work had been in the doldrums. The climate in the art world was
changing rapidly. Caro had chosen his moment well. Yet even as his
darts were thrown, Moore was returning to form. The two-piece series
was under way. In 1960–1 he completed a major bronze, seven feet
long, which movingly fused together three recurring obsessions: reclining
figure, mother and child, internal and external forms. In this *Reclining
Mother and Child*, the pierced, hollowed-out, and almost abstract mother
cradles her tough little abstract infant in a wonderfully tender protective
gesture. Then in 1961 came another stylistic breakthrough: the use of
thin, sharp forms. He had always admired the shapes of bones, some
knuckly and jointed, others lightweight, fine yet strong, like the breast-
bones of birds. Some he found buried in the garden, some he even saved
from the stewpot. One such bone led him to make *Seated Woman: Thin
Neck* early in 1961, then to use the same thinness throughout a figure.

The result was *Standing Figure: Knife-Edge*. The original maquette
consisted simply of a piece of sawn shoulder bone a few inches long, with
a bit of plasticine added for the head, and another to form a base [128].

He gave it for enlargement to a young sculptor of French Canadian origins, Roland Piché, who lived about forty miles away in Essex and at this stage did some contracted-out work for Henry. 'I remember the plasticine head fell off as I was carrying it and I had to pop it back on,' he recalled.[27] From such modest origins one of Moore's most attractive conceptions [129] sprang; but as Piché pointed out, it was not just a matter of sticking a piece of plasticine on a bone fragment: 'It's the ability to recognize that matters and the connection that makes the metaphor work.' Piché's enlargement was to just over five feet tall; then it was almost doubled in height and an edition of seven was made of each size. With its upwards-rising, almost dancing movement it is reminiscent of the so-called *Victory of Samothrace* in the Louvre, and at one stage Moore called it Winged Victory. The contrast between the knife-edged torso and the more rugged lower part provides intriguing alternations of thick and thin as the viewer moves around it.

Few of Moore's works depend more heavily for their full impact on the right setting. When the author visited the Hirshhorn Museum in Washington, a cast of the smaller size was looking waif-like and forlorn by the disused fountain in the courtyard; and it is hard to believe that the large version is ideally sited in the lobby of the MCA tower at Universal City, Hollywood. This elegant if slightly sweet piece, which seems ready to soar off into the air, needs a natural setting for its completion. In Greenwich Park it looks superb against the sky and a staggering view of London; it probably looks very happy against trees in a carefully created setting in St Stephen's Green Park in Dublin where, amid the usual controversy, it was unveiled in Moore's presence in 1967 as a memorial to the poet W. B. Yeats; and if the proud owner is to be believed, it looks marvellous in the garden at Winston Salem of Gordon Hanes, a North Carolina businessman. Sending the sculptor some photographs of the bronze, he wrote:

> As you see from the long shots taken under the oak tree, she bursts upon the viewer as you drive in and drop down a small hill. She is revealed feet first coming up until she stands alone and magnificent against the evergreen tree background. The feeling she engenders of awe and wonder and excitement and the funny flipover in the stomach I have felt with only one other sculpture ...[28]

Hanes went on to describe how, as a boy, he had been taken to the Louvre by an English teacher and they had come upon that same famous *Victory* (or Nike) *of Samothrace*, and his heart had stood still. 'Little did I dream that some day I would live with a sculpture that is, to me, as beautiful and as strong and as moving as that ancient Greek work.'

That aesthetic thrill was, in essence, what great sculpture was about. Looking for it, experiencing it, and coming back for more drew people in their tens of thousands to Moore exhibitions all over the world. For those lucky or determined enough to buy one of his works, there was the added excitement of ownership, even if often at considerable financial sacrifice. Any man who could give so much pleasure was fortunate, and Henry knew it. Such appreciative letters – and he received hundreds from his admirers – and the testimony of his friends meant much to him. The philistines might bay, fellow artists or critics might snipe. The struggle to produce good work was its own reward, the appreciation of public and friends a welcome bonus.

Chapter XV

The Lincoln Center piece
1962–5

Looking back at Moore's immensely long career, it is striking how many of his best-known large public bronzes date from the later part of it. How late is 'late Moore' when he went on working into his early eighties? The emergence of the first two-piece figure in 1959 seemed to mark a moment of regeneration. Alan Bowness sees the completion of the Unesco figure in 1958 as the watershed, marking the end of a period in which Moore had regarded himself as a public sculptor, conscious of his social role, and the beginning of a new, more personal late period. From then on, in Bowness's interpretation, Moore was more inclined to please himself, exploiting the possibilities of working on a grand scale now open to him as a successful sculptor, indifferent to fashion and caring little what others might think.[1]

This theory, though persuasive, abounds in paradoxes. If Moore's late work is more personal, it is more personal to Moore rather than to the public, since the average Moore fancier would probably consider a work like the *King and Queen* or *Warrior with Shield* more personal than the increasingly abstract pieces on which the sculptor was now to embark. It is also undeniable that the more emphasis Henry laid on the form rather than the content of his work, the more ideally suited it came to be as a foil to modern architecture. Even one of his giantesses might not be able to stand up to a strong building. Writ sufficiently large, the rounded geometry of his later abstractions added the softening touch that so often seemed desirable for the new corporation headquarters, arts centre or campus. Thus the more personal, in Bowness's sense, the work became, the more liable it was to be prominently displayed in public.

In the three fertile years of 1962 to 1965, Moore was to produce a wide range of fresh conceptions which were either created with a contemporary architectural setting in mind or which sooner or later, for better or for worse, were inserted into one. The two-piece reclining figure for the Lincoln Center [136] was a straightforward commission. Others, like the *Knife-Edge Two Piece* [131]; the *Arch* [138]; the *Locking Piece* [135]; the *Archer* [139]; and *Nuclear Energy* [144] all became associated with specific architectural settings. These works have a toughness, a muscularity seen only fleetingly since the 1930s. In a number of them, as in much of Moore's later work, there is also a strongly erotic note which had been held in abeyance since the *Upright Motives*. They are very masculine.

Of no work was this truer than of the one which dominated the years 1962 to 1964: the *Reclining Figure* for the Lincoln Center, the most dynamic of Moore's two-piece interpretations of his favourite theme and, at twenty-eight feet tall and eighteen feet long, the largest – though in terms of mass and man-hours the Unesco figure is a comfortable winner. This unique bronze was commissioned for the new Lincoln Center for the Performing Arts, then being built on a fourteen-acre site in mid-town New York. Four buildings designed by different architects were to provide accommodation for opera, drama, dance, theatre, concerts, film festivals, and a library, grouped around a plaza. On one side of this open space, in front of the Vivian Beaumont Theater and Library Building, there was to be a large pool in whose waters a substantial piece of sculpture would be reflected.

The chairman of the Center's three-man art committee was Frank Stanton, President of CBS Inc., known as a perfectionist with a deep interest in design. He was supported by René d'Harnoncourt, director of the Museum of Modern Art, and Andrew Ritchie, director of the Yale University Art Gallery. At Stanton's first meeting in November 1961 with the principal architects – among them Eero Saarinen and Gordon Bunshaft of Skidmore, Owings and Merrill, who were working together on the Vivian Beaumont building, Philip Johnson and Wallace Harrison (who had done the UN building in New York) – Moore was the unanimous first choice for the pool sculpture. However, when they later met again to confirm their decision, one by one the architects reported that other clients of theirs wanted a Moore in or near a building being designed or nearing completion.[2] Johnson had approached Moore already for a piece or pieces for his beautiful Seagram building. Bunshaft had visited the sculptor for the first time that spring in connection with a new downtown headquarters building for the Chase Manhattan Bank, and Henry had done some maquettes unsuitable for a sixty-storey building (Dubuffet's *Four Trees*, eventually chosen, was around forty feet high).

Anxious to head off these rival projects, Stanton hastened to Hoglands in December 1961. When he had explained his mission, Moore commented: 'Now I know why I was getting all those calls from architects in New York!' Stanton unrolled the plans in the sitting room and Henry exclaimed about the pool: 'It's as big as a cricket pitch!' (a tennis court would be nearer). Soon afterwards he had a massive nosebleed, and Irina remarked: 'Henry, you know that always happens when you get excited!' Stanton was asked to stay to lunch, a rare compliment to a stranger, and went back to New York feeling encouraged.

Though he kept in touch, much of the action now passed to Bunshaft, a large man with a gentle manner who was to become a close friend of the sculptor. Moore went out to New York in early March 1962, partly to see the site, partly to visit Philip Johnson, and partly in connection with a forthcoming first exhibition at Knoedler's. At Henry's insistence, Bunshaft accompanied him to Philip Johnson's country home, and on the way persuaded the sculptor that Johnson's idea of two Moores balancing each other by the Seagram building would make them look like candelabra.[3]

Before long the Lincoln Center commission was clinched and the fee agreed: $240,000, to come from the $1 million given to the Center specifically for the visual arts by the Albert A. List Foundation, List being a New Englander who had transformed a coal company into a wide-ranging conglomerate. The fee was to cover all costs. There were no restrictions on Moore's artistic freedom, and the chance to do something coming out of water was an attractive challenge. He suggested a two-part sculpture, and the idea was accepted. If they liked the outcome, they could have it.

In summer 1962 he made some small maquettes, enlarging the two that seemed most suitable to almost half the final size. Experiments in a small swimming pool built for Mary suggested that one rose more effectively from the water. Stanton and Bunshaft agreed with his choice, so he was ready to press on with the final enlargement. First, however, some practical difficulties had to be solved. He needed not only a studio big enough to take an object so vast, but some way of viewing it – in natural light – from all angles and from a considerable distance, since it would ultimately be seen in the middle of a largish pool. So he had built what looked like a Meccano-set hangar for a private plane, covered with transparent plastic which could be rolled up at the sides in fine weather. Around it he marked the size of the pool and of the plaza, and even ensured that the plaster model would face the sun at the same angle as in New York.[4]

With the help of four or five assistants, work was also proceeding on other major enlargements, such as the *Three-Piece Reclining Figure* (Bridge Prop), the *Locking Piece*, the *Archer*, and the large elmwood reclining figure. Disaster nearly struck the full-sized plaster model of the Lincoln Center piece in autumn 1963. Doubling the half-sized model produced an eight-fold increase in volume, and the crisis came when the two assistants involved, Robert Holding and Geoffrey Greetham, applied too much plaster to the top of the forward-leaning torso. Cracks appeared at the bending point, and the top part had to be propped up with a wooden support. Then, as the temperature dropped with unseasonal sharpness in December, there loomed the prospect of the water content of the fresh plaster freezing in the unheated hangar, causing the figure to shatter. An old stove with a gargantuan appetite for coal was rushed in and disaster averted.

Enlargement on this scale creates its own distortions, since the same parts will be viewed from a different perspective. In this instance the neck and head, which from below now looked shorter than intended, had to be made about a foot longer than the mathematical enlargement. Not until August 1964 was the great labour finished. Hermann Noack and several of his artisans arrived from Berlin to saw up and pack the torso section in eleven pieces for safe transport to Berlin, and a few weeks later Henry and his assistants did the same for the leg section. Before the two parts could be cast in bronze they had to be cut into sixty-five smaller pieces which would eventually be welded together.

It took Noack and his men almost a year to complete the task and patinate the bronze, which comes out penny-bright, down to a soft, greenish brown. Finally in July 1965 it was shipped by barge to Hamburg and thence by air to New York, where the two huge crates were dumped on the uncompleted plaza of the Lincoln Center. Two weeks earlier the New York City Art Commission had only narrowly (by five votes to four) approved its installation, along with a Sandy Calder stabile due to be sited 200 feet off. Opposing them both, the Parks Commissioner, Newbold Morris, observed that if he were forty years younger than his sixty-two years, he would 'go sit on a park bench and cry'.[5]

That summer of 1965, Henry and Irina had been staying at the Hotel Byron in Forte dei Marmi. Before flying to New York for the installation he spent a night in Rome. There he met Wolfgang Fischer, who was to accompany him in the absence on holiday of his father Harry. 'Have you seen the Giacometti exhibition at the Tate?' Fischer junior asked brightly over dinner, after they had clip-clopped over the Tiber in a horse and buggy to Trastevere. 'Yes, good but over-rated,' Moore replied. 'The famous dog with the hanging ears, for example. It's a copy from a Greek vase ... his elongation of the figure is Mediterranean art from the era before Greek sculpture. If only the critics went more often to the British Museum, they could put all this into historical perspective ... the great success of Giacometti in England comes from the painterly qualities of his sculpture.'[6]

A week in New York

Relaxing with the chianti, Henry mused aloud to Fischer that perhaps the week in New York would be the worst in his life. He had no real idea whether the proportions of the sculpture and the buildings would be right, he said. The position in the pool might not work, and the light might be wrong. Reality seemed pleasantly distant as they travelled first class across the Atlantic, soothed by TWA's caviar and vodka, Châteaubriand steak and burgundy, and a war film featuring that keen Moore-collector, Sophia Loren. Stanton and Bunshaft were at Kennedy Airport to meet them and ensure a swift, VIP passage through customs.

By now Moore was treated like royalty on such trips, with Fischer (normally Harry, this time Wolfgang) acting as equerry: buying tickets, briefing the chauffeur of the big black Lincoln limousine, taking him shopping, keeping cash at the ready for his needs, dishing out tips. In addition Fischer had to keep his ears open for all potentially useful gossip from the world of collectors, dealers, patrons, and architects, and prevent Henry from straying too far into the genial opposition camp of Knoedler's: Marlborough Fine Art had opened its own New York branch in 1963, as noted, and Knoedler's were in turn determined not to lose their grip on Moore's American market.

Next morning they all assembled at the Lincoln Center site. From the Stanhope Hotel there were Fischer, Hermann Noack, and an artisan called Grabert; then came the top-level triumvirate of Bunshaft, Stanton and Moore, who had been staying in a comfortable apartment provided by Knoedler's; two or three senior officials from the Lincoln Center; television teams and a CBS film crew covering the life history of the sculpture in a film called Henry Moore: Man of Form;[7] newspaper and magazine reporters and art critics. As for the two huge bronzes, they remained in their crates. The pool was in no state to receive them.

Though it had been lined with lead before being covered with the black, reflecting tiles, water had leaked into the offices below. The water's exit point was easy enough to see; where it went in was impossible to discover. Luckily no one then knew that the leaks would take three years to cure, during most of which time the pool would remain dry.

Moore's first reaction on seeing the site was of relief at the relative simplicity of the architectural background, he told John Canaday of the *New York Times*. But he was still anxious that his work would be dwarfed by its setting, and hoped that when installed, its reflection would give the viewer the impression of looking up into cave-like forms.[8] On the second day Noack and his assistant Grabert, maddened by the prevailing inactivity – was this the usual American tempo? – unpacked the two great bronze pieces to see what further work might be necessary on them. Moore was taken on a tour of the other Lincoln Center buildings, and signed a contract covering copyright and reproduction rights. By the following day he too was getting more and more impatient. That evening the two pieces were at last winched and bolted into position on their concrete supports. Fearing that his sculpture would sit too low in the water, Moore had earlier that day arranged for it to be raised several inches; a mistake, since the water level was never to be high enough.

When Henry returned to the site, slightly tipsy after dinner with the munificent Albert and Vera List, the great reclining figure was there, in position albeit waterless, and spotlit from the roof of the uncompleted Metropolitan Opera building. He was delighted, and walked round and round it, saying 'Yes, I think that will do.'[9] He climbed a staircase to see how it would look from there. 'Yes, it does look like a rock,' he exclaimed with pleasure. The Lists' young daughter was, however, not so impressed. Pointing to the torso end, she very audibly told the sculptor: 'I think this square part under the head is wrong. It does not fit. I don't like it!' The smiles of the Lists' guests, who had assembled admiringly, froze. Moore was equal to the occasion, laughing and saying: 'She is just like my daughter Mary, just like her!' And turning to her father he added: 'I always tell Mary not to get married too young. How old are you?' he asked the child. 'I am fourteen.' 'That's fine. You should wait to marry for another ten years.' To this she firmly countered: 'I don't think I can wait that long.'[10]

That weekend Moore relaxed at the art-filled home in the Hamptons, outside New York, of Gordon and Nina Bunshaft before flying back to Italy. Only a day or so after returning to Perry Green he was back in New

York for the formal inauguration of his work. The city was experiencing a severe drought, but enough water was acquired to give the reclining figure a reflection and to turn the arch under the torso into an elongated oval. Music was played, 500 guests assembled on folding chairs by the pool, while Henry sat with leading dignitaries on a platform at one end. Among old friends present were Kenneth Clark and Joseph Hirshhorn. Frank Stanton spoke briefly and elegantly, quoting a fulsome Clark dictum: 'If I had to send one man to another planet to represent the human race, it would be Henry Moore.' The city's Mayor Wagner presented Moore with a medallion on which was inscribed: 'To Henry Moore, one of the great creative geniuses of our time; his dynamic achievements are cultural expressions of universal significance and importance.'[11] The sculptor thanked him and everyone else in a one-line speech. Had there not been a newspaper strike at the time, there might have been some protests, since when the Vivian Beaumont Theater was opened a month later, a group of artists picketed the building with signs saying 'Insult to American sculptors – no Moore.'[12] On that basis, the president of the Lincoln Center commented, American composers should picket the Philharmonic Hall every time a work by Beethoven was performed.[13]

The chauvinist outburst was untypical, and Moore's bronze received a favourable press, unlike the center as a whole, which critics tended to consider over-conservative in design. For Ada Louise Huxtable of the *New York Times*, the strong, structural good looks of the theatre building with its pool and Henry Moore sculpture offered 'the only honestly contemporary vista in the place'; and in the same feature, John Canaday said the bronze 'occupies its pool so naturally it might have grown there'.[14]

Henry's assumption that the water would soon reach its correct level was unfortunately not fulfilled. To his great annoyance, the pool continued to be beset by problems. Even when these were resolved, the fact remained that his sculpture had been set too high. The error was not corrected until 1982–3, when the reclining figure was, in consultation with Moore, set eight inches lower in the water, and the bronze itself – not one of Noack's more robust castings – received some much-needed attention at the hands of the art restorers Christine Roussel Inc. As a form of anchorage, small openings had been made in the two sections, it transpired, and (apparently after Noack's departure) seven cubic yards of cement had been pumped in. This had held entering rain water or condensate at various internal levels. The water froze in New York's fierce winters, expanded and burst many of the welded bronze seams.

When Christine Roussel showed Moore photographs of the work in progress, he was so pleased that he asked how he could help. The Lincoln Center always needed money, he was told. 'Would £100,000 help?' he asked. It would, and with the good offices of the Henry Moore Foundation, it did.[15]

The floodlighting took rather fewer years to perfect, and a fine moonlit effect was eventually achieved. Despite all the tribulations, which again scarred the sculptor's attitude to architectural projects, the end product must be adjudged a considerable success. Like many of Moore's best works, the Lincoln Center *Reclining Figure* can be interpreted in several different ways. The torso is a mother looming over a boulder-like child. It is a male figure, legs parted, body braced for a thrust into the cleft bent temptingly below. It is a cliff rearing up over a stone island. Crackling with energy, it remained for Gordon Bunshaft 'probably the best piece Henry ever did'.[16] Much of its success is undoubtedly due to its being designed and tailored to a specific site, and it remained the only casting.

Two casts were made of the working model. One went to Vera List, who in autumn 1985 gave it to the new museum for the visual arts at the Massachusetts Institute of Technology named after herself and her husband. The other Henry retained, lending it on a long-term basis to the new Charing Cross Hospital in Hammersmith, west London, whose architect (Ralph Tubbs) he knew. In Hammersmith they do things rather differently from New York. Welcoming it in 1975 with the headline 'Our next mystery object is ... a work of art!' the *Acton Gazette*'s photograph showed a man pointing to the bronze rising from a small ornamental pool in front of the hospital, captioned: ' "Don't ask me what it is, mate, I'm only the head porter," says a mystified Mr Thomas Holder.'[17] All too near the road and pavement, it stands forlorn, etched against parked cars and plate glass by the hospital's front entrance. It must be among the worst-sited Moores in the Western world.

The sculptor's enthusiasm for working with Bunshaft, undampened by water problems and warmed by their developing friendship, was boosted by a visit immediately after the New York inauguration to the architect's native Buffalo, near the Niagara Falls. Moore had been urged to make the detour by Seymour Knox, the diminutive Maecenas of the Albright-Knox Art Gallery, in order to see the modern section of the collection in the wing designed by Bunshaft. The museum is remarkable for having just one, two or three of the finest examples of work by twentieth-century masters, rather than a larger, more uneven spread. Its Moore holdings, the first great elmwood reclining figure, the elmwood

Upright Internal/External Forms of 1953–4, and the first two-piece reclining figure, were typically selective. After inspecting both the old masters and the modern works, which are particularly well lit, Henry pronounced it 'a beautiful gallery – one of the nicest I've seen.'[18] An architect who could produce a museum building of that quality earned his respect. On his way home from Buffalo, Moore stopped briefly in Chicago to discuss a very large project at the university, to which we will come later. In his mid-sixties, his involvement with the USA was intensifying.

Honours and committees

There was not to be a major Moore in central London (the Time-Life carving apart) until 1967, though further out the London County Council did its best to make good the omission. In 1962 it installed a *Draped Seated Woman* on its Stifford Estate in Stepney, east London, where local children welcomed it as a climbing frame and target for bottle-throwing;[19] and the following year the LCC purchased, for £8,000, a cast of *Two-Piece Reclining Figure No. 3* for its Brandon Housing Estate in Southwark, south of the Thames. For the moment, honours were forthcoming, important commissions in England not.

The first honour to be bestowed might seem minor, but Moore prized it highly. In July 1962 he had returned to Castleford to be made a Freeman of his home town. It was his first visit since, just twenty years previously, he had spent those two weeks down the mines with his drawing pad. Before receiving the Freedom, he went back to Temple Street elementary school and was shown an old punishment book recording that he had received two strokes of the cane, for teasing some girls. The ceremony then took place in the assembly hall of Castleford Grammar School, as it now was, and he shared the honour with Jesse Dowding, a former chairman of the urban council who had worked forty years at the coal-face. Looking around the familiar old hall as the sonorous phrases about his international fame flowed from the mayor, Alderman Jack Smart, Henry might have spotted his old school friend Frank Ambler, now the school's deputy headmaster. For once Moore was obliged to make a proper speech of thanks in reply, and he spent some time hymning the beauties of the local slag heaps, those geometric, man-made mountains which, he reckoned, had made their impact on his work.[20] With the Freedom came a scroll, and an inscribed silver rose bowl.

His next honour came from Italy and took the not unwelcome form of cash. He learned that he had been awarded the Feltrinelli Prize by the sages of the ancient National Academy of the Lincei in Rome in May 1963. It was worth £14,400 (about £72,000 today), and President Segni of Italy himself performed the award ceremony at a full session of the academy that December.[21]

In August 1963 came the most distinguished of British honours, the Order of Merit. When, to general surprise, Graham Sutherland had pipped Moore to it in 1960, the sculptor had cabled: 'It's the very top of all.' Had Moore not received the CH in 1955, he might well have joined the Order of Merit earlier: the one inevitably delayed the other. Like the Garter, the Thistle and the Victorian Order, the OM is the unfettered and personal gift of the sovereign, its holders – never more than twenty-four – being 'such persons, being subjects of Our Crown, as may have rendered exceptionally meritorious service in Our Navy and Our Army or towards the advancement of Art, Literature and Science.' Although much discussed as a desirable innovation by Queen Victoria, it was instituted by King Edward VII in 1902, shortly after his accession, prompting a Cabinet minister of the day to comment to Lord Curzon: 'It is for savants and soldiers. Its chief objects are that it is worn around the neck and puts Edward VII on a par with Frederick the Great who invented a similar one!'[22] Of that, too, Moore was to become a member. Those whom he and the historian G. P. Gooch, aged ninety, now joined included Winston Churchill, the Poet Laureate John Masefield, the philosopher and mathematician Bertrand Russell, the architect Basil Spence, and the aged Bohemian painter Augustus John.

News of the honour came to Henry while on holiday in Dubrovnik, Yugoslavia. Uncharacteristically, he had arranged to go for a change of scene with Irina, Mary, now seventeen, and the erudite and amusing Cork Street art dealer, Heinz Roland of Roland, Browse and Delbanco and his wife Lilian. They had taken a boat from Venice to Split, subsequently staying at the Hotel Excelsior in Dubrovnik. Henry had left instructions with his secretary Betty Tinsley at Hoglands that no mail was to be forwarded. Yet there was a fat letter with big seals on it from Buckingham Palace. It stated that if he agreed to accept the honour, he should send a telegram saying 'Yes Moore' (or 'No Moore') to the Lord Chamberlain. Roland recalled: 'When Henry handed in a telegram saying 'Yes Moore', addressed to Buckingham Palace, the porter thought we were drunk.'[23] They went out to celebrate, and when they returned to the Excelsior they *were* a bit tight. Henry and Heinz danced together as the orchestra played *Ave Maria*.

At Kotor the bay had a backcloth of mountains and the trapped heat brought the temperature to a painful 40° centigrade. On Corfu, where the two families had separate bungalows, Henry kept saying: 'What wonderful olive trees! I must draw them,' but it was Mary who got out her sketchbook. Periodically the sculptor revealed the capacity for anxiety which lurked beneath his affability. When Roland had swum from the shore at Dubrovnik to a none-too-near island, he was beside himself with worry, Roland soon discovered. On Corfu he was reduced to a similar state when Mary, a lively and attractive girl, went off one evening with a Greek youth on the back of his motorcycle and stayed out late. The anxiety was natural, the extent of it striking. He was a possessive father.

The holiday was voted a success, and the following summer they went off again together, this time on a touring holiday through France. Moore showed a high degree of touristic zeal in visiting the interiors of châteaux, and Roland was struck by the liveliness of his mind. 'Now how many inhabitants do we think this town has, and what is its main industry?' he might say. They made their guesses and wrote them down before looking up the answers. 'He was always anxious to learn,' Roland recalled affectionately.[24] Yet the dealer had never met an artist so preoccupied with his position after his death. 'Who do you think is the greatest?' Moore would ask, and Roland sensed that the reply he wanted was: 'Michelangelo, Rodin, and Moore.' The obsession tinged his view of other sculptors. Brancusi was great, important, yes, but his range was too narrow, and the same went for Giacometti. From the Loire they revisited the caves of the Dordogne, then crossed the Cévennes and made their way down to Collioure, south of Perpignan, whence the Moores returned by public transport.

A few selected entries from Moore's typically crowded engagement diary for the subsequent weeks will show, pace Anthony Caro, just how far from being isolated at Hoglands he was. Between 13 September and 1 October, for example, he received a party of sixteen Czechs at home, a warm-up for an exhibition in Prague; met the architect Lord Llewellyn Davies on the piazza of The Times newspaper to discuss a project for a sundial; had dinner with Miró at the Tate Gallery; went with Graham Greene to the first night of Greene's play Carving a Statue, which was about a sculptor (after a party at the Ritz Hotel the author took Henry and Irina on a tour of Soho); dined with Maurice Ash; welcomed the dealer Charles Gimpel with Leigh Block, an important Chicago collector; lunched with Lawrence Gowing, principal of Chelsea School of Art, in

London and attended a Royal Fine Art Commission meeting; entertained the painter Ceri Richards and his wife Frances, old friends; attended an Arts Council meeting, lunched with Harry Fischer, and dined with the King's Road framer Alfred Hecht; and attended a meeting of National Gallery trustees after lunching with Tony Keswick and Philip Hendy at the Savoy Hotel.

The monthly meetings of the National Gallery's fifteen trustees were at least as stimulating as the Tate Gallery's equivalents, and involved none of the legwork of keeping in touch with contemporary artistic output. The trustees were a similar blend, drawn from art historians, artists, city gentlemen, and aristocrats who might, as Tony Keswick put it, be accustomed to coming down in the morning and seeing a Rembrandt or a Velasquez over their breakfast.[25] Lord Salisbury and the Duke of Devonshire came into this category; and naturally the art historians, like Sir Brinsley Ford and Denis Mahon, were specialists in Old Masters.

Moore was a trustee with only very short breaks from 1955, when he joined as the Tate's representative, to 1974. Although in these years no controversy reached quite such epic proportions as the Tate row of 1952–4, there was no lack of internal and public debate. Among the main issues with which Moore and his colleagues had to deal were: a re-crudescence of protests, at their fiercest in the late 1940s, over the National Gallery's picture-cleaning policy; the future of the magnificent Impressionist collection of Sir Hugh Lane, bequeathed both to the National Gallery and, in an unsigned codicil before he went down with the *Lusitania*, to the Dublin Municipal Gallery; the theft of Goya's *Portrait of the Duke of Wellington* in 1961, a few days after it had been acquired for the nation; the possibility of imposing admission charges; and, inevitably, a succession of controversial acquisitions, despite the inadequacy – lamented in every annual report – of purchase grants from the Treasury and the lack of fiscal inducements to donors.

Sir Philip Hendy, who was the National Gallery's director until 1967, was a bonny fighter, and Moore supported him during the often bitter cleaning controversy. The sculptor also came out publicly in his old friend's defence over two major acquisitions which attracted newspaper attention. The first, in 1961, was of two large, late Renoirs, *La Danseuse au tambourin* and *La Danseuse aux castagnettes*. 'Whoever doesn't like those girls doesn't understand what Renoir was trying to do,' Henry later wrote.[26] David Carritt, then the *Evening Standard*'s art critic, saw Moore's influence behind the purchase. So *that* was why the pictures were bought, he mischievously but probably not entirely inaccurately speculated: they might not be beautiful or typical, but they were the only Renoir girls who might have sat for Henry Moore. It seemed tough, he added, that future generations should be landed with these colossally expensive pictures (almost £200,000, now equivalent to some £1,200,000, for the pair) because they resembled the work of England's greatest twentieth-century sculptor.[27]

It all depended whether one liked late Renoir, of which the dancers were magnificent examples. Moore did, in part undoubtedly because it had the same monumentality which he hoped his own work had. So, *a fortiori*, he liked late Cézanne, and when four years later Hendy pulled off the considerable coup of acquiring one of the *Grandes Baigneuses* from an heir of Auguste Pellerin, Henry was on hand to sing its praises. There had been some startled comment at the price of £475,000 (around £2,500,000 today), and Hendy shrewdly installed the sculptor at the press view of this demanding work. To the *Observer*'s Nigel Gosling, Moore said he found its qualities even more interesting than those of the version in the Barnes Collection: with its drastic removal of the pastoral setting and the concentration of the figures, compressed into a narrow plane like seals on a ledge, 'it seems to express the big things about painting';[28] and to Eric Newton of the *Guardian* he praised its imperturbable dignity and monumentality – 'that strange quality that only the greatest artists possess'.[29]

Broadly speaking, Henry's fellow trustees recall him as an extremely valuable colleague whose views carried great weight, especially on such matters as hanging, lighting, wall decoration and, naturally, the artistic merits of possible acquisitions. As in other similar forums, he was not one to lead discussions, but he spoke quite frequently and did not mince his words, was always constructive and often persuasive. He was perhaps rather too inclined to support Philip Hendy, who was regarded by some of the more conservative art historians as not altogether sound and often eccentric in his ideas.[30] As we have seen, he believed in loyalty, and mutual support played a strong role in the Hendy–Moore friendship.

Moore's life on the high plateau of fame and success may seem enviable: satisfying creative work interspersed with agreeable, high-level contacts both at home and in London, and almost everywhere the acknowledgement of his achievements. But of course it was not as straightforward as that. Work might not be going well. He was sometimes in pain from an ankle which he had damaged playing tennis with Mary and then neglected. Dealers and collectors could be importunate, there were endless letters always waiting to be answered, difficulties over exhibitions, and much else. Sometimes he would seek refuge with local friends: intelligent, sympathetic people, but in the main not very interested in his sort of art. One such couple recalled:

> He used to come here in moments of strain, sometimes his face all pinched. He might ring up and say 'Can I come, I've had an awful day.' Then half-way through dinner, after he had drunk a bit, he would start telling corny Yorkshire stories ... He recalled, for example, that when they were living on top of each other in their little house in Castleford, he would hear his Dad saying to his mother 'Give us a little bit, then,' and she would blow out the candle. So for ever after he associated the expression 'Give us a little bit' with – blowing out candles! Our friends were always saying 'You know Henry Moore, do ask us to dinner with them one evening.' We never did. Perhaps that's one of the reasons they liked to come here.[31]

When the same friends went to dinner at Hoglands, usually with other people, there was generally an enormous joint of lamb, beef or ham. On almost the first such occasion, Henry started carving, then asked his friend to take over – 'You do it, I can't carve.' They started laughing, but their host could not see any connection between carving cooked meat and sculpting.

Despite their by now considerable income, the Moores continued to live in most ways quite modestly and frugally. Their only concession to affluence had been to get Frank Farnham to add, in 1959–60, a sitting-room extension to the back of the house and to begin gradually to cover the small wall-space not consisting of windows overlooking the garden with fine paintings and drawings: a Vuillard landscape, two magnificent pastels of women at their toilette by Degas, a sumptuous head and shoulders of a girl by Courbet.

Relations with assistants

The Yorkshire respect for money was noticeable in the working area. For example, when he was an assistant, Darryl Hill had been amazed to be asked to pull old nails out of boards so they could be re-used, yet a large sum might be spent on a new tool. With Roland Piché, Moore would negotiate the sums he owed for contracted-out work down to the nearest penny when Piché was all for rounding it up or down; but once he said, pointing to some artefact in his collection, 'I'll double your fee if you can tell me where this comes from.'[32]

The assistants, with whom Moore now inevitably had a much more distant relationship, tended to feel under-appreciated and underpaid: their enlargements were, after all, helping the sculptor to make big money from his bronzes, they could argue. Dissatisfaction came to a head in 1964, when several major sculptures were being enlarged at the same time, and no less than six assistants were working on them: Bob Holding, the most experienced; Yeheskiel Yardini, a gangling Israeli; Ronnie Robertson-Swann, a cocky, intelligent Australian; and three young Britons, Geoff Greetham, Derek Howarth, and Hylton Stockwell. A complaint was lodged through one of their number with Moore about the level of their wages. Henry agreed to a meeting with all of them, at which they explained that since he was in the supertax bracket, any additional pay could be offset against his tax bill, and so would cost him nothing. They were not impressed when Moore countered that he believed it was important for young artists to be impecunious. Even so, he increased their money.

Of those present, Hylton Stockwell was the most rebellious. 'After five years of being a student, here we were still in bronze,' he recalled. 'I had no objection to bronze as such, but the way of working – the emphasis on volume, the big gesture, the monumental: that kind of approach seemed sterile.'[33] One day not long afterwards he brought in an air pistol and with Ronnie Robertson-Swann started taking pot shots at old bits of plaster and even at the lights. Frank Farnham, the carpenter-neighbour, noticed signs of damage (though they had missed the light bulbs) and alerted Moore, who came down and asked whose gun had been used. Henry was so furious that Howarth, an innocent bystander, feared he might have a heart attack.[34] At first they were all sacked, but when the facts were established, only Stockwell left. Of the forty-odd assistants who served for a significant length of time at Hoglands, he seems to have been the only one to be fired on the spot. Others not included in that approximate total were encouraged to leave by gentler methods when their shortcomings were revealed.

In these very productive years between 1961 and 1964, bones – thick ones and thin ones – inspired many of Moore's most interesting pieces, such as *Standing Figure: Knife Edge*; *Large Torso: Arch*; *Knife Edge Two Piece*; *Nuclear Energy*, and *Locking Piece*. This last was an impressively tough and three-dimensional bronze, originally cast in 1962 at three feet six inches high, and it was not misnamed: the two parts have to be turned as well as lifted to be separated, resembling from some angles a grimly copulating pair of old turtles. On different occasions the sculptor has said it was inspired by two pebbles with which he was playing, and which seemed to fit and lock together, and by a sawn fragment of bone with a socket and joint found in the garden, a likelier explanation.[35]

In 1963, when Henry was in the throes of the Lincoln Center project, the architect Gordon Bunshaft asked him if he had anything suitable for the front of the new headquarters in Brussels of the Banque Lambert, designed by his firm Skidmore, Owings and Merrill. It had taken eight years to build, the Lambert family was interested in contemporary art, and the new young chairman, Baron Léon Lambert, liked the idea of a Henry Moore. The sculptor suggested that the large version of the *Locking Piece* might be suitable: they could perhaps try out the plaster cast in Brussels, painted to resemble bronze, when it was on its way by road to Noack's foundry in Berlin.

Two assistants from Hoglands went out to the Belgian capital, and they were just fixing it up on a fake base in front of the attractively ribbed building when Moore and Bunshaft arrived by car. 'Gordon, the building is too strong,' the sculptor exclaimed. 'It has a strong pattern. The sculpture gets lost!' 'It's probably not big enough,' the architect replied pragmatically. 'But let's go ahead, as it's much better than not having anything there.'[36] Baron Lambert was delighted with it, and asked whether it could be a unique bronze and become known as the *Banque Lambert Piece*. Moore told him he would like to have a cast for himself, which he would give to the Tate Gallery (as was done: it now stands on the Embankment opposite the gallery). That was agreed, but then Moore had a third cast made, which ended up in The Hague. One day Lambert spotted a photograph of it there in a newspaper, and telephoned Bunshaft angrily to ask what was going on. Moore had to be brought in to pacify him. The name of Lambert never adhered to the *Locking Piece*.

Some episodes in Moore's life defy chronological or thematic treatment. That display of realism offers as good a bridge as any to a thoroughly Yorkshire weekend which Henry and Irina spent in August 1963 – even if the setting was Warwickshire. As happened occasionally, they were invited by Jack and Jacquetta Priestley to stay at Kissing Tree House, their Georgian home near Stratford-upon-Avon. A third Yorkshireman was present, the well-known astronomer Fred Hoyle and his wife Barbara. The weekend coincided with a charity cricket match pitting Yorkshire against their traditional arch-enemy, Lancashire, which had been organized by the actress Peggy Ashcroft and was in turn sparked by the Royal

Shakespeare Company's famous production of Shakespeare's Wars of the Roses plays. The great cricketers Len Hutton and Cyril Washbrook, both retired, were captaining Yorkshire and Lancashire respectively. Hearing of this from Peggy Ashcroft, the Priestleys decided to ask the two veteran cricketers to lunch. Before they all went off to the match afterwards, Priestley called out: 'Let's have a picture of the four Yorkshiremen!' Taking the group, probably with the novelist's camera, Barbara Hoyle commented: 'A pride of Yorkshiremen!', to which Cyril Washbrook added with feeling: 'A boast of Yorkshiremen, more likely!' Whereupon he was pulled in, and all five were snapped together, Washbrook in the middle. Lady Hoyle, as she became, recalled Henry saying during the weekend that in his early days he had done so much carving that his hands 'began to feel like hooves'.[37]

Another anecdote, more character-revealing, concerned a visit to London by the then Indian Prime Minister Jawaharlal Nehru a few years earlier. Julian Huxley, who knew many famous men, had invited him to lunch. Nehru expressed a desire to meet the great sculptor, but Henry turned down the invitation, because he and Irina were due to visit Mary at her school, Cranborne Chase, that day. Then he thought: 'Mary would like to meet Nehru, let's accept.'[38] A tale of imaginative parental devotion? Or endearingly cussed-Yorkshire refusal to be impressed by the great? Or of immodest and unimaginative indifference to a statesman who had led a great nation to independence? Perhaps a mixture of all three, with the Yorkshire element uppermost.

On another occasion, Moore was put in a difficult situation by Prince Philip. It was after one of those Buckingham Palace luncheons at which the guests represent a cross-section of distinguished endeavour. There was the famous former athlete Harold Abrahams; the editor of the *Manchester Guardian*, Alastair Hetherington; a banker; a jockey; the Clerk of the House of Commons; and, rather tactlessly, Professor Thomas Bodkin, the Birmingham University art historian who so loathed Moore's work.[39] Over coffee, according to a newspaper report, Prince Philip asked the sculptor: 'Would you like to design a fountain for me? I'm rather dissatisfied with the one we've got at Windsor.' Henry replied that he was 'not really a fountain man' – fountains, much as he liked them, had rather complicated waterworks and were really for specialists.[40] According to a version he later gave to his niece Ann Garrould, he added: 'Why don't you design it and I'll sign it!'[41]

Prince Philip showed less appreciation of Moore's work a few years later, when presenting three small Moore bronzes as Zoological Society prizes. Solly Zuckerman, Henry's old friend from the 1930s, was the society's honorary secretary and thought contemporary sculpture would make a more interesting prize than a medal or book. Sidney Bernstein, of the Granada entertainment empire, suggested Zuckerman should approach Moore, and offered £2,000 for the cost of casting. Moore agreed to make three of his small animal pieces available. *Bird* (1955) became the T. H. Huxley award for an outstandingly original doctoral thesis; *Animal Form* (1959) became the Stamford Raffles award for work by an amateur or professional zoologist; while *Animal Head* (1956), a tough, rather expressionistic work, became the Prince Philip prize for practical work by a sixth-former in animal ecology. When the Queen's husband, then known for his asperity, handed over 'his' prize, he remarked that it looked like 'a monkey's gallstone':[42] had he, one wonders, been dipping into Zuckerman's *Functional Affinities of Man, Monkeys and Apes?* The Moore bronzes were awarded as prizes for six years, by which time Lord Zuckerman realized they had become disproportionately valuable (and costly to insure). Previous recipients had to give an undertaking not to sell them. With the sculptor's permission Zuckerman disposed of the three remaining Moores to raise funds for a cheaper artist to be commissioned. 'The one we chose was Lis Frink – and the same thing happened again!' he recalled.[43] Meanwhile eighteen zoologists had acquired a notable heirloom.

Those who admired Moore could be as tactless as those who did not. When opening the second large exhibition of his work to be shown at the Wakefield City Art Gallery (in August 1963), Sir Colin Anderson, then chairman of the Tate's trustees, told his Yorkshire audience: 'Anyone who feels himself resisting Moore's work is being very stupid. Do not get angry with this kind of work, and do not treat it with scorn. Anger and scorn in the face of such things are really masks for one's inability to compete with it.' Proud hackles rose, and even national newspapers reported local reactions.[44] These divided along predictable lines, and all the gallery's attendance records were broken. A few weeks earlier, by contrast, a show of smaller Moores held in the Arts Council's gallery in Cardiff, south Wales, attracted only fifty people in its first ten days, from a population of more than a quarter of a million.[45] It must have been a record for lack of interest.

An almost ideal Moore exhibition was held in the ancient Norfolk city of King's Lynn during its fourteenth festival, in July 1964. With the help of Patrick Phillips of the Leicester Galleries, Henry sited a dozen substantial bronzes outside, in courtyards, churchyards, and on terraces and lawns, and at night they were spotlit to great effect. The *Glenkiln Cross* looked particularly fine in the churchyard of St Margaret's, while *Standing Figure: Knife Edge* dominated a terrace at the Guildhall overlooking the river Ouse. The idea may have come to him from seeing some of his bronzes the previous year displayed in the streets and squares of Spoleto during that beautiful city's music festival. In King's Lynn, smaller sculptures and drawings were shown in the long refectory hall of Thoresby College, built in the sixteenth century for chantry priests. It must have been among the most beautiful exhibitions of his career.

Henry's first show at Knoedler's in New York, in June 1964, was a more conventional affair, devoted mainly to bronzes of the last decade. Most of the reviews were warm, but perhaps the most thoughtful came from Brian O'Doherty in the *New York Times*. Over-deified in the 1940s and 1950s, Moore was between two reputations that sometimes overlapped, he wrote. For many he was the man who had revived an art dead in England for 400 years to become one of the greatest twentieth-century sculptors. For others he was a good but overrated sculptor, of importance in the 1930s and 1940s, whose recent work was inflated and portentous, thus eroding his best earlier achievement by revealing its defects. O'Doherty criticized what he called the gigantism of the later work, especially the two-piece reclining figures, as self-conscious, rhetorical, and seeking to force expressiveness through size. The main metaphor, of body as rock formation, could seem like a parody of itself, just as its inertness made it seem more like cliff and rock than anything else, and so lose its power.[46]

O'Doherty's comments summarized the two poles of critical reaction to Moore's work at this period, in England as well as America. He could equally well have written that Henry was between a number of reputations: those for and against in the art world, mainly for coherent reasons; the reactions of the broad public, conscious mainly perhaps of his international fame; and the growing admiration of American collectors and businessmen, for whom the sculptor was becoming the acceptable face of modern art. This last group was to be a source of comfort in the coming years as the assaults of the younger generation reached their maximum intensity.

Chapter XVI

Toronto and the Tate Gift

1965–74 (i)

To get to the top is tough, to stay there tougher still. Henry Moore had both stamina and resilience, and he would need them in the next two or three years. It was hard to be a grand old man in the late 1960s. Youth was in the ascendant, with student revolts across the Western world reaching their peak in France and Germany in 1968. Even in Britain's relatively unmilitant student body there was a taste for a share of power, and for younger artists, all accepted standards had become suspect. For England's brightest young sculptors, Moore was now old hat, even if his role in making the country sculpture-conscious was grudgingly acknowledged.

The strength of Anthony Caro's influence was in evidence at the *New Generation* exhibition at the Whitechapel Gallery in March 1965, virtually all the nine young sculptors being shown having studied or taught with him at the St Martin's School of Art. There was a nursery feel about these bright and cheerful pieces scattered about the floor and often painted in vivid, appealing colours. Here was the opposite of Moore's preoccupation with the human figure and organic forms. Even the popular newspapers noticed that something was happening. 'I'm against nature,' Roland Piché, who was one of the exhibitors, told a *Daily Mail* reporter; 'Moore is on its side.'[1] In the *Financial Times*, Paul Grinke said that Caro's work had

> spelled the end of the tactile surface and made the twin processes of carving and modelling redundant. Subject matter, the tyranny of the pedestal and the plinth and the texture of the material no longer mattered ... Caro could now achieve a free play of sturdy tailor-made metal shapes, mutually dependent and exacting in their clean-cut purity of form and colour.[2]

For the next decade experimental sculpture would take some very odd and devious paths. Often it was the thought that counted: a walk through a landscape, a pile of bricks, even Bruce McLean pretending to be a Henry Moore reclining figure, all these were considered to be a form of sculpture, however ephemeral. Like Dada art before and after the First World War, it was anti-authoritarian, and it sought to remove the borderlines between life and art. Beside some of his students' works, even Caro seemed positively traditional, and before long, John Russell would be telling *Sunday Times* readers that good judges had been calling Caro 'the best sculptor in the world' and 'the best English artist since Turner'.[3]

Even though Russell was commenting on the curious gap between Caro's critical reputation and the average public reaction to his work – that it was something the builders had left behind – Henry must have rubbed his eyes in disbelief on seeing those fulsome phrases traditionally associated with his own name attributed to his ex-assistant. The public's mystification when faced with Caro's work and its incredulity that such a conceptual creation as Carl André's famous pile of bricks could be called art ultimately worked in Moore's favour. How reassuringly sculptural his bronzes now looked! By a pleasing irony, newspaper stories mocking the creations of younger artists, as they had once mocked his, made his own work seem the more acceptable.

It is impossible to know whether these shifts in the climate of opinion made any impact on his approach to the task in hand, but certainly the coming years were to be among his most fruitful. Moving freely between his more abstract mode and a renewed interest in the reclining figure, he produced such notable pieces as the *Archer*, *Nuclear Energy*, *Large Two Forms*, *Three Rings*, *Three Piece: Vertebrae*, *Spindle Piece*, *Square Form with Cut*, *Sheep Piece* and *Hill Arches*. If some of these bronzes have a pumped-up look in their largest versions, others undoubtedly gain by sheer size. The erotic note struck in the previous decade remains to the fore. *Two Piece Sculpture No. 7 – Pipe* is the most obviously phallic, but there is a recurring sense of upward-straining or outward-thrusting members or of actual or imminent coupling in these bronzes. Moore's work was evidence that while late middle age may involve a reduction in sexual activity, it does not necessarily diminish the sexual drive. The same period also yielded some of his best graphics, and saw a return to carving.

Periodically through these years the sculptor and his work were the subject of controversies which would have tested the nerve of much younger men. In most instances his own generosity and human warmth ensured a happy outcome. The most prolonged and remarkable of these

sagas was centred on the smoothly virile piece called the *Archer*. The
story shows how, by shaping some plaster in his studio at Hoglands,
Henry could set off a chain of events which, in this instance, helped
to change the image of dull, dreary Toronto and eventually to make
it a point of pilgrimage for the student or devoted admirer of his
work.

Its origins went back to 1958, when the Finnish architect Viljo Revell
won the biggest architectural competition in the world, for the design of
a new city hall and civic square for the booming but still provincial and
stuffy Canadian city. The most striking feature of Revell's design was the
curved shape of the two towers of the proposed city hall; even today they
retain their capacity to surprise, although time, acid rain, and the blinds
and curtains needed to screen out the sun have not been kind to them.
Moore had met Revell through their mutual friend, the architectural
writer J. M. Richards, and when the Finn decided that the huge square
required a major piece of sculpture, it was a Henry Moore he wanted.
Showing a certain disregard for Torontonian sensitivities, he put the idea
to Henry on a visit to Perry Green, without consulting the civic authorities
and with no authority to commit them to a Moore sculpture. Plans and
models of the square were examined, and the *Archer* (formally called *Three
Way Piece No 2: Archer*) was selected as the best bet. A fee of $120,000
(then around £42,000) was discussed.

In retrospect, it is evident that Revell should have initiated a process
of education and persuasion before announcing that he wanted to commission Moore and had been having discussions with the sculptor to that
end. Though provision for 'embellishment' of the scheme had been made
within the overall budget of $24.5 million, the money had to be released
by the council's Board of Control. In mid-March 1966 an impassioned
debate took place in the new city hall, which had been opened the
previous year. Baffled aldermen giggled as they passed a colour photograph of the *Archer* among themselves 'like schoolboys with the latest
copy of *Rogue*', as a local columnist later commented.[4] One alderman,
Fred Beavis, shouted 'How much art and culture can we stand? How
much culture are we going to have pushed down our throats?' Another
opponent, William Dennison, believed that 'standards of what constitutes
art should be guided basically by what the most people enjoy and take
pleasure in' – a definition which would have eliminated much twentieth-
century art from museums. Another alderman's wife told him, 'If you
vote for this, don't bother coming home.'[5] A statement that Moore was
the greatest sculptor since Michelangelo was said to have antagonized

members of the Italian community. When it came to a vote, the *Archer* was rejected by thirteen to ten.

For Toronto's mayor Philip Givens, however, the Moore sculpture had become a symbol. As he put it: 'Toronto was a hick town, and I was interested in seeing that it turned the corner of becoming a great metropolis. Having a Henry Moore work was to be the dawn of a new era.'[6] Givens had been mayor since 1963, the battle for the modernist city hall and square having been won by a predecessor, Nathan Phillips, after whom the square was named. Short of stature, lively and outspoken, Givens was an unorthodox politician of great humour and intelligence. Knowing he was a skilled fund-raiser, he now decided to fight the rejection of the *Archer* and raise the money himself.

In a wealthy but philistine city like the old Toronto, lovers of contemporary art are likely to be a close-knit group. The Toronto art establishment was mainly composed of wealthy businessmen and their wives, some Jewish (as was Givens), others as White Anglo-Saxon Protestant as the city's traditions. Among the more prominent collectors were the financier Sam Zacks, and his knowledgeable wife Ayala; Signy Eaton, the attractive wife of John David Eaton of the department store chain; Bud Feheley, who ran a large graphic design company; and Edmund Bovey, president of the Northern and Central Gas Corporation. In the Blair Laing gallery the city had a sole commercial outpost of the modern spirit, where Moore, Hepworth, Armitage, and Marini had all been shown. Givens knew other city personalities would also be sympathetic – like John Parkin, who had been an associate architect with Revell. Sure enough, a day after the negative vote Givens heard from Parkin that an industrial designer called Clair Stewart had called him to say: 'I don't want to be the only damn fool in Toronto, but I and my family will give $20,000 to save the Moore for Toronto. Will you set the wheels in motion ...?'[7]

A committee was formed to raise the full $120,000, headed by the distinguished lawyer, J. Keiller MacKay, a former Lieutenant-Governor of Ontario. Jo Hirshhorn, whose uranium interests were in Canada, helped to ensure that the bronze remained available by reassuring Moore that all would be well. Within five weeks $70,000 had been raised, with substantial contributions from the Eatons and the Maclean Foundation. Feeling confident enough to ring Moore himself, Givens found him quite caught up in the drama, and happy to await the outcome. After hearing a first-hand account of the great debate in Toronto not long afterwards (over lunch at the Athenaeum with Roloff Beny, a Toronto photographer), Henry offered to trim his price to $100,000, providing he could make a second cast for the National Gallery in West Berlin, designed by Mies van der Rohe, a concession from which he benefited even more than Toronto. In early June, Blair Laing, visiting England, was able to tell the sculptor that the $100,000 had been raised and give him a cheque for the first instalment.

The *Archer* had made its début, albeit only as a duplicate plaster cast, in June 1965 at an evening of theatrical homage to T. S. Eliot, whose memorial service four months earlier had attracted a striking concentration of literary and artistic figures (including Moore) to Westminster Abbey. Among those taking part at the Globe Theatre were Laurence Olivier, Paul Scofield, Igor Stravinsky, and Groucho Marx, who read the ballad of 'Gus the Theatre Cat'. Too busy to design a backcloth, as suggested, Henry had taken a plaster cast of the cast of the *Archer*, which he thought could be used as décor. When the curtain went up after an overture specially composed by Stravinsky had been played, the deadwhite *Archer* made a full revolution in silence on a rotating plinth. Through the evening, as Olivier, Scofield and other actors read extracts from Eliot's work and performed *Sweeney Agonistes*, its position and lighting were altered. Henry at least found it a moving experience, and it made him think there was a future for real sculpture on stage.[8]

A year later, the ten-and-a-half-feet-tall polished bronze having been completed by Noack, it was shown for the first time in exhibition in Sonsbeek Park, Arnhem, Holland. Roloff Beny photographed Moore inspecting it: 'A big moment for a great artist – and us,' the *Toronto Star* proclaimed a trifle sycophantically next morning.[9] Mayor Givens was impatient to get the sculpture to Toronto and in place before the forthcoming municipal elections, as a vindication of what he had done. Some of his opponents felt he was being provocative. 'We had a big military parade and an unveiling,' he recalled. 'It was like the unveiling of the golden calf in the desert in front of the Israelites.'[10] Some 10,000 Torontonians watched the ceremony on 26 October 1966, to the quickening strains of the band of the Royal Regiment of Canada and of the Metro Toronto Police Pipe Band. 'Posterity will remember tonight,' Givens told the crowd. 'The philistines have retreated in disorder.' The crowd applauded as a blue shroud was pulled off the *Archer* to reveal the orangey-gold bronze gleaming in the spotlights, its bulk impressive at close quarters. Even William Dennison, who had led the opposition, conceded it had some 'very impressive qualities'.[11] A satirical sculpture featuring a bicycle wheel mounted on an old bedstead was paraded in protest by fifty university students, only to be smashed by mounted police.

Givens had been too pro-Moore for his own political good. A few weeks later he was resoundingly defeated in the municipal elections, by the same William Dennison and, bizarrely, with a third candidate called Archer splitting the vote. In the election campaign Givens had been labelled the art-loving big-spender, and he had great difficulty in convincing taxpayers that they had not contributed a cent towards the Moore sculpture. Dennison presented himself as a man of caution, anxious to hold down public spending and taxes. Looking back on the campaign, Givens said: 'This is a WASP, stingy, frugal town. They held it against me, and I lost. Moore wrote to me that he felt bad. Everybody felt bad. But now that my kids are grown up, they say "Gee, Dad, you fought your fight for something you believed in," which makes me feel good.' Later Givens went as a member of the federal parliament to Ottawa, but, after a row with the Prime Minister Pierre Trudeau, resigned and returned to Toronto. There he became a police commissioner and, eventually, a civil trial judge.

Moore himself had been obliged to miss the unveiling ceremony by his first and only trip to Israel, where his work was being shown under British Council auspices at the Israel Museum in Jerusalem (then being directed by Dr Sandberg from the Stedelijk in Amsterdam) and at the Tel Aviv Museum. Henry's visit, his furthest eastwards, clinched his feeling of having a special relationship with the spiritual home of many of his keenest collectors. His four-day stay included lunch with Jerusalem's durable mayor Teddy Kollek, a memorable session with schoolchildren in the educational wing of the Israel Museum and, from Tel Aviv with that museum's director Dr Haim Gamzu, a trip through the Negev desert to the Dead Sea. Margaret MacLeod of the British Council had a dip in its slimily salty and notoriously buoyant waters, but the sculptor decided against the experience. He did, however, talk to a camel driver, who lamented that he did not yet have enough camels to get married.[12]

The gift to the Tate

Shortly before Moore made his first visit to Toronto in March 1967, he became embroiled in a controversy in London which almost certainly redounded to the Canadian city's benefit. Once again the capacity of his work to create drama and stir passions was to be vividly demonstrated. The chain of events started on 26 February, when the *Sunday Telegraph*'s art critic, Edwin Mullins, announced that Henry Moore, 'the world's leading sculptor', had offered to give between twenty and thirty of his major works to the nation. They would probably go to the Tate Gallery, he wrote. It would be the most important gift since Turner left the contents of his studio to the nation in 1851, and a special Moore gallery might have to be built under the Tate's long-delayed rebuilding scheme. The sculptor was anxious that the nation should have a complete range of his works, Mullins said.

The proposed gift was not in fact a sudden decision. Moore's idea of adding to the Tate's substantial holdings of his work had been mentioned to Sir John Rothenstein in 1960, according to the latter's memoirs. Henry had authorized the Tate's director to give the trustees the good news at his last board meeting four years later.[13] Norman Reid, who thereupon succeeded Sir John, recalled that the sculptor had also discussed the proposed gift with him before he took over in 1964, talking of a 'substantial' body of work, and had made an initial list of some two dozen pieces.[14] Both directors realized that such a gift would be impossible to display until the Tate gained its extension, and so the date of the handover was left open.

Mullin's story aroused great interest. The *Daily Express* rather surprisingly called Moore's gesture 'an act of generosity beyond the power of princes to equal', and called for a 'suitably splendid setting for these works of genius' to be provided. Moore told the *New York Times* that 'if the gallery puts up a special wing with a complete unity of its own, I shall be pleased. But I am not laying down any conditions.'[15]

Consciously or unconsciously, his generosity may have been partly prompted by a desire to pre-empt history's judgement on his work, and reflected his anxiety, noted on holiday by Heinz Roland, to join the Pantheon of the great. The first to point this out was the former president of the Royal Academy, Sir Charles Wheeler, who seemed to think Moore *had* attached some conditions to his offer. No means of tilting the scales of time had yet been discovered, he wrote to *The Times*. Values changed, and 'great' works of today might well become the bronze oddities of tomorrow: in his youth, the works of George Frederick Watts, OM, RA had filled several of the Tate's galleries, and now presumably filled the basement. The gift should be accepted, but without strings.[16]

Other correspondents, and some leader writers, wondered whether the over-stocked Tate was the best place for the Moores. London's parks and other prominent sites were suggested, and the continuing lack of Moore bronzes in central London was repeatedly lamented. Moore himself, when pressed, favoured the riverside terraces by the Royal Festival Hall.[17] At that stage he feared his work would be lost in a London park, and that a sculpture park at Hoglands would be little visited. A *Times* correspondent nicely suggested that since the sculptor liked desolate natural settings, why not Salisbury Plain? 'Moorehenge might well surpass Stonehenge and Woodhenge in popularity and public esteem.'[18]

It was at this delicate juncture, when the Tate's capacity to absorb his benefaction was far from certain, that Henry flew to Toronto *en route* for Montreal, to advise on the siting of his *Locking Piece* at Expo '67, and New York, where the Brooklyn Museum was showing his work. On the way out he paused in Ottawa, where one of his bronzes formed part of a centennial gift from the British government to Canada and its new National Library. Greeted at Toronto airport by the ex-mayor Philip Givens he remarked: 'It's heartening to meet a man who would jeopardize his political position for a work of art.'[19]

The main event of the visit was a reception given by the *Archer* activists in his honour at the new city hall: a seminal occasion, it transpired, thanks to a contributor to the *Archer* fund, J. Allan Ross, a former president of the P. K. Wrigley chewing-gum firm. In the middle of the reception he came over to Givens and rather coarsely suggested: 'Why don't you ask the old guy what he's going to do with all his sculpture? Maybe we can get it after he dies.' 'Look, Allan, *you* go over and ask him,' Givens countered. To the latter's amazement, Ross did just that, Givens recalled:

> I thought Moore would flip, but he took it in his stride, and said: 'Well, you know, I'm British' – which was the understatement of the day – 'and I feel I owe a debt to the country I come from … however, I don't think the Tate is going to be big enough to handle all my work. There may be something remaining, and with regard to that, perhaps something might be possible.'[20]

Next morning the sculptor was quoted as saying: 'I'd like the sculpture to go to London for sentimental reasons, but offers from someone else might help the Tate Gallery to make up its mind.'[21] Suddenly the idea of a Henry Moore gallery in Toronto was in the air, with Ross saying he might contribute $500,000 towards its erection.[22] Others, he believed, might contribute too. Indeed, the fateful conversation had been overheard by Sam Zacks, president of the Art Gallery of Ontario, and its director William Withrow. They were introduced to Moore, and were swift to appreciate how perfect the timing of a Moore gift would be. So was another prominent Toronto businessman, Edmund Bovey, shortly to succeed Zacks in the chair. As at the Tate, expansion was planned. A promise of Moores, exciting in itself, would also be a perfect lever for extracting additional funding from the provincial government. Over lunch that second day, these wealthy and friendly pillars of the Toronto art establishment continued to explore, with Henry, the possibility of a Moore centre in the city.[23] The sculptor liked the openness and enthusiasm of the Torontonians. When he departed after little more than twenty-four hours, they had been given grounds for hope. As for Henry, he could use their interest to put pressure on the Tate if it showed signs of ungrateful quibbling.

Even in London his generosity swiftly proved to have had a laxative effect on the Treasury. A few weeks after his return from North America, the Prime Minister announced – ironically, at the annual Royal Academy dinner – that the government would provide £200,000 towards the cost of housing the works offered by Henry Moore providing the trustees raised a similar sum towards the proposed extension. 'We are all deeply impressed by the generosity of Mr Moore,' he said.[24] But the way he had blurred together the display of the Moores and the funding of the Tate extension was to prove very troublesome.

Not everyone was delighted by the Labour government's largesse. A disgusted *Daily Mirror* reader complained: 'It seems that children with holes in their hearts are less important than sculptures with holes in their middles.'[25] The unkindest cut came from forty-one younger artists, mostly well known, who wrote collectively to *The Times* to protest against this allocation of funds. Since the signatories of such letters are always listed alphabetically, it was described as being 'from Mr Craigie Aitchison and others', though poor Aitchison, a gentle soul, had nothing to do with the drafting or organization of the letter. 'I had joined the Marlborough Gallery earlier that year, and they never forgave me because of it,' he recalled. 'I left two years later.'[26]

The heavyweight signatories included Derek Boshier, Anthony Caro, Patrick Caulfield, Bernard and Harold Cohen, Elisabeth Frink, Howard Hodgkin, Allen Jones, Phillip King, Eduardo Paolozzi, Tim Scott, Joe Tilson, William Tucker, William Turnbull, Euan Uglow, Gillian Wise and Bryan Young. The Tate had only limited space in which to expand and fulfil its role as 'the only permanent manifestation of a living culture', they wrote in inert, committee-style prose. London would not achieve its proper place 'as an organic part of our world by devoting itself so massively to the work of a single artist':

Whoever is picked out for this exceptional place will necessarily seem to represent the triumph of modern art in our society. The radical nature of art in the twentieth century is inconsistent with the notion of an heroic and monumental role for the artist and any attempt to predetermine greatness for an individual in a publicly financed form of permanent enshrinement is a move we as artists repudiate.[27]

This public disavowal of his chosen path of greatness and the suggestion that he was trying to ensure himself a measure of immortality greatly hurt Moore. The wound was the deeper for being inflicted with the co-operation of two former assistants whom he had esteemed and liked, Caro and King, and by others he had known and taught, like Paolozzi and Frink. To Moore the letter reeked of ingratitude and disloyalty, and amounted to a public rejection. Had he not almost single-handed made British sculpture a credible force across the world? Had he not taught for twenty years and served on committees in the name of the art they all believed in? Was this to be his thanks for his act of generosity?

When Caro and King learned how hurt and angry Henry was, they drove down to Hoglands together and assured him they had not meant the letter as a personal thing. Caro said his wife Sheila had advised him not to sign. 'You should have done what Sheila said,' Henry replied.[28] Re-reading the letter recently, Caro considered it 'absolute crap – anti-heroic and all that stuff'. Phillip King explained: 'The fear was that the Tate would be flooded with Henry Moores and there wouldn't be room for everyone else: there was a rumour that Henry Moore was going to take over all the new space. It was more addressed to the Tate than to anyone else.'[29]

Caro and King told Moore that Bernard Cohen had been the chief instigator of the letter: he had muscled them into it. 'To say that I was made the fall guy is putting it mildly,' Cohen recalled. 'I was one of a considerable number of people responsible. We each went around with letters to be signed; the division of labour was geographical and on the basis of friends. Between six and eight people had met for the drafting of the first and second letters' (the first was scrapped as inaccurate, on David Sylvester's advice):

Everyone was very shocked at the time that Moore, who had always insisted on the importance of open space as a setting for his sculpture, should accept the idea of an enclosed space like the Tate; and we had waited patiently for a museum that would house the best of

twentieth-century art. Now it appeared we were not going to get
it. Instead Harold Wilson had said the money would be used for a
Henry Moore museum....[30]

That was a distortion of the Prime Minister's words. But if the latter had
made it clearer that the £200,000 towards housing the Moore gift was
to be *additional* to the sum earmarked for the Tate extension, much
misunderstanding and distress could have been avoided.

Moore's friends sprang to defend him: Philip Hendy with a rather feeble
letter to *The Times* suggesting that Moore was indeed a heroic and
monumental artist who was 'acknowledged throughout the world as
proof of humanity's potential greatness'; Kenneth Clark with a letter
from Florence, the city of Giotto, Donatello, Masaccio, da Vinci, and
Michelangelo (as he put it), where the historian 'cannot help wondering
if great art has ever been or ever will be "inconsistent with the heroic
role for the artist". If we believe that Henry Moore has fulfilled this role
in our own day we are surely right to make his work available to posterity
in a worthy manner.'[31] Anthony Lousada, chairman of the Tate's
trustees, tried belatedly to set the record straight by emphasizing that the
matching £200,000 to be raised by the Tate would go to the extension
and not to housing the Moores.[32] The only really cogent letter came
from the painter Victor Pasmore, who regretted that the younger avant-
garde should write 'in terms which one would expect from a Board of
Public Authorities', consequently exuding something of a hypocritical
air.[33]

In the circumstances, the fears of the signatories seem reasonable, even
if their prose and argumentation were inept and graceless. In fact no
special provision was made for housing the Moore gift (though it will be if
the Tate acquires an additional building for twentieth-century sculpture).
Instead, the sculptor suggested that it should only become effective when
exhibition space had been increased by fifty per cent. Difficulties with the
atmospheric controls delayed the opening of the extension until May
1979, and the gift of thirty-five sculptures was handed over in time to
be shown as a celebration of Henry's eightieth birthday in summer 1978.

Just a few days after the letter of the forty-one disgruntled artists had
appeared in *The Times*, Sam Zacks had written as the president of the Art
Gallery of Ontario to Moore formally to state that the AGO was planning
a large extension of its buildings and would be interested in having a
separate Moore Gallery, for which a sum in excess of $1,000,000 could
be raised:

125, 126, 127. Moore at work on
Reclining Figure, 1959–64, 90 inches
long, elmwood, Henry Moore Foundation:
the fifth of the elmwood reclining figures

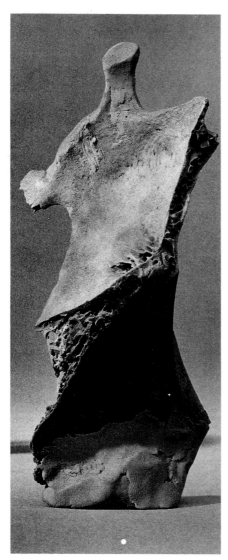

128. The original model – a piece of bone topped and tailed with plasticine additions – for *Standing Figure: Knife Edge* of 1961

129. Moore with the large version of *Standing Figure: Knife Edge*, 1961, 112 inches high, bronze. In the right setting, its dancing grace gives the heart a lift

130. *Three Piece Reclining Figure No. 1*, 1961–2, 113 inches long, bronze. For many admirers, such rugged, primeval Moores compare unfavourably with the smoother and more abstract bronzes which followed

131. *Knife Edge Two Piece*, 1962–5, 12 feet long by 7 feet high, bronze, as sited opposite the Houses of Parliament, London: a gift of the Contemporary Art Society. Highly polished, enigmatic and elegant, it contrasts strongly with the two- and three-piece reclining figures

132. Irina Moore at home, May 1963

133. Four Yorkshiremen and one Lancastrian: (left to right) Fred Hoyle, astronomer; J. B. Priestley, novelist and playwright; Cyril Washbrook, Lancashire batsman; Moore; Len Hutton, the legendary Yorkshire cricketer; at Stratford-upon-Avon, August 1963

134. At the dedication of the Lincoln Center piece: (left to right) John D. Rockefeller III, Albert List, Moore, Vera List, William Schuman and Frank Stanton, New York, 21 September 1965

135. *Locking Piece*, 1963–4, $115\frac{1}{2}$ inches high, bronze. The large version being moved at Hoglands

136. Lincoln Center *Reclining Figure*,
1963–5, 28 feet long, 18 feet high, bronze,
before the water level was corrected

137. Two of Moore's assistants, Ronnie
Robertson-Swann (left), and Derek
Howarth, making an armature for *Three
Way Piece No. 1: Points* of 1964–5. The
tips of the arrows mark the outer
perimeter of the sculpture. The arrows
are tied on with strips of hessian dipped in
plaster to avoid the use of nails

138. Moore with Alfred Barr, former
director of the Museum of Modern Art in
New York, in the Museum's sculpture
garden in September 1965, seen through
Large Torso: Arch, 1962–3, 78$\frac{1}{2}$ inches
high, bronze, the smaller version

139. The unveiling on 26 October 1966 in Toronto of *The Archer* (*Three Way Piece No. 2: Archer*, 1964–5, 134 inches long and 128 inches high, bronze). Moore was visiting Israel at the time

141. Joe Hirshhorn, who bought more than 50 of Moore's sculptures, in 1966

140. Moore outside the new building of *The Times*, London, with (left to right): Kenneth (later Lord) Thomson, Gavin Astor, Sir William Haley (former editor), the architect Richard (later Lord) Llewellyn-Davies, and *Sundial*, 1965–6, 144 inches high, bronze, after the unveiling, 23 November 1967

142. *Top*, (left to right) Alan Wilkinson, curator of the Moore Centre, Mary Moore, Henry Moore and William Withrow, director of the Art Gallery of Ontario, during the installation of the Moore Gallery, October 1974

143. *Above*, a view of some of the original plasters in the Moore Gallery: (left to right) *Nuclear Energy, Two Piece Reclining Figure No. 1, Glenkiln Cross, Draped Reclining Figure, Reclining Figure (Lincoln Center)*, and *Upright Motive No. 8*

144. Moore (*right*) directing operations as *Nuclear Energy* (1964–6, 144 inches high, bronze) is lowered into position at Chicago University, December 1967

145. Moore at a Henraux marble quarry in the Carrara Mountains in Italy, about 30 minutes' drive from his villa

146. *The Archer* in Nathan Philips Square, Toronto, seen against the curved towers of Viljo Revell's City Hall

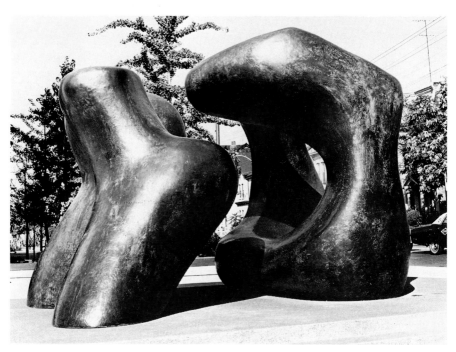

147. *Large Two Forms*, 1966–9, 20 feet long, bronze, outside the Art Gallery of Ontario. Like *The Archer*, it has become a focal point for group and portrait photographs

148. *Two Piece Sculpture No. 7: Pipe*, 1966, 37 inches long, bronze. A working model-sized sculpture of a particularly phallic nature

149. *Large Totem Head*, 1968, 96 inches high, bronze, seen here at Hoglands, more controversially sited at Nuremberg in West Germany

150. *Above*, Moore with Sir Kenneth Clark at a reception in London, November 1969

151. *Above right*, Moore with Queen Juliana of the Netherlands when receiving the Erasmus Prize at Arnhem in May 1968. Next to him are two previous winners, Marc Chagall and (face half visible) Oskar Kokoschka

152. *Right*, Moore at the London premiere in early 1969 of the film *Funny Girl* with its star Barbra Streisand. It was produced by his friend Ray Stark. Behind is David Frost, a 1960s television personality

153. *Below right*, Moore with Mary in the garden of the villa at Forte dei Marmi, around 1966

154. *Bottom*, Henry playing boules with Irina on the beach at Forte dei Marmi, 1969

155. *Above left*, (left to right) Jacques Lipchitz, Henry Moore and Marino Marini, three of the world's leading sculptors together in Italy in 1970. *Photograph by Karsh of Ottawa*

156. *Left*, making light of a broken *Upright Motive* in polystyrene, Hoglands, around 1969

157. *Top*, a page from *Sheep Sketchbook*, 1972, $8\frac{1}{4}$ inches by 9 inches, ball-point pen. To Moore's surprise, the related etchings were a great success

158. *Above*, found objects in the maquette studio at Hoglands, and a broken model for the *Times Sundial*, probably late 1960s

159. Moore etching on to the plate from the elephant skull given him by Juliette Huxley, 1969

160. Moore with Naum Gabo and Dame Barbara Hepworth at a memorial presentation for Sir Herbert Read at the Tate Gallery, London 1970

161. Moore with Sophia
Loren, a discriminating
collector, in 1972. Between
them is Moore's *Figure* of
1933–4, 30 inches high,
Corsehill stone

162. Joan Miró, then aged 80, on a visit to Hoglands in 1973

163. *Sheep Piece* 1971–2, 18 feet high, bronze, at Hoglands. A sexual encounter between two forms, rated among his finest bronzes by some good judges

I would like to point out that a handsome Moore Gallery and sculpture court on the site of our own gallery would be most meaningful, not only to Toronto, but to this whole continent which holds your work in the highest esteem. In the city there are close to one hundred pieces of your works, and many would be donated to the gallery and added to the ones you might donate, so we could assemble a very imposing group of your creations.[34]

The contrast between supportive, enthusiastic Canadians and ungrateful, niggardly Britons could scarcely have been more heavily underlined. The Tate did not get less as a result, but Moore's desire to be generous to Toronto was reinforced. There was further proof of the Canadian city's devotion that October when a touring British Council show of Moore's recent work was amplified with forty items borrowed from local collectors like the Eatons, Zacks, and Feheleys. Press comment was warm: the show had, it was generally agreed, turned a British week into a Henry Moore week and given his work and reputation a new resonance.

Serious discussions about the mooted Moore Gallery were held that December, when the sculptor spent a couple of nights in Toronto on the way back from unveiling his *Nuclear Energy* piece in Chicago. The project was at that delicate stage in which each party was looking for a commitment from the other before taking action. Moore gave an assurance that he would deliver the goods if proposals for housing the sculpture and related matters could be agreed before too long. The Premier of Ontario, John Robarts, had indicated that provincial funds would be available for the overall expansion programme providing the private sector contributed generously. John Parkin, the architect, who had been associated with the AGO for thirty-two years, was to design the Moore Gallery in consultation with Moore. It all seemed very promising.

The whole ambitious venture moved a step nearer fruition in spring 1968, when most of the major players in the drama happened to be in London: the Zacks, the Boveys, William Withrow, even John Robarts and his wife, who agreed to come to a dinner arranged by Bovey at the White Tower restaurant providing he was not asked for a commitment for money in front of Henry Moore. There would be no talk of money, he was assured, but he would really enjoy meeting Henry Moore. And so he did, as Bovey recalled:

We had Henry and John Robarts sitting together in the middle of a big oblong table in a private room, and they got on famously, telling each other jokes and really having a lot of fun. At the end we were singing Yorkshire songs [Toronto's original name was York]. It was a really useful thing, and they both told me independently afterwards how well they thought of each other.[35]

The University of Toronto played its small part in May 1968 by awarding Moore an honorary degree in law, for which he made a brief trip, his third; and through that summer both sides progressively firmed up their commitments during visits to Hoglands. Yet there was nothing formal in writing until the autumn when, after a celebratory lunch at the Café Royal in London, Moore and Bovey – now president of the AGO – signed an agreement in the presence of the sculptor's solicitor. In December Bovey announced in Toronto that Moore would be giving a 'large and representative selection of his private collection', which would be housed in a new wing. It was just two and a half years since the seminal importuning by Allan Ross during Moore's first visit.

Moore as amateur architect

A novel and welcome aspect of the Toronto exercise from Henry's viewpoint was that John Parkin, who was designing the entire expansion programme, was happy to allow him to play the amateur architect. This he did with relish, concentrating on the lighting of the large Moore Gallery, the most important room in the proposed Henry Moore Sculpture Centre. Most art galleries are lit with paintings in mind. Here was a chance to achieve an ideal light for sculpture. That, Moore believed, should come either from the top or the side, roughly at right angles to the horizontal or vertical elements of the forms. Paintings, by contrast, required above all an even light: if stronger at the top, it would distort the lower tonal values.[36] He gave his pedagogic streak full rein one day in January 1969 when he took Parkin and the AGO's director William Withrow on a tour of London museums and galleries to show how it should and should not be done. They visited the recently opened Hayward Gallery, which he disliked, the Tate, British Museum, Serpentine Gallery, and Whitechapel Gallery, which he liked best. 'He was so preoccupied with the light that he didn't really see much else, good or bad,' Withrow recalled.[37]

Yet the dimensions too, were important, and affected the light. Parkin remembered long discussions of possible permutations:

The main room was to be 5,000 square feet: 50 × 100 feet, a double rectangle. Henry decided that. The first idea was to have the whole ceiling translucent, then only the central part. The question of the ceiling height became a matter of endless concern, whether fifteen or sixteen feet clear of all obstructions. At one stage we had a light-coloured floor and dark walls. In the final evolution it was the opposite, light walls and dark floor, and the dimensions were slightly increased.[38]

In pondering the composition of his gift to Toronto, Moore had concluded that a large part of it should consist of the original plasters from which the bronzes had been cast. They were his true originals: once the assistants had done the basic work, he had finished them with his own hands. The Tate would not have room for them, though Norman Reid had asked for a couple of key ones; yet they needed a safe home to ensure that there was no posthumous mass reproduction, as happened with many of Rodin's. 'It is taking longer than I expected to sort out the sharing of work between the Tate and Toronto,' Moore wrote to Parkin in February 1968. 'There will be a great many smaller plasters and bronzes ... but in some cases ten of these would take up the same room as a large one.'[39]

Before long the AGO hadgained a valuable recruit. This was Alan Wilkinson, a young Canadian who in early 1969 had begun to study Moore's drawings at the Courtauld Institute of Art in London for his second-year MA thesis, and was taken on that autumn to be what Withrow called 'our man in Much Hadham'. Two years earlier Wilkinson had met Moore briefly in Canada through a cousin working at Hoglands as an assistant, and he had paid a quick visit to Perry Green on arrival in England in September 1967. His supervisor at the Courtauld was Alan Bowness, who in spring 1969 arranged for him to visit his subject. He went armed with twenty questions in order of importance, assuming he would never see Moore again:

> The hour was up and I had got to question fifteen and thought, Oh dear, this is the end; but he was so kind, and said come back next week. As it turned out, I could go whenever I liked, look through the drawings and feed him my ten questions a week. I ended up working a couple of days a week for him, helping him with the photographs and archives.[40]

His theme was mentioned to Withrow by the director of the Courtauld Institute, Sir Anthony Blunt. For years Blunt had been retained by the

AGO, as he had been earlier by the National Gallery of Canada in Ottawa, to advise on acquisitions, exhibitions and so forth, Canada then being short of such expertise at the highest levels. When Withrow and Zacks visited him in London and said they were looking for a future curator of the Moore Centre, he said: 'There is a young Canadian here...'[41]

At that stage there was an initial list of thirty or forty sculptures and plasters, Wilkinson recalled, and it was his job to fill it out as much as possible, for example with maquettes, drawings, and graphics, of which no mention had been made in the contract. The first substantial work which he obtained, a working model version of *Three Piece Vertebrae*, was handed over when construction began, as a form of deposit; and when Wilkinson subsequently went over to Toronto he would take several maquettes wrapped up in his briefcase as a gesture of faith from Henry.

Moore's generosity was probably increased by an episode which caused Wilkinson great anguish. In parallel with his thesis the young Canadian had been formally commissioned to write a book, his first, for Thames and Hudson on Moore's drawings. Both Moore and the Neuraths, founders of the publishing house, thought it would be useful if Sir Kenneth Clark did a short introduction. So the completed manuscript was sent off to the great man. After an increasingly worrying wait of almost a year, Clark produced some 8,000 words, enough to serve as a complete text. The commercial logic was inexorable: Clark was very famous, Wilkinson entirely unknown. One day in 1973 Moore said to him: 'Well Alan, I'm afraid K. Clark has written this and we can't have both of you and you will have to drop out.'[42] Wilkinson was furious, and felt betrayed. 'I did sense a change in Moore's attitude,' he recalled. 'I am sure he felt badly, but couldn't resist the name of his friend K. Clark as the author of my book.' He could have taken legal action, but the opening of the Moore Centre was approaching, and litigation might have ended his friendship with the sculptor.

Even a Moore loyalist like Philip Hendy thought the incident deplorable, and Moore's feelings of guilt almost certainly boosted the number of items dispatched from Hoglands to Toronto. By 1974 these totalled 101 original plasters and bronzes, 57 drawings and some 200 graphics. Wilkinson could scarcely believe Moore's generosity. On one memorable day he was allowed to take away fifty-seven drawings from a selection of seventy which he had laid out on the sitting-room floor; on another it was forty-odd plaster maquettes.

'Clark's book emerged in 1974, lavishly produced and with a some-what disingenuous preface: 'Some time ago, with the approval of Henry

Moore, I was asked to write an introduction to a selection of his drawings ... when I began to go through the five hundred or so photographs ... I realized that a short introduction to such a large volume would be disproportionate and unhelpful ... '[43] There was no mention of Wilkinson's text, research or selection of the photographs of the drawings. But the Canadian survived his exposure to Yorkshire realism and reckoned that the catalogue which he later produced for the AGO and for Moore's revelatory eightieth-birthday exhibition of drawings at the Tate was the better for the extra work he had been able to do.

Back at the front line in Toronto, Bovey led the private sector fund-raising for the new buildings, of which the Moore Centre would be a part. Individuals and local corporations contributed more than $3 million, then a record for a cultural project in Toronto, the provincial government stumped up $12.5 million, and even the federal government contributed $4 million soon after the completion of stage one of the building programme. The first shipment of seventeen original plasters from Hoglands arrived in September 1973, while construction was still in progress. The following May, Moore called in to inspect on the way back from a trip to New York, and helped position a twenty-foot-high bronze, *Large Two Forms* [147], dating from the late 1960s, outside the gallery. Wilkinson had seen it being enlarged at Hoglands and thought it would look well on the site provided by Parkin. There its smoothly sensual curves serve as a comfortable resting place for passers-by. Like the *Archer* a few hundred yards away, it is also a favourite spot for amateur portrait photography, and children love diving in and out of its holes.

The AGO's expansion made it five times larger than the original building. Within it the Moore Centre consisted of the large Moore Gallery, approached by a sloping ramp or from a more conventional L-shaped gallery named after Irina Moore, intended for drawings, graphics, and items in small display cases, and a 150-seat lecture theatre. Among other new facilities were two exhibition galleries named after Sam Zacks, who to Moore's sorrow had meanwhile died, and his wife Ayala: much of their fine collection of nineteenth- and twentieth-century works was now integrated into the AGO's main collection. The total cost of the new facilities was around $18 million, and Moore's gift alone was valued at $15 million.

The sculptor himself arrived with Irina and their daughter Mary a good week before the official opening, in time to supervise the siting of the larger plasters in the main gallery. Three assistants, John Farnham, Michel Muller, and Malcolm Woodward, who had spent the best part of a year repairing the plasters, came along too. Displaying the greyish-white originals in the carefully contrived space was far from easy, even when the less interesting ones had been winnowed out. Eventually twenty-six went on show. Perhaps unexpectedly, the effect was strikingly sepulchral.

The day of the opening of the new extension, 26 October 1974, was sunny and crisply autumnal. It was both a domestic and an international occasion, the Torontonians leavened with foreign museum directors, critics, and dealers. One Briton invited to see the custom-built Moore shrine was the Tate's director Norman Reid, who was startled to spot among the plasters the 1951 Festival of Britain *Reclining Figure*. He had been most anxious to secure this for the Tate as part of the Moore gift, only to find that it had been promised to an Australian gallery. The Tate's claim had, he thought, prevailed – yet here it was! Conveying his surprise to Henry with a cocked eyebrow, he was assured all was well: 'I had another made for them,' the sculptor explained, no doubt with a slightly guilty giggle.[44] The Tate duly got the original.

The celebrations were marked by the first peal of bells for twenty-five years from the nearby church of St Patrick's and a skirl of pipes from the 48th Highland Regiment. Moore contributed briefly and rather inaudibly to ninety minutes of speeches, after which a jazz band and some comedians loosened up the constrained atmosphere. Then the doors were opened to the general public. Only a small picket of protesters tried to spoil the festive atmosphere with placards proclaiming 'Art is for the white, for the rich, for the elite', and denouncing the attention paid to Moore at the expense of Canadian artists.

The critics liked the new extension; but some, like Hilton Kramer of the *New York Times*, found the main gallery a little bleak, fascinating though the plasters were.[45] John Russell of the *Sunday Times* was struck by their spectral quality: to him they looked as if they had been 'dug from a tomb with their gravecloths still fresh and white'.[46] Bryan Robertson, the former director of the Whitechapel Gallery in London and an expert on presentation, reckoned it was a 'fine, simple gallery', and the extension was 'all exactly as it should be'.[47] It was generally agreed that the additions had made the AGO a museum not to be missed, and that the Moore Centre would be a necessary point of pilgrimage for Moore scholars.

And so it has remained. Further gifts and purchases from Moore and from commercial dealers along with donations from collectors have brought the number of items by Moore there to around 900, including

132 sculptures, 73 drawings, and some 700 graphics. That is the largest number of Moore works in any one public institution, but it would be a trickier task to assess the relative value of the Moore holdings of the Tate, the Hirshhorn Museum in Washington, and the AGO. In the realm of scholarship the latter now has competition from the Leeds City Art Gallery and its Henry Moore Centre for the Study of Sculpture. What makes the AGO's Moores unique is not just their sheer number but the fact that most of them are actually *on view*. A museum like the Tate Gallery, and even the Hirshhorn, can only show a fraction of its holdings at any one time. The visitor to Toronto, however, can study a catholic selection of Moore's work in many media, most notably those ghostly plasters of some of his major bronzes. They make an eerie and unforgettable spectacle.

If Toronto city council had not voted against the purchase of the *Archer*, it is most unlikely that the Moore Centre would be there. The AGO's extension would have been smaller and probably later, and the transformation of Toronto into today's handsome, lively, and relatively sophisticated city would have been that much slower. Like some overweight cupid or transatlantic Eros, the *Archer* fired his arrows at the heart of Torontonians, and won many of them for contemporary art.

Chapter XVII

Towards apotheosis in Florence
1965–72 (ii)

As the Arabs say, the dogs may bark, but the caravan moves on. If the early to mid-1960s saw Moore's reputation sink to its nadir with younger artists and critics, the thinking public scarcely noticed. The events in Toronto (to which those in this chapter run parallel) were only possible because a few resolute individuals believed in the lasting value of his work. In London any sour taste left by *The Times* letter was soon to be erased by a seventieth-birthday exhibition at the Tate Gallery which was the high-water mark of his fame in his own country. Four years later came the climactic event of his career: a vast retrospective show in Florence which gave his name a new resonance across the Continent.

The Florence triumph and all it meant to Moore and to the way his work was seen would almost certainly never have taken place if the sculptor had not put down firm roots in Tuscany. As we have seen, since completing the Unesco carving at Querceta in 1958 he had spent a few weeks of most summers on holiday in Forte dei Marmi with Irina and Mary, alleviating his leisure with some carving. Then in 1965, probably with help from his Feltrinelli prize money, he purchased a tiny shack of his own in a plot of land from a local painter friend, Arturo Cavalli. It consisted of just two rooms, a central space for cooking and eating, a lavatory and wash-basin (but no bathroom), and was situated about ten minutes' walk up the Via Civitali from the seafront, on the Viareggio side of Forte dei Marmi. The nearest large town is Lucca. Pisa is about forty-five minutes' drive away, Florence just over an hour.

A year later Henry and Irina had a medium-sized bungalow built next to the original tiny shack, which was thereafter used for guests, with one room sometimes serving as a drawing studio. The new house was unpretentious to a fault: a red-tiled, squarish building, plain but not quite ugly. Inside it is refreshingly cool, with travertine floors and a spacious living room furnished with tweed-covered armchairs and sofa. Metal beds in the two and a half bedrooms strike an institutional note, but kitchen and bathroom are comfortably proportioned. The neighbouring houses are Mediterranean-suburban. The backdrop of mountains is magnificent on a clear day; yet the visitor is bound to think: 'With all that money, why this?'

For Moore, it worked perfectly. It was near the beach and the marble works at Querceta. Forte dei Marmi itself is a pleasant, clean resort largely free of English, American or German tourists. Henry soon devised a routine. It usually involved a few hours' work at Henraux in the morning, from which he would return in his open Mini-Moke to join Irina and Mary for a swim and sunbathe at Laura's, one of the immaculately tended private beaches. Sometimes they would have a picnic lunch there, or return to the house. Some social life might follow: visiting friends might come for a drink or tea, and all too frequently there would be someone anxious to get a drawing or sculpture at a reduced price from him. In the evening they might go to one of the town's many excellent restaurants. Sometimes friends like the Hendys would come and stay, or Mary might have someone along.

Around 1970 Moore bought a much more obviously desirable house about forty-five minutes away in the beautiful hilltop village of Camaiore. He and Irina never used it, and foreign exchange difficulties nearly resulted in its being sold to Sir Denis Hamilton, then editor-in-chief of Times Newspapers and an old friend. In the end it went to Mary, and Sir Denis bought a house in the hamlet above Camaiore called Pieve di Camaiore, where his nearest neighbour was Jacques Lipchitz. Marino Marini still had a studio in Forte, and sometimes the Hamiltons would ask the Moores and the Marinis to supper. They would forgather on the veranda, Sir Denis recalled, with Lipchitz telling stories about Picasso and his own years in Paris (from 1909 to 1941), and Marini contributing little English but a great sense of fun. On the edge of the trio was Hamilton, 'the lowly scribbler, trying to take part in argument with the three greatest living sculptors in the world'.[1] The relative proximity of Moore and Marini in Forte had led the Italian to execute a small portrait head of his English contemporary: not, alas, one of his better efforts in that genre, and a poor likeness.

With a firm base now in Forte dei Marmi, Moore took to spending a good six weeks every summer – usually August and a week either side – in Italy. One by-product was an increased flow of marble and stone carvings from Henraux. After the six-year gap caused by the Unesco

project, he had first reverted to carving in 1964. The results, *Two Forms*
and *Oval Sculpture*, were table-sized pieces in white marble, abstracted
from the human form. In 1965 there followed a small, suave white
marble version of the *Archer*, and in subsequent years a steady procession
of carvings large and small, some original conceptions, others marble or
stone versions of bronzes. All these late carvings were executed by the
skilled Henraux artisans with a decreasing level of supervision from
Moore. As a result they have a cool, uninvolved look very different from
the intense glow of the early carvings. It suits the larger, more abstract
pieces, but gives an inert, manufactured look to some of the more figurative ones.

In 1967, the year of the Tate Gift controversy, Moore's Italian connections led to his first proper venture into stage design. The occasion
was the tenth Festival of Two Worlds at Spoleto, no great distance from
Forte dei Marmi, organized by the American-Italian composer Gian-
Carlo Menotti. Menotti had suggested that a contemporary sculptor like
Giacomo Manzù might be commissioned to design the sets for Mozart's
opera *Don Giovanni*. When Manzù declined, Menotti's friend, the art
historian and critic Giovanni Carandente, suggested that Moore should
be asked, having become friendly with Henry through his sculpture show
in Spoleto in 1962. Somewhat reluctantly the sculptor now agreed that
sets might be made which were based on his works: the spectacle of the
Archer at the Eliot evening had after all been inspiriting. When Menotti
visited Hoglands, Moore said his participation must not be announced
until he had seen the sets completed, mounted and lit on stage.[2]

Carandente and Moore next chose some suitable works: a reclining
figure, the *Falling Warrior*, some *Helmets*, the *Arch*, shelter drawings and
the mysterious drawing *Crowd Looking at a Tied-Up Object*, of 1942 (for
the scene with the Commendatore).[3] Carandente, who later became
Italy's Inspector General of Fine Arts, took Henry several times from Forte
to Spoleto in June 1967 to supervise the progress of the sets. These
included polyurethane replicas of the chosen sculptures, some painted as
bronzes, others as marble, and painted décor adapted from his drawings.
Menotti recalled that Moore was hard to please, shaking his head again
and again, and objecting to the spacing or dimensions of the different
elements: a wall was too high or low, a sculpture too much to left or
right:

After we had come to despair that he would ever approve the
production, his assistant timidly suggested that I should sit Mr

Moore always in the same seat in the stalls, so that he would always get the same perspective of the stage. The trick worked, and to this day we call that seat 'la poltrona di Moore'.[4]

Eventually the sculptor saw some rehearsals and said: 'It is very nice. You can use my name.' When shown in mid-July 1967, the production was loved or loathed by the critics (*The Times* called it 'ugly and perverse'); but Menotti considered the experience 'perhaps the highlight' of his career as a producer, and Carandente even called the production 'the most memorable in the history of modern theatre décor'. Moore turned down all other requests to design sets for operas or plays, such as one from the Royal Opera House, Covent Garden, to do Wagner's *Ring* cycle, fearing that 'if one got one's coat-tails into the mangle of the theatre, one would be drawn bodily in'.[5]

The Times Sundial

As we have seen, Moore not infrequently overcame his reluctance to accept commissions, with all their restrictions on his freedom and time-consuming consultations. Usually the result more than justified the effort, at least in artistic terms. One step into the unknown produced a genuine Moore novelty: the *Sundial* [140]. Gavin Astor, president of Times Newspapers, thought the forecourt of the proposed new building for the old Thunderer at Blackfriars, a stone's throw from the Thames, needed a sculpture, related perhaps to the idea of time. The chief architect involved, Richard Llewellyn-Davies, proposed a sundial – perhaps, he suggested after doing some homework, a heliochronometer, consisting of a bar which threw its shadow on a calibrated scale and gave, theoretically, a far more accurate reading than the conventional flèche variety. Astor thought it a great idea: but who should execute it? Llewellyn-Davies sat on the Royal Fine Art Commission with Moore, and suggested him. Rather surprisingly, Henry accepted the commission without demur when the architect and his partner, John Weeks, visited Hoglands, armed with plans and diagrams of the machines, around 1962.[6]

A few months later Moore produced what looked like a superior re-draw of the diagrams, and later a maquette which everyone thought marvellous. The possibility of making the heliochronometer adjustable, either by hand or clockwork, was examined but rejected as too complicated, as was a plan to stand it in a pool of water. A full-sized, twelve-feet-high wood model was then made by Frank Farnham at Hoglands, checked, photographed, and dispatched to Noack in Berlin for casting: close liaison and a visit from Henry were required to ensure that the calibrations were correctly marked. *The Times* reproduced a photograph of the model, with a comment from Moore that it was a 'nice, clean object'.[7] This prompted the humorist A. P. Herbert, who had recently published a book called *Sundials, or Fun with the Sun*, to build a mock-up with two half-hoops from an old whisky barrel and a piece of string, and to calculate that owing to the differences between Sun Time, Greenwich Mean Time and the time shown on Big Ben, the heliochronometer would always be between forty-five and seventy-five minutes wrong: hence, unbeknown to 'APH', the idea of having an adjusting mechanism.[8] Eventually a panel was affixed to the base of the Moore-chronometer explaining the difference between solar and clock time.

On 23 November 1967 the unique bronze cast was unveiled, having been carefully positioned in the south-facing courtyard with advice from Dr F. A. B. Ward of the Science Museum, who had acted as technical consultant. Sadly, not a ray of sunshine penetrated to New Printing House Square on that grey autumn morning. Among those present were Moore; Sir William Haley, the former editor of *The Times*; Gavin Astor; Kenneth (later Lord) Thomson, son of *The Times*'s Canadian-born pro-prietor (and the author, then a *Times* employee).

On its raised circular platform the Moore *Sundial* looked very handsome against a decent if bland building, though its impact was reduced by that roving enemy of modern sculpture, the motor car: the ban on parking in the piazza was soon flouted. Then in early 1974 *The Times* sold the building, sundial and all, to the *Observer* newspaper, previously just a tenant in the right-hand wing, and moved to a pseudo-Venetian building in Gray's Inn Road, north of Fleet Street. A few months later that summer, to the dismay of Moore, Astor, Denis Hamilton and many others, the sundial vanished. It had never occurred to them that the management of the Sunday newspaper might not share their view that it was an integral part of the property, designed specifically for that spot. Tristan Jones, then the *Observer*'s general manager, was stung by the widespread idea that something underhand had been done:

> The sale included the Henry Moore ... but I didn't want it. Being a good philistine, it struck me as quite pointless. So I had no hesitation in flogging it, in consultation with others, which meant those entitled to be consulted. They did not include Gavin Astor or

Henry Moore. The only people I felt I should consult were our own directors and trustees. They agreed with me: what should we want with a thing like that? It didn't appear to have any significance for the *Observer*.[9]

The sundial, last seen on the back of a lorry heading south, was discovered in the entrance courtyard of IBM's Arthur K. Watson International Education Centre in La Hulpe, on the outskirts of Brussels, a distinguished contemporary building by the Danish architect Jørgen Bo. Recently it was relocated in a specially designed plaza in front of a new extension there; but Bo admits that the centre's woodland setting is not ideal for such a piece.[10] The sale to IBM was effected by the London dealer Thomas Gibson, a neat coup by any standards. *The Times* was left with a twenty-two-inch-high cast of the working model, of which an edition of no less than twenty was made, perhaps to compensate for the uniqueness of the sundial itself. At the old Blackfriars building, now mainly occupied by an American bank, a miniature raised garden with several handsome trees has replaced the sundial: a much less original but in some ways more effective foil to the architecture.

Nuclear Energy for Chicago

Another commission, unveiled a few weeks after *The Times Sundial*, required real courage, loaded as it was with disagreeable associations. The origins of one of Moore's biggest projects went back to November 1963, when he received a letter from Professor William McNeill, head of the history department of the University of Chicago. NcNeill was chairing a committee charged with commemorating the achievement of the Italian-born American physicist Enrico Fermi. On 2 December 1942 Fermi had achieved the first controlled nuclear chain reaction in the improbable setting of a converted subterranean squash court on the university campus. The building had since been torn down and weeds had taken over the waste ground. Only a plaque on a chain fence recorded the fell deed. With the twenty-fifth anniversary approaching, a fitting memorial seemed to be required.

The idea of a competition was rejected, since leading sculptors notoriously disliked competing with their juniors. Lipchitz turned down a direct approach, declaring after visiting the site: 'Don't make me pregnant until you have a down payment.'[11] Since they had no money in hand, that ruled him out. So McNeill wrote to Moore, telling him that the sculpture would be a monument to man's triumphs, 'charged with high hope and profound fear, just as every triumphant breakthrough has always been'.[12] As a confirmed supporter of the Campaign for Nuclear Disarmament, Henry was understandably stunned by the implications of the theme as well as the difficulties of finding a suitable sculptural metaphor. None the less, perhaps because he was tempted by the prospect of being associated with so portentous a step, he replied on 2 December 1963:

> I realize what a tremendous happening that was, and that a monu-
> ment for such a triumphant breakthrough may be called for. It
> seems an enormous event in man's history, and a worthy memorial
> for it would be a great responsibility and not easy to do. However, it
> would be a great challenge and something I might like to consider.[13]

Later that month, when he was still in the toils of the Lincoln Center commission, Moore received McNeill and two other committee members at Hoglands. Before long he showed his visitors a six-inch-high maquette which he had made a few days earlier, dome-shaped and clearly related to his earlier helmet series. The Chicagoans found it hard to envisage how it might look enlarged to twelve feet, but left feeling confident of their host's ability to produce a worthy memorial. There was no commitment. 'I will make it anyway,' the sculptor said. 'If you like it you may have it for the site': a pleasant contrast to Lipchitz's attitude.

A comprehensive fee of $200,000 was agreed, just $40,000 less than for the Lincoln Center two-part figure. 'All of us must be satisfied,' Moore wrote in February 1964 when discussing the terms and timing, 'that it is a worthy monument for the great event it would commemorate – and this can only be known when the work is taking shape in its full size.'[14] A plaster working model of about four feet high was completed that August and cast early the following year. On seeing photographs in black and white and colour, the university committee agreed 'unanimously and enthusiastically' to recommend the purchase and erection of the statue.

The upper part of the sculpture, Moore explained to McNeill in a further letter in May 1965, was connected with the mushroom cloud of an atomic explosion, and also with the shape and eye sockets of a human skull. The lower half was architectural, the arched cavities and domed interior being reminiscent of a church or cathedral. 'The whole sculpture was meant to have a kind of contained power and force,' he wrote.[15] The London art critics, however, were unimpressed when the bronze working model was shown in a double bill with Francis Bacon's paintings at

Marlborough Fine Art's New London Gallery in July 1965. Edwin Mullins of the *Sunday Telegraph* considered it 'a brutish thing, based on a confused and pretentious idea' – to make visual comparisons between a mushroom cloud and a man's head was rather forced and faintly ludicrous.[16] The *Guardian's* Norbert Lynton called it 'a prosaic image inflated beyond its formal capacity': Moore had, he regretted, become a victim of world-wide renown. A world avid for his work was all too easily satisfied with what it got.[17]

Moore visited Chicago for the first time that September following the Lincoln Center unveiling. At a lunch given for him by members of the university it was suggested that the commission should be called *Nuclear Energy* rather than, as hitherto, *Atom Piece*, since that was uncomfortably close to Atom Peace. The suggestion was adopted. Raising the necessary funds was proving difficult, but eventually a large grant was obtained from the Ferguson fund, set up to endow Chicago with public sculpture – thanks mainly to the refusal of one of its trustees to see the money used for a large piece by a Communist, Picasso, intended for a new civic centre.[18]

The great bronze with its polished dome or cranium was completed in good time by Noack, checked in Berlin by Moore in late August 1967, and shipped to Chicago by barge and freighter. Accompanied by Harry Fischer, the sculptor arrived in Chicago on 29 November to supervise the installation and take part in the twenty-fifth anniversary celebrations of Fermi's feat. A show of one hundred of Moore's sculptures and drawings, drawn from local sources, had been mounted by the university's Renaissance Society for the occasion (many were from the collection of Joel Starrels, later bequeathed to the university). Work on a new library was proceeding in the vicinity of the sculpture's site, but the pedestal of polished black Norwegian granite was ready to receive its burden.

It was always a moment of high drama when a major bronze was hoisted aloft and then gently lowered into place. Noack had provided a large eye bolt to be inserted into the top of the sculpture, as well as a bronze disc which screwed in to plug the hole: 'that final touch of thoughtfulness', Henry commented admiringly to the assistant university architect, Mikkel Hansen.[19] The press gathered around to catch the action as the bronze was swung in a high arc. Hansen sensed the pressure on Moore as the sculptor had it picked up and lowered again and again, striving to get the position right. They paused for a break, pretending the job was done, then completed it without the snapping of cameras. A nasty scratch to the polished dome caught the light. Moore requested some liver of sulphate, which no one had heard of; but a secretary traced a phial of the brown crystals. Henry dissolved one, and with a brush took the shine off the scratch.

The day of the unveiling, 2 December, was bitterly cold, but it was warmed by a sense of making history. Among the thousand or more people who gathered for the unveiling were thirty of the scientists, or their widows, who had been present when Dr Fermi had ordered the final control rod to be pulled from the uranium pile, thus touching off the first man-made nuclear reaction. That morning they were addressed over closed-circuit television by Presidents Lyndon Johnson of the USA and Giuseppe Saragat of Italy. Now they gazed up at the huge sculpture swathed in tarpaulin which pulsed and flapped noisly in the wind. Behind the wrapped sculpture, a high-school band dressed in blue and gold stood at attention. In the near-freezing mist, Harry Fischer feared for the health of his sixty-nine-year-old charge. Then at 3.36 p.m., twenty-five years to the minute after Fermi had given his momentous order from his control room on the old squash-court balcony, his widow Laura Fermi, the president of Chicago University, George Beadle, and Henry Moore pulled on cords which tugged off the tarpaulin, and there stood *Nuclear Energy*, gleaming brightly despite the dull weather, a sinister image for a sinister event.[20]

Achievements of a very different order had been celebrated just five weeks earlier in Dublin with the unveiling by the Prime Minister Jack Lynch of Moore's *Standing Figure: Knife Edge* as a memorial to the poet W. B. Yeats. Three Irish poets read extracts from Yeats's verse, and Moore chatted to the poet's widow, whose son and daughter were also present. 'Art knows no frontiers,' the *Irish Times* commented in a tactful allusion to Anglo-Irish conflicts, 'and yesterday a great artist in one medium did homage to another.'[21] A few days later, in this autumn of unveilings, central London at last acquired a prominently sited Moore when the Minister of Public Building and Works, Robert Mellish, did the honours for the large version of *Knife Edge Two Piece* in Abingdon Street Garden by the Houses of Parliament. In 1970 the bronze was moved to an even more prominent site on the immaculate strip of lawn opposite Barry and Pugin's neo-Gothic masterpiece, to whose intricacies its svelte and polished elegance offered the perfect foil. Since it was a gift from the Contemporary Art Society, no public money was involved. That did not prevent a Conservative backbencher, Neil Marten, from asking in the Commons why 'this lovely part of Westminster should be littered with something that looks like a crashed unidentified flying object'. Mellish, to his credit, replied: 'Since I am not clear what the Hon. Member is referring to, I am unable to answer his question.'[22] The *Locking Piece* was, as noted, unveiled a few hundred yards further west, in Riverwalk Gardens just beyond the Tate, in July 1968.

Finally, another Moore novelty: a stone and bronze memorial plaque which he designed for the headstone of the grave of the poet Edith Sitwell, at the request of her brothers Osbert and Sacheverell Sitwell. Dame Edith, a convert to Roman Catholicism, had died in 1964. Moore's plaque is set above the text of a short poem about the unity of past and present, youth and age, death and life, and shows a child's hand clasping an adult's: sentimental but touching. Henry attended the service of dedication, an ecumenical affair, on 11 November 1967 at the village church of Weedon Lois, near the ancestral Sitwell home of Weston Hall in Northamptonshire.

Coming as they did less than six months after the outburst in *The Times* of the forty-one younger artists about the Tate gift, these unveilings and dedications in the USA and England, coupled with the firming-up of the Toronto gallery project, must have done much to restore Moore's self-esteem. Then in December 1967 he heard that he had been awarded the Erasmus Prize, given for achievements in fields not covered by Nobel prizes. Previous winners, chosen by a board of Dutchmen advised by an international committee, had included Sir Herbert Read, Charlie Chaplin, and Ingmar Bergman. It was worth roughly £11,500 (around £55,000 today), tax-free: the Inland Revenue distinguished between prizes awarded for work submitted, as at biennales, and those which came out of the blue, like this and Moore's earlier Feltrinelli Prize. Moore went to Arnhem to receive it from Prince Bernhard on 3 May 1968, accompanied by Mary – Irina had broken a leg – and Sir Kenneth Clark. Queen Juliana and Princess Beatrix were also present: a daunting occasion for speech-making. Moore announced that he would probably spend part of the money on studios for young sculptors in Britain or Italy. In fact he gave £5,000–£6,000 to SPACE, a charity set up later that year mainly by the painters Bridget Riley and Peter Sedgley, to provide studio space in London for professional artists, and to give them help in establishing their own studios. It is still very active.

An interview with the Dutch newspaper *De Waarheid* after the cere-mony found Moore in immodest mood. 'All great artists created their best work at the end of their lives,' he said. 'Being famous makes no difference. If you need constant encouragement, that is weakness of character.'[23] Having enjoyed the steady support of powerful men for

about forty years, he was not well placed to judge. The country which
had given birth to the severities of Mondrian and de Stijl took Moore to
its heart: to coincide with the prize, the Kröller-Müller Museum in Otterlo
staged a big exhibition of his work with the British Council (seventy-one
sculptures, forty-four drawings). Though not easy to reach, it drew
50,000 visitors in a month before moving on to Germany.

Within a few weeks Moore was to be richly honoured in his own
country. The Arts Council had been canvassing ideas for his seventieth-
birthday exhibition since 1964: should it inaugurate the Hayward
Gallery, being built for exhibitions near the Royal Festival Hall? Should
much of it be out of doors, perhaps in Battersea Park? Or should the Tate
have it? The Tate's claims prevailed; and David Sylvester, who had done
so well with Moore's 1951 retrospective, was the sculptor's own choice
to do justice to his three score years and ten. The unlovely Hayward
Gallery was opened by the Queen on 9 July 1968, making a strong start
with a Matisse exhibition: the rival Moore attraction across the Thames
opened a week later, stayed open a week longer and attracted a slightly
higher total but lower average attendance – 124,081 people in sixty-seven
days, as against 114,214 for Matisse in sixty days. At a celebratory dinner
given by the trustees of the Tate, Jo Hirshhorn presented the director,
Norman Reid, with a cheque for $30,000 as a token of his friendship with
Moore. 'They can do anything with it they like,' he told the author.
'Henry is one of the greats of the twentieth century, and a lovely simple
human being. I wanted to do something in his name.'[24]

Other transatlantic admirers gathered in London, and Gordon Bunshaft
gave a dinner at the Ritz Hotel at which, he decided, a wine made in the
year of Moore's birth should be served. Baron Lambert was invited,
providing he could bring a bottle of 1898 Mouton-Rothschild from
Philippe de Rothschild. Before long Bunshaft received a call from Rothschild's Bank to say that a magnum was being dispatched; but it must not
be opened until just before being served. In the event it had a little
bouquet, but went flat almost instantly. Everyone drank a thimbleful.[25]
The evening, however, sparkled. Among those present were the James
Johnson Sweeneys, the Seymour Knoxes, the Hirshhorns and even Sturgis
Ingersoll, the Philadelphian collector who had visited Moore in 1934.
Sylvester too was there, and Mary, now an attractive twenty-two-year-
old Oxford graduate.

One of the strengths of the Tate exhibition was the number of early
carvings lent by collectors in deference to Moore's seventieth birthday.
For the rest, Sylvester's selection favoured semi-abstract work over the

more naturalistic pieces. Though he tried in vain to borrow the North-ampton *Madonna and Child*, which he greatly admired, he omitted the large version of the *King and Queen*. Bronzes were separated from carvings, the latter being sparsely deployed in three rooms benefiting from natural lighting.

Moore made one suggestion which turned out to be a mistake. Large, late bronzes were to be shown on the Tate's back lawn (since built over), and would be seen from many angles against a background of parked cars. 'Henry said that nothing is so unsatisfactory for a background as cars, parked or moving,' Sylvester recalled. 'He insisted we build a wooden fence inside the railings, and even paid about £3,000 for it out of his own money. But it didn't work, and looked bloody awful – cheap and ramshackle.'[26] Once again, the sculptor left the selection of works entirely to Sylvester: partly, the latter felt, because Moore believed that an artist is not necessarily the best judge of his own work, and – as a corollary – should not censor it as he does it. Moore's unevenness as a sculptor has never troubled Sylvester, who believes that an artist should be judged by his best work. 'An artist who produces one A-plus work is better than an artist who produces fifty A works.'

The London critics rose to the challenge of striking a balance, as the *Guardian*'s Norbert Lynton put it, between unquestioning admiration and those who, partly in reaction, found his work weak, derivative or limited. While preferring the early carvings, he reckoned the sculptor's status was secure, since he had found a viable marriage between classical concepts, distortion, and abstraction.[27] Guy Brett of *The Times*, who also saw the thirties carvings as a high point, reckoned the show made most theories about Moore seem over-simplifications.[28] Recent bronzes and carvings from Italy also drew praise.

A gulf yawned, yet again, between the relatively cautious endorsement of the critics and the reactions of the press as a whole. Two days before Moore's birthday on 30 July, the *Observer* headlined an interview by John Gale 'A Visit to the Greatest Living Englishman'. In the front porch of Hoglands, readers learned, the tallest of several pairs of gumboots had the name 'Henry' inked inside; they belonged, Gale raptly revealed, 'to a man often described as the greatest living Englishman'.[29] Often? Perhaps this was a corruption of Clark's 'Moore as ideal emissary to another planet' theory. A *Daily Mirror* profile called him the Colossus of Perry Green. 'Moore's career is characterized by the dignity and humility of a great artist ... not only in the man but in his work, Moore is a colossus,' Mike Molloy wrote.[30]

The theme of greatness was taken up. 'Henry Moore, OM, is seventy today,' a *Guardian* editorial said on 30 July, 'and people are calling him the greatest living Englishman':

> It is an excellent thing that a sculptor should be recognized for once in England as a great man. There is no need to vote Moore the greatest anything. It would be enough and a pleasant change for England to be remembered by someone who is not an Admiral or a General or a war-winning politician.

Philip Hendy, who knew just how unhumble Moore could be, provided an astringent touch at the start of a friendly tribute in *The Times*. The sculptor had on one occasion, he related, described a common acquaintance as the most conceited man he knew. 'Bar one,' said his friend (probably Hendy himself). 'Who's that?' 'You, Henry. Don't tell me you have ever thought of yourself as anything but the greatest sculptor alive.' There was a momentary cloud of introspection, then the sun came out brighter than ever: 'Oh well,' said Moore, denying nothing, 'I suppose it depends on how you show it!'[31]

Perhaps the friend had been Herbert Read. From him there could be no more tributes. That June, Moore had paid a visit to his stalwart supporter's sickbed in the Yorkshire village of Stonegrave, from which he had latterly commuted. Five days later Sir Herbert died, aged seventy-four. Before long Moore and Barbara Hepworth together bought a portrait of the critic and poet painted by Patrick Heron and gave it to the National Portrait Gallery; and in March 1970, with Ben Nicholson and Naum Gabo, they each gave one of their works to the Tate in Read's memory. The tribute was well merited. No one had done as much, most valuably in the 1930s, to promote their reputations across the English-speaking world in a steady flow of books, catalogue essays, articles and, after the Second World War, in lectures. On international committees, at biennales, virtually wherever high-level decisions were being taken about how money for art should be spent or prizes and commissions awarded, Read had been a loyal and tireless advocate of their work. They owed him much, not least for his friendship.

Moore's Tate retrospective in 1968 marked the moment when the sheer weight of his achievement, and the quality of his recent work, turned the tables on his critics. For the next decade his reputation remained on a pinnacle virtually beyond the reach of his detractors. It no longer mattered that his work meant little or nothing to younger artists. As the avant-garde fractured into dozens of movements, such as

minimalism ('minimal art is for minimal minds'. Henry liked to say),
Moore's sculpture became a reassuring part of modern life: striking,
recognizable, sturdily contemporary, something we could be proud of.
His prices too, for many people a yardstick of success, were soaring. In
the late 1960s, a major bronze was fetching £50,000–£70,000, and a
good drawing around £5,000, enabling the *Daily Express*'s William
Hickey column to crow: 'Moore, I predict, will chalk up £1 million a
year':[32] a broad-brush estimate, but not entirely improbable in terms of
gross revenue. The upper tax rates had not yet climbed to their punitive
levels of the mid-1970s. Certainly the Moores were now rich. Their
way of life remained unchanged, though Henry might stay in the Ritz
overnight in London rather than the Rembrandt Hotel, and was slightly
readier to jump into a taxi.

Some money went into property, including a few acres adjoining the
bottom of the park-like garden and studios. At the far end of a large field
acquired in 1967 there was a pyramid of gravel and clay excavated from
a gravel pit. Moore had it bulldozed so that it formed a harmoniously
shaped mound screening off the disused pit and attendant dumped refuse.
Having always admired sculpture or sculptural ruins which were raised
against the sky, like those of the Acropolis or at Delphi, he came to see
the hill as an ideal site on which to achieve a similar effect.

By good chance he had, in 1968, been introduced by a former assistant,
Derek Howarth, to the use of polystyrene as a medium for making
enlargements. It was feather-light and could be carved with hot wire like
cheese. Howarth had first encountered it in 1964, and since leaving
Hoglands had become proficient in using it for theatrical work. One day
he arrived with some props painted like stone carvings in the back of his
car. Pretending they were heavy, he made to pass one to Moore, who
protested 'Oh no, I can't take that' – only to realize that there was no
weight at all. When Howarth explained it could be bought in blocks of
eight by four or sixteen by four, Henry quickly saw how much time and
expense it could save.[33]

With advice from Howarth, the Hoglands assistants now knocked up
polystyrene replicas of the *Glenkiln Cross* and two other *Upright Motives*
to see if they might meet the challenge of the hill. They took about two
days each to complete rather than the two months that an old-style
armature of wood and scrim covered in plaster would have required. The
hill defeated them, however, as it subsequently defeated a mock-up of the
large *Arch*, or *Spindle Piece* with its outward-pointing, bee-sting breasts,
and even the gravidly sensual *Sheep Piece* of 1971–2, as this large bronze

was to be called after becoming a rubbing and sheltering post for sheep in the field itself. Some of Moore's most discriminating critics, like Anthony Caro and David Sylvester, consider the *Sheep Piece* to be one of his finest works; and so it sometimes seems, when well-sited, beautifully polished, and seen in the right frame of mind. On other occasions it can seem portentously sexual, with its suggestions of a ram mounting a ewe or of a lamb nuzzling its mother. Moore's sculpture is like that: it changes each time you see it, and the sculptor would not have wanted it otherwise. One consequence is that it is quite easy to go right off a piece, especially from among the large bronzes, which earlier seemed telling and impressive.

Other works may, by contrast, grow on one, like for example the creation most closely associated with the mound and its challenge: *Hill Arches* (of 1972–3) [167], an uncharacteristically complex four-part piece, involving three stirrup-like shapes, two of which arch towards each other, with the third leaning recumbent against one of them. Between the two upright arches is a large bronze ball, egg or sphere. Here, too, there are sexual and protective overtones, but rather gentler. One cast, as we shall see, ended up in a controversial location in Vienna, while another graces an island in a lake at the headquarters in Moline, Illinois, of Deere and Company. It did not, however, look good on the mound at Hoglands, which remained unadorned. Probably it was too far from likely viewing points. Even the mightiest piece was dwarfed by the distance and made to seem spindly or squat.

Graphic ventures

Graphics were among Moore's other preoccupations – and money-spinners – at this time. In the 1960s there was a boom in all forms of original prints: lithographs, etchings, drypoints, aquatints and other variants executed by the artist in the medium in which they were eventually published (usually as an edition of not more than 250 signed prints). Such graphics enabled the less well-off collector to buy an original, authenticated work of art which would at least keep its value, and often appreciate sharply.

Moore had probably been too obsessed with his carvings and drawing to become involved in all the exciting lithographic activity focused around the Curwen and Baynard presses in London in the 1930s, despite the involvement of friends like Piper, Sutherland, Bawden, Ravilious, and Paul Nash. His only ventures were a couple of unpublished woodcuts done in 1931 and a lithograph, *Spanish Prisoner* [63], showing a caged

head behind barbed wire: this was intended for sale to raise money for
Republican soldiers who had fled to France and been interned, but it was
never editioned.

Moore's first major effort as a graphic artist resulted from an invitation
in 1949 from the persuasive Brenda Rawnsley, of School Prints, to design
some lithographs which could be printed cheaply to bring images of real
quality to English schools. Not only Moore but Picasso and Braque,
among others on either side of the Channel, agreed to do so. They used
a technique perfected by the Ipswich printers W. S. Cowell, which enabled
the artist to work in his or her own studio, registering different colours
on a single plastic sheet. Moore did seven lithographs in this way, though
only four were editioned, for some reason in runs of fifty.[34]

Older, traditional forms of lithography used a technique of drawing on
grainy limestone, later zinc, with a greasy crayon or liquid, the image
being locked into the granular surface of the stone. For the image to be
printed the right way round, it had to be drawn in reverse, one of several
inhibiting factors. In the last quarter-century various highly sophisticated
alternative techniques have been evolved. The Curwen Press, with which
Henry worked for many years, favoured a complicated process known as
diazo, which required him to use ink or wash on transparent film, the
images being transferred to the diazo plate by ultra-violet light.[35] Perhaps
it is the indirectness of the working methods which gives many of Moore's
lithographs, highly decorative though they may be, a somewhat flat
and perfunctory look, as if the virtuoso was playing around with the
possibilities of the medium without becoming unduly involved.

Since each lithograph (sometimes a group of them) involved a publisher
and a printer – occasionally they were the same – and since many art
galleries were anxious to cash in on Moore's reputation and the print
boom, much coming and going at Hoglands was involved. From London
came Stanley Jones, the master printer at the Curwen Press and an
outstandingly nice man; and Bernhard Baer of the Ganymed Press, who
carried perfectionism further than most. From the Continent, there was
Felix Man, a tetchy photojournalist who had turned to publishing and
had a tie-up with the Galerie Wolfgang Ketterer in Stuttgart; Gérald
Cramer, immensely tall, pernickety and persevering, who commissioned
prints for his specialist gallery in Geneva and eventually published (with
his son Patrick) the four volumes of Moore's collected graphic work; and
from Zurich, the younger and more relaxed Wolfensberger brothers, Edi
and Ruedi, who have a gallery and printing works in the unappealing
Bederstrasse. The latter enlivened their visits to Hoglands with a round

of ping-pong with Moore. As a lithographer, they found him a brilliant technician. 'He knew exactly what you wanted, and he was very lively, gentle and accommodating,' Ruedi recalled.[36] On one occasion Wolfensberger took over some proofs and at Heathrow airport collected someone else's identical suitcase. On opening it, there were pyjamas and shirts instead of proofs. 'Henry went very quickly to the telephone and in about ten minutes had located the right suitcase and had a taxi deliver it.' The Wolfensbergers printed Moore's black and white Stonehenge sequence of 1972–3, which was among his more impressive lithographic ventures.

Etching was Moore's preferred graphic medium, though his output in it was much smaller. Perhaps because etching remains a much more direct technique than lithography, it seemed to capture his heart as well his head. The basic technique of etching remains unchanged: a copper plate is covered with an acid-resistant ground, on which the artist draws with a needle, exposing the copper where a line is required. The lines are then bitten out in an acid bath in successive immersions, according to the strength of line required, completed parts being 'stopped-out' with an acid-resistant varnish. Henry was given some early lessons in the subtleties of how much ink to use, 'wiping-off' and so in 1951 by the painter Merlyn Evans, an experienced practitioner. A handful of rather slight works resulted there and then, and his interest in the medium seemed to wilt. Between 1963, when a harsh winter made work on sculpture difficult, and 1966, he completed some forty lithographs but only a few more etchings, which were unimpressive.

Then in 1967 he was introduced by Cramer of Geneva and Alistair Grant, professor in printing at the Royal College of Art, to the great Parisian master printer and etching specialist Jacques Frélaut, of Frélaut and Lacourière near the Sacré-Coeur. Grant and Frélaut took a copper plate covered with ground down to Hoglands, then proofs were made at the Royal College; the plate might then be taken back for more work to be done: it was somewhat laborious, but eight interesting etchings were eventually printed by Frélaut in Paris (in 1971, to save all that toing and froing, Grant set up a little Starwheel press for proofing in a studio at Hoglands).[37] In 1969, *Ideas for Sculpture in Landscape*, and *Projects for Hill Sculpture* marked a significant advance in confidence and technique without suggesting that a masterpiece might be in the offing – the *Elephant Skull album* of 1969 and 1970, a virtuoso yet deeply felt outpouring which ranks high among Moore's works on paper.

The skull in question had come to Henry via his old friends Sir Julian and Juliette Huxley. Staying at the Mount Kenya Club in the early 1960s, they discovered that its wealthy American owner, Ray Ryan, was in despair because the wild animals which his guests came to see were being poached. The Huxleys promised to mention the matter to Kenya's President Jomo Kenyatta when they saw him shortly. In gratitude Ryan offered to make them members of his safari club, but Juliette Huxley said that what she had always wanted was a real elephant skull. 'You shall have one,' said Ryan. 'Tomorrow we have to shoot a rogue elephant, and I'll send you the skull' – which he did.

For about two years the skull decorated a corner of the Huxley's Hampstead garden on a rotating table, and in 1965 Henry came to see it. He had been working on the smaller version of *Nuclear Energy*, and noticed an affinity. Juliette Huxley, who was Swiss-born and had been taught to sculpt by John Skeaping, could see he was very interested:

> About six or nine months later we drove to see Henry, and in the car on the way I said 'I think I will give my elephant skull to Henry.' Soon after we arrived, Julian got out and told Henry as he came to greet us: 'We have decided to give you our elephant skull.' Henry sent along a lorry next day, and they took it complete with the rotating table I had had made. He had it beautifully cleaned and polished, so that it now looks like ivory: it was getting a bit mossy and mouldy, and a wren had built a nest where the neck connects with the vertebrae. . .[38]

She was saddened that henceforward Moore would always say he had been given the skull by 'my old friend Julian Huxley' – though to do the egocentric biologist justice, he gave his wife full credit for both the acquisition and the gift in his memoirs.[39]

Initially, the sculptor simply kept the skull as the most impressive item in his vast collection of natural objects such as stones, shells, bones, and driftwood – his 'library of natural forms', as he called it. One day Gérald Cramer arrived from Geneva and asked if Moore had done the etchings he had promised. Henry had done nothing, and Irina, who had come to love the skull while cleaning it up, suggested he should tackle it as a theme.[40]

Once he began, Moore became so fascinated that he produced not just a few etchings, but thirty-seven, exploring the skull's outline, its tunnels and cavities, recesses and eye sockets. Under his etching needle they became valleys, gorges, caves and mountains, Doric columns and underground dungeons. His previous etchings had been based on drawings.

Now he was exploring a new subject, communicating directly on to the plate with the wonderfully fine line of the etching needle, which he used to create striking contrasts of light and shade with much Seurat-like cross-hatching. Magnificently printed by Frélaut in Paris, the engravings made their debut at Cramer's gallery in Geneva in December 1970 before being shown to uniformly enthusiastic reviews in Paris, London (Marlborough Graphics), Munich and New York. *The* (London) *Times* showed a photograph of the sculptor with his hands inside the skull, captioned to its shame 'Henry Moore putting finishing touches to a sculpture, "Elephant Skull"' – a correction appeared next day. The *Daily Express* typically calculated that the 115 sets of the etchings would bring him £234,000 'in the next few days', as if printing costs, the publisher's slice and so on did not exist.[41] Even so, graphics at this level could be very lucrative for all concerned.

The *Elephant Skull album* was followed by the more obviously appealing and vastly popular sequence devoted to the sheep which, at a tap on the window of one of Moore's studios, would come and stare inquisitively at him from a few feet away, practically demanding to be drawn. The preparatory sketchbook, mainly executed in ballpoint, enjoyed great success when published in facsimile form not long afterwards.

Moore himself emerged in March 1970 as co-author, with the painter and sculptor Michael Ayrton, of a handsome Thames and Hudson publication devoted to the thirteenth-century Italian sculptor Giovanni Pisano. Many visits to Pisa, not far from Forte dei Marmi, had convinced Henry that Pisano's path-breaking ability to express in sculptural form his understanding of life and people made him among the ten greatest artists in European history.[42] Dining with Walter and Eva Neurath of Thames and Hudson at their holiday home in Camaiore, he lamented that there was no book which gave Pisano his due. Walter Neurath suggested his firm should fill the gap.

Soon afterwards, Michael and Elisabeth Ayrton came to see the Moores in Italy. The sight of Pisano's work in Pisa in 1947 had made Ayrton want to take up sculpture. Four years later he had moved to Essex and invited Moore, whom he had met in Hampstead in 1940, to lunch to see his first few pieces. Henry had been very encouraging, Elisabeth Ayrton recalled, describing one piece in particular as 'not half bad'. A friendship developed. Ayrton was intelligent, erudite, and articulate, and there were usually lots of bright children around (one of whom became Penny Leach, the child-care expert). Henry once stood on his head for them on a paving stone outside the house. They wrote in chalk to commemorate the feat,

'Henry Moore stood on his head here.' Short-lived though it was, he was proud of the inscription.[43] Ayrton, a fine draughtsman, did a number of pencil drawings of Moore, one of which showed him playing ping-pong, at which he hated to be beaten. Neither normally counted fellow artists among his friends.

Being a fluent writer with half a dozen publications to his credit, ranging in theme from Hogarth to Greek mythology, Ayrton was enthusiastic about the idea of a Pisano book. They decided to write half each, but since Moore found words a painful medium, he later not surprisingly restricted himself to dictating a foreword on to a tape-recorder and to showing the photographer Ilario Bessi how he thought sculpture should be photographed.[44] The book received a warm press, and the *Sunday Times* published a long extract from Moore's introduction.[45] Michael Ayrton died only five years later of a coronary, aged fifty-four. Had Moore passed away at the same age, in 1952, he would have missed thirty years of productive life. His work would have stopped at the *King and Queen*, and the creative rebirth of the 1960s would have been denied him.

The *New York Times*'s Hilton Kramer, one of the few English-language art critics of real intellectual stature, had grasped the quality of Moore's recent work when, in April 1970, seventeen marble and stone carvings were shown at Knoedler's and forty-three bronzes at Marlborough's New York branch on 57th Street: a rare joint venture between rivals. For years, Kramer wrote, Moore had found himself in the testing position of being ignored by the young and adored by the Establishment. He saw these two large, handsome exhibitions as a 'triumphant confirmation' of the artist's greatness, establishing the 1960s as 'the finest period in Mr Moore's long and copious oeuvre since the 1930s'.[46] As an antidote, within a few months Paul Overy was describing Epstein at his best as 'infinitely better than either Moore or Hepworth', whose work had become 'mostly pretty bad, overblown and insensitive'; nine months later, reviewing Henri Laurens at the Hayward Gallery in London, he concluded that the French artist was 'far finer' than Moore.[47]

There were soon to be changes in Moore's commercial arrangements. In 1971, amid all the politicking which followed the sale of Knoedler's in New York to Dr Armand Hammer and Dr Maury Leibovitz, he transferred his consigned works to Wildenstein's, whose large operation at 64th Street Harry Brooks had joined three years earlier. That same autumn Harry Fischer left Marlborough Fine Art in London to set up his own gallery, Fischer Fine Art, almost opposite Christie's in King Street, St James's. With Frank Lloyd concentrating on making the New York branch a success story, relations between the two ex-Viennese had become intolerably strained. Moore agreed to support Fischer by giving him a proportion of his output; but he liked to keep as many eggs in as many baskets as possible, and remained friendly with Marlborough in Bond Street. Fischer Fine Art opened in June 1972, one of the top attractions of a fine, mixed, inaugural show being the 1945 elmwood reclining figure for which Fischer had paid his record $260,000 (£101,562) at auction in New York a few months previously.

In the non-commercial sector, Moore's work continued to boost Britain's image abroad through the efforts of the British Council. Commerce and culture were not always totally separate: sixty-five Moore sculptures and thirty-two drawings provided an artistic patina to British Week (an official sales promotion drive) in Tokyo in autumn 1969. 'As a supporting event ... it was exactly the right thing in the right place,' the council's representative in the Japanese capital reported enthusiastically.[48] The show, sponsored by Mainichi newspapers, was the first major one-man exhibition by a British artist in Japan and one of the first attractions of the new Museum of Modern Art, where it was seen by almost 50,000 people in forty-one days. In Osaka and Nagoya afterwards, though crammed into department store galleries, it averaged 3,000 visitors a day.

After a successful showing in Hong Kong, a reduced version drawn mainly from Moore's own holdings was sent by the British Council in 1971 to Iran and Turkey. The exhibitions in Iran were seen as part of the celebrations of the 2,500th anniversary of the Persian monarchy which culminated in the grotesquely grandiose homage to the Shah in Persepolis that October. Queen Farah's attendance at the Moore opening in Tehran in early May ensured wide publicity. So enthusiastic was she about Moore's work that she bought four substantial bronzes, including a working-model version of *Oval with Points*, and two maquettes. From Tehran the show went to Isfahan and then to Shiraz, where it attracted a dismal 730 visitors in two weeks. After a hazardous journey by road and rail the Moore sculptures and drawings showed much greater pulling power in Istanbul: some 10,000 Turks managed the trip out to the Museum of Painting and Sculpture overlooking the Bosphorus.[49]

Moore's own travels in this period took him to Prague in spring 1969, to New York in spring 1970 for the Knoedler-Marlborough double exhibition, and to Vienna in spring 1971. Despite the crushing a year earlier of Dubček's experiment in 'socialism with a human face', the British Council had decided to go ahead with an exhibition in Prague of British painting from Hogarth to Turner, perhaps to cheer up the poor

Czechs. Moore's work had been shown there (and in Bratislava, the same show going on to Bucharest and Israel) in 1966, but without the sculptor's presence. The 1969 visit seems to have been at the suggestion of Sir Kenneth Clark, who was adding lustre to the opening at the Valdštejn Gallery. Moore took along a cast of a sensual, semi-abstract bronze completed the previous year, *Two Piece Sculpture No. 10: Interlocking*, for presentation to the National Gallery in Prague. The British ambassador lent them his Rolls-Royce to visit notable collections and see the glories of the city in comfort.

The idea of having a major Moore bronze in Vienna had been hatched when the painter Georg Eisler, then president of the Vienna Secession, and senior Viennese museum officials were in London in 1969 to discuss a Secession show for the Royal Academy. Deciding to start at the top, the scheme's supporters had hit upon a site in the middle of a pond being created by a Danish landscape architect in front of the great baroque Karlskirche. Moore went over to see it with Wolfgang Fischer, stayed at the famous Sacher Hotel, saw Richard Strauss's *Der Rosenkavalier* and was royally entertained over two full days. Among the artists he met were the sculptors Fritz Wotruba and Alfred Hrdlicka, who wrote a charming article about Moore's visit to his studio, likening him to a welter weight boxer who was yet world champion of all classes.[50] The Karlskirche arrangements were not clinched until 1973, *Hill Arches* being installed there in 1978.

By now the inauguration of big Moore bronzes in the USA had become so frequent as to be of purely local interest in most instances. For example, the Seattle First Bank in January 1971 acquired a cast of *Three Piece Sculpture: Vertebrae* for $165,000 via Harry Brooks in New York and a San Francisco dealer, Paule Anglim. It was set in a reflecting pool as a humanizing touch for the bank's austere new headquarters. Whether he liked it or not, Moore's big bronzes were the perfect foil to the architecture of big business. If the building was good, it was hard to say no even if he was consulted. In the last resort, if a company bought a Moore, it was free to do with it what it wished.

The sculptor's first direct involvement with the brilliant Chinese-American architect I. M. Pei sprang from a very different project. Pei had been commissioned to design a library for a key site in Columbus, Indiana (population 27,000), a town once dubbed the Athens of the Prairie on account of the quality of its architecture. Much of this was attributable to the patronage of J. Irwin Miller, chairman of the local Cummins Engine Co. Pei now persuaded Miller to pay for a large Moore which, he felt, was needed to pull together the new library and two other distinguished buildings with which it formed a square.

It remained to find the right piece in consultation with Moore. On his first visit to Hoglands, the architect explained the site and the role the bronze would play. As a candidate Pei proposed a larger version of *Large Torso: Arch*, which he had admired in the sculpture garden of the Museum of Modern Art in New York. The *Arch* had invited entry, and Pei's daughter had enjoyed herself running in and out of it. But the space framed by the six-foot-six-inch-high cast was too small for an adult. They talked about the scale of the buildings and of the square in Columbus, Pei recalled:

> In a very short time Henry came up with the idea that it should be high enough and wide enough for say two persons to walk through hand in hand, but not so wide that it would encourage a car to drive through. That started the dimensions – we decided it should be six to eight feet wide.[51]

Proportionately enlarged, the height came out at about twenty feet; and so, very rapidly, it was decided. While sculptor and architect enjoyed a cup of tea, two assistants produced a rough mock-up in polystyrene. 'Jolly good,' said Henry when he saw it, and that was it.

To enable him properly to inspect the completed cast in open surroundings, as Moore insisted on doing, Noack suggested they should have it taken to Berlin's Tiergarten. The dimensions of the vehicle required to carry the huge bronze were such that the operation had to be carried out between 1 a.m. and 3 a.m., to avoid traffic chaos. The *Arch* made the journey with an escort of three police cars, blue lights flashing, and four motorcycle outriders. Having been approved by the sculptor, the cast faced a long voyage by barge through the GDR to Hamburg, thence by sea to New Orleans, by barge again up the Mississippi, then overland from the Kentucky bank of the Ohio river to Columbus, where it was bolted into place on 15 April 1971, with Irwin Miller and several classes of children watching. Pei's imaginative view of the role of sculpture in architecture, his knowledgeable enthusiasm for Moore's work, and his delightful personality encouraged Henry to work with him again on the *Dallas Piece* and the gigantic version of *Knife Edge Two Piece* for the National Gallery's East Building in Washington.

Both Pei and Gordon Bunshaft helped Moore to achieve a happier relationship with architecture in the later part of his life. Because they became close friends and because he respected their buildings, working with them became a collaborative act in which the sculptor kept his freedom of manoeuvre and did not feel diminished or used. Perhaps, too, he sensed that as his own work became larger, it became in some instances quasi-architectural: the *Arch* itself, for example, looks at its best (as in the travertine version in Hyde Park, London) when framing sky and nature, like a fragment of the Parthenon. For the greatest show of his life, now imminent, he had a fibreglass version made of the great bone-like structure.

Triumph in Florence

In retrospect, the Florence exhibition which Princess Margaret opened on 20 May 1972 stands out as a kind of apotheosis, with news of its magnificence spreading around the world. Yet at the time it seemed a tremendous gamble to show a foreign artist, however famous, in the Forte di Belvedere, on the outskirts of the city; and for Moore, to be shown in such a setting. Would enough people make the journey out to the great fortress designed by Michelangelo? In the event, 345,000 did so before it closed on 8 October, an average of 2,500 a day. On the last day there were more than 7,000.

The initial idea seems to have been put to the Mayor of Florence, Luciano Bausi, by Moore's friend, the Florentine dealer Maria Luigi Guaita of the Il Bisonte gallery. Bausi was enthusiastic, and became the driving force of the enterprise. The British Council threw in its own vast experience and made it a joint Anglo-Italian venture. Partly to help obtain funds from the Italian government, various committees were set up with exactly matching British and Italian members. Henry's friend the art historian Giovanni Carandente became the central co-ordinator and catalogue editor, while Piero Micheli, the city's architect, took charge of the complicated physical arrangements.

Michelangelo's great citadel itself seemed at first a mixed blessing. Moore was to observe: 'No better site for showing sculpture in the open air, in relationship to architecture and to a town, could be found anywhere in the world.' Yet its own awesome grandeur and monumentality made it a frightening competitor.[52] Built to withstand force, its severe geometry exuded a force of its own. The hillside setting was equally breathtaking. From the grassy promontories within the fortress there were panoramic views of the city, dominated by Brunelleschi's sculpturesque cathedral dome, and in other directions the eye ranged over ancient olive groves and orchards punctuated by the dark verticals of cypresses out to distant mountains beyond.

In no other major exhibition of his career was Moore as intimately involved in the arrangements. Many of the 289 exhibits (168 sculptures, 121 works on paper) came from his own, Irina's and Mary's collections. He even wrote letters to some important potential lenders, like Sophia Loren and Carlo Ponti: an invitation to dinner with them resulted when the whole team was in Rome in late February 1972 for a press conference. Two cars picked them up (Bausi, Micheli, Carandente, Guaita and others), and they climbed through fir trees to an old villa on a hill outside Rome: very much a family home, but with fine paintings including some Bacons and small Renoirs on the walls, and Moore's two rediscovered early *jardinières* on either side of the sitting-room fireplace. The Ponti collection included some prime early Moore carvings, which were duly lent.

After that short preliminary trip to Florence and Rome, Henry and Irina returned to Florence on 1 May, settling into a service flat in the Palazzo Benci down by the river Arno, where they were well looked after. At one stage they spent a few days in Camaiore with their friends Brigitte and Gottfried Fischer, who had steered the Fischer Verlag to new prosperity after the Second World War. Henry's main concern at the Belvedere was the disposition of the forty-odd large pieces being shown on the various levels of grass terraces within the fort. To have strung them out in a line on the edge of the parapet overlooking the city roofscape would have been easy but inadequate.

Because of the narrowness of the archway giving access to the Belvedere at ground level and the slipperiness of the cobbles, every piece and packing case had to be hoisted up and over the top battlements by crane. To aid further manoeuvres up there, a small truck and crane had themselves been lifted up. It took a full week just to get the exhibits into the edifice. The vehicle bearing the *Three Piece: Vertebrae*, which the Israel Museum had lent, was so large that it got stuck against the porch of a house *en route*, even though a detour had been made. A second truck was sent to the further side of the house and the cases were transferred.[53] The giant, 180-ton Carrara marble version of *Square Form with Cut* [166], fresh from the Henraux works, had to be hoisted up in its fifty to sixty component pieces, then reassembled layer by layer like a stone wall. The smaller works, drawings and graphics were installed in the three-storey sixteenth-century building at the peak of the citadel, whose restoration was being completed as the show was mounted. There were fears that the wax in such mixed-media drawings as the shelter studies might melt in the summer heat under the roof on the top floor, since there were no climatic controls. 'They all turned to me and said "Decide!"' Margaret McLeod of the British Council recalled.[54] Some monitoring equipment was located, and the shelter drawings were moved to a lower, cooler room, where they were also seen to better effect.

Harold Acton, the writer and collector, looked in from time to time from his villa La Pietra, joining the party for a dinner given by Carandente in the kitchen of the vast and empty castle of Cafaggiolo, about twenty miles from Florence. His own house guests, Princess Margaret and her husband Lord Snowdon, were there too, as was the sculptor Lynn Chadwick.[55] Generally Moore would eat with a group of helpers at one of the pleasant trattorias in the area, especially La Beppa at the foot of the Belvedere. When his American friends like Jo Hirshhorn, Seymour Knox, the Bunshafts, and Harry Brooks began to arrive, there were some splashier celebrations.

Yet it was not an entirely agreeable period. Apart from the frustrations of not getting on with his 'real' work and the importunings of journalists and photographers, Moore had been suffering bouts of mild depression. This was traced to a minor but lasting diabetic condition. Once corrective measures were taken, his normal cheerfulness returned, with Irina having henceforward to keep an eye on his sugar intake. He was also troubled by a rheumatic knee. For added warmth in the sometimes cool spring weather he borrowed some long underpants from an Italian gardener who heard of his trouble. 'I'm all right, I've got the gardener's underpants on,' he would call out when someone advised him to take it steady on a stone staircase.[56] He was after all rising seventy-four, and his age was at last beginning to show.

The evening of the alfresco opening at the Belvedere was cold and damp. A fanfare of trumpets greeted Princess Margaret as she arrived to an escort of guards in medieval uniforms. After long speeches by the mayor, the education minister and the director-general of the British Council, Sir John Henniker, all of which were translated, the brevity of Princess Margaret's opening words was much appreciated. The floodlit sculptures looked magnificent against the city's floodlit monuments, but it was too chilly to savour the spectacle. Many in the audience of some 2,000 people wore raincoats for warmth, and when the speeches were over there was a rush for the doors of the main building more for warmth than for art. However, only Moore and the royal and official parties were allowed in.

Fears of inadequate attendance were soon proved groundless. The

Italian press, which had earlier reflected criticisms that the first living artist to be given a major show in the Belvedere should be a foreigner, was overwhelmingly enthusiastic. Long queues formed on the first morning, and by the second the entire stock of 3,000 copies of Carandente's not inexpensive catalogue (5,000 lire, or £3·50, now worth around £12) had sold out. Extra guards had to be hired, and at one stage entrance tickets ran out. Even Carandente was taken aback by the success.[57]

It was, as Moore's Much Hadham friend John Thompson, then deputy editor of the *Sunday Telegraph*, observed, 'a stunning climax to the career of the miner's son from Yorkshire who first found his way to Florence as a student in 1925, and whose imagination has been stirred ever since by the magnificence of the Florentine achievement'.[58] To the young Moore who stalked the streets of Florence in 1925 it would have seemed the wildest of dreams, John Russell mused in the *Sunday Times*, that his work would one day fill the Belvedere and overflow on to its lawns.[59]

It was not all rapturous praise. As usual the critics were impressed by the works of the 1930s; but the post-war bronzes were seen to stand up to their beautiful setting with mixed success. For Guy Brett of *The Times*, the simplifications involved in producing the largest pieces seemed to smooth away internal energy, giving them the static feeling of immense relics.[60] Michael Shepherd of the *Sunday Telegraph* found insufficient content in the large *Arch*, in the *Locking Piece* and in *Square Form with Cut*, and considered the *Three Piece Vertebrae* [178], whose 'bony, warrior-like shapes lord it on a rampart as if they would earn themselves a place in the Piazza della Signoria itself', the triumph of the show.[61] In the *New York Times*, Hilton Kramer observed penetratingly that Moore's work of the 1930s was an exploration of an interior universe, crowded with troubled and sometimes violent feelings which had no place in his later work. For this, the sculptor had chosen a form of public speech, eliminating the language of the private self. The later work was devoid of violence, pastoral, the massive interlocking forms embracing each other with an easy lyricism and occupying the earth with a delicious sense of organic harmony: a public expression of an essentially benevolent emotion. It was this sense of well-being which the younger generation of artists and critics could not forgive, he wrote.[62]

Moore remained in Florence for a week after the opening. On 27 May, on the eve of his return to Perry Green with Irina, the Italian President, Giovanni Leone, paid an official visit to the exhibition, and afterwards at a private ceremony made Moore a Cavaliere di Gran Croce dell'Ordine al

Merito (the Germans followed suit that August with their highest honour for services to science and the arts, the order Pour le Mérite). The exhibition had been due to close on 29 September, and on the 27th the President of the Senate in Rome, Amintore Fanfani, presented Henry with a gold medal to mark its success. Then it was learned that Britain's Prime Minister Edward Heath wanted to see it on 4 October after political talks in Rome, and it was extended for a week. Moore duly escorted Heath around.

The Florence exhibition was not just a triumph but produced a subtle shift in the way Moore's work was seen by his admirers. From now on he was considered not just a modern master but as one whose work represented artistic continuity and a dialogue with the past, so absent from what Hilton Kramer called the 'heartless' new movements of the art scene.[63] Moore had long believed he stood in the great European tradition. Seeing his work in that ancient and magnificent setting in Florence, others now saw the logic of his claim.

Chapter XVIII

Becoming an institution

1973–9

In these seven years which led beyond his eightieth birthday, Moore remained very active and productive. Counting one cast of each edition of bronzes and excluding drawings and graphics, his output ran to 150 sculptures. Stylistically they are marked by a swing away from the abstractions of the 1960s and back to the quintessential themes of earlier years: mother and child, reclining figure, helmet head, even a falling warrior for the West German city of Goslar. Compared with the grand creations of the previous decade, these bronzes and carvings – it was a busy period for the Henraux artisans – suggest an autumn mellowness. Moore seemed at last to be worrying less about being considered great: ironically, the death of Picasso in April 1973 led to him being periodically invoked as the 'greatest living artist' as well as the greatest living sculptor. Safe on its peak, his reputation was now beyond the fire of younger artists, among whom a strong reaction against abstraction was gaining strength.

The danger for Moore was rather that a higher degree of acceptance in the afterglow of the Florence exhibition would give his work a kind of critical invisibility. As an admirer put it, his sculpture had become so much part of the landscape that a considerable effort was required actually to see it.[1] For the general public the danger of over-familiarity was less acute, and the celebration of his seventy-fifth and eightieth birthdays gave a new intimacy to his relationship with Londoners. In the same period a very successful exhibition in Zurich and the public installation of about eighteen 'important' Moores in the USA and Continental Europe underlined his pre-eminence as a creator of monumental outdoor bronzes. Across the Western world the environmentalist spirit was growing. Moore's work, full of landscape and organic references, brought a sense of nature to the heart of large cities. To those who saw life on earth as an interdependent whole, his vision was very relevant.

Until he was over eighty Moore remained fit enough to make dozens of short but exhausting trips abroad to help locate or unveil a work, to supervise or attend the opening of a Moore exhibition. His personality remained generally free of the excessive *gravitas* of old age: at seventy-five John Russell saw him as 'unaffected, convivial, outstandingly loyal to his friends, forthright in his opinions, and with something in him of the schoolboy just let out of school'.[2] He could also on occasion be dogmatic and repetitious, but the reminiscences about his early days, however familiar to his intimates, came out with every sign of freshness.

Yet while his health and stamina remained remarkable, he was increasingly vulnerable to mishaps. In spring 1973 he suffered a mild bout of pleurisy in the left lung, which confined him to bed and made him cancel appointments for two weeks. Irina believed it stemmed from having to get out of a bath to answer the telephone in Luxembourg, thus catching a chill which went to his lungs. He was in the Grand Duchy for the opening of an exhibition of his work in a new wing of the main public museum. The Luxembourgeois, accustomed to the somewhat bland abstractions of the current Ecole de Paris painters, were much struck by the grandeur and strength of his work. If only 4,000 saw it over four weeks, it had to be remembered that the country's population of 340,000 was less than the attendance at the Florence exhibition.

A more serious setback occurred the following January when Henry fell while getting out of the bath at Hoglands, injuring his back and breaking the ankle which he had already damaged playing tennis. Though not confined to bed, he was subsequently limited to sedentary work for at least a month – to the benefit of his output of graphics – and was from then on more dependent on a stick for support. Worse, by taking the strain off his affected ankle when walking he damaged his back. It was perhaps comforting that an intact version of himself had recently gone on view at Madame Tussaud's. In January 1973 he had been measured with callipers and photographed, eyes and hair being matched for colour and texture. Moore was intrigued by the techniques used. First he was modelled in clay, then a plaster mould was made from the clay model. The mould was then used to make his body in fibreglass and his exposed head and hands in wax. Henry supplied some old clothes, including a pair of black shoes for which he searched in vain afterwards. He went to inspect his *alter ego* in December 1973, and the model Moore was revealed next day, leaning casually against a pillar just behind a seated Picasso. As a picture in *The Times* of the two Moores demonstrated, the likeness was very good.[3]

Picasso's death (shortly followed by that of Lipchitz) drew a guarded tribute from Moore. Picasso was probably one of the most naturally gifted artists since Raphael, he said, and had influenced artists forty years younger, and also those of today, without their knowing it. 'He was a remarkable phenomenon and changed the way people see things.'[4] One senses a number of ifs and buts hovering unspoken. Later Henry said of him: 'If you are as clever as that, there are shortcomings.'[5] Was Picasso too protean, too virtuoso, too productive for his own good? For someone as competitive as Moore, he undoubtedly was. Such prodigious gifts were hard to forgive. Worse still, Picasso achieved greatness while flouting conventional morality.

Henry's seventy-fifth birthday on 30 July 1973 was a muted affair, with the Tate's seventieth-birthday tribute and the Florence exhibition still fresh in many memories. The biggest exhibition linked to it was at the County Museum of Art in Los Angeles, with Moore's friend and ardent admirer Henry Seldis, of the *Los Angeles Times*, as guest curator. The hundred sculptures and twenty-six works on paper were drawn mainly from Californian museums and private collections. The biggest lender was the food manufacturer Norton Simon, with seventeen sculptures from his private collection, his foundation, and his museum in Pasadena. Billy Wilder, and Jack Warner's daughter Mrs Stanley Sheinbaum were among many show-business contributors. Moore was represented by daughter Mary, who was a hit with the local press.

The French, normally reluctant to honour foreign artists, welcomed Moore to one of their inner sanctums in November 1973 when he became an associate member of the Académie des Beaux-Arts, known for some reason as a *membre de l'Institut*. Moore had been sponsored by Daniel Wildenstein, the Parisian dealer, collector and racehorse owner. Several preliminary trips to Paris were involved for fittings of the pasha-like green and gold uniform, and in London a ceremonial sword was made, with hilt and head designed by the sculptor in conjunction with Cartier, the jewellers; Wilkinson, the swordsmiths; and Max Harari, head of Wildenstein's London branch. The hilt was in rough silver, with a small Moore-like bronze head. When Henry first strapped it on, the weight was such that the tail-end went straight up into the air. So they had the silver hollowed out.[6] Eventually Moore got stuck in a traffic jam on the way to the ceremony and was late. In his speech of acceptance he reminisced (in English) about his many visits to France from the First World War onwards. The Académie mounted a show of his graphic work, and *Le Monde* celebrated both events with an appreciative profile.

Daniel Wildenstein was then on good terms with the Pompidou government, and President Pompidou was an enthusiast for contemporary art. Probably through this combination of circumstances, Moore was asked whether he would like to produce something really monumental to balance the Arc de Triomphe at the far end of the avenue culminating in the futuristic, high-rise development known as La Défense. He took the opportunity of this visit to inspect the proposed site, but eventually declined the challenge, offering instead to provide a sculpture for one of the new zones. No doubt he sensed it was more an architectural than a sculptural task, and his experience of large projects had not on the whole been encouraging. Even so, to be offered such a project in Paris was no mean compliment.

The London branch of Wildenstein's unwittingly introduced to the Moore orbit the young American, Raymond Danowski, who was to become Mary Moore's husband. Danowski had been working in a gallery off Bond Street, and was taken on by Max Harari in 1973, at a point when Daniel Wildenstein had agreed that the London branch might try venturing into contemporary American painting as a back-up for the dwindling supply of good Impressionists. Being *au fait* with New York's art scene, Danowski seemed well qualified. Then Wildenstein changed his mind, which left the new recruit as an ordinary salesman, with Moore the only major contemporary artist in England with whom the gallery was associated.

Danowski paid one or two visits to Hoglands on business in autumn and winter 1973. In the following May he and Mary were virtually thrown together when they represented Wildenstein's and Moore *père* respectively at an exhibition of Henry's drawings organized by the gallery in Tokyo. The impact was dramatic. Mary was twenty-eight, Danowski thirty. Her way of life and taste in boyfriends tended to the Bohemian. The current one was the poet Brian Patten, of whom Henry had a higher opinion than of most: indeed, Mary's way of life probably represented a reaction or revolt against her father's protectiveness, doting affection, addiction to routine, and deep respect for the social fabric. Danowski was very different, an urbane charmer who enjoyed high living and had been previously married in the USA, with two daughters and a son.

From Tokyo the two young people vanished, surfacing eventually in San Francisco and then New York. They were away for more than a month. Since Danowski was still employed by Wildenstein's, Harari was not pleased. When the prodigals returned, Mary seemed to have discovered the joys of spending money. Clothes and cars were upgraded, and a farmhouse near Hoglands called Minges, which Henry and Irina had made available, was soon being lavishly done up. Since Moore had given his daughter a large number of his drawings and bronzes (major pieces were by now fetching around £100,000 each), there was an almost limitless source of funds; and since not all these gifts had been very clearly documented, some friction over sales was inevitable.

At first Moore seems to have found Danowski a refreshing contrast to many of Mary's previous boyfriends. He was not only presentable but genuinely interested in contemporary art. He also had some good ideas. One was that Moore should stop quixotically handing over the bulk of his earnings to the Inland Revenue. Under the Labour government, surtax was nearing its peak of eighty-three per cent of earned income, and the rates on investment income were even higher. According to a letter which he was to write to Mrs Thatcher apropos of the British Council soon after she became Prime Minister in 1979, in the ten years between 1967 and 1977 he paid a total of £4,350,621 in tax, the figure for 1975 alone being £1,031,275 – while the British Council received less than £1,000,000 to spend on organizing exhibitions abroad in the same decade. Nine-tenths of his income had come from sales abroad, thanks in no small measure to the British Council's help in making his work known overseas, he wrote.[7]

Since around 1960 his friend Maurice Ash had been advising him to divert a larger proportion of his income from tax. But so far action had been taken only against the looming threat of death duties, with the setting up in 1972 of a Henry Moore Trust, generally known as the Hoglands Trust. This was to be administered by the Tate Gallery, the trustees being the director, Sir Norman Reid or successor, three or four Tate trustees, and a Moore nominee, in this case Maurice Ash. The main aim was to prevent the estate being broken up and partly sold to pay death duties. Instead it would become a sculpture park where Moore's work could be admired in the setting in which it had been conceived. Land and sculpture belonging to the artist were transferred to the trust, with £250,000 for future funding. By dint of being chairman of the Tate's trustees, the Oxford historian, Alan Bullock, became chairman.

When Mary and Raymond were married in summer 1976, nothing had changed: Moore remained self-employed and a heavy taxpayer, but the future of the estate had been assured. The marriage took place on 24 June at Bishop's Stortford register office, a few miles from Perry Green.

Henry, Irina and two friends were present – probably not quite the occasion they had envisaged for Mary. The marriage certificate gave Danowski's profession as art dealer, his father's as warehouseman. When the *Sunday Express*'s gossip columnist discovered that the wedding had taken place, Danowski told him:

> The nice thing about my marriage is that I am now part of a good family life. I get on very well with Mr Moore. He is a very human person . . . I am not career-oriented. I don't do anything very specific now apart from my interest in trees. I would call myself an amateur arboriculturalist.[8]

This last reference was to a large number of trees which he and Mary had bought to plant at Minges, and showed a nice touch of humour. It was engaging too that he was so open about his lack of interest in earning a living. There were two coincidences in Mary's choice of husband: first, that his name was Raymond, as Henry's father's and eldest brother's had been; and secondly, that he should, like Irina, have been of East European origin.

Danowski had not in fact been idle, having put forward some grandiose plans for a new Henry Moore Foundation, in whose development Moore at first saw his son-in-law playing an active role. 'Raymond's going to do this,' he would tell visitors, or 'Raymond plans to do that . . .' Not long after the marriage, Norman Reid was surprised to receive a telephone call from Henry saying 'Look, nothing has changed, but I am going to make a family foundation, as Mary is now married.' It would not interfere with existing arrangements, 'but we thought it would be a good thing to have a family thing as well'.[9] Its members would probably be Irina, Mary, Raymond, and Lord Goodman, the solicitor whom Moore regarded as the wisest adviser on worldly matters.

It was typical of Henry to announce something like that over the telephone; that was often his preferred way of doing business. In fact the Henry Moore Trust remained in existence, but with a sole trustee, the Henry Moore Foundation, as the new entity was called. Under the new arrangements, from January 1977 the profits from Moore's work went to the Foundation via a newly created subsidiary, Raymond Spencer Ltd, as the managing director of which he was paid a salary. The aims of the body were to conserve the work and reputation of Henry Moore and the setting in which the work was created, and to assist the arts in general and sculpture in particular. As such they were a blend of altruism and enlightened self-interest, and led, as we shall see, to an impressive spread of often imaginative benefactions.

At first Henry found it hard to reconcile himself to the idea that his money should be disbursed on the trustees' say-so, and he seemed anxious to have it hoarded up. When told that a charity was obliged by law to spend its income, he was unimpressed. Then he realized the capital from his earnings, no longer depleted by tax, was running into millions, and his attitude changed. Ironically that coincided with a ruling that trustees *could* accumulate income.

The Danowski plan for a large sculpture park on farmland near Hoglands had been submitted to the local authorities for planning permission, to the alarm of the local population. Already uneasy over Moore's purchase of a dozen properties on and around Perry Green, they became openly hostile when, in March 1978, details of the projected 190-acre sculpture park became known: 180 acres of 'high-quality' agricultural land to be taken out of use, residential property to be adapted for storage or display, and much demolition and construction, a hostel being among the proposed new buildings.

Fears of coaches bringing up to 100,000 visitors a year, with hot-dog stands and heavy traffic shattering the peace of the hamlet, surfaced vividly at a meeting in the parish hall. 'Villagers Hammer Moore Sculpture Park Plan', a *Guardian* headline reported with evident relish.[10] Mary Moore pointed out to the press that she and her husband would be staying on, and had no desire to live next to a Woburn Park. Some 3,000 visitors already came every year by appointment, she said: that was probably an over-estimate of the coachloads of art lovers from museums, schools, and other bodies which periodically descended on Hoglands. The East Hertfordshire Planning Committee reacted by suggesting a reduction of the proposed area and the elimination of the suggested hostel, presumably intended for students. Moore was upset by the ill-will which the proposal had created. Though by English standards the scheme had shown signs of *folie de grandeur*, the sculptor seemed insensitive to local feeling in giving it his approval: he after all had lived there for more than thirty-five years, while Danowski was new to the area. Eventually most elements of the plan were quietly shelved.

Ironically, just when Moore was endeavouring to secure the future of his home, part of his past was being wiped out. There had been controversy off and on since 1966 over the birthplace of Castleford's most famous son at 30 Roundhill Road. First the row centred on whether it should be marked by an official plaque. When the council took no action,

'I've found his teddy bear.' *Skyrack Express*,
Tadcaster, Yorkshire, 22 February 1974

the current owner, a miner called Harold Higgins, had one made. Then
came the possibility of the house being demolished as part of a slum
clearance scheme. Moore stilled protests by saying that he would not like
sentiment to stand in the way of progress.[11] Progress duly took its course
on 15 February 1974, when three other houses were demolished with
No. 30. A small garden created on the site was soon reduced by vandalism
to a wasteland.

When Moore was nearing his seventy-fifth birthday and between his
bout of pleurisy and his broken ankle, he bravely accepted an invitation
to illustrate or interpret some poems by his old acquaintance W. H.
Auden. The idea came from Véra Russell, whose suggestions were not
easily ignored and who had known Auden since the 1930s. Over lunch at
Hoglands she, Auden, Moore, and Mark Cornwall-Jones of the Petersburg
Press discussed the idea; then poet and sculptor met again in Vienna
almost a year later, in September 1973, during Moore's second visit to
discuss the Karlskirche project. Auden, who lived at Kirchstetten outside
Vienna, came in his carpet slippers to a reception which Chancellor
Kreisky himself gave to celebrate the clinching of arrangements for the
big Moore bronze. Georg Eisler remembered seeing the two Yorkshiremen,
the exile and the stay-at-home, facing each other across a table, the
poet's lined and furrowed face resembling a relief map of lower Austria.[12]

Ten days later Auden died of a heart attack, aged sixty-six. Next day,
from memory and as a tribute, Moore drew some thumbnail sketches
consisting almost entirely of the lines on that battered visage. Auden's
death gave the lithograph project a fresh poignancy. Since the poems
showed a strong sense of the spirit of place, Moore soon fixed on the
Yorkshire landscape as the strongest link between them. The resulting

dark and mysterious images of hills, crevasses, tunnels, mill-streams, and vestigial figures are among his most moving and original graphic works. The twenty lithographs were exhibited in the prints and drawings gallery of the British Museum in spring 1974, along with works which Moore regarded as loosely related. It was a wonderful chance to pay off the debt which he felt he owed the British Museum as a formative influence, and once again to place himself in the grandest mainstream of European art. His guiding light in executing the lithographs, he admitted, had been Seurat and his 'black' drawings, of which he lent two of his own examples. From the British Museum's own vast holdings he chose *inter alia* three drawings by Michelangelo, four by Rembrandt, and two by that master of mystery, Odilon Redon. From his own earlier work he gave a first proper airing since the war to his mining drawings, whose value in preparing him for his more recent graphic ventures he had at last come to appreciate. His famous wartime drawing, *Crowd Looking at a Tied-Up Object*, was lent by Lord Clark. With selected Auden manuscripts and biographical photographs, the exhibition provided a true insight into two outstanding imaginations.

The Palumbo altar

Another commission which was completed at about the same time as the lithographs resulted in the only altar to be designed by Moore. It was initiated by Peter Palumbo, a London property developer with a passion for great architecture (as he saw it) and a keen interest in collecting contemporary art. Strong religious convictions had led him to become a patron and churchwarden of St Stephen Walbrook in the heart of the City, a miniature St Paul's Cathedral regarded as one of Christopher Wren's smaller-scale masterpieces. The church had been badly damaged by enemy bombs in the Second World War, and Palumbo spent much time and money in planning its restoration.

In 1967 he had the idea that Moore was the perfect artist to design a circular altar to be placed directly under the church's celebrated dome, with the congregation seated around it. Perhaps surprisingly, the sculptor reacted very positively when the suggestion was broached to him by Palumbo's friend Harry Fischer: it seemed to be a beautiful idea and a wonderful church, he told Fischer.[13] He visited St Stephen's in May 1968 and got on well with Palumbo. There was even some talk of installing one of the largest-sized casts of the *Arch* in the controversial redevelopment of Mansion House Square, complete with a Mies van der Rohe tower block, which the developer was already trying to bring to fruition (it was finally turned down by the planning authorities in 1985).

Like so many commissions, this altar project was to be fraught with complications and delays. To obtain a 'faculty' (ecclesiastical planning consent) for the altar, a petition had to be made to the Chancellor of the Diocese through the archdeacon. It was all reminiscent of a Trollope novel. The archdeacon, Sam Woodhouse, was sympathetic. Others would inevitably be hostile to such a mixing of old and new. The difficulties ahead were compounded by the serving of a Dangerous Structure Notice on the floor of the church. The appointment in early 1972 of Robert Potter, a prominent architect later to become Surveyor of the Fabric of St Paul's Cathedral, coincided with the emergence of Moore's first drawings of the altar. When a polystyrene mock-up was tried out in the church in March that year, it struck the rector, the Revd Chad Varah, as 'right and inevitable'.[14]

From then on, progress was relatively swift, on the sculptural if not the legal-ecclesiastical front. The altar, eight feet in diameter and almost three and a half feet high, was carved at the Henraux works, along with the 'footpace' designed by Moore: a stepped platform, also of travertine, in the middle of which the altar would stand and from which communion would be dispensed to communicants kneeling on the step. Altar and footpace, together weighing some ten tons, were shipped to England early in 1973. When the Diocesan Advisory Committee first considered the question of the faculty in March 1975, on the basis of photographs, doubts were expressed, but judgement was postponed pending work on crypt and floor. The final vote was not taken until January 1983, after a visit to inspect the unique object at Hoglands, where it was being kept. It was lost by eight to seven, on the chairman's casting vote. Those opposed felt that Moore's work might have suited an earlier style of architecture, like Gothic, but was at odds with Wren's.

A petition for this ruling to be overturned was now made to the Consistory Court of the Diocese of London. In order that architectural and other experts could form their own judgement on a factual basis, the massive altar – flat on top, but with subtly moulded flanks – was brought into the church in early 1986 at a cost of £33,000, almost half as much as its would-be donor had paid for it [170]. Although restoration work was still far from complete, it looked extraordinarily dramatic under Wren's great dome. Indeed, among the arguments of those opposing it was that the altar would be too dominant and do violence to the church's geometry, and that it was not stylistically 'congruent' with its setting.

They also claimed that to site it centrally was to deny Wren's vision of the church as auditorium, with attention focused on the pulpit.

At the legal hearing the altar's supporters argued in essence that it was a fine thing in itself, that its central positioning was consonant with modern liturgical practice, and that it would enhance the church. The Chancellor, George Newsom QC, was clearly sympathetic to the negative arguments, but dismissed the petition for the altar's installation on a fine point of ecclesiastical law: an altar must be a table, and since Moore's carving could not be described as a table in the normal sense of a raised surface supported on legs or a central pillar, it could not be an altar. Having lost the second round, the rector and his backers lodged an appeal with the Court of Ecclesiastical Causes Reserved. In February 1987 the court, composed of three bishops and two High Court judges and sitting for only the second time in its twenty-three-year history, ruled that such a legless, solid slab could indeed be considered a Holy Table, and allowed the appeal – with the rider that the altar was of superb quality. Palumbo and Moore were vindicated, and the final stages of the church's restoration could proceed as planned.

Zurich connections

So often the subject of controversy, Moore's work had never before been at the centre of legal proceedings, quaint though they might be. Yet even abroad devious tactics had sometimes to be adopted to gain acceptance for the public siting of a Moore sculpture. The story of how the Zurich suburb of Zollikon got its *Falling Warrior* in 1959, for example, provides a strange preface to Moore's interesting relationship with Switzerland's financial capital. Among the city's many collectors were two brothers, Hans and Walter Bechtler, specializing respectively in twentieth-century painting and sculpture. Together they had endowed a foundation which, like a private version of the Contemporary Art Society, presented works of art to communities which might otherwise have shunned them.

On a visit to Perry Green in 1956, Walter Bechtler was so struck by the preliminary plaster of the *Falling Warrior* that he indented for a cast on the spot. Shortly after he received it, he offered it to the Zollikon authorities: it seemed a perfect début for the foundation. Understandably, the officials who inspected it prone in his garden by the lake found it baffling. There was then no public Moore in Switzerland outside the Zurich and Basle museums. Might its theme make it suitable for their cemetery, they eventually suggested? Bechtler could not accept such a banishment. He had in mind a lakeside site then being re-landscaped. The impasse was broken when the architect concerned discovered that three pioneering Finnish aviators had been killed in 1920 when their amphibious plane crashed in the lake *en route* from north Italy to Finland. The *Falling Warrior* was unveiled with great panoply as their memorial on 6 September 1959, to the great benefit of Swiss-Finnish relations.[15]

Moore's relationship with Zurich, much closer than with any single German city, was to culminate in one of the most successful shows of his career and in the placing of a cast of *Sheep Piece* [163] by the lake which gives the city so much of its character. Yet private lives too were changed by contact with his work, an interaction perfectly exemplified by his dealings with a well-known Zurich lawyer, Willy Staehelin, and his wife Marina.

To the amazement of their friends, who feared they might be over-reaching themselves, the Staehelins had in the 1950s commissioned Marcel Breuer, by then a famous figure in New York, to design them a house on a superb lakeside site at Feldmeilen, on the city's outskirts. They were already familiar with Moore's work when they went to see Breuer in 1956. He later showed them photographs of the Unesco building in Paris, which he had co-designed, with its sentinel-like Moore, and said he could envisage a Moore sculpture on the front lawn of their new home. Before long the Staehelins visited Henry at Perry Green with Harry Fischer, finding him very gentle and not at all the big star: coming upon him in his little maquette studio, they felt as if they had gone down into some Wagnerian mountain to see a dwarf shaping his clay.

Starting with a Unesco-related reclining figure, they eventually bought four large bronzes; six bronzes of working-model size; six bronze maquettes; and two substantial marble carvings. One of the latter was a three-foot-high version in red travertine of *Two Forms*, which the play-wright Edward Albee had originally hoped to buy from Marlborough Fine Art; the other, a poignantly simple *Torso*. Both dated from 1966. Moore helped choose the final location of each piece, and had the base of *Two Forms* raised so that it was silhouetted against the lake, a stirring sight. When he came to stay one wet weekend in 1970, he said on arrival: 'You are no doubt worried what to do with me all weekend, but don't worry, I shall just look at my sculptures'; and he did spend part of it trudging around with an umbrella studying his offspring.[16]

Like the lives of many people who seem to have everything, the Staehelins' was touched by tragedy in 1973, when their daughter, Barbara, died in an accident in Munich. It would be some consolation, her desolated parents felt, if one of Moore's figures could watch over her mortal remains, buried in a beautifully kept cemetery not far away at Meilen. They already owned a cast of *Upright Motive No. 7*, and hoped a cast of *Glenkiln Cross* might be available. All had been sold, however, and they settled for *Upright Motive No. 2*, which stands there on a grassy knoll against a background of larch, birch, and pine, looking out to the distant lake. There is no inscription, and none is needed: this Moore offers consolation not just to the Staehelins but to all those ready to receive it.

The Staehelins have work by other sculptors, above all Henri Laurens, four of whose rhythmic bronzes are set in a little flood-lit, plant-filled courtyard within Breuer's L-shaped, single-storey design, and some fine paintings. But only with Moore and his sculpture did they forge so life-enhancing a relationship. 'We live in a marriage of Breuer and Moore,' Willy Staehelin commented over lunch on the terrace by the swimming pool. 'Our sculptures speak to each other across the garden.'[17]

For nine years Staehelin was chairman of the Friends of the Zurich Kunsthaus museum. Among those whom he entertained at his home and who were impressed by the Moores was his successor in that position, Dr Hanspeter Bruderer, executive vice-president of Elektrowatt, a huge industrial and engineering holding company. In exchange for permission to build their new lakeside headquarters one storey higher than the usual limit, the firm had given the city some land in front of the new building, and planned furthermore to provide a sculpture for the adjacent park: probably something by a Swiss sculptor, perhaps Zurich's own admirable Max Bill.

That idea was abandoned in the recession following the oil price rises of 1973, but Bruderer continued to cherish it. Having fallen in love with the *Sheep Piece* on a visit to Perry Green with Edi Wolfensberger in summer 1974, he decided – rather as Mayor Givens had in Toronto – to try to raise enough money privately to purchase it for the city and the lakeside park. He reckoned he needed 50,000 Swiss francs each from a dozen citizens, and approached Staehelin first. 'If you put yourself at the head of the list, you can put me down as No. 2,' the lawyer replied. No immortality or even short-term glory was on offer, since the exercise was to be anonymous, but contributions were tax-deductible. To his surprise, Bruderer had his money and more within four weeks.[18]

Theoretically the choice of sculpture was still open, but the *Sheep Piece* was duly selected – with Moore's co-operation – when a group of the sponsors visited Perry Green. Later Bruderer, Henry, and Irina chose its final resting place in the park, for which a small, grassed hillock was created, the better to etch the great bronze's sensual forms against the lake. It was installed there when the big Moore exhibition was held in the same park in summer 1976. It has since been vandalized at least twice with paint. When the author inspected it, one haunch bore a Communist poster summoning a demonstration on the coming May Day.

One evening, Bruderer recalled, Henry and Irina came to dinner at his home with the Wolfensbergers. When they were all quite merry, Henry suggested: 'I would like to know what was important to you all at the age of sixteen. Irina, you start.' When the naturally diffident Irina proffered a memory, Moore put in: 'No, I don't think that's what you told me, you can be quite open here.' His own contribution: lying under a trees in an orchard near school in Castleford catching glimpses of girls' thighs. Entirely convincing. A few years later, when Bruderer was celebrating his sixtieth birthday, and still chairman of the Friends, Moore presented the original plaster of *Reclining Figure: Angles*, a recent work, to the Kunsthaus to show his admiration and warm connections with the city, and in appreciation of the interest shown in the 1976 exhibition.

In fact the private organization which mounted this show, the Zurich Forum, was viewed rather snootily by the city's art establishment, of which Staehelin and Bruderer were pillars. With its aim of making the arts (and not just the fine arts) available to those deprived of them by social, economic or geographical factors, it was bound to be considered leftish. As for Moore, he was evidently torn between admiration for its idealism and for the courage of its staff in organizing such an exhibition of around 280 items, and anxiety – fuelled by the scepticism of his Zurich friends – that the usual high standards for such installations would not be met.

At the outset he was outstandingly generous, the Forum's founder Georg Müller recalled, welcoming them to Perry Green and lending maquettes and allied objects without even seeming to count them.[19] But when the sculptor went to Zurich in late May 1976 for the installation of the *Sheep Piece* and to help in the final stages of the exhibition's installation, he seemed depressed by the Forum's modest resources, and left two days before the opening.

True to the Forum's popularizing mission, the show was billed as Expo Henry Moore. The larger sculptures could be seen free of charge in the park itself. Smaller pieces and the 150 drawings and graphics were displayed in a huge three-part tent, for which an entrance charge was made. Far from being criticized for any shortcomings in presentation, the exhibition received a very friendly and extensive press: German newspapers from as far afield as Hamburg carried striking photographs of the *King and Queen*, the *Arch*, *Sheep Piece*, and others outlined against the lake. A sour note was struck only towards the end, when technicians involved in the nearby production of an operetta used the *Arch* literally as a Mooring – for an electric cable, compounding their sin by hanging a sign on it pointing to the toilets. The fibreglass *Arch* was quickly moved. An estimated half million people saw the alfresco Moores during June, July and August, while 74,000 visited the tented section and 13,000 expensive catalogues were sold. It was a remarkable success for almost wholly inexperienced organizers, and it transformed the Forum's reputation. The citizens of Zurich felt a sense of loss when those powerful yet friendly presences were removed from the lakeside. The *Sheep Piece* remained, a lasting reminder of how Moore had been brought to the people.

At no other stage of the sculptor's life were so many of his bronzes being installed in European and American cities as in the mid- to late 1970s. Coincidentally, another cast of *Sheep Piece* had come to rest a fortnight before the installation of its Zurich sister, in a park adjacent to the Nelson Gallery of Art in Kansas City, Missouri, after much public debate about its siting. Among the cities to benefit between 1974 and 1979 were: in the USA, Baltimore, Boston, Kansas City, Washington, Dallas, Houston, Little Rock; in West Germany, Bielefeld, Goslar, Nuremberg and Bonn; in Scandinavia, Oslo in Norway, Gävle in Sweden, and Humlebaeck in Denmark; elsewhere on the Continent, Luxembourg, Zurich, and Vienna; and London (Greenwich Park). These installations represented the peak of Moore's popularity as a creator of monumental bronzes suitable for architectural and landscape settings.

In 1975 Moore's old friend and only serious English competitor of his own generation, Barbara Hepworth, died in a fire at her home in St Ives, Cornwall, aged seventy-two. Her international reputation had reached its zenith in the mid-1960s with the unveiling at United Nations head-quarters in New York of her large bronze memorial to the UN's late Secretary-General, Dag Hammarskjöld. Though she employed two assist-ants, her output was a fraction of Moore's, not least because carvings formed a much higher proportion of the total. John Read happened to be at Hoglands making one of his films about Moore when the news of Hepworth's tragic death came through. Soon afterwards his brother Tom, a BBC radio producer, rang to ask whether Moore would be prepared to record a brief tribute. John Read put the request to Henry, but he did not feel able to oblige, seemingly from sheer lack of admiration for her work.[20]

In the following year Kenneth Clark's wife Jane died, three years after suffering a stroke which paralysed her down one side. Henry had been an outstandingly solicitous and understanding friend, telephoning and visiting with an unselfishness which would have done credit to a much less busy man. He had always been fond of Jane Clark, sensing that it was her warmth and thoughtfulness which had prompted many of Clark's acts of generosity, especially in the late thirties and forties. In her will she left the first shelter sketchbook, which Henry had given her after the war, to the British Museum. Another sad loss was of Harry Fischer, dealer and friend, who had done so much for Moore in the German-speaking world. The sculptor attended the funeral in Hampstead.

Such sorrows were inevitable as Moore neared eighty. There was the occasional compensation, such as the birth on 1 February 1977 of a first grandchild, Gus. He and Irina had long wanted to be grandparents, Moore candidly told the *Daily Mail*, and were very excited: every day they went to see the child and to hold him, as a photograph nicely entitled 'A chip off the old block!' testified.[21] Gus was much doted upon by his grandparents, and a rash of small bronze children began to appear, climbing over reclining mothers, among the late bronzes. When some Zurich friends, Paul and Margrit Hahnloser, came to Hoglands at this stage to make a purchase, they chose a maquette of a seated woman, only to find that Henry had made a baby for it in a different colour and finish, and wanted to fix it into her arms with a screw. They asked him not to.[22] Somehow the link between life and art was too strong. The mawkish tots were like bronze snapshots.

In the mid- to late 1970s, the reclining figure was once again the dominant theme, featuring in more than two dozen versions ranging from the nearly abstract to a degree of naturalism not seen since the 1950s. Except perhaps in the huge *Three Piece Reclining Figure: Draped* of 1975 (almost fifteen feet long) [171], the eroticism of the sixties and early seventies is in abeyance. In its stead there is frequently a seductively sinuous suavity: *Broken Figure*, for example, is irresistibly tactile in black marble. The level of productivity and inventiveness would have been remarkable in a much younger man; yet Moore was rising eighty, and contending with a steady flow of visitors, numerous short trips abroad, and several big exhibitions of his work. Between 1976 and 1978 he even risked a last elmwood carving: *Reclining Figure: Holes* [172], just over seven feet long. Despite being carved entirely by his assistants, it is a compelling restatement of his greatest theme, and was eventually lent to the Metropolitan Museum in New York.

The more famous Henry became, the more letters he received from

interested and, occasionally, disinterested parties. Not a few were from
unknown admirers, like a New Yorker expressing his gratitude for the
'joy and excitement you have given me by your creativity'. Excitement
was a recurring theme, especially from those who had met Moore on a
tour of Hoglands. Naturally there were many business letters from dealers
and collectors. Cheeky requests for co-operation came in regularly. One
young man wanted to mint a 'decision coin', to be flipped on suitable
occasions, with 'yes' and 'no' on either side. Would Moore consider
designing the two faces? Another optimist, a publisher of 'little books',
wanted a drawing from Moore to illustrate a two-line poem allegedly
written by John Betjeman, W. H. Auden, and Louis MacNeice, which
went:

> I often think that I would like
> To be the saddle of a bike.

Then there were requests for parties to visit Hoglands from local
associations of artists, architects, and many other groups, and more
exotic ones such as the Norwegian Club's Ladies Group, or the Wives of
the Council and Technical Committee of the International Skating Union.
As indicated earlier, the answer to many of these was positive, the
resulting coachloads sometimes being shown around by a sculptor-assist-
ant. To all the many requests for him to speak he said no. Of the would-
be scroungers, not many had the effrontery (or candour) of the English
doctor who wrote:

> For those of us who are very intelligent, but have no genius, I think
> there is both admiration and resentment of those such as yourself.
> I delight in the fruits of your talent, but I am in anguish that I have
> no genius as well ... One expects someone so extraordinarily lucky
> in his gifts to be as perfect a human being as he is perfect in his
> work ... If I had money to spare ... I would willingly spend it on
> works of art at the market price, but I do not and thus must pester
> you ...

Moore doubtless gave him short shrift. Gently he declined an American
girl who offered to model for him at Forte dei Marmi ('my body is not
unlike those as your sculptures' (sic)) saying he no longer drew from life.

Moore at the Orangerie, Paris

The next big exhibition after Zurich was at the Orangerie and in the
adjacent Tuileries Gardens in Paris in summer 1977, following a formal

application from the French to the British Council. It was directed by Dominique Bozo, then of the Musée d'Art Moderne, later director of the Centre Pompidou. Moore was much involved in the selection of the exhibits, and spent two weeks in Paris up to the opening. Among living sculptors, only Giacometti (Swiss, but a Paris resident) had been shown in that setting, back in 1969, and Moore knew the difficulties he faced. Michel Ragon described them vividly in *Les Nouvelles Littéraires*:

> Is Henry Moore known in France? No. It must be said that he has never lived in France, and if an artist has not lived in France for at least ten years, he is considered negligible in French artistic circles.[23]

Yet Moore's earlier shows in Paris had been well received even if not well attended, and Francis Bacon's retrospective at the Grand Palais in 1971 had been an outstanding success. So too now was Moore's major exhibition of 116 sculptures and a similar number of drawings, with graphics being shown at the Bibliothèque Nationale. In just under four months it attracted 120,000 visitors, a few thousand more than Giacometti over the same period, though less than half a big Cézanne exhibition. Thousands more passers-by could see the seven monumental pieces in the oddly formal setting of the Tuileries Gardens from the Place de la Concorde and even from across the Seine.

The critics were generally enthusiastic, seeing the Paris exhibition as a worthy successor to those in Florence and Zurich, and emphasizing Moore's blending of tradition and innovation, fantasy and monumentality. *Le Monde* gave him a full page, which included a long interview.[24] The British critics, many of whom made the trip to Paris, were in turn impressed by the discreet didacticism of the thematic presentation. The most notable dissenter was again Paul Overy of *The Times*. The shelter drawings were sentimental and slack, he heretically reckoned. The disastrous rise in Moore's international reputation had led him to produce gigantic, overblown sculptures. Reaction against his inflated reputation in the 1960s had led to overpraise of Caro and his disciples.[25] A more extreme version of these arguments covered three columns of *Die Welt* from the pen of Werner Spies. Deploring the superlatives heaped on Moore's work, he called him a shameless plunderer of other artists' ideas in his desperate search for originality, who fell back on a banal compromise between classical and modern, figurative and abstract, and whose humourlessness was mistaken for power.[26]

Such views were a healthy corrective to the often unselective praise of some of Moore's admirers, notably the mighty trinity of Read, Clark, and

Hendy. In defending him in the earlier, embattled days from the assaults of the philistines and in using their powerful positions to buttress Moore's own status and reputation, they did much to promote the Moore name, but they also sowed the seeds of reaction.

At the cruder end anger took the form of vandalism. In the Tuileries such words as 'hideous', 'grotesque', and 'absurd' were daubed on one of the large works, fortunately a fibreglass cast. That September a large cast of *Three Way Piece: Points*, lent by Mary Moore for a site outside the British Council's headquarters in Spring Gardens, off Trafalgar Square, was toppled from its base and quite badly split and dented. Two years earlier a cast of the *Glenkiln Cross* was first daubed in red paint and wrapped in paper, then knocked over: all this on the lawn outside St Albans Cathedral in Hertfordshire. Moore's smoother bronzes are frequently blighted by graffiti. When the author last saw the *Archer* in West Berlin, outside the National Gallery, it was covered in obscenities, not just written on in ballpoint or felt-tipped pens, but often scored right through the patina.

Though perhaps more a form of tribute than of vandalism, thefts and fakes of Moore's works have been not uncommon. Thefts have generally been of small bronzes from under-supervised commercial galleries, though quite recently a heavy early piece in concrete was removed in broad daylight from the Mayor Gallery in Cork Street. It was found more than a year later in a left-luggage locker in Liverpool Street Station after a drugs tip-off. Moore only started consistently initialling and numbering his casts (e.g., Moore 3/6, for the third of six casts) around 1965. Thieves would sometimes obliterate the number to frustrate identification.

Fakes sometimes caused trouble to the big auction houses. Usually they were extra casts made from existing small or medium-sized bronzes. Due to shrinkage they would be slightly smaller than the original, and such details as facial features (if any) would be slightly blurred. One family group which was sent to Christie's for sale had to be compared side by side with a true version in the collection of the property developer Charles Clore to establish that it was 'wrong'. An apparent fake might be simply a work done in the style of Henry Moore, not necessarily with the aim of deception in the first instance. As for replicas of his work, Moore hated them. Periodically American museums sought his permission to sell plaster or bronze versions of Moores in their collections, sometimes of reduced size, seeing such facsimiles as an educationally and commercially valuable spin-off, like a van Gogh print. They were surprised and upset when Moore emphatically denied permission or, as in one instance, demanded compensation when the deed had been done. There could be no quality control over such ventures, and he believed they cheapened the originals and caused confusion.

Genuinely creative and licenced reinterpretations of his work, such as tapestries, were another matter. The first four Moore tapestries were executed from drawings in the early 1970s by a Scottish weaver from Black Isle, in Ross and Cromarty. A few years later Mary and Raymond Danowski were impressed by an exhibition of tapestries created by students of West Dean College in Sussex, funded by the great collector of surrealism, Edward James. A sequence of eight Moore tapestries resulted. They were shown to great effect at the Victoria and Albert Museum in 1980 and subsequently in New Zealand, the USA, and Canada.

When uncertainty arose over whether they belonged to Henry, Mary or the Foundation, Moore commissioned a further five, and eventually five more. Their destination was a great sixteenth-century aisled barn which the sculptor had had moved at great expense from a farm six miles from Perry Green to the studio area at Hoglands. The farm had been bought as an investment, and the barn was reconstructed with a new tile roof, new clapboard external walls, a superb timber floor, two lavatories and hot air heating. Henry's original aim was to preserve a beautiful traditional building, but the result was a potential lecture hall or library for the Foundation. With half a dozen large (generally about seven by five feet) tapestries on the walls – subtle interpretations of some of Moore's tenderest drawings – and the magnificent beams aloft, it would make a dramatically beautiful setting for a musical recital.

A further five Moore tapestries were later commissioned by Fischer Fine Art, four being sold to the Kansan collector George Ablah. This patronage enabled West Dean College to set up a permanent studio and take on a steady team of weavers. So far they have completed some two dozen Moore tapestries as well as others for artists such as John Piper and Howard Hodgkin. Compared with similar operations in France and even in Edinburgh, the Sussex venture is small-scale, but it scores in quality and sensitivity.

As his eightieth birthday approached, Moore remained very active. In 1977 he paid three visits each to Paris and Berlin, and also went to Oslo, Copenhagen, Vienna, Bonn, Frankfurt, and Florence for openings, sitings, unveilings and the like. During five weeks in Forte dei Marmi he experienced the worst storm to have hit the area in living memory. Thousands of trees were blown down, and two fell on the house in the Via Civitali. Damage was slight.

Shortly after his return he took part in a reunion arranged by the Queen of the twenty-four members she had appointed to the Order of Merit, to mark its seventy-fifth anniversary. Twenty-one were fit enough to attend the service of thanksgiving in the Chapel Royal at St James's Palace, followed by luncheon at Buckingham Palace. Among Henry's friends there were J. B. Priestley, Lord Clark, the choreographer Sir Frederick Ashton, Professor Dorothy Hodgkin, Lord Zuckerman, and Graham Sutherland. In a group photograph taken in the Music Room in Buckingham Palace, Sutherland sat as doyen on the Queen's right, with Moore sandwiched between Prince Philip and Lord Mountbatten as the next senior on her left.

To Washington, Dallas and Houston

The following year was no less exhausting, with his eightieth birthday being celebrated amid trips to Vienna, Washington, Paris, Oslo, and Bonn, with nine days in early December taking him to Dallas, Houston, Wichita, Chicago and New York.

The trip to Washington, in May, and by Concorde for the first time, was for the installation of a king-sized and 'flopped' version of *Knife Edge Two Piece* at the top of the entrance steps of I. M. Pei's masterpiece, the new East Building of the National Gallery. Glinting welcomingly there, it must be seen by more people than any other of Moore's works, since some five million a year pass it by.

The idea of installing a major Moore on a prominent site on the Pennsylvania Avenue side of the new building was put to the sculptor in 1972. A few months later the necessary funds were pledged by the foundation set up by Washington's leading philanthropists, Morris and Gwendolyn Cafritz, who had made a fortune in real estate in the 1950s and 1960s. Three years later Moore belatedly proposed *Spindle Piece* as a candidate. J. Carter Brown, the director of the National Gallery, tactfully asked whether Moore might create something specially for the spot, thus touching a raw nerve. 'I have never done that,' Henry replied, far from accurately. A sculpture should be an entity in itself, and should look well in a variety of situations, he told the director, just as a person showed different aspects of his personality in different situations – otherwise sculpture became a kind of applied art. On the other hand, he agreed it must be right in scale, material, texture, general mass and form, and siting.[27]

The sculptor had called in on his way to Dallas in April 1976, in both cases to inspect the proposed locations for his pieces. Superbly prominent though it was, the spot chosen by Pei on the north side of Pennsylvania Avenue in Washington lacked one vital ingredient: sunlight. Moore turned it down, the *Spindle Piece* was re-routed to the North Carolina Museum of Art in Raleigh, and he and Pei decided on the outside porch of the East Building entrance as the new location. Pei helped choose the *Two Piece Knife Edge* as a substitute, suggesting that its two parts should be interchanged or flopped, as he liked to put it.

The new configuration, which Moore tried out in a svelte small-scale model now in the National Gallery, suited the site better and made it more of a unique piece, duly dubbed *Two Piece Mirror Knife Edge* by Carter Brown. Minor excitements along the way included a dock strike in England which theatened to delay delivery from Southampton. On 12 May 1978 Moore arrived and helped guide the two eighteen-feet-tall sections into place. Huge though they were, wind tests had shown that a very strong anchorage was needed, and they were bolted into place by lowering a man through a hatch at the top of each of the bronze pieces. The East Building was opened by President Carter two weeks later. Inside the spectacular concourse area a cryptic and sombre Moore carving in travertine, *Stone Memorial* of 1969 – like the building, donated by Paul Mellon – stands under its spiritual opposite, a vast Calder mobile. Near an almost garishly brilliant tapestry by Miró a sculpture by Moore's former assistant Anthony Caro perches bizarrely on a high shelf.

Even in diplomatic circles a Moore bronze was now a prestige object, as an episode at the British Embassy in Washington illustrates. For the Queen's Bicentennial visit in 1976 the ambassador, Sir Peter Ramsbotham, and his wife Frances planned a big reception in the embassy garden following a banquet in the ballroom at which President Ford was to be the main guest. Sir Peter recalled:

> It was felt necessary to have some eye-catching point at the bottom
> of the garden to which I could lead the Queen and President, with
> Prince Philip and Mrs Ford, and whence they could each proceed,
> on different circuits, back to the steps of the main house, greeting
> the 3,000 guests already waiting in the garden.[28]

Moore and Lady Ramsbotham had got on very well on an earlier occasion, and she suggested that one of his works might provide the right focus of interest. Moore responded to the idea, and a cast of *Vertebrae* was shipped out and assembled at the bottom of the garden under his supervision. The Queen's comments on seeing it are not known, but when the comedian Bob Hope subsequently spotted the great golden bronzes after being presented with an honorary knighthood by Sir Peter, he commented: 'Gee, that reminds me of Sammy Davis's cufflinks!'

Moore owed his warm relations with Dallas to I. M. Pei. The architect, whose work was also popular in Houston, had been commissioned in the early 1970s to design a new city hall for Dallas. He came up with a startling 400-feet-long, wedge-shaped construction, its eight storeys of glass and concrete sloping forward from a narrow base. Once again Pei suggested that a Moore sculpture should complement the severe calligraphy of his design. An executive jet was sent to Washington to collect the sculptor, who arrived to see the site with Irina, Mary, and Raymond Danowski. He pronounced Pei's building 'great, bold, magnificent'.[29] His sculpture would need to be about thirty feet high, he reckoned, and offer a contrast to the sharp contours and crisp outline of the city hall. Eventually he decided that *Three Piece: Vertebrae* would best fit the bill. Pei again proposed that the component parts should be rearranged: if they were grouped in a triangular cluster rather than strung out in a line, people would be able to walk through the sculpture on the piazza in front of the city hall, and thus become more involved with it. Moore was happy to fall in with the suggestion.

The city's newspapers, the *Dallas Morning News* and *Dallas Times Herald*, were sympathetic to the idea of a large civic Moore, but the commission soon sparked a vigorous debate. The views of the traditionalist, 'I-know-what-I-like' school were expressed by councillor William Cothrum, who had scrutinized some of Moore's work elsewhere and announced that he preferred to be able to understand what he was looking at.[30] Dallas's modern art enthusiasts blushed as his remarks received national press coverage: it was all too reminiscent of the fifties, when the Dallas Museum of Fine Arts bowed to protests and removed a Picasso from view. Much had changed in Dallas since then, however. Contemporary art now had many powerful patrons.

Prominent among them were Margaret MacDermott and Raymond and Patsy Nasher, who had helped entertain Moore on his first visit. Mrs MacDermott's late husband Eugene had been one of the founders of Texas Instruments. Everything in her smallish house, from the rugs to the Monets, reflected her quietly perfect taste, typified by a little Moore carving of a girl, done in alabaster in 1931 and originally bought by Eton's future headmaster Robert Birley for £30. Her patronage ranged across the city's vigorous cultural life, and she now played a behind-the-scenes role in rallying private money for the public Moore. The main donor was Fritz Hawn, a real-estate dealer, who volunteered first $200,000 and eventually $300,000, in memory of his wife Mildred. A further $50,000 came from other sources.

The Nashers owned an outstandingly wide-ranging collection of contemporary sculpture which coincidentally included a working-model version of *Three Piece: Vertebrae*. In 1965 Nasher had opened in Dallas one of the earliest and handsomest galleria-style shopping centres in the USA, called NorthPark. He and his wife had paid pilgrimages to Perry Green. Anxious to share their enthusiasm and help educate public taste, they had regularly shown items from their collection indoors and outdoors at NorthPark, and in summer 1977 included their cast of *Vertebrae* with several other Moores in a small exhibition there.

Before the three huge pieces destined for the city hall arrived in Dallas in autumn 1978, the ground had been further prepared with a barrage of newspaper stories and interviews with Moore himself. In an imaginative gesture, the public was allowed to inspect and watch as craftsmen from the Morris Singer foundry completed the welding and patination in an old hangar at Love Field airport. In early December the sculptor arrived with I. M. Pei to supervise the installation of the *Dallas Piece* [169], as it was tactfully renamed. For Moore, seeing a major work in front of a powerful example of contemporary architecture was a testing moment. All too frequently he felt that he and the architect had not got the scale right, and that the sculpture looked like 'a little ornament pinned on to a lady's dress'.[31] This time he was well pleased with the effect.

Finally it was the turn of the people to give their verdict. Since no city funds were involved, they could afford to take a relatively relaxed view. Here are half a dozen comments:

'That's some hunk of gold! I'm glad we have it.'

'Oh my God! Is this a junkyard?'

'A pretty classy pigeon perch.'

'I'm just a normal human being and it doesn't make sense to me.'

'I'm coming back for another look. I want to like it.'

'Dallas should be proud of this thing.'[32]

Some saw a likeness to a group of seals, and Moore himself detected a resemblance to a whale emerging from water. As long as comparisons were with the natural world, he was happy. In this case, local reactions delighted him, and he inscribed a large photograph of the sculpture *in situ* 'For the people of Dallas, with much affection and admiration, from Henry Moore.' It dominated the front page of the *Dallas Morning News* next day. Small wonder that he is so warmly remembered there.

Not all his Texan contacts were as pleasant. While in Dallas in 1978 he also paid a flying visit to Houston, which has more public sculpture than Dallas and an even more dramatic skyline. His aim was to inspect a site for *Large Spindle Piece* in Tranquillity Park, a small garden intended to be associated with the first landing on the moon. It turned out to be hemmed in by tower blocks and to have a car park immediately underneath, so that only diminutive trees and shrubs could be planted in the shallow soil. Moore was driven there direct from the airport, to be greeted by press and television reporters who followed him around with boom microphones, and a man serving whiskies.

When he saw the location he said to the dealer who was accompanying him: 'You're kidding!' To the press he was tactful, but the site was turned down.[33] Eventually, after various photographs of possible locations had been shown to him at home in England, *Spindle Piece* ended up on a strip of park between two freeways well clear of downtown Houston. Soon after its installation it was attacked by a large black man who went berserk with a heavy chain. The dent was still visible several years later. Numerous smaller Moore bronzes led quiet lives in private houses and gardens in Houston, but with them and their owners the sculptor had little contact.

Eightieth-birthday salute

With two major Tate Gallery retrospectives and such recent triumphs as the shows in Florence, Zurich, and Paris fresh in many memories, Moore's eightieth birthday on 30 July 1978 posed a challenge. How could it be worthily celebrated in his own country in a way which contributed something new to an understanding of his work? Moore's native Yorkshire was on its mettle as well as London. The idea of staging a big exhibition in Bradford, some twenty miles from Castleford, was the joint inspiration of Véra Russell and the city's lord mayor Paul Hockney, brother of the painter. It was Moore's idea to have it opened by Bradford's most famous son, J. B. Priestley. This was done on 31 March 1978 at Cartwright Hall, where 100 sculptures and 120 works on paper made it the largest Moore show to be held in Britain outside London. Moore had himself helped site eight large bronzes in the adjacent Lister Park. Together sculptor and writer carved a birthday cake inscribed in icing 'Love from Yorkshire'.[34] Reviews were warm ('Henry, the show is a birthday cracker,' a local paper announced), though both Overy in *The Times* and William Feaver in the *Observer* repeated their preference for the smaller works, especially the carvings.[35]

In London there was a double salute, with drawings at the Tate and sculpture at the Serpentine Gallery in Kensington Gardens. On David Sylvester's inspired suggestion, the emphasis there was to be on large bronzes shown outside amid the natural beauties of the park. The Tate show was much the biggest to date of Moore's drawings, ranging from the *Head of an Old Man*, done as a student in 1921, to a drawing of the artist's own hands from 1977. The 261 items had been assembled, analysed, and catalogued by Dr Alan Wilkinson in Toronto and first shown there before touring Japan and opening in London in late June. Though underplayed in many of the reviews, they were for many a revelation of the fecundity and intensity of Moore's imagination, of the virtuosity of his draughtsmanship, and sombre tenderness of his vision. At the same time the Tate showed the Moore Gift, which had been handed over a year ahead of the opening of the troubled extension, along with its earlier Moore acquisitions.

At the Serpentine, Sylvester (again on behalf of the Arts Council) concentrated on late carvings inside that pretty gallery, and on late bronzes outside in its leafy environs. Londoners had never seen anything like these giant bronzes skilfully disposed in parkland. When the show was three weeks old and the critics had expressed their admiration for this piece and their doubts about that one, a remarkable public debate opened first in *The Times*'s letter columns and then in the *Evening Standard*. To see our greatest sculptor's work in such a setting enriched the quality of life in the city, the Old Master dealer Roy Miles wrote.[36] Another correspondent suggested that *Hill Arches* [167], over which children delighted to climb and slide, might be bought by public subscription. There were some dissenting voices, but the *Evening Standard* took up the idea. The Serpentine show had brought Moore's work to the attention of people who never ventured into museums or galleries, an editorial commented, and the response of children refuted arguments that modern art is meaningless and remote. Part of the exhibition, it suggested (as if the works were in public ownership) should be left behind as a monument to our greatest artist.[37]

The idea found widespread favour, though several regular dog-walkers made it clear they encouraged their charges to lift their legs long and copiously against bronzes which they considered incongruous and grotesque. The newspaper's campaign and the public support for it encouraged Moore to present a travertine version of the large fibreglass *Arch* so successfully sited by the lake. When completed it was brought over from

Forte dei Marmi in seven sections, erected by an Italian artisan and unveiled on 1 October 1980 by the then Environment Secretary, Michael Heseltine, with Moore present.

Not only the big bronzes affected people deeply. In *The Times* Paddy Kitchen described how not one member of the public had, while she was watching, walked past the still unfinished large elmwood *Reclining Figure: Holes* without touching it, and one young man almost embraced it.[38] Early carvings had meanwhile been shown at Fischer Fine Art, and once again the critics compared their compactness and contained energy favourably with the relative blandness of the late, monumental bronzes. Such strictures, though doubtless valid aesthetically, missed one point: the early work was mainly for indoors, while the later, outdoor pieces had achieved a new relationship for contemporary sculpture both with nature and with the non-museum-going public.

The later stone and marble carvings, all done in Italy, do not give the same feelings as the early ones of having been wrested from their resistant block in an inspiring struggle between artist and material. Too often, one feels, Moore had selected a bronze and said: 'Let's have this in marble – a little bigger, perhaps.' *Draped Reclining Figure* of 1978, for example, works well as a smallish bronze of just over three feet long. In travertine at just over twice the length, it looks vacuous and inert.

By now Moore's supervision was restricted to the last stages of carving by the Henraux artisans. The most articulate of the trio, Giulio Cardini, who reckoned in 1983 that he had carved or helped carve at least fifty Moores since 1964, recalled:

> Moore would send us a model. We would start enlarging it to a certain stage, then he would come over here and say how it should be finished. More recently he came at a later stage, when it was almost completed. Sometimes he might base suggestions for change on the model, sometimes he might suggest a departure from the model.[39]

In Pietrasanta another master craftsman, Sem Ghelardini, reckoned it was not the extent of supervision by the artist which mattered, but the degree of rapport with the artisan. Between 1968 and 1974 Ghelardini did half a dozen or more pieces for Moore with a colleague, at a time when the sculptor was uneasy about a change of management at Henraux. For some of them Moore never came at all, he said, yet it was 'fine'.[40] Ghelardini executed the twenty-six-feet-long travertine version of *Reclining Connected Forms* which was installed in Baltimore in 1974. Having

worked with many 'important' artists, including Miró and Chagall, he
still believed Moore was the greatest. 'It's all a matter of planes and
volumes, getting the light on one plane and not on another, a matter of
a millimetre or two,' he observed. 'Michelangelo was called the singer of
volumes. Moore knows how to use volumes.'

There are many views on the morality of using artisans, and most
sculptors will be severely critical of those who exercise less supervision
than they do themselves. Some will send a little plasticine model a few
inches long in a box and never go near Italy, later taking delivery of a
huge version which owes a great deal to the interpretation of the artisan.
Some sculptors claim to be able to walk around an exhibition identifying
which craftsman worked on which pieces. At the other end of the scale,
a sculptor may use the craftsmen solely to do the initial roughing out.
Moore would defend himself by drawing analogies with architects not
constructing the buildings they designed, or composers leaving others to
interpret their music, arguments which he applied equally to his use of
assistants at Hoglands. How much does it matter by which methods the
end product is achieved, providing it emerges as intended? The answer
is surely, not much. Yet one has only to compare an early Moore carving
with a late equivalent done at Querceta to appreciate the difference in
involvement. On one occasion Moore farmed out two pieces to be done
in travertine to a director who had left Henraux. The artisan employed
naughtily did an identical copy of each for himself. Moore was so annoyed
that when he heard they were for sale in Rome, he hurried down there
and attacked one with a hammer. He had done no work himself on any
of them. The only difference was that the rogue version had not been
authorized.

While the late bronzes were making their impact in Kensington
Gardens, the children's favourite, *Hill Arches*, was the subject of controversy in Vienna. Henry had returned to the Austrian capital in the
previous summer to finalize the location of the huge and complex piece.
Not wanting it to compete with the frontal view of the Karlskirche, a
church he found more beautiful each time he saw it, he suggested it
should be moved over to the left of the newly created pond, where its
two great bronze arches echoed the curves of the Karlskirche's cupola
[167]. It was installed under Moore's supervision in April 1978: his
fourth visit to a city he had come to love. As at the Lincoln Center, the
water was initially too shallow and the lining tiles needed to be painted
black to maximize the reflection; but these matters were swiftly put right.
Local reaction was, however, hostile, newspapers being inundated with

complaints that the sculpture spoiled the view of the historic church. The row soon passed over. Not for nothing had Henry insisted on a spring installation, when the sun was shining and people were feeling cheerful. The Viennese were moreover getting a bargain: the bronze's value was estimated at £230,000. Moore was charging only the cost of casting and freight. That represented a gift of about £200,000.

That year his work first penetrated the Arab world when the mayor of Jedda in Saudi Arabia, Mohammed Said Farsi, bought the first of four large bronzes which were placed beside the corniche of El-Hamra over the next two years. The mayor, an engineer, had come to know Moore's work through visits to England, books and discussions with friends in Europe. His first contacts were through a Spanish architect, Julio Lafuente, and Sir Leslie Martin, with whom he visited Hoglands in late 1978.[41] Since Islam forbids the representation of the human figure in art – a reaction against the worship of idols which Mohammed had found at Mecca – the sculptures had to be more or less abstract. Those chosen were *Large Spindle Piece, Large Oval with Points, Upright Motive No. 2*, and *Three Piece Reclining Figure No. 1* [130]. The last may look like a trisected dinosaur, but is certainly related to the human figure. Over the years Farsi and his colleagues had also worked with such sculptors as César, Arp, Pomodoro, and Lipchitz.

Another monumental bronze, *Large Two Forms*, which had been intended for Jedda, was re-routed to Bonn, the West German capital, and led to a warm personal relationship between Moore and the Chancellor, Helmut Schmidt. The possibility of placing a large Moore bronze in the forecourt of the grimly contemporary new three-storey chancellery building (Bundeskanzleramt) had first been mooted in 1975, after the Swiss sculptor, Max Bill, had put forward some unsatisfactory proposals. Chancellor Schmidt, who had inherited the plans for the building from the government of Willy Brandt, called for the appointment of a jury. It was almost unanimous in picking Moore.

Since no one at the chancellery knew Moore, it was felt that the Chancellor himself should write and invite him over. Schmidt, a connoisseur of the Expressionists with a particular love for Emil Nolde's work, said with uncharacteristic diffidence: 'He's such an important man, I can't just write to him and ask him to come!'[42] He nerved himself to do so in spring 1977, however, and the two men met in the federal capital when Moore was returning from one of his visits to Noack in Berlin. Although it was an almost Mediterranean day, the sculptor was visibly taken aback by the bleakness of the chancellery building and of its

164. *Two Piece Reclining Figure: Points*, 1969–70, 144 inches long, bronze, seen at the great Florence exhibition of 1972. Again, the erotic element is to the fore

165. *The Arch* 1969, 20 feet high, fibreglass, at the Florence exhibition. A bronze cast is in Columbus, Indiana, and a travertine version in Kensington Gardens, London

166. *Large Square Form with Cut*, 1969–71, 17 feet 10 inches high, Rio Serra marble, seen against Brunelleschi's cathedral at the Florence exhibition; now in the Tuscan city of Prato

167. *Hill Arches*, 1973, 18 feet long, bronze, in front of the Karlskirche in Vienna: a baroque sculpture for a baroque church, Moore maintained

168. The architect I. M. Pei and Moore applaud each other in delight after the inauguration of the *Dallas Piece*, Dallas, May 1978

169. *Dallas Piece*, 1977–8, approximately 40 feet long, bronze, in front of I. M. Pei's new Dallas City Hall. This unique cast is an enlarged, rearranged version of *Three Piece Sculpture: Vertebrae*

170. Moore's altar for the church of St Stephen Walbrook in the City of London, 1973, 8 feet in diameter, 41 inches high, travertine, as seen by its ecclesiastical judges in 1986, when the Wren church was still being restored

171. *Three Piece Reclining Figure: Draped*, 1975, 14 feet 8 inches long, bronze. A strong late work, particularly well sited at the Louisiana Museum at Humlebaek in Denmark; also at the Massachusetts Institute of Technology in Boston, and on loan to the Court of European Justice in Luxembourg

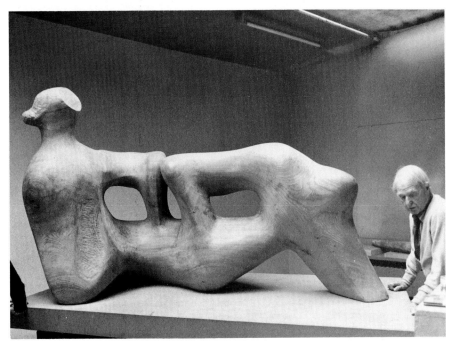

172. *Reclining Figure: Holes*, 1975–8, $87\frac{1}{2}$ inches long, the last major elmwood carving, Metropolitan Museum, New York (loan from Henry Moore Foundation)

173. *Reclining Figure*, 1938–83, bronze. Seen here at Hoglands, this 35 foot long bronze is now outside the Overseas Chinese Banking Corporation in Singapore. When first cast in lead it was 13 inches long.

174. *Reclining Woman: Elbow*, 1981, 87 inches long, bronze, a cast of which reclines outside the Leeds City Art Gallery. It was one of Moore's last substantial works

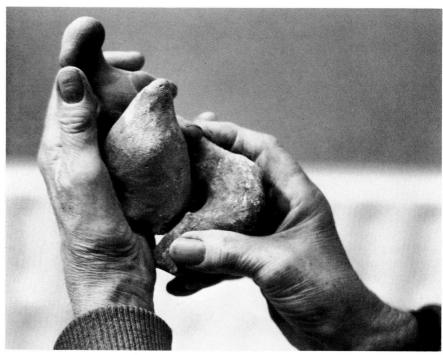

175, 176. Old hands of an old master

177. An 80th birthday portrait by Frank Herrmann

178. *Three Piece Sculpture: Vertebrae*, 1968–9, approximately 24 feet long, bronze, being enjoyed in Kensington Gardens, London, during Moore's 80th birthday exhibition there in June 1978. The children are from Rhyl primary school, London NW5

179. Moore with Bruno Kreisky, the Austrian Chancellor (right), and W. H. Auden (with cigarette), Vienna, September 1973

180. Moore with his first grandchild Gus and daughter Mary, February 1977: a 'chip off the old block'

181. Irina Moore, Mary and Raymond Danowski and Ann Garrould in the garden at Forte dei Marmi, mid-1970s

182. The West German Chancellor, Helmut Schmidt, with Moore in London after presenting him with the Grand Cross of the Order of Merit at the embassy in Belgrave Square, SW1, 14 April 1980

183. Members of the Order of Merit in the Music Room, Buckingham Palace, 17 November 1972: (left to right standing) Lord Todd, J. B. Priestley, Lord Hinton, Sir Alan Hodgkin, Sir George Edwards, Lord Penney, Sir Isaiah Berlin, Harold Macmillan, Lord Clark, Sir Ronald Syme, Sir Frederick Ashton, Lord Franks; (seated) Dame Veronica Wedgwood, Sir William Walton, Professor Dorothy Hodgkin, Graham Sutherland, Her Majesty the Queen, Prince Philip, Henry Moore, Earl Mountbatten, Lord Zuckerman, Malcolm MacDonald

184. Moore laying the foundation stone of the Henry Moore Sculpture Gallery at the Leeds City Art Gallery, 10 April 1980

185. Moore drawing in his favourite studio at Hoglands in 1982, aged 84

186. Moore after the dedication at St Paul's Cathedral of his *Mother and Child* (1983, 7 feet high, travertine) with the Dean of St Paul's, Dr Alan Webster (centre) and the Revd Philip Buckler, sacrist, London, March 1984. The carving was done by the artisans of Henraux in Italy

187. Henry Moore photographed in the sitting room at Hoglands by David Finn about six months before his death in 1986

188. Before his operation in summer 1983, walking was difficult for Moore; after it, impossible. He is seen here in late 1982 with one of his tapestries in the aisled barn at Hoglands

189. Watched by Frank Farnham, Moore passes a carrot to Charlie the donkey at Allens Green on one of their regular afternoon drives through the lanes of Hertfordshire, January 1985

190. François Mitterrand, the French President, investing Moore as a Commander of the Legion of Honour at Hoglands, October 1985, with Moore's niece Ann Garrould (right)

191. *Interior Form*, 1951–81, 16 feet
3 inches high, bronze, at the Henry Moore
Sculpture Reserve, Arden House, New
York State, inaugurated in 1986 (loan
from the Henry Moore Foundation)

forecourt, then decorated with some low brick walls resembling tank blocks; and he was startled to be told that no funds had been allocated. Might a loan be possible? he was asked in the capital of the economic miracle. Moore stalled, suggesting the Chancellor might visit Hoglands next time he was in London. That was done, rather dramatically by helicopter, after an EEC summit conference in London in July.

Further letters were subsequently exchanged, but nothing happened for eighteen months. The site was evidently a stumbling block. To break the impasse, the Chancellor urged his cultural adviser, Erich Milleker, to tackle Moore, which he did, taking along the director-general of museums from the nearby city of Cologne for support. Milleker recalled:

> We discussed the situation in Moore's sitting room. He saw what we wanted, but played a little naïf, as if he didn't really understand. We recapitulated. He said, 'It's really that this building is so strong, it's very difficult to set anything against it: there wouldn't be any harmony.' He was too polite to say that he found everything dreadful.[43]

Moore recommended them to see whether there was anything they liked in the Kensington Gardens exhibition. Eventually, having toyed with *Sheep Piece*, they proposed *Large Two Forms*, only to be told that all casts had been sold or promised. Might Noack not do another one? a despairing Milleker innocently asked. The sculptor replied swiftly: 'If I sell a piece and someone pays a specific price, he must know how many casts there are and that no more will be made.' Less scrupulously, he mused whether *Large Two Forms* was after all suitable for an Arab client (Mayor Farsi in Jedda), since it undoubtedly had human forms in it. Milleker left thinking that once again nothing would happen; but a couple of months later Moore telephoned to say that he had reached an understanding with the architect of the Saudi Arabian project. In the course of a second visit to Bonn he offered to lend *Large Two Forms* for two years, providing transport and installation costs were paid. In discussing a precise location the decision was taken to grass over most of the forecourt and create a low mound for the bronze in the middle: Schmidt had to spend hours in parliament and in committee explaining the logic of it all.

A plan to save money by using the army to transport the bronze was abandoned, though not before the military had submitted eighteen alternative methods, including helicopter: in an emergency the sculpture would have to be jettisoned, it was explained. Moore came over in summer 1979 to supervise the installation and ensure the correct relationship of the two pieces. He returned three weeks later on 19 September for the opening, which coincided with a state visit by President Pertini of Italy. As Henry's plane touched down at Cologne airport, it was announced that no one should leave the aircraft until Henry Moore had done so. Everyone turned around to see where this Henry Moore was – and so did Moore.[44] That was real modesty. He was whisked straight to the state luncheon for Signor Pertini, and thence to a small show of his work which had been thoughtfully arranged as a flanking measure near the chancellery.

It is hard to imagine a bronze by a foreign artist like, say, Picasso, being installed in a forecourt of No. 10 Downing Street, were there such a space, or even in the rear garden. When Schmidt was asked why an English rather than German artist had been honoured, he replied that Germans could not allow themselves such chauvinistic attitudes: European culture had always crossed national boundaries. Besides, Moore was half a citizen of the Federal Republic because he was a member of the order Pour le Mérite, a holder of the Bundesverdienstkreuz with star, a member of the Berlin Academy of Arts, and for twenty years had had his bronzes cast by the Berlin firm of Noack.[45] The Moore piece was indeed widely accepted as a good solution to a difficult problem. Despite the sculptor's fears, it seems to gain by the brilliance of its highly polished finish against the dark greeny grey of the chancellery 'bunker'.

There was little opposition when two years later Schmidt took the further risk of seeking parliament's approval to buy it for the nation. Moore named a friendly (by his standards) price of £122,000, fixed in sterling at a time when the pound was relatively weak. The bronze even played a role in a diplomatic exchange between Herr Schmidt and Margaret Thatcher when the new Prime Minister came to Bonn to haggle over Britain's contribution to the EEC budget. Trying to deflect her obdurate logic, Schmidt alluded to the sculpture's significance in Anglo-German cultural relations. Mrs Thatcher countered that there was also a Moore outside the House of Commons, but it was much smaller: indeed, the difference almost perfectly reflected the relative sizes of the German and British gross national products ...[46] (with a population of similar size and fewer natural resources, West Germany then produced goods worth twice as much as Britain).

By this stage, any major city in the Federal Republic felt pretty naked without its civic Moore. But when a cast of the eight-foot-tall *Large Totem Head* [149] arrived in a pedestrian street of Nuremberg's medieval quarter without warning in late 1979, reactions were mainly hostile. The largely abstract, though to some eyes decidedly clitoral, bronze was a gift to the ity from the huge Karstadt department store chain. There seemed to be no control over such gifts, complained a local sculptor, Michael Prechtl: 'Somebody makes a present, and there it is' ('*Es stiftet einer was, und dann steht's halt da.*')[47] Others thought the sculpture needed more space than the narrow street provided, and some local artists were hurt that their work had not been considered.

Henry's eighty-first year ended with a visit from the actress Lauren Bacall to Hoglands, lunch with Kenneth Clark and his new, half-French wife Nolwen in London, an office party in the new headquarters of the Henry Moore Foundation at Dane Tree House, next to Hoglands, and a visit from Mary, Raymond and grandson Gus on Boxing Day.

Lauren Bacall had become interested in Moore's work in the fifties in California, had bought a maquette or two, and been thrilled by the Florence exhibition. When she enthused about it three years later to Robert Lewin of the Brook Street Gallery in London, he told her how welcoming Moore was to those interested in his work, and promptly called Perry Green. Moore was out, but next morning the telephone rang in her hotel room, she recalled:

> The operator said Henry Moore was on the phone. I could not believe it. I said 'Is this really Henry Moore?' and he said, 'Is this really Lauren Bacall?' I felt twelve years old, I was so excited.[48]

Moore seemed excited himself when he subsequently showed the actress around his studios. She found him 'absolutely adorable' and from then on never came to London without visiting Hoglands, often with one of her sons. Anxious not to take advantage of her friendship, she bought most of her Moores from dealers: several maquettes, a larger reclining figure and numerous lithographs. 'I am surrounded by Henry Moore in my daily life,' she said proudly, 'and feel his strength and vitality always.'

In that she spoke for many. Yet sadly the artist's strength and vitality with which his work was generally imbued, was now beginning to ebb. Working late in the most distant studio on the last day of 1979 because he wanted to date something with that year, he lost his way back. It was very dark, he had forgotten his torch, and snow covered the path. When he fetched up at the house after wandering around for half an hour, his teeth were chattering with cold and he contracted a mild case of hypothermia. For a few days he was quite seriously ill. Thereafter he always worked in the nearer studios on winter evenings. His good fortune was beginning to desert him, and not just in matters of health.

Chapter XIX

Pain and good works

1980–6

Recent history is always the most difficult to write. Emotional scars may be fresh, and not enough time has elapsed for a sense of perspective to be gained. That is certainly true of the last six years of Henry Moore's life. Had he died around the beginning of 1980, aged eighty-one, he would have been spared much unhappiness, pain and physical decline.

The decade was still young when there occurred the most upsetting episode of his adult life. In March 1980 his daughter Mary and her husband Raymond Danowski suddenly and unexpectedly departed from Minges, their farmhouse near Hoglands, to live in South Africa. Gus, so doted on by his grandfather and now just over three years old, naturally went too. Henry was stricken. 'If I had to give anyone a single piece of advice, it would be "Don't have just one child," ' he told a friend. It was two years before they saw Mary again, by which time Gus had, in January 1981, acquired a sister, Jane. A third child, to Moore's pride and delight named Henry, followed in December 1984.

In retrospect, Mary and Raymond's decision to put several thousand miles between themselves and Hoglands was not without logic. Although there must have been many benefits and excitements in younger days from being the daughter of someone as famous and respected at home and abroad as Moore, the offspring of household names notoriously have a tough time establishing their own identity. To be known as Henry Moore's daughter must have become cumulatively oppressive and frustrating, even if in reality her hold over him was strong.

It was no secret to anyone working at or within earshot of Hoglands that father and daughter had an often stormy relationship. Moore's temper could be very short: perhaps it was the Irish in him. He lost it periodically with those who worked for him, and more frequently with his daughter. The sound of them shouting at each other had been a familiar source of mild embarrassment to those nearby.

His fame aside, Moore cannot have been an easy father. All parents are tempted to regard their children as an extension of themselves. Henry, preoccupied as he was, for all his apparent modesty, with his pre-eminence, tended to regard Mary as another of his creations, if the only animate one, and resented it when she did not behave as her maker would have wished. It was as if one of his major themes, mother and child, had turned sour on him. For friends and admirers his tendency to dogmatic generalization and to assume that he was always right was acceptable, even admirable as the homespun philosophizing of a great man. For a spirited, intelligent, and gifted daughter – Mary had by this time illustrated several children's books – it must have been hard to stomach. Perhaps too there had been some resentment on her part, conscious or unconscious but thoroughly understandable, at being packed off in early adolescence by seemingly fond parents to a distant boarding school. Irina's temperament complemented Henry's in many ways, but as a mother her undemonstrativeness cannot have made confidences easy.

Equally, it was never going to be less than very difficult to be Moore's son-in-law. Henry had always been prone to cut Mary's boyfriends down to size. Though Raymond was very different from them and had, as noted, got off to a good start, his relations with Moore had deteriorated. 'If Mary loves him, what can you do?' the sculptor would say resignedly to his assistants. For a man as frugal and hard-working as Moore, Danowski's confessed lack of 'career-orientation' and his prodigal way with money (a green Rolls-Royce, an Aston Martin, no expense spared in doing up Minges) were hard to take. There had latterly been a dispute over the ownership of certain sculptures by Moore which had been exported to Switzerland. To ensure their return the sculptor had had to pay out a considerable sum. That fraught episode had done nothing to promote harmony within the family.

Danowski has given the author only a few clues as to why they departed for Cape Town in March 1980. The idea of a move had been discussed with lawyers for a couple of years, he said. 'We had a lot of things on our plate. We felt we were too caught up in being the family of a famous person. It was affecting our lives. We felt we were revolving around his courtiers, and we wanted to have a normal life.'[1] Whatever other factors played their part – and Britain's taxation levels were prob-ably among them – the choice of South Africa could scarcely have been unhappier. For decades Moore had been signing letters to *The Times*

protesting against the latest horrors of the *apartheid* system. He would
not have dreamt of visiting the country, let alone of living there.

Raymond and Mary had been to Cape Town in 1978 and had liked it.
Returning there in spring 1980, they first lived in an hotel, and then
bought a finely situated house. 'We had friends there, and I was interested
in the political climate,' Danowski said. They could have gone to the
USA, he reflected, but there were drug problems in American schools.
They did not want to go to some tax bolt-hole like Monte Carlo. Perhaps
they should have gone to France, he said. In the event they stayed more
than five years in South Africa, returning to England in September 1985
and buying a house in Dorset in south-west England, a good three-hour
drive from Perry Green. The breach in Henry's family life had not lasted
long, but it had hurt. A concept of happiness had been shattered.

To maintain a family presence within the Foundation, where these
events had their reverberations, Henry invited his niece Ann Garrould to
join the team and help provide direction. As the daughter of his sister
Mary, the former Norfolk headmistress, and god-daughter of Alice
Gostick, Ann provided a double link with his childhood. She had studied
at the Courtauld Institute in London, and although Moore had a low
opinion of art historians and disliked the academic approach to art, it
helped that she knew the techniques of scholarship and could marshal
arguments to support her opinions. Henry had invited her to work for
him in 1971, but she had reckoned her two children needed her. When
Mary departed, she accepted a second invitation, subsequently playing a
full part in organizing exhibitions, dealing with visitors, representing her
uncle abroad, and compiling a catalogue of his drawings. The other staff
members at that time were Betty Tinsley, Henry's fiercely loyal personal
assistant since 1957; David Mitchinson, who had arrived in 1968 fresh
from Bath Academy of Art and looked after publications (including
catalogues, graphics, records and so on); and sometimes another
assistant.

Henry continued to pay the price of survival with the loss of old friends.
Of the famous four, Gregory and Read had gone first. In September 1980
it was Philip Hendy's turn, aged seventy-nine. Partly paralysed by a
stroke, Sir Philip had spent the last nine months of his life in hospital in
Oxford, unable to talk but eager to hear news. Loyal as ever, Moore made
the cross-country journey three or four times to commune with him. The
last survivor was Kenneth Clark, who died in May 1983, aged seventy-
six. Though not well himself and unable to walk or stand for any length
of time, Moore attended the funeral, and – moved to tears – threw the

first handful of soil on to the lowered coffin from his wheelchair. Contrary
to some earlier indications that the Tate would benefit, Clark bequeathed
most of his Moore drawings to the British Museum. Another blow was the
death in 1980 of Marino Marini, and in November 1981 Irina's mother
died, aged ninety-three, in the Paris nursing home in which Henry had
supported her. Much of her later life had been spent in Spain and France.

In 1981 Moore had lost one of his closest American friends, Jo Hirshhorn, who was also one of the biggest collectors of his work. Being one
of ten children brought up in Brooklyn by his widowed immigrant Latvian
mother, Hirshhorn came from an even more impoverished background
than Moore. By the age of seventeen he had become a successful broker
on the New York stock exchange. His big business coup came in the late
1940s with his discovery of the Blind River uranium deposits in Canada.
His second wife was an artist and helped develop his relatively conventional taste in art. Before long he became famous for buying in bulk
but with discrimination, and for a Levantine enthusiasm for bargaining.

He had first met Moore in the 1950s, and when he married his third
wife Olga it was in front of the *Glenkiln Cross* in the garden of his home
in Greenwich, New York. By the time he died aged eighty-two there were
fifty-five Moore sculptures, including four carvings, among the 12,000
cataloguable works of art, antiquities and furniture which he had
amassed. More than 7,000 of these – some 5,000 paintings and 2,000
sculptures – were handed over in 1974 to form the basis of the Hirshhorn
Museum in Washington. The circular building, resembling an armoured
doughnut raised on pillars, was designed by another of Moore's closest
American friends, Gordon Bunshaft. Outside the entrance on Independence Avenue a fine cast of the phallic *Two Piece Reclining Figure:
Points* stands guard, while in the foyer the *King and Queen* commands the
eye with its hieratic dignity. Moore had loved Hirshhorn's enthusiasm,
his warmth and his Damon Runyonesque delivery and wit. Among
collectors of twentieth-century art, he had no equal in his day.

At Hoglands, the show went on. Moore's three long-serving though
still underpaid assistants, Michel Muller, originally from Alsace, Malcolm
Woodward (another Yorkshire miner's son), and John Farnham, son of
neighbour Frank Farnham, enlarged the maquettes which Moore could
still make, and sometimes a not fully exploited earlier work too. Now
that all revenue went to the Foundation, quality control became less
rigorous. Since the money was going to a good cause, how it was earned
perhaps seemed less important. Sometimes when an assistant struck a
difficulty in enlarging which needed resolving – perhaps hands which

needed greater definition – Moore would now say 'You have a go.' Though some big prestige pieces were still done, they were less remunerative, and the small working models produced a better return than the six- or seven-foot size, being much quicker to enlarge and, even proportionately, much cheaper to have cast in bronze.

Among the few major pieces to emerge was *Two Piece Reclining Figure: Cut* of 1980, later called *Architecture Prize*, since the nine bronzes in maquette size became part of the $100,000 Pritzker Architecture Prize funded by the Hyatt Foundation under its president Jay A. Pritzker. The first winner was Moore's old friend Philip Johnson, then aged seventy-four. A sixteen-foot cast of this tough, angular piece was installed on a site outside the new Palais des Congrès in Strasbourg in 1981, after a row over its cost of £155,000: for a Moore of those dimensions, a real bargain.

Around 1979–80 there was a sharp increase in Moore's prices, partly because Danowski, with his knowledge of the New York scene, reckoned the bullish art market could absorb it. When a cast of *Three Piece Reclining Figure No. 1* of 1962 fetched $310,000 at Sotheby's in New York in November 1981, it was an auction record for the work of a living artist. That was soon eclipsed by the $1,265,000 paid the following year by Thomas Gibson for the 1946 elmwood reclining figure, as mentioned earlier. In the same saleroom in autumn 1983 a mixed-media drawing of the (Stevenage) *Family Group* went for $310,000 (£227,333) as a result of competitive bidding by two owners of the bronze.

The Henry Moore Foundation had also entered the drawings market in 1977, buying over the next decade some forty Moore drawings to fill gaps in the chronological sequence of its holdings. Among them was a fine shelter drawing which Juliette Huxley felt obliged to part with in late 1982. Her sense of guilt was increased when it went for £36,000 at Sotheby's in London. 'It fetched an awful lot,' she told Henry when she rang him to explain why she had sold it. 'I know,' he replied. 'I bought it.'[2] That was not strictly true, but he tended to equate the Foundation with himself.

Broadly speaking, prices had increased almost tenfold over the past twenty years, with a spurt over the last five. At the Knoedler exhibition of 1962 the asking price for *Composition* of 1934 was $6,500. In 1983 Harry Brooks sold it at Wildenstein in New York for $85,000. In 1962 the asking price for *Upright Motive No. 5* was $25,000. In 1983 it was $180,000. Even the wealthy city of Hamburg found it hard to muster the £162,000 required in summer 1980 to acquire *Reclining Figure: Hand* of 1976/9 from a commercial show very successfully held partly out of doors in the appropriately named Moorweide (Moor meadow).

Sadly the sculptor was not fit enough to revisit San Francisco in September 1980 for the opening of the Davies Symphony Hall at the Performing Arts Center, in front of which reposed his *Four Piece Reclining Figure* of 1972. But he did make it to Castleford that summer for the unveiling of his *Draped Reclining Figure*, which he was presenting to his home town in fulfilment of an old promise. It had been sited on one of those specially created mounds on a small lawn outside the town's new Civic Centre. It was the first time, he told a large crowd, that he had unveiled one of his own works. He paid tribute to his parents and teachers, and said: 'If I had the chance I wouldn't exchange being brought up in Castleford.'[3] He was given a miner's lamp as a memento of his visit.

A symbolic Madrid show

Despite his growing infirmity, Moore was set to return to Madrid in spring 1981 for the first time since 1935: as if to demonstrate that superlatives had not yet been exhausted, the British Council was putting on the biggest of all Moore exhibitions, consisting of nearly 600 works divided almost equally between sculpture and works on paper. It was, moreover, to be the first major exhibition devoted to a living foreign artist since Franco's death in 1975 and the successful restoration of democracy. For the Spaniards, who were conscious that Moore had signed the manifesto against non-intervention during the Civil War, it was a symbol of their return to the cultural mainstream of Europe: 'Henry Moore turns Madrid into the cultural capital of Europe,' the Madrid newspaper *Ya* proudly proclaimed, while *El Pais* saw an even wider significance: 'Spain is rightly now entering the world cultural arena, and the public are following this with attention and interest,' it commented.[4]

Moore had stayed away from Spain on principle during the long years of Franco, and was looking forward to the Madrid opening. But about two days before they were due to depart, he telephoned Margaret McLeod, who was now deputy director of the British Council's art department, to say he felt he could not make the trip. One reason for his decision was his dislike of meeting a lot of people unless he could stand to greet them, which he could no longer do. McLeod had to pass the news to the Duke of Gloucester, who had agreed to open the exhibition with the Spanish minister for culture. Disappointingly, no member of the Spanish royal family attended the opening, perhaps because the security services remained edgy after the attempted coup staged in the Cortes by

Francoist hotheads that February. Queen Sophia more than made amends when she came to London in 1983 for the opening of the Murillo exhibition at the Royal Academy. Henry was prevented by ill health from attending a dinner given for her at the Spanish Embassy in Belgrave Square, so she came to see him at Perry Green the next day.

The Madrid exhibition had been two years in the making, and was superbly laid out in the Palacio Velasquez, the Palacio Cristal and the Retiro Park, along thematic lines: even British critics, flown there by the British Council, felt they had seen Moore afresh. More than a quarter of a million Spaniards poured in over three months, after which the exhibition moved for six weeks to the no less handsome setting of the Gulbenkian Foundation's building and gardens in Lisbon, of which Sir Leslie Martin was the chief architect. Less confidently than Spain, Portugal too had emerged from dictatorship, and the desire to catch up with European culture was strong. Some 17,000 people, including the Prime Minister, saw the show in the first week. A reduced version went finally to the Miró Foundation's building, designed by the famous Catalan architect Josep Lluis Sert high on the Monjuich Hill overlooking Barcelona. Though recently ill, Miró made a special trip from his home in Majorca, and was delighted by what he saw. Little more than a year later he too was dead.[5]

Another noteworthy though infinitely smaller British Council venture took Moore's work to Eastern Europe again that summer when sculptures, drawings, and prints, mainly from Perry Green, made their début in the Bulgarian capital of Sofia. To judge by the opening speech of the deputy chairman of the Committee for Culture, Mr Berbenliev, even in that redoubt of Marxist orthodoxy Moore's work was beginning to look reassuringly established:

> Henry Moore is one of the few artists to remain true to himself and to avoid the exaggerated enthusiasm for searching for new forms of plastic expression. Above all he deals with the human figure ... the sculptor Moore has created new perceptions of the relationship between the human body, matter and space which coincide with the ideas of the present century.[6]

The goodwill generated across the ideological divide by this show had been boosted at Hoglands shortly before its opening when Henry presented the Bulgarian ambassador with a working-model-sized cast of *Helmet Head No. 6*, of 1975, as a gift for the National Gallery in Sofia, marking the 1,300th anniversary of the country's existence.

Most days now found the sculptor sitting in a battered old square wooden chair covered in yellow foam rubber in his graphics studio at the bottom of the garden. Work remained a drug and helped take his mind off the pain from his back. Probably thanks to his affection for grandson Gus, the mother and child theme was to the fore among the new drawings and maquettes, and they were imbued with a new tenderness: even the sheep which he began to draw again seemed to be done with an awareness that the ovine lot had its bitter moments. The earlier sheep had been plump, contented, well-kempt. Those of the early eighties had a shaggy, melancholy mien.

Among earlier works which were now further enlarged were *Spindle Piece* and the famous *Upright Internal/External Forms*. At the Henraux works the *Spindle Piece* was bumped up to sixteen feet in travertine for the new Pavillon Hotel in Miami, five feet taller than the largest bronze version. It was shipped over in five segments and assembled *in situ* by two of the Querceta artisans. By such ventures Moore enriched the Foundation if not his own reputation.

From the various transformations of *Upright Internal/External Forms* alone he must have made as much money as many artists do in a decade or more. The piece started as a seven-inch-high maquette in 1951, from which an edition of seven bronzes was made. That year it was enlarged to working-model size at just over two feet high: again there was an edition of seven. Then came the 'life-size' bronze version at six feet seven inches, of which three were made. The elmwood version of 1954, acquired as noted by the Albright-Knox Art Gallery, stood just under eight feet tall. That remarkable carving was dearly loved by Gordon Bunshaft, and when one of his partners was designing a huge office building in Chicago, Bunshaft recommended a twenty-five-feet-high version of the same work for its lofty glass lobby.[7]

Henry liked the idea, since the piece would be seen from different angles from each of the building's first three floors. The resulting cast was supposed to be unique, Bunshaft recalled, but Moore took the sixteen-feet three-inches-tall interior piece and had another cast made. That ended up in a pool in front of the British Embassy in Rome, a spot for which – unbeknown to the ambassador who revived the idea – its architect Sir Basil Spence had originally envisaged a Moore sculpture.[8] Not content with that, Moore then issued six casts of the same interior piece as a new sculpture of working-model size, a further six as a two-foot-tall maquette, and five more at sixteen feet three inches. Yet he could seriously assure visiting journalists that he was 'fed up with the business of art' and just wanted to get on with his work, as he did in an enjoyably tetchy interview with Jeffrey Robinson in the *International Herald Tribune* in May 1982.[9]

The most remarkable of these enlargements resulted from the fourth and final collaboration with I. M. Pei. The Chinese-born architect had designed a new headquarters in Singapore for the Overseas Chinese Banking Corporation. On completion in 1976 it was, at fifty-two storeys, the tallest building on the island and a symbol of the new Singapore. A few years after the opening Pei succeeded in his ambition of gaining some open space among the clutter of shops and houses at the base, on which he could site the first major sculptural commission in the Far East, as he believed it would be.

He approached Moore without optimism, since the sculptor had told him that he was doing no more large pieces: they were time-consuming and not profitable, and he was concentrating on drawings for the Foundation. But it would make a difference, he conceded, if it were not a new piece.[10] So the architect combed through the catalogue of all Moore's output, finally fixing on a thirteen-inch-long lead reclining figure of 1938 which had later been cast in bronze in an edition of three. 'It's a very *open* piece,' he explained:

> The negative space is almost more important and more prominent than the positive volumes. It means you will have surprises when you walk into this piece. If you have a cube or a sphere, it doesn't matter how much you enlarge it, it's still the same. With a piece you can enter, it becomes something new. I thought Henry would be taken by that.[11]

The lead original in the Museum of Modern Art in New York would be too soft to work from, but Pei traced a bronze cast to the Peggy Guggenheim collection in Venice. On Moore's recommendation, he had two plaster casts made from it: they could be exported from Italy without all the paperwork required for a work of art. With the sculptor's approval and the blessing of the chairman of the Singapore bank, Tan Ching Tuan, work began first on enlarging and then casting the piece at the Morris Singer foundry in Hampshire. The final product [173], finished in a new, slightly ruddy bronze, was by far Moore's largest reclining figure, measuring thirty-four feet long and almost fourteen feet tall, weighing in at four tons and costing its purchaser £375,000. A giant could walk under the left armpit. Pei felt it none the less had just the lightness and sensuality to complement his strong masculine building.

It is virtually impossible to judge so special a piece outside its intended setting. When Moore had a second cast made for the Foundation and installed it in the *Sheep Piece* field near his studios, it looked like something from *Gulliver's Travels*, and merged conspicuously less well with nature than more solid works: perhaps a case of nature abhorring a vacuum. In Singapore, where it was installed in 1984, its initial impact was spoiled by a low car park in the background, destined to be screened out with trees. Pei likes to think of the great bronze performing a missionary role in spreading the message of contemporary art in the Far East, winning over a world in which the new gods of Western culture and big business are still challenged by the old gods of the Orient.

The Moore gospel had in fact already spread, perhaps via Japan, to South Korea, where an economic miracle at least as remarkable as Singapore's was taking place. One of the three great commercial groups which had helped to regenerate the country's economy following the Korean War was the Samsung conglomerate headed by Lee Byong Chol (sometimes called Byung-Chull Lee). Chairman Lee had started in business in the late 1930s, but his enterprises collapsed under the impact of the country's north-south conflict. Subsequently restarting with sugar and textiles, he then branched into heavy industry and electronics in the 1970s, later adding computers, aircraft engines, and other high technology ventures. By the 1980s the group employed some 100,000 people.

In 1982 the Ho-Am Museum, funded by the Samsung Foundation of Art and Culture, had opened twenty-five miles outside the capital of Seoul. A Henry Moore exhibition, of fifty-two sculptures and eighty drawings and graphics, formed its second attraction, after an opening show of its permanent collection of Oriental and Western paintings, sculpture, pottery, porcelain, and coins. The Moore items were drawn from the Foundation's own holdings, with the Korea Broadcasting System and a daily newspaper partly sponsoring the event. It attracted 70,500 visitors, a respectable total given the not very convenient location.[12]

Before long two large recent reclining figures by Moore joined the ten Rodins and 100 other sculptures in the permanent collection. Not to be outdone, one of Lee Byong Chol's rivals, Kim Woo Chong of the Daewoo group, also acquired a large, recent reclining figure: if you wanted an archetypal Moore which proclaimed that you had made it, a reclining figure it had to be.

These Korean dabblings, welcome though they were, paled beside the coup of the Mokichi Okada Association's new Museum of Art at Atami in Japan in acquiring, as mentioned earlier, Mary Moore's cast of the *King and Queen*, the most sought-after of all Moore's bronzes. Okada, who died in 1955, founded one of the many new religions which sprang up in the spiritual vacuum created by Japan's defeat in the Second World War. The personality cult devoted to him as a latter-day messiah appeals to few Westerners, from the available evidence; but the museum financed and built by his believers is remarkable. Opened in March 1982, it is dedicated to the idea that man's highest creativity springs from nature's beauty, and so the two are best experienced together.

The museum lies fifty-five minutes by Bullet Train from Tokyo, and is constructed from honey-coloured stone on a pine-clad bluff 1,000 feet above the Pacific Ocean. Museum and art centre are reached by a four-stage escalator set in tunnels through the rock. The last escalator debouches on to a broad terrace, in the centre of which sit the *King and Queen*, gazing out to sea with their backs to the steps leading up to the museum. The space inside is devoted mainly to an austerely uncluttered display of masterpieces of Oriental art, with only token representation of Western painting and sculpture: a late Monet of water lilies, an unusually slim Maillol bronze, each originally shown with a room to itself. So here too Moore was carrying a torch for Western culture: a silver lining perhaps in the cloud represented by the sale of a cast which he wished he had kept for the Foundation.

The Leeds Centre

Restricted as he now was in his movements and social life, Henry derived great satisfaction from the Foundation's more important activities. The most notable of these was its contribution to the expansion and reju-venation of the Leeds City Art Gallery, which he had remembered as a 'pretty poor affair' in his two years at the nearby art school.[13] The collection had since been transformed by a sequence of first-class directors from Philip Hendy onwards, but the building on its coveted site next to the city hall was now too small and in a poor, even dangerous state. Fortunately the city council's leisure services committee was chaired between 1976 and 1980 by Dr Jeffrey Sherwin, a man of great energy with a passion for the fine arts: he and the director of the Leeds galleries, Robert Rowe, made a strong partnership.

Dr Sherwin conceived the idea that the gallery should be expanded forwards over Centenary Street, a narrow road which was used mainly for parking, and into the so-called Garden of Rest, a paved area by the city's main thoroughfare in which some modern sculpture, including work by Moore and Hepworth, had been shown in Rowe's first exhibition as director in 1958. With city funds tight, the funding of this scheme to the tune of £1.5 million would not be easy. Sherwin had another idea: to install a pub in the basement of the adjacent library and use the rent as part of the financial backing. The first approach to Moore came from Rowe and Sherwin in autumn 1975 in the form of a request to allow the pub to be called The Henry Moore. It was a way of drawing him in.

At first the sculptor wanted to give his name only to the new sculpture gallery envisaged for the ground floor of the extension, and paid a visit shortly afterwards to see the site. When the Foundation had been set up a year or so later, Mary and Raymond suggested that part of the existing building should be converted into a centre for the study of sculpture. Moore and the trustees approved the idea, giving £300,000 on condition that it was created and that Sir Leslie Martin should act as architectural adviser.[14] The foundation added £20,000 for furnishings, while the Arts Council eventually contributed an unprecedentedly generous £150,000, delighted no doubt that a bold spirit of enterprise and self-help should have seized an English institution. Local businessmen and other sources helped make up the balance.

Thus did Leeds gain a handsomely refurbished gallery with a special section within it ponderously called the Henry Moore Centre for the Study of Sculpture, and also an extension housing *inter alia* the Henry Moore Sculpture Gallery. The pub was eventually called Stumps, in deference to local enthusiasm for cricket. An idea in delightfully bad taste from the brewery, that plaster replicas of Moore's most celebrated works should be installed in niches as part of the décor, was firmly squashed. The study centre was to be run by Dr Terry Friedman, an American with a Ph.D. from the Courtauld Institute who later became the gallery's Principal Keeper too. Its aim continues to be to inform the public of the achievements of all sorts of sculptors through its library facilities, lectures in its own lecture theatre, publications, and exhibitions. Its first publication was a study of Moore's antithesis, the late Victorian, neo-classical British sculptor Hamo Thornycroft, by his daughter Elfrida Manning. In gratitude for the help she had received, Mrs Manning bequeathed to the centre a superb archive of diaries, letters, sketches, and other material.

Moore visited Leeds again briefly in April 1980 to lay the foundation stone of the Moore Sculpture Gallery, and kept in touch with progress. He returned in July 1981 for a topping-out ceremony and to receive the freedom of the city – the first artist to do so. In November 1982 he was back again, this time for the inauguration ceremony in which the Queen herself opened the extended and revamped galleries. Though confined for most of his visit to his wheelchair (which gave him a much lower viewing point for works of art), he was able to have several conversations with the Queen and presented her with a copy of his facsimile *Sheep Sketch Book*, inscribed: 'To Her Majesty – with deepest respect, admiration and affection, from your loyal subject Henry Moore.'[15] Ex-Chancellor Helmut Schmidt, as he had been for a few weeks since losing a vote of confidence in the Bundestag in early October, had accepted Moore's invitation to the opening, and was there with his wife. Coincidentally, his predecessor Willy Brandt was in Leeds a few days later to receive an honorary degree. For the miner's son born a few miles away eighty-four years earlier, it was quite a day.

There were many parallels between the evolution of the study centre in Leeds and of the Henry Moore Centre in Toronto, with Dr Sherwin – like Mayor Givens – generating funds and enthusiasm, while Robert Rowe combined the roles of William Withrow and Alan Wilkinson. Once again the sculptor was touched by the enthusiasm and generosity of the local people, and in this case there was a direct link with his early years. Leeds gained more Moore money, Toronto more works: a suggestion by Mary Moore that a selection of early pieces should be presented to Leeds by the Foundation was never implemented. The Foundation did however make over a major recent bronze: the imposingly sensual *Reclining Woman: Elbow* [174], completed in 1981 and arguably Moore's last significant new sculpture, reclines in front of the new extension just as *Large Two Forms* rears up on its cramped site in front of the Art Gallery of Ontario.

Thanks to Philip Hendy, however, Leeds scored with the great stone *Reclining Figure* of 1929, acquired in 1941 and joined five years later by the stone *Maternity* of 1924. Rowe acquired a three-piece reclining figure (*Bridge Prop*) from Moore in the 1960s for the cost of the foundry bill, and latterly the Foundation helped with the purchase of the 1936 *Mother and Child* carving which so enraged Roland Penrose's Hampstead neighbours in the late thirties, and of a 1929 concrete mask. A number of maquettes, both in plaster and bronze, have been lent. The two major carvings were among the highlights of the study centre's inaugural exhibition, devoted solely to pre-1940 carvings and shown with a handful of inspirational objects from the British Museum, thus again emphasizing Moore's links with earlier cultures. An impressively researched catalogue struck the right scholarly yet readable note.

Although the study centre is part of Leeds City Art Galleries and comes under their director, it is largely funded by an annual grant from the

Foundation in Perry Green, a situation which could perhaps one day create divided loyalties. The final phase in the gallery's expansion was concluded in May 1986 with the opening of a further extension at the back. The new wing, to which the Henry Moore Foundation contributed £600,000, included temporary exhibition space, water-colour galleries, print room, art workshop, restaurant, conservation studios, stores, and additional offices. In this most dramatic expansion and reanimation of a provincial gallery in recent times in England, Moore money had played an indispensable role.

Whereas in Leeds the name of Henry Moore was prominent, much of the Foundation's funding was discreet to the point of near-anonymity: supporting exhibitions, endowing bursaries, contributing to the acquisition of notable works of art for the nation, and many other worthy causes. With the capital climbing beyond £20 million, the income alone soon exceeded £1 million a year. Among the trustees of this increasingly formidable instrument were Sir Denis Hamilton, Maurice Ash, Bernard Meadows, Sir Leslie Martin, Alan Bowness, and Margaret McLeod following her retirement from the British Council. Lord Goodman was chairman. Unlike some trustees, he shared Henry's view that a good meeting was a short meeting. Mary and Raymond Danowski, who had contributed some valuable ideas, ceased to be trustees on their departure for South Africa.

Shortly before the Leeds opening in late November 1982, Henry had paid a twenty-four-hour visit to West Berlin which was to be his last trip abroad. The main aim was to examine the possibility of doing a vast enlargement at Noack's of a slight piece called *Divided Oval: Butterfly*, of 1967, for Sutton Place in Surrey, the former home of Jean Paul Getty. Unfortunately the imaginative schemes of the new American owner, Stanley Seeger, who had bought the property in 1980, proved to be too lavish for the available funds, and in 1986 Sutton Place was back on the market. Meanwhile *Butterfly*, whose ninefold enlargement had been executed by a specialist firm in Berlin, was emerging painfully from its chrysalis in seventy-eight separate pieces. In terms of surface area it was among the largest of Moore's bronzes, and gave Noack many headaches. At the time of writing its final home remained in doubt. Henry's penultimate overseas trip, which also lasted twenty-four hours, had been to Forte dei Marmi in August to receive the freedom of the town: a farewell with honour indeed. Since then his villa there has been used by relatives and friends, and has been bequeathed to the Foundation.

Cultural diplomacy in Latin America

It was one of Moore's wishes at this late stage of his life that his work should be shown again and on a grand scale in Mexico, source of so much of his early inspiration. In addition to the small shows of 1950, already mentioned, followed by his visit in 1953, there had been an exhibition of thirty-two sculptures and forty-two drawings in Mexico City in 1964 which aroused great enthusiasm. When the Duke of Edinburgh visited the country later that summer he presented to President Mateos on behalf of the British government a Moore reclining figure of 1933 which the sculptor had made available at a greatly reduced price. It was eventually displayed in the Museo de Arte Moderno in Mexico City; and it was in the same museum that President Lopez Portillo opened a full-scale, British Council-backed Moore exhibition of 145 sculptures, 88 drawings and 46 graphics on 4 November 1982. Attendance was in the Florence, Zurich, and Madrid class: 400,000 and more visitors in three months. Side-shows of mime, singing, guitar playing, and contemporary dance flourished, and Moore's links with Mexican art were a recurring theme of several hundred press articles devoted to the event.

The 1964 show had gone on to Caracas, the Venezuelan capital, Rio de Janeiro in Brazil, and the Argentinian capital, Buenos Aires, where it no doubt helped counteract some of the damage to Anglo-Argentinian relations caused by the long-running dispute over the sovereignty of the Falkland Islands. In spring 1982 this had led to war between the two countries, culminating in the defeat and demise of General Galtieri's military junta. Despite that gain for democracy, the David and Goliath struggle had badly damaged Britain's reputation throughout Latin America. It was a perfect moment for cultural diplomacy. Fortuitously, 1983 was the bicentenary year of the birth of Simon Bolívar, who had liberated Venezuela, Colombia, Panama, Ecuador, Peru, and Bolivia from Spanish rule, supported by Britain alone among the major powers.

A weighty British contribution to the bicentenary celebrations was evidently called for, and an important Henry Moore exhibition plus a visit from the London Festival Ballet were chosen as the main ingredients. Arrangements were made for the Mexico City show to travel on to Caracas, where it was opened in early March 1983 by President Luis Herrera Campins, at the Museo de Arte Contemporaneo. Fears that the President might stay away because of the 'Falklands factor' were confounded, and the Venezuelan public followed his lead: around

245,000 of them saw the show in two and a half months, one in seventy of the population. Thanks partly to a front-page feature in the newspaper *El Nacional*, 20,000 people saw the exhibition on its last day, which must have been a record of sorts.

As had been done successfully in Mexico, a separate group of a dozen Moore maquettes with about forty drawings and graphics was sent at the same time to six regional cities in which contemporary European art was rarely glimpsed, with gratifying results. In the gallery at Barquesimeto the rooms used were renamed the Moore Galleries, as a tribute to the huge attendance and improved temperature, humidity, and security controls on which the British Council had insisted. Some who had seen their first Moores in their local capital went to Caracas for a full immersion. For example, a housewife from Ciudad Bolívar drove 800 miles with her husband and children for this once-in-a-lifetime experience. There were tours for the blind (as in Mexico City), with a museum staff member producing a catalogue in braille, and tours even for soldiers and policemen. Two former presidents, the opposition's presidential candidate and several Cabinet members were among the visitors.[16]

Someone told Sofia Imber, the director of the Caracas museum and a well-known television personality, that only the Beatles at their peak could have created a comparable stir and earned as much goodwill for Britain. 'We don't agree with that remark,' she wrote to Sir John Burgh, the director-general of the British Council, 'but only because we are certain that Henry Moore has actually made a greater stir, and has had a much deeper impact than the Beatles ever could.'[17] The Venezuelan media, she added, had unanimously recognized the Moore show as the 'most important and best executed ever presented in this country'. For the British Council it was good value too, being seen by almost a quarter of a million people for an outlay of £210,000 (mainly paid by the Venezuelan authorities and sponsors), while the Festival Ballet, also hugely successful, could be seen by only 25,000 for twice the cost.

Moore's ability to attract more than 650,000 people to his exhibitions in Mexico and Venezuela suggested that even if he was out of touch with the contemporary international avant-garde, he was more in tune with the spirit of the times than young artists might like to think. His work still gave off the full frisson of modernity, yet it was clearly related to humanity and to nature, it was moving and sensual, and it was recognizably sculpture. For all that the public was now grateful.

In Moore's eighty-fifth year even the Parisian critics seemed anxious to prove that they had taken him to their flinty hearts. When in February

1983 the Galerie Maeght put on a show consisting mainly of bronzes and drawings of the past two years, they were eloquent in their praise of the serenity, freedom, tenderness and poetry of these octogenarian works. A similar reaction greeted an eighty-fifth birthday exhibition, again mainly of recent bronzes and drawings, at Marlborough Fine Art in London in July. The *Evening Standard*'s Richard Cork saw a symbolism shot through with pathos in the skeletal drawings of trees, and a new sense of vulnerability in the drawings and bronzes on the mother and child theme. Tackling Moore for the first time in what a correspondent later called a birthday clobbering, the *Guardian*'s young critic Waldemar Januszczak found that the intensity of these drawings showed up the 'flaccid monumentality' of the large outdoor sculpture, as seen in another birthday show in and around the Great Hall of Winchester Castle.[18]

New York's tribute

Much the most substantial tribute took place at the Metropolitan Museum in New York. Organized by the chairman of the twentieth-century department, William Lieberman, it was the biggest show of Moore's work in the USA since the 1946 retrospective at the Museum of Modern Art, when Lieberman had been the great Barr's assistant. His aim now was primarily to correct the prevalent view of Moore as the creator of monumental outdoor bronzes and of little else, and as an artist who had become old hat.[19] Lack of outdoor space to display large pieces was a further reason to play them down and to play up the early carvings. Some of those which Lieberman succeeded in borrowing from little-known American collectors had been bought long ago from Valentin and never seen since, even in photographic form. In all there were sixty-four pieces executed between 1922 and 1940, and no less than twenty-six war drawings.

Since Moore was too infirm to go to New York to discuss the layout of the exhibition, Lieberman had taken a scale model of the Lehman wing to Perry Green. The resulting presentation, on two floors, was widely agreed to be a work of art in itself, and the critics were duly impressed by the early sculptures. The impact was felt well beyond the metropolis, with the art critic of the *Dallas Morning News*, for example, writing: 'Thanks to this show ... Moore will be as keenly appreciated for his intimate statements as for his public accomplishments.'[20]

The exhibition was sponsored by Gould Inc., a Chicago electronics firm which a few years earlier had acquired a cast of Moore's *Large Two Forms* for its new headquarters campus, and one or two other items. The firm had found its Moores to be 'symbols of its commitment to innovation and exploration', the chairman William T. Ylvisaker said in a prefatory catalogue note. 'The continuing interplay of forms and spaces which one experiences in a Moore sculpture stimulates our imagination and encourages us to seek new approaches in our research laboratories and our training centers as well as in the management of our business.'[21] This led a writer in the *Toronto Globe and Mail*, William Bentley Mays, to speculate whether the Henry Moore effect on Gould's $1.6 billion sales could be quantified. With refreshing cynicism he described Moore's work as 'perhaps the most pervasive artistic status symbol in the developed capitalist world' during its expansionist phase of the sixties and seventies. In front of corporate headquarters, civic buildings, and cultural centres his sculpture provided 'prestigious emotional relief' from the sterility of modernist architecture, and stood as 'mute tribute to the worldly-wise internationalism' of his business patrons.[22]

Despite the provocative veneer Mays was saying much the same as a Jungian interpreter like Neumann: that Moore's archetypal forms with their earth-mother associations help to redress the masculine and aggressive forces dominating Western civilization. If businessmen who paraded their Moores in public were proclaiming their sophistication to the world, was that a serious sin? There is often only a thin line between boasting, sharing one's enthusiasms, and evangelizing. Americans largely lack the great British fear of being thought to show off.

Among Moore's most energetic friends in the American business world was David Finn, chairman and co-founder of the large New York public-relations firm Ruder Finn & Rotman, who was also an amateur painter and a professional photographer of sculpture. By the early 1980s he had illustrated some two dozen books, including *Sculpture and Environment*, a massive compilation of photographs of Moore's major pieces in outdoor sites around the world, with comments from the sculptor.[23] He was among those collectors of Moore's work who was keen for others to share his pleasure in it, and he was prepared to take considerable trouble towards that end.

Among the projects to which he contributed time and money was the creation of Columbia University's Henry Moore Sculpture Reserve at Arden House, Harriman, in upstate New York. When this was inaugurated in May 1983 by the university's president, Michael Sovern, it had been ten years in the making. 'We wanted to use the knowledge we gained from seeing Henry's work in so many different environments to help create one environment in which his sculpture would be ideally sited,' Finn recalled.[24] Originally Brown University, at Providence, Rhode Island, where three of Finn's children had studied, was to have benefited. But eventually the potential hazards of the site, which included border difficulties, the possible construction of oil tanks across a bay, and the future of a Nike missile site on the 500-acre property, were considered to outweigh the advantages.

Discussions with Columbia, which by chance had given Moore an honorary degree three years earlier, began in 1977. Although itself located in New York City, the university had in 1950 been presented by Governor Averell Harriman with his former family seat, Arden House, and its 450-acre estate some forty-eight miles to the north. The house subsequently became an international conference centre, the grounds a magnificent, protected wilderness. From its walks and trails the visitor might observe deer, fox, beaver, birds of prey, and grouse, while a 1,700-foot ridge of the Ramopo mountains gives dramatic views of a forested valley and two lakes. Henry was much taken by its beauty when Finn escorted him there on his last visit to the USA in 1978. 'It is like being in Scotland,' he observed, 'but so close to New York!'[25] The reserve was officially declared open in autumn 1986, with several works on long-term loan from the Henry Moore Foundation, and others in prospect, not least from the Finns.

This potentially inspiring venture could be considered one of the many offspring of Sir William Keswick's inspired siting of sculpture on his Scottish estate in the 1950s. Photographs of his moorland Moores had gone around the world, helping for example to inspire the Storm King Art Center at Mountainville, again in upstate New York, in the late 1960s. The London County Council's open-air sculpture shows, rapidly emulated abroad, had also played their part in spreading the concept of the sculpture park. So too had Moore's own insistence that nature made the best setting for his work. In Britain the idea took root more slowly than in the USA or on the Continent, but the early 1980s saw a sudden flowering of sculpture parks. Among the larger ones were the Yorkshire Sculpture Park near Wakefield and the Welsh Sculpture Park near Port Talbot which, along with more modest ventures at Sutton Manor in Hampshire and Portland in Dorset, opened in 1983. That year was indeed to be a sort of unofficial Sculpture Year, culminating in a huge Arts Council exhibition called *The Sculpture Show* at the Hayward and Serpentine galleries, among whose sponsors was the Henry Moore Foundation.

The evolution of sculpture over the last two decades into a virtually free form was there brilliantly epitomized by David Mach's huge assemblage in the shape of a submarine of 6,000 used tyres. The notoriety which this work achieved almost rivalled that of the American sculptor Carl André's pile of bricks at the Tate Gallery when the public suddenly awoke to its charms in 1976, four years after its acquisition. Controversy turned to tragedy when an incensed art-lover (or hater?) tried to set fire to the rubber submarine and himself perished in the flames.

The cult of the found object, originally associated by the surrealists with natural objects, had joined forces with the anarchism of the Dada movement and run amok. By the 1980s, any old man-made rubbish, from a used sanitary pad to a slashed armchair or a disused fridge or washing machine, could be more or less wittily presented as a form of sculpture. It was little wonder that to many artists and a few critics Moore now seemed an anachronism, and that to an increasingly large part of the public his work had become a welcome refuge from the inanities of what passed for the modern spirit: a kind of sculptural Sir Edward Elgar, as an American critic called him, and not by chance the great Edwardian composer was coming back into fashion.[26] Moore's belief that art must represent human values was being vindicated by the spiritual nullity of work which aimed no higher than mental or visual titillation. In sculpture the pendulum would surely swing back towards feeling, form, and the past just as it was swinging in painting. From New York to Paris and Düsseldorf, the wave of abstraction which had unfurled over the Western world from the mid-1950s to the mid-1970s was receding. So-called hyper-realism, in which the painter laboured minutely to simulate the effects of colour photography, was perhaps an extreme form of reaction. It was succeeded by the heavily commercialized revival of the Germanic expressionism of the 1920s and 1930s, in Italy by the re-creation or apeing of Old Masters, and in England by a Chagall-like preoccupation with strange beasts.

Old age is often cruel. Moore had become a frail figure, upset for a long time at being bereft of his daughter Mary and her children, and physically in constant pain. His visits to London were rare. One was in June 1983, to see the Tate Gallery's superb summer exhibition, *The Essential Cubism*, whose main organizer was Douglas Cooper. The Tate's director Alan Bowness wheeled him around. Three weeks later, in mid-July, he was due to visit the British Museum for a private viewing of the Goulandris collection of Cycladic art, but on the day before he was seized with severe pains in his back, and had to retire to bed. Something was seriously wrong, and on 8 August he was taken to Addenbrooke's Hospital in Cambridge, a major teaching hospital which was handier than anything equivalent in London.

There he underwent a prostate operation to remove a blockage to the urinary flow, a familiar problem in old age. There is no guarantee of success in this operation, partly because the scar tissue can form into an obstruction to the urethra. In that event the body starts to retain its waste products and the entire system is in danger of being poisoned, with potentially fatal results. In Moore's case, all did not go well, but the worst was avoided. He returned to Hoglands on 17 August, a week after the operation and at a stage when its outcome was still uncertain. Twelve days later he returned as an emergency case. To relieve the flow of urine a catheter was inserted, but his system was slow to recover, and for more than a week he seemed to be in danger of slipping away. Those who visited him regularly – they included Irina, his niece Ann Garrould, Bernard Meadows, and the Leslie Martins, who lived nearby – found it impossible to get through to his mind. He seemed to be losing interest in remaining alive.

Word that Henry was seriously ill spread quickly. Messages of concern and goodwill flowed in from the art world, while in Fleet Street newspaper obituaries were hastily updated. Some of the sculptor's American friends were afraid that British medicine would not be equal to the hour. David Finn flew from New York to London, and having put himself in the picture telephoned Bill Ylvisaker of Gould Inc., thinking that the latter's polo-playing contacts with the Duke of Edinburgh and Prince Charles might prove useful. Ylvisaker called Buckingham Palace and spoke to Prince Charles's private secretary, who after checking with the heir-apparent telephoned Addenbrooke's to express the royal concern for Moore's health. Whether all this made any difference is doubtful: the hospital does its best for all its patients regardless of their fame and was fully aware of Moore's identity.

In the event it was Mary who probably saved her father's life with some inspired common sense. Having arrived in England from South Africa on 7 September, almost a month after the initial operation, she saw that if he was to be remotivated, he must be taken back home to Hoglands. That was done on 12 September, and before long he began to rally. When the author paid a visit a month later, he was lying in a bed which had been installed in the sitting room. There he could contemplate the fine paintings and artefacts which he and Irina had collected and the garden which Irina had so lovingly created, visible from both sides of the room and at the end. He looked emaciated and pale, the face drawn and strangely noble, wasted arms thin upon the sheets, not unlike a marble knight recumbent upon a medieval tomb. 'I have lived a long time, long enough,' he said when congratulated on his recovery. 'I suppose I've been lucky in being able to work with so few breaks.' Two days earlier Irina had had a fall in the house and feared she had broken a leg which had only just recovered from another recent fracture. But this time it was 'only' her wrist.

Moore had by then begun doing some drawing and modelling with plasticine, propped up against the pillows in bed, and had even been down to the studios in his wheelchair to see how work was progressing: the huge Singapore piece was the main task in hand. A few months earlier, foreseeing either illness or a fatal mishap, he had asked his old friend and assistant Bernard Meadows, previously a very active trustee, to take on extra duties as a consultant to the Foundation. From now on Meadows would be available to ensure that any remaining enlargements were carried out as he thought Moore would have wished, and to take decisions or give advice where needed on the siting of major pieces (as for example in the New York parks show of the Ablah collection) and generally to act as Henry's *alter ego*.

Before long Moore's resilience began to reassert itself. Some of the sparkle returned to his eyes, and his greeting regained its familiar warmth, giving visitors the impression they were just the person he had been hoping to see. A new routine was established. A nurse would help him dress in the morning, and he would transfer from his bed to an adjacent chair. Visitors sat on the bed, sometimes competing with the television set a few yards in front of him. Henry loved to hear what his friends had been up to, and they soon realized just how much their visits cheered him. Most mornings one or two would come in for a half-hour or more to reminisce about old times. Moore's memory having faded rapidly since his operation, he was often pleased and surprised to learn of all the things he had done and to be reminded of the places he had visited. What a fortunate life he had had, he would comment, and how lucky he had been in his friends. At noon he would generally suggest a drink, and take a little whisky himself. Irina would come into the sitting room at about this stage, and often he would turn to her for names and other information. After lunch he would be taken for a drive, generally by Frank Farnham, otherwise by Wilfred Holmes, a local hire-car driver. Beautiful though the view was from his perch in the sitting room, he grew bored with it and loved a change of scene. On these drives, often through the estates of friendly local landowners like the Buxtons and Normans, he saw more of the local countryside than at any other time during his forty-five years in Hertfordshire. A favourite stopping point was at Allen's Green, where he would feed carrots to a donkey belonging to the village pub. 'He really loved that old donkey,' Frank Farnham recalled. 'Its name was Brandy, but we renamed it Charlie at his suggestion.'[27]

To alleviate his enforced inactivity there ebbed and flowed into the sitting room of Hoglands dealers, publishers, journalists, museum officials, collectors and others whom he knew more or less well, who would be escorted in to say hello for a few minutes, and sometimes much longer. Activity at the Foundation's headquarters at Dane Tree House next door ranged from the hectic to the relatively slack. Much depended on how many exhibitions loomed. In 1983, a very busy year, there were seventeen around the world for which it was primarily responsible. Even if the British Council were the prime organizer, the Foundation and its holdings of Moore's work would be involved. If the show was important, Ann Garrould or David Mitchinson would go out to ensure that high standards of presentation were maintained, a task requiring considerable tact.

With the trustees taking decisions about grants, the rest of the Foundation functioned much as a scholarly art gallery might do. When not preoccupied with exhibitions, Ann Garrould worked on a catalogue of Moore's drawings, a Sisyphean task which others had previously attempted, while David Mitchinson did the same for the later graphics, in partnership with Gérald Cramer's son Patrick. The result was the fourth and last volume of the collected graphics, published in 1986. At the final count Moore's drawings ran to almost 5,500 items, and graphics to 719. The grand total of sculptures was just over 1,000 separate pieces, counting one cast of each different version of the same piece. Allowing for single items like carvings and editions of up to nine, there are probably about 5,000 Moore sculptures in existence.

For visitors to Hoglands the attractions included the small sculpture park down by the studios, and the studios themselves. Even without the chance of glimpsing the great man, these continued to attract around 2,000 people by appointment each year, generally by coach. Normally Ann Garrould would show them around and explain Moore's working methods. The maquette studio with its little plaster or clay models and array of found objects like flints, shells, bones of oddly shaped pieces of wood, was particularly popular.

Most day-to-day business was handled by Betty Tinsley. Having been with Moore for almost thirty years, she had become more a personal assistant than a secretary, dictating letters to Anne Unthank. Mrs Tinsley had long been a kind of human memory bank representing the continuity in Henry's business life and friendships. His debt to her sense of loyalty, her humour, and common sense was immense. Every famous artist needs someone who can see off the importunate, the opportunists, the phonies, and the bores. Betty Tinsley was good at that too, thus sparing Irina the task. Living nearby on Perry Green, she was always available.

Only a major exhibition could now lure Moore to London. Among those which he visited were *English Romanesque Art* at the Hayward Gallery, the paintings of George Stubbs at the Tate, Neopolitan painting and Benin bronzes at the Royal Academy. By 1985 not even the major Renoir exhibition at the Hayward could draw him to the capital. The effort had become too great. One visit, the first after his operation, was exceptional in being for the consecration of his last commission, a *Madonna and Child* for St Paul's Cathedral [186]. The Dean, Dr Alan Webster, had long been a Moore admirer. As Dean of Norwich Cathedral he had in 1976 persuaded the sculptor to lend a cast of the *Glenkiln Cross* for a lawn within the cloisters. Moving to St Paul's two years later, he determined to secure a Moore for Wren's masterpiece. One day he mentioned his ambition to Sir Denis Hamilton, whom he knew.[28]

Sir Denis succeeded in firing Henry's enthusiasm with a vision of a Moore in London's most famous cathedral, and subsequently showed him possible sites in the crypt and in a bay not far from the high altar. Henry could think of no suitable existing piece, but accepted the Dean's idea that a Madonna-like mother and child would be appropriate. Suddenly it seemed an exciting challenge. That evening he telephoned Hamilton and said: 'I have had no tea and supper, I can't get this Madonna and Child out of my mind. It may be my last work, and I want it to give the feel of having a religious connotation.'[29] Each evening he telephoned to report progress, until he had made four maquettes. They were enlarged to working-model size and one was selected and dispatched to the Henraux studio in Italy, Moore having decided that travertine would be more suitable than bronze for such a site.

The author happened to be present in August 1983 when the two blocks of stone arrived there, one for the Madonna, one for the child. The polystyrene model looked unimpressive, and it was hard to believe that anything worthy would emerge. Such fears were at least partly confounded by the result. This final and very simplified version of Moore's first theme exudes a restrained tenderness, with the mother leaning protectively over her child. The carving, which stands seven feet tall, was installed in the cathedral's north choir aisle, not far from the main altar, in March 1984. In the course of his visit for the dedication at the end of the month he accepted the advice of Sir Roy Strong, who was present in an advisory capacity, that it should be raised on a higher base. Newspaper photographs of him with the *Madonna and Child* brought home the heavy toll taken by his operation.

That October he received the singular honour of a visit from the French head of state, President François Mitterrand, to Hoglands to bestow on him the order of Commander of the Legion of Honour. Like Chancellor Schmidt, the President came by helicopter from London, where he had been the guest of the Queen. Following a bomb scare at a French Embassy reception a couple of days previously, security was tight at the sculptor's home. First came the Essex police with their sniffer dogs, then the Hertfordshire police with long-handled mirrors to search under cars, then a couple of fire engines to stand by. There was some dismay when the local garbage collectors effortlessly penetrated the *cordon sanitaire* on their weekly round. Two helicopters brought in the President and his entourage, which included the ambassador M. de Margerie, formerly head of France's museums and a Moore admirer. When the machines had landed in the field with the *Sheep Piece* and the Singapore giantess, Bernard Meadows and Ann Garrould advanced as the greeting party towards the further, more imposing helicopter, only for the Mitterrands to emerge from the nearer one and wait for them to return. After a tour of studios and garden, they repaired to the Hoglands sitting room. Someone had discovered that it was the President's sixty-sixth birthday, so Henry gave him a drawing of a reclining figure in exchange for the Legion of Honour. 'Don't I get a uniform as well?' he asked when the order was placed around his neck, and three times he repeated '*J'aime Paris.*' When asked by the President which French sculptor had influenced him, he replied: 'Rodin, of course.' Was there someone more recent he admired, he was asked. 'Giacometti,' Henry replied, 'but he was Swiss, of course.'

In deference to his age and poor health, Moore's reputation had entered a kind of honoured critical limbo. Demand for his sculpture and drawings remained brisk, his prices high, but his work had receded from the forefront of debate. However, those who plan big exhibitions are obliged, like those who book top opera singers or instrumentalists, to think two or three years ahead. Among them was Sir Hugh Casson, president of the Royal Academy. He and his colleagues were booking their exhibition

rooms for 1988, when Henry would be ninety. How better to clinch the
RA's identification with the mainstream of contemporary British art than
to mount a major Moore retrospective? When Sir Hugh put the idea to
him by letter, Moore at first said he was not interested: he had not forgiven
the RA for its failure to support the embattled Epstein between the wars.
No doubt the Munnings attacks still rankled too. Sir Hugh persisted, and
Bernard Meadows was a sympathetic intermediary. They had both known
Casson for years, and Moore recognized that the RA had undergone a
transformation in its attitudes, which Casson had accelerated. Many
leading artists now belonged, and the RA's exhibitions were the best in
London. Henry had been particularly struck by the Benin bronzes. So it
was agreed: there would be a full-scale Moore exhibition at Burlington
House in October 1988, three months after his ninetieth birthday.

In mid-1986 it seemed improbable but just possible that he would survive to witness that event. He was in fair shape for his eighty-eighth
birthday on 30 July, which was celebrated with a small party of Foundation
staff and other assistants and helpers, gathered around his chair in the sitting room. One of his targets had always been to match Michelangelo's
age of eighty-nine, but that too he was to be denied. About a week after his
birthday a decline set in. He no longer felt equal to the afternoon drive,
and became progressively weaker and more disorientated. His last outside
visitors were his oldest friends, from whom his great fame had somewhat
separated him: Raymond Coxon, who had recently celebrated his ninetieth birthday, and his wife Gin, the great love of Moore's early manhood.
The Coxons, who had remained spry enough to enjoy a visit to the USA
a few months previously, were saddened to find him so evidently near
the end. But Henry had sufficient spirit left to urge Gin to kiss him goodbye
on the mouth, which she tenderly did.

Death came peacefully a few days later, at 2 a.m. on Sunday 31 August.
His daughter Mary was with him at the end. Although his last three
years had been sad, he and his family were fortunate that he was spared
the onset of senility. The spark of that tremendous vitality may have
glowed very feebly towards the end, but it was never quite extinguished,
and the great charm of his character continued to shine through.

The news of his death was not released until around 1 p.m. that
Sunday; time enough for daily newspapers to top and tail their oft-revised
and updated obituaries, but short notice for fresh tributes to be written
for Monday's editions. Many of those published in London touched on
Moore's stature as man as well as artist. 'Since the death of Sir Winston
Churchill, Henry Moore has been the most internationally acclaimed of

Englishmen, honoured by every civilized country in the world,' the *Daily Telegraph* wrote in a leading article, adding that he had attained a stature 'almost unknown in the history of British artists'. In the *Guardian*, Norbert Lynton went so far as to say that 'time will show which was his greater achievement, his life or his art'. In *The Times* the director of the Tate Gallery, Alan Bowness, said that no artist had ever acquired such total mastery of three-dimensional form. With his death, he concluded, we had lost 'one of the greatest Englishmen of our time'.

From east to west and north to south across the globe, newspapers paid their tributes, drawing attention now to the story of the miner's son who became world famous, now to the universality of his appeal and its roots in the fundamental themes of man's existence, now to the way in which, as *Die Welt* put it, 'he made space an artistic event'. Superlatives were in general employed with restraint: *The Times* hedged its bets by calling him 'an outstanding figure among modern British sculptors and an artist of international reputation'. With a full-page obituary, the *New York Times* treated his death like that of a major statesman. John Russell, who wrote it, called him 'a sculptor pre-eminent in twentieth-century art'.[30] Moore's preferred label would probably have been 'the greatest sculptor since Rodin' – with no qualification or equivocation.

The funeral was held three days later at the tiny parish church of Perry Green, a few hundred yards from Hoglands, and there too his mortal remains were buried. Apart from Irina, Mary, Raymond and their children, the family was also represented by Henry's sole surviving sister, Betty Howarth and her daughter, and by his other nieces Ann Garrould and Aline Reed, daughter of his brother Raymond. His sister Betty died a few weeks later after breaking a leg, just short of her ninety-second birthday. In addition to the staff and most of the trustees of the Henry Moore Foundation and some local employees, there were a few close and mainly local friends, including Sir William Keswick.

The nation's tribute, a 'service of thanksgiving for the life and work of Henry Moore OM CH 1898–1986', took place at noon on 18 November at Westminster Abbey. It was a remarkable occasion, with the Royal Philharmonic Orchestra conducted by Sir Georg Solti and the soprano Felicity Lott helping to provide the music, an address from Sir Stephen Spender, and the Duke of Gloucester and the actress Dame Peggy Ashcroft reading the lessons. Lord Zuckerman OM represented the Queen, and the Prime Minister herself, Margaret Thatcher, paid her own tribute to Moore's character and achievement by attending: she had a personal link with his work, since every three months Ann Garrould had gone to

No. 10 Downing Street to provide a fresh drawing for an alcove in a ground-floor corridor, where it hung above a smallish reclining figure; while the garden at Chequers, the Prime Minister's country seat, boasts a six-foot-high bronze called *Figure in a Shelter*.

All too many of Henry's closest friends had preceded him to the grave, but among his surviving contemporaries present were the Coxons, John and Myfanwy Piper, and Lord Houghton, with whom he had joined the Civil Service Rifles in 1917. Other close friends from earlier days included Sir Robert and Lady Sainsbury, Lady Hendy, and Sir James and Lady Richards, and among more recent ones the New York architects Gordon Bunshaft and I. M. Pei. It was perhaps sad that relatively few artists were present (apart from Piper and the Coxons, they included Anthony Caro, Patrick Heron, Tom Phillips, and William Turnbull), and that representatives of organizations with which Henry had been connected should have outnumbered friends. None the less, even if the emotional temperature never rose very high, it was a moving hour and a worthy farewell.

In the studios at Hoglands all work on enlargements had ceased on Moore's death, as stipulated by the sculptor: a sensible and necessary decision even if it gave the rather misleading impression that he had exercised some supervision in the three years following his prostate operation. It is true that from time to time an assistant would bring a working-model-sized piece into the sitting room and stand it on a table for him to see; and on occasion a large polystyrene model was trundled to the window for his inspection. But Moore was in no state to suggest or make any changes. 'Very good my boy,' he might say, pleased to know that the good work was going on.

There was no cause for Moore's passing to affect the Foundation's involvement in British Council exhibitions abroad. Just a month previously the largest Moore show to be held in the Far East returned from Japan, having earlier created a stir in Hong Kong. The first Moore exhibition to be held in India was scheduled for New Delhi in October 1987, with a less substantial show of smaller works touring such cities as Madras, Bombay, and Calcutta for a longer period. The capacity of Moore's work to amaze, delight, and startle new audiences shows no sign of diminishing.

An artist's death does not necessarily boost the value of his work, but it seemed to do so in Moore's case. Other factors, like a weak dollar, soaring stock-exchange prices and an impending increase in the capital gains tax rate in the USA, may also have been at work. Moore had been buried only a month when it was reported that George Ablah, the Kansan oil and property man, had sold sixteen of his hundred Moores for more than $10 million. The buyer was Nobutaka Shikanai, founder of the Hakone Open Air Museum in Japan, who planned to use his new acquisitions to establish a Henry Moore Garden there.[31] A few weeks later Ablah sold a further fifty-seven Moores, this time to the Hall Family Foundation of Kansas City, whose assets derive mainly from Hallmark greeting cards. The price was $20 million, the bronzes being intended for loan to the Nelson-Atkins Museum of Art in Kansas City.[32] So having paid $22 million for his hundred Moores, Ablah had made an $8 million profit and still had twenty-seven works in hand: some compensation for falling oil prices. Then in a feverish week in November 1986 in which the two big auction houses sold paintings and sculpture worth some $120 million in New York, Moore's *Reclining Figure* (Festival) of 1951 went for a personal record of $1.76 million, a figure which needed to be compared for perspective with $3.6 million paid for a painting by Jasper Johns happily entitled *Out the Window*.[33]

In the long term it seems likely that time will winnow Moore's best work from the less good and the bad, and that even the best will be subject to the fluctuations of taste and fashion to which all big reputations in the creative field are prey. Among the greatest enthusiasts there have been wide differences of view about the relative merits of, for example, his early and late work. The same is true among admirers of the big late bronzes. In art criticism there are no absolute standards. Judgement is ultimately a matter of taste.

The author's experience in the course of four years of continued exposure to the work may well reflect a typical evolution of attitudes. I started with a strong affection for the *King and Queen*, the Northampton *Madonna and Child*, the Dartington *Memorial Figure*, the family group maquettes and many of the pre-1950 drawings. Much of the very early work seemed unduly primitive, while that of the 1930s was either baffling or too plugged in to Paris – Moore's version of what Giacometti, Lipchitz, Laurens *et al.* were doing. The late work seemed patchy and often too big for its own good.

Closer acquaintance brought an appreciation of the unforced grandeur of many of the early carvings, of their intelligence, inventiveness, intensity and vitality. In several senses Moore was at that stage a force of nature, in tune with its forms and its materials, and inexhaustibly fertile in his imagination and creativity, as his drawings also demonstrated. The Leeds reclining figure and the elmwood carvings on the same theme, including those done after the Second World War, remain his greatest achievements. The drawings up to the shelter studies, whether from the life, studies for sculpture or works of pure imagination, are often of great power and haunting beauty. In all these creations there is a sense of mystery, of communion with the forces of the universe. Our own imaginations are roused and challenged by the audacity of Moore's imagination.

On this analysis, his creative force was at its peak between 1929 and 1941, when he was in his early forties, and still appreciated by only a small minority of art lovers. The shelter drawings marked his break-through to a wider public and a first falling-off in quality, the reasons for their popularity being the cause of the decline. They saw the first intrusion of Moore the moralist, portraying and ennobling the suffering of the people, showing his compassion with an epic touch. The mining drawings, more direct and less self-conscious and prettified, are relatively underrated.

From the Northampton *Madonna and Child* through to the family groups, the *King and Queen*, the wounded warriors and the multitudinous daughters of the Unesco figure, the mood of uplift recurs. All these semi-narrative works owed much to Moore's vision of himself, conscious or not, as a great public artist. There is something almost Victorian in the way they demand the emotional involvement of the spectator, and the public reacted accordingly, though often with violent hostility. During the same period – from 1944 to the 1950s – Moore intermittently produced work true to his tougher spirit, such as the 1945 elmwood reclining figure, the 1951 Festival figure and the *Glenkiln Cross*.

With the two- and three-piece reclining figures of 1959–65 he returns to the greater emotional detachment of the 1930s, when the first such figures were produced. Although at first arresting in their majestic and rugged bulk, most of these come to seem too crude an analogy between female form and landscape. It is as if Moore had been impressed by what Neumann had written about him. Yet at the same time he was winning his way through to such remarkable semi-abstract creations as *Standing Figure: Knife Edge*, *Locking Piece*, *Three Piece: Vertebrae* and *Sheep Piece*. All these work very well at full size. Others, like *Spindle Piece* and *Square Form with Cut*, have a pumped-up look, and are more convincing in smaller versions. None the less, from this phase lasting from 1959 to around 1974 date many of Moore's best-known monumental creations. To have created significant works of art on that vast scale is a remarkable achieve-ment. They became the natural first choice for major architectural sites across the developed free world. It had never been done before, and it may be a long time before it is done as well again.

In the last decade of his active life he reverted to the great themes of the twenties and thirties, the mother and child and reclining figure, and to a more naturalistic style. Gigantism is restricted to a few specifically public pieces, and to commissioned enlargements of earlier works. At their best the products of this mellow period are very pleasing, even if the quality is uneven.

It is true, yet an over-simplification, to say that Moore's success derives in large measure from the universality of his main themes: mother and child, reclining earth mother, foetus and womb. The themes themselves were not original, but he managed to endow them with many layers of meaning and so evoke a complex range of responses. It was extraordinarily clever to have evolved a style which was highly individual yet which, by fusing together so much from primitive and Western art, appealed both to tribal and to more sophisticated instincts. In essence his themes were man, nature, and sex. The sexual drive of his sculpture is the source of much of its power and energy. It is a hymn to the life force and its irresistible thrust, echoing the Romantic preoccupation with man's relationship to nature, anticipating contemporary anxieties about the rape of the earth's natural resources and our environment, offering us a bridge back to the old intuitive relationship. Stressing as he did the harmony between his work and nature, it was perverse of him (and others) to talk of himself as a humanist: if humanism still stands for anything, it is surely for the value of individual endeavour outside the framework of organized beliefs. There is more of Zen Buddhism than of humanism in Moore's sculpture, which no doubt helps explain its growing popularity in Japan. As an artist he was not interested in individuals. Even his more naturalistic figures have only rudimentary features.

In bringing man and nature together in his creations he captured the spirit of the times in a truer and profounder way than has been appreciated, as indeed have a few other sculptors like Barbara Hepworth and Isamo Noguchi, the Japanese-American, on a smaller scale. Another great achievement was to popularize the idea of contemporary sculpture, especially outdoor sculpture, around the world. His fame became a form of evangelizing. It is true that he was more powerfully promoted by an official body, the British Council, than any other artist of this century; but the Council's efforts would soon have been curtailed or halted had not the response been so remarkable. Britain and the reputation of British art gained much thereby. At home his fame brought sculpture into the centre of the national stage and raised many curtains for younger generations of practitioners. Given the lowly status of artists in Britain, it was no small feat to have been called the greatest living Englishman and, on death, the most honoured abroad since Churchill. The integrity of his character and his dedication to his work were an example to fellow artists everywhere.

He left behind two monuments: his sculpture and the Henry Moore Foundation, whose capital at the time of his death had risen to some £40 million, derived from sales since its establishment in early 1977, helped by the initial half a million pounds and the performance of the stock market. The Foundation's holdings of Moore's work, running to some 640 sculptures and 1,438 drawings, would be worth a good deal more. It seems likely that its grants and donations will continue for many generations to remind people of the scale of his achievement. If the trustees' plans are fulfilled, this unique body will be playing a more prominent part in Britain's cultural life, its organization strengthened by the appointment of a director and an administrator. It was also hoped that eventually a larger display of Moore's work would be possible on land behind Hoglands. If the necessary land can be acquired, access could be arranged from the B1004 road from Ware to Much Hadham. Perry Green would then be unaffected by any increased traffic.

Seen in retrospect, Moore's life has an impressive coherence, almost a look of inevitability, as if the Castleford lad was predestined for greatness. How deceptive that is. Only a combination of good fortune – he could so easily have been killed or maimed at the battle of Cambrai – determination, steadfastness, hard work, intelligence, creativity, and a rare endowment of ability enabled him to get to the top and stay there. He would certainly not have achieved as much without Irina's steadying influence. She was his antidote to the calls of wealth and fame, sustaining and restraining. Henry Moore was a man of vaulting ambition, determined to be the world's greatest living sculptor. In his own day he was widely recognized as such. If there is a life hereafter, he will be following the judgements of posterity closely. But he can surely be confident that his best work will have an enduring place in the history of Western civilization. Long may they both last.

Notes

Chapter I (pages 19 to 35)

1. Herbert Chesshyre, Chester Herald, College of Arms, to RB, letters 26 June 1985 and 26 March 1986, reporting on genealogical researches commissioned by the Henry Moore Foundation.
2. I. Hill, Castleford Borough Librarian, historical note August 1960, Castleford Public Library (quoting unnamed source).
3. Ann Garrould and Aline Reed (HM's nieces) to RB, interviews August 1983; Betty Howarth, HM's sister, to RB, interview Epping, December 1982.
4. Aline Reed to RB, interview Norfolk, August 1983.
5. Donald Hall, *Henry Moore* (London: Victor Gollancz, 1966), p. 30.
6. HM to John Heilpern, *Observer* magazine, 30 April 1972.
7. HM to RB, November 1982.
8. Betty Howarth to RB, loc. cit.
9. *Pontefract and Castleford Express*, 30 January 1904.
10. Herbert Read, *Henry Moore*, (London: Thames and Hudson, 1965), p. 13
11. Betty Howarth to RB, loc. cit.
12. Ibid.
13. HM to RB, January 1984.
14. *The Times*, 29 July 1978.
15. Betty Howarth to RB, loc. cit.
16. Frank Ambler to RB, interview Leeds, November 1984.
17. Aline Reed, loc. cit; John Read, *Henry Moore – one Yorkshireman looks at his world*, BBC TV, 1967.
18. *Henry Moore: Early Carvings 1920–40*, (article by Ann Garrould), Leeds City Art Gallery (catalogue), November 1982, p. 13.
19. Read, p. 20; Garrould, p. 14; Hall, p. 32.
20. Read, p. 21; *Le Monde* (interview with HM), 12 May 1977.
21. John Russell, *Henry Moore*, (London: Allen Lane, 1968), (revised edn. Pelican, 1973), p. 18; Ambler, loc. cit.
22. Russell, p. 19; Hall, p. 158.
23. John Read film, loc. cit; Hall, p. 159.
24. HM to RB, November 1982.
25. (Various), *Castleford Secondary School – the first fifty years*, 1957.
26. Quoted without source in the same booklet.
27. Ambler to RB, loc. cit.
28. Winnie Testin to RB, letter dated 24 November 1984.
29. Read, op. cit. p. 23.
30. Paul Asquith, the current owner, kindly showed the author around in November 1984.
31. Read, op. cit., p. 18.
32. HM to John Read; *Henry Moore at 80*, BBC TV, July 1978; and to RB, March 1984.
33. Winnie Testin to RB, loc. cit.

34. HM to John Read, loc. cit.
35. HM in *Henry Moore*, photographed and edited by John Hedgecoe, words by Henry Moore (London: Thomas

Nelson, 1968), p. 33.

36. Winnie Testin to RB, loc. cit. Connie McOwat to RB, letters dated 21 November and 1 December 1984.

Chapter II (*pages 36 to 47*)

1. Russell, op. cit. p. 20.
2. Herbert Read, *The Contrary Experience* (London: Faber and Faber, 1963).
3. Lord Houghton to RB, interview London, June 1983.
4. Garrould, op. cit., p. 16, based on a letter to Miss Gostick.
5. Lord Houghton to RB, loc. cit.
6. William Packer, *Henry Moore*, an illustrated biography (London: Weidenfeld and Nicolson, 1985), p. 28.
7. Miss Gostick's letters from HM were bequeathed to his niece Ann Garrould. Most of them were kindly lent to the author.
8. Undated letter, probably 19 March 1917 from internal evidence.
9. Garrould, Leeds catalogue, p. 16.
10. Undated letter, probably late April/early May.
11. Undated letter, later in May.
12. Undated letter, probably June.
13. Packer, op. cit., p. 29 quoting Captain Davenport, *History of the Prince of Wales's Own Civil Service Rifles*, 1921, p. 374.
14. HM to Albert Wainwright, letter dated 30 September, 1917 (courtesy of Wakefield City Art Gallery and Museum)
15. HM to Miss Gostick, letter dated 6 October 1917.
16. Ibid., 19 October 1917.
17. Packer, drawing on Davenport, op. cit., pp. 30–1.

18. A. H. Maude (ed.), *The History of the 47th London Division 1914–19* (London: Amalgamated Press, 1922), quoted by Packer, op. cit., p. 33.
19. HM to RB, 8 June 1984.
20. Hall, op. cit., p. 36.
21. Davenport, op. cit., vol. 2, p. 166.
22. War Diary at Public Record Office, Kew.
23. Davenport, op. cit., p. 167.
24. Read, op. cit., p. 28.
25. HM to Alice Gostick, 9 January 1918.
26. Lord Houghton to RB, loc. cit.
27. Ibid.
28. HM to RB, *The Times*, 10 July 1978.
29. HM to RB, February 1984.
30. Wainwright's letter is dated 2 January 1918, clearly a mistake for 1919.
31. Hedgecoe, op. cit., p. 33.
32. Ibid.
33. Catalogue of exhibition of Albert Wainwright's life and work, Wakefield City Art Gallery, December 1980–February 1981, p. 22. Two snapshots showing the four of them are thought to date from summer 1919.
34. J. J. Sweeney, *Henry Moore*, statement in *Partisan Review*, vol. XIV No. 2, New York, March–April 1947.

Chapter III (*pages 48 to 58*)

1. HM to J. J. Sweeney, *Partisan Review*, loc. cit.

2. Russell, op. cit., p. 21.
3. Raymond Coxon to RB, interview

London, February 1983.

4. HM to RB, 7 March 1983.

5. Donald Hall, 'An interview with Henry Moore', American *Horizon*, vol. III, No. 2, November 1960.

6. Alan Wilkinson, *The Drawings of Henry Moore* (Courtauld Institute thesis) (New York and London: Garland Publishing, 1983), p. 3.

7. HM to RB, March 1983.

8. Coxon to RB, loc. cit.

9. HM's student notes are in the archive of the Henry Moore Centre for the Study of Sculpture at the Leeds City Art Gallery.

10. HM to RB, March 1983.

11. Raymond Coxon to RB, loc. cit.

12. E. J. Winfield to RB, interview Castleford, November 1984 (also most helpful on Castleford in the 1910s and 1920s).

13. Common Room Notes, RCA, spring 1922.

14. *Narayana and Bhataryan* was performed at the Henry Moore Centre for the Study of Sculpture at the Leeds City Art Gallery on 23 November 1984 by students of the Crewe and Alsager College of Higher Education.

15. Connie Hardy to RB, letter dated 1 December 1984.

16. Donald Hall, *Horizon* interview, op. cit.

17. Russell, op. cit., p. 21. The translation was published in London in 1914.

18. Oliver Brown, *Exhibition* (London: Evelyn Adams and Mackay, 1968), pp. 63–4

19. Ann Garrould, op. cit., p. 17.

20. Geoffrey Shakerley, *Henry Moore: Sculptures in Landscape* (London: Studio Vista, 1978). Text by Stephen Spender, p. 11.

21. Quoted by Russell, op. cit., p. 21, without source.

22. Herbert Read, op. cit., p. 31.

23. Oxford University Press, 1981: paperback edition, pp. 70–3.

24. Russell, op. cit., p. 24.

25. Hedgecoe, op. cit., p. 33.

26. Both figures were presented to the Leeds City Art Gallery in 1973 by a contemporary and friend of Henry's, Jocelyn Horner.

27. Donald Hall, *Horizon* interview, op. cit.

Chapter IV (pages 59 to 81)

1. John Russell, op. cit., p. 22.

2. John and Véra Russell, 'Conversations with Henry Moore', *Sunday Times*, 17 and 24 December 1961.

3. Royal College of Art magazine, February 1921.

4. William Rothenstein, *Men and Memories II* (London: Faber and Faber, p. 223.

5. HM to Stephen Spender, letter quoted in Spender's introduction to *The Stonehenge Suite – 15 Lithographs and Etchings* (London: Ganymede Original Editions, 1974).

6. HM to Jocelyn Horner, letter dated

29 October (Henry Moore Centre archives, Leeds).

7. Henry Moore, 'Primitive Art', *Listener*, vol. XXV, No. 641, 24 August 1941, p. 598–9.

8. Sweeney, *Partisan Review*, op. cit.

9. Hedgecoe, op. cit., p. 33.

10. Ibid.

11. HM to John and Véra Russell, transcript of *Sunday Times* interviews, p. 91.

12. *Henry Moore at the British Museum*, text by Henry Moore, pictures by David Finn (London: British Museum Publications, 1981), p. 125.

13. Ibid.
14. Henry Moore, 'Primitive Art', *Listener*, 24 August 1941, pp. 598–9.
15. Hedgecoe, p. 45.
16. Coxon to RB, loc. cit.
17. John and Véra Russell, *Sunday Times*, loc. cit.
18. Alan Wilkinson thesis, op. cit., p. 18.
19. John and Véra Russell, loc. cit.
20. John Rewald, *Gazette des Beaux Arts*, 1975, pp. 163–8.
21. John and Véra Russell, loc. cit.
22. Raymond and Gin Coxon to RB, loc. cit.
23. Ibid.
24. John and Véra Russell, loc. cit.
25. Fragment of letter to Wainwright dated 'A Sunday morning in late October', in Wakefield City Art Gallery archive.
26. Ann Garrould, op. cit., p. 20.
27. Betty Howarth to RB, loc. cit., (her fiancé Rowland Howarth supported Mary Moore that night).
28. Mr and Mrs Alfred Cohen to RB, interview August 1983.
29. John and Véra Russell, op. cit.
30. HM to RB, 28 May 1983.
31. John Russell, op. cit., p. 28.
32. Ezra Pound, *Gaudier-Brzeska*: a memoir (London: New Directions, 1974), p. 9.
33. Henry Moore, statement in *Architectural Association Journal*, vol. XLV, pp. 408–13, London, 1930.
34. From a review in *The Egotist*, 1914, quoted in Herbert Read, op. cit., p. 34.
35. Hedgecoe, op. cit., p. 45.
36. Herbert Read, op. cit., pp. 32–3; HM to RB, 7 March 1983; Coxon to RB, loc. cit.; John and Véra Russell, loc. cit.
37. Hedgecoe, op. cit., p. 34.
38. HM to RB, 22 July 1982; also recalled by Sir John Rothenstein to RB, interview, November 1984.
39. Hedgecoe, op. cit., p. 37. Comparative value of the pound based on official figures of its purchasing power then and now.
40. Rutherston later offered his collection to Bradford, which spurned it. In 1925 the bulk of it went to Manchester, where a new art gallery was projected but never built. He died in 1927. HM's undated letter is at Leeds City Art Gallery.
41. Donald Hall, op. cit., p. 53.
42. Christopher Neve, *Leon Underwood* (London: Thames and Hudson, 1974), p. 74.
43. Hedgecoe, p. 50.
44. *Yorkshire Post*, 1 February 1929; 'Henry Moore, a Yorkshire Sculptor'; an article prompted by his first major commission, for London Transport's new headquarters, stating that he had previously been represented by the 'keystone' heads at Wembley.
45. HM at the BM, op. cit. p. 104. According to Bernard Meadows, who witnessed it, the accident happened in 1939 with another adze which Moore had bought.
46. Hedgecoe, pp. 34–5.
47. HM to RB, 7 March 1983.
48. John Russell, op. cit., p. 35.
49. *Henry Moore: the Language of Sculpture*, BBC, 1973, written and directed by John Read, script pp. 10–11.
50. HM to RB, 7 March 1983.
51. *Henry Moore*, BBC, loc. cit.
52. Letter dated 8 February 1925.
53. E.g. HM to Alan Wilkinson, op. cit., p. 18.
54. Letter dated 12 March 1925, quoted John Rothenstein, *Modern English Painters: Lewis to Moore* (London: Eyre and Spottiswood, 1956).
55. Henry Moore: 'Primitive Art', *Listener*, 24 August 1941, pp. 598–9.
56. Giorgio Vasari, *Lives of the Artists*, (trans. George Bull), a selection (London: Penguin, 1965), p. 131.
57. John and Véra Russell, *Sunday Times*, loc. cit.
58. HM to RB, 28 March 1983.
59. Helen Binyon, *Eric Ravilious: Memoir of an Artist* (London: Lutterworth

Press, 1983), p. 30–1; A. Wilkinson, op. cit., p. 33.

60. *Observer* magazine, 30 April 1972, John Heilpern interview with HM.
61. Gin Coxon to RB, loc. cit.
62. HM to RB, 28 March 1983.

63. Hedgecoe, p. 42.
64. Both letters reproduced in Hedgecoe, p. 42.
65. To John Heilpern, *Observer* magazine, loc. cit.

Chapter V (*pages 82 to 96*)

1. J. J. Sweeney, op. cit., 1947.
2. Letter to Gin Coxon, dated 19 August 1925.
3. Letter dated Saturday afternoon, but by content clearly around 4–5 August 1925.
4. Letter to Gin dated 3 September 1925.
5. Henry Moore, *Sculpture & Drawings 1921–48*, ed. David Sylvester, (London: Lund Humphries, 1944, revised 1957), p.3.
6. Jacob Epstein: *An Autobiography* (London: Hulton Press, 1955), pp. 107–11.
7. *Sunday Times*, 23 August 1959 (obituary article by HM).
8. Ibid.
9. Donald Hall, op. cit., p. 59.
10. Jack Clarkson to RB, letters dated 12 and 22 April 1985. Clarkson later became Principal of Newcastle-under-Lyme School of Art.
11. Alma Ramsey to RB, letters 3 and 26 January 1985.
12. Elizabeth Collins to RB, interview London, March 1985.
13. Quoted in display at the Alfred Gilbert exhibition, Royal Academy, London, March–June 1986.
14. A. Wilkinson, op. cit., p. 205.
15. John Russell, op. cit., p. 42.
16. Herbert Read, op. cit., p. 59.
17. John and Véra Russell, loc. cit.
18. *The Times*, 21 January 1928.
19. *Observer*, 29 January 1928.
20. *Daily Herald*, 26 January 1928.
21. *Yorkshire Evening Post*, 28 January 1928.

22. *Morning Post*, 28 January 1928.
23. *Westminster Gazette*, 26 January 1928.
24. *Yorkshire Evening Post*, 28 January 1928.
25. *Evening Standard*, 1 March 1928.
26. *The New Age*, 14 June 1928.
27. 'Sculpture in the Open Air', a talk by Henry Moore, British Council, London, 1955 (in *Henry Moore on Sculpture*, ed. Philip James (London: Macdonald, 1966–8), p. 97. The St James relief was originally called *North Wind* (in Herbert Read's 1934 monograph) and is on the north side of the building. But Moore later believed he had portrayed the gentler West Wind.
28. Jack Clarkson recalled this, letter to RB, dated 12 April 1985.
29. Richard Cork: 'Overhead Sculpture for the Underground Railway', in catalogue to exhibition *British Sculpture in the Twentieth Century* (London: Whitechapel Art Gallery, 1981), p. 98.
30. Aline Reed to RB, interview 29 August 1983.
31. *Evening Standard*, 29 January 1929.
32. *The Times*, 5 April 1929.
33. *Morning Post*, 13 April 1929.
34. *Daily Telegraph*, 24 May 1929.
35. Richard Cork. op. cit., p. 98.
36. *Daily Express*, 24 November 1964; *Sunday Telegraph*, 29 November 1964.
37. *The Times*, 17 December 1964.

Chapter VI (pages 97 to 117)

1. Donald Hall, op. cit., p. 65.
2. HM to RB, 4 July 1978.
3. Irina Moore to RB, 4 May 1983.
4. Dennis Bult-Francis to RB, interview London, 20 February 1986.
5. Stephen Spender *In Irina's Garden*, a memoir by IM (London: Thames and Hudson, 1986), p. 49.
6. Dennis Bult-Francis to RB, loc. cit.
7. Dick Hosking to RB, letter dated 26 January 1985.
8. IM in Spender, p. 50.
9. IM to RB, loc. cit.
10. Dennis Bult-Francis, who attended, to RB, loc. cit.
11. IM and HM to RB, 4 May 1983.
12. Donald Hall, op. cit., p. 67.
13. IM and HM to RB, loc. cit. Sister Betty thought so too.
14. IM/Spender, op. cit., p. 50.
15. Barbara Hepworth, *A Pictorial Autobiography* (London: Thames and Hudson, 1970), p. 20.
16. HM to RB, 11 October 1982.
17. J. P.Hodin,*BarbaraHepworth*(London: Lund Humphries, 1961), p. 12.
18. John Russell, op. cit., p. 82.
19. Lord Zuckerman to RB, interview London, 3 April 1984.
20. *Liverpool Echo*, 14 June 1929. The show was put on by the Sandon Studios Society at Bluecoat Chambers.
21. Wilkinson thesis, p. 263.
22. Herbert Read, op. cit., p. 72.
23. Robert Melville, *Henry Moore, Sculpture & Drawings 1921–1969* (New York: Harry Abrams, 1970), pp. 10–11.
24. From Fry's 'Essay in Aesthetics', quoted John Russell, op. cit., p. 44.
25. Erich Neumann,*The Archetypal World of Henry Moore* (London: Routledge and Kegan Paul, 1959), p. 17.
26. Henry Moore and John Hedgecoe, *My Ideas, Inspiration and Life as an Artist* (London: Ebury Press, 1986), p. 62.
27. *Morning Post*, 13 May 1930. See also *Daily News*, 5 May 1930.
28. *Scotsman*, 3 June 1930.
29. Desmond Zwemmer, son of Anton, to RB, interview, London, March 1983.
30. *Evening Standard*, 20 November 1930.
31. R. H. Wilenski to HM, letter dated 11 June 1930 (courtesy University of Victoria BC).
32. HM to Wilenski, letter dated 6 December 1930.
33. *Morning Post*, 13 December 1930.
34. *Evening News*, 1 January 1931.
35. HM to Christopher Crosman, Albright-Knox Gallery, Buffalo, unpublished MS, September 1976.
36. Herbert Read, op. cit., p. 35.
37. Ibid.
38. *The Times*, 29 July 1957.
39. Donald Hall, p. 78.
40. Ibid., and interview Raymond Coxon, loc. cit.
41. Reproduced in Packer, p. 125
42. Oliver Brown, *Exhibition*, a memoir, p. 150.
43. *The Times* 13 April 1931.
44. *Manchester Guardian*, 13 April 1931.
45. *Observer*, 12 April 1931.
46. *Jewish Chronicle*, 1 May 1931.
47. *Morning Post*, 11 April 1931.
48. *Daily Mirror*, 14 April 1931.
49. *Bournemouth Echo*, 12 May 1931.
50. Herbert Read, *The Contrary Experience* (London: Faber and Faber, 1963), p. 207.
51. Transcript of John and Véra Russell interview, p. 147.
52. Ibid.
53. *Listener*, 22 April 1931.
54. Current reprint Faber and Faber paperback,London,1982,pp.252–7.
55. Oliver Brown, op. cit., p. 151.
56. Dr Heinz Spielmann, of the Museum für Kunst und Gewerbe, to RB, letters dated 16, 28 February and 1 March 1984.

57. *70 Years of Henry Moore*, ed. David Mitchinson, catalogue of exhibition at Rijksmuseum Kröller-Müller, Otterlo, May–July 1968 (unpaginated: reproduced under the year 1931).

58. From material provided by Dr Spielmann, as in note 56.

59. Francis Hawcroft, Principal Keeper at the Whitworth Art Gallery to RB,

letters dated 13 and 20 June 1959, and *French Nineteenth-Century Drawings in the Whitworth Art Gallery*, catalogue published by the gallery in 1981, article by Michael Clarke, pp. 4–5.

60. Dorothy Crighton, current owner of Jasmine Cottage, to RB, interview October 1983.

61. HM and IM to RB, 16 March 1984.

Chapter VII (*pages 118 to 142*)

1. *The Seven and Five Society 1920–35*, catalogue introduction by Mark Glazebrook, Michael Parkin Fine Art Ltd, January–February 1980.

2. Quoted in *Decade 1920–30*, Arts Council catalogue, 1970, p. 22.

3. *Scotsman*, 15 February 1932.

4. Quoted by Glazebrook, op. cit.

5. *Henry Moore at Home*, BBC 2 TV film written and directed by John Read, London, 1973, transcript, p.8.

6. John Russell, op. cit., p. 57.

7. Barbara Hepworth, op. cit., pp. 22–3.

8. *Studio*, September 1932; *Yorkshire Post*, 15 July 1932.

9. Sir Robert Sainsbury to RB, interview London, May 1983.

10. Graham Sutherland, 'Welsh Sketchbook' (letter to Colin Anderson), *Horizon*, No. 28, London, 1942.

11. Henry Moore, 'The Sculptor Speaks', article in *Listener*, 18 August 1937; 'Henry Moore Talking', conversation with David Sylvester, *Listener*, 29 August 1963; Hedgecoe, op. cit., p. 100.

12. David Mitchinson, Leeds catalogue, 1982, op. cit., p. 35.

13. HM to RB, 24 July 1979.

14. Called *Recent Developments in British Painting*.

15. *The Times*, 2 June 1933.

16. Mark Glazebrook, *Unit One*, *Spirit of the 30s*, Mayor Gallery, June 1984, introduction, p. 15.

17. *Unit One*, edited by Herbert Read (London: Cassell, 1934), p. 12.

18. Henry Moore, 'The Sculptor Speaks', quoted in Philip James, op. cit., p. 62.

19. To Mark Glazebrook, op. cit., p. 19; and to RB, 24 July 1979.

20. Undated letter in Tate archives.

21. Quoted in Frances Spalding, *British Art Since 1900* (London: Thames and Hudson, 1986), p. 110

22. *The Times*, 4 November 1933.

23. *Spectator*, 19 November 1933.

24. *Homage to Henry Moore* (London: A. Zwemmer Ltd, 1972), reminiscence by HM, pp. 21–2; Read's text reproduced pp. 23–40.

25. Desmond Zwemmer to RB, interview London, 9 March 1983.

26. As for note 24.

27. *Spectator*, 1 February 1935.

28. Sir James Richards to RB, interview 7 March 1984.

29. Jack Pritchard, *View from a Long Chair* (London: Routledge and Kegan Paul, 1984), pp. 78–127.

30. HM to Henry Seldis, *Los Angeles Times*, 28 July 1968.

31. Geoffrey Grigson to RB, interview Wiltshire, 14 August 1984.

32. Stephen Spender to RB, interview London, July 1983.

33. Geoffrey Shakerley, *Henry Moore, Sculpture in Landscape* (London: Studio Vista, 1978), introduction by Stephen Spender, p. 11.

34. HM to RB, July 1982.

35. HM to RB, 28 March 1983.
36. Article in the *Listener* by HM, 18 August 1937.
37. As for note 35.
38. Raymond Coxon to RB, letter dated 7 July 1937.
39. The trip has hitherto been erroneously dated to 1936, the year the Spanish Civil War broke out.
40. To Donald Hall, op. cit., p. 83.
41. HM to the Coxons, letter dated 8 September 1935. The acquisition of this house has previously been wrongly dated to 1934.
42. Statement by HM in catalogue of Kent County Council Biennial exhibition, Folkestone, July–August 1983.
43. To David Sylvester, *Sculpture and Drawings by Henry Moore*, catalogue, Tate Gallery exhibition, London, May–July 1951.
44. Jack Hepworth to RB, letter dated 25 September 1985.
45. Bernard Meadows to RB, interview London, 20 May 1983.
46. Ibid.
47. HM to Donald Hall, interview in *Horizon*, New York, November 1960.
48. HM to Gordon Washburn, letter dated 1 May 1939 (Albright-Knox Gallery archives).
49. Henry Seldis, *Henry Moore in America* (New York: Praeger, 1973), p. 37.
50. Ibid, p. 36.
51. Ibid, pp. 65, 107 and 53 respectively.
52. Leeds catalogue, 1982, op. cit., p. 34 (David Mitchinson essay).
53. Henry Moore, 'The Sculptor Speaks', *Listener*, loc. cit. 1937.

Chapter VIII (pages 143 to 166)

1. A. J. P. Taylor, *English History 1914–45* (London: Oxford University Press, 1965/Pelican Books, 1970), p. 485.
2. Undated letter, probably lateish 1936.
3. *AIA, The Story of the Artists International Association 1933–53*, edited by Lynda Morris and Robert Radford (Oxford: The Museum of Modern Art, 1983), p. 2.
4. HM to RB, April 1984.
5. *AIA*, op. cit., p. 28.
6. Montagu Slater in *Left Review*, January 1936 (cited in AIA history), p. 29.
7. Quoted in AIA history, op. cit., p. 41. Front page reproduced in Otterlo catalogue under 1936.
8. HM to John and Véra Russell, transcript, op. cit. Also *Daily Worker*, 31 January 1938; *Edinburgh Evening News*, 31 January 1938.
9. *Reynolds News*, 30 January 1938.
10. Spender to RB, interview Provence, July 1983.
11. *Yorkshire Post*, 31 March 1938.
12. *AIA*, op. cit., p. 54.
13. Reprinted in *British Surrealism Fifty Years On*, Mayor Gallery, London, March–April 1986.
14. Quoted in virtually any dictionary of art.
15. Quoted by Michel Rémy in *British Surrealism Fifty Years On*, op. cit., p. 13.
16. Quoted in *AIA*, op. cit., p. 41.
17. Quoted in Frances Spalding, *British Art Since 1900* (London: Thames and Hudson, 1986), p. 117.
18. John Piper to RB, interview Berkshire, July 1984.
19. Published by Gerald Howe, London.
20. *Listener*, 18 August 1937, pp. 338–40.
21. Herbert Read, 'A Nest of Gentle Artists', *Apollo*, September 1962.
22. Published by Faber and Faber.
23. This passage is virtually identical to the last paragraph of Moore's contribution to *Unit One*, of 1934, op. cit.

24. David Hall, op. cit., p. 90 (quoting an unnamed magazine article.
25. Hedgecoe, op. cit., p. 105.
26. Carlton Lake, 'Henry Moore's World', article in *Atlantic Monthly*, Boston, January 1962.
27. Bernard Meadows to RB, interview London, 10 June 1983.
28. Dirk Bogarde, *A Postillion Struck by Lightning* (London: Chatto & Windus, 1977), p. 226.
29. Letter dated 14 September 1937.
30. Serge Chermayeff to RB, letter dated 28 March 1984.
31. Henry Moore, 'Sculpture in the Open Air', a talk recorded by the British Council in 1955 in London.
32. As for note 30.
33. Explained in letter from HM to Kenneth Clark, dated 15 March 1939.
34. Meadows to RB, interview London, June 1983.
35. Kenneth Clark, *Another Part of the Wood* (London: John Murray, 1974), p. 256.
36. Kathleen Sutherland to RB during his preparation of *Graham Sutherland: A Biography* (London: Faber and Faber, 1982).
37. Postcard from HM to KC, 11 September 1938; letter dated 29 November 1938.
38. Clark, op. cit.
39. Berthold Lubetkin to RB, letter dated 13 April 1984.
40. André Breton, 'Artistic Genesis and Perspective of Surrealism,' 1941, republished in *Le Surréalisme et la peinture* (Paris: Gallimard, 1965), translated by Simon Watson Taylor and published in the UK in 1972 by Macdonald & Co, p. 73.
41. Letter to the dealer Frank Lloyd of Marlborough Fine Art, dated 24 June 1965 (courtesy of Detroit Museum of Art).
42. Henry Seldis, op. cit., p. 51.
43. Gordon Onslow-Ford to RB, letter dated 20 December 1985.
44. As for notes 42 and 43, and letter from Gilbert Lloyd of Marlborough Fine Art to RB, dated 19 June 1985.
45. Erich Neumann, *The Archetypal World of Henry Moore* (London: Routledge and Kegan Paul, 1959), pp. 78–9.
46. John Russell, op. cit., pp. 129–30.
47. Roland Penrose, *Scrapbook 1900–1981* (London: Thames and Hudson, 1981), p. 103.
48. Ibid, p. 102 (author's comment).
49. Henry Moore, 'Sculpture in the Open Air', loc. cit.
50. *Daily Telegraph*, 24 March 1938.
51. *Daily Mail*, 8 April 1938.
52. Sir Robert Sainsbury to RB, interview London, May 1983.
53. Sir John Rothenstein to RB, interview London, January 1984.
54. Letter dated 26 March 1939.
55. Letters dated 8 and 13 April, 1939.
56. Letter from HM to Kenneth Clark dated 22 February 1939.

Chapter IX (*pages 167 to 193*)

1. *Scotsman*, 5 November 1935.
2. *The Times*, 3 November 1936.
3. HM to Kenneth Clark, letter dated 1 October 1939.
4. *The Times*, 13 February 1940.
5. Quoted in *British Surrealism Fifty Years On*, op. cit., p. 17.
6. Hiram Winterbotham to RB, letter dated 17 August 1984.
7. Published by Secker and Warburg in a limited edition, 1945.
8. Joan Wyndham, *Love Lessons* (London: William Heinemann, 1985), p. 48.
9. Ibid., entries on pp. 60, 70 and 80 respectively.
10. Hedgecoe, op. cit., p. 134.
11. Erich Neumann, op. cit., p. 60.
12. Donald Hall, op. cit., p. 104.

13. Hedgecoe, op. cit., p. 140.
14. HM to J.J. Sweeney, statement in *Partisan Review*, March 1947, op. cit.
15. Letters from E. M. O'R. Dickey, dated 5 January and 24 April 1941 (Courtesy of the Imperial War Museum).
16. Letter from E. M. O'R. Dickey, dated 14 August 1941.
17. Stephen Spender, *The Thirties and After* (London: Collins, 1978), p. 91.
18. *Sunday Times*, 18 May 1941.
19. John Russell, op. cit. p. 112.
20. To RB circa 1984, and no doubt to many others.
21. *The Drawings of Henry Moore*, Alan Wilkinson, op. cit., p. 36.
22. Interview with Auriol Stevens, *Guardian*, 5 May 1969.
23. HM to Philip Hendy, letter dated 4 December 1938 (courtesy of Leeds City Art Gallery).
24. Kenneth Clark, *The Other Half*, London: John Murray, 1977, p. 44.
25. *Yorkshire Observer*, 26 July 1941.
26. *Harrogate Advertiser*, 24 January 1942.
27. HM to Dickey, letter dated 9 September 1941 (IWM).
28. HM to Alan Wilkinson, January 1972, quoted in Tate catalogue, p. 37.
29. Auden/Moore Poems – catalogue of British Museum exhibition, 1974, section III (no pagination).
30. As for note 28.
31. HM to Herbert Read, letter dated 29 December 1941.
32. HM to Herbert Read, letter dated 10 January 1942.
33. *Illustrated*, 24 January 1942.
34. Letter from HM to E. D. Averill, 11 December 1964, quoted in 'HM on Sculpture', op. cit., p. 218.
35. HM statement to J.J. Sweeney, *Partisan Review*, op. cit.
36. Neumann, op. cit., pp. 64–5.
37. *Daily Herald*, 29 October 1942.
38. IM to RB, 4 May 1983.
39. The book cited is *Kulturgeschichte Afrikas* by Frobenius (1933): Dr

Wilkinson's Tate catalogue, p. 36.
40. Henry Seldis, op. cit., pp. 54–5.
41. See *Artist and Maecenas, A tribute to Curt Valentin*, catalogue of exhibition at Marlborough-Gerson Gallery, New York, November 1963.
42. *New York Sun*, 15 May 1943.
43. Grace Clements in *Art & Architecture*, September 1943.
44. Letter dated 27 July 1943, Public Record Office, Kew, London.
45. Walter Hussey, *Patron of Art* (London: Weidenfeld and Nicolson, 1985), an autobiographical memoir fully describing this and other commissions; this ref., p. 23.
46. Ibid., p. 28.
47. Ibid., p. 33.
48. Kenneth Clark, *The Other Half*, op. cit., p. 39.
49. Hussey, op. cit., p. 41.
50. Quoted in Hussey, p. 45
51. *Northampton Independent*, 15 November 1946.
52. Walter Hussey to RB, interview London, December 1982.
53. Ibid.
54. Hussey, op. cit., p. 48.
55. Geoffrey Grigson, *Henry Moore* (London: Penguin, 1944), p. 12.
56. *The Times Educational Supplement*, 27 May 1944.
57. Jill Craigie, *Sunday Times* magazine, 9 November 1986 and to RB, interview London, February 1981.
58. Dorothy Bimrose, *Digswell: A Matter Done*. The story of the Digswell Arts Trust, with a foreword by Henry Moore (Welwyn Garden City: Digswell Arts Trust, 1964).
59. *Educator Extraordinary*, by Harry Rée (London: Longman, 1973; and Peter Owen, 1985), p. 72.
60. Herbert Read, op. cit., p. 164.
61. HM to Tom Hopkinson, 'How a Sculptor Works', *Books and Art*, London, November 1957.
62. HM to John Heilpern, interview *Observer* magazine, loc. cit.
63. Ann Garrould to RB, April 1985.

Chapter X (*pages 194 to 215*)

1. Michael Young, *The Elmhirsts of Dartington* (London: Routledge and Kegan Paul, 1982), p. 247. The report was published by Political and Economic Planning (PEP).
2. *Mid-Devon Times*, 3 August 1968.
3. Dame Elisabeth Frink to RB, letter March 1985.
4. Shelley Fausset to RB, interview London, February 1985.
5. Respectively Hedgecoe, p. 171, and to Denys Sutton, *New York Times*, 23 March 1959.
6. Kenneth Clark, *The Nude* (London: John Murray, 1956), pp. 356–7.
7. John Russell, op. cit., p. 136.
8. Neumann, op. cit., p. 117.
9. Herbert Read, op. cit., p. 176.
10. Wilkinson, Tate catalogue, p. 44. The book was Ernst Fuhrmann's *Peru II* (1922).
11. Ann Garrould to RB, October 1985.
12. Letters to RB from William McVey, dated 18 May 1985, and from Susan Waller, curator of Cranbrook Academy of Art, dated 26 March 1985.
13. Thomas Gibson to RB, interview May 1986. The sale was on 21 May 1982.
14. *Observer*, 20 October 1946.
15. Vincent Price to RB, undated letter summer 1984.
16. Sir John Rothenstein, *Brave Day, Hideous Night* (London: Hamish Hamilton, 1966), pp. 186–95.
17. Kenneth Clark, *The Other Half*, op. cit., pp. 71–2.
18. Rothenstein, op. cit., pp. 43–6.
19. HM to RB, May 1984.
20. Theodora FitzGibbon to RB, letter dated 28 April 1984.
21. *Yorkshire Evening Post*, 26 October 1945.
22. HM to RB, April 1984.
23. Antony Bell (later chairman of Lund Humphries) to RB, interview January 1985.
24. HM and IM to RB, 6 April 1984.
25. Dorothy Miller to RB, interview New York, November 1983; and Sam Hunter's introduction to *The Museum of Modern Art, New York* (Harry Abrams in association with MOMA, 1985), p. 22.
26. Seldis, op. cit., p. 75.
27. As for note 25.
28. To John Russell, *New York Times*, 11 July 1979.
29. Ibid.
30. Seldis, op. cit., p. 79.
31. Seldis, op. cit., pp. 77–9.
32. Seldis, op. cit., p. 74.
33. William Lieberman to RB, interview New York, December 1983.
34. Dorothy Miller to RB, loc. cit.
35. *New York Times*, 18 December 1946.
36. *New York World Telegram*, 21 December 1946.
37. *New York Daily Worker*, 5 January 1947.
38. *Art News*, December 1946, quoted by Seldis, p. 83.
39. HM to Seldis, op. cit., pp. 76–7.
40. Alfred Cohen to RB, letter dated 4 September 1983.
41. *Melbourne Age*, 7 February 1948; *Melbourne Herald*, 3 March 1948.
42. *Melbourne Argus*, 2 March 1948.
43. *Sun*, and Sydney *Morning Herald*, both of 5 December 1947.
44. British Council files, Public Record Office, Kew, London.
45. HM, 'Sculpture in the Open Air', op. cit.
46. Fausset to RB, loc. cit.
47. Neumann, op. cit., pp. 94–5.
48. Russell, op. cit., p. 136.
49. Lady Strauss to RB, interview London, June 1985.
50. *Yorkshire Evening Post*, 14 May 1948.
51. *The Times*, 17 May 1986.
52. *New Statesman*, 29 May 1948; and *Spectator*, 21 May 1948.
53. British Council files, PRO, Kew.

54. John Rothenstein, *Brave Day, Hideous Night*, pp. 201–2.
55. G. C. Argan to RB, letter dated 14 March 1985.
56. Kenneth Clark, *The Nude*, op. cit., p. 355.
57. Rothenstein, op. cit., p. 202.
58. Ibid., p. 203.

59. HM to Barry Penrose, *Art for Money's Sake*, BBC 2, 8 April 1976.
60. British Council files, PRO.
61. Rothenstein, op. cit., pp. 203–4.
62. Margaret Barr to RB, letter dated 19 January 1985.
63. *Manchester Guardian*, 15 June 1948.

Chapter XI (*pages 216 to 236*)

1. *The Times, Daily Express*, etc., 29 April 1949; *Independent*, 18 December 1986 (review).
2. *Yorkshire Post*, 30 April 1949.
3. J. M. Richards, *Memoirs of an Unjust Fella* (London: Weidenfeld and Nicolson, 1980), p. 228.
4. *Daily Telegraph* comment, 30 July 1949.
5. *Yorkshire Post*, 9 April 1949.
6. *Yorkshire Post*, 9 May 1949.
7. British Council reports.
8. *Libre Belgique*, 14 October 1949 (author's translation).
9. Reuter report in *Yorkshire Post*, 10 October 1949.
10. Kenneth Clark, *Another Part of the Wood*, op. cit., p. 121.
11. Quoted in British Council report.
12. Geoffrey Grigson, *Recollections, Mainly of Artists and Writers* (London: Chatto and Windus, 1984), pp. 97–8.
13. British Council reports.
14. *Die Welt*, 22 March 1950.
15. *Rheinische Post*, 30 April 1950.
16. Cressida Ridley, widow of the lost son, to RB, letter dated 25 June 1984; and Brian Toll, rector of Claydon and Barham, letter 16 May 1984.
17. Stuart Maclure, *Educational Developments and School Building* (London: Longman, 1984), p. 45.
18. Eugene Rosenberg to RB, interview London, September 1984.
19. HM 'Sculpture in the Open Air', loc. cit.

20. HM to Dorothy Miller at MOMA, letter dated 31 January 1951 (courtesy of MOMA).
21. *Daily Graphic*, 3 November 1950.
22. *Daily Dispatch*, 3 November 1950.
23. *Financial Times*, 30 October 1950.
24. David Finn, Henry Moore, *Sculpture and Environment* (London: Thames and Hudson, 1977), p. 263.
25. John Russell, op. cit., pp. 134 and 135.
26. *Sunday Times*, 6 September 1949.
27. Sir William Keswick to RB, interview Essex, March 1984.
28. HM to Jane and K. Clark, letter dated 30 April 1954.
29. As for note 27.
30. HM to David Sylvester, quoted in Tate Gallery catalogue, 1951.
31. Henry Moore, 'Sculpture in the Open Air', 1955, op. cit.
32. Robert Clatworthy RA to RB, interview London, December 1985.
33. Anthony Caro to RB, interview London, 1983 April.
34. Ibid.
35. HM to K. and Jane Clark, letter dated 28 February 1951.
36. HM to John and Véra Russell, *Sunday Times*, 17 and 24 December 1961.
37. British Council reports.
38. *Art News*, January 1951.
39. Arts Council archives (commissioning letter dated 24 May 1949).
40. David Finn, op. cit., p. 287.
41. Hedgecoe, op. cit., p. 197.
42. *Yorkshire Post*, 8 and 12 November 1951.

43. David Sylvester to RB, interview London, January 1985.
44. *Burlington Magazine*, June 1948, pp. 158–65; and July 1948, pp. 189–95.
45. As for note 43.

46. *The Times*, 2 May 1951.
47. *Observer*, 13 May and 24 June 1951.
48. *Sunday Times*, 13 May 1951.
49. John Read to RB, interview London, October 1983.

Chapter XII (*pages 237 to 256*)

1. HM to Gordon Smith, letter 31 October 1955 (Smith had recently succeeded Andrew Ritchie as director of the Albright-Knox Gallery).
2. Ibid.
3. Neumann, op. cit., p. 128.
4. Hedgecoe, op. cit., p. 221.
5. Henry Moore: *Complete Sculpture*, ed. Alan Bowness (London: Lund Humphries, 1977), vol IV, p. 8.
6. David Sylvester to RB, interview London, January 1985.
7. Hedgecoe, op. cit., p. 221.
8. *New York Times*, 17 October 1954.
9. David Astor to RB, interview London, May 1986.
10. Sir William Keswick to RB, loc. cit.
11. Francis Brennan to RB, letter 11 July 1984.
12. 'Sculpture in the Open Air', op. cit.; Hedgecoe, p. 213; and Seldis, p. 179.
13. Francis Brennan to RB, loc. cit.
14. Ibid.
15. 'Sculpture in the Open Air', loc. cit.
16. Hedgecoe, op. cit., p. 213.
17. *Daily Telegraph*, 5 March 1954.
18. *Bristol Evening Post* etc., 27 May 1954.
19. *Birmingham Gazette*, 13 March 1955.
20. Unsourced letter, Philip James, op. cit., p. 250.
21. Neumann, op. cit., p. 119.
22. HM to Herbert Read, letter 26 April 1952. Read received a cheque for his help.
23. Text reproduced in Philip James, op. cit., pp. 84–90.
24. Basil Spence, *Phoenix at Coventry* (London: Geoffrey Bles, 1962), p. 67.
25. Anthony Blee to RB, interview London, February 1985.

26. John Rothenstein, *Time's Thievish Progress* (London: Cassell, 1970), p. 78.
27. Ronald Alley, Catalogue of the Tate Gallery's collection of Modern (Foreign) Art, Tate Gallery, 1981.
28. Sir Norman Reid to RB, interview London, June 1984.
29. For a fuller account, see John Rothenstein's autobiographical volume *Brave Day, Hideous Night*, and the author's biography of Graham Sutherland, op. cit.
30. Norman Reid to RB, loc. cit.
31. HM to RB, July 1979.
32. Rothenstein, *Brave Morning, Hideous Night*, op. cit., p. 368.
33. Gabo to HM, letter 15 April 1953, Tate Gallery archives.
34. HM to Gabo, 30 December 1952; *Evening Standard*, 1 February 1952.
35. HM to Gabo, letter 25 May 1953, Tate archives.
36. To Valter Zanini, *O Tempo*, 11 December 1953.
37. British Council report (BC archives).
38. *Diario di São Paulo*, 15 December 1953; *Ultima Hora*, 2 February 1954.
39. HM to Mathias Goeritz, letter 2 January 1950.
40. Article by Iola Vidrio, publication unknown, quoted in British Council report.
41. Mathias Goeritz to RB, letters May and June 1985. Other material from Lynndon Clough and Walter Plumb, letters May and March 1985.
42. Goeritz to RB, loc. cit.
43. Marino Marini in *Artist and Maecenas*,

A Tribute to Curt Valentin, op. cit, p. 17.

44. Ibid, p. 14, letter dated 13 September 1954.

45. *Toronto Globe and Mail*, 22 October 1966.

46. Ralph Colin to RB, interview New York, December 1983.

47. Quoted by Seldis, op. cit., p. 136.

48. *Partisan Review*, January–February 1955 issue, quoted by Seldis, op. cit., p. 147.

49. Donald Hall, op. cit., p. 136.

50. Harry Brooks to RB, interview New York, December 1983.

Chapter XIII (*pages 257 to 275*)

1. Patrick Heron, 'Americans at the Tate', *Arts*, New York, March 1956, quoted in Frances Spalding, op. cit., p. 185.

2. HM in catalogue of exhibition at Rijksmuseum Kröller-Müller Otterlo, 1965.

3. John Russell, op. cit., p. 173.

4. To Donald Hall, op. cit., 137.

5. J. W. C. Boks to RB, letter 25 September 1985.

6. Herbert Read, op. cit., p. 203.

7. Hedgecoe, op. cit., p. 274.

8. *Yorkshire Post*, 9 June 1955.

9. HM in *New York Herald Tribune*, 16 April 1976.

10. *Sunday Telegraph*, 5 June 1977.

11. Darryl Hill to RB, interview London, June 1985.

12. *The Times*, 18 May 1956.

13. Minutes of the first meeting, 16–18 May 1955 (courtesy Unesco archives).

14. Pierre Marcel to RB, interview Paris, July 1983.

15. To David Finn, op. cit., p. 100.

16. To John O'Connor, *Wall St Journal*, 17 April 1970.

17. Dated 2 May 1957.

18. Marcel's memory, confirmed by a scribbled note on the final instalment of £5,400.

19. HM to Carlton Lake, op. cit., p. 43.

20. Dr Gabriele Lavaggi, chairman of Henraux in recent years to RB, interview at Querceta, July 1983.

21. To Yorick Blumenfeld, *Geo magazine*, New York, June 1980.

22. To John Hedgecoe, op. cit., p. 416. HM's engagement diaries of 1957–8 are missing.

23. *Sunday Dispatch*, 29 December 1957.

24. *The Times*, 4 March 1958.

25. *La Nazione Italiana*, 27 April 1958.

26. *The Times*, 17 October 1958; June reference from *Daily Express*, 24 June 1958.

27. *Daily Express*, 21 October 1958.

28. *The Times*, 17 October 1958.

29. HM to Hanns Swarzenski, curator of European decorative arts and sculpture at Boston Museum of Arts, letter 5 November 1958 (courtesy of the Boston Museum).

30. Herbert Read, op. cit., p. 214.

31. John Russell, op. cit., p. 192.

32. IM to RB, February 1984.

33. British Council archives.

34. *Daily Telegraph*, 19 September 1956.

35. *Otago Daily Times*, 19 September 1956.

36. British Council reports and *Hawkes Bay Herald Tribune*, 22 September 1956.

37. *Eastern Province Herald*, 8 May 1957.

38. British Council reports.

39. D. Finn, op. cit., p. 272; Hedgecoe, op. cit., p. 278.

40. The author, who lived nearby, was present on numerous such occasions.

41. Maurice Ash to RB, interview Devon, April 1983.

42. IM to RB, September 1985.

43. A summary of conversations and correspondence in 1985–6.

44. *Homage to Henry Moore* (various contributors), ed. G. di San Lazzaro, (London: A. Zwemmer, 1972), p. 41.
45. *Observer*, 4 May 1958.
46. Alluded to in the *Observer*, 9 November 1958, quoted in the official record of the session (courtesy Auschwitz Museum).
47. Information from the Auschwitz Museum.
48. *Coventry Evening Telegraph*, 9 November 1959.
49. *Zycie Warszawy*, 22 October 1959, quoted in British Council report.
50. British Council archives.
51. Documentation from Carol Schwartz, union archivist, letter to RB, February 1985. Henry Hill died just before the author had established his identity.
52. Henry Seldis, art critic of the *Los Angeles Times*, op. cit., p. 206.

Chapter XIV (*pages 276 to 292*)

1. Capital punishment, *Manchester Guardian*, 26 August 1955; Hungarian intellectuals, *The Times*, 16 November 1956; Treason Trials, *Guardian*, 4 February 1957; nuclear testing, *Daily Worker*, 30 July 1958; Benn, *Yorkshire Post*, 21 April 1961; Immigrants, *Guardian*, 25 January 1962; Mexican intellectuals, meeting Caxton Hall, 20 June 1962; diplomatic bachelors, *Observer*, 2 February 1964; Polish intellectuals, *The Times*, 18 April 1964; Covent Garden, *Evening Standard*, 27 April 1964.
2. *The CND Story*, edited by John Minnion and Philip Bolsover (London: Allison and Busby, 1983), pp. 14–21.
3. HM to the Russells, transcript, op. cit., p. 43.
4. HM to RB, February 1984.
5. Fischer to Henry Seldis, op. cit., p. 123.
6. Hermann Noack III to RB, interview Berlin, October 1984.
7. Heinz Ohff, *Noack: Die Geschichte einer Bildgiesser-Dynastie* (published in Berlin by Noack for seventieth anniversary of the firm, 1967).
8. As for note 6.
9. *Observer*, 31 May 1959.
10. HM to Hedgecoe, op. cit., p. 338.
11. HM to Huw Wheldon, *Monitor*, an anthology (London: Macdonald, 1962), quoted in Philip James, op. cit., p. 274. The Seurat is now in the Tate Gallery.
12. Phillip King to RB, interview London, December 1984; Phillip King, 'Henry Moore, the working day', article in catalogue for 'Head-Helmet', an exhibition at the Arts Centre, Durham, June 1982.
13. John Farnham to RB, interview Perry Green, April 1984.
14. Hedgecoe, op. cit., p. 476.
15. Epstein: *Sunday Times*, 23 August 1959; Gregory: *The Times*, 19 February 1959.
16. *Time* magazine, 21 September 1959.
17. Peter Powell to RB, interview Bristol, February 1985.
18. Letter from Alfred Hentzen to HM, 28 July 1973, (courtesy Kunsthalle).
19. British Council reports.
20. *Der Tagesspiegel*, 30 July 1961. Grohmann's book, *The Art of Henry Moore*, is published by Harry Abrams, New York.
21. British Council report, and letter from Bryan Swingler, BC representative in Berlin, to RB, 15 February 1985.
22. *Sunday Graphic*, 13 December 1959.
23. *Stuttgarter Zeitung*, 1 May 1961.
24. *Irish Times*, 1 April 1954; *Irish Press*, 15 April 1954; *Irish Times*, 8 May 1956.
25. *Observer*, 27 November 1960.

26. *The Times*, 28 November 1960.
27. Roland Piché to RB, interview London, February 1986.

28. Gordon Hanes to HM, 25 July 1978 (courtesy of G. Hanes).

Chapter XV (*pages 293 to 311*)

1. Alan Bowness, introduction to *Henry Moore: Complete Sculpture*, vol IV, p. 8.
2. Frank Stanton to RB, letter 21 February 1984.
3. Gordon Bunshaft to RB, interview New York, November 1983.
4. David Hall, p. 164 (Hall was in attendance for much of this period).
5. *Daily Telegraph*, 14 July 1965.
6. From Wolfgang Fischer's diaries, with kind permission, translation by RB.
7. Broadcast in USA, 5 October 1965; in UK, 18 April 1966 (BBC 1).
8. *New York Times*, 25 August 1965.
9. As for note 6.
10. Ibid.
11. *The Times*, 22 September 1965.
12. *Daily Telegraph*, 23 October 1965.
13. Press statement, 16 November 1965.
14. *New York Times*, 25 September 1966.
15. John Pollis of Christine Roussel Inc. to RB, letter 8 February 1984.
16. As for note 3.
17. *Acton Gazette*, 26 June 1975.
18. *Buffalo Evening News*, 23 September 1965.
19. *East London Advertiser*, 17 October 1980; *Observer*, 14 April 1963.
20. *Pontefract and Castleford Express*, 6 July 1962; *Yorkshire Evening Post*, 29 and 30 June 1962; Donald Hall, p. 154.
21. *The Times*, 13 May and 6 December 1963.
22. *Interdisciplinary Science Reviews*, September 1983, p. 209, ('The Chosen Few', article by Anthony Michaelis). St John Brodrick, Secretary of State for War, to Lord Curzon, Viceroy of India.

23. Heinz Roland to RB, interview London, October 1982.
24. Ibid.
25. Sir William Keswick to RB, loc. cit.
26. Quoted in Philip James, op. cit., p. 187, source unknown.
27. *Evening Standard*, 24 May 1981.
28. *Observer*, 17 January 1965.
29. *Guardian*, 16 January 1965.
30. Letters from Andrew Forge, Martin Froy, Nancy Woodall, Sir Edward Playfair, the Duke of Devonshire, Lord Plymouth and interviews with Sir William Keswick and Sir Brinsley Ford.
31. The source's husband insists on anonymity for fear of seeming to trade on their friendship.
32. Interviews with Hill and Piché, loc. cit.
33. Hylton Stockwell to RB, interview London, April 1985.
34. Derek Howarth to RB, interview Hertfordshire, June 1985.
35. Warren Forma, *Five British Sculptors* (New York: Grossman, 1964), quoted Philip James, p. 144; Hedgecoe, op. cit., p. 456.
36. Gordon Bunshaft to RB, loc. cit.
37. Jacquetta Priestley to RB, letter 23 January 1984; Sir Fred Hoyle to RB, letter 28 February 1984.
38. Donald Hall, op. cit., p. 153; Seldis, op. cit., p. 121.
39. *The Times* court page, 12 December 1958.
40. *Daily Sketch*, 6 March 1960.
41. Ann Garrould to RB, June 1986.
42. *Daily Mirror*, 28 April 1962.
43. Lord Zuckerman to RB, interview London, April 1984.
44. *The Times*, 12 August 1963;

Wakefield Express, 17 August 1963;
Daily Mirror, 19 August 1963.

45. *Western Daily Mail*, 3 July 1963.
46. *New York Times*, 14 June 1964.

Chapter XVI (*pages 312 to 329*)

1. *Daily Mail* ('reporting on Whizz Kids in Sculpture'), 11 March 1965.
2. *Financial Times*, 15 November 1965 (review of work at Kasmin Gallery).
3. *Sunday Times*, 26 January 1969.
4. *Toronto Daily Star*, 24 March 1966.
5. Ibid., 3 May 1966.
6. Philip Givens to RB, interview Toronto, August 1982.
7. John Parkin to RB, interview Toronto, August 1982.
8. *Evening Standard*, 4 February 1965; Hedgecoe, op. cit., p. 487; *The Times*, 14 June.
9. *Toronto Star*, 28 May 1966.
10. As for note 6.
11. *Toronto Globe and Mail*, 28 October 1966.
12. Margaret McLeod to RB, interview London, January 1985.
13. Rothenstein, *Time's Thievish Progress*, op. cit., pp. 201–3.
14. Sir Norman Reid to RB, interview London, June 1984.
15. *Daily Express, New York Times*, 28 February 1967.
16. *The Times*, 1 March 1967.
17. *Observer*, 5 March 1967.
18. *The Times*, 7 March 1967.
19. *Toronto Star*, 14 March 1967.
20. Givens to RB, loc. cit.
21. *Toronto Daily Star*, 16 March 1967.
22. *Toronto Globe and Mail*, 16 March 1967.
23. Valerie Ross, 'The Wooing of Henry Moore', *Toronto Life*, July 1975, p. 11.
24. *Financial Times*, 27 April 1967.
25. *Daily Mirror*, 1 May 1967.
26. Craigie Aitchison to RB, letter dated 8 March 1985.
27. *The Times*, 26 May 1967. Signatories not already mentioned were: David Annesley, Gillian Ayres, Anthony Benjamin, Garth Evans, Sheila Fell, Patrick George, Anthony Hill, Malcolm Hughes, Gwyther Irwin, Tess Jaray, Michael Kidner, John Latham, Francis Morland, Henry Mundy, Myles Murphy, John Plumb, Peter Sedgley, Peter Snow, Peter Startup, Marc Vaux, Brian Wall, Anthony Wishaw.
28. Anthony Caro to RB, loc. cit.
29. Phillip King to RB, loc. cit.
30. Bernard Cohen to RB, telephone interview, January 1985.
31. *The Times*, 27 May (Hendy) and 2 June (Clark), 1967.
32. *The Times*, 27 May 1967.
33. *The Times*, 1 June 1967.
34. Quoted by Valerie Ross, loc. cit.
35. Edmund Bovey to RB, interview Toronto, August 1982.
36. HM to RB, July 1982.
37. William Withrow to RB, interview Toronto, August 1982.
38. John Parkin to RB, loc. cit.
39. HM to Parkin, letter 13 February 1969.
40. Alan Wilkinson to RB, interview Toronto, August 1982.
41. William Withrow to RB, loc. cit.
42. As for note 40.
43. Kenneth Clark, *Henry Moore Drawings* (London: Thames and Hudson, 1974), p. 7.
44. Norman Reid to RB, loc. cit.
45. *New York Times*, 24 October 1974.
46. *Sunday Times*, 3 November 1974.
47. *The Times*, 2 November 1974.

Chapter XVII (pages 330 to 357)

1. Sir Denis Hamilton to RB, interview London, October 1983.
2. Gian-Carlo Menotti to RB, letter dated 27 August 1984.
3. Giovanni Carandente to RB, letter dated 21 May 1985.
4. As for note 2.
5. To John and Véra Russell, interview transcript, loc. cit., p. 18.
6. John Weeks to RB, interview London, June 1984.
7. *The Times*, 12 August 1967.
8. *The Times* Diary, 16 August and 16 October 1967.
9. Tristan Jones to RB, telephone interview, June 1984.
10. Professor Jørgen Bo to RB, letter dated 12 April 1985.
11. Professor William McNeill to RB, letter dated 15 March 1985.
12. McNeill to HM, letter dated 14 November 1963, quoted in *Chicago Today*, winter 1966, pp. 11–14.
13. Ibid.
14. HM to McNeill, 18 February 1964.
15. HM to McNeill, 24 May 1965.
16. *Sunday Telegraph*, 1 August 1965.
17. *Guardian*, 29 July 1965.
18. Prof. McNeill to RB, loc. cit.
19. Mikkel Hansen to RB, letter dated 10 September 1985.
20. Letters from Hansen and McNeill, *Chicago Sun Times*, 3 December 1967, and Muriel Beadle, *Where Has All the Ivy Gone* (New York: Doubleday, 1972), p. 349.
21. *Irish Times*, 27 October 1967.
22. *Daily Express*, 7 November 1967; *Daily Telegraph*, 19 November 1967.
23. *De Waarheid*, 4 May 1968.
24. *The Times* Diary, 18 July 1968.
25. Gordon Bunshaft to RB, loc. cit.
26. David Sylvester to RB, loc. cit.
27. *Guardian*, 18 July 1968.
28. *The Times*, 18 July 1968.
29. *Observer*, 28 July 1968.
30. *Daily Mirror*, 17 July 1968.
31. *The Times*, 13 July 1968.

32. *Daily Express*, 20 November 1968.
33. Derek Howarth to RB, loc. cit.
34. *Henry Moore, The Graphic Work*, vol 1, ed. Gérald Cramer, Alistair Grant and David Mitchinson (Geneva: Gérald Cramer, 1977) – foreword, unnumbered pages.
35. Pat Gilmour, *Henry Moore, Graphics in the Making* (London: Tate Gallery, 1975), pp. 14–15.
36. Ruedi Wolfensberger to RB, interview Zurich, October 1982.
37. Alistair Grant to RB, interview London, February 1985.
38. Lady Huxley to RB, interview London, September 1984.
39. Julian Huxley, *Memories II* (London: George Allen and Unwin, 1973), p. 253.
40. IM and HM to RB, April 1984.
41. *The Times*, 26 May 1971; *Daily Express* 22 May 1971.
42. Michael Ayrton and Henry Moore, *Giovanni Pisano* (London: Thames and Hudson, 1970), pp. 7–11.
43. Elisabeth Ayrton to RB, interview Gloucestershire, February 1985.
44. HM to Kenneth Clark, letter dated January 1970.
45. *Sunday Times*, 8 March 1970.
46. *New York Times*, 15 April 1970.
47. *Financial Times*, 21 August 1970; *The Times*, 25 May 1971.
48. British Council archives.
49. British Council reports.
50. *Die Presse*, 13 April 1971.
51. I. M. Pei to RB, loc. cit.
52. Statement by HM to Mayor Bausi on opening day.
53. Margaret McLeod of the British Council to RB, loc. cit.
54. Ibid.
55. Sir Harold Acton to RB, letter dated 16 November 1984.
56. John Thompson in *Sunday Telegraph*, 14 May 1972.
57. British Council reports; letter from Carandente to RB, 21 May 1985.

58. As for note 56.
59. *Sunday Times*, 21 May 1972.
60. *The Times*, 20 May 1972.

61. *Sunday Telegraph*, 4 June 1972.
62. *New York Times*, 20 June 1972.
63. *New York Times*, 25 June 1972.

Chapter XVIII (*pages 358 to 389*)

1. Ian Gibson, *International Herald Tribune*, 14 May 1977.
2. *Los Angeles Times*, 30 September 1986.
3. Juliet Simpkins, Mme Tussauds, to RB, 28 January 1985; *The Times*, 24 December 1973.
4. *The Times*, 9 April 1973.
5. *Sunday Times*, 12 July 1981.
6. Max Harari to RB, interview London, May 1984.
7. *Sunday Telegraph*, 7 September 1986.
8. *Sunday Express*, 25 July 1976.
9. Sir Norman Reid to RB, loc. cit.
10. *Guardian*, 18 March 1977.
11. *Yorkshire Evening Post*, 7 April 1971.
12. Georg Eisler to RB, loc. cit.
13. Harry Fischer to Peter Palumbo, letter dated 9 January 1968.
14. Chad Varah to HM, 23 March 1972.
15. *Sammlungen Hans und Walter Bechtler*, Kunsthaus Zürich, August 1982, pp. 189–92; Walter Bechtler to RB, interview Zurich, May 1983.
16. Willy and Marina Staehelin to RB, interview Zurich, May 1983.
17. Ibid.
18. H.P. Bruderer to RB, interview Zurich, May 1983.
19. Georg Müller to RB, letter dated 8 January 1985.
20. John Reed to RB, 16 March 1987.
21. *Daily Mail*, 15 February 1977.
22. Margrit Hahnloser to RB, interview Zurich, May 1983.
23. *Les Nouvelles Littéraires*, 18 May 1977.
24. *Le Monde*, 12 May 1977.
25. *The Times*, 14 June 1977.
26. *Die Welt*, 28 June 1977.

27. J. Carter Brown, memo on visit to HM, 23 June 1975 (National Gallery archives).
28. Sir Peter Ramsbotham to RB, letter dated 12 December 1985.
29. *Dallas Morning News*, 16 April 1976.
30. *Dallas Morning News*, 9 July 1976.
31. *Dallas Morning News*, 4 December 1978.
32. *Dallas Morning News* and *Dallas Times Herald*, 5 December 1978.
33. Janie Lee, dealer, and Charles Tapley, designer of Tranquillity Park, to RB, Houston, November 1985.
34. *Bradford Telegraph and Argus*, 1 April 1978.
35. Ibid., 3 April 1978; *The Times*, 16 May 1978; *Observer*, 9 April 1978.
36. *The Times*, July 1978.
37. *Evening Standard*, 10 October 1978.
38. *The Times*, 12 July 1978.
39. Giulio Cardini to RB, interview Querceta, July 1983.
40. Sem Ghelardini to RB, interview Pietrasanta, July 1983.
41. M.S. Farsi to RB, letter (undated), summer 1985.
42. Erich Milleker, to RB, interview Bonn, June 1983.
43. Ibid.
44. Recalled by Sir Robert Sainsbury to RB, loc. cit.
45. *Neue Ruhr Zeitung*, 21 September 1979.
46. (Winter 1979–80) *Financial Times*, 7 September 1981 (post-purchase).
47. *Nürnberger Zeitung*, 5 December 1979.
48. Lauren Bacall to RB, letter dated 17 August 1984.

Chapter XIX (*pages 390 to 421*)

1. Raymond Danowski to RB, September 1986.
2. Lady Huxley to RB, loc. cit.
3. *Pontefract and Castleford Express*, 12 June 1980.
4. *Ya*, 21 May 1981; *El Pais*, 21 May 1981.
5. British Council archives.
6. Ibid., (BC translation).
7. Gordon Bunshaft to RB, loc. cit.
8. Sir Ronald Arculus to RB, interview London, March 1985.
9. *International Herald Tribune*, 8 May 1982 ('Henry Moore, Self-Cast Monument').
10. I. M. Pei to RB, loc. cit.
11. Ibid.
12. Chongsun Rhi, chief curator, to RB, letter dated 8 October 1985.
13. HM to RB, November 1982.
14. Robert Rowe to RB, interview Leeds, November 1982.
15. *Yorkshire Post*, 27 November 1982.
16. British Council reports and Foreign Office sources.
17. *Sunday Times*, 3 July 1983.
18. *Guardian*, 6 July 1983.
19. William Lieberman to RB, interview New York, December 1983.
20. Janet Kutner, *Dallas Morning News*, 8 June 1983.
21. William S Lieberman, *Henry Moore: Sixty Years of His Art* (New York: Thames and Hudson and the Metropolitan Museum of Art, 1983), p. 7.
22. *Toronto Globe and Mail*, 7 May 1983.
23. David Finn, *Sculpture & Environment*, foreword by Kenneth Clark, commentaries by Henry Moore (London: Thames and Hudson, 1977).
24. David Finn to RB, letter dated 5 March 1985.
25. Quotes in Columbia University booklet, 2 May 1985.
26. Vivien Raynor in the *New York Times*, 29 August 1983.
27. Frank Farnham to RB, interview December 1986.
28. Dr Alan Webster to RB, interview London, March 1984.
29. Sir Denis Hamilton to RB, loc. cit.
30. All quotations from obituaries etc., 1 September except Bowness in *The Times*, 2 September 1986.
31. *New York Times*, 2 October 1986.
32. *Independent*, London, 24 November 1986.
33. *Time* magazine, 1 December 1986.

Short bibliography

The following are some of the books which the author found most useful:

Herbert Read, *Henry Moore*, London: Thames and Hudson, 1965

John Russell, *Henry Moore*, London: Allen Lane, The Penguin Press, 1968, revised edition Pelican 1973

Donald Hall, *Henry Moore*, London: Victor Gollancz, 1966

John Hedgecoe and Henry Moore, *Henry Moore*, London: Thomas Nelson, 1968

Henry Seldis, *Henry Moore in America*, New York: Praeger, 1973

William Packer, *Henry Moore*, London: Weidenfeld and Nicolson, 1985

Alan Wilkinson, *The Drawings of Henry Moore*, New York and London: Garland Publishing, 1983

Philip James (ed.), *Henry Moore on Sculpture*, London: Macdonald, 1966

Henry Moore: Complete Sculpture, London: Lund Humphries and Zwemmer
  Vol. I, 1921–1948 (Sculpture & Drawings) ed. Herbert Read, 1944, revised 1957, ed. David Sylvester
  Vol. II, 1949–1954, ed. David Sylvester, 1955
  Vol. III, 1955–1964, ed. Alan Bowness, 1965
  Vol. IV, 1964–1973, ed. Alan Bowness, 1977
  Vol. V, 1974–1980, ed. Alan Bowness, 1983
  (Vol. VI in preparation)

Henry Moore and David Finn, *Henry Moore at the British Museum*, London: British Museum Publications, 1981

David Finn and Henry Moore, *Sculpture and Environment*, London: Thames and Hudson, 1977

Kenneth Clark, *Henry Moore Drawings*, London: Thames and Hudson, 1974

Henry Moore: The Graphic Work
    Vol. I, 1931–1972, ed. Gérald Cramer, Alistair Grant and David Mitchinson, Gérald Cramer, Geneva, 1973
    Vol. II, 1973–1975, ed. Gérald Cramer, Alistair Grant and David Mitchinson, Gérald Cramer, Geneva, 1976
    Vol. III, 1976–1979, ed. Patrick Cramer, Alistair Grant and David Mitchinson, Patrick Cramer, Geneva, 1980
    Vol. IV, 1980–1984, ed. Patrick Cramer, Alistair Grant and David Mitchinson, Patrick Cramer, Geneva, 1986

David Mitchinson (ed.), *Henry Moore Sculpture*, London: Macmillan, 1981

Erich Neumann, *The Archetypal World of Henry Moore*, trans. R. F. C. Hull, London: Routledge and Kegan Paul, 1959

Geoffrey Shakerley and Stephen Spender, *Henry Moore: Sculptures in Landscape*, London: Studio Vista, 1978

Homage to Henry Moore (various contributors, ed. G. di San Lazzaro), London: Zwemmer, 1972

Michael Ayrton and Henry Moore, *Giovanni Pisano, Sculptor*, London: Thames and Hudson, 1969

Sandy Nairne and Nicholas Serota (eds.), *British Sculpture in the Twentieth Century*, London: Whitechapel Art Gallery, 1981

Frances Spalding, *British Art Since 1900*, London: Thames and Hudson, 1986

Oliver Brown, *Exhibition*, London: Evelyn, Adams and Mackay, 1968

Jack Pritchard, *View from a Long Chair*, London: Routledge & Kegan Paul, 1984

Kenneth Clark, *Another Part of the Wood*, London: John Murray, 1974

Kenneth Clark, *The Other Half*, London: John Murray, 1977

Walter Hussey, *Patron of Art*, London: Weidenfeld and Nicolson, 1985

John Rothenstein, *Brave Day, Hideous Night*, London: Hamish Hamilton, 1966

William Rothenstein, *Men and Memories*, vols. I and II, London: Faber and Faber, 1931 and 1932

Herbert Read, *A Concise History of Modern Sculpture*, London: Thames and Hudson, 1964

Mary Banham and Bevis Hillier (eds.), *A Tonic to the Nation: The Festival of Britain 1951*, London: Thames and Hudson, 1976

Richard Shone, *The Century of Change*, London: Phaidon Press, 1977

J. P. Hodin, *Barbara Hepworth*, London: Lund Humphries, 1961

List of illustrations and acknowledgements for photographs

Between page 64 and page 65

Between page 128 and page 129

Between page 192 and page 193

134. The dedication of the Lincoln Center piece, New York, 21 September 1965 (*Keystone Press Agency Inc., New York; photo: Bob Serating, New York*)

135. *Locking Piece*, 1963–4, bronze (*HMF*)

136. Lincoln Center *Reclining Figure*, 1963–5, bronze (*photo: Errol Jackson, London*)

137. Two of Moore's assistants, Ronnie Robertson-Swann and Derek Howarth, making an armature for *Three Way Piece No. 1: Points* of 1964–5 (*photo: Errol Jackson, London*)

138. Moore with Alfred Barr, September 1965, seen through *Large Torso: Arch*, 1962–3, bronze (*HMF; photo: Frederick A. Praeger, New York*)

139. The unveiling on 26 October 1966 in Toronto of *Three Way Piece No. 2: Archer*, 1964–5, bronze (*photo: The Globe and Mail, Toronto*)

140. Moore outside the new building of *The Times* with *Sundial*, 1965–6, bronze (*Times Newspapers*)

141. Jo Hirshhorn in 1966 (*HMF; photo: Charles Gimpel, London*)

142. The installation of the Moore Gallery, October 1974 (*Art Gallery of Ontario, Toronto*)

143. Original plasters in the Moore Gallery (*Art Gallery of Ontario, Toronto*)

144. Moore directing operations as *Nuclear Energy*, 1964–6, is lowered into position at Chicago University, December 1967 (*University of Chicago; HMF*)

145. Moore at Henraux marble quarry in the Carrara Mountains in Italy (*HMF; photo: John Hedgecoe*)

146. The *Archer* in Nathan Philips Square, Toronto (*Art Gallery of Ontario, Toronto*)

147. *Large Two Forms*, 1966–9, bronze, outside the Art Gallery of Ontario (*Art Gallery of Ontario, Toronto; photo: Bo Boustedt*)

148. *Two Piece Sculpture No. 7: Pipe*, 1966, bronze (*HMF*)

149. *Large Totem Head*, 1968, bronze (*HMF*)

150. Moore with Sir Kenneth Clark at a reception in London, November 1969 (*HMF*)

151. Moore with Queen Juliana of the Netherlands when receiving the Erasmus Prize at Arnhem in May 1968 (*HMF; photo: National Foto Persbureau, Amsterdam*)

152. Moore at the London première in early 1969 of the film *Funny Girl* (*HMF; photo: Pic Photos, London*)

153. Moore with Mary in the garden of the villa at Forte dei Marmi, around 1966 (*HMF: photo: Ugo Mulas, Milan*)

154. Henry playing boules with Irina on the beach at Forte dei Marmi, 1969, aged 71 (*photo: Errol Jackson, London*)

155. Jacques Lipchitz, Henry Moore and Marino Marini (*Camera Press Ltd., London; photo: Karsh of Ottawa*)

156. Making light of a broken *Upright Motive* around 1969 (*Keystone Press Agency Ltd, London; HMF; photo: Chris Ware*)

157. A page from *Sheep Sketch Book*, 1972 (*private collection; HMF*)

158. Found objects in the maquette studio at Hoglands, probably late 1960s (*HMF*)

159. Moore etching on to the plate from the elephant skull given to him by Juliette Huxley, 1969 (*photo: Errol Jackson, London*)

160. Moore with Naum Gabo and Dame Barbara Hepworth at a memorial presentation for Sir Herbert Read at the Tate Gallery, London 1970 (*HMF*)

161. Moore with Sophia Loren in 1972 (*HMF; photo: Tazio Secchiaroli*)

162. Joan Miró, then aged 80, on a visit to Hoglands in 1973 (*HMF*)

163. *Sheep Piece*, 1971–2, bronze (*photo: Errol Jackson, London*)

Between page 384 and page 385

164. *Two Piece Reclining Figure: Points*, 1969–70, bronze (*photo: Errol Jackson, London*)

165. The *Arch*, 1969, fibreglass (*photo: Errol Jackson, London*)

166. At the great Florence exhibition of 1972: *Large Square Form with Cut*, 1969–71, Rio Serra marble (*HMF; photo: Errol Jackson, London*)

167. *Hill Arches*, 1973, in front of the Karlskirche in Vienna (*photo: Errol Jackson, London*)

168. The architect I. M. Pei and Moore after the inauguration of the *Dallas Piece*, Dallas, May 1978 (*photo: Jim Murray Film, Dallas*)

169. *Dallas Piece*, 1977–8, bronze, in front of I.M. Pei's new Dallas City Hall (*photo: Nathaniel Liberman, New York*)

170. Moore's altar for the church of St Stephen Walbrook in the City of London, 1973

171. *Three Piece Reclining Figure: Draped*, 1975, bronze (*HMF*)

172. *Reclining Figure: Holes*, 1975–8, elmwood (*HMF*)

173. *Reclining Figure*, 1938–83, bronze (*HMF*)

174. *Reclining Woman: Elbow*, 1981, bronze (*HMF*)

HMF = Henry Moore Foundation

Index